EVERYMAN,
I WILL GO WITH THEE,
AND BE THY GUIDE,
IN THY MOST NEED
TO GO BY THY SIDE

THE BOOK OF COMMON PRAYER

1662 VERSION

INCLUDES APPENDICES FROM THE 1549
VERSION AND OTHER COMMEMORATIONS

WITH AN INTRODUCTION
BY DIARMAID MacCULLOCH

EVERYMAN'S LIBRARY

241

First included in Everyman's Library, 1999
Extracts from The Book of Common Prayer, 1662 Version, the rights
in which are vested in the Crown, are reproduced by permission of
the Crown's Patentee, Cambridge University Press

Introduction © Diarmaid MacCulloch, 1999
Bibliography and Chronology © Everyman's Library, 1999
Typography by Peter B. Willberg

www.everymanslibrary.co.uk

ISBN 978-1-85715-241-8

A CIP catalogue record for this book is available from the
British Library

Published by Everyman's Library,
50 Albemarle Street, London W1S 4DB.

Distributed by Penguin Random House UK,
20 Vauxhall Bridge Road, London SW1V 2SA.

This edition includes the various amendments to the
Book of Common Prayer of 1662 that are contained in the
following measures:

Clergy (Ordination and Miscellaneous Provisions) Measure 1964
Prayer Book (Miscellaneous Provisions) Measure 1965
Prayer Book (Further Provisions) Measure 1968

Typeset in the UK by AccComputing, North Barrow, Somerset
Printed and bound in Germany by GGP Media GmbH, Pössneck

THE BOOK OF
COMMON PRAYER

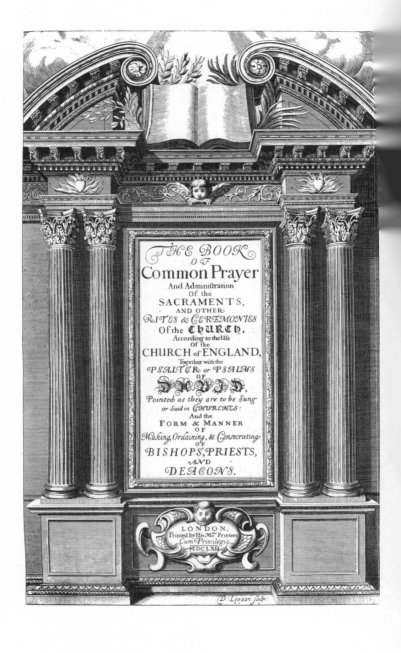

THE BOOK
OF
Common Prayer
And Administration
Of the
SACRAMENTS,
AND OTHER
RITES & CEREMONIES
Of the CHURCH,
According to the Use
Of the
CHURCH of ENGLAND,
Together with the
PSALTER or PSALMS
OF
DAVID,
Pointed as they are to be Sung
or Said in CHURCHES:
And the
FORM & MANNER
OF
Making, Ordaining, & Consecrating
OF
BISHOPS, PRIESTS,
AND
DEACONS.

LONDON,
Printed by His Majᵗⁱᵉˢ Printers
Cum Privilegio
MDCLXII.

D: Loggan sculp:

GENERAL CONTENTS

INTRODUCTION

THE Book of Common Prayer is one of the most important books in the English language. This is not because it is an incomparable road to heaven (though some still find it to be), nor even because it remains in formal terms the standard liturgy through which the established Church of England leads a nation in worshipping God. Rather, it is important as one of a handful of texts to have decided the future of a world language. These key texts emerged in a small northern European kingdom in the sixteenth century, and they are threefold: beside the Prayer Book, masterminded by Thomas Cranmer (1489–1556), they consist of the Bible as translated from Hebrew, Greek and Latin by William Tyndale (*c.* 1490–1536) and Miles Coverdale (1488–1568), and the plays of William Shakespeare (1564–1616). Together, these have shaped sound patterns and speech structures through which billions of the human race communicate with each other.

Among these three sources of world English, the Prayer Book has a unique place, because it is a piece of theatre designed to be performed by an entire people, week by week, day by day. Tyndale's Bible is intended to be read by the faithful, or to be listened to at home or in church. Shakespeare's plays allow a company of actors to act out before an audience the triumphs, the comedy and tragedy of human life. The Prayer Book has all these purposes and intentions, yet it combines them in a drama of human life and destiny where all those present have a speaking part. 'The Lord be with you', is the greeting from the leader of worship at morning and evening prayer, and since the year 1549 back has come the greeting response from the people, 'And with thy spirit'. 'Lift up your hearts', says the priest as the drama of the holy communion gathers pace: 'We lift them up unto the Lord' is the reply. For several centuries, the people in church admittedly had a cheerleader or spokesman in the performance, the parish clerk. In many ancient English parish churches there are pulpits in three decks for parson and clerk the parson sat in his deck above the clerk, in the Prayer Book dialogue of God's service, before he climbed up to the third pulpit deck to take the worship further in his sermon. The sermon would be an exploration of the English biblical text which Tyndale pioneered, and which was read in sequence throughout the Prayer Book's year.

The Prayer Book in History

To understand why this book was created, we go back to the sixteenth century. In 1500 all Europe, as far east as what are now the Baltic states, Poland, Slovakia, Hungary and Croatia, was united by a single culture and by a single branch of the Christian church. It was led by those who spoke Latin as their natural language, and by one symbolic head, the Bishop of Rome (the Pope). Over the century, this western Latin church fell apart in a complex sequence of bitter ideological battles, which we call the Reformation. The Reformation upheavals represented the greatest fault-line to appear in Christian culture since the Latin and Greek halves of the Roman empire had gone their separate ways a thousand years earlier. The cause was a deep disagreement about how human beings could be saved to eternal life, how they might exercise the saving power of God in the world – arguments even about what it was to be human. Ranged on one side were traditional church leaders who stressed the authority of their institution, and its power to create the body and blood of God out of bread and wine, in the eucharistic service known as the mass. Lined up against them was a great variety of protestors (many of them also clergy) who saw these claims as bogus. They said that a great many beliefs and doctrines proclaimed by the western church were distortions of true Christianity as seen in the Bible, and that the church authorities had sought to usurp God's power. They regarded the mass used by the Roman Church as the centrepiece of a huge confidence trick. Because of one very specific political protest made in 1529 by a group of German princes, the challengers came to be known as Protestants.

One central Protestant aim was to give back ordinary people their full part in worship. The medieval western church had maintained the use of Latin for the liturgy. Latin had been the universal language of the western Roman empire, and it was still understood and regularly used in everyday life by educated people; however, it could be seen as excluding or marginalizing the large majority of Europeans who were not educated. So in England the coming of the Reformation brought a liturgy in English, the Book of Common Prayer. It was not called 'Common Prayer' for nothing: it was meant to be prayer shared in common. In areas of the Tudor realms which spoke a different language, the book was translated accordingly: French for the Channel Isles, Welsh for Wales, and (disastrously belated), Gaelic for the Gaelic-speaking parts of Ireland. It could even be used in Latin where Latin was the normal language: Oxford and Cambridge colleges and some major schools like Eton.

In England, the Reformation was begun in the reign of Henry VIII (1509–47), when the king was blocked by the Pope in his efforts to have his marriage to Queen Catherine of Aragon declared null and void. Pious, intensely egocentric and opinionated, Henry became convinced that the Pope's obstinacy was a devilish conspiracy against God's wish that the king should get what he wanted. So he broke with Rome, just at the moment when a significant faction among his clergy were becoming excited by the Reformation's explosion of religious energy on the continent. Henry chose one of these clergy, a diplomat and Cambridge don called Thomas Cranmer, to be his Archbishop of Canterbury, because he liked and trusted Cranmer and knew that he was determined to see through the annulment of the Aragon marriage.

Thus Cranmer came to the highest position in the church, with his own agenda for religious revolution, which did not always coincide with the king's eccentric mixture of religious beliefs. Two of his chief priorities were to see the Bible published in English, and the worship of the church changed from Latin to English. With the powerful help of Cranmer's friend and collaborator, the king's chief minister Thomas Cromwell, a version of Tyndale's and Coverdale's English Bible translation was legalized, and then a further revision of it was given official status (the so-called 'Great Bible') in 1539. At the same time, Cranmer started reshaping the Latin services of the medieval church into English. Henry was not enthusiastic for the idea, and so while the old king lived, the only part of this work to be made public and official was the Litany, the solemn recitation of prayers in dialogue by priest and people, usually walking in procession. This is substantially still the Litany to be found in this book.

When Henry's young son became King Edward VI in 1547, government fell into the hands of a group of Protestant noblemen who were Cranmer's close colleagues. Now he could make much more progress with his plans. In particular, he had come to radical conclusions about the church's central act of worship, the Eucharist. Along with many Protestant reformers (the main exception being the rather conservative Martin Luther), he no longer believed that bread and wine could turn physically into the body and blood of Christ on every eucharistic table in Christendom. Christ's body was in heaven at the right hand of God, and it was blasphemous to suppose that he could be elsewhere. Accordingly, for Cranmer, what happened in the Eucharist was that Christ called believers up to him in heaven, rather than coming down to them himself in bodily form into bread and wine. If he was present in the service, it was in spiritual form, a gift provided only for those faithful whom God had chosen. People who were damned would have no experience of his presence, even if they were attending communion. It is this 'spiritual presence' view of the Eucharist which underpinned Cranmer's remodelling of the Prayer Book.

The archbishop's changes were slowed up only by the need to conciliate still powerful religious conservatives, and to avoid too much trouble with the large proportion of Edward's subjects who were bewildered by religious change. Accordingly, he introduced his work in stages. First, in 1548, he created 'an order of communion', an English rite to be inserted in the old Latin mass, so that at every Eucharist, the people were exhorted to

:ome forward and then received the consecrated bread and wine
(over the previous five centuries, most laypeople had communi-
:ated as infrequently as once a year, and even then, only received
the bread). This order is still substantially embedded in the text
of the communion service. Then in 1549 came the first version
of the Prayer Book, the entire liturgy presented in English.

In order to get the reluctant consent of conservative politicians, the book was not a wholehearted break with the past. In
the justifications for change given in its preface (the section of
the book now headed 'Concerning the Service of the Church'),
the emphasis was on the complexity of the old services, the
confused way in which they presented the text of scripture, and
the variety of service patterns ('uses') even within the single
kingdom of England. 'From henceforth all the whole Realm
shall have but one Use.' Besides drawing heavily on the liturgies
created by Protestant reformers in Europe, Cranmer adapted
the medieval use customary at Salisbury Cathedral and which
had become widely popular in England, the 'Sarum Use'. His
theme of uniformity was taken up a few years later by the
Roman Catholic Church (that part of the old western church
which remained loyal to the Pope): at the Council of Trent, it
created a single eucharistic rite for the whole Roman Church,
the Tridentine mass, as the centrepiece of a whole range of
standardized services.

Cranmer's new book attracted mixed reactions. In Devon and
Cornwall in 1549, popular anger about it became full-scale rebellion, which the government brutally repressed; the rebels fam-
ously called the new communion service 'a Christmas game'
because it was in English. However, in eastern and southern
England, where there were widespread popular disturbances
over a variety of other grievances, the protestors gladly used
the new Prayer Book. Thereafter, Cranmer and King Edward's
government were emboldened to go further. Cranmer was
annoyed that more subtle conservatives, in particular his long-
standing rival Stephen Gardiner the Bishop of Winchester, were
saying that the 1549 Prayer Book was perfectly capable of being
used just like the old services, and could be understood as

expressing the old theology; this was not at all what Cranmer had intended. Accordingly, by 1552 he had drastically revised the book to express his ideas more emphatically. The changes are most obvious in the communion service, when compared with that of 1549 (see appendix). Even the title of the service has changed. In 1549, three different theological identities were on offer: 'The Supper of the Lord and the Holy Communion, commonly called the Mass'. Now even that last very grudging inclusion of the traditional name 'mass' was suppressed, and the service restructured to remove any idea that the bread and wine could be identified with the body and blood of Christ. The shape of this service remains essentially intact, although the 1662 revision of the book made small modifications, designed to make it possible to hold a more positive view of how the bread and wine showed forth the presence of God.

Equally revolutionary was Cranmer's 1552 restructuring of his 1549 funeral service (see appendix). One of the great issues of the Reformation was the power which the old church claimed to exercise over death and the departed. Medieval theology saw three possibilities for the human soul after death; in a few cases of exceptional sanctity, the soul might be ready for heaven, while for the truly wicked, there was no doubt that hell beckoned, but for most humans, neither especially bad nor especially good, the likely fate was a time of purging, punishment and refining, in a state known as purgatory. The attraction of the doctrine of purgatory was that it gave hope to humanity: purgatory was a prelude to heaven, and therefore a chance for ordinary fallible people to achieve eternal bliss. Moreover, the old church increasingly maintained that it was possible to lessen one's time in purgatory by doing good works in earthly life, among which were prayers, especially the powerful prayer of the mass. The living could also pray for the dead in purgatory, and thus do good to both parties. In some sense, the living could influence the fate of the dead. It was a compelling idea which the reformers, Cranmer among them, detested and were determined to combat.

The old funeral service therefore needed drastic revision in order to remove the idea that performing it might help the dead n any way. In the halfway-house book of 1549 there were still traces of the old ethos – psalms to recite, a direct address by the priest to the corpse, the possibility of celebrating a Eucharist as part of the funeral – but in 1552 all that changed. The historian Eamon Duffy comments that 'the oddest feature of the 1552 rite is the disappearance of the corpse from it ... at the moment of committal in 1552, the minister turns not towards the corpse, but away from it, to the living congregation around the grave'.* The church in England thus surrendered its power over death back to the Lord of life and death in heaven: it was a move of perfect theological consistency in Cranmer's terms, but one which also rather sidestepped the problem of whether or not the deceased had been chosen by God for salvation. It has ceased to satisfy the pastoral needs of modern Anglicanism.

Cranmer's 1552 book was used for less than a year before young King Edward died (probably of pneumonia); his Catholic half-sister Mary restored the entire old church and imprisoned Archbishop Cranmer on charges of treason and heresy. Probably if Edward had lived, Cranmer would have changed the Prayer Book still further. Instead he was burned at the stake, a hesitant, reluctant but ultimately an heroic martyr for the Reformation in England. Mary's reign lasted a mere five years (cancer, not pneumonia, this time), and the final long-lived Tudor, Elizabeth I, brought back a Protestant church – with it, Cranmer's Prayer Book, hardly altered. With further modifications, made in 1662 when the episcopal Church of England had been recreated after Charles II had returned from civil war exile, the book achieved its final form. It was accompanied by a doctrinal statement lightly revised by Elizabeth's bishops from a production of Edward's reign: the Thirty-Nine Articles, included in this book, and still recognized as an essential part of the church's historic inheritance.

The Prayer Book remained the only legal form of worship in the established churches of England, Wales and Ireland down to the twentieth century, when in common with all the churches

*E. Duffy, *The Stripping of the Altars: Traditional Religion in England 1400–1580*, Yale University Press, 1992 (pp. 473–5).

of the west, extensive experiments with new liturgies began The *Alternative Service Book* of the Church of England still proclaims by its name that the Prayer Book remains the standard by which all the church's worship is to be judged. Nevertheless, when this new book was first introduced in 1980, it announced a very modern guiding principle that 'revision and adaptation of the church's worship are continuous processes, and that any liturgy, no matter how timeless its qualities, also belongs to a particular period and culture'. Cranmer, lacking our belief in progress, provided a more pessimistic spin on the idea of development in his 1549 preface: 'There was never any thing by the wit of man so well devised, or so sure established, which in continuance of time hath not been corrupted.' He saw his work in terms of restoration, not improvement.

Within the British Isles, the Prayer Book is primarily the property of English culture. In Wales, despite the fine early translation of the book into Welsh, much Welsh religious life later became channelled into Protestant nonconformity, which until recently was the central expression of Welsh cultural identity. In Ireland, the established Protestant church emerged as a minority body from the political and religious confusion of the sixteenth century, and it has remained so. In Scotland, a hamfisted attempt by Charles I's government to force a version of the Prayer Book onto the Kirk in 1637 provoked violence and fury which led to the Scots waging successful war on Charles's other kingdom, England. After this unpromising start, only a small and disestablished Scottish Episcopal Church cherished the book in later years. Yet in the untidy fashion of history, in the eighteenth century, this Scottish church and its distinctive version of the Prayer Book had an effect on a major branch of the English church which found itself stranded in the newly-independent United States of America. The bitterness of the American War of Independence made it difficult at first for the newly-created 'Protestant Episcopal Church of the United States of America' to find a sensible way of relating to the Church of England, so the little disestablished sister-church in Scotland stepped into the vacuum, consecrating the first

American bishops and influencing the first American Episcopalian Prayer Book in 1789. Two-thirds of those who had signed the Declaration of Independence in 1776, and two-thirds of those who signed the American Constitution, were Episcopalians, whose devotional life had been formed by the 1662 Book of Common Prayer.

Alongside the British and American story is that of the second British empire: the new ventures of British power throughout the world once the first empire in north America had been lost. In the century after George III's loss of his thirteen American colonies, Britain reasserted itself as a world power, with a new colonial empire of extraordinary geographical extent: Africa, Asia, Australasia. The Church of England was to be found working throughout this empire, and eventually beyond it. Alongside it, the Episcopal Church of the United States also undertook missions across the globe. What started nearly half a millennium ago as Henry VIII's quarrel with the Pope in a single corner of Europe, has now turned into a worldwide family of churches, now known by a descriptive family name hardly used before the nineteenth century: the 'Anglican Communion'. There is no pope or patriarch to exercise authority in this dispersed and highly diverse collection of churches: no common bond apart from the recognition of each other's clerical ministers, based on the memory of a shared history and the identity which it has created. That shared memory is symbolized especially by the practice of worship according to the tradition first created by Thomas Cranmer in the Tudor age. The Book of Common Prayer, in a flurry of different guises and versions, still gives unity to Anglicanism, one of the major elements of the Christian mosaic.

The Content of the Book

The preface of the book, explaining the motives behind its compilation, opens with a section written by the 1662 revisers. Their first thought was to hammer home an idea of Anglicanism as deliberately occupying the centre ground, a notion which has become familiar to later Anglicanism, but which would have seemed very controversial in Cranmer's revolutionary church a century before: 'It hath been the wisdom of the Church of England, ever since the first compiling of her Publick Liturgy, to keep the mean between the two extremes.' This sense of being a middle way (*via media*) is one which the Anglican Communion has come to cherish, seeing itself as standing between Protestantism and Roman Catholicism – not a notion which Cranmer would have cherished! Yet there is indeed a sense of an old world shaping a new if one considers the helpful tables at the beginning of the book. The 'Calendar' of the church's year from Advent through the interminable Sundays after Trinity is (particularly since the 1662 revision) respectably strewn with special sacred occasions: saints' days (saints from the New Testament, the early church and the history of England), plus the ancient feasts and seasons of the Christian year, like Christmas, Easter, Lent, the Ascension of Jesus, Lammastide. While pruning what it saw as Roman excess, Anglicanism has preserved this rhythm of festival and fast where many Protestants have rejected it.

The first two services are the regular performance of prayer, praise and scripture readings for morning and evening: mattins and evensong. Day by day during the course of any one month, they provide for the recital of the entire 150 psalms, which are set out later in the book with useful notes to show on which day each is to be used. It is worth noticing that these psalms are still presented in the language of Miles Coverdale from the 1539 Great Bible, not in the later version of the 'Authorized' or 'King James' Bible of 1611. So in psalm 23, 'The Lord is my shepherd: therefore can I lack nothing' – not 'The Lord is my shepherd; I shall not want'. As the round of the psalms is repeated, the whole of human experience of the divine unfolds: not just awe or praise, but bewilderment, anger and even downright savagery. That is why it is so important that the psalter is recited all through, not making any cuts to avoid offending our modern squeamishness. Human beings are there, warts and all.

At the heart of the book is its holy communion service. Cranmer unsuccessfully tried to ensure that this would become he chief service of each Sunday in the parishes of England, and ne would have been pleased to know this has become the norm n Anglican worship today. Preceding the service itself is the complete cycle of biblical readings at communion for the year, together with a short seasonal prayer for every Sunday and every major holy day. These prayers are the collects: eighty-four in all, although there are further examples elsewhere in the book. They may be considered the ultimate examples of Cranmer's genius: for the most part they translate much older Latin originals, but many are his alone, and all exhibit his skill in expressing themes, moods and profound theological ideas with an almost haiku-like brevity. They are witness to Cranmer's belief (not shared by all reformers of his age) that God may not appreciate torrents of words when approached by humanity.

The following services mark the stages of human life, from birth to death. First are the church's liturgies of membership: baptism, commonly conveyed in infancy in the Anglican tradition, and the one sacrament whose validity is recognized across the divides of Christendom – then confirmation, a cere-mony in which the grace of baptism is reaffirmed as a child reaches more mature years. Logically linked to this is a short course of doctrinal instruction in question and answer form, the catechism: a favourite educational device in the Reformation's bitter battles of ideas. Marriage follows: a service Englished by England's first married archbishop, and the first liturgy in Chris-tian history officially to affirm that marriage could be enjoyable for human beings – 'for the mutual society, help, and comfort, that the one ought to have of the other'. At the heart of it are ancient words which had always been spoken in English since the early middle ages, for they are the words by which the couple pledge themselves to each other. These are possibly the oldest phrases regularly to be used by modern English speakers.

There follow rites for coping with sickness and death, and also a thanksgiving for women for surviving childbirth, a process more closely linked to sickness and death in Cranmer's age than in the modern west. Next a service interestingly neglected in modern Anglicanism: a service of cursing, or commination. Let adulterers, drunkards and contract killers, not to mention he tha[t] removeth his neighbour's landmark, beware. The round of services ends more cheerfully with various services appended to the original book. The first, 'Forms of Prayer to be used at Sea', reflects the emergence of England as a major naval power during the seventeenth century. The form for ordaining the three clerical orders of the church (which is known as the Ordinal), was originally published separately in 1550. Finally, the commemorative thanksgiving for the anniversary of the reigning sovereign's accession is a reminder that the Church of England still has the monarch as its supreme governor; indeed the convention that the interior of every English parish church should display the royal arms is still widely observed.

For many years there were more state services, until Queen Victoria decided that they had had their day; they are here given in the appendix. They were written to commemorate major milestones in the history of the Stuart royal family: Guy Fawkes' enterprising effort to remove James I and Parliament at one fiery stroke, the beheading of Charles I after the English civil wars, and the return of his son Charles II to the thrones of Britain eleven years later. Curiously, the most momentous event in later English history never received equal commemoration: the 'Glorious Revolution' of 1688, in which the nation's leaders decided that they had had enough of Catholic James II. The Church of England, like many leading politicians at the time, was never quite sure how to justify James's removal, and it seems to have decided to leave well alone, rather than cause unseemly argument in church services by creating a new liturgy of thanksgiving for the *fait accompli*.

The Legacy of the Prayer Book

It was a sheer accident that a functionary of Henry VIII, chosen to be archbishop to sort out a marital difficulty, turned out to be a gourmet of words when he was set to produce a form of worship for the kingdom. His gift was precisely appropriate. Cranmer could not write poetry – and luckily, he knew it, once sadly confessing in a letter to King Henry that he had a tin ear for verse. His insight is amply confirmed by his one venture into poetry, a translation in his Ordinal of a Latin hymn, which was so awful that it had to be replaced in 1662 by John Cosin's lovely verses 'Come Holy Ghost, our souls inspire'. In formal prose, however – that which was needed for the liturgy – Cranmer was a master, having an exact ear for sentences which could be repeated a hundred, a thousand times, and contain no infelicity or sudden jarring note. He was not ashamed to borrow other people's texts and then tweak them patiently until they would bear a shape capable of withstanding the remorseless repetition which liturgy demands.

Cranmer deliberately intended the language of the book to be sonorous and slightly archaic: he had no intention of letting his liturgy be sneered at for being modish or inferior to the old Latin. This archaic quality was highly significant for the future of English: it saved it from being hijacked by the pompous Latin and Greek vocabulary beloved by many of Cranmer's scholarly contemporaries. Two factors make the sixteenth century crucial for very many European languages: first the spread of printing technology, which created standardized texts in large quantities and therefore tended to standardize modes of expression, and second the scholarly movement known as humanism, which seized European universities and enjoyed enormous intellectual prestige. Humanists were enthusiastic for the culture of ancient Greece and Rome, and excitedly imported all sorts of words from Greek and Latin in order to extend the range and flexibility of vernacular languages.

Sometimes this humanist effort was genuinely enriching. Often, however, it produced overblown, embarrassingly showy results: undiscriminating praise is often lavished on Tudor English, which in reality could be self-important and broken-backed. Cranmer, however, protected the Prayer Book from humanist excess by his consciously old-fashioned diction. A competent humanist scholar himself and a notable innovator in language when he thought it appropriate, he was nevertheless fastidious in what he took from humanist vocabulary, only occasionally striking a false note or making a verbal gamble with the future which did not pay off. So one of his collects in the Ordinal may bring pleasurable bafflement to idle perusers of the Prayer Book during service-time when it urges God to 'prevent us in all our doings': 'go before' is a meaning of 'prevent' which has long decayed. Perhaps Cranmer edited the Ordinal in more of a hurry than usual – for another phrase in it, 'the immarcescible crown of glory', needed to be calmed down in 1662 to 'the never-fading crown of glory'. Such examples are rare. The English language's veneer of humanist borrowings, over its matrix of Anglo-Saxon with Norman-French reinforcement, has to a great extent been fixed by Cranmer's linguistic restraint.

There is more to the Prayer Book than merely its words. It provides the English roots of a multi-faceted religious tradition, which despite its international dimension, still resonates with the images of St Augustine's cathedral at Canterbury; of country churchyards where rooks caw in the trees; of small intimate communities sheltering under northern hills; of neighbouring parish churches which (with Anglican contrariness) may treat Cranmer's liturgy either with illogically Tridentine ceremonial splendour, or with a savage austerity worthy of Geneva. Moreover, without knowledge of the Prayer Book and its thought-world, so much of English literature makes less sense. John Donne, George Herbert, Laurence Sterne, Jonathan Swift, John and Charles Wesley, Gilbert White, were parsons: so were the fathers of Jane Austen, the Brontës, and Dorothy L. Sayers. T. S. Eliot came to England and adopted Anglican spirituality, finding fresh inspiration in the Book of Common Prayer. A. N. Wilson, in elegiac mood, has thus meditated on Anglican culture's central place in English identity: 'decking the church for Christmas; arranging the flowers, and the flower rotas; laughing at the eccentricities of bishops and curates and the congregations committed to their charge: such stuff would seem to have little to do with true religion to the new noddle Born Again believer. But for centuries it formed a part of the fabric of our national life.'*

*A. N. Wilson, *The Faber Book of Church and Clergy*, Faber and Faber, 1992 (p.viii).

The Book of Common Prayer, pivotal to all these minor and comfortable intersections between the sacred and the everyday, was intended as an approach to the divine. Perhaps the Prayer Book text is now most often experienced in the setting of choral evensong in the cathedral tradition: something of an irony, because Thomas Cranmer had little affection for either cathedrals or their choirs. Cranmer's attitude is all the more unfortunate because some of the best English music of the last four hundred years has been written for the performance of evensong. Moreover, the Prayer Book's author would also be alarmed by another facet of 'evensong spirituality': its continuing popularity in an age of agnosticism and religious doubt. Here is an unintended function for Cranmer's evening texts. For those who find the classical picture of the Christian God unbelievable or alien, this Anglican performance of patterned liturgical beauty may provide a window on seriousness. Less strident and less excluding than the Christian invitation to approach the eucharistic table, evensong's understated presentation of the sacred may yet be the solace of those who find other, more demonstrative, expressions of Christianity beyond their powers of assent.

It is indeed worth pondering the lessons which the Prayer Book might offer to those now seeking to express Christian aspirations in liturgy. That acute observer of religious change in the modern world, Don Cupitt, expressed himself trenchantly about the liturgical books which have sought to improve on Cranmer's forms:

The Book of Common Prayer (1662) gives a rather vivid impression of the cultural and political world that produced it. Its replacement, the *Alternative Service Book* (1980), floats in a social vacuum, its pages containing no reference anywhere to any of the distinctive features of modern civilization ... The book moves in a Heritage limbo, pseudo-traditional and outside real history. In relation to the lives we are actually living and what is making news at the end of the twentieth century, the ASB services are the purest fantasy. Morally speaking, we might just as well be spending our time in church reading *The Lord of the Rings*.[*]

[*] D. Cupitt, *Radicals and the Future of the Church*, S.C.M. Press, London, 1989 (pp. 138–9).

Can new forms of worship speak to modern society as powerfully as the Book of Common Prayer has done for four centuries? It is the central document of a culture which has produced a treasure-house of literature, enshrined indeed here in Everyman's Library. The Prayer Book is myth, in the profoundest and truest sense of the word. It remains to be seen what, if anything, can replace it.

Diarmaid MacCulloch

DIARMAID MacCULLOCH is Senior Tutor at St Cross College, Oxford. His works include *Thomas Cranmer: A Life*, *The Reign of Henry VIII: Politics, Policy and Piety* and *Building a Godly Realm: The Establishment of English Protestantism 1558–1603*.

SELECT BIBLIOGRAPHY

F. E. BRIGHTMAN, *The English Rite*, 2 vols., Rivingtons, 1915. A monumental survey comparing all the versions and showing the sources of the text.

D. E. W. HARRISON, *Common Prayer in the Church of England*, S.P.C.K., London, 1969. A sensible brief introduction to history and recent practice.

M. J. HATCHETT, *Commentary on the American Prayer Book*, Harper Collins, 1995. An excellent commentary, on the Prayer Book as well as its American successor.

W. K. LOWTHER CLARKE and C. HARRIS, eds., *Liturgy and Worship: A Companion to the Prayer Books of the Anglican Communion*, S.P.C.K., London, 1932. A standard work of reference.

D. MACCULLOCH, *Thomas Cranmer: A Life*, Yale University Press, 1996. The latest biography.

J. MALTBY, *Prayer Book and People in Elizabethan and Early Stuart England*, Cambridge University Press, 1998. The reception of the Prayer Book by the English people.

J. R. H. MOORMAN, *A History of the Church in England*, A. & C. Black, 1953. Provides the historical background.

E. C. RATCLIFF, *The Booke of Common Prayer of the Church of England: its Making and Revisions 1549–1661*, S.P.C.K., London, 1949. Has eighty reproductions of the original texts.

M. SHEPHERD, *Oxford American Prayer Book Commentary*, Oxford University Press, 1950.

CHRONOLOGY

HISTORY OF THE PRAYER BOOK AND HISTORICAL BACKGROUND	LITERARY CONTEXT
1485 Accession of Henry VII after battle of Bosworth: the first Tudor monarch.	
1489 Thomas Cranmer born, Aslockton, Nottinghamshire.	
1509 Accession of Henry VIII. Marriage to Catherine of Aragon. Birth of John Calvin.	Erasmus in England: Latin translation of New Testament (Cambridge).
1511 Henry VIII joins Holy League against France.	Erasmus: *The Praise of Folly*.
1516 Birth of Princess Mary.	Sir Thomas More: *Utopia*. Erasmus: *Institution of a Christian Prince*; Greek New Testament (Basle).
1517 Luther publishes his 95 theses against indulgences at Wittenberg.	
1519 Charles V elected Holy Roman Emperor.	
1520 Francis I and Henry VIII at the Field of the Cloth of Gold. English followers of Luther at Cambridge include Tyndale and Latimer.	Martin Luther: *Christian Liberty, The Reformation of the Christian Estate, The Babylonian Captivity of the Church*.
1521 Henry VIII made Defender of the Faith. Diet of Worms: Luther condemned. In England, his books burned.	Henry VIII: *Assertio Septem Sacramentum*.
1522 Charles V and Henry in alliance against France.	Luther: German translation of the New Testament. Huldreich Zwingli: *Archeteles*.
1523 Zwingli reforms Zurich.	Lefèvre d'Etaples: French New Testament. More: *Responsio ad Lutherum*.
1524 Erasmus persuaded to attack Luther on free will.	Luther: Hymnbook.
1525 Charles V defeats French at Pavia. German peasants' revolt crushed.	William Tyndale, in collaboration with William Roy: first English translation of the New Testament (Cologne). Luther: *Bondage of the Will*.
1527 Sack of Rome by imperial army. Henry VIII seeks papal annulment of marriage to Catherine of Aragon. Reformation in Sweden. Cranmer part of royal embassy to Charles V in Spain.	Martin Bucer: *Commentary on St Matthew*. Death of Machiavelli.

	HISTORY OF THE PRAYER BOOK AND HISTORICAL BACKGROUND	LITERARY CONTEXT
1528	Reformation in Basle and Berne; Bucer reforms Strassburg.	Tyndale: *Obedience of a Christian Man*. Jerome Barlow: *The Burial of the Mass*. Simon Fish: *Supplication of the Beggars*. Castiglione: *The Courtier*. Erasmus: *Ciceronianus*.
1529	Henry VIII fails to get annulment granted by Pope. Cranmer joins royal theological team arguing for marriage annulment; becomes chaplain to Boleyn family. Fall of Wolsey. Sir Thomas More appointed Lord Chancellor. Reformation Parliament opens.	More: *Dialogue Concerning Heresies*, *Supplication of Souls*. Luther: Catechism. Tyndale and Coverdale: translation of Genesis.
1530	Persecution of reformers: Tyndale denounced as heretic, existing translations of Bible burned. Diet of Augsburg presented with Lutheran confession. Cranmer on embassy in Rome; made rector of Bredon (Worcestershire).	Tyndale: *The Practice of Prelates*. Zwingli: *De Providentia Dei*, *Fidei ratio*. George Joyce: *Garden of the Soul*.
1531	First evangelical martyrs burned in England. Praemunire charge against clergy. Rise of Thomas Cromwell. In France, evangelicals protected by Marguerite of Navarre. Death of Zwingli. German Protestants form League of Schmalkalden. Cranmer makes contact with Martin Bucer.	Cranmer's translation of Henry VIII's case for marriage annulment, *Academiarum Censurae*, as *Determinations of the Universities*. Machiavelli: *Discourses*. Sir Thomas Elyot: *The Book called the Governor*. Tyndale: *An Answer to Sir Thomas More*.
1532	Latimer tried for heresy. Submission of the Clergy. Resignation of More. Death of Archbishop Warham. Cranmer marries niece of a Lutheran theologian in Nuremberg.	More: *Confutation of Tyndale's Answer*. *The Glass of the Truth* (authors include Henry VIII). Calvin: *De Clementia*. Machiavelli: *The Prince*. Rabelais: *Pantagruel*.
1533	Cranmer appointed Archbishop of Canterbury. Act in Restraint of Appeals signals break with Rome. Cranmer marries Henry to Anne Boleyn and grants annulment of Aragon marriage. Birth of Elizabeth. Persecution of Protestants in France.	More: second part of the *Confutation*; *Apology*. Birth of Montaigne. John Leland begins antiquarian book collection from monastic libraries.

	HISTORY OF THE PRAYER BOOK AND HISTORICAL BACKGROUND	LITERARY CONTEXT
1534	Act of Supremacy. Treason Act. First evangelical bishops appointed. Execution of Elizabeth Barton. Trials of Fisher and More. Anabaptists take over Münster. Loyola founds Jesuit Order.	Rabelais: *Gargantua*.
1535	Executions of Fisher, More and other Catholics opposed to Royal Supremacy. End of Anabaptist rule in Münster. Miles Coverdale produces first complete English Bible (which is also the first authorized translation): psalter used in all subsequent Prayer Books.	More: *Dialogue of Comfort*. Gardiner: *De vera obedientia* (defends Supremacy).
1536	Dissolution of smaller monasteries. Death of Catherine of Aragon. Execution of Anne Boleyn. Henry VIII marries Jane Seymour. Pilgrimage of Grace.	Calvin: *Institutes of a Christian Religion*. Thomas Starkey: *An Exhortation to the people instructing them to unity and obedience*. Elyot: *The Castle of Health*. Marot: French translation of the Psalms. Reginald Pole: *De Conservanda Ecclesiae* (opposes Supremacy). Death of Erasmus and Tyndale.
1537	Birth of Edward, Prince of Wales. 'Bishops' Book' (doctrinal statement for Church of England); compilation led by Cranmer. Denmark becomes Protestant.	
1538	Major English shrines destroyed; friaries dissolved. Anabaptists persecuted in England. Cranmer begins translating parts of liturgy into English.	Elyot: Latin–English *Dictionary*.
1539	Counter-reformatory Act of Six Articles drives many evangelicals abroad.	Coverdale's revised 'Great' Bible.
1540	Dissolution of monasteries completed. Fall of Cromwell ends pro-Protestant policy. Henry has marriage to Anne of Cleves annulled, marries Catherine Howard.	
1542	Catherine Howard executed on information from Cranmer.	
1543	Henry marries Catherine Parr. 'King's Book', a more conservative doctrinal statement for Church of	

	HISTORY OF THE PRAYER BOOK AND HISTORICAL BACKGROUND	LITERARY CONTEXT
1543 cont	England. Hermann von Wied, Archbishop of Cologne, produces *Pia Consultatio*, a major source for Prayer Book.	
1544	Litany in English published.	
1545	First meeting of the Council of Trent.	
1546	Death of Luther. Cranmer abandons Lutheran views on Eucharist.	
1547	Death of Henry VIII. Accession of Edward VI: regency council under Protestant Somerset. Protestant refugees return. Charles V defeats German Protestants. All chantries dissolved; heresy laws abolished.	*Book of Homilies*, edited by Cranmer.
1548	English introduced into the mass as 'the Holy Communion'.	
1549	Act of Uniformity. First English Book of Common Prayer. West Country Rebellion against Prayer Book. John Dudley seizes power (made Duke of Northumberland 1551).	Thomas Smith: *Discourse of the Commonweal*.
1550	Stone altars replaced by wooden tables.	Cranmer: *Defence of the Sacrament*.
1551	Miles Coverdale appointed Bishop of Exeter. Martin Bucer dies.	Bucer: *De Regno Christi* (proposals to reform English Church). Cranmer: *Answer to Gardiner* on the Eucharist.
1552	Act of Uniformity and Second Prayer Book.	Ronsard: *Amours*.
1553	Forty-Two Articles state official church doctrine. Death of Edward VI. Accession of Mary I. Prayer Book declared illegal.	
1554	Wyatt's Rebellion. Execution of Lady Jane Grey. Mary marries Philip II of Spain. Return of Cardinal Pole. Roman Catholicism restored.	Sebastian Castellio: *De Haereticis*.
1555	Persecution of heretics begins. Hooper, Latimer and Ridley burned.	
1556	Cranmer burned. Abdication of Charles V.	
1558	Loss of Calais to French. Death of Mary. Accession of Elizabeth I.	John Knox: *First Blast of the Trumpet against the Monstrous Regiment of Women*. Marguerite de Navarre: *Heptameron*.

HISTORY OF THE PRAYER BOOK AND HISTORICAL BACKGROUND	LITERARY CONTEXT
'559 Supremacy Act declares Elizabeth Supreme Governor. Act of Uniformity reintroduces 1552 Prayer Book, slightly modified. Marian exiles return; some Catholics deprived of livings flee. In Scotland, Protestants rebel against French Regent. First Protestant Synod at Paris.	Calvin: *Confessio Gallicana*. *Mirror for Magistrates* (first of many editions).
1560 Death of Melanchthon.	Geneva Bible (translated by English Protestant exiles).
1561 Mary Stuart returns to Scotland.	
1563 Thirty-Nine Articles (modified version of 1553 Forty-Two Articles). End of the Council of Trent. End of the first French war of religion (begun in 1562).	John Foxe: *Book of Martyrs*. Second *Book of Homilies*.
1564 Death of Calvin. Beginning of Vestiarian controversy.	Birth of Shakespeare and Marlowe.
1566 Revolt of the Netherlands.	
1568 Mary Queen of Scots escapes to England. William Allen founds English Catholic college at Douai.	'Bishops' Bible. Vasari: *Lives of the Artists* (second edition). Death of Miles Coverdale.
1569 Catholic Northern Rebellion.	
1570 Pius V excommunicates Elizabeth.	
1571 Ridolfi Plot. Treason Act. Puritan 'Admonition' to Parliament demands reform of Prayer Book. Turks defeated at Lepanto.	
1572 Dutch rebels capture Holland and Zealand. Massacre of St Bartholomew's Day in France.	Whitgift's *Answer* to the Admonition.
1573 Second Puritan 'Admonition'.	Cartwright's *Reply*: first literary debate between Puritans and Anglicans. Tasso: *Aminta*. Birth of John Donne.
1574 First Catholic missionaries arrive from Douai. (College moves to Rheims in 1578.)	Whitgift: *Defence of the Answer*. Walter Travers: *Book of Discipline*.
1577 Archbishop Grindal refuses to stop 'prophesyings' and is suspended.	
1580 First Jesuit missionaries arrive from Rome led by Edmund Campion and Robert Parsons.	

	HISTORY OF THE PRAYER BOOK AND HISTORICAL BACKGROUND	LITERARY CONTEXT
1581	Increased penalties on recusants. Campion and others executed.	John Newton's translation of Seneca's *Ten Tragedies*. Barnaby Rich: *Apolonius and Silla*
1582		New Testament printed in Rheims by Catholic exiles.
1583	Anti-Puritan Whitgift becomes Archbishop of Canterbury. Throckmorton Plot.	
1584	Assassination of William of Orange. Henry of Navarre becomes heir to French throne.	Reginald Scott: *The Discovery of Witchcraft*. Giordano Bruno in England. Death of Pierre de Ronsard.
1585	England sends military aid to Dutch. Babington Plot begins. Philip II helps Catholics in French civil war.	
1587	Execution of Mary Queen of Scots.	Holinshed: *Chronicles of England, Scotland and Ireland*.
1588	Defeat of the Spanish Armada. Entire Bible translation in Welsh published. Death of the Earl of Leicester, patron of Puritans and playwrights. Puritan 'Marprelate' propaganda campaign.	First Puritan Martin Marprelate tracts printed. Thomas Kyd: *The Spanish Tragedy*. William Byrd: *Psalms, Sonnets and Songs*.
1589	Failure of Portugal expedition. Henry III of France assassinated. English military aid sent to Henry IV. Marlowe's tutor, Francis Ket, burned for unitarian views. Cartwright and other Presbyterians imprisoned.	Shakespeare's first plays performed. Marlowe: *The Jew of Malta* performed. Hakluyt: *Principal Navigations, Voyages and Discoveries of the English nation*.
1590	Puritan printing press discovered and shut down. Leaders imprisoned.	Nashe: *An Almond for a Parrot* (Marprelate tract). Sidney: 'New' *Arcadia*. Spenser: *The Faerie Queene*, Books i–iii.
1593	Persecution of Separatists: Penry, possibly one of the Marprelate writers, executed. Marlowe arrested on blasphemy charges and murdered. Henry IV re-converts to Catholicism to unite France.	Shakespeare: *Venus and Adonis*. Nashe: *Christ's Tears over Jerusalem*. Birth of Herbert and Walton.
1594	Henry IV accepted as King in France. Rebellion in Ireland. Ralegh accused of blasphemy.	Hooker: *Of the Laws of Ecclesiastical Policy*, Books i–iv. Nashe: *The Terror of the Night* and *The Unfortunate Traveller*. Greene: *Friar Bacon and Friar Bungay*. Marlowe: *Edward II*. Shakespeare: *Rape of Lucrece*.

	HISTORY OF THE PRAYER BOOK AND HISTORICAL BACKGROUND	LITERARY CONTEXT
1595	Lambeth Articles. Execution of Jesuit missionary and poet Robert Southwell. Irish Rebellion. France at war with Spain.	Southwell: *Poems.* Sidney: *Defence of Poesy.* Spenser: *Amoretti, Epithalamion.* Death of Tasso and Kyd.
1596	England allies with France against Spain. Robert Cecil appointed Secretary of State.	Spenser: *Faerie Queene*, Books iv–vi. Ralegh: *Discovery of the Empire of Guiana.* Birth of Descartes.
1597	The government suppresses *The Isle of Dogs*, imprisons the authors, Jonson and Nashe, and closes the London theatres. They soon re-open.	Hooker: *Ecclesiastical Laws* completed. Bacon: *Essays.* Shakespeare: *1 Henry IV, Richard II, Richard III, Romeo and Juliet.* Dowland: *First Book of Songs.*
1598	Edict of Nantes. Peace between France and Spain. Irish defeat English. Essex appointed Lord Deputy.	James VI of Scotland: *The True Law of Free Monarchies.* Sidney: *Works.* Chapman and Marlowe: *Hero and Leander.*
1599	Failure of campaign in Ireland. Essex disgraced. Government suppresses satirical writings; burns pamphlets by Nashe.	Dekker: *The Shoemaker's Holiday.* Death of Spenser.
1600		Shakespeare: *Henry V, The Merchant of Venice, A Midsummer Night's Dream, Much Ado About Nothing.* Death of Hooker.
1601	Essex's rebellion and execution. Spanish invasion of Ireland. Monopolies debate.	Shakespeare: *The Phoenix and the Turtle, Troilus and Cressida.* Death of Nashe. Lancelot Andrewes appointed Dean of Westminster Abbey.
1603	Death of Elizabeth. Accession of James I. Millenary Petition: Puritans demand reform of Church.	Shakespeare: *Hamlet.* Florio, tr. Montaigne's *Essays.*
1604	Peace with Spain. Hampton Court Conference. Revised Prayer Book.	Shakespeare: *Othello, Measure for Measure.*
1605	Gunpowder Plot. Persecution of Catholics.	Bacon: *The Advancement of Learning.* Cervantes: *Don Quixote.* Birth of Sir Thomas Browne.
1607	First successful English colony founded in Virginia. Plantation of Ulster by Protestant Scots and English begins.	Tourneur: *The Revenger's Tragedy.* Jonson: *Volpone.*
1608		Shakespeare: *King Lear.* Birth of Milton.

	HISTORY OF THE PRAYER BOOK AND HISTORICAL BACKGROUND	LITERARY CONTEXT
1609	Truce between Spain and the Netherlands. Catholic League in Germany. Galileo and Kepler's astronomical discoveries announced.	Shakespeare: *Sonnets*. Donne: *The Expiration*.
1610	Parliament submits the Petition of Grievances. In Holland, followers of Jacobus Arminius present 'Remonstrance'. Assassination of Henry IV.	Donne: *Pseudo-Martyr*. English New Testament completes Douai and Rheims Bible.
1611	James I dissolves his first Parliament. He denounces Arminian teaching in Holland. Inquisition begins investigating Galileo. Authorized version of Bible published.	Chapman, tr. *Iliad* completed. Tourneur: *The Atheist's Tragedy*.
1612	Death of Henry, Prince of Wales. Last recorded burning of heretics in England. First Baptist congregation in England.	Webster: *The White Devil*. Jonson: *The Alchemist*. Middleton: *Women Beware Women* performed. Orlando Gibbons: *Madrigals, Motets*.
1613	Marriage of Princess Elizabeth to Protestant Frederick, Elector Palatine.	Donne writes *Good Friday*, *Epithalamion*. Birth of Crashaw.
1616	Ralegh released from the Tower to lead Guiana expedition. Harvey expounds theory of the circulation of the blood.	Death of Shakespeare. James I: *Works*. Jonson: *Works*. Chapman, tr. *The Whole Works of Homer*.
1618	Execution of Ralegh. Book of Sports. Beginning of Thirty Years' War. Synod of Dort condemns Arminian doctrine.	Birth of Lovelace and Cowley.
1620	Spanish invade the Palatinate: James incenses public opinion by failing to intervene. Settlement of Pilgrim Fathers at Plymouth, Massachusetts.	Death of Campion. Birth of Evelyn.
1621	Bacon impeached. Religious war in France.	Donne appointed Dean of St Paul's. Birth of Marvell.
1622	James I's *Direction to Preachers* aims to suppress Calvinist preaching.	Herbert: *Latin Orations*. Birth of Henry Vaughan.
1623	Prince Charles and the Duke of Buckingham's abortive visit to Madrid.	Shakespeare: First Folio. Birth of Blaise Pascal.
1624	Birth of George Fox, founder of the Society of Friends.	Donne: *Devotions upon Emergent Occasions*. Edward Herbert: *De Veritate*.

HISTORY OF THE PRAYER BOOK AND HISTORICAL BACKGROUND	LITERARY CONTEXT
1625 Death of James I. Accession of Charles I. Marriage to Catholic Henrietta Maria of France.	Bacon: *Translations of Certain Psalms.*
1626 Pym leads attacks in Parliament on Buckingham and Arminianism.	Donne: *Five Sermons.*
1627 Failure of La Rochelle expedition. Forced Loan and Five Knights case.	Bacon: *New Atlantis.*
1628 Assassination of Buckingham. Laud appointed Bishop of London. Petition of Right. Charles I's Declaration to promote religious conformity.	Harvey: *De Motu Cordis.* Birth of Bunyan.
1629 Dissolution of Parliament. Beginning of Eleven Years' Personal Rule.	Andrewes: *XCVI Sermons.* Pemble: *A Plea for Grace* attacks Arminianism.
1631 Sack of Magdeburg by imperial army. Growth of Catholicism at English Court.	Death of Donne. Birth of Dryden. Cresacre More: *Life and Death of Thomas More.* James Shirley: *The Traitor.*
1633 Laud appointed Archbishop of Canterbury. Opposition to Arminian innovations in the Church. Book of Sports re-issued: widespread offence. Wentworth (created Earl of Strafford 1639) appointed Lord Deputy in Ireland. Inquisition condemns Galileo. In France, Jansenism is established at Port-Royal.	George Herbert: *The Temple.* Death of Herbert. Donne: *Poems.* Quarles: *Divine Poems.* Prynne: *Histrio-Mastix.* Ford: *'Tis Pity She's a Whore.*
1637 Ship Money case. Attempt to impose Book of Common Prayer on Scotland (based on 1549 version) causes riots in protest.	Bishop Williams: *The Holy Table: Name and Thing* attacks Laudian altar. Milton: *Comus.*
1638 Scottish National Covenant against Prayer Book. Prelude to first Bishops' War in 1639.	Cowley: *Love's Riddle.* Milton: *Lycidas.* Suckling: *Aglaura.* Carew: *Psalms* set by Henry Lawes.
1640 Short Parliament. Second Bishops' War. Long Parliament. Root and Branch petition calls for abolition of episcopacy. Laud imprisoned.	Donne: *LXXX Sermons* prefaced by Walton's *Life of Donne.* Carew: *Poems.*
1641 Execution of Strafford. Irish Rebellion. Grand Remonstrance against arbitrary government.	Milton: *Of Reformation* attacks episcopacy.
1642 Beginning of the Civil War. Birth of Isaac Newton.	Milton: *The Reason of Church Government.*

	HISTORY OF THE PRAYER BOOK AND HISTORICAL BACKGROUND	LITERARY CONTEXT
1643	Solemn League and Covenant. Scotland enters the war.	Browne: *Religio Medici*. Milton: *The Doctrine and Discipline of Divorce*.
1645	Laud executed. The New Model Army defeats the Royalists.	Milton: *Poems*. Waller: *Poems*.
1646	Charles I surrenders to the Scots, who hand him over to Parliament. Episcopacy abolished. John Lilburne leads the Levellers in London.	Crashaw: *Steps to the Temple*. Edwards: *Gangraena* attacks sectaries.
1647	The Army's Peace Proposals. Growth of Leveller movement in the Army. The Putney Debates.	Cowley: *The Mistress*.
1648	The Second Civil War breaks out. Pride's Purge. The end of the Thirty Years' War.	Winstanley: *The Breaking of the Day of God*. Walwyn: *The Bloody Project*. Fanshawe, tr. *Il Pastor Fido* and original poems.
1649	The trial and execution of Charles I. England is declared a Commonwealth. Cromwell defeats Leveller mutinies and crushes the Irish rebellion. Winstanley founds the Digger community.	More Leveller pamphlets by Lilburne, Walwyn and Overton. Charles I (?): *Eikon Basilike*. Milton: *Eikonoklastes*, *The Tenure of Kings and Magistrates*. Lovelace: *Lucasta*. Death of Crashaw.
c.1650	The first meetings of the Society of Friends.	
1650	In Wales, Welsh-speaking preachers are introduced. The Fifth Monarchists are formed.	Vaughan: *Silex Scintillans*. Marvell: *An Horatian Ode upon Cromwell's Return from Ireland*.
1651	Defeat and flight of Charles II.	Hobbes: *Leviathan*. Milton: *Pro populo anglicano defensio*. Cartwright: *Poems*.
1652		Winstanley: *The Law of Freedom in a Platform*.
1653	Protectorate established under Cromwell. Religious toleration extended to all Puritans except Fifth Monarchists and Quakers.	Izaac Walton: *The Compleat Angler*. Marvell writes *The Bermudas*.
1656	Cromwell allows Jews back into England. Birth of Edmund Halley.	Harrington: *Oceana*. Davenant: *The Siege of Rhodes*.
1658	Death of Cromwell. Struggle for government settlement between Parliament and the army.	Browne: *Hydriotaphia*, *The Garden of Cyrus*. Marvell: *A Poem upon the Death of His Highness the Lord Protector*.
1660	Convention Parliament recalls the King. His Declaration of Breda offers religious toleration.	Milton: *The Ready and Easy Way to Establish a Free Commonwealth*.

	HISTORY OF THE PRAYER BOOK AND HISTORICAL BACKGROUND	LITERARY CONTEXT
1660 cont	Restoration of the monarchy and episcopacy. The Royal Society founded.	Milton imprisoned for a short time and his books burned. The Baptist Bunyan imprisoned until 1672. Theatres re-open.
1661	Corporation Act inaugurates the Clarendon Code, aimed at excluding nonconformists from government. Louis XIV assumes personal rule in France.	Boyle: *The Sceptical Chemist.*
1662	Act of Uniformity and new Prayer Book (modified form of 1559); about a thousand clergy deprived. Anglican opposition forces Charles II to withdraw his first Declaration of Indulgence, offering toleration to Protestant and Catholic dissenters.	Samuel Butler: *Hudibras.* Stanley: *History of Philosophy.* Death of Pascal.
1666	Final outbreaks of the Plague (since 1665). The Great Fire of London.	Bunyan: *Grace Abounding.* Molière: *Le Misanthrope.*
1667	War of Devolution between France and Spain. End of Third Dutch War. Fall of Clarendon.	Milton: *Paradise Lost.* Dryden: *Annus Mirabilis.* Sprat: *History of the Royal Society.* Birth of Defoe and Swift.
1668		Dryden: *Essay of Dramatic Poetry.* Cowley: *Works.*
1669		William Penn: *No Cross, No Crown.*
1670	The secret Treaty of Dover between Charles II and Louis XIV.	Dryden: *The Conquest of Granada.* Walton: *Lives of Donne, Wotton, Hooker, Herbert.* Birth of Congreve.
1671		Milton: *Paradise Regained, Samson Agonistes.*
1672		Bunyan: *Pilgrim's Progress,* Part 1.
1673	The Test Act excludes Roman Catholics from public office.	Traherne: *Roman Forgeries.* Molière: *La Malade imaginaire.* Death of Molière.
1674		Death of Milton, Herrick, Traherne.
1675	Wren begins rebuilding St Paul's Cathedral.	Wycherley: *The Country Wife.*
1677	Marriage of William of Orange, Protestant leader of Europe against France, to Mary, elder daughter of the Catholic James, Duke of York.	Dryden: *All for Love.* Aphra Behn: *The Rover.* Racine: *Phèdre.*

	HISTORY OF THE PRAYER BOOK AND HISTORICAL BACKGROUND	LITERARY CONTEXT
1678	The Popish Plot spreads anti-Catholic fears.	Bunyan: *Pilgrim's Progress*, Part 2. Death of Marvell. Birth of Farquhar.
1679	The Exclusion Crisis: Whigs attempt to exclude James and secure a Protestant succession.	Burnet: *History of the Reformation*. Death of Hobbes.
1680		Bunyan: *The Life and Death of Mr Badman*. Burnet: *Life and Death of the Earl of Rochester* (inspired by his deathbed conversion). Filmer: *Patriarcha* (Tory-Anglican political theory).
1681	Dissolution of the Oxford Parliament: Charles II defeats the Exclusionists.	Dryden: *Absalom and Achitophel*. Nevil: *Plato Redivivus*. Marvell: *Poems*.
1682		Dryden: *The Medal, Religio Laici*. Otway: *Venice Preserved*.
1683	The Rye House Plot ends in the arrest of leading Whigs.	
1685	Death of Charles II (after converting to Catholicism in accordance with the Treaty of Dover). Accession of James II. Monmouth's rebellion and execution. James arouses opposition by the use of his dispensing power. Louis XIV revokes the Edict of Nantes: Huguenot refugees arrive in England.	Dryden: *Ode to the Memory of Mrs Anne Killigrew*.
1687	James II's Declaration of Indulgence.	Dryden: *The Hind and the Panther, Song for St Cecilia's Day*. Newton: *Principia*. Halifax: *Letter to a Dissenter*.
1688	Second Declaration of Indulgence opposed by majority of Anglicans. Trial and acquittal of the Seven Bishops. The birth of an heir to James prompts the invitation of seven Whig and Anglican Tory peers to William of Orange to invade.	Dryden: *Britannia Rediviva* (on the birth of the Roman Catholic prince). Halifax: *Character of a Trimmer*. Behn: *Oroonoko*.
1689	William and Mary are crowned joint sovereigns and promise to maintain 'the Protestant Reformed Religion established by law'. Parliament produces the Bill of Rights and the Toleration Act, which grants limited toleration to all Protestant dissenters.	Death of Aphra Behn. Birth of Richardson.

THE BOOK OF

COMMON PRAYER

and

ADMINISTRATION OF THE SACRAMENTS

and other rites and ceremonies of the
church according to the use of

THE CHURCH OF ENGLAND

together with
The Psalter or Psalms of David
pointed as they are to be sung or said
in churches

and the form or manner of making,
ordaining, and consecrating of
Bishops, Priests, and Deacons

THE BOOK OF

COMMON
PRAYER

as Revised and Settled at the
Savoy Conference
Anno 1662.　14 Charles II.

THE CONTENTS

3

THE PREFACE

IT hath been the wisdom of the Church of *England*, ever since the first compiling of her Publick Liturgy, to keep the mean between the two extremes, of too much stiffness in refusing, and of too much easiness in admitting any variation from it. For, as on the one side common experience sheweth, that where a change hath been made of things advisedly established (no evident necessity so requiring) sundry inconveniences have thereupon ensued; and those many times more and greater than the evils, that were intended to be remedied by such change: So on the other side, the particular Forms of Divine worship, and the Rites and Ceremonies appointed to be used therein, being things in their own nature indifferent, and alterable, and so acknowledged; it is but reasonable, that upon weighty and important considerations, according to the various exigency of times and occasions, such changes and alterations should be made therein, as to those that are in place of Authority should from time to time seem either necessary or expedient. Accordingly we find, that in the Reigns of several Princes of blessed memory since the Reformation, the Church, upon just and weighty considerations her thereunto moving, hath yielded to make such alterations in some particulars, as in their respective times were thought convenient: Yet so, as that the main Body and Essentials of it (as well in the chiefest materials, as in the frame and order thereof) have still continued the same unto this day, and do yet stand firm and unshaken, notwithstanding all the vain attempts and impetuous assaults made against it, by such men as are given to change, and have always discovered a greater regard to their own private fancies and interests, than to that duty they owe to the publick.

By what undue means, and for what mischievous purposes the use of the Liturgy (though enjoined by the Laws of the Land, and those Laws never yet repealed) came, during the late unhappy confusions, to be discontinued, is too well known to the world, and we are not willing here to remember. But when upon His Majesty's happy Restoration, it seemed probable, that amongst other things, the use of the Liturgy also would return of course (the same having never been legally abolished) unless some timely means were used to prevent it; those men who under the late usurped powers had made it a great part of their business to render the people disaffected thereunto, saw themselves in point of reputation and interest concerned (unless they would freely acknowledge themselves to have erred, which such men are very hardly brought to do) with their utmost endeavours to hinder the restitution thereof. In order whereunto divers Pamphlets were published against the Book of *Common Prayer*, the old Objections mustered up, with the addition of some new ones, more than formerly had been made, to make the number swell. In fine, great importunities were used to His Sacred Majesty, that the said Book might be revised, and such Alterations therein, and Additions thereunto made, as should be thought requisite for the ease of tender Consciences: whereunto His Majesty, out of his pious inclination to give satisfaction (so far as could be reasonably expected) to all his subjects of what persuasion soever, did graciously condescend.

In which review we have endeavoured to observe the like moderation, as we find to have been used in the like case in former times. And therefore of the sundry Alterations proposed unto us, we have rejected all such as were either of dangerous consequence (as secretly striking at some established Doctrine, or laudable Practice of the Church of *England*, or indeed of the whole Catholick Church of Christ) or else of no consequence at all, but utterly frivolous and vain. But such Alterations as were tendered to us (by what persons, under what pretences, or to what purpose soever so tendered) as seemed to us in any degree requisite or expedient, we have willingly, and of our own accord assented unto: not enforced so to do by any strength of Argument, convincing us of the necessity of making the said Alterations: For we are fully persuaded in our judgements (and we here profess it to the world) that the Book, as it stood before established by Law, doth not contain in it any thing contrary to the Word of God, or to sound Doctrine, or which a godly man may not with a good Conscience use and submit unto, or which is not fairly defensible against any that shall oppose the same; if it shall be allowed such just and favourable construction as in common Equity ought to be allowed to all human Writings, especially such as are set forth by Authority, and even to the very best translations of the holy Scripture itself.

Our general aim therefore in this undertaking was, not to gratify this or that party in any their unreasonable demands; but to do that, which to our best understandings we conceived might most tend to the preservation of Peace and Unity in the Church; the procuring of Reverence, and exciting of Piety and Devotion in the Publick Worship of God; and the cutting off occasion from them that seek occasion of cavil or quarrel against the Liturgy of the Church. And as to the several variations from the former Book, whether by Alteration, Addition, or otherwise, it shall suffice to give this general account, That most of the Alterations were made, either first, for the better direction of them that are to officiate in any part of Divine Service; which is chiefly done in the Calendars and Rubricks: Or secondly, for the more proper expressing of some words or phrases of ancient usage in terms more suitable to the language of the present times, and the clearer explanation of some other words and phrases, that were either of doubtful signification, or otherwise liable to misconstruction: Or thirdly, for a more perfect rendering of such portions of holy Scripture, as are inserted into the Liturgy; which, in the Epistles and Gospels especially, and in sundry other places, are now ordered to be read according to the last Translation: and that it was thought convenient, that some Prayers and Thanksgivings, fitted to special occasions, should be added in their due places; particularly for those at Sea, together with an office for the Baptism of such as are of Riper Years: which, although not so necessary when the former Book was compiled, yet by the growth of Anabaptism, through the licentiousness of the late times crept in amongst us, is now become necessary, and may be always useful for the baptizing of Natives in our Plantations, and others converted to the Faith.

If any man, who shall desire a more particular account of the several Alterations in any part of the Liturgy, shall take the pains to compare the present Book with the former; we doubt not but the reason of the change may easily appear.

And having thus endeavoured to discharge our duties in this weighty affair, as in the sight of God, and to approve our sincerity therein (so far as lay in us) to the consciences of all men; although we know it impossible (in such variety of apprehensions, humours, and interests, as are in the world) to please all; nor can expect that men of factious, peevish, and perverse spirits should be satisfied with any thing that can be done in this kind by any other than themselves: Yet we have good hope, that what is here presented, and hath been by the Convocations of both Provinces with great diligence examined and approved, will be also well accepted and approved by all sober, peaceable, and truly conscientious Sons of the Church of *England*.

CONCERNING THE
SERVICE OF THE CHURCH

THERE was never any thing by the wit of man so well devised, or so sure established, which in continuance of time hath not been corrupted: As, among other things, it may plainly appear by the Common Prayers in the Church, commonly called *Divine Service*. The first original and ground whereof if a man would search out by the ancient Fathers, he shall find, that the same was not ordained but of a good purpose, and for a great advancement of godliness. For they so ordered the matter, that all the whole Bible (or the greatest part thereof) should be read over once every year; intending thereby, that the Clergy, and especially such as were Ministers in the congregation, should (by often reading, and meditation in God's word) be stirred up to godliness themselves, and be more able to exhort others by wholesome doctrine, and to confute them that were adversaries to the truth; and further, that the people (by daily hearing of holy Scripture read in the Church) might continually profit more and more in the knowledge of God, and be the more inflamed with the love of his true Religion.

But these many years passed, this godly and decent order of the ancient Fathers hath been so altered, broken, and neglected, by planting in uncertain Stories, and Legends, with multitude of Responds, Verses, vain Repetitions, Commemorations, and Synodals; that commonly when any Book of the Bible was begun, after three or four Chapters were read out, all the rest were unread. And in this sort the Book of *Isaiah* was begun in *Advent*, and the Book of *Genesis* in *Septuagesima*; but they were only begun, and never read through: After like sort were other Books of holy Scripture used. And moreover, whereas Saint *Paul* would have such language spoken to the people in the Church, as they might understand, and have profit by hearing the same; The Service in this Church of *England* these many years hath been read in Latin to the people, which they understand not; so that they have heard with their ears only, and their heart, spirit, and mind, have not been edified thereby. And furthermore, notwithstanding that the ancient Fathers have divided the *Psalms* into seven Portions, whereof every one was called a *Nocturn*: Now of late time a few of them have been daily said, and the rest utterly omitted. Moreover, the number and hardness of the Rules called the *Pie*, and the manifold changings of the Service, was the cause, that to turn the Book only was so hard and intricate a matter, that many times there was more business to find out what should be read, than to read it when it was found out.

These inconveniences therefore considered, here is set forth such an Order, whereby the same shall be redressed. And for a readiness in this matter, here is drawn out a Calendar for that purpose, which is plain and easy to be understood; wherein (so much as may be) the reading of holy Scripture is so set forth, that all things shall be done in order, without breaking one piece from another. For this cause be cut off Anthems, Responds, Invitatories, and such like things as did break the continual course of the reading of the Scripture.

Yet, because there is no remedy, but that of necessity there must be some Rules; therefore certain Rules are here set forth;

which, as they are few in number, so they are plain and easy to be understood. So that here you have an Order for Prayer, and for the reading of the holy Scripture, much agreeable to the mind and purpose of the old Fathers, and a great deal more profitable and commodious, than that which of late was used. It is more profitable, because here are left out many things, whereof some are untrue, some uncertain, some vain and superstitious; and nothing is ordained to be read, but the very pure Word of God, the holy Scriptures, or that which is agreeable to the same; and that in such a Language and Order as is most easy and plain for the understanding both of the Readers and Hearers. It is also more commodious, both for the shortness thereof, and for the plainness of the Order, and for that the Rules be few and easy.

And whereas heretofore there hath been great diversity in saying and singing in Churches within this Realm; some following *Salisbury* Use, some *Hereford* Use, and some the Use of *Bangor*, some of *York*, some of *Lincoln*; now from henceforth all the whole Realm shall have but one Use.

And forasmuch as nothing can be so plainly set forth, but doubts may arise in the use and practice of the same; to appease all such diversity (if any arise) and for the resolution of all doubts, concerning the manner how to understand, do, and execute, the things contained in this Book; the parties that so doubt, or diversely take any thing, shall alway resort to the Bishop of the Diocese, who by his discretion shall take order for the quieting and appeasing of the same; so that the same order be not contrary to any thing contained in this Book. And if the Bishop of the Diocese be in doubt, then he may send for the resolution thereof to the Archbishop.

THOUGH it be appointed, That all things shall be read and sung in the Church in the *English* Tongue, to the end that the Congregation may be thereby edified; yet it is not meant, but that when men say Morning and Evening Prayer privately, they may say the same in any language that they themselves do understand.

And all Priests and Deacons are to say daily the Morning and Evening Prayer either privately or openly, not being let by sickness, or some other urgent cause.

And the Curate that ministereth in every Parish-Church or Chapel, being at home, and not being otherwise reasonably hindered, shall say the same in the Parish-Church or Chapel where he ministereth, and shall cause a Bell to be tolled thereunto a convenient time before he begin, that the people may come to hear God's Word, and to pray with him.

OF CEREMONIES
WHY SOME BE ABOLISHED, AND SOME RETAINED

OF such Ceremonies as be used in the Church, and have had their beginning by the institution of man, some at the first were of godly intent and purpose devised, and yet at length turned to vanity and superstition: some entered into the Church by undiscreet devotion, and such a zeal as was without knowledge; and for because they were winked at in the beginning, they grew daily to more and more abuses, which not only for their unprofitableness, but also because they have much blinded the people, and obscured the glory of God, are worthy to be cut away, and clean rejected: other there be, which although they have been devised by man, yet it is thought good to reserve them still, as well for a decent order in the Church, (for the which they were first devised) as because they pertain to edification, whereunto all things done in the Church (as the Apostle teacheth) ought to be referred.

And although the keeping or omitting of a Ceremony, in itself considered, is but a small thing; yet the wilful and contemptuous transgression and breaking of a common order and discipline is no small offence before God, *Let all things be done among you*, saith Saint *Paul*, *in a seemly and due order*: The appointment of the which order pertaineth not to private men; therefore no man ought to take in hand, nor presume to appoint or alter any publick or common Order in Christ's Church except he be lawfully called and authorized thereunto.

And whereas in this our time, the minds of men are so diverse, that some think it a great matter of conscience to depart from a piece of the least of their Ceremonies, they be so addicted to their old customs; and again on the other side, some be so new-fangled, that they would innovate all things, and so despise the old, that nothing can like them, but that is new: it was thought expedient, not so much to have respect how to please and satisfy either of these parties, as how to please God, and profit them both. And yet lest any man should be offended, whom good reason might satisfy, here be certain causes rendered, why some of the accustomed Ceremonies be put away, and some retained and kept still.

Some are put away, because the great excess and multitude of them hath so increased in these latter days, that the burden of them was intolerable; whereof Saint *Augustine* in his time complained, that they were grown to such a number that the estate of Christian people was in worse case concerning that matter, than were the Jews. And he counselled that such yoke and burden should be taken away, as time would serve quietly to do it. But what would Saint *Augustine* have said, if he had seen the Ceremonies of late days used among us; whereunto the multitude used in his time was not to be compared? This our excessive multitude of Ceremonies was so great, and many of them so dark, that they did more confound and darken, than declare and set forth Christ's benefits unto us. And besides this, Christ's Gospel is not a Ceremonial Law, (as much of *Moses*' Law was,) but it is a Religion to serve God, not in bondage of the figure or shadow, but in the freedom of the Spirit; being content only with those Ceremonies which do Serve to a decent Order and godly Discipline, and such as be apt to stir up the dull mind of man to the remembrance of his duty to God, by some notable and special signification, whereby he might be edified. Furthermore, the most weighty cause of the abolishment of certain Ceremonies was, That they were so far abused, partly by the superstitious blindness of the rude and unlearned, and partly by the unsatiable avarice of such as sought more their own lucre, than the glory of God, that the abuses could not well be taken away, the thing remaining still.

But now as concerning those persons, which peradventure will be offended, for that some of the old Ceremonies are retained still: If they consider that without some Ceremonies it is not possible to keep any Order, or quiet Discipline in the Church, they shall easily perceive just cause to reform their judgements. And if they think much, that any of the old do remain, and would rather have all devised anew: then such men granting some Ceremonies convenient to be had, surely where the old may be well used, there they cannot reasonably reprove the old only for their age, without bewraying of their own folly. For in such a case they ought rather to have reverence unto them for their antiquity, if they will declare themselves to be more studious of unity and concord, than of innovations and new-fangleness, which (as much as may be with the true setting forth of Christ's Religion) is always to be eschewed. Furthermore, such shall have no just cause with the Ceremonies reserved to be offended. For as those be taken away which were most abused, and did burden men's consciences without any cause; so the other that remain, are retained for a discipline and order, which (upon just causes) may be altered and changed, and therefore are not to be esteemed equal with God's Law. And moreover, they be neither dark nor dumb Ceremonies, but are so set forth, that every man may understand what they do mean, and to what use they do serve. So that it is not like that they in time to come should be abused as other have been. And in these our doings we condemn no other Nations, nor prescribe any thing but to our own people only: For we think it convenient that every Country should use such Ceremonies as they shall think best to the setting forth of God's honour and glory, and to the reducing of the people to a most perfect and godly living, without error or superstition; and that they should put away other things, which from time to time they perceive to be most abused, as in men's ordinances it often chanceth diversely in divers countries.

RULES TO ORDER
THE SERVICE

1. When some other greater Holy Day falls on Ash Wednesday, on Passion Sunday, on Palm Sunday or one of the fourteen days following, on Ascension Day, or on Whitsunday or on one of the seven days following, it shall be transferred as appropriate to the Friday after Ash Wednesday, or the Tuesday after Passion Sunday, or the Tuesday after Easter 1, or the Friday after Ascension Day, or the Tuesday after Trinity Sunday: except that if Easter Day falls on April 22nd, 24th or 25th, the festival of St Philip and St James shall be observed on the Tuesday of the week following Easter 1, and the festival of St Mark shall be observed on the Thursday of that week.

2. On any Sunday other than Passion Sunday, Palm Sunday, Easter Day, Easter 1, Whitsunday and Trinity Sunday, the service of the Sunday may be replaced by that of a greater Holy Day falling on the Sunday, or of a patronal or dedication festival, or of a Harvest Thanksgiving, or of a baptism or confirmation; or it shall be permissible to transfer a greater Holy Day falling on a Sunday to the following Tuesday, except that St Stephen's Day, Epiphany and All Saints' Day may not be so transferred.

The Annunciation of the Blessed Virgin Mary shall be transferred in accordance with Rule 1 only when it falls on Passion Sunday, on Palm Sunday or one of the fourteen days following.

3. A lesser Holy Day shall lapse if it falls on any Sunday, on Ash Wednesday, on Palm Sunday or any of the fourteen days following, on Ascension Day, or on Whitsunday or any of the seven days following. A lesser Holy Day shall lapse when a greater Holy Day is transferred to the date appointed for it, but the collect of the lesser Holy Day may be used as a memorial. But when a lesser Holy Day is observed as a patronal festival, it may be treated as a greater Holy Day and observed in accordance with rules 1, 2 and 6; it shall take precedence over other greater Holy Days falling on or transferred to the same day.

4. When a greater or lesser Holy Day falls on an Ember Day or a Rogation Day, the service appointed for the Holy Day shall be said and the collect only of the Ember Day or Rogation Day shall be said as a memorial.

5. Except when other provision is made, the collect of the Sunday is to be used on the remaining days of the week; but the collect of Christmas Day, Ash Wednesday and Ascension Day shall be used on the weekdays which follow when no other provision is made.

The collect of every Sunday except Easter Day shall be said at evening prayer on the Saturday evening before; and the collect of other Holy Days except Christmas Day shall be said at evening prayer on the evening before; except that at evening prayer on Christmas Day, Ash Wednesday, Ascension Day and All Saints' Day the collect of the day only shall be said.

6. A service for evening prayer appointed for a greater Holy Day or for a patronal or dedication festival may be used either on the evening of the Holy Day or on the previous evening, or if circumstances require it this service may be held on both evenings; except that on St Stephen's Day, St John's Day, the Innocents' Day, Ash Wednesday, Ascension Day, or All Saints' Day, it may be said on the evening of the Holy Day only.

THE ORDER
HOW THE PSALTER IS APPOINTED TO BE READ

THE Psalter shall be read through once every Month, as it is there appointed, both for Morning and Evening Prayer. But in *February* it shall be read only to the twenty-eighth, or twenty-ninth day of the Month.

And, whereas *January*, *March*, *May*, *July*, *August*, *October*, and *December* have One-and-thirty days apiece; It is ordered, that the same Psalms shall be read the last day of the said months, which were read the day before: So that the Psalter may begin again the first day of the next month ensuing.

And, whereas the 119th Psalm is divided into twenty-two portions, and is over-long to be read at one time; It is so ordered, that at one time shall not be read above four or five of the said portions.

And at the end of every Psalm, and of every such part of the 119th Psalm, shall be repeated this Hymn,

Glory be to the Father, and to the Son: and to the Holy Ghost;

As it was in the beginning, is now, and ever shall be: world without end. Amen.

NOTE, That the Psalter followeth the Division of the Hebrews, and the Translation of the great English Bible, set forth and used in the time of King *Henry* the Eighth, and *Edward* the Sixth.

THE ORDER

HOW THE REST OF HOLY SCRIPTURE IS APPOINTED TO BE READ

THE Old Testament is appointed for the First Lessons at Morning and Evening Prayer, so as the most part thereof will be read every year once, as in the Calendar is appointed.

The New Testament is appointed for the Second Lessons at Morning and Evening Prayer, and shall be read over orderly every year twice, once in the morning and once in the evening, besides the Epistles and Gospels, except the Apocalypse, out of which there are only certain Lessons appointed at the end of the year, and certain Proper Lessons appointed upon divers feasts.

And to know what Lessons shall be read every day, look for the day of the Month in the Calendar following, and there ye shall find the chapters and portions of chapters that shall be read for the Lessons, both at Morning and Evening Prayer, except only the moveable feasts, which are not in the Calendar, and the immoveable, where there is a blank left in the column of Lessons, the Proper Lessons for all which days are to be found in the Table of Proper Lessons.

If Evening Prayer is said at two different times in the same place of worship on any Sunday (except a Sunday for which alternative Second Lessons are specially appointed in the Table,) the Second Lesson at the second time may, at the discretion of the minister, be any chapter from the four Gospels, or any Lesson appointed in the Table of Lessons from the four Gospels.

Upon occasions, to be approved by the Ordinary, other Lessons may, with his consent, be substituted for those which are appointed in the Calendar.

And note, That whensoever Proper Psalms or Lessons are appointed, then the Psalms and Lessons of ordinary course appointed in the Psalter and Calendar (if they be different) shall be omitted for that time.

Note also, That upon occasions to be appointed by the Ordinary, other Psalms may, with his consent, be substituted for those appointed in the Psalter.

If any of the Holy-days for which Proper Lessons are appointed in the Table fall upon a Sunday which is the first Sunday in Advent, Easter Day, Whitsunday, or Trinity Sunday, the Lessons appointed for such Sunday shall be read, but if it fall upon any other Sunday, the Lessons appointed either for the Sunday or for the Holy-day may be read at the discretion of the minister.

NOTE also, That the Collect, Epistle, and Gospel appointed for the Sunday shall serve all the week after, where it is not in this Book otherwise ordered.

PROPER LESSONS

TO BE READ AT

MORNING AND EVENING PRAYER ON THE SUNDAYS AND OTHER HOLY-DAYS THROUGHOUT THE YEAR

LESSONS PROPER FOR SUNDAYS

	MATTINS	EVENSONG	
Sundays of Advent			
The First	Isaiah 1	Isaiah 2	or Isaiah 4, *v.* 2
Second	5	11, to *v.* 11	or 24
Third	25	26	or 28, *v.* 5 to *v.* 19
Fourth	30, to *v.* 27	32	or 33, *v.* 2 to *v.* 23
Sundays after Christmas			
The First	Isaiah 35	Isaiah 38	or Isaiah 40
Second	42	43	or 44
Sundays after the Epiphany			
The First	Isaiah 51	Isaiah 52, *v.* 13 & 53	or Isaiah 54
Second	55	57	or 61
Third	62	65	or 66
Fourth	Job 27	Job 28	or Job 29
Fifth	Proverbs 1	Proverbs 3	or Proverbs 8
Sixth	9	11	15
Septuagesima	Gen. 1 & 2, to *v.* 4	Genesis 2, *v.* 4	or Job 38
Second Lesson	Rev. 21, to *v.* 9	Rev. 21, *v.* 9 to 22, *v.* 6	
Sexagesima	Genesis 3	Genesis 6	or Genesis 8
Quinquagesima	Gen. 9, to *v.* 20	Genesis 12	or Genesis 13
Sundays in Lent			
The First	Gen. 19, *v.* 12 to 30	Gen. 22, to *v.* 20	or Genesis 23
Second	27, to *v.* 41	28	or 32
Third	37	39	or 40
Fourth	42	43	or 45
Fifth	Exodus 3	Exodus 5	or Exod. 6, to *v.* 14
Sixth	9	10	or 11
Second Lesson	Matthew 26	Luke 19, *v.* 28	or Luke 20, *v.* 9 to *v.* 21
Easter Day	Exod. 12, to *v.* 29	Exod. 12, *v.* 29	or Exodus 14
Second Lesson	Rev. 1, *v.* 10 to *v.* 19	John 20, *v.* 11 to *v.* 19	or Revelation 5
Sundays after Easter			
The First	Num. 16, to *v.* 36	Num. 16, *v.* 36	or Num. 17, to *v.* 12
Second Lesson	1 Cor. 15, to *v.* 29	Jn. 20, *v.* 24 to *v.* 30	
Second	Num. 20, to *v.* 14	Num. 20, *v.* 14 to 23 [21, *v.* 10	or 21, *v.* 10
Third	22	23	or 24
Fourth	Deut. 4, to *v.* 23	Deut. 4, *v.* 23 to *v.* 41	or Deut. 5
Fifth	6	9	or 10

	MATTINS	EVENSONG	
Sunday after *Ascension Day*	Deut. 30	Deut. 34	or Joshua 1
Whitsunday	Deut. 16, to *v.* 18	Isaiah 11	or Ezek. 36, *v.* 25
Second Lesson	Romans 8, to *v.* 18	Gal. 5, *v.* 16	or Acts 18, *v.* 24 to 19, *v.* 21
Trinity Sunday	Isa. 6, to *v.* 11	Gen. 18	or Gen. 1 & 2, to *v.* 4
Second Lesson	Rev. 1, to *v.* 9	Eph. 4, to *v.* 17	or Matthew 3

Sundays after Trinity

	MATTINS	EVENSONG	
The First	Joshua 3, *v.* 7 to 4, *v.* 15	Joshua 5, *v.* 13 to 6, *v.* 21	or Joshua 24
Second	Judges 4	Judges 5	or Judges 6, *v.* 11
Third	1 Sam. 2, to *v.* 27	1 Samuel 3	or 1 Sam. 4, to *v.* 19
Fourth	12	13	or Ruth 1
Fifth	15, to *v.* 24	16	or 1 Samuel 17
Sixth	2 Samuel 1	2 Sam. 12, to *v.* 24	or 2 Samuel 18
Seventh	1 Chron. 21	1 Chron. 22	or 1 Chron. 28, to *v.* 21
Eighth	29, *v.* 9 to *v.* 29	2 Chron. 1	or 1 Kings 3
Ninth	1 Kings 10, to *v.* 25	1 Kings 11, to *v.* 15	or 11, *v.* 26
Tenth	12	13	or 17
Eleventh	18	19	or 21
Twelfth	22, to *v.* 41	2 Kings 2, to *v.* 16	or 2 Kings 4, *v.* 8 to *v.* 38
Thirteenth	2 Kings 5	6, to *v.* 24	or 7
Fourteenth	9	10, to *v.* 32	or 13
Fifteenth	18	19	or 23, to *v.* 31
Sixteenth	2 Chron. 36	Nehemiah 1 & 2, to *v.* 9	or Nehemiah 8
Seventeenth	Jeremiah 5	Jeremiah 22	or Jeremiah 35
Eighteenth	36	Ezekiel 2	or Ezek. 13, to *v.* 17
Nineteenth	Ezekiel 14	18	or 24, *v.* 15
Twentieth	34	37	or Daniel 1
Twenty-first	Daniel 3	Daniel 4	or 5
Twenty-second	6	7, *v.* 9	or 12
Twenty-third	Hosea 14	Joel 2, *v.* 21	or Joel 3, *v.* 9
Twenty-fourth	Amos 3	Amos 5	or Amos 9
Twenty-fifth	Micah 4 & 5, to *v.* 8	Micah 6	or Micah 7
Twenty-sixth	Habakkuk 2	Habakkuk 3	or Zephaniah 3
Twenty-seventh	Eccles. 11 & 12	Hag. 2, to *v.* 10	or Malachi 3 & 4

Note.—That the Lessons appointed in the above Table for the Twenty-seventh Sunday after Trinity shall always be read on the Sunday next before Advent.

LESSONS PROPER FOR HOLY-DAYS

	MATTINS	EVENSONG
S. Andrew		
First Lesson	Isaiah 54	Isaiah 65, to *v.* 17
Second Lesson	John 1, *v.* 35 to *v.* 43	John 12, *v.* 20 to *v.* 42
S. Thomas		
First Lesson	Job 42, to *v.* 7	Isaiah 35
Second Lesson	John 20, *v.* 19 to *v.* 24	John 14, to *v.* 8
Nativity of Christ		
First Lesson	Isaiah 9, to *v.* 8	Isaiah 7, *v.* 10 to *v.* 17
Second Lesson	Luke 2, to *v.* 15	Titus 3. *v.* 4 to *v.* 9
S. Stephen		
First Lesson	Genesis 4, to *v.* 11	2 Chr. 24, *v.* 15 to *v.* 23
Second Lesson	Acts 6	Acts 8, to *v.* 9
S. John Evangelist		
First Lesson	Exodus 33, *v.* 9	Isaiah 6
Second Lesson	John 13, *v.* 23 to *v.* 36	Revelation 1
Innocents' Day		
First Lesson	Jeremiah 31, to *v.* 18	Baruch 4, *v.* 21 to *v.* 31
Circumcision		
First Lesson	Genesis 17, *v.* 9	Deuteronomy 10, *v.* 12
Second Lesson	Romans 2, *v.* 17	Col. 2, *v.* 8 to *v.* 18
Epiphany		
First Lesson	Isaiah 60	Isaiah 49, *v.* 13 to *v.* 24
Second Lesson	Luke 3, *v.* 15 to *v.* 23	John 2, to *v.* 12
Conversion of S. Paul		
First Lesson	Isaiah 49, to *v.* 13	Jeremiah 1, to *v.* 11
Second Lesson	Galatians 1, *v.* 11	Acts 26, to *v.* 21
Purification of Virgin Mary		
First Lesson	Exodus 13, to *v.* 17	Haggai 2, to *v.* 10
S. Matthias		
First Lesson	1 Sam. 2, *v.* 27 to *v.* 36	Isaiah 22, *v.* 15
Annunciation of our Lady		
First Lesson	Genesis 3, to *v.* 16	Isaiah 52, *v.* 7 to *v.* 13
Ash Wednesday		
First Lesson	Isaiah 58, to *v.* 13	Jonah 3
Second Lesson	Mark 2, *v.* 13 to *v.* 23	Heb. 12, *v.* 3 to *v.* 18
Monday before Easter		
First Lesson	Lam. 1, to *v.* 15	Lam. 2, *v.* 13
Second Lesson	John 14, to *v.* 15	John 14, *v.* 15
Tuesday before Easter		
First Lesson	Lam. 3, to *v.* 34	Lam. 3, *v.* 34
Second Lesson	John 15, to *v.* 14	John 15, *v.* 14
Wednesday before Easter		
First Lesson	Lam. 4, to *v.* 21	Daniel 9, *v.* 20
Second Lesson	John 16, to *v.* 16	John 16, *v.* 16
Thursday before Easter		
First Lesson	Hosea 13, to *v.* 15	Hosea 14
Second Lesson	John 17	John 13, to *v.* 36
Good Friday		
First Lesson	Genesis 22, to *v.* 20	Isaiah 52, *v.* 13, & 53
Second Lesson	John 18	1 Peter 2
Easter Even		
First Lesson	Zechariah 9	Hosea 5, *v.* 8 to 6, *v.* 4
Second Lesson	Luke 23, *v.* 50	Roman 6, to *v.* 14

	MATTINS	EVENSONG
Monday in Easter Week		
First Lesson	Exodus 15, to *v.* 22	Canticles 2, *v.* 10
Second Lesson	Luke 24, to *v.* 13	Matthew 28, to *v.* 10
Tuesday in Easter Week		
First Lesson	2 Kings 13, *v.* 14 to *v.* 22	Ezekiel 37, to *v.* 15
Second Lesson	John 21, to *v.* 15	John 21, *v.* 15
S. Mark		
First Lesson	Isaiah 62, *v.* 6	Ezekiel 1, to *v.* 15
S. Philip and S. James		
First Lesson	Isaiah 61	Zechariah 4
Second Lesson	John 1, *v.* 43	
Ascension Day		
First Lesson	Daniel 7, *v.* 9 to *v.* 15	2 Kings 2, to *v.* 16
Second Lesson	Luke 24, *v.* 44	Hebrews 4
Monday in Whitsun Week		
First Lesson	Genesis 11, to *v.* 10	Num. 11, *v.* 16 to *v.* 31
Second Lesson	1 Cor. 12, to *v.* 14	1 Cor. 12, *v.* 27, & 13
Tuesday in Whitsun Week		
First Lesson	Joel 2, *v.* 21	Micah 4, to *v.* 8
Second Lesson	1 Thess. 5, *v.* 12 to *v.* 24	1 John 4, to *v.* 14
S. Barnabas		
First Lesson	Deut. 33, to *v.* 12	Nahum 1
Second Lesson	Acts 4, *v.* 31	Acts 14, *v.* 8
S. John Baptist		
First Lesson	Malachi 3, to *v.* 7	Malachi 4
Second Lesson	Matthew 3	Matthew 14, to *v.* 13
S. Peter		
First Lesson	Ezekiel 3, *v.* 4 to *v.* 15	Zechariah 3
Second Lesson	John 21, *v.* 15 to *v.* 23	Acts 4, *v.* 8 to *v.* 23
S. James		
First Lesson	2 Kings 1, to *v.* 16	Jer. 26, *v.* 8 to *v.* 16
Second Lesson	Luke 9, *v.* 51 to *v.* 57	
S. Bartholomew		
First Lesson	Gen. 28, *v.* 10 to *v.* 18	Deut. 18, *v.* 15
S. Matthew		
First Lesson	1 Kings 19, *v.* 15	1 Chron. 29, to *v.* 20
S. Michael		
First Lesson	Genesis 32	Daniel 10, *v.* 4
Second Lesson	Acts 12, *v.* 5 to *v.* 18	Revelation 14, *v.* 14
S. Luke		
First Lesson	Isaiah 55	Ecclus. 38, to *v.* 15
S. Simon and S. Jude		
First Lesson	Isaiah 28, *v.* 9 to *v.* 17	Jer. 3, *v.* 12 to *v.* 19
All Saints		
First Lesson	Wisdom 3, to *v.* 10	Wisdom 5, to *v.* 17
Second Lesson	Heb. 11, *v.* 33, & 12, to *v.* 7	Rev. 19, to *v.* 17

PROPER PSALMS ON CERTAIN DAYS

	MATTINS	EVENSONG
Christmas Day	Psalm 19, 45, 85	Psalm 89, 110, 132
Ash Wednesday	6, 32, 38	102, 130, 143
Good Friday	22, 40, 54	69, 88
Easter Day	2, 57, 111	113, 114, 118
Ascension Day	8, 15, 21	24, 47, 108
Whitsunday	48, 68	104, 145

THE CALENDAR: WITH THE TABLE OF LESSONS

JANUARY hath xxxi Days	MORNING PRAYER 1st Lesson	2nd Lesson	EVENING PRAYER 1st Lesson	2nd Lesson
1 A *Cirumcision of our Lord*				
2 b	Genesis 1, to *v.* 20	Matt. 1, *v.* 18	Gen. 1, *v.* 20 to 2, *v.* 4	Acts 1
3 c	2, *v.* 4	2	3, to *v.* 20	2, to *v.* 22
4 d	3, *v.* 20 to 4, *v.* 16	3	4, *v.* 16	2, *v.* 22
5 e	5, to *v.* 28	4, to *v.* 23	5, *v.* 28 to 6, *v.* 9	3
6 f *Epiphany of our Lord*				
7 g	6, *v.* 9	4, *v.* 23 to 5, *v.* 13	7	4, to *v.* 32
8 A Lucian, Priest and Martyr	8	5, *v.* 13 to *v.* 33	9, to *v.* 20	4, *v.* 32 to 5, *v.* 17
9 b	11, to *v.* 10	5, *v.* 33	12	5, *v.* 17
10 c	13	6, to *v.* 19	14	6
11 d	15	6, *v.* 19 to 7, *v.* 7	16	7, to *v.* 35
12 e	17, to *v.* 23	7, *v.* 7	18, to *v.* 17	7, *v.* 35 to 8, *v.* 5
13 f Hilary, Bishop and Confessor	18, *v.* 17	8, to *v.* 18	19, *v.* 12 to *v.* 30	8, *v.* 5 to *v.* 26
14 g	20	8, *v.* 18	21, to *v.* 22	8, *v.* 26
15 A	21, *v.* 33 to 22, *v.* 20	9, to *v.* 18	23	9, to *v.* 23
16 b	24, to *v.* 29	9, *v.* 18	24, *v.* 29 to *v.* 52	9, *v.* 23
17 c	24, *v.* 52	10, to *v.* 24	25, *v.* 5 to *v.* 19	10, to *v.* 24
18 d Prisca, Roman Virgin and Martyr	25, *v.* 19	10, *v.* 24	26, to *v.* 18	10, *v.* 24
19 e	26, *v.* 18	11	27, to *v.* 30	11
20 f Fabian, Bp of Rome and Martyr	27, *v.* 30	12, to *v.* 22	28	12
21 g Agnes, Roman Virgin and Martyr	29, to *v.* 21	12, *v.* 22	31, to *v.* 25	13, to *v.* 26
22 A Vincent, Spanish Deacon and Martyr	31, *v.* 36	13, to *v.* 24	32, to *v.* 22	13, *v.* 26
23 b	32, *v.* 22	13, *v.* 24 to *v.* 53	33	14
24 c	35, to *v.* 21	13, *v.* 53 to 14, *v.* 13	37, to *v.* 12	15, to *v.* 30
25 d *Conversion of S. Paul*				
26 e	37, *v.* 12	14, *v.* 13	39	15, *v.* 30 to 16, *v.* 16
27 f	40	15, to *v.* 21	41, to *v.* 17	16, *v.* 16
28 g	41, *v.* 17 to *v.* 53	15, *v.* 21	41, *v.* 53 to 42, *v.* 25	17, to *v.* 16
29 A	42, *v.* 25	16, to *v.* 24	43, to *v.* 25	17, *v.* 16
30 b	43, *v.* 25 to 44, *v.* 14	16, *v.* 24 to 17, *v.* 14	44, *v.* 14	18, to *v.* 24
31 c	45, to *v.* 25	17, *v.* 14	45, *v.* 25 to 46, *v.* 8	18, *v.* 24 to 19, *v.* 21

FEBRUARY hath xxviii Days In Leap Year 29 Days	MORNING PRAYER *1st Lesson*	*2nd Lesson*	EVENING PRAYER *1st Lesson*	*2nd Lesson*
1 d Fast	Gen. 46, *v.* 26 to 47, *v.* 13	Matthew 18, 10 *v.* 21	Gen. 47, *v.* 13	Acts 19, *v.* 21
2 e *Purification of* *Mary the Blessed Virgin*		18, *v.* 21 to 19, *v.* 3		20, to *v.* 17
3 f Blasius, an Armenian Bp and Martyr	48	19, *v.* 3 to *v.* 27	49	20, *v.* 17
4 g	50	19, *v.* 27 to 20, *v.* 17	Exodus 1	21, to *v.* 17
5 A Agatha, a Sicilian Virgin and Martyr	Exodus 2	20, *v.* 17	3	21, *v.* 17 to *v.* 37
6 b	4, to *v.* 24	21, to *v.* 23	4, *v.* 27 to 5, *v.* 15	21, *v.* 37 to 22, *v.* 23
7 c	5, *v.* 15 to 6, *v.* 14	21, *v.* 23	6, *v.* 28 to 7, *v.* 14	22, *v.* 23 to 23, *v.* 12
8 d	7, *v.* 14	22, to *v.* 15	8, to *v.* 20	23, *v.* 12
9 e	8, *v.* 20 to 9, *v.* 13	22, *v.* 15 to *v.* 41	9, *v.* 13	24
10 f	10, to *v.* 21	22, *v.* 41 to 23, *v.* 13	10, *v.* 21, & 11	25
11 g	12, to *v.* 21	23, *v.* 13	12, *v.* 21 to *v.* 43	26
12 A	12, *v.* 43 to 13, *v.* 17	24, to *v.* 29	13, *v.* 17 to 14, *v.* 10	27, to *v.* 18
13 b	14, *v.* 10	24, *v.* 29	15, to *v.* 22	27, *v.* 18
14 c Valentine, Bp and Martyr	15, *v.* 22 to 16, *v.* 11	25, to *v.* 31	16, *v.* 11	28, to *v.* 17
15 d	17	25, *v.* 31	18	28, *v.* 17
16 e	19	26, to *v.* 31	20, to *v.* 22	Romans 1
17 f	21, to *v.* 18	26, *v.* 31 to *v.* 57	22, *v.* 21 to 23, *v.* 10	2, to *v.* 17
18 g	23, *v.* 14	26, *v.* 57	24	2, *v.* 17
19 A	25, to *v.* 23	27, to *v.* 27	28, to *v.* 13	3
20 b	28, *v.* 29 to *v.* 42	27, *v.* 27 to *v.* 57	29, *v.* 35 to 30, *v.* 11	4
21 c	31	27, *v.* 57	32, to *v.* 15	5
22 d	32, *v.* 15	28	33, to *v.* 12	6
23 e Fast	33, *v.* 12 to 34, *v.* 10	Mark 1, to *v.* 21	34, *v.* 10 to *v.* 27	7
24 f *S. Matthias,* Apostle and Martyr		1, *v.* 21		8, to *v.* 18
25 g	34, *v.* 27	2, to *v.* 23	35, *v.* 29 to 36, *v.* 8	8, *v.* 18
26 A	39, *v.* 30	2, *v.* 23 to 3, *v.* 13	40, to *v.* 17	9, to *v.* 19
27 b	40, *v.* 17	3, *v.* 13	Lev. 9, *v.* 22 to 10, *v.* 12	9, *v.* 19
28 c	Leviticus 14, to *v.* 23	4, to *v.* 35	16, to *v.* 23	10
29	19, to *v.* 19	Matthew 7	19, *v.* 30 to 20, *v.* 9	12

MARCH hath xxxi Days	MORNING PRAYER 1st Lesson	2nd Lesson	EVENING PRAYER 1st Lesson	2nd Lesson
1 d David, Archb. of Menevia	Leviticus 25, to *v.* 18	Mk. 4, *v.* 35 to 5, *v.* 21	Leviticus 25, *v.* 18 to *v.* 44	Romans 11, to *v.* 25
2 e Cedde, or Chad, Bp of Litchfield	26, to *v.* 21	5, *v.* 21	26, *v.* 21	11, *v.* 25
3 f	Numbers 6	6, to *v.* 14	Num. 9, *v.* 15 to 10, *v.* 11	12
4 g	10, *v.* 11	6, *v.* 14 to *v.* 30	11, to *v.* 24	13
5 A	11, *v.* 24	6, *v.* 30	12	14, & 15, to *v.* 8
6 b	13, *v.* 17	7, to *v.* 24	14, to *v.* 26	15, *v.* 8
7 c Perpetua, Mauritanian Martyr	14, *v.* 26	7, *v.* 24 to 8, *v.* 10	16, to *v.* 23	16
8 d	16, *v.* 23	8, *v.* 10 to 9, *v.* 2	17	1 Cor. 1, to *v.* 26
9 e	20, to *v.* 14	9, *v.* 2 to *v.* 30	20, *v.* 14	1, *v.* 26, & 2
10 f	21, to *v.* 10	9, *v.* 30	21, *v.* 10 to *v.* 32	3
11 g	22, to *v.* 22	10, to *v.* 32	22, *v.* 22	4, to *v.* 18
12 A Gregorius Mag., Bp of Rome & Conf.	23	10, *v.* 32	24	4, *v.* 18, & 5
13 b	25	11, to *v.* 27	27, *v.* 12	6
14 c	Deut. 1, to *v.* 19	11, *v.* 27 to 12, *v.* 13	Deut. 1, *v.* 19	7, to *v.* 25
15 d	2, to *v.* 26	12, *v.* 13 to *v.* 35	2, *v.* 26 to 3, *v.* 18	7, *v.* 25
16 e	3, *v.* 18	12, *v.* 35 to 13, *v.* 14	4, to *v.* 25	8
17 f	4, *v.* 25 to *v.* 41	13, *v.* 14	5, to *v.* 22	9
18 g Edward, King of the W. Saxons	5, *v.* 22	14, to *v.* 27	6	10, & 11, *v.* 1
19 A	7, to *v.* 12	14, *v.* 27 to *v.* 53	7, *v.* 12	11, *v.* 2 to *v.* 17
20 b	8	14, *v.* 53	10, *v.* 8	11, *v.* 17
21 c Benedict, Abbot	11, to *v.* 18	15, to *v.* 42	11, *v.* 18	12, to *v.* 28
22 d	15, to *v.* 16	15, *v.* 42, & 16	17, *v.* 8	12, *v.* 28, & 13
23 e	18, *v.* 9	Luke 1, to *v.* 26	24, *v.* 5	14, to *v.* 20
24 f Fast	26	1, *v.* 26 to *v.* 46	27	14, *v.* 20
25 g *Annunciation of Mary*		1, *v.* 46		15, to *v.* 35
26 A	28, to *v.* 15	2, to *v.* 21	28, *v.* 15 to *v.* 47	15, *v.* 35
27 b	28, *v.* 47	2, *v.* 21	29, *v.* 9	16
28 c	30	3, to *v.* 23	31, to *v.* 14	2 Cor. 1, to *v.* 23
29 d	31, *v.* 14 to *v.* 30	4, to *v.* 16	31, *v.* 30 to 32, *v.* 44	1, *v.* 23 to 2, *v.* 14
30 e	32, *v.* 44	4, *v.* 16	33	2, *v.* 14, & 3
31 f	34	5, to *v.* 17	Joshua 1	4

25

hath xxx Days		MORNING PRAYER		EVENING PRAYER	
		1st Lesson	*2nd Lesson*	*1st Lesson*	*2nd Lesson*
1 g		Joshua 2	Luke 5, *v.* 17	Joshua 3	2 Cor. 5
2 A		4	6, to *v.* 20	5	6, & 7, *v.* 1
3 b	Richard, Bp of Chichester	6	6, *v.* 20	7	7, *v.* 2
4 c	Ambrose, Bp of Millan	9, *v.* 3	7, to *v.* 24	10, to *v.* 16	8
5 d		21, *v.* 43 to 22, *v.* 11	7, to *v.* 24	22, *v.* 11	9
6 e		23	8, to *v.* 26	24	10
7 f		Judges 2	8, *v.* 26	Judges 4	11, to *v.* 30
8 g		5	9, to *v.* 28	6, to *v.* 24	11, *v.* 30 to 12, *v.* 14
9 A		6, *v.* 24	9, *v.* 28 to *v.* 51	7	12, *v.* 14, & 13
10 b		8, *v.* 32 to 9, *v.* 25	9, *v.* 51 to 10, *v.* 17	10	Galatians 1
11 c		11, to *v.* 29	10, *v.* 17	11, *v.* 29	2
12 d		13	11, to *v.* 29	14	3
13 e		15	11, *v.* 29	16	4, to *v.* 21
14 f		Ruth 1	12, to *v.* 35	Ruth 2	4, *v.* 21 to 5, *v.* 13
15 g		3	12, *v.* 35	4	5, *v.* 13
16 A		1 Samuel 1	13, to *v.* 18	1 Samuel 2, to *v.* 21	6
17 b		2, *v.* 21	13, *v.* 18	3	Ephesians 1
18 c		4	14, to *v.* 25	5	2
19 d	Alphege, Archb. of Canterbury	6	14, *v.* 25 to 15, *v.* 11	7	3
20 e		8	15, *v.* 11	9	4, to *v.* 25
21 f		10	16	11	4, *v.* 25 to 5, *v.* 22
22 g		12	17, to *v.* 20	13	5, *v.*22 to 6, *v.* 10
23 A	S. George, Martyr	14, to *v.* 24	17, *v.* 20	14, *v.* 24 to *v.* 47	6, *v.* 10
24 b		15	18, to *v.* 31	16	Philippians 1
25 c	*S. Mark*, Evang. and Martyr		18, *v.* 31 to 19, *v.* 11		2
26 d		17, to *v.* 31	19, *v.* 11 to *v.* 28	17, *v.* 31 to *v.* 55	3
27 e		17, *v.* 55 to 18, *v.* 17	19, *v.* 28	19	4
28 f		20, to *v.* 18	20, to *v.* 27	20, *v.* 18	Col. 1, to *v.* 21
29 g		21	20, *v.* 27 to 21, *v.* 5	22	1, *v.* 21 to 2, *v.* 8
30 A		23	21, *v.* 5	24, & 25, *v.* 1	2, *v.* 8

MAY hath xxxi Days	MORNING PRAYER *1st Lesson*	*2nd Lesson*	EVENING PRAYER *1st Lesson*	*2nd Lesson*
1 b *S. Philip and S. James*, Ap. & M.				Col. 3, to *v.* 18
2 c	1 Samuel 26	Luke 22, to *v.* 31	1 Samuel 28, *v.* 3	3, *v.* 18 to 4, *v.* 7
3 d Invention of the Cross	31	22, *v.* 31 to *v.* 54	2 Samuel 1	4, *v.* 7
4 e	2 Samuel 3, *v.* 17	22, *v.* 54	4	1 Thess. 1
5 f	6	23, to *v.* 26	7, to *v.* 18	2
6 g S. John Evang. ante portam Latinam	7, *v.* 18	23, *v.* 26 to *v.* 50	9	3
7 A	11	23, *v.* 50 to 24, *v.* 13	12, to *v.* 24	4
8 b	13, *v.* 38 to 14, *v.* 26	24, *v.* 13	15, to *v.* 16	5
9 c	15, *v.* 16	John 1, to *v.* 29	16, to *v.* 15	2 Thess. 1
10 d	16, *v.* 15 to 17, *v.* 24	1, *v.* 29	17, *v.* 24 to 18, *v.* 18	2
11 e	18, *v.* 18	2	19, to *v.* 24	3
12 f	19, *v.* 24	3, to *v.* 22	21, to *v.* 15	1 Timothy 1, to *v.* 18
13 g	23, to *v.* 24	3, *v.* 22	24	1, *v.* 18, & 2
14 A	1 Kings 1, to *v.* 28	4, to *v.* 31	1 Kings 1, *v.* 28 to *v.* 49	3
15 b	1 Chron. 29, *v.* 10	4, *v.* 31	3	4
16 c	1 Kings 4, *v.* 20	5, to *v.* 24	5	5
17 d	6, to *v.* 15	5, *v.* 24	8, to *v.* 22	6
18 e	8, *v.* 22 to *v.* 54	6, to *v.* 22	8, *v.* 54 to 9, *v.* 10	2 Timothy 1
19 f Dunstan, Archb. of Canterbury	10	6, *v.* 22 to *v.* 41	11, to *v.* 26	2
20 g	11, *v.* 26	6, *v.* 41	12, to *v.* 25	3
21 A	12, *v.* 25 to 13, *v.* 11	7, to *v.* 25	13, *v.* 11	4
22 b	14, to *v.* 21	7, *v.* 25	15, *v.* 25 to 16, *v.* 8	Titus 1
23 c	16, *v.* 8	8, to *v.* 31	17	2
24 d	18, to *v.* 17	8, *v.* 31	18, *v.* 17	3
25 e	19	9, to *v.* 39	21	Philemon
26 f Augustine, the first Archb. of Canterbury	22, to *v.* 41	9, *v.* 39 to 10, *v.* 22	2 King 1	Hebrews 1
27 g Venerable Bede, Presbyter	2 Kings 2	10, *v.* 22	4, *v.* 8	2, & 3, to *v.* 7
28 A	5	11, to *v.* 17	6, to *v.* 24	3, *v.* 7 to 4, *v.* 14
29 b	6, *v.* 24	11, *v.* 17 to *v.* 47	7	4, *v.* 14, & 5
30 c	8, to *v.* 16	11, *v.* 47 to 12, *v.* 20	9	6
31 d	10, to *v.* 18	12, *v.* 20	10, *v.* 18	7

Day			Morning 1st Lesson	Morning 2nd Lesson	Evening 1st Lesson	Evening 2nd Lesson
1	e	Nicomede, Roman Priest & Martyr	2 Kings 13 to v. 21	John 13, to v. 21	2 Kings 17, to v. 24	Hebrews 8
2	f		17, v. 24	13, v. 21	2 Chron. 12	9
3	g		2 Chron. 13	14	14	10, to v. 19
4	A		15	15	16, & 17, to v. 14	10, v. 19
5	b	Boniface, Bp of Mentz & Martyr	19	16, to v. 16	20, to v. 31	11, to v. 17
6	c		20, v. 31, & 21	16, v. 16	22	11, v. 17
7	d		23	17	24	12
8	e		25	18, to v. 28	26, & 27	13
9	f		28	18, v. 28	2 Kings 18, to v. 9	James 1
10	g		29, v. 3 to v. 21	19, to v. 25	2 Chron. 30, & 31, v. 1	2
11	A	*S. Barnabas*, Apostle and Martyr				
12	b		2 Kings 18, v. 13	19, v. 25	2 Kings 19, to v. 20	3
13	c		19, v. 20	20, to v. 19	20	4
14	d		Is. 38, v. 9 to v. 21	20, v. 19	2 Chron. 33	5
15	e		2 Kings 22	21	2 Kings 23, to v. 21	1 Peter 1, to v. 22
16	f		23, v. 21 to 24, v. 8	Acts 1	24, v. 8 to 25, v. 8	1, v. 22 to 2, v. 11
17	g	S. Alban, Martyr	25, v. 8	2, to v. 22	Ezra 1, & 3	2, v. 11 to 3, v. 8
18	A		Ezra 4	2, v. 22	5	3, v. 8 to 4, v. 7
19	b		7	3	8, v. 15	4, v. 7
20	c	Translation of Edward, King of the W. Saxons	9	4, to v. 32	10, to v.20	5
21	d		Nehemiah 1	4, v. 32 to 5, v. 17	Nehemiah 2	2 Peter 1
22	e		4	5, v. 17	5	2
23	f	Fast	6, & 7, to v. 5	6	7, v. 73 & 8	3
24	g	*Nativity of S. John Baptist*				
25	A		13, to v. 15	7, to v. 35	13, v. 15	1 John 1
26	b		Esther 1	7, v. 35 to 8, v. 5	Esther 2, v. 15, & 3	2, to v. 15
27	c		4	8, v. 5 to v. 26	5	2, v.15
28	d	Fast	6	8, v. 26	7	3, to v. 16
29	e	*S. Peter*, Apostle and Martyr				
30	f		Job 1	9, to v. 23	Job 2	3, v. 16 to 4, v. 7

		MORNING PRAYER		EVENING PRAYER	
		1st Lesson	*2nd Lesson*	*1st Lesson*	*2nd Lesson*
1	g		Job 3	Acts 9, *v.* 23	Job 4	1 John 4, *v.* 7
2	A	Visitation of the Blessed Virgin Mary	5	10, to *v.* 24	6	5
3	b		7	10, *v.* 24	9	2 John
4	c	Transl. of S. Martin, Bp & Confessor	10	11	11	3 John
5	d		12	12	13	Jude
6	e		14	13, to *v.* 26	16	Matt. 1, *v.* 18
7	f		17	13, *v.* 26	19	2
8	g		21	14	22, *v.* 12 to *v.* 29	3
9	A		23	15, to *v.* 30	24	4, to *v.* 23
10	b		25, & 26	15, *v.* 30 to 16, *v.* 16	27	4, *v.* 23 to 5, *v.* 13
11	c		28	16, *v.* 16	29, & 30, *v.* 1	5, *v.* 13 to *v.* 33
12	d		30, *v.* 12 to *v.* 27	17, to *v.* 16	31, *v.* 13	5, *v.* 33
13	e		32	17, *v.* 16	38, to *v.* 39	6, to *v.* 19
14	f		38, *v.* 39, & 39	18, to *v.* 24	40	6, *v.* 19 to 7, *v.* 7
15	g	Swithun, Bp of Winchester, Translation	41	18, *v.* 24 to 19, *v.* 21	42	7, *v.* 7
16	A		Proverbs 1, to *v.* 20	19, *v.* 21	Proverbs 1, *v.* 20	8, to *v.* 18
17	b		2	20, to *v.* 17	3, to *v.* 27	8, *v.* 18
18	c		3, *v.* 27 to 4, *v.* 20	20, *v.* 17	4, *v.* 20 to 5, *v.* 15	9, to *v.* 18
19	d		5, *v.* 15	21, to *v.* 17	6, to *v.* 20	90, *v.* 18
20	e	Margaret, V. & M. at Antioch	7	21, *v.* 17 to *v.* 37	8	10, to *v.* 24
21	f		9	21, *v.* 37 to 22, *v.* 23	10, *v.* 16	10, *v.* 24
22	g	S. Mary Magdalen	11, to *v.* 15	22, *v.* 23 to 23, *v.* 12	11, *v.* 15	11
23	A		12, *v.* 10	23, *v.* 12	13	12, to *v.* 22
24	b	Fast	14, *v.* 9 to *v.* 28	24	14, *v.* 28 to 15, *v.* 18	12, *v.* 22
25	c	*S. James*, Apostle and Martyr				13, to *v.* 24
26	d	S. Anne, Mother to the B. V. Mary	15, *v.* 18	25	16, to *v.* 20	13, *v.* 24 to *v.* 53
27	e		16, *v.* 31 to 17, *v.* 18	26	18, *v.* 10	13, *v.* 53 to 14, *v.* 13
28	f		19, *v.* 13	27	20, to *v.* 23	14, *v.* 13
29	g		21, to *v.* 17	28, to *v.* 17	22, to *v.* 17	15, to *v.* 21
30	A		23, *v.* 10	28, *v.* 17	24, *v.* 21	15, *v.* 21
31	b		25	Romans 1	26, to *v.* 21	16, to *v.* 24

		Morning 1st	Morning 2nd	Evening 1st	Evening 2nd
1 c	Lammas Day	Proverbs 27, to *v.* 23	Romans 2, to *v.* 17	Proverbs 28, to *v.* 15	Matthew 16, *v.* 24 to 17, *v.* 14
2 d		30, to *v.* 18	2, *v.* 17	31, *v.* 10	17, *v.* 14
3 e		Eccles. 1	3	Eccles. 2, to *v.* 12	18, to *v.* 21
4 f		3	4	4	18, *v.* 21 to 19, *v.* 3
5 g		5	5	6	19, *v.* 3 to *v.* 27
6 A	Transfiguration of our Lord	7	6	8	19, *v.* 27 to 20, *v.* 17
7 b	Name of Jesus	9	7	11	20, *v.* 17
8 c		12	8, to *v.* 18	Jeremiah 1	21, to *v.* 23
9 d		Jeremiah 2, to *v.* 14	8, *v.* 18	5, to *v.* 19	21, *v.* 23
10 e	S. Laurence, Archd. of Rome and Martyr	5, *v.* 19	9, to *v.* 19	6, to *v.* 22	22, to *v.* 15
11 f		7, to *v.* 17	9, *v.* 19	8, *v.* 4	22, *v.* 15 to *v.* 41
12 g		9, to *v.* 17	10	13, *v.* 8 to *v.* 24	22, *v.* 41 to 23, *v.* 13
13 A		15	11, to *v.* 25	17, to *v.* 19	23, *v.* 13
14 b		18, to *v.* 18	11, *v.* 25	19	24, to *v.* 29
15 c		21	12	22, to *v.* 13	24, *v.* 29
16 d		22, *v.* 13	13	23, to *v.* 16	25, to *v.* 31
17 e		24	14, & 15, to *v.* 8	25, to *v.* 15	25, *v.* 31
18 f		26	15, *v.* 8	28	26, to *v.* 31
19 g		29, *v.* 4 to *v.* 20	16	30	26, *v.* 31 to *v.* 57
20 A		31, to *v.* 15	1 Cor. 1, to *v.* 26	31, *v.* 15 to *v.* 38	26, *v.* 57
21 b		33, to *v.* 14	1, *v.* 26, & 2	33, *v.* 14	27, to *v.* 27
22 c		35	3	36, to *v.* 14	27, *v.* 27 to *v.* 57
23 d	Fast	36, *v.* 14	4, to *v.* 18	38, to *v.* 14	27, *v.* 57
24 e	S. *Bartholomew*, Apostle and Martyr		4, *v.* 18, & 5		28
25 f		38, *v.* 14	6	39	Mark 1, to *v.* 21
26 g		50, to *v.* 21	7, to *v.* 25	51, *v.* 54	1, *v.* 21
27 A		Ezekiel 1, to *v.* 15	7, *v.* 25	Ezekiel 1, *v.* 15	2, to *v.* 23
28 b	S. Augustine, Bp of Hippo, Conf., & Doct.	2	8	3, to *v.* 15	2, *v.* 23 to 3, *v.* 13
29 c	Beheading of S. John Baptist	3, *v.* 15	9	8	3, *v.* 13
30 d		9	10, & 11, *v.* 1	11, *v.* 14	4, to *v.* 35
31 e		12, *v.* 17	11, *v.* 2 to *v.* 17	13, to *v.* 17	4, *v.* 35 to 5, *v.* 21

Day		1st Lesson (M)	2nd Lesson (M)	1st Lesson (E)	2nd Lesson (E)
1 f	Giles, Abbot and Confessor	Ezekiel 13, v. 17	1 Cor. 11, v. 17	Ezekiel 14, to v. 12	Mark 5, v. 21
2 g		14, v. 12	12, to v. 28	16, v. 44	6, to v. 14
3 A		18, to v. 19	12, v. 28, & 13	18, v. 19	6, v. 14 to v. 30
4 b		20, to v. 18	14, to v. 20	20, v. 18 to v. 33	6, v. 30
5 c		20, v. 33 to v. 44	14, v. 20	22, v. 23	7, to v. 24
6 d		24, v. 15	15, to v. 35	26	7, v. 24 to 8, v. 10
7 e	Evurtius, Bp of Orleans	27, to v. 26	15, v. 35	27, v. 26	8, v. 10 to 9, v. 2
8 f	Nativity of the B. V. Mary	28, to v. 20	16	31	9, v. 2 to v. 30
9 g		32, to v. 17	2 Cor. 1, to v. 23	33, to v. 21	9, v. 30
10 A		33, v. 21	1, v. 23 to 2, v. 14	34, to v. 17	10, to v. 32
11 b		34, v. 17	2, v. 14, & 3	36, v. 16 to v. 33	10, v. 32
12 c		37, to v. 15	4	37, v. 15	11, to v. 27
13 d		47, to v. 13	5	Daniel 1	11, to v. 27 to 12, v. 13
14 e	Holy Cross Day	Daniel 2, to v. 24	6, & 7, v. 1	2, v. 24	12, v. 13 to v. 35
15 f		3	7, v. 2	4, to v. 19	12, v. 35 to 13, v. 14
16 g		4, v. 19	8	5, to v. 17	13, v. 14
17 A	Lambert, Bp and Martyr	5, v. 17	9	6	14, to v. 27
18 b		7, to v. 15	10	7, v. 15	14, v. 27 to v. 53
19 c		9, to v. 20	11, to v. 30	9, v. 20	14, v. 53
20 d	Fast	10, to v. 20	11, v. 30 to 12, v. 14	12	15, to v. 42
21 e	*S. Matthew, Ap., Evang., and M.*		12, v. 14, & 13		15, v. 42, & 16
22 f		Hosea 2, v. 14	Galatians 1	Hosea 4, to v. 13	Luke 1, to v. 26
23 g		5, v. 8 to 6, v. 7	2	7, v. 8	1, v. 26 to v. 57
24 A		8	3	9	1, v. 57
25 b		10	4, to v. 21	11, & 12, to v. 7	2, to v. 21
26 c	S. Cyprian, Archb. of Carthage & M.	13, to v. 15	4, v. 21 to 5, v. 13	14	2, v. 21
27 d		Joel 1	5, v. 13	Joel 2, to v. 15	3, to v. 23
28 e		2, v. 15 to v. 28	6	2, v. 28 to 3, v. 9	4, to v. 16
29 f	*S. Michael and all Angels*				
30 g	S. Hierome, Pr., Conf., & Doct.	3, v. 9	Ephesians 1	Amos 1, & 2, to v. 4	4, v. 16

		Morning 1st	Morning 2nd	Evening 1st	Evening 2nd
1 A	Remigius, Bp of Rhemes	Amos 2, *v.* 4 to 3, *v.* 9	Ephesians 2	Amos 4, *v.* 4	Luke 5, to *v.* 17
2 b		5, to *v.* 18	3	5, *v.* 18 to 6, *v.* 9	5, *v.* 17
3 c		7	4, to *v.* 25	8	6, to *v.* 20
4 d		9	4, *v.* 25 to 5, *v.* 22	Obadiah	6, *v.* 20
5 e		Jonah 1	5, *v.* 22 to 6, *v.* 10	Jonah 2	7, to *v.* 24
6 f	Faith, Virgin and Martyr	3	6, *v.* 10	4	7, *v.* 24
7 g		Micah 1, to *v.* 10	Philippians 1	Micah 2	8, to *v.* 26
8 A		3	2	4	8, *v.* 26
9 b	S. Denys, Areopagite, Bp & Martyr	5	3	6	9, to *v.* 28
10 c		7	4	Nahum 1	9, *v.* 28 to *v.* 51
11 d		Nahum 2	Col. 1, to *v.* 21	3	9, *v.* 51 to 10, *v.* 17
12 e		Habakkuk 1	1, *v.* 21 to 2, *v.* 8	Habakkuk 2	10, *v.* 17
13 f	Transl. of King Edward Conf.	3	2, *v.* 8	Zephaniah 1, to *v.* 14	11, to *v.* 29
14 g		Zeph. 1, *v.*14 to 2, *v.* 4	3, to *v.* 18	2, *v.* 4	11. *v.* 29
15 A		3	3, *v.* 18, & 4	Haggai 1	12, to *v.* 35
16 b		Haggai 2, to *v.* 10	1 Thess. 1	2, *v.* 10	12, *v.* 35
17 c	Etheldrede, Virgin	Zechariah 1, to *v.* 18	2	Zechariah 1, *v.* 18, & 2	13, to *v.* 18
18 d	*S. Luke,* Evangelist		3		13, *v.* 18
19 e		3	4	4	14, to *v.* 25
20 f		5	5	6	14, *v.* 25 to 15, *v.* 11
21 g		7	2 Thess. 1	8, to *v.* 14	15, *v.* 11
22 A		8, *v.* 14	2	9, *v.* 9	16
23 b		10	3	11	17, to *v.* 20
24 c		12	1 Timothy 1, to *v.* 18	13	17, *v.* 20
25 d	Crispin, Martyr	14	1, *v.* 18, & 2	Malachi 1	18, to *v.* 31
26 e		Malachi 2	3	3, to *v.* 13	18, *v.* 31 to 19, *v.* 11
27 f	Fast	3, *v.* 13, & 4	4	Wisdom 1	19, *v.* 11 to *v.* 28
28 g	*S. Simon* & *S. Jude,* Ap. & Martyr		5		19, *v.* 28
29 A		Wisdom 2	6	4, *v.* 7	20, to *v.* 27
30 b		6, to *v.* 22	2 Timothy 1	6, *v.* 22 to 7, *v.* 15	20, *v.* 27 to 21, *v.* 5
31 c	Fast	7, *v.* 15	2	8, to *v.* 19	21, *v.* 5

NOVEMBER hath xxx Days	MORNING PRAYER *1st Lesson*	*2nd Lesson*	EVENING PRAYER *1st Lesson*	*2nd Lesson*
1 d *All Saints' Day*				
2 e	Wisdom 9	2 Timothy 3	Wisdom 11, to *v.* 15	Luke 22, to *v.* 31
3 f	11, *v.* 15 to 12, *v.* 3	4	17	22, *v.* 31 to *v.* 54
4 g	Ecclus. 1 to *v.* 14	Titus 1	Ecclus. 2	22, *v.* 54
5 A	3, *v.* 17 to *v.* 30	2	4, *v.* 10	23, to *v.* 26
6 b Leonard, Confessor	5	3	7, *v.* 27	23, *v.* 26 to *v.* 50
7 c	10, *v.* 18	Philemon	14, to *v.* 20	23, *v.* 50 to 24, *v.* 13
8 d	15, *v.* 9	Hebrews 1	16, *v.* 17	24, *v.* 13
9 e	18, to *v.* 15	2, & 3, to *v.* 7	18, *v.* 15	John 1, to *v.* 29
10 f	19, *v.* 13	3, *v.* 7 to 4, *v.* 14	22, *v.* 6 to, *v.* 24	1, *v.* 29
11 g S. Martin, Bp and Confessor	24, to *v.* 24	4, *v.* 14, & 5	24, *v.* 24	2
12 A	33, *v.* 7 to *v.* 23	6	34, *v.* 15	3, to *v.* 22
13 b Britius, Bishop	35	7	37, *v.* 8 to *v.* 19	3, *v.* 22
14 c	39, to *v.* 13	8	39, *v.* 13	4, to *v.* 31
15 d Machutus, Bp	41, to *v.* 14	9	42, *v.* 15	4, *v.* 31
16 e	44, to *v.* 16	10, to *v.* 19	50, to *v.* 25	5, to *v.* 24
17 f Hugh, Bp of Lincoln	51, *v.* 10	10, *v.* 19	Baruch 4, to *v.* 21	5, *v.* 24
18 g	Baruch 4, *v.* 36, & 5	11, to *v.* 17	Isaiah 1, to *v.* 21	6, to *v.* 22
19 A	Isaiah 1, *v.* 21	11, *v.* 17	2	6, *v.* 22 to *v.* 41
20 b Edmund, King and Martyr	3, to *v.* 16	12	4, *v.* 2	6, *v.* 41
21 c	5, to *v.* 18	13	5, *v.* 18	7, to *v.* 25
22 d Cecilia, Virgin and Martyr	6	James 1	7, to *v.* 17	7, *v.* 25
23 e S. Clement I, Bp of Rome & Martyr	8, *v.* 5 to *v.* 18	2	8, *v.* 18 to 9, *v.* 8	8, to *v.* 31
24 f	9, *v.* 8 to 10, *v.* 5	3	10, *v.* 5 to *v.* 20	8, *v.* 31
25 g Catherine, Virgin and Martyr	10, *v.* 20	4	11, to *v.* 10	9, to *v.* 39
26 A	11, *v.* 10	5	12	9, *v.* 39 to 10, *v.* 22
27 b	13	1 Peter 1, to *v.* 22	14, to *v.* 24	10, *v.* 22
28 c	17	1, *v.* 22 to 2, *v.* 11	18	11, to *v.* 17
29 d Fast	19, to *v.* 16	2, *v.* 11 to 3, *v.* 8	19, *v.* 16	11, *v.* 17 to *v.* 47
30 e *S. Andrew*, Ap. and Martyr				

DECEMBER hath xxxi Days	MORNING PRAYER 1st Lesson	2nd Lesson	EVENING PRAYER 1st Lesson	2nd Lesson
1 f	Isaiah 21, to v. 13	1 Peter 3, v. 8 to 4, v. 7	Isaiah 22, to v. 15	John 11, v. 47 to 12, v. 20
2 g	22, v. 15	4, v. 7	23	12, v. 20
3 A	24	5	25	13, to v. 21
4 b	26, to v. 20	2 Peter 1	26, v. 20, & 27	13, v. 21
5 c	28, to v. 14	2	28, v. 14	14
6 d Nicolas, Bp of Myra in Lycia	29, to v. 9	3	29, v. 9	15
7 e	30, to v. 18	1 John 1	30, v. 18	16, to v. 16
8 f Conception of the B. V. Mary	31	2, to v. 15	32	16, v. 16
9 g	33	2, v. 15	34	17
10 A	35	3, to v. 16	40, to v. 12	18, to v. 28
11 b	40, v. 12	3, v. 16 to 4, v. 7	41, to v. 17	18, v. 28
12 c	41, v. 17	4, v. 7	42, to v. 18	19, to v. 25
13 d Lucy, Virgin and Martyr	42, v. 18 to 43, v. 8	5	43, v. 8	19, v. 25
14 e	44, to v. 21	2 John	44, v. 21 to 45, v. 8	20, to v. 19
15 f	45, v. 8	3 John	46	20, v. 19
16 g O Sapientia	47	Jude	48	21
17 A	49, to v. 13	Revelation 1	49, v. 13	Revelation 2, to v. 18
18 b	50	2, v. 18 to 3, v. 7	51, to v. 9	3, v. 7
19 c	51, v. 9	4	52, to v. 13	5
20 d Fast	52, v. 13, & 53	6	54	7
21 e *S. Thomas*, Ap. and Martyr				
22 f	55	8	56	10
23 g	57	11	58	12
24 A Fast	59	14	60	15
25 b *Christmas Day*				
26 c *S. Stephen*, the first Martyr				
27 d *S. John*, Apostle and Evang.				
28 e *Innocents' Day*		16		18
29 f	61	19, to v. 11	62	19, v. 11
30 g	63	20	64, & 65, to v. 8	21, to v. 15
31 A Silvester, Bp of Rome	65, v. 8	21, v. 15 to 22, v. 6	66	22, v.6

REVISED TABLE OF LESSONS MEASURE, 1922

13 Geo. 5. No. 3

A Measure passed by the National Assembly of the Church of England to amend the Law relating to the Tables of Lessons contained in the Prayer Book. [*4 August* 1922]

1. On and after the First Sunday in Advent next after the passing of this Measure the Tables of Lessons contained in the Schedule to this Measure may be followed at the discretion of the Minister in lieu of the Table of Proper Lessons and the Table of Daily First and Second Lessons contained in the second part of the Schedule to the Prayer Book (Tables of Lessons) Act 1871 and thereby directed to be printed and published in the Book of Common Prayer of the Church of England:

Provided that when the Tables of Lessons contained in the Schedule to this Measure have once been adopted in any Church or Chapel the same Tables shall there be continuously followed at least until the end of the ecclesiastical year.

2. In this Measure the expression 'Minister' means the rector, vicar or perpetual curate of a parish or the curate in charge of a parish.

3. This Measure may be cited as the Revised Tables of Lessons Measure, 1922.

EXCEPT on Septuagesima Sunday, and the Sunday next before Advent, on every Sunday on which Lessons from the Gospels are provided both for Mattins and Evensong, one of such Lessons shall always be read.

It is convenient that, when alternative Lessons are provided, choice be exercised according to some scheme of consecutive reading.

THE REVISED TABLES OF LESSONS
1922

	MORNING PRAYER	EVENING PRAYER
Advent Sunday	(1) Isaiah 1, 1-20	(1) Isaiah 2, or Isaiah 1, 18-end
	(2) John 3, 1-21, or 1 Thess. 4, 13–5, 11	(2) Matt. 24, 1-28 or Rev. 14, 13–15, 4
M.	(1) Isaiah 3, 1-15	(1) Isaiah 4, 2-end
	(2) Mark 1, 1-20	(2) James 1
Tu.	(1) Isaiah 5, 1-17	(1) Isaiah 5, 18-end
	(2) Mark 1, 21-end	(2) James 2, 1-13
W.	(1) Isaiah 6	(1) Isaiah 8, 16–9, 7
	(2) Mark 2, 1-22	(2) James 2, 14-end
Th.	(1) Isaiah 9, 8–10, 4	(1) Isaiah 10, 5-23
	(2) Mark 2, 23–3, 12	(2) James 3
F.	(1) Isaiah 10, 24–11, 9	(1) Isaiah 11, 10–12 end
	(2) Mark 3, 13-end	(2) James 4
S.	(1) Isaiah 13, 1–14, 2	(1) Isaiah 14, 3-27
	(2) Mark 4, 1-20	(2) James 5
Second Sunday in Advent	(1) Isaiah 5	(1) Isaiah 10, 33–11, 9, or Isaiah 11, 10–12 end
	(2) John 5, 19-40, or 2 Peter 3, 1-14	(2) Matt. 24, 29-end, or Rev. 20 and 21, 1-8
M.	(1) Isaiah 17	(1) Isaiah 18
	(2) Mark 4, 21-end	(2) 1 Peter 1, 1-21
Tu.	(1) Isaiah 19, 1-17	(1) Isaiah 19, 18-end
	(2) Mark 5, 1-20	(2) 1 Peter 1, 22–2, 10
W.	(1) Isaiah 21, 1-12	(1) Isaiah 22, 1-14
	(2) Mark 5, 21-end	(2) 1 Peter 2, 11–3, 7
Th.	(1) Isaiah 24	(1) Isaiah 28, 1-13
	(2) Mark 6, 1-13	(2) 1 Peter 3, 8–4, 6
F.	(1) Isaiah 28, 14-end	(1) Isaiah 29, 1-14
	(2) Mark 6, 14-29	(2) 1 Peter 4, 7-end
S.	(1) Isaiah 29, 15-end	(1) Isaiah 30, 1-18
	(2) Mark 6, 30-end	(2) 1 Peter 5
Third Sunday in Advent	(1) Isaiah 25, 1-9	(1) Isaiah 26, or Isaiah 28, 1-22
	(2) Luke 3, 1-17, or 1 Tim. 1, 12–2, 7	(2) Matt. 25, 1-30, or Rev. 21, 9–22, 5
M.	(1) Isaiah 30, 19-end	(1) Isaiah 31
	(2) Mark 7, 1-23	(2) 1 John 1, 1–2, 6
Tu.	(1) Isaiah 38, 1-20	(1) Isaiah 40, 1-11
	(2) Mark 7, 24–8, 10	(2) 1 John 2, 7-end
Ember Day W.	(1) Isaiah 40, 12-end	(1) Isaiah 41
	(2) Mark 8, 11–9, 1	(2) 1 John 3
Th.	(1) Isaiah 42, 1-17	(1) Isaiah 42, 18–43, 13
	(2) Mark 9, 2-32	(2) 1 John 4
Ember Day F.	(1) Isaiah 43, 14–44, 5	(1) Isaiah 44, 6-23
	(2) Mark 9, 33-end	(2) 1 John 5
Ember Day S.	(1) Isaiah 44, 24–45, 13	(1) Isaiah 45, 14-end
	(2) Mark 10, 1-31	(2) 2 John

Fourth Sunday in Advent	(1) Isaiah 32, 1-18	(1) Isaiah 33, 2-22, or Isaiah 35
	(2) Luke 1, 26-45, or 2 Tim. 3, 14–4, 8	(2) Matt. 25, 31-end, or Rev. 22, 6-end
M.	(1) Isaiah 46	(1) Isaiah 47
	(2) Mark 10, 32-end	(2) 3 John
Tu.	(1) Isaiah 48	(1) Isaiah 50, 4-10
	(2) Mark 11, 1-26	(2) Jude
W.	(1) Isaiah 51, 1-16	(1) Isaiah 51, 17–52, 12
	(2) Mark 11, 27–12, 12	(2) 2 Peter 1
Th.	(1) Isaiah 52, 13–53 end	(1) Isaiah 54
	(2) Mark 12, 13-34	(2) 2 Peter 2
F.	(1) Isaiah 56, 1-8	(1) Isaiah 57, 15-end
	(2) Mark 12, 35–13, 13	(2) 2 Peter 3
S.	(1) Isaiah 59	
	(2) Mark 13, 14-end	
Christmas Eve		(1) Zechariah 2, 10-end
		(2) Titus 2, 11–3, 7
Christmas Day	(1) Isaiah 9, 2-7	(1) Isaiah 7, 10-14
	(2) Luke 2, 1-20	(2) 1 John 4, 7-end
S. Stephen	(1) Genesis 4, 1-10	(1) 2 Chron. 24, 15-22
	(2) Acts 6	(2) Acts 7, 54–8, 4
S. John Evangelist	(1) Exodus 33, 9-19	(1) Isaiah 6, 1-8
	(2) John 13, 21-35	(2) 1 John 5, 1-12
Innocents' Day	(1) Jeremiah 31, 1-17	(1) Isaiah 49, 14-25
	(2) Matthew 18, 1-10	(2) Mark 10, 13-16
*Sunday after Christmas Day	(1) Isaiah 40, 1-11	(1) Isaiah 40, 12-end, or Isaiah 41, 1-20
	(2) Luke 2, 22-40, or Colossians 1, 1-20	(2) John 10, 1-16, or Philippians 2, 1-11
December 29	(1) Isaiah 55	(1) Isaiah 60, 1-12
	(2) Luke 12, 1-21	(2) Colossians 2, 6-17
December 30	(1) Isaiah 60, 13-end	(1) Isaiah 61
	(2) Luke 12, 22-34	(2) Colossians 3, 1-17
December 31	(1) Isaiah 62	(1) Deut. 10, 12–11, 1
	(2) Luke 12, 35-48	(2) Luke 21, 25-36
Circumcision	(1) Genesis 17, 1-13	(1) Deuteronomy 30
	(2) Romans 2, 17-end	(2) Romans 13
*Second Sunday after Christmas	(1) Isaiah 42, 1-16	(1) Isaiah 43, 1-13, or Isaiah 43, 14–44, 5
	(2) Matthew 6, 19-end, or Ephesians 1	(2) Matthew 7, 13-27, or 1 John 3
January 2	(1) Isaiah 63, 1-6	(1) Isaiah 63, 7-end
	(2) Matthew 1, 18-end	(2) 1 Thessalonians 1
⅛⅛⅛January 3	(1) Isaiah 64	(1) Isaiah 65, 1-16
	(2) Matthew 2	(2) 1 Thess. 2, 1-16
January 4	(1) Isaiah 65, 17-end	(1) Isaiah 66, 1-9
	(2) Matthew 3, 1–4, 11	(2) 1 Thess. 2, 17–3 end
January 5	(1) Isaiah 66, 10-end	(1) Isaiah 49, 1-13
	(2) Matthew 4, 12–5, 16	(2) Romans 15, 8-21

*Note.—The Lessons of the Sunday after Christmas will be read only when December 29, 30, or 31 is a Sunday, and in the last case the Morning Lessons only.

The Lessons of the Second Sunday after Christmas will be read only when January 2, 3, 4, or 5 is a Sunday, and in the last case the Morning Lessons only.

	MORNING PRAYER	EVENING PRAYER
Epiphany	(1) Isaiah 60	(1) Isaiah 61
	(2) Luke 3, 15-22	(2) John 2, 1-11
M.	(1) Hosea 2, 14-end	(1) Hosea 4, 1-11
Week	(2) Matthew 5, 17-end	(2) 1 Thess. 4, 1-12
days Tu.	(1) Hosea 5, 8–6, 6	(1) Hosea 8
between	(2) Matthew 6, 1-18	(2) 1 Thess. 4, 13–5, 11
Epiphany W.	(1) Hosea 9	(1) Hosea 10
and the	(2) Matthew 6, 19-end	(2) 1 Thess. 5, 12-end
First Th.	(1) Hosea 11	(1) Hosea 12
Sunday	(2) Matthew 7	(2) 2 Thessalonians 1
after F.	(1) Hosea 13, 1-14	(1) Hosea 14
Epiphany	(2) Matthew 8, 1-17	(2) 2 Thessalonians 2
S.	(1) Joel 1	(1) Joel 2, 1-14
	(2) Matthew 8, 18-end	(2) 2 Thessalonians 3
First Sunday	(1) Isaiah 44, 6-end	(1) Isaiah 45, or
after Epiphany		Isaiah 48
	(2) John 1, 19-34, or	(2) John 4, 1-42, or
	Ephesians 2	Col. 1, 21–2, 7
M.	(1) Joel 2, 15-end	(1) Joel 3
	(2) Matthew 9, 1-17	(2) Galatians 1
Tu.	(1) Amos 1	(1) Amos 2
	(2) Matthew 9, 18-34	(2) Galatians 2
W.	(1) Amos 3	(1) Amos 4
	(2) Matthew 9, 35–10, 23	(2) Galatians 3
Th.	(1) Amos 5	(1) Amos 6
	(2) Matthew 10, 24-end	(2) Galatians 4, 1–5, 1
F.	(1) Amos 7	(1) Amos 8
	(2) Matthew 11	(2) Galatians 5, 2-end
S.	(1) Amos 9	(1) Obadiah
	(2) Matthew 12, 1-21	(2) Galatians 6
Second Sunday	(1) Isaiah 49, 1-13	(1) Isaiah 49, 14-end, or
after Epiphany		Isaiah 50, 4-10
	(2) Luke 4, 16-30, or	(2) John 12, 20-end, or
	James 1	1 Thess. 1, 1–2, 12
M.	(1) Jonah 1 and 2	(1) Jonah 3 and 4
	(2) Matthew 12, 22-end	(2) 1 Cor. 1, 1-25
Tu.	(1) Micah 1	(1) Micah 2
	(2) Matthew 13, 1-23	(2) 1 Cor. 1, 26–2 end
W.	(1) Micah 3	(1) Micah 4, 1–5, 1
	(2) Matthew 13, 24-43	(2) 1 Corinthians 3
Th.	(1) Micah 5, 2-end	(1) Micah 6
	(2) Matthew 13, 44-end	(2) 1 Cor. 4, 1-17
F.	(1) Micah 7	(1) Nahum 1
	(2) Matthew 14	(2) 1 Cor. 4, 18–5 end
S.	(1) Nahum 2	(1) Nahum 3
	(2) Matthew 15, 1-28	(2) 1 Corinthians 6
Third Sunday	(1) Hosea 11, 1–12, 6	(1) Hosea 14, or
after Epiphany		Joel 2, 15-end
	(2) John 2, or	(2) John 6, 22-40, or
	James 2	Galatians 1
M.	(1) Habakkuk 1	(1) Habakkuk 2
	(2) 1 Corinthians 7	(2) 1 Corinthians 8

Tu.	(1) Habakkuk 3, 2-end	(1) Zephaniah 1
	(2) 1 Corinthians 9	(2) 1 Cor. 10, 1–11, 1
W.	(1) Zephaniah 2	(1) Zephaniah 3
	(2) 1 Cor. 11, 2-end	(2) 1 Cor. 12, 1-27
Th.	(1) Zechariah 11	(1) Zechariah 13
	(2) 1 Cor. 12, 27–13 end	(2) 1 Cor. 14, 1-19
F.	(1) Malachi 1	(1) Malachi 2, 1-16
	(2) 1 Cor. 14, 20-end	(2) 1 Cor. 15, 1-34
S.	(1) Mal. 2, 17–3, 12	(1) Mal. 3, 13–4, end
	(2) 1 Cor. 15, 35-end	(2) 1 Corinthians 16
Fourth Sunday after Epiphany	(1) Amos 3	(1) Amos 4, 4-end, or Amos 5, 1-24
	(2) John 3, 22-end, or James 3	(2) John 6, 41-end, or 1 Cor. 1, 1-25
M.	(1) Jeremiah 1	(1) Jeremiah 2, 1-13
	(2) 2 Cor. 1, 1–2, 11	(2) 2 Cor. 2, 12–3 end
Tu.	(1) Jeremiah 4, 1-18	(1) Jeremiah 5, 1-19
	(2) 2 Corinthians 4	(2) 2 Corinthians 5
W.	(1) Jeremiah 5, 20-end	(1) Jeremiah 6, 1-21
	(2) 2 Cor. 5, 20–7, 1	(2) 2 Cor. 7, 2-end
Th.	(1) Jeremiah 7, 1-28	(1) Jeremiah 8
	(2) 2 Corinthians 8	(2) 2 Corinthians 9
F.	(1) Jeremiah 9, 1-24	(1) Jeremiah 10
	(2) 2 Corinthians 10	(2) 2 Corinthians 11
S.	(1) Jeremiah 14	(1) Jeremiah 15
	(2) 2 Cor. 12, 1-13	(2) 2 Cor. 12, 14–13 end
Fifth Sunday after Epiphany	(1) Amos 7	(1) Amos 8, or Amos 9
	(2) John 4, 43-end, or James 4	(2) John 7, 14-36, or 1 Cor. 1, 26–2 end
M.	(1) Jeremiah 17, 1-18	(1) Jeremiah 17, 19-end
	(2) Acts 15, 1-29	(2) Acts 15, 30–16, 5
Tu.	(1) Jeremiah 18, 1-17	(1) Jeremiah 20
	(2) Acts 16, 6-end	(2) Acts 17, 1-15
W.	(1) Jeremiah 23, 9-32	(1) Jeremiah 30, 1-22
	(2) Acts 17, 16-end	(2) Acts 18, 1-23
Th.	(1) Jeremiah 31, 1-20	(1) Jeremiah 31, 23-end
	(2) Acts 18, 24–19, 7	(2) Acts 19, 8-20
F.	(1) Jeremiah 33, 1-13	(1) Jeremiah 33, 14-end
	(2) Acts 19, 21-end	(2) Acts 20, 1-16
S.	(1) Ezekiel 1	(1) Ezekiel 11, 1-13
	(2) Acts 20, 17-end	(2) Acts 21, 1-16
Sixth Sunday after Epiphany	(1) Micah 2	(1) Micah 3, or Micah 5, 2-end
	(2) John 5, 24-end or James 5	(2) John 7, 37–8, 11, or 1 Corinthians 3
M.	(1) Ezekiel 12, 17-end	(1) Ezekiel 15
	(2) Acts 21, 17-36	(2) Acts 21, 37–22, 22
Tu.	(1) Ezekiel 17	(1) Ezekiel 20, 27-44
	(2) Acts 22, 23–23, 11	(2) Acts 23, 12-end
W.	(1) Ezekiel 24, 15-end	(1) Ezekiel 27
	(2) Acts 24, 1-23	(2) Acts 24, 24–25, 12
Th.	(1) Ezekiel 31	(1) Ezekiel 33, 1-20
	(2) Acts 25, 13-end	(2) Acts 26

		MORNING PRAYER	EVENING PRAYER
F.	(1)	Ezekiel 36, 22-end	(1) Ezekiel 37, 15-end
	(2)	Acts 27, 1-26	(2) Acts 27, 27-end
S.	(1)	Ezekiel 43, 1-9	(1) Ezekiel 47, 1-12
	(2)	Acts 28, 1-15	(2) Acts 28, 16-end
Septuagesima	(1)	Genesis 1, 1–2, 3	(1) Genesis 2, 4-end, or Jeremaiah 10, 1-16
	(2)	John 1, 1-18, or Rev. 21, 1-14	(2) Mark 10, 1-16, or Rev. 21, 15–22, 5
M.	(1)	Genesis 3	(1) Genesis 4, 1-16
	(2)	Matthew 15, 29–16, 12	(2) Romans 1
Tu.	(1)	Genesis 6, 5-end	(1) Genesis 7
	(2)	Matthew 16, 13-end	(2) Romans 2
W.	(1)	Genesis 18, 1-14	(1) Genesis 8, 15–9, 17
	(2)	Matthew 17, 1-23	(2) Romans 3
Th.	(1)	Genesis 11, 1-9	(1) Genesis 11, 27–12, 10
	(2)	Matthew 17, 24–18, 14	(2) Romans 4
F.	(1)	Genesis 13	(1) Genesis 14
	(2)	Matthew 18, 15-end	(2) Romans 5
S.	(1)	Genesis 15	(1) Genesis 16
	(2)	Matthew 19, 1-15	(2) Romans 6
Sexagesima	(1)	Genesis 3	(1) Genesis 6, 5-end, or Genesis 8, 15–9, 17, or Ecclus. 15, 11-end
	(2)	Mark 9, 33-end, or 1 Corinthians 6	(2) Luke 17, 20-end, or 1 Cor. 10, 1-24
M.	(1)	Genesis 17, 1-22	(1) Genesis 18
	(2)	Matthew 19, 16–20, 16	(2) Romans 7
Tu.	(1)	Genesis 19, 1-3, 12-29	(1) Genesis 21
	(2)	Matthew 20, 17-end	(2) Romans 8, 1-17
W.	(1)	Genesis 22, 1-19	(1) Genesis 23
	(2)	Matthew 21, 1-22	(2) Romans 8, 18-end
Th.	(1)	Genesis 24, 1-28	(1) Genesis 24, 29-end
	(2)	Matthew 21, 23-end	(2) Romans 9
F.	(1)	Genesis 25, 7-11, 19-end	(1) Genesis 26, 1-5, 12-end
	(2)	Matthew 22, 1-33	(2) Romans 10
S.	(1)	Genesis 27, 1-40	(1) Genesis 27, 41–28 end
	(2)	Matthew 22, 34–23, 12	(2) Romans 11
Quinquagesima	(1)	Genesis 12, 1-8, or Ecclus. 1, 1-13	(1) Genesis 13, or Genesis 15, 1-18, or Ecclus. 1, 14-end
	(2)	Matthew 5, 1-16, or 1 Cor. 12, 4-end	(2) Luke 10, 25-37, or 2 Cor. 1, 1-22
M.	(1)	Genesis 29, 1-20	(1) Genesis 31, 1-9, 14-21
	(2)	Matthew 23, 13-end	(2) Romans 12
Tu.	(1)	Genesis 31, 22–32, 2	(1) Genesis 32, 3-30
	(2)	Matthew 24, 1-28	(2) Romans 13
Ash Wednesday	(1)	Isaiah 58	(1) Jonah 3, or Prayer of Manasses
	(2)	Mark 2, 13-22	(2) Heb. 3, 12–4, 13
Th.	(1)	Genesis 33	(1) Genesis 35, 1-20
	(2)	Matthew 24, 29-end	(2) Romans 14
F.	(1)	Genesis 37	(1) Genesis 40
	(2)	Matthew 25, 1-30	(2) Romans 15
S.	(1)	Genesis 41, 1-40	(1) Genesis 41, 41-end
	(2)	Matthew 25, 31-end	(2) Romans 16

	MORNING PRAYER	EVENING PRAYER
First Sunday in Lent	(1) Genesis 18, or Ecclesiasticus 2	(1) Genesis 21, 1-21, or Genesis 22, 1-19, or Baruch 3, 1-14
	(2) Matthew 3, or Hebrews 6	(2) Mark 14, 1-26, or 2 Corinthians 4
M.	(1) Genesis 42	(1) Genesis 43
	(2) Matthew 26, 1-30	(2) Philippians 1
Tu.	(1) Genesis 44	(1) Genesis 45, 1-15
	(2) Matthew 26, 31-56	(2) Philippians 2
Ember Day W.	(1) Genesis 45, 16–46, 7	(1) Genesis 46, 26–47, 12
	(2) Matthew 26, 57-end	(2) Philippians 3
Th.	(1) Genesis 47, 13-end	(1) Genesis 48
	(2) Matthew 27, 1-26	(2) Philippians 4
Ember Day F.	(1) Genesis 49, 1-32	(1) Genesis 49, 33–50 end
	(2) Matthew 27, 27-56	(2) Colossians 1, 1-20
Ember Day S.	(1) Exodus 1, 1-14, 22–2, 10	(1) Exodus 2, 11-22
	(2) Matthew 27, 57–28 end	(2) Col. 1, 21–2, 7
Second Sunday in Lent	(1) Genesis 27, 1-40, or Ecclus. 4, 11-28	(1) Genesis 28, 10-end, or Genesis 32, 3-30, or Ecclus. 5, 1-14
	(2) Matthew 9, 1-17, or Hebrews 6, 11-end	(2) Mark 14, 27-52, or 2 Corinthians 5
M.	(1) Exodus 2, 23–3 end	(1) Exodus 4, 1-23
	(2) John 1, 1-28	(2) Colossians 2, 8–3, 11
Tu.	(1) Exodus 4, 27–6, 1	(1) Exodus 6, 2-13 and 7, 1-7
	(2) John 1, 29-end	(2) Colossians 3, 12–4, 1
W.	(1) Exodus 7, 8-end	(1) Exodus 8, 1-19
	(2) John 2	(2) Colossians 4, 2-end
Th.	(1) Exodus 8, 20–9, 12	(1) Exodus 9, 13-end
	(2) John 3, 1-21	(2) Philemon
F.	(1) Exodus 10, 1-20	(1) Exodus 10, 21–11 end
	(2) John 3, 22-end	(2) Ephesians 1
S.	(1) Exodus 12, 1-20	(1) Exodus 12, 21-36
	(2) John 4, 1-26	(2) Ephesians 2
Third Sunday in Lent	(1) Genesis 37, or Ecclus. 10, 12-24	(1) Genesis 39, or Genesis 42, or Ecclus. 17, 1-26
	(2) Matthew 18, 1-14, or Heb. 10, 19-end	(2) Mark 14, 53-end, or 2 Cor. 5, 20–7, 1
M.	(1) Exodus 12, 37-end	(1) Exodus 13, 1-16
	(2) John 4, 27-end	(2) Ephesians 3
Tu.	(1) Exodus 13, 17–14, 14	(1) Exodus 14, 15-end
	(2) John 5, 1-23	(2) Ephesians 4, 1-16
W.	(1) Exodus 15, 1-26	(1) Exodus 15, 27–16, 35
	(2) John 5, 24-end	(2) Ephesians 4, 17-30
Th.	(1) Exodus 17	(1) Exodus 18
	(2) John 6, 1-21	(2) Ephesians 4, 31–5, 21
F.	(1) Exodus 19	(1) Exodus 20, 1-21
	(2) John 6, 22-40	(2) Ephesians 5, 22–6, 9
S.	(1) Exodus 22, 20–23, 17	(1) Exodus 23, 18-end
	(2) John 6, 41-end	(2) Ephesians 6, 10-end

		MORNING PRAYER	EVENING PRAYER

Fourth Sunday in Lent
(1) Genesis 43, or Ecclus. 27, 30–28, 9
(2) Luke 15, or Hebrews 12

(1) Genesis 44, 1–45, 8, or Genesis 45, 16–46, 7, or Ecclus. 34, 13-end
(2) Mark 15, 1-21, or 2 Corinthians 9

M.
(1) Exodus 24
(2) John 7, 1-24

(1) Exodus 25, 1-22
(2) 1 Timothy 1, 1-17

Tu.
(1) Exodus 28, 1-4, 29-41
(2) John 7, 25-end

(1) Exodus 29, 38–30, 16
(2) 1 Timothy 1, 18–2 end

W.
(1) Exodus 32
(2) John 8, 1-30

(1) Exodus 33
(2) 1 Timothy 3

Th.
(1) Exodus 34
(2) John 8, 31-end

(1) Exodus 35, 20–36, 7
(2) 1 Timothy 4

F.
(1) Exodus 40, 17-end
(2) John 9

(1) Leviticus 6, 8-end
(2) 1 Timothy 5

S.
(1) Lev. 19, 1-18, 30-end
(2) John 10, 1-21

(1) Leviticus 25, 1-24
(2) 1 Timothy 6

Fifth Sunday in Lent
(1) Exodus 2, 23–3 end
(2) Matthew 20, 17-28, or Hebrews 13, 1-21

(1) Exodus 4, 1–23, or Exodus 4, 27–6, 1
(2) Mark 15, 22-end, or 2 Cor. 11, 16–12, 10

M.
(1) Numbers 6
(2) John 10, 22-end

(1) Numbers 9, 15-end, and 10, 29-end
(2) Titus 1, 1–2, 8

Tu.
(1) Numbers 11, 10-33
(2) John 11, 1-44

(1) Numbers 12
(2) Titus 2, 9–3 end

W.
(1) Numbers 13, 1-3, 17-end
(2) John 11, 45-end

(1) Numbers 14, 1-25
(2) 2 Timothy 1

Th.
(1) Numbers 16, 1-35
(2) John 12, 1-19

(1) Numbers 16, 36–17 end
(2) 2 Timothy 2

F.
(1) Numbers 20
(2) John 12, 20-end

(1) Numbers 22, 1-35
(2) 2 Timothy 3

S.
(1) Numbers 22, 36–23, 26
(2) John 13

(1) Numbers 23, 27–24 end
(2) 2 Timothy 4

Palm Sunday
(1) Isaiah 52, 13–53 end
(2) Matthew 26

(1) Exodus 10, 21–11 end, or Isaiah 59, 12-end
(2) Luke 19, 29-end, or John 12, 1-19

M.
(1) Lam. 1, 1-12
(2) John 14, 1-14

(1) Lam. 3, 1-42
(2) John 14, 15-end

Tu.
(1) Isaiah 42, 1-9
(2) John 15, 1-16

(1) Wisdom 2, 1, 12-end
(2) John 15, 17-end

W.
(1) Numbers 21, 4-9
(2) John 16, 1-15

(1) Leviticus 16, 2-24
(2) John 16, 16-end

Th.
(1) Exodus 24, 1-11
(2) John 17

(1) Exodus 16, 2-15
(2) John 13, 1-35

Good Friday
(1) Genesis 22, 1-18
(2) John 18

(1) Isaiah 52, 13–53 end
(2) John 19, 31-end, or 1 Peter 2, 11-end

Easter Eve
(1) Zechariah 9, 9-12
(2) Luke 23, 50-end

(1) Job 19, 21-27
(2) John 2, 13-22

43

Easter Day	(1) Exodus 12, 1-14	(1) Isaiah 51, 1-16, or Exodus 14
	(2) Rev. 1, 4-18	(2) John 20, 1-23, or Romans 6, 1-13
M.	(1) Exodus 15, 1-18	(1) Isaiah 12
	(2) Luke 24, 1-12	(2) 1 Peter 1, 1-12
Tu.	(1) Isaiah 25, 1-9	(1) Isaiah 26, 1-19
	(2) Matthew 28, 1-10	(2) 1 Peter 1, 13-end
W.	(1) Isaiah 61	(1) Canticles 2, 8-end
	(2) John 21, 1-14	(2) Rev. 7, 9-end
Th.	(1) 1 Kings 17, 8-end	(1) Daniel 12
	(2) Mark 5, 21-end	(2) 1 Thess. 4, 13-end
F.	(1) 2 Kings 4, 8-37	(1) Zeph. 3, 14-end
	(2) Luke 7, 11-17	(2) Acts 17, 16-31
S.	(1) Jeremiah 31, 1-14	(1) Micah 7, 7-end
	(2) John 11, 17-44	(2) Acts 26, 1-23
First Sunday after Easter	(1) Isaiah 52, 1-12	(1) Isaiah 54, or Ezekiel 37, 1-14
	(2) Luke 24, 13-35, or 1 Cor. 15, 1-28	(2) John 20, 24-end, or Revelation 5
M.	(1) Deut. 6, 3-18	(1) Deut. 1, 19-end
	(2) Acts 1, 1-14	(2) Acts 1, 15-end
Tu.	(1) Deut. 2, 1-25	(1) Deut. 2, 26-3, 5
	(2) Acts 2, 1-21	(2) Acts 2, 22-end
W.	(1) Deut. 3, 18-end	(1) Deut. 4, 1-24
	(2) Acts 3, 1-4, 4	(2) Acts 4, 5-31
Th.	(1) Deut. 4, 25-40	(1) Deut. 5, 1-21
	(2) Acts 4, 32-5, 11	(2) Acts 5, 12-6, 7
F.	(1) Deut. 5, 22-end	(1) Deuteronomy 6
	(2) Acts 6, 8-7, 16	(2) Acts 7, 17-34
S.	(1) Deut. 7, 1-11	(1) Deut. 7, 12-end
	(2) Acts 7, 35-8, 4	(2) Acts 8, 4-25
Second Sunday after Easter	(1) Exodus 16, 2-15, or Isaiah 55	(1) Exodus 32, or Exodus 33, 7-end, or Isaiah 56, 1-8
	(2) John 5, 19-29, or 1 Cor. 15, 35-end	(2) John 21, or Phil. 3, 7-end
M.	(1) Deuteronomy 8	(1) Deut. 9, 1-10
	(2) Acts 8, 26-end	(2) Acts 9, 1-31
Tu.	(1) Deut. 9, 11-end	(1) Deuteronomy 10
	(2) Acts 9, 32-end	(2) Acts 10, 1-23
W.	(1) Deut. 11, 1-12	(1) Deut. 11, 13-end
	(2) Acts 10, 24-end	(2) Acts 11, 1-18
Th.	(1) Deut. 12, 1-14	(1) Deut. 15, 1-18
	(2) Acts 11, 19-end	(2) Acts 12, 1-24
F.	(1) Deut. 16, 1-20	(1) Deut. 17, 8-end
	(2) Acts 12, 25-13, 12	(2) Acts 13, 13-43
S.	(1) Deut. 18, 9-end	(1) Deuteronomy 19
	(2) Acts 13, 44-14, 7	(2) Acts 14, 8-end
Third Sunday after Easter	(1) Num. 22, 1-35, or Isaiah 57, 15-end	(1) Num. 22, 36-23, 26, or Num. 23, 27-24 end, or Isaiah 59
	(2) Mark 5, 21-end, or Acts 2, 22-end	(2) John 11, 1-44, or Revelation 2, 1-17

M.	(1) Deut. 21, 22–22, 8	(1) Deut. 24, 5-end
	(2) Acts 15, 1-21	(2) Acts 15, 22-35
Tu.	(1) Deuteronomy 26	(1) Deut. 28, 58-end
	(2) Acts 15, 36–16, 5	(2) Acts 16, 6-end
W.	(1) Deut. 29, 10-end	(1) Deuteronomy 30
	(2) Acts 17, 1-15	(2) Acts 17, 16-end
Th.	(1) Deut. 31, 1-13	(1) Deut. 31, 14-29
	(2) Acts 18, 1-23	(2) Acts 18, 24–19, 7
F.	(1) Deut. 31, 30–32, 14	(1) Deut. 32, 15-47
	(2) Acts 19, 8–20	(2) Acts 19, 21-end
S.	(1) Deuteronomy 33	(1) Deut. 32, 48-end, and 34
	(2) Acts 20, 1-16	(2) Acts 20, 17-end
Fourth Sunday after Easter	(1) Deut. 4, 1-24, or Isaiah 60	(1) Deut. 4, 25-40, or Deuteronomy 5, or Isaiah 61
	(2) Luke 16, 19-end, or Acts 3	(2) Luke 7, 1-35, or Rev. 2, 18–3, 6
M.	(1) Joshua 1	(1) Joshua 2
	(2) Acts 21, 1-16	(2) Acts 21, 17-36
Tu.	(1) Joshua 3	(1) Joshua 4, 1–5, 1
	(2) Acts 21, 37–22, 22	(2) Acts 22, 23–23, 11
W.	(1) Joshua 5, 13–6, 20	(1) Joshua 7
	(2) Acts 23, 12-end	(2) Acts 24, 1-23
Th.	(1) Joshua 9, 3-end	(1) Joshua 10, 1-15
	(2) Acts 24, 24–25, 12	(2) Acts 25, 13-end
F.	(1) Joshua 21, 43–22, 8	(1) Joshua 22, 9-end
	(2) Acts 26	(2) Acts 27
S.	(1) Joshua 23	(1) Joshua 24, 1-28
	(2) Acts 28, 1-15	(2) Acts 28, 16-end
Fifth Sunday after Easter	(1) Deuteronomy 6, or Isaiah 62	(1) Deuteronomy 8, or Deut. 10, 12–11, 1, or Isaiah 63, 7-end
	(2) Luke 20, 27–21, 4, or Acts 4, 1-33	(2) John 6, 47-69, or Revelation 3, 7-end
M.	(1) Deut. 7, 6-13	(1) Deut. 11, 8-21
Rogation Days	(2) Matthew 6, 5-18	(2) Matthew 6, 19-end
Tu.	(1) Deut. 28, 1-14	(1) 1 Kings 8, 22-43
	(2) Luke 5, 1-11	(2) James 5, 1-18
W.	(1) Joel 2, 21-27	(1) Song of Three Children 29-37
	(2) John 6, 22-40	(2) Luke 24, 36-end
Ascension Day	(1) 2 Kings 2, 1-15	(1) Daniel 7, 9-10, 13-14
	(2) Ephesians 4, 1-16	(2) Hebrews 1
F.	(1) Judges 2, 6-end	(1) Judges 4
	(2) Hebrews 2	(2) Hebrews 3
S.	(1) Judges 5	(1) Judges 6, 1-24
	(2) Hebrews 4, 1-13	(2) Hebrews 4, 14–5, 10
Sunday after Ascension	(1) Deuteronomy 26, or Isaiah 64	(1) Deuteronomy 30, or Deuteronomy 34, or Isaiah 65, 17-end
	(2) John 14, 1-14, or Ephesians 1, 3-end	(2) John 16, 5-end, or Acts 1, 1-14

		MORNING PRAYER	EVENING PRAYER
M.		(1) Judges 6, 25-end	(1) Judges 7
		(2) Hebrews 5, 11–6 end	(2) Hebrews 7
Tu.		(1) Judges 8, 32–9, 24	(1) Judges 10, 17–11, 28
		(2) Hebrews 8	(2) Hebrews 9, 1-14
W.		(1) Judges 11, 29–12, 7	(1) Judges 13
		(2) Hebrews 9, 15-end	(2) Hebrews 10, 1-18
Th.		(1) Judges 14	(1) Judges 16, 4-end
		(2) Hebrews 10, 19-end	(2) Hebrews 11
F.		(1) Ruth 1	(1) Ruth 2
		(2) Hebrews 12, 1-13	(2) Hebrews 12, 14-end
S.		(1) Ruth 4, 1-17	(1) Deut. 16, 9-12
		(2) Hebrews 13	(2) Luke 11, 1-13
Whitsunday		(1) Joel 2, 28-end	(1) Isaiah 11, 1-9, or Ezekiel 36, 22-36
		(2) Romans 8, 1-17	(2) Romans 8, 18-end, or Gal. 5, 13-end
M.		(1) Ezekiel 11, 14-20	(1) Wisdom 1, 1-7
		(2) Acts 2, 12-36	(2) Acts 2, 37-end
Tu.		(1) Ezekiel 37, 1-14	(1) Wisdom 7, 15–8, 1
		(2) 1 Cor. 12, 1-13	(2) 1 Cor. 12, 27–13 end
Ember Day	W.	(1) 1 Kings 19, 1-18	(1) Wisdom 9
		(2) 1 Corinthians 2	(2) 1 Corinthians 3
	Th.	(1) 2 Samuel 23, 1-5	(1) Exodus 35, 30–36, 1
		(2) Ephesians 6, 10-20	(2) Acts 18, 24–19, 7
Ember Day	F.	(1) Num. 11, 16-17, 24-29	(1) Jeremiah 31, 31-34
		(2) 2 Cor. 5, 14–6, 10	(2) 2 Corinthians 3
Ember Day	S.	(1) Num. 27, 15-end	(1) Isaiah 61
		(2) Matt. 9, 35–10, 20	(2) Acts 20, 17-35
Trinity Sunday		(1) Isaiah 6, 1-18	(1) Exodus 34, 1-10, or Num. 6, 22-end, or Isaiah 40, 12-end
		(2) Mark 1, 1-11, or 1 Peter 1, 1-12	(2) Matt. 28, 16-end, or Ephesians 3
M.		(1) 1 Samuel 1	(1) 1 Samuel 2, 1-21
		(2) James 1	(2) Luke 1, 1-23
Tu.		(1) 1 Samuel 2, 22-end	(1) 1 Samuel 3
		(2) James 2, 1-13	(2) Luke 1, 24-56
W.		(1) 1 Samuel 4	(1) 1 Samuel 7
		(2) James 2, 14-end	(2) Luke 1, 57-end
Th.		(1) 1 Samuel 8	(1) 1 Samuel 9, 1-25
		(2) James 3	(2) Matthew 1, 18-end
F.		(1) 1 Samuel 9, 26–10, 16	(1) 1 Samuel 10, 17-end
		(2) James 4	(2) Luke 2, 1-39
S.		(1) 1 Samuel 11	(1) 1 Samuel 12
		(2) James 5	(2) Matthew 2
First Sunday after Trinity		(1) Joshua 1, or Job 1	(1) Joshua 5, 13–6, 20, or Joshua 24, or Job 2
		(2) Mark 2, 1-22, or Romans 1	(2) Matthew 1, 18-end, or Acts 8, 26-end
M.		(1) 1 Samuel 13	(1) 1 Samuel 14, 1-23
		(2) 1 Peter 1, 1-21	(2) Luke 2, 40-end

		MORNING PRAYER	EVENING PRAYER
Tu.	(1)	1 Samuel 14, 24-48	(1) 1 Samuel 15
	(2)	1 Peter 1, 22–2, 10	(2) Luke 3, 1-22
W.	(1)	1 Samuel 16	(1) 1 Samuel 17, 1-30
	(2)	1 Peter 2, 11–3, 7	(2) Luke 4, 1-30
Th.	(1)	1 Samuel 17, 31-54	(1) 1 Samuel 17, 55–18, 16
	(2)	1 Peter 3, 8–4, 6	(2) Luke 5, 1-11
F.	(1)	1 Samuel 19	(1) 1 Samuel 20, 1-17
	(2)	1 Peter 4, 7-end	(2) Mark 1, 21-39
S.	(1)	1 Samuel 20, 18-end	(1) 1 Samuel 21, 1–22, 5
	(2)	1 Peter 5	(2) Mark 1, 40–2, 12
Second Sunday after Trinity	(1)	Judges 4 or 5, or Job 3	(1) Judges 6, 33–7, 23, or Ruth 1, or Job 5, 6-end
	(2)	Mark 2, 23–3, 19, or Romans 5	(2) Matthew 2, or Acts 9, 1-31
M.	(1)	1 Samuel 22, 6-end	(1) 1 Samuel 23
	(2)	2 Peter 1	(2) Luke 5, 27-end
Tu.	(1)	1 Samuel 24	(1) 1 Samuel 25, 2-42
	(2)	2 Peter 2	(2) Luke 6, 1-19
W.	(1)	1 Samuel 26	(1) 1 Samuel 28, 3-end
	(2)	2 Peter 3	(2) Matthew 5, 1-16
Th.	(1)	1 Samuel 31	(1) 2 Samuel 1
	(2)	Jude	(2) Matthew 5, 17-end
F.	(1)	2 Samuel 2, 1–3, 1	(1) 2 Samuel 3, 17-end
	(2)	1 John 1, 1–2, 6	(2) Matthew 6, 1-23
S.	(1)	2 Sam. 5, 1-12, 17-end	(1) 2 Samuel 6
	(2)	1 John 2, 7-end	(2) Matthew 7
Third Sunday after Trinity	(1)	1 Samuel 1, or Job 19	(1) 1 Samuel 2, 1-21, or 1 Samuel 3, or Job 28
	(2)	Mark 4, 1-29, or Romans 6	(2) Matt. 4, 23–5, 16, or Acts 10
M.	(1)	2 Samuel 7	(1) 2 Samuel 9
	(2)	1 John 3, 1-12	(2) Luke 7, 1-17
Tu.	(1)	2 Samuel 11	(1) 2 Samuel 12, 1-23
	(2)	1 John 3, 13–4, 6	(2) Matthew 11, 2-end
W.	(1)	2 Samuel 13, 38–14, 24	(1) 2 Samuel 14, 25–15, 12
	(2)	1 John 4, 7-end	(2) Luke 7, 36–8, 3
Th.	(1)	2 Samuel 15, 13-end	(1) 2 Samuel 16, 1-19
	(2)	1 John 5	(2) Matthew 12, 22-end
F.	(1)	2 Samuel 17, 1-23	(1) 2 Samuel 17, 24–18, 18
	(2)	2 John	(2) Matthew 13, 1-23
S.	(1)	2 Samuel 18, 19-end	(1) 2 Samuel 19, 1-23
	(2)	3 John	(2) Matthew 13, 24-43
Fourth Sunday after Trinity	(1)	1 Samuel 12, or Job 29	(1) 1 Samuel 15, 1-31, or 1 Samuel 16, or Job 38
	(2)	Mark 6, 1-32, or Romans 12	(2) Matthew 5, 17-end, or Acts 13, 1-26
M.	(1)	2 Samuel 19, 24-end	(1) 2 Samuel 23, 1-17
	(2)	1 Thessalonians 1	(2) Matthew 13, 44-end

Tu.	(1) 2 Samuel 24	(1) 1 Kings 1, 5-31
	(2) 1 Thess. 2, 1-16	(2) Mark 4, 35–5, 20
W.	(1) 1 Kings 1, 32-end	(1) 1 Chron. 22, 2-end
	(2) 1 Thess. 2, 17–3 end	(2) Mark 5, 21-end
Th.	(1) 1 Chron. 28, 1-10	(1) 1 Chron. 28, 20–29, 9
	(2) 1 Thess. 4, 1-12	(2) Matthew 9, 27–10, 23
F.	(1) 1 Chron. 29, 10-end	(1) 1 Kings 3
	(2) 1 Thess. 4, 13–5, 11	(2) Matthew 10, 24-end
S.	(1) 1 Kings 4, 21-end	(1) 1 Kings 5
	(2) 1 Thess. 5, 12-end	(2) Mark 6, 7-44
Fifth Sunday after Trinity	(1) 1 Samuel 17, 1-54, or Wisdom 1	(1) 1 Samuel 20, 1-17, or 1 Samuel 26, or Wisdom 2
	(2) Mark 6, 53–7, 23, or Romans 13	(2) Matthew 6, or Acts 14
M.	(1) 1 Kings 6, 1-14	(1) 1 Kings 1, 21
	(2) 2 Thessalonians 1	(2) Matthew 14, 22-end
Tu.	(1) 1 Kings 8, 22-53	(1) 1 Kings 8, 54–9, 9
	(2) 2 Thessalonians 2	(2) Mark 8, 1-26
W.	(1) 1 Kings 10	(1) 1 Kings 11, 1-13
	(2) 2 Thessalonians 3	(2) Matthew 16, 13-end
Th.	(1) 1 Kings 11, 26-end	(1) 1 Kings 12, 1-24
	(2) Galatians 1	(2) Matthew 17
F.	(1) 1 Kings 12, 25–13, 10	(1) 1 Kings 13, 11-end
	(2) Galatians 2	(2) Mark 9, 33-end
S.	(1) 1 Kings 14, 1-20	(1) 2 Chronicles 12
	(2) Galatians 3	(2) Matthew 18, 12-end
Sixth Sunday after Trinity	(1) 2 Samuel 1, or Wisdom 3, 1-9	(1) 2 Samuel 7, or 2 Samuel 12, 1-23, or Wisdom 4, 7-14
	(2) Mark 7, 24–8, 10 or Romans 14, 1–15, 7	(2) Matthew 7, or Acts 15, 1-31
M.	(1) 2 Chronicles 13	(1) 2 Chronicles 14
	(2) Galatians 4, 1–5, 1	(2) Luke 9, 51-end
Tu.	(1) 2 Chronicles 15	(1) 2 Chronicles 16
	(2) Galatians 5, 2-end	(2) Luke 10, 1-22
W.	(1) 1 Kings 16, 15-end	(1) 1 Kings 17
	(2) Galatians 6	(2) Luke 10, 23–11, 13
Th.	(1) 1 Kings 18, 1-16	(1) 1 Kings 18, 17-end
	(2) 1 Cor. 1, 1-25	(2) Luke 12, 1-34
F.	(1) 1 Kings 19	(1) 1 Kings 21
	(2) 1 Cor. 1, 26–2 end	(2) Luke 12, 35-end
S.	(1) 1 Kings 22, 1-40	(1) 2 Chronicles 20, 1-30
	(2) 1 Corinthians 3	(2) Luke 13
Seventh Sunday after Trinity	(1) 2 Samuel 18, or Wisdom 5, 1-16	(1) 1 Kings 3, or 1 Kings 8, 22-61, or Wisdom 6, 1-11
	(2) Mark 9, 2-32, or Philippians 1	(2) Matt. 9, 35–10, 23, or Acts 16, 6-end
M.	(1) 2 Kings 1	(1) 2 Kings 2, 1-22
	(2) 1 Cor. 4, 1-17	(2) Luke 14, 1-33

Tu.	(1) 2 Kings 4, 1-37	(1) 2 Kings 5
	(2) 1 Cor. 4, 18–5 end	(2) Luke 15
W.	(1) 2 Kings 6, 1-23	(1) 2 Kings 6, 24–7, 2
	(2) 1 Corinthians 6	(2) Luke 16
Th.	(1) 2 Kings 7, 3-end	(1) 2 Kings 8, 1-15
	(2) 1 Corinthians 7	(2) Luke 17
F.	(1) 2 Kings 9	(1) 2 Kings 11, 1-20
	(2) 1 Corinthians 8	(2) Luke 18, 1-14
S.	(1) 2 Kings 11, 21–12 end	(1) 2 Kings 13
	(2) 1 Corinthians 9	(2) Matthew 20, 1-16
Eighth Sunday after Trinity	(1) 1 Kings 10, 1-13, or Wisdom 6, 12-end	(1) 1 Kings 12, or 1 Kings 13, 1-32, or Wisdom 7, 15–8, 1
	(2) Mark 10, 1-31, or Philippians 2	(2) Matt. 10, 24-end, or Acts 17, 16-end
M.	(1) 2 Kings 14	(1) 2 Chronicles 26
	(2) 1 Cor. 10, 1–11, 1	(2) Mark 10, 32-end
Tu.	(1) 2 Kings 15, 17-end	(1) 2 Kings 16
	(2) 1 Cor. 11, 2-end	(2) Luke 19, 1-28
W.	(1) Isaiah 7, 1-17	(1) Isaiah 8, 1-18
	(2) 1 Cor. 12, 1-27	(2) Luke 19, 29-44
Th.	(1) 2 Kings 17, 1-23	(1) 2 Kings 17, 24-end
	(2) 1 Cor. 12, 27–13 end	(2) Mark 11, 11-12, 12
F.	(1) 2 Kings 18, 1-8	(1) 2 Chronicles 30
	(2) 1 Cor. 14, 1-19	(2) Matthew 22, 1-22
S.	(1) 2 Kings 18, 13-end	(1) 2 Kings 19
	(2) 1 Cor. 14, 20-end	(2) Matthew 22, 23-end
Ninth Sunday after Trinity	(1) 2 Kings 17, or Wisdom 11, 21–12, 2	(1) 1 Kings 18, or 1 Kings 19, or Wisdom 12, 12-21
	(2) Luke 1, 1-25, or Philippians 3	(2) Matthew 11, or Acts 20, 17-end
M.	(1) 2 Kings 20	(1) 2 Chronicles 33
	(2) 1 Cor. 15, 1-34	(2) Matthew 23
Tu.	(1) 2 Kings 22	(1) 2 Kings 23, 1-20
	(2) 1 Cor. 15, 35-end	(2) Mark 12, 41–13, 13
W.	(1) 2 Kings 23, 21-35	(1) 2 Kings 23, 36–24, 17
	(2) 1 Corinthians 16	(2) Mark 13, 14-end
Th.	(1) 2 Kings 24, 18–25, 7	(1) 2 Kings 25, 8-end
	(2) 2 Cor. 1, 1-22	(2) Matthew 25, 1-30
F.	(1) Jeremiah 19	(1) Jeremiah 21, 1-10
	(2) 2 Cor. 1, 23–2 end	(2) Matthew 25, 31-end
S.	(1) Jeremiah 22, 20–23, 8	(1) Jeremiah 24
	(2) 2 Corinthians 3	(2) Mark 14, 1-26
Tenth Sunday after Trinity	(1) 1 Kings 21, or Ecclus. 3, 17-29	(1) 1 Kings 22, 1-40, or 2 Kings 4, 8-37, or Ecclus. 11, 7-28
	(2) Luke 1, 26-56, or Philippians 4	(2) Matt. 13, 24-52, or Acts 27

M.	(1) Jeremiah 25, 1-14	(1) Jeremiah 27, 2-end
	(2) 2 Corinthians 4	(2) Mark 14, 27-52
Tu.	(1) Jeremiah 28	(1) Jeremiah 29, 1-20
	(2) 2 Corinthians 5	(2) Mark 14, 53-end
W.	(1) Jeremiah 32, 1-25	(1) Jeremiah 32, 26-end
	(2) 2 Cor. 5, 20–7, 1	(2) Mark 15, 1-41
Th.	(1) Jeremiah 33	(1) Jeremiah 34, 8-end
	(2) 2 Cor. 7, 2-end	(2) Luke 23, 33-end
F.	(1) Jeremiah 37	(1) Jeremiah 38, 1-13
	(2) 2 Corinthians 8	(2) Mark 15, 42–16 end
S.	(1) Jeremiah 38, 14-end	(1) Jeremiah 39
	(2) 2 Corinthians 9	(2) Luke 24, 13-end
Eleventh Sunday after Trinity	(1) 2 Kings 5, or Ecclus. 18, 1-14	(1) 2 Kings 6, 8-23 or 2 Kings 17, 1-23, or Ecclus. 38, 24-end
	(2) Luke 1, 57-end, or Col. 3, 12–4, 6	(2) Matt. 16, 13-end, or Acts 28
M.	(1) Jeremiah 40	(1) Jeremiah 41
	(2) 2 Corinthians 10	(2) John 1, 1-28
Tu.	(1) Jeremiah 42	(1) Jeremiah 43
	(2) 2 Corinthians 11	(2) John 1, 29-end
W.	(1) Jeremiah 44, 1-14	(1) Jeremiah 44, 15-end
	(2) 2 Corinthians 12, 1-13	(2) John 2
Th.	(1) Ezekiel 2	(1) Ezekiel 3, 4-end
	(2) 2 Cor. 12, 14–13 end	(2) John 3, 1-21
F.	(1) Ezekiel 8	(1) Ezekiel 9
	(2) Romans 1	(2) John 3, 22-end
S.	(1) Ezekiel 11, 14-end	(1) Ezekiel 33, 21-end
	(2) Romans 2, 1–16	(2) John 4, 1-26
Twelfth Sunday after Trinity	(1) 2 Kings 18, 13-end, or Micah 6	(1) 2 Kings 19, or Isaiah 38, 1-20, or Micah 7
	(2) Luke 4, 1-15, or Philemon	(2) Matt. 18, 15-end, or Ephesians 1
M.	(1) Ezra 1	(1) Ezra 3
	(2) Romans 2, 17-end	(2) John 4, 27-end
Tu.	(1) Ezra 4	(1) Haggai 1, 1–2, 9
	(2) Romans 3	(2) John 5, 1-23
W.	(1) Zechariah 1, 1-17	(1) Zech. 1, 18–2 end
	(2) Romans 4	(2) John 5, 24-end
Th.	(1) Zechariah 3	(1) Zechariah 4
	(2) Romans 5	(2) John 6, 1-21
F.	(1) Zechariah 6, 9-end	(1) Haggai 2, 10-end
	(2) Romans 6	(2) John 6, 22-40
S.	(1) Ezra 5	(1) Ezra 6
	(2) Romans 7	(2) John 6, 41-end
Thirteenth Sunday after Trinity	(1) 2 Kings 22, or Habakkuk 2, 1-14	(1) 2 Kings 23, 1-30, or 2 Chron. 36, 1-21, or Habakkuk 3, 2-end
	(2) Luke 4, 31–5, 11, or 1 Timothy 6	(2) Matt. 20, 1-28, or Ephesians 2
M.	(1) Zechariah 7	(1) Zechariah 8
	(2) Romans 8, 1-17	(2) John 7, 1-24

	MORNING PRAYER	EVENING PRAYER
Tu.	(1) Ezra 7	(1) Ezra 8, 15-end
	(2) Romans 8, 18-end	(2) John 7, 25-end
W.	(1) Ezra 9	(1) Ezra 10, 1-19
	(2) Romans 9	(2) John 8, 1-30
Th.	(1) Nehemiah 1	(1) Nehemiah 2
	(2) Romans 10	(2) John 8, 31-end
F.	(1) Nehemiah 4	(1) Nehemiah 5
	(2) Romans 11, 1-24	(2) John 9
S.	(1) Nehemiah 6, 1–7, 4	(1) Nehemiah 8
	(2) Romans 11, 25-end	(2) John 10, 1-21
Fourteenth Sunday after Trinity	(1) Ezra 1, 1–8 and 3, or Zephaniah 1	(1) Neh. 1, 1–2, 8, or Daniel 1, or Zephaniah 3
	(2) Luke 7, 36-end, or 1 Corinthians 13	(2) Matt. 21, 23-end, or Ephesians 4, 1-24
M.	(1) Nehemiah 9, 1-23	(1) Nehemiah 9, 24-end
	(2) Romans 12	(2) John 10, 22-end
Tu.	(1) Nehemiah 13	(1) Daniel 2, 1-24
	(2) Romans 13	(2) John 11, 1-44
W.	(1) Daniel 2, 25-end	(1) Daniel 4, 1-18
	(2) Romans 14	(2) John 11, 45-end
Th.	(1) Daniel 4, 19-end	(1) Daniel 7, 9-end
	(2) Romans 15, 1-13	(2) John 12, 1-19
F.	(1) Daniel 9, 1-19	(1) Daniel 9, 20-end
	(2) Romans 15, 14-end	(2) John 12, 20-end
S.	(1) Daniel 10	(1) Daniel 12
	(2) Romans 16	(2) John 13
Fifteenth Sunday after Trinity	(1) Daniel 3	(1) Daniel 5, or Daniel 6
	(2) Luke 9, 57–10, 24, or 2 Timothy 1	(2) Matthew 28, or Ephes. 4, 25–5, 21
M.	(1) Esther 1	(1) Esth. 2, 5-11, 15-end
	(2) Philippians 1, 1-11	(2) John 14, 1-14
Tu.	(1) Esther 3	(1) Esther 4
	(2) Philippians 1, 12-end	(2) John 14, 15-end
W.	(1) Esther 5	(1) Esther 6 and 7
	(2) Philippians 2, 1-11	(2) John 15
Th.	(1) 1 Maccabees 1, 1-19	(1) 1 Maccabees 1, 20-40
	(2) Philippians 2, 12-end	(2) John 16, 1-15
F.	(1) 1 Maccabees 1, 41-end	(1) 1 Maccabees 2, 1-28
	(2) Philippians 3	(2) John 16, 16-end
S.	(1) 1 Maccabees 2, 29-48	(1) 1 Maccabees 2, 49-end
	(2) Philippians 4	(2) John 17
Sixteenth Sunday after Trinity	(1) Jeremiah 5, 1-19	(1) Jeremiah 5, 20-end, or Jeremiah 7, 1-15
	(2) Luke 11, 1-28, or Titus 2, 1–3, 7	(2) John 8, 12-30, or Ephes. 5, 22–6, 9
M.	(1) 1 Macc. 3, 1-26	(1) 1 Macc. 3, 27-41
	(2) Colossians 1, 1-20	(2) John 18, 1-27
Tu.	(1) 1 Macc. 3, 42-end	(1) 1 Macc. 4, 1-25
	(2) Col. 1, 21–2, 7	(2) John 18, 28-end

	MORNING PRAYER	EVENING PRAYER
W.	(1) 1 Macc. 4, 26-35	(1) 1 Macc. 4, 36-end
	(2) Colossians 2, 8-19	(2) John 19, 1-30
Th.	(1) 1 Macc. 6, 1-17	(1) 1 Macc. 6, 18-47
	(2) Col. 2, 20–3, 11	(2) John 19, 31-end
F.	(1) 1 Macc. 7, 1-20	(1) 1 Macc. 7, 21-end
	(2) Col, 3, 12–4, 1	(2) John 20 [14, 4-15
S.	(1) 1 Macc. 9, 1-22	(1) 1 Macc. 13, 41-end &
	(2) Col. 4, 2-end	(2) John 21
Seventeenth Sunday after Trinity	(1) Jeremiah 17, 5-14	(1) Jeremiah 18, 1-17, or Jeremiah 22, 1-19
	(2) Luke 11, 29-end, or 1 Peter 1, 1-21	(2) John 8, 31-end, or Ephesians 6, 10-end
M.	(1) Job 1	(1) Job 2
	(2) Philemon	(2) Luke 1, 1-23
Tu.	(1) Job 3	(1) Job 4
	(2) Ephesians 1, 1-14	(2) Luke 1, 24-56
W.	(1) Job 5	(1) Job 6
	(2) Ephesians 1, 15-end	(2) Luke 1, 57-end
Th.	(1) Job 7	(1) Job 8
	(2) Ephesians 2, 1–10	(2) Luke 2, 1-21
F.	(1) Job 9	(1) Job 10
	(2) Ephesians 2, 11-end	(2) Luke 2, 22-end
S.	(1) Job 11	(1) Job 12
	(2) Ephesians 3	(2) Luke 3, 1-22
Eighteenth Sunday after Trinity	(1) Jeremiah 26	(1) Jeremiah 30, 1-3, 10-22, or Jeremiah 31, 1-20
	(2) Luke 12, 1-34, or 1 Peter 1, 22–2, 10	(2) John 13, or 1 John 1, 1–2, 11
M.	(1) Job 13	(1) Job 14
	(2) Ephesians 4, 1-16	(2) Luke 4, 1-30
Tu.	(1) Job 15, 1-16	(1) Job 16, 1–17, 2
	(2) Ephesians 4, 17-30	(2) Luke 4, 31-end
W.	(1) Job 17, 3-end	(1) Job 18
	(2) Ephesians 4, 31–5, 21	(2) Luke 5, 1-16
Th.	(1) Job 19	(1) Job 21
	(2) Ephesians 5, 22-end	(2) Luke 5, 17-end
F.	(1) Job 22	(1) Job 23
	(2) Ephesians 6, 1-9	(2) Luke 6, 1-19
S.	(1) Job 24	(1) Job 25, 1–26 end
	(2) Ephesians 6, 10-end	(2) Luke 6, 20-38
Nineteenth Sunday after Trinity	(1) Jeremiah 31, 23-37	(1) Jeremiah 35, or Jeremiah 36
	(2) Luke 12, 35-end, or 1 Peter 2, 11–3, 7	(2) John 14, or 1 John 2, 12-end
M.	(1) Job 27	(1) Job 28
	(2) 1 Timothy 1, 1-17	(2) Luke 6, 39–7, 10
Tu.	(1) Job 29, 1–30, 1	(1) Job 31, 13-end
	(2) 1 Timothy 1, 18–2 end	(2) Luke 7, 11-35
W.	(1) Job 32	(1) Job 33
	(2) 1 Timothy 3	(2) Luke 7, 36-end
Th.	(1) Job 38, 1-21	(1) Job 38, 22-end
	(2) 1 Timothy 4	(2) Luke 8, 1-21

F.	(1) Job 39	(1) Job 40
	(2) 1 Timothy 5	(2) Luke 8, 22-end
S.	(1) Job 41	(1) Job 42
	(2) 1 Timothy 6	(2) Luke 9, 1-17
Twentieth Sunday after Trinity	(1) Ezekiel 2	(1) Ezekiel 3, 4-21, or Ezekiel 13, 1-16
	(2) Luke 13, or 1 Peter 3, 8–4, 6	(2) John 15, or 1 John 3
M.	(1) Proverbs 1, 1-19	(1) Proverbs 1, 20-end
	(2) Titus 1, 1–2, 8	(2) Luke 9, 18-50
Tu.	(1) Proverbs 2	(1) Proverbs 3, 1-26
	(2) Titus 2, 9–3 end	(2) Luke 9, 51-end
W.	(1) Proverbs 3, 27–4, 19	(1) Proverbs 4, 20–5, 14
	(2) 2 Timothy 1	(2) Luke 10, 1-24
Th.	(1) Proverbs 6, 1-19	(1) Proverbs 8
	(2) 2 Timothy 2	(2) Luke 10, 25-end
F.	(1) Proverbs 9	(1) Proverbs 10, 1-22
	(2) 2 Timothy 3	(2) Luke 11, 1-28
S.	(1) Proverbs 11, 1-25	(1) Proverbs 12, 10-end
	(2) 2 Timothy 4	(2) Luke 11, 29-end
Twenty-first Sunday after Trinity	(1) Ezekiel 14	(1) Ezekiel 18, 1-4, 19-end, or Ezekiel 33, 1-20
	(2) Luke 14, 1-24, or 1 Peter 4, 7–5, 11	(2) John 16, or 1 John 4
M.	(1) Proverbs 14, 9-27	(1) Proverbs 15, 18-end
	(2) Luke 12, 1-34	(2) Luke 12, 35-53
Tu.	(1) Proverbs 16, 31–17, 17	(1) Proverbs 18, 10-end
	(2) Luke 12, 54–13, 9	(2) Luke 13, 10-end
W.	(1) Proverbs 20, 1-22	(1) Proverbs 22, 1-16
	(2) Luke 14, 1-24	(2) Luke 14, 25–15, 10
Th.	(1) Proverbs 24, 23-end	(1) Proverbs 25
	(2) Luke 15, 11-end	(2) Luke 16
F.	(1) Proverbs 26, 12-end	(1) Proverbs 27, 1-22
	(2) Luke 17, 1-19	(2) Luke 17, 20-end
S.	(1) Proverbs 30, 1-16	(1) Proverbs 31, 10-end
	(2) Luke 18, 1-30	(2) Luke 18, 31–19, 10
Twenty-second Sunday after Trinity	(1) Ezekiel 34, 1-16	(1) Ezekiel 34, 17-end, or Ezekiel 37, 15-end
	(2) Luke 14, 25–15, 10 or 2 Peter 1	(2) John 17, or 1 John 5
M.	(1) Ecclesiastes 1	(1) Ecclesiastes 2, 1-23
	(2) Luke 19, 11-28	(2) Luke 19, 29-end
Tu.	(1) Ecclesiastes 3, 1-15	(1) Ecclesiastes 3, 16–4, 6
	(2) Luke 20, 1-26	(2) Luke 20, 27–21, 4
W.	(1) Ecclesiastes 4, 7-end	(1) Ecclesiastes 5
	(2) Luke 21, 5-end	(2) Luke 22, 1-38
Th.	(1) Ecclesiastes 6	(1) Ecclesiastes 7, 1-14
	(2) Luke 22, 39-53	(2) Luke 22, 54-end
F.	(1) Ecclesiastes 7, 15-end	(1) Ecclesiastes 8
	(2) Luke 23, 1-25	(2) Luke 23, 26-49
S.	(1) Ecclesiastes 9	(1) Ecclesiastes 10, 5-18
	(2) Luke 23, 50–24, 12	(2) Luke 24, 13-end

	MORNING PRAYER	EVENING PRAYER
Twenty-third Sunday after Trinity	(1) Prov. 1, 20-end, or 1 Macc. 1, 1-28	(1) Proverbs 2, or Proverbs 3, 1-26, or 1 Macc. 2, 29-48
	(2) Luke 16, or 1 Cor. 1, 1-25	(2) John 9, or 1 Corinthians 13
M.	(1) Ecclus. 1, 1-10	(1) Ecclus. 1, 11-end
	(2) Acts 1	(2) Acts 2, 1-21
Tu.	(1) Ecclesiasticus 2	(1) Ecclus. 3, 17-29
	(2) Acts 2, 22-end	(2) Acts 3, 1–4, 4
W.	(1) Ecclus. 4, 11-28	(1) Ecclus. 4, 29–6, 1
	(2) Acts 4, 5-31	(2) Acts 4, 32–5, 11
Th.	(1) Ecclus. 6, 14-31	(1) Ecclus. 7, 27-end
	(2) Acts 5, 12–6, 7	(2) Acts 6, 8–7, 16
F.	(1) Ecclus. 10, 6-8, 12-24	(1) Ecclus. 11, 7-28
	(2) Acts 7, 17-34	(2) Acts 7, 35–8, 4
S.	(1) Ecclus. 14, 20–15, 10	(1) Ecclus. 15, 11-end
	(2) Acts 8, 4-25	(2) Acts 8, 26-end
Twenty-fourth Sunday after Trinity	(1) Proverbs 8, 1-21, or 1 Macc. 2, 49-end	(1) Proverbs 8, 1, 22-end, or Proverbs 9, or 1 Maccabees 3, 1-26
	(2) Luke 17, 1-19, or 1 Cor. 1, 26– 2 end	(2) John 10, or James 3
M.	(1) Ecclus. 16, 17-end	(1) Ecclus. 17, 1-24
	(2) Acts 9, 1-31	(2) Acts 9, 32-end
Tu.	(1) Ecclus. 18, 1-14	(1) Ecclus. 19, 13-end
	(2) Acts 10, 1-23	(2) Acts 10, 24-end
W.	(1) Ecclus. 21, 1-17	(1) Ecclus. 22, 6-22
	(2) Acts 11, 1-18	(2) Acts 11, 19-end
Th.	(1) Ecclus. 22, 27–23, 15	(1) Ecclus. 24, 1-22
	(2) Acts 12, 1-24	(2) Acts 12, 25–13, 12
F.	(1) Ecclus. 24, 23-end	(1) Ecclus. 27, 30–28, 9
	(2) Acts 13, 13-43	(2) Acts 13, 44–14, 7
S.	(1) Ecclus. 31, 1-11	(1) Ecclus. 34, 9-end
	(2) Acts 14, 8-end	(2) Acts 15, 1-21
Twenty-fifth Sunday after Trinity	(1) Proverbs 13, or 1 Macc. 4, 1-25	(1) Proverbs 14, 31–15, 17, or Proverbs 16, 1-19, or 1 Macc. 4, 26-35
	(2) Luke 22, 1-38, or 1 Corinthians 3	(2) Luke 22, 39-end, or James 4
M.	(1) Ecclesiasticus 35	(1) Ecclus. 37, 7-15
	(2) Acts 15, 22-35	(2) Acts 15, 36–16, 5
Tu.	(1) Ecclus. 38, 1-14	(1) Ecclus. 38, 24-end
	(2) Acts 16, 6-end	(2) Acts 17, 1-15
W.	(1) Ecclus. 39, 1-11	(1) Ecclus. 39, 13-end
	(2) Acts 17, 16-end	(2) Acts 18, 1-23
Th.	(1) Ecclus. 42, 15-end	(1) Ecclus. 43, 1-12
	(2) Acts 18, 24–19, 7	(2) Acts 19, 8-20

*Note.—Instead of the Lessons set down for this and the three following weeks, the Lessons which were omitted in the weeks after the Epiphany may be read. Provided only that the Lessons set down for the Sunday and week next before Advent be always read.

	Morning Prayer	Evening Prayer
F.	(1) Ecclus. 43, 13-end	(1) Ecclus. 50, 1-24
	(2) Acts 19, 21-end	(2) Acts 20, 1-16
S.	(1) Ecclus. 51, 1-12	(1) Ecclus. 51, 13-end
	(2) Acts 20, 17-end	(2) Acts 21, 1-16
Twenty-sixth Sunday after Trinity	(1) Proverbs 23, 15-end, or 1 Macc. 4, 36-end	(1) Prov. 24, 23-end, or Prov. 31, 10-end, or 1 Macc. 14, 4-15
	(2) Luke 23, 1-25, or Jude	(2) Luke 23, 26-end, or James 5
M.	(1) Tobit 4, 5-19	(1) Tobit 13
	(2) Acts 21, 17-36	(2) Acts 21, 37–22, 22
Tu.	(1) Baruch 1, 15–2, 10	(1) Baruch 2, 11-end
	(2) Acts 22, 23–23, 11	(2) Acts 23, 12-end
W.	(1) Baruch 3, 1-8	(1) Baruch 3, 9-end
	(2) Acts 24, 1-23	(2) Acts 24, 24–25, 12
Th.	(1) Baruch 4, 21-30	(1) Baruch 4, 36–5 end
	(2) Acts 25, 13-end	(2) Acts 26
F.	(1) 2 Macc. 4, 7-17	(1) 2 Macc. 6, 12-end
	(2) Acts 27, 1-26	(2) Acts 27, 27-end
S.	(1) 2 Macc. 7, 1-19	(1) 2 Macc. 7, 20-41
	(2) Acts 28, 1-15	(2) Acts 28, 16-end
Sunday next before Advent	(1) Eccles. 11 and 12	(1) Haggai 2, 1-9, or Malachi 3 and 4
	(2) John 19, 13-end, or Hebrews 11, 1-16	(2) John 20, or Heb. 11, 17–12, 2, or Luke 15, 11-end
M.	(1) Wisdom 1	(1) Wisdom 2
	(2) Revelation 1	(2) Revelation 2
Tu.	(1) Wisdom 3, 1-9	(1) Wisdom 4, 7-end
	(2) Revelation 3	(2) Revelation 4
W.	(1) Wisdom 5, 1-16	(1) Wisdom 6, 1-21
	(2) Revelation 5	(2) Revelation 6
Th.	(1) Wisdom 7, 15–8, 4	(1) Wisdom 8, 5-18
	(2) Revelation 7	(2) Rev. 10 and 11, 1-14
F.	(1) Wisdom 8, 21–9 end	(1) Wisdom 10, 15–11, 10
	(2) Revelation 11, 15–12 end	(2) Revelation 14, 1-13
S.	(1) Wisdom 11, 21–12, 2	(1) Wisdom 12, 12-21
	(2) Revelation 18	(2) Revelation 19, 1-16

LESSONS PROPER FOR HOLY-DAYS NOT INCLUDED IN THE FOREGOING TABLE

		FIRST EVENSONG		MATTINS		SECOND EVENSONG	
		1st Lesson	2nd Lesson	1st Lesson	2nd Lesson	1st Lesson	2nd Lesson
S. Andrew	Nov. 30	Ecclus. 14, 20–end	John 1, 35–42	Zechariah 8, 20–end	John 12, 20–32	Ezekiel 47, 1–12	1 Corinthians 1, 18–end
S. Thomas	Dec. 21	2 Sam. 15, 17–21	John 11, 1–16	Job 42, 1–6	John 14, 1–7	Isaiah 35	1 Peter 1, 3–9
Conversion of S. Paul	Jan. 25	Jeremiah 1, 4–10	Acts 26, 1–23	Isaiah 49, 1–13	Gal. 1, 11–end	Isa. 45, 18–end	Phil. 3, 1–14
Purification of the Virgin Mary	Feb. 2	Exod. 13, 11–16	Galatians 4, 1–7	1 Sam. 1, 21–end	Heb. 10, 1–10	Haggai 2, 1–9	Rom. 12, 1–5
S. Matthias	Feb. 24	Isaiah 22, 15–22	John 15, 1–16	1 Sam. 2, 27–35	Matt. 7, 15–27	1 Sam. 16, 1–13	Acts 20, 17–35
Annunciation of our Lady	Mar. 25	Genesis 3, 1–15	Rom. 5, 12–21	Isaiah 52, 7–12	Heb. 2, 5–end	1 Sam. 2, 1–11	Matt. 1, 18–23
S. Mark	April 25	Ezekiel 1	Acts 12, 25—13, 13	Ecclus. 51, 13–end	Acts 15, 35–end	Isaiah 62, 6–end	2 Timothy 4, 1–11
S. Philip and S. James	May 1	Prov. 4, 10–18	John 1, 43–end	Job 23, 1–12	John 6, 1–14	Isaiah 30, 15–21	John 17, 1–8
S. Barnabas	June 11	Job 29, 11–16	Acts 4, 32–end	Jer. 9, 23, 24	Acts 9, 26–31	Isaiah 42, 5–12	Acts 14, 8–end
S. John Baptist	June 24	Malachi 3, 1–6	Luke 1, 5–23	Ecclus. 48, 1–10	Luke 3, 1–20	Malachi 4	Matt. 11, 2–19
S. Peter	June 29	Ezekiel 2, 1–7	Acts 3	Ezekiel 3, 4–11	Acts 11, 1–18	Ezek. 34, 11–16	John 21, 15–22
S. Mary Magdalen	July 22	Proverbs 31, 10–end	Luke 8, 1–3	Isaiah 52, 7–10	John 20, 1–10	Zephaniah 3, 14–end	Mark 15, 40—16, 7
S. James	July 25	2 Kings 1, 1–15	Luke 9, 46–56	Jeremiah 45	Mark 1, 14–20	Jer. 26, 1–15	Mark 5, 21–end
Transfiguration	Aug. 6	Exod. 24, 12–end	Luke 9, 28–45	Exod. 34, 29–end	2 Corinthians 3	1 Kings 19, 1–16	2 Pet. 1, 12–end
S. Bartholomew	Aug. 24	Gen. 28, 10–17	John 1, 43–end	Ecclus. 39, 1–10	Matt. 10, 1–15	Deut. 18, 15–19	Matt. 10, 16–22
S. Matthew	Sept. 21	1 Kings 19, 15–end	Matthew 6, 19–end	Proverbs 3, 1–18	Matthew 19, 16–end	1 Chronicles 29, 9–17	1 Timothy 6, 6–19
S. Michael	Sept. 29	Ezekiel 10, 8–end	Revelation 5	2 Kings 6, 8–17	Acts 12, 1–11	Daniel 10, 4–end	Matt. 13, 24–30, 36–43
S. Luke	Oct. 18	Isaiah 55	Luke 1, 1–4	Isaiah 61, 1–6	Acts 16, 6–18	Ecclus. 38, 1–14	Col. 4, 7–end
S. Simon and S. Jude	Oct. 28	Isaiah 28, 9–16	Eph. 2, 11–end	Ecclus. 2	Luke 6, 12–23	1 Macc. 2, 42–66	Jude 17–end
All Saints	Nov. 1	Wisdom 3, 1–9	Heb. 11, 32—12, 2	Wisdom 5, 1–16	Revelation 19, 6–10	Ecclus. 44, 1–15	Revelation 7, 9–end

TABLES AND RULES

FOR THE MOVEABLE AND IMMOVEABLE FEASTS TOGETHER WITH THE DAYS OF FASTING AND ABSTINENCE THROUGH THE WHOLE YEAR

RULES TO KNOW WHEN THE MOVEABLE FEASTS AND HOLY-DAYS BEGIN

E*ASTER DAY* (on which the rest depend) is always the First *Sunday* after the Full Moon which happens upon, or next after, the Twenty-first Day of *March*; and if the Full Moon happens upon a *Sunday*, *Easter Day* is the *Sunday* after.

Advent Sunday is always the nearest *Sunday* to the Feast of *S. Andrew*, whether before or after.

| *Septuagesima* *Sexagesima* *Quinquagesima* *Quadragesima* | *Sunday* is | Nine Eight Seven Six | Weeks before *Easter*. |

| *Rogation Sunday* *Ascension Day* *Whitsunday* *Trinity Sunday* | is | Five Weeks Forty Days Seven Weeks Eight Weeks | after *Easter*. |

A TABLE OF ALL THE FEASTS
THAT ARE TO BE OBSERVED IN THE
CHURCH OF ENGLAND
THROUGHOUT THE YEAR

All Sundays in the Year.

The Days of the Feasts of
- The Circumcision of our Lord JESUS CHRIST.
- The Epiphany.
- The Conversion of *S. Paul*.
- The Purification of the Blessed Virgin.
- *S. Matthias* the Apostle.
- The Annunciation of the Blessed Virgin.
- *S. Mark* the Evangelist.
- *S. Philip* and *S. James* the Apostles.
- The Ascension of our Lord JESUS CHRIST.
- *S. Barnabas*.
- The Nativity of *S. John* Baptist.

The Days of the Feasts of
- *S. Peter* the Apostle.
- *S. James* the Apostle.
- *S. Bartholomew* the Apostle.
- *S. Matthew* the Apostle.
- *S. Michael* and all Angels.
- *S. Luke* the Evangelist.
- *S. Simon* and *S. Jude* the Apostles.
- All Saints.
- *S. Andrew* the Apostle.
- *S. Thomas* the Apostle.
- The NATIVITY of our LORD.
- *S. Stephen* the Martyr.
- *S. John* the Evangelist.
- The Holy Innocents.

Monday and *Tuesday* in *Easter Week*.
Monday and *Tuesday* in *Whitsun Week*.

A TABLE

OF THE

VIGILS, FASTS, AND DAYS OF ABSTINENCE

TO BE OBSERVED IN THE YEAR

The Evens or Vigils before

{

The Nativity of our Lord.
The Purification of the Blessed Virgin *Mary*.
The Annunciation of the Blessed Virgin.
Easter Day.
Ascension Day.
Pentecost.
S. Matthias.
S. John Baptist.
S. Peter.
S. James.
S. Bartholomew.
S. Matthew.
S. Simon and *S. Jude.*
S. Andrew.
S. Thomas.
All Saints.

NOTE, That if any of these Feast-Days fall upon a *Monday*, then the Vigil or Fast-Day shall be kept upon the *Saturday*, and not upon the *Sunday* next before it.

DAYS OF FASTING, OR ABSTINENCE

I. The Forty Days of Lent.

II. The Ember Days at the Four Seasons, being the *Wednesday, Friday,* and *Saturday* after . . . .

{

1. The First *Sunday* in Lent.
2. The Feast of *Pentecost.*
3. *September* 14.
4. *December* 13.

III. The Three *Rogation Days*, being the *Monday, Tuesday,* and *Wednesday,* before *Holy Thursday,* or the *Ascension* of our LORD.

IV. All the *Fridays* in the Year, except CHRISTMAS DAY.

A SOLEMN DAY

FOR WHICH
A PARTICULAR SERVICE IS APPOINTED

The Anniversary of the Day of the Accession of the Reigning Sovereign.

A TABLE TO FIND EASTER DAY

FROM THE PRESENT TIME TILL THE YEAR 2199 INCLUSIVE ACCORDING TO THE FOREGOING CALENDAR

Golden Number	Day of the Month	Sunday Letter
	March 21	C
XIV	——— 22	D
III	——— 23	E
	——— 24	F
XI	——— 25	G
	——— 26	A
XIX	——— 27	B
VIII	——— 28	C
	——— 29	D
XVI	——— 30	E
V	——— 31	F
	April 1	G
XIII	——— 2	A
II	——— 3	B
	——— 4	C
X	——— 5	D
	——— 6	E
XVIII	——— 7	F
VII	——— 8	G
	——— 9	A
XV	——— 10	B
IV	——— 11	C
	——— 12	D
XII	——— 13	E
I	——— 14	F
	——— 15	G
IX	——— 16	A
XVII	——— 17	B
VI	——— 18	C
	——— 19	D
	——— 20	E
	——— 21	F
	——— 22	G
	——— 23	A
	——— 24	B
	——— 25	C

THIS Table contains so much of the Calendar as is necessary for the determining of *Easter*; to find which, look for the Golden Number of the year in the first column of the Table, against which stands the day of the Paschal Full Moon; then look in the third column for the Sunday Letter, next after the day of the Full Moon, and the day of the Month standing against that Sunday Letter is *Easter Day*. If the Full Moon happens upon a Sunday, then (according to the first rule) the next Sunday after is *Easter Day*.

To find the Golden Number, or Prime, add one to the Year of our Lord, and then divide by 19; the remainder, if any, is the Golden Number; but if nothing remaineth, then 19 is the Golden Number.

To find the Dominical or Sunday Letter, according to the Calendar,

until the year 2099 inclusive,	0 A
add to the Year of our Lord its	1 G
fourth part, omitting fractions;	2 F
and also the number 6: Divide	3 E
the sum by 7; and if there is no	4 D
remainder, then A is the Sun-	5 C
day Letter: But if any number	6 B

remaineth, then the Letter standing against that number in the small annexed Table is the Sunday Letter.

For the next following Century, that is, from the year 2100 until the year 2199 inclusive, add to the current year its fourth part, and also the number 5, and then divide by 7, and proceed as in the last Rule.

NOTE, That in all Bissextile or Leap-Years, the Letter found as above will be the Sunday Letter, from the intercalated day exclusive to the end of the year.

ANOTHER TABLE TO FIND EASTER

TILL THE YEAR 2199 INCLUSIVE

Golden Number	SUNDAY LETTERS						
	A	B	C	D	E	F	G
I	April 16	17	18	19	20	21	15
II	April 9	10	4	5	6	7	8
III	Mar. 26	27	28	29	30	24	25
IV	April 16	17	18	12	13	14	15
V	April 2	3	4	5	6	7	1
VI	April 23	24	25	19	20	21	22
VII	April 9	10	11	12	13	14	15
VIII	April 2	3	4	Mar. 29	30	31	April 1
IX	April 23	17	18	19	20	21	22
X	April 9	10	11	12	6	7	8
XI	Mar. 26	27	28	29	30	31	April 1
XII	April 16	17	18	19	20	14	15
XIII	April 9	3	4	5	6	7	8
XIV	Mar. 26	27	28	29	23	24	25
XV	April 16	17	11	12	13	14	15
XVI	April 2	3	4	5	6	Mar. 31	April 1
XVII	April 23	24	18	19	20	21	22
XVIII	April 9	10	11	12	13	14	8
XIX	April 2	3	Mar. 28	29	30	31	April 1

To make use of the preceding Table, find the Sunday Letter for the Year in the uppermost Line, and the Golden Number, or Prime, in the Column of Golden Numbers, and against the Prime, in the same Line under the Sunday Letter, you have the Day of the Month on which EASTER falleth that year. But Note, that the Name of the Month is set on the Left Hand, or just with the Figure, and followeth not, as in other Tables, by Descent, but Collateral.

A TABLE TO FIND EASTER

FROM THE YEAR 2200 TO THE YEAR 2299
INCLUSIVE

Golden Number	Day of the Month	Sunday Letter
VI	March 21	C
	—— 22	D
XIV	—— 23	E
III	—— 24	F
	—— 25	G
XI	—— 26	A
	—— 27	B
XIX	—— 28	C
VIII	—— 29	D
	—— 30	E
XVI	—— 31	F
V	April 1	G
	—— 2	A
XIII	—— 3	B
II	—— 4	C
	—— 5	D
X	—— 6	E
	—— 7	F
XVIII	—— 8	G
VII	—— 9	A
	—— 10	B
XV	—— 11	C
IV	—— 12	D
	—— 13	E
XII	—— 14	F
I	—— 15	G
	—— 16	A
IX	—— 17	B
XVII	—— 18	C
	—— 19	D
	—— 20	E
	—— 21	F
	—— 22	G
	—— 23	A
	—— 24	B
	—— 25	C

THE Golden Numbers in the foregoing Calendar will point out the Days of the Paschal Full Moons, till the Year of our Lord 2200; at which Time, in order that the Ecclesiastical Full Moons may fall nearly on the same Days with the real Full Moons, the Golden Numbers must be removed to different Days of the Calendar, as is done in the annexed Table, which contains so much of the Calendar then to be used, as is necessary for finding the Paschal Full Moons, and the Feast of *Easter*, from the Year 2200, to the Year 2299 inclusive. This Table is to be made use of, in all respects, as the first Table before inserted, for finding *Easter* till the Year 2199.

A TABLE OF THE MOVEABLE FEASTS

FOR ONE HUNDRED AND SEVEN YEARS
ACCORDING TO THE FOREGOING CALENDAR

The Year of Our Lord	Golden Number	The Epact	Sunday Letter	Sundays after Epiphany	Septuagesima Sunday	The First Day of Lent	Easter Day	Rogation Sunday	Ascension Day	Whitsunday	Sundays after Trinity	
1999	V	13	C	3	Jan. 31	Feb. 17	Apr. 4	May 9	May 13	May 23	25	N
2000	VI	24	BA	6	Feb. 20	Mar. 8	— 23	— 28	Jun. 1	Jun. 11	23	D
2001	VII	5	G	5	— 11	Feb. 28	— 15	— 20	May 24	— 3	24	—
2002	VIII	16	F	2	Jan. 27	— 13	Mar. 31	— 5	— 9	May 19	26	—
2003	IX	27	E	5	Feb. 16	Mar. 5	Apr. 20	— 25	— 29	Jun. 8	23	N
2004	X	8	DC	4	— 8	Feb. 25	— 11	— 16	— 20	May 30	24	—
2005	XI	19	B	2	Jan. 23	— 9	Mar. 27	— 1	— 5	— 15	26	—
2006	XII	0	A	5	Feb. 12	Mar. 1	Apr. 16	— 21	— 25	Jun. 4	24	De
2007	XIII	11	G	4	— 4	Feb. 21	— 8	— 13	— 17	May 27	25	—
2008	XIV	22	FE	1	Jan. 20	— 6	Mar. 23	Apr. 27	— 1	— 11	27	No
2009	XV	3	D	4	Feb. 8	— 25	Apr. 12	May 17	— 21	— 31	24	—
2010	XVI	14	C	3	Jan. 31	— 17	— 4	— 9	— 13	— 23	25	—
2011	XVII	26	B	6	Feb. 20	Mar. 9	— 24	— 29	Jun. 2	Jun. 12	22	—
2012	XVIII	6	AG	4	— 5	Feb. 22	— 8	— 13	May 17	May 27	25	De
2013	XIX	17	F	2	Jan. 27	— 13	Mar. 31	— 5	— 9	— 19	26	—
2014	I	29	E	5	Feb. 16	Mar. 5	Apr. 20	— 25	— 29	Jun. 8	23	No
2015	II	10	D	3	— 1	Feb. 18	— 5	— 10	— 14	May 24	25	—
2016	III	21	CB	2	Jan. 24	— 10	Mar. 27	— 1	— 5	— 15	26	—
2017	IV	2	A	5	Feb. 12	Mar. 1	Apr. 16	— 21	— 25	Jun. 4	24	Dec
2018	V	13	G	3	Jan. 28	Feb. 14	— 1	— 6	— 10	May 20	26	—
2019	VI	24	F	5	Feb. 17	Mar. 6	— 21	— 26	— 30	Jun. 9	23	—
2020	VII	5	ED	4	— 9	Feb. 26	— 12	— 17	— 21	May 31	24	Nov
2021	VIII	16	C	3	Jan. 31	— 17	— 4	— 9	— 13	— 23	25	—
2022	IX	27	B	5	Feb. 13	Mar. 2	— 17	— 22	— 26	Jun. 5	23	—
2023	X	8	A	4	— 5	Feb. 22	— 9	— 14	— 18	May 28	25	Dec
2024	XI	19	GF	3	Jan. 28	Feb. 14	Mar. 31	May 5	May 9	May 19	26	Dec.
2025	XII	0	E	5	Feb. 16	Mar. 5	Apr. 20	— 25	— 29	Jun. 8	23	Nov.
2026	XIII	11	D	3	— 1	Feb. 18	— 5	— 10	— 14	May 24	25	—
2027	XIV	22	C	2	Jan. 24	— 10	Mar. 28	— 2	— 6	— 16	26	—
2028	XV	3	BA	5	Feb. 13	Mar. 1	Apr. 16	— 21	— 25	Jun. 4	24	Dec.
2029	XVI	14	G	3	Jan. 28	Feb. 14	— 1	— 6	— 10	May 20	26	—
2030	XVII	26	F	5	Feb. 17	Mar. 6	— 21	— 26	— 30	Jun. 9	23	—
2031	XVIII	6	E	4	— 9	Feb. 26	— 13	— 18	— 22	— 1	24	Nov.
2032	XIX	17	DC	2	Jan. 25	— 11	Mar. 28	— 2	— 6	May 16	26	—
2033	I	29	B	5	Feb. 13	Mar. 2	Apr. 17	— 22	— 26	Jun. 5	23	—
2034	II	10	A	4	— 5	Feb. 22	— 9	— 14	— 18	May 28	25	Dec.
2035	III	21	G	2	Jan. 21	— 7	Mar. 25	Apr. 29	— 3	— 13	27	—
2036	IV	2	FE	4	Feb. 10	— 27	Apr. 13	May 18	— 22	Jun. 1	24	Nov.:
2037	V	13	D	3	— 1	— 18	— 5	— 10	— 14	May 24	25	— 2
2038	VI	24	C	6	— 21	Mar. 10	— 25	— 30	Jun. 3	Jun. 13	22	— 2
2039	VII	5	B	4	— 6	Feb. 23	— 10	— 15	May 19	May 29	24	— 2

A TABLE OF THE MOVEABLE FEASTS

FOR ONE HUNDRED AND SEVEN YEARS
ACCORDING TO THE FOREGOING CALENDAR

	Golden Number	The Epact	Sunday Letter	Sundays after Epiphany	Septuagesima Sunday	The First Day of Lent	Easter Day	Rogation Sunday	Ascension Day	Whitsunday	Sundays after Trinity	Advent Sunday
ɔ	VIII	16	AG	3	Jan. 29	— 15	— 1	— 6	— 10	— 20	26	Dec. 2
ı	IX	27	F	5	Feb. 17	Mar. 6	— 21	— 26	— 30	Jun. 9	23	— 1
2	X	8	E	3	— 2	Feb. 19	— 6	— 11	— 15	May 25	25	Nov.30
3	XI	19	D	2	Jan. 25	— 11	Mar. 29	— 3	— 7	— 17	26	— 29
4	XII	o	CB	5	Feb. 14	Mar. 2	Apr. 17	— 22	— 26	Jun. 5	23	— 27
5	XIII	11	A	4	— 5	Feb. 22	— 9	— 14	— 18	May 28	25	Dec. 3
6	XIV	22	G	2	Jan. 21	— 7	Mar. 25	Apr. 29	— 3	— 13	27	— 2
7	XV	3	F	4	Feb. 10	— 27	Apr. 14	May 19	— 23	Jun. 2	24	— 1
8	XVI	14	ED	3	— 2	— 19	— 5	— 10	— 14	May 24	25	Nov.29
9	XVII	26	C	5	— 14	Mar. 3	— 18	— 23	— 27	Jun. 6	23	— 28
50	XVIII	6	B	4	— 6	Feb. 23	— 10	— 15	— 19	May 29	24	— 27
51	XIX	17	A	3	Jan. 29	— 15	— 2	— 7	— 11	— 21	26	Dec. 3
52	I	29	GF	6	Feb. 18	Mar. 6	— 21	— 26	— 30	Jun. 9	23	— 1
53	II	10	E	3	— 2	Feb. 19	— 6	— 11	— 15	May 25	25	Nov.30
54	III	21	D	2	Jan. 25	— 11	Mar. 29	— 3	— 7	— 17	26	— 29
55	IV	2	C	5	Feb. 14	Mar. 3	Apr. 18	— 23	— 27	Jun. 6	23	— 28
56	V	13	BA	3	Jan. 30	Feb. 16	— 2	— 7	— 11	May 21	26	Dec. 3
57	VI	24	G	6	Feb. 18	Mar. 7	— 22	— 27	— 31	Jun. 10	23	— 2
58	VII	5	F	4	— 10	Feb. 27	— 14	— 19	— 23	— 2	24	— 1
59	VIII	16	E	2	Jan. 26	— 12	Mar. 30	— 4	— 8	May 18	26	Nov.30
60	IX	27	DC	5	Feb. 15	Mar. 3	Apr. 18	— 23	— 27	Jun. 6	23	— 28
61	X	8	B	4	— 6	Feb. 23	— 10	— 15	— 19	May 29	24	— 27
62	XI	19	A	2	Jan. 22	— 8	Mar. 26	Apr. 30	— 4	— 14	27	Dec. 3
63	XII	o	G	5	Feb. 11	— 28	Apr. 15	May 20	— 24	Jun. 3	24	— 2
64	XIII	11	FE	3	— 3	— 20	— 6	— 11	— 15	May 25	25	Nov.30
65	XIV	22	D	2	Jan. 25	Feb. 11	Mar. 29	May 3	May 7	May 17	26	Nov.29
66	XV	3	C	4	Feb. 7	— 24	Apr. 11	— 16	— 20	— 30	24	— 28
67	XVI	14	B	3	Jan. 30	— 16	— 3	— 8	— 12	— 22	25	— 27
68	XVII	26	AG	6	Feb. 19	Mar. 7	— 22	— 27	— 31	Jun. 10	23	Dec. 2
69	XVIII	6	F	4	— 10	Feb. 27	— 14	— 19	— 23	— 2	24	— 1
70	XIX	17	E	2	Jan. 26	— 12	Mar. 30	— 4	— 8	May 18	26	Nov.30
71	I	29	D	5	Feb. 15	Mar. 4	Apr. 19	— 24	— 28	Jun. 7	23	— 29
72	II	10	CB	4	— 7	Feb. 24	— 10	— 15	— 19	May 29	24	— 27
73	III	21	A	2	Jan. 22	— 8	Mar. 26	Apr. 30	— 4	— 14	27	Dec. 3
74	IV	2	G	5	Feb. 11	— 28	Apr. 15	May 20	— 24	Jun. 3	24	— 2
75	V	13	F	3	— 3	— 20	— 7	— 12	— 16	May 26	25	— 1
2076	VI	24	ED	5	— 16	Mar. 4	— 19	— 24	— 28	Jun. 7	23	Nov.29
2077	VII	5	C	4	— 7	Feb. 24	— 11	— 16	— 20	May 30	24	— 28
2078	VIII	16	B	3	Jan. 30	— 16	— 3	— 8	— 12	— 22	25	— 27
2079	IX	27	A	6	Feb. 19	Mar. 8	— 23	— 28	Jun. 1	Jun. 11	23	Dec. 3
2080	X	8	GF	4	— 4	Feb. 21	— 7	— 12	May 16	May 26	25	— 1

A TABLE OF THE MOVEABLE FEASTS

FOR ONE HUNDRED AND SEVEN YEARS
ACCORDING TO THE FOREGOING CALENDAR

The Year of Our Lord	Golden Number	The Epact	Sunday Letter	Sundays after Epiphany	Septuagesima Sunday	The First Day of Lent	Easter Day	Rogation Sunday	Ascension Day	Whitsunday	Sundays after Trinity	A...
2081	XI	19	E	2	Jan. 26	— 12	Mar. 30	— 4	— 8	— 18	26	Ne
2082	XII	0	D	5	Feb. 15	Mar. 4	Apr. 19	— 24	— 28	Jun. 7	23	—
2083	XIII	11	C	3	Jan. 31	Feb. 17	— 4	— 9	— 13	May 23	25	—
2084	XIV	22	BA	2	— 23	— 9	Mar. 26	Apr. 30	— 4	— 14	27	De
2085	XV	3	G	5	Feb. 11	— 28	Apr. 15	May 20	— 24	Jun. 3	24	—
2086	XVI	14	F	2	Jan. 27	— 13	Mar. 31	— 5	— 9	May 19	26	—
2087	XVII	26	E	5	Feb. 16	Mar. 5	Apr. 20	— 25	— 29	Jun. 8	23	No
2088	XVIII	6	DC	4	— 8	Feb. 25	— 11	— 16	— 20	May 30	24	—
2089	XIX	17	B	3	Jan. 30	— 16	— 3	— 8	— 12	— 22	25	—
2090	I	29	A	5	Feb. 12	Mar. 1	— 16	— 21	— 25	Jun. 4	24	Dee
2091	II	10	G	4	— 4	Feb. 21	— 8	— 13	— 17	May 27	25	—
2092	III	21	FE	2	Jan. 27	— 13	Mar. 30	— 4	— 8	— 18	26	Nov
2093	IV	2	D	4	Feb. 8	— 25	Apr. 12	— 17	— 21	— 31	24	—
2094	V	13	C	3	Jan. 31	— 17	— 4	— 9	— 13	— 23	25	—
2095	VI	24	B	6	Feb. 20	Mar. 9	— 24	— 29	Jun. 2	Jun. 12	22	—
2096	VII	5	AG	5	— 12	Feb. 29	— 15	— 20	May 24	— 3	24	Dec
2097	VIII	16	F	2	Jan. 27	— 13	Mar. 31	— 5	— 9	May 19	26	—
2098	IX	27	E	5	Feb. 16	Mar. 5	Apr. 20	— 25	— 29	Jun. 8	23	Nov.
2099	X	8	D	4	— 8	Feb. 25	— 12	— 17	— 21	May 31	24	—
2100	XI	19	C	2	Jan. 24	— 10	Mar. 28	— 2	— 6	— 16	26	—
2101	XII	0	B	5	Feb. 13	Mar. 2	Apr. 17	— 22	— 26	Jun. 5	23	—
2102	XIII	11	A	4	— 5	Feb. 22	— 9	— 14	— 18	May 28	25	Dec.
2103	XIV	22	G	2	Jan. 21	— 7	Mar. 25	Apr. 29	— 3	— 13	27	—
2104	XV	3	FE	4	Feb. 10	— 27	Apr. 13	May 18	— 22	Jun. 1	24	Nov.
2105	XVI	14	D	3	Feb. 1	— 18	— 5	— 10	— 14	May 24	25	—

A TABLE OF THE MOVEABLE FEASTS

ACCORDING TO THE SEVERAL DAYS THAT EASTER CAN POSSIBLY FALL UPON

Easter Day	Sundays after Epiphany	Septuagesima Sunday	The First Day of Lent	Rogation Sunday	Ascension Day	Whitsunday	Sundays after Trinity	Advent Sunday
Mar. 22	1	Jan. 18	Feb. 4	Apr. 26	Apr. 30	May 10	27	Nov. 29
— 23	1	— 19	— 5	— 27	May 1	— 11	27	— 30
— 24	1	— 20	— 6	— 28	— 2	— 12	27	Dec. 1
— 25	2	— 21	— 7	— 29	— 3	— 13	27	— 2
— 26	2	— 22	— 8	— 30	— 4	— 14	27	— 3
— 27	2	— 23	— 9	May 1	— 5	— 15	26	Nov. 27
— 28	2	— 24	— 10	— 2	— 6	— 16	26	— 28
— 29	2	— 25	— 11	— 3	— 7	— 17	26	— 29
— 30	2	— 26	— 12	— 4	— 8	— 18	26	— 30
— 31	2	— 27	— 13	— 5	— 9	— 19	26	Dec. 1
Apr. 1	3	— 28	— 14	— 6	— 10	— 20	26	— 2
— 2	3	— 29	— 15	— 7	— 11	— 21	26	— 3
— 3	3	— 30	— 16	— 8	— 12	— 22	25	Nov. 27
— 4	3	— 31	— 17	— 9	— 13	— 23	25	— 28
— 5	3	Feb. 1	— 18	— 10	— 14	— 24	25	— 29
— 6	3	— 2	— 19	— 11	— 15	— 25	25	— 30
— 7	3	— 3	— 20	— 12	— 16	— 26	25	Dec. 1
— 8	4	— 4	— 21	— 13	— 17	— 27	25	— 2
— 9	4	— 5	— 22	— 14	— 18	— 28	25	— 3
— 10	4	— 6	— 23	— 15	— 19	— 29	24	Nov. 27
— 11	4	— 7	— 24	— 16	— 20	— 30	24	— 28
— 12	4	— 8	— 25	— 17	— 21	— 31	24	— 29
— 13	4	— 9	— 26	— 18	— 22	June 1	24	— 30
— 14	4	— 10	— 27	— 19	— 23	— 2	24	Dec. 1
— 15	5	— 11	— 28	— 20	— 24	— 3	24	— 2
— 16	5	— 12	Mar. 1	— 21	— 25	— 4	24	— 3
— 17	5	— 13	— 2	— 22	— 26	— 5	23	Nov. 27
— 18	5	— 14	— 3	— 23	— 27	— 6	23	— 28
— 19	5	— 15	— 4	— 24	— 28	— 7	23	— 29
— 20	5	— 16	— 5	— 25	— 29	— 8	23	— 30
— 21	5	— 17	— 6	— 26	— 30	— 9	23	Dec. 1
— 22	6	— 18	— 7	— 27	— 31	— 10	23	— 2
— 23	6	— 19	— 8	— 28	June 1	— 11	23	— 3
— 24	6	— 20	— 9	— 29	— 2	— 12	22	Nov. 27
— 25	6	— 21	— 10	— 30	— 3	— 13	22	— 28

NOTE, That in a Bissextile or Leap-Year, the Number of *Sundays* after Epiphany will be the same, as if *Easter Day* had fallen One Day later than it really does. And for the same reason, One Day must, in every Leap-Year, be added to the Day of the Month given by the Table for *Septuagesima* Sunday: And the like must be done for the First Day of *Lent* (commonly called *Ash Wednesday*) unless the Table gives some Day in the Month of *March* for it; for in that case, the Day given by the Table is the right Day.

GENERAL TABLES FOR FINDING THE DOMINICAL OR SUNDAY LETTER, AND THE PLACES OF THE GOLDEN NUMBERS IN THE CALENDAR

TABLE I

6	5	4	3	2	1	0
B	C	D	E	F	G	A
				1600	1700	1800
1900 2000	2100	2200	2300 2400	2500	2600	2700 2800
2900	3000	3100 3200	3300	3400	3500 3600	3700
3800	3900 4000	4100	4200	4300 4400	4500	4600
4700 4800	4900	5000	5100 5200	5300	5400	5500 5600
5700	5800	5900 6000	6100	6200	6300 6400	6500
6600	6700 6800	6900	7000	7100 7200	7300	7400
7500 7600 8500	7700 &c.	7800	7900 8000	8100	8200	8300 8400

To find the Dominical or Sunday Letter for any given Year of our Lord, add to the year its fourth part, omitting fractions; and also the number, which in Table I standeth at the top of the column, wherein the number of hundreds contained in that given year is found: Divide the sum by 7, and if there is no remainder, then A is the Sunday Letter; but if any number remaineth, then the Letter, which standeth under that number at the top of the Table, is the Sunday Letter.

TABLE II

1	2	3	1	2	3	1	2	3	1	2	3	1	2	3
	Years of our Lord			Years of our Lord			Years of our Lord			Years of our Lord			Years of our Lord	
B	1600	0		3000	6	B	4400	12		5800	18	B	7200	24
	1700	1		3100	7		4500	13		5900	19		7300	25
	1800	1	B	3200	7		4600	13	B	6000	19		7400	25
	1900	2		3300	7		4700	14		6100	19		7500	26
B	2000	2		3400	8	B	4800	14		6200	20	B	7600	26
	2100	2		3500	9		4900	14		6300	21		7700	26
	2200	3	B	3600	8		5000	15	B	6400	20		7800	27
	2300	4		3700	9		5100	16		6500	21		7900	28
B	2400	3		3800	10	B	5200	15		6600	22	B	8000	27
	2500	4		3900	10		5300	16		6700	23		8100	28
	2600	5	B	4000	10		5400	17	B	6800	22		8200	29
	2700	5		4100	11		5500	17		6900	23		8300	29
B	2800	5		4200	12	B	5600	17		7000	24	B	8400	29
	2900	6		4300	12		5700	18		7100	24		8500 &c.	0

To find the Month and Days of the Month to which the Golden Numbers ought to be prefixed in the Calendar, in any given Year of our Lord, consisting of entire hundred years, and in all the intermediate years betwixt that and the next hundredth year following, look in the second column of Table II for the given year, consisting of entire hundreds, and note the number or cypher which stands against it in the third column; then, in Table III look for the same number in the column under any given Golden Number, which when you have found, guide your eye side-ways to the left hand, and in the first column you will find the Month and Day to which that Golden Number ought to be prefixed in the Calendar, during that period of one hundred years.

The letter B prefixed to certain hundredth years in Table II denotes those years which are still to be accounted Bissextile or Leap-Years in the New Calendar; whereas all the other hundredth years are to be accounted only common years.

66

The Golden Numbers

Paschal Full Moon	Sunday Letter	1	2	3	4	5	6	7	8	9	10	11	12	13	14	15	16	17	18	19
March 21	C	8	19	0	11	22	3	14	25	6	17	28	9	20	1	12	23	4	15	26
March 22	D	9	20	1	12	23	4	15	26	7	18	29	10	21	2	13	24	5	16	27
March 23	E	10	21	2	13	24	5	16	27	8	19	0	11	22	3	14	25	6	17	28
March 24	F	11	22	3	14	25	6	17	28	9	20	1	12	23	4	15	26	7	18	29
March 25	G	12	23	4	15	26	7	18	29	10	21	2	13	24	5	16	27	8	19	0
March 26	A	13	24	5	16	27	8	19	0	11	22	3	14	25	6	17	28	9	20	1
March 27	B	14	25	6	17	28	9	20	1	12	23	4	15	26	7	18	29	10	21	2
March 28	C	15	26	7	18	29	10	21	2	13	24	5	16	27	8	19	0	11	22	3
March 29	D	16	27	8	19	0	11	22	3	14	25	6	17	28	9	20	1	12	23	4
March 30	E	17	28	9	20	1	12	23	4	15	26	7	18	29	10	21	2	13	24	5
March 31	F	18	29	10	21	2	13	24	5	16	27	8	19	0	11	22	3	14	25	6
April 1	G	19	0	11	22	3	14	25	6	17	28	9	20	1	12	23	4	15	26	7
April 2	A	20	1	12	23	4	15	26	7	18	29	10	21	2	13	24	5	16	27	8
April 3	B	21	2	13	24	5	16	27	8	19	0	11	22	3	14	25	6	17	28	9
April 4	C	22	3	14	25	6	17	28	9	20	1	12	23	4	15	26	7	18	29	10
April 5	D	23	4	15	26	7	18	29	10	21	2	13	24	5	16	27	8	19	0	11
April 6	E	24	5	16	27	8	19	0	11	22	3	14	25	6	17	28	9	20	1	12
April 7	F	25	6	17	28	9	20	1	12	23	4	15	26	7	18	29	10	21	2	13
April 8	G	26	7	18	29	10	21	2	13	24	5	16	27	8	19	0	11	22	3	14
April 9	A	27	8	19	0	11	22	3	14	25	6	17	28	9	20	1	12	23	4	15
April 10	B	28	9	20	1	12	23	4	15	26	7	18	29	10	21	2	13	24	5	16
April 11	C	29	10	21	2	13	24	5	16	27	8	19	0	11	22	3	14	25	6	17
April 12	D	0	11	22	3	14	25	6	17	28	9	20	1	12	23	4	15	26	7	18
April 13	E	1	12	23	4	15	26	7	18	29	10	21	2	13	24	5	16	27	8	19
April 14	F	2	13	24	5	16	27	8	19	0	11	22	3	14	25	6	17	28	9	20
April 15	G	3	14	25	6	17	28	9	20	1	12	23	4	15	26	7	18	29	10	21
April 16	A	4	15	26	7	18	29	10	21	2	13	24	5	16	27	8	19	0	11	22
April 17	B	5	16	27	8	19	0	11	22	3	14	25	6	17	28	9	20	1	12	23
April 18	C	6	17	28	9	20	1	12	23	4	15	26	7	18	29	10	21	2	13	24
April 18	C	7	18	29	10	21	2	13	24	5	16	27	8	19	0	11	22	3	14	25

THE ORDER FOR

MORNING AND EVENING PRAYER

DAILY TO BE SAID AND USED THROUGHOUT THE YEAR

THE Morning and Evening Prayer shall be used in the accustomed Place of the Church, Chapel, or Chancel; except it shall be otherwise determined by the Ordinary of the Place. And the Chancels shall remain as they have done in times past.

And here is to be noted, that such Ornaments of the Church, and of the Ministers thereof at all times of their Ministration, shall be retained, and be in use, as were in this Church of *England* by the Authority of Parliament, in the Second Year of the Reign of King *Edward* the Sixth.

Readers and such other lay persons as may be authorised by the Bishop of the diocese may, at the invitation of the Minister of the parish, or, where the Cure is vacant, or the Minister is incapacitated, at the invitation of the Churchwardens, say or sing Morning or Evening Prayer (save for the Absolution); and in case of need, where no clerk in Holy Orders or Reader or lay person authorised as aforesaid is available, the Minister or (failing him) the Churchwardens shall arrange for some suitable lay person to say or sing Morning or Evening Prayer (save for the Absolution).

THE ORDER FOR
MORNING PRAYER
DAILY THROUGHOUT
THE YEAR

At the beginning of Morning Prayer the Minister shall read with a loud voice some one or more of these Sentences of the Scriptures that follow. And then he shall say that which is written after the said Sentences.

WHEN the wicked man turneth away from his wickedness that he hath committed, and doeth that which is lawful and right, he shall save his soul alive. *Ezek.* 18. 27.

I acknowledge my transgressions, and my sin is ever before me. *Psalm* 51. 3.

Hide thy face from my sins, and blot out all mine iniquities. *Psalm* 51. 9.

The sacrifices of God are a broken spirit: a broken and a contrite heart, O God, thou wilt not despise. *Psalm* 51. 17.

Rend your heart, and not your garments, and turn unto the Lord your God: for he is gracious and merciful, slow to anger, and of great kindness, and repenteth him of the evil. *Joel* 2. 13.

To the Lord our God belong mercies and forgivenesses, though we have rebelled against him: neither have we obeyed the voice of the Lord our God, to walk in his laws which he set before us. *Dan.* 9. 9, 10.

O Lord, correct me, but with judgement; not in thine anger, lest thou bring me to nothing. *Jer.* 10. 24. *Psalm* 6. 1.

Repent ye; for the Kingdom of heaven is at hand. *S. Matth.* 3. 2.

I will arise and go to my father, and will say unto him, Father, I have sinned against heaven, and before thee, and am no more worthy to be called thy son. *S. Luke* 15. 18, 19.

Enter not into judgement with thy servant, O Lord; for in thy sight shall no man living be justified.   *Psalm* 143. 2.

If we say that we have no sin, we deceive ourselves, and the truth is not in us: but if we confess our sins, he is faithful and just to forgive us our sins, and to cleanse us from all unrighteousness.

     1 *S. John* 1. 8, 9.

DEARLY beloved brethren, the Scripture moveth us in sundry places to acknowledge and confess our manifold sins and wickedness; and that we should not dissemble nor cloke them before the face of Almighty God our heavenly Father; but confess them with an humble, lowly, penitent, and obedient heart; to the end that we may obtain forgiveness of the same, by his infinite goodness and mercy. And although we ought at all times humbly to acknowledge our sins before God; yet ought we most chiefly so to do, when we assemble and meet together to render thanks for the great benefits that we have received at his hands, to set forth his most worthy praise, to hear his most holy Word, and to ask those things which are requisite and necessary, as well for the body as the soul. Wherefore I pray and beseech you, as many as are here present, to accompany me with a pure heart and humble voice unto the throne of the heavenly grace, saying after me:

A general Confession to be said of the whole Congregation after the Minister, all kneeling.

ALMIGHTY and most merciful Father, We have erred and strayed from thy ways like lost sheep, We have followed too much the devices and desires of our own hearts, We have offended against thy holy laws, We have left undone those things which we ought to have done, And we have done those things which we ought not to have done, And there is no health in us: But thou, O Lord, have mercy upon us miserable offenders; Spare thou them, O God, which confess their faults, Restore thou them that are penitent, According to thy promises declared unto mankind in Christ Jesu our Lord: And grant, O most merciful Father, for his sake, That we may hereafter live a godly, righteous, and sober life, To the glory of thy holy Name. Amen.

The Absolution or Remission of sins to be pronounced by the Priest alone, standing: the people still kneeling.

ALMIGHTY God, the Father of our Lord Jesus Christ, who desireth not the death of a sinner, but rather that he may turn from his wickedness and live; and hath given power and commandment to his Ministers, to declare and pronounce to his people, being penitent, the Absolution and Remission of their sins: He pardoneth and absolveth all them that truly repent and unfeignedly believe his holy Gospel. Wherefore let us beseech him to grant us true repentance and his Holy Spirit, that those things may please him which we do at this present, and that the rest of our life hereafter may be pure and holy; so that at the last we may come to his eternal joy; through Jesus Christ our Lord.

The people shall answer here, and at the end of all other prayers,

Amen.

If no priest be present the person saying the Service shall read the Collect for the Twenty-First Sunday after Trinity, that person and the people still kneeling.

Then the Minister shall kneel, and say the Lord's Prayer with an audible voice: the people also kneeling, and repeating it with him, both here, and wheresoever else it is used in Divine Service.

OUR Father which art in heaven, Hallowed be thy Name, Thy kingdom come, Thy will be done, in earth as it is in heaven. Give us this day our daily bread; And forgive us our trespasses, As we forgive them that trespass against us; And lead us not into temptation, But deliver us from evil. For thine is the kingdom, the power, and the glory, For ever and ever. *Amen.*

Then likewise he shall say,

O Lord, open thou our lips.
Answer. And our mouth shall shew forth thy praise.
Priest. O God, make speed to save us.
Answer. O Lord, make haste to help us.

Here, all standing up, the Priest shall say,

Glory be to the Father, and to the Son: and to the Holy Ghost;
Answer. As it was in the beginning, is now and ever shall be:
world without end. Amen.
Priest. Praise ye the Lord.
Answer. The Lord's Name be praised.

*Then shall be said or sung this Psalm following: Except on
Easter Day, upon which another Anthem is appointed: and
on the nineteenth day of every month it is not to be read here,
but in the ordinary course of the Psalms.*

VENITE, EXULTEMUS DOMINO
Psalm 95

O COME, let us sing unto the Lord: let us heartily rejoice in
the strength of our salvation.

Let us come before his presence with thanksgiving: and shew
ourselves glad in him with psalms.

For the Lord is a great God: and a great King above all gods.

In his hand are all the corners of the earth: and the strength
of the hills is his also.

The sea is his, and he made it: and his hands prepared the
dry land.

O come, let us worship, and fall down: and kneel before the
Lord our Maker.

For he is the Lord our God: and we are the people of his
pasture, and the sheep of his hand.

To day if ye will hear his voice, harden not your hearts: as in
the provocation, and as in the day of temptation in the wilderness;

When your fathers tempted me: proved me, and saw my works.

Forty years long was I grieved with this generation, and said: It is a people that do err in their hearts, for they have not known my ways.

Unto whom I sware in my wrath: that they should not enter into my rest.

Glory be to the Father, and to the Son: and to the Holy Ghost; As it was in the beginning, is now, and ever shall be: world without end. Amen.

Then shall follow the Psalms in order as they be appointed. And at the end of every Psalm throughout the year, and likewise in the end of Benedicite, Benedictus, Magnificat, and Nunc dimittis, shall be repeated,

Glory be to the Father, and to the Son: and to the Holy Ghost; *Answer.* As it was in the beginning, is now, and ever shall be: world without end. Amen.

Then shall be read distinctly with an audible voice the First Lesson, taken out of the Old Testament as is appointed in the Calendar: Except there be proper Lessons assigned for that day: He that readeth so standing and turning himself, as he may best be heard of all such as are present. And after that shall be said or sung, in English, the Hymn called Te Deum Laudamus, daily throughout the year.

Note that before every Lesson the Minister shall say, Here beginneth such a Chapter, *or* Verse of such a Chapter, of such a Book: *And after every Lesson,* Here endeth the First, *or* the Second Lesson.

TE DEUM LAUDAMUS

WE praise thee, O God: we acknowledge thee to be the Lord.

All the earth doth worship thee: the Father everlasting.

To thee all Angels cry aloud: the heavens and all the power therein.

To thee Cherubin and Seraphin: continually do cry,

Holy, Holy, Holy: Lord God of Sabaoth;

Heaven and earth are full of the Majesty: of thy glory.

The glorious company of the Apostles: praise thee.

The goodly fellowship of the Prophets: praise thee.

The noble army of Martyrs: praise thee.

The holy Church throughout all the world: doth acknowledge thee;

The Father: of an infinite Majesty;

Thine honourable, true: and only Son;

Also the Holy Ghost: the Comforter.

Thou art the King of glory: O Christ.

Thou art the everlasting Son: of the Father.

When thou tookest upon thee to deliver man: thou didst not abhor the Virgin's womb.

When thou hadst overcome the sharpness of death: thou didst open the kingdom of heaven to all believers.

Thou sittest at the right hand of God: in the glory of the Father.

We believe that thou shalt come: to be our Judge.

We therefore pray thee, help thy servants: whom thou hast redeemed with thy precious blood.

Make them to be numbered with thy Saints: in glory everlasting.

O Lord, save thy people: and bless thine heritage.

Govern them: and lift them up for ever.

Day by day: we magnify thee;

And we worship thy Name: ever world without end.

Vouchsafe, O Lord: to keep us this day without sin.

O Lord, have mercy upon us: have mercy upon us.

O Lord, let thy mercy lighten upon us: as our trust is in thee.

O Lord, in thee have I trusted: let me never be confounded.

Or this Canticle,

BENEDICITE, OMNIA OPERA

O ALL ye Works of the Lord, bless ye the Lord: praise him, and magnify him for ever.

O ye Angels of the Lord, bless ye the Lord: praise him, and magnify him for ever.

O ye Heavens, bless ye the Lord: praise him, and magnify him for ever.

O ye Waters that be above the Firmament, bless ye the Lord: praise him, and magnify him for ever.

O all ye Powers of the Lord, bless ye the Lord: praise him, and magnify him for ever.

O ye Sun and Moon, bless ye the Lord: praise him, and magnify him for ever.

O ye Stars of Heaven, bless ye the Lord: praise him, and magnify him for ever.

O ye Showers and Dew, bless ye the Lord: praise him, and magnify him for ever.

O ye Winds of God, bless ye the Lord: praise him, and magnify him for ever.

O ye Fire and Heat, bless ye the Lord: praise him, and magnify him for ever.

O ye Winter and Summer, bless ye the Lord: praise him, and magnify him for ever.

O ye Dews and Frosts, bless ye the Lord: praise him, and magnify him for ever.

O ye Frost and Cold, bless ye the Lord: praise him, and magnify him for ever.

O ye Ice and Snow, bless ye the Lord: praise him, and magnify him for ever.

O ye Nights and Days, bless ye the Lord: praise him, and magnify him for ever.

O ye Light and Darkness, bless ye the Lord: praise him, and magnify him for ever.

O ye Lightnings and Clouds, bless ye the Lord: praise him, and magnify him for ever.

O let the Earth bless the Lord: yea, let it praise him, and magnify him for ever.

O ye Mountains and Hills, bless ye the Lord: praise him, and magnify him for ever.

O all ye Green Things upon the Earth, bless ye the Lord: praise him, and magnify him for ever.

O ye Wells, bless ye the Lord: praise him, and magnify him for ever.

O ye Seas and Floods, bless ye the Lord: praise him, and magnify him for ever.

O ye Whales, and all that move in the Waters, bless ye the Lord: praise him, and magnify him for ever.

O all ye Fowls of the Air, bless ye the Lord: praise him, and magnify him for ever.

O all ye Beasts and Cattle, bless ye the Lord: praise him, and magnify him for ever.

O ye Children of Men, bless ye the Lord: praise him, and magnify him for ever.

O let Israel bless the Lord: praise him, and magnify him for ever.

O ye Priests of the Lord, bless ye the Lord: praise him, and magnify him for ever.

O ye Servants of the Lord, bless ye the Lord: praise him, and magnify him for ever.

O ye Spirits and Souls of the Righteous, bless ye the Lord: praise him, and magnify him for ever.

O ye holy and humble Men of heart, bless ye the Lord: praise him, and magnify him for ever.

O Ananias, Azarias, and Misael, bless ye the Lord: praise him, and magnify him for ever.

Glory be to the Father, and to the Son: and to the Holy Ghost;

As it was in the beginning, is now, and ever shall be: world without end. Amen.

Then shall be read in like manner the Second Lesson, taken out of the New Testament. And after that the Hymn follow-ing: Except when that shall happen to be read in the Chapter for the day, or for the Gospel on Saint John Baptist's Day.

BENEDICTUS
S. Luke 1. 68

BLESSED be the Lord God of Israel: for he hath visited, and redeemed his people;

And hath raised up a mighty salvation for us: in the house of his servant David;

As he spake by the mouth of his holy Prophets: which have been since the world began;

That we should be saved from our enemies: and from the hands of all that hate us;

To perform the mercy promised to our forefathers: and to remember his holy covenant;

To perform the oath which he sware to our forefather Abraham: that he would give us;

That we being delivered out of the hands of our enemies: might serve him without fear;

In holiness and righteousness before him: all the days of our life.

And thou, child, shalt be called the Prophet of the Highest: for thou shalt go before the face of the Lord to prepare his ways;

To give knowledge of salvation unto his people: for the remission of their sins;

Through the tender mercy of our God: whereby the day-spring from on high hath visited us;

To give light to them that sit in darkness, and in the shadow of death: and to guide our feet into the way of peace.

Glory be to the Father, and to the Son: and to the Holy Ghost;

As it was in the beginning, is now, and ever shall be: world without end. Amen.

Or this Psalm,

JUBILATE DEO
Psalm 100

O BE joyful in the Lord, all ye lands: serve the Lord with gladness, and come before his presence with a song.

Be ye sure that the Lord he is God: it is he that hath made us, and not we ourselves; we are his people, and the sheep of his pasture.

O go your way into his gates with thanksgiving, and into his courts with praise: be thankful unto him, and speak good of his Name.

For the Lord is gracious, his mercy is everlasting: and his truth endureth from generation to generation.

Glory be to the Father, and to the Son: and to the Holy Ghost;

As it was in the beginning, is now, and ever shall be: world without end. Amen.

Then shall be sung or said the Apostles' Creed, by the Minister and the people standing: Except only such days as the Creed of Saint Athanasius is appointed to be read.

I BELIEVE in God the Father Almighty, Maker of heaven and earth:

And in Jesus Christ his only Son our Lord, Who was conceived by the Holy Ghost, Born of the Virgin Mary, Suffered under Pontius Pilate, Was crucified, dead, and buried: He descended into hell; The third day he rose again from the dead; He ascended into heaven, And sitteth on the right hand of God the Father Almighty; From thence he shall come to judge the quick and the dead.

I believe in the Holy Ghost; The holy Catholick Church; The Communion of Saints; The Forgiveness of sins; The Resurrection of the body, And the life everlasting. Amen.

And after that these Prayers following, all devoutly kneeling: the Minister first pronouncing with a loud voice,

The Lord be with you.
Answer. And with thy spirit.
  Minister. Let us pray.
Lord, have mercy upon us.
  Christ, have mercy upon us.
Lord, have mercy upon us.

Then the Minister, Clerks, and people shall say the Lord's Prayer with a loud voice.

OUR Father which art in heaven, Hallowed be thy Name, Thy kingdom come, Thy will be done, in earth as it is in heaven. Give us this day our daily bread; And forgive us our trespasses, As we forgive them that trespass against us; And lead us not into temptation, But deliver us from evil. Amen.

Then the Priest standing up shall say,

O Lord, shew thy mercy upon us.
Answer. And grant us thy salvation.
Priest. O Lord, save the Queen.
Answer. And mercifully hear us when we call upon thee.
Priest. Endue thy Ministers with righteousness.
Answer. And make thy chosen people joyful.
Priest. O Lord, save thy people.
Answer. And bless thine inheritance.
Priest. Give peace in our time, O Lord.
Answer. Because there is none other that fighteth for us, but only thou, O God.
Priest. O God, make clean our hearts within us.
Answer. And take not thy Holy Spirit from us.

Then shall follow three Collects: The first of the day, which shall be the same that is appointed at the Communion: The second for Peace: The third for Grace to live well. And the two last Collects shall never alter, but daily be said at Morning Prayer throughout all the year, as followeth, all kneeling.

The Second Collect, for Peace.

O GOD, who art the author of peace and lover of concord, in knowledge of whom standeth our eternal life, whose service is perfect freedom: Defend us thy humble servants in all assaults of our enemies; that we, surely trusting in thy defence, may not fear the power of any adversaries; through the might of Jesus Christ our Lord. *Amen.*

The Third Collect, for Grace.

O LORD our heavenly Father, Almighty and everlasting God, who hast safely brought us to the beginning of this day: Defend us in the same with thy mighty power; and grant that this day we fall into no sin, neither run into any kind of danger; but that all our doings may be ordered by thy governance, to do always that is righteous in thy sight; through Jesus Christ our Lord. *Amen.*

In Quires and Places where they sing here followeth the Anthem.

Then these five Prayers following are to be read here: Except when the Litany is read; and then only the two last are to be read, as they are there placed.

A Prayer for the Queen's Majesty.

O LORD our heavenly Father, high and mighty, King of kings, Lord of lords, the only Ruler of princes, who dost from thy throne behold all the dwellers upon earth: Most heartily we beseech thee with thy favour to behold our most gracious Sovereign Lady, Queen *ELIZABETH*; and so replenish her with the grace of thy Holy Spirit, that she may alway incline to thy will, and walk in thy way: Endue her plenteously with heavenly gifts; grant her in health and wealth long to live; strengthen her that she may vanquish and overcome all her enemies, and finally after this life she may attain everlasting joy and felicity; through Jesus Christ our Lord. *Amen.*

A Prayer for the Royal Family.

ALMIGHTY God, the fountain of all goodness, we humbly beseech thee to bless *Philip* Duke of *Edinburgh*, *Charles* Prince of *Wales*, and all the Royal Family: Endue them with thy Holy Spirit; enrich them with thy heavenly grace; prosper them with all happiness; and bring them to thine everlasting kingdom; through Jesus Christ our Lord. *Amen.*

A Prayer for the Clergy and People.

ALMIGHTY and everlasting God, who alone workest great marvels: Send down upon our Bishops and Curates, and all Congregations committed to their charge, the healthful Spirit of thy grace; and that they may truly please thee, pour upon them the continual dew of thy blessing. Grant this, O Lord, for the honour of our Advocate and Mediator, Jesus Christ. *Amen.*

A Prayer of Saint Chrysostom.

ALMIGHTY God, who hast given us grace at this time with one accord to make our common supplications unto thee; and dost promise that when two or three are gathered together in thy Name thou wilt grant their requests: Fulfil now, O Lord, the desires and petitions of thy servants, as may be most expedient for them; granting us in this world knowledge of thy truth, and in the world to come life everlasting. *Amen.*

2 Corinthians 13.

THE grace of our Lord Jesus Christ, and the love of God, and the fellowship of the Holy Ghost, be with us all evermore. *Amen.*

Here endeth the Order of Morning Prayer throughout the Year.

THE ORDER FOR
EVENING PRAYER
DAILY THROUGHOUT
THE YEAR

At the beginning of Evening Prayer the Minister shall read with a loud voice some one or more of these Sentences of the Scriptures that follow. And then he shall say that which is written after the said Sentences.

WHEN the wicked man turneth away from his wickedness that he hath committed, and doeth that which is lawful and right, he shall save his soul alive. *Ezek.* 18. 27.

I acknowledge my transgressions, and my sin is ever before me. *Psalm* 51. 3.

Hide thy face from my sins, and blot out all mine iniquities. *Psalm* 51. 9.

The sacrifices of God are a broken spirit: a broken and a contrite heart, O God, thou wilt not despise. *Psalm* 51. 17.

Rend your heart, and not your garments, and turn unto the Lord your God: for he is gracious and merciful, slow to anger, and of great kindness, and repenteth him of the evil. *Joel* 2. 13.

To the Lord our God belong mercies and forgivenesses, though we have rebelled against him: neither have we obeyed the voice of the Lord our God, to walk in his laws which he set before us. *Dan.* 9. 9, 10.

O Lord, correct me, but with judgement; not in thine anger, lest thou bring me to nothing. *Jer.* 10. 24. *Psalm* 6. 1.

Repent ye; for the Kingdom of heaven is at hand. *S. Matth.* 3. 2.

I will arise and go to my father, and will say unto him, Father, I have sinned against heaven, and before thee, and am no more worthy to be called thy son. *S. Luke* 15. 18, 19.

Enter not into judgement with thy servant, O Lord; for in

hy sight shall no man living be justified. *Psalm* 143. 2.

    If we say that we have no sin, we deceive ourselves, and the truth is not in us: but if we confess our sins, he is faithful and just to forgive us our sins, and to cleanse us from all unrighteousness.

1 S. John 1. 8, 9.

DEARLY beloved brethren, the Scripture moveth us in sundry places to acknowledge and confess our manifold sins and wickedness; and that we should not dissemble nor cloke them before the face of Almighty God our heavenly Father; but confess them with an humble, lowly, penitent, and obedient heart; to the end that we may obtain forgiveness of the same, by his infinite goodness and mercy. And although we ought at all times humbly to acknowledge our sins before God; yet ought we most chiefly so to do, when we assemble and meet together to render thanks for the great benefits that we have received at his hands, to set forth his most worthy praise, to hear his most holy Word, and to ask those things which are requisite and necessary, as well for the body as the soul. Wherefore I pray and beseech you, as many as are here present, to accompany me with a pure heart and humble voice unto the throne of the heavenly grace, saying after me:

    A general Confession to be said of the whole Congregation after the Minister, all kneeling.

ALMIGHTY and most merciful Father, We have erred and strayed from thy ways like lost sheep, We have followed too much the devices and desires of our own hearts, We have offended against thy holy laws, We have left undone those things which we ought to have done, And we have done those things which we ought not to have done, And there is no health in us: But thou, O Lord, have mercy upon us miserable offenders; Spare thou them, O God, which confess their faults, Restore thou them that are penitent, According to thy promises declared unto mankind in Christ Jesu our Lord: And grant, O most merciful Father, for his sake, That we may hereafter live a godly, righteous, and sober life, To the glory of thy holy Name Amen.

The Absolution or Remission of sins to be pronounced by the Priest alone, standing: the people still kneeling.

ALMIGHTY God, the Father of our Lord Jesus Christ, who desireth not the death of a sinner, but rather that he may turn from his wickedness and live; and hath given power and commandment to his Ministers, to declare and pronounce to his people, being penitent, the Absolution and Remission of their sins: He pardoneth and absolveth all them that truly repent and unfeignedly believe his holy Gospel. Wherefore let us beseech him to grant us true repentance and his Holy Spirit, that those things may please him which we do at this present, and that the rest of our life hereafter may be pure and holy; so that at the last we may come to his eternal joy; through Jesus Christ our Lord. *Amen.*

If no priest be present the person saying the Service shall read the Collect for the Twenty-First Sunday after Trinity, that person and the people still kneeling.

Then the Minister shall kneel, and say the Lord's Prayer: the people also kneeling, and repeating it with him.

OUR Father which art in heaven, Hallowed be thy Name, Thy kingdom come, Thy will be done, in earth as it is in heaven. Give us this day our daily bread; And forgive us our trespasses, As we forgive them that trespass against us; And lead us not into temptation, But deliver us from evil. For thine is the kingdom, the power, and the glory, For ever and ever. Amen.

Then likewise he shall say,

O Lord, open thou our lips.
Answer. And our mouth shall shew forth thy praise.
Priest. O God, make speed to save us.
Answer. O Lord, make haste to help us.

Here, all standing up, the Priest shall say,

Glory be to the Father, and to the Son: and to the Holy Ghost;
Answer. As it was in the beginning, is now, and ever shall be:
world without end. Amen.

Priest. Praise ye the Lord.

Answer. The Lord's Name be praised.

Then shall be said or sung the Psalms in order as they be appointed. Then a Lesson of the Old Testament, as is appointed. And after that Magnificat (or the Song of the Blessed Virgin Mary) in English, as followeth.

MAGNIFICAT
S. Luke 1

My soul doth magnify the Lord: and my spirit hath rejoiced in God my Saviour.

For he hath regarded: the lowliness of his hand-maiden.

For behold, from henceforth: all generations shall call me blessed.

For he that is mighty hath magnified me: and holy is his Name.

And his mercy is on them that fear him: throughout all generations.

He hath shewed strength with his arm: he hath scattered the proud in the imagination of their hearts.

He hath put down the mighty from their seat: and hath exalted the humble and meek.

He hath filled the hungry with good things: and the rich he hath sent empty away.

He remembering his mercy hath holpen his servant Israel: as he promised to our forefathers, Abraham and his seed for ever.

Glory be to the Father, and to the Son: and to the Holy Ghost;

As it was in the beginning, is now, and ever shall be: world without end. Amen.

Or else this Psalm: Except it be on the nineteenth day of the month, when it is read in the ordinary course of the Psalms.

CANTATE DOMINO
Psalm 98

O SING unto the Lord a new song: for he hath done marvellous things.

With his own right hand, and with his holy arm: hath he gotten himself the victory.

The Lord declared his salvation: his righteousness hath he openly shewed in the sight of the heathen.

He hath remembered his mercy and truth toward the house of Israel: and all the ends of the world have seen the salvation of our God.

Shew yourselves joyful unto the Lord, all ye lands: sing, rejoice, and give thanks.

Praise the Lord upon the harp: sing to the harp with a psalm of thanksgiving.

With trumpets also and shawms: O shew yourselves joyful before the Lord the King.

Let the sea make a noise, and all that therein is: the round world, and they that dwell therein.

Let the floods clap their hands, and let the hills be joyful together before the Lord: for he cometh to judge the earth.

With righteousness shall he judge the world: and the people with equity.

Glory be to the Father, and to the Son: and to the Holy Ghost;

As it was in the beginning, is now, and ever shall be: world without end. Amen.

Then a Lesson of the New Testament, as it is appointed. And after that Nunc dimittis (or the Song of Simeon) in English, as followeth.

NUNC DIMITTIS
S. Luke 2. 29

LORD, now lettest thou thy servant depart in peace: according to thy word.

For mine eyes have seen: thy salvation;

Which thou hast prepared: before the face of all people;

To be a light to lighten the Gentiles: and to be the glory of thy people Israel.

Glory be to the Father, and to the Son: and to the Holy Ghost;

As it was in the beginning, is now, and ever shall be: world without end. Amen.

Or else this Psalm: Except it be on the twelfth day of the month.

DEUS MISEREATUR
Psalm 67

GOD be merciful unto us, and bless us: and shew us the light of his countenance, and be merciful unto us:

That thy way may be known upon earth: thy saving health among all nations.

Let the people praise thee, O God: yea, let all the people praise thee.

O let the nations rejoice and be glad: for thou shalt judge the folk righteously, and govern the nations upon earth.

Let the people praise thee, O God: yea, let all the people praise thee.

Then shall the earth bring forth her increase: and God, even our own God, shall give us his blessing.

God shall bless us: and all the ends of the world shall fear him.

Glory be to the Father, and to the Son: and to the Holy Ghost;

As it was in the beginning, is now, and ever shall be: world without end. Amen.

Then shall be said or sung the Apostles' Creed, by the Minister and the people standing.

I BELIEVE in God the Father Almighty, Maker of heaven and earth:

And in Jesus Christ his only Son our Lord, Who was conceived by the Holy Ghost, Born of the Virgin Mary, Suffered under Pontius Pilate, Was crucified, dead, and buried: He descended into hell; The third day he rose again from the dead; He ascended into heaven, And sitteth on the right hand of God the Father Almighty; From thence he shall come to judge the quick and the dead.

I believe in the Holy Ghost; The holy Catholick Church; The Communion of Saints; The Forgiveness of sins; The Resurrection of the body, And the life everlasting. Amen.

And after that these Prayers following, all devoutly kneeling: the Minister first pronouncing with a loud voice,

The Lord be with you.
Answer. And with thy spirit.
Minister. Let us pray.
Lord, have mercy upon us.
Christ, have mercy upon us.
Lord, have mercy upon us.

Then the Minister, Clerks, and people shall say the Lord's Prayer with a loud voice.

OUR Father which art in heaven, Hallowed be thy Name, Thy kingdom come, Thy will be done, in earth as it is in heaven. Give us this day our daily bread; And forgive us our trespasses, As we forgive them that trespass against us; And lead us not into temptation, But deliver us from evil. Amen.

Then the Priest standing up shall say,

O Lord, shew thy mercy upon us.
Answer. And grant us thy salvation.
Priest. O Lord, save the Queen.
Answer. And mercifully hear us when we call upon thee.
Priest. Endue thy Ministers with righteousness.
Answer. And make thy chosen people joyful.
Priest. O Lord, save thy people.
Answer. And bless thine inheritance.
Priest. Give peace in our time, O Lord.
Answer. Because there is none other that fighteth for us, but only thou, O God.
Priest. O God, make clean our hearts within us.
Answer. And take not thy Holy Spirit from us.

Then shall follow three Collects: The first of the day: The second for Peace: The third for Aid against all Perils, as here-after followeth: which two last Collects shall be daily said at Evening Prayer without alteration.

The Second Collect at Evening Prayer.

O GOD, from whom all holy desires, all good counsels, and all just works do proceed: Give unto thy servants that peace which the world cannot give; that both our hearts may be set to obey thy commandments, and also that by thee we being defended from the fear of our enemies may pass our time in rest and quietness; through the merits of Jesus Christ our Saviour. *Amen.*

The Third Collect, for Aid against all Perils.

LIGHTEN our darkness, we beseech thee, O Lord; and by thy great mercy defend us from all perils and dangers of this night; for the love of thy only Son, our Saviour Jesus Christ. *Amen.*

In Quires and Places where they sing here followeth the Anthem.

A Prayer for the Queen's Majesty.

O LORD our heavenly Father, high and mighty, King of kings, Lord of lords, the only Ruler of princes, who dost from thy throne behold all the dwellers upon earth: Most heartily we beseech thee with thy favour to behold our most gracious Sovereign Lady, Queen *ELIZABETH*; and so replenish her with the grace of thy Holy Spirit, that she may alway incline to thy will, and walk in thy way: Endue her plenteously with heavenly gifts; grant her in health and wealth long to live; strengthen her that she may vanquish and overcome all her enemies, and finally after this life she may attain everlasting joy and felicity; through Jesus Christ our Lord. *Amen.*

A Prayer for the Royal Family.

ALMIGHTY God, the fountain of all goodness, we humbly beseech thee to bless *Philip* Duke of *Edinburgh*, *Charles* Prince of *Wales*, and all the Royal Family: Endue them with thy Holy Spirit; enrich them with thy heavenly grace; prosper them with all happiness; and bring them to thine everlasting kingdom; through Jesus Christ our Lord. *Amen.*

A Prayer for the Clergy and People.

ALMIGHTY and everlasting God, who alone workest great marvels: Send down upon our Bishops and Curates, and all Congregations committed to their charge, the healthful Spirit of thy grace; and that they may truly please thee, pour upon them the continual dew of thy blessing. Grant this, O Lord, for the honour of our Advocate and Mediator, Jesus Christ. *Amen.*

A Prayer of Saint Chrysostom.

ALMIGHTY God, who hast given us grace at this time with one accord to make our common supplications unto thee; and dost promise that when two or three are gathered together in thy

Name thou wilt grant their requests: Fulfil now, O Lord, the desires and petitions of thy servants, as may be most expedient for them; granting us in this world knowledge of thy truth, and in the world to come life everlasting. *Amen.*

2 *Corinthians* 13.

THE grace of our Lord Jesus Christ, and the love of God, and the fellowship of the Holy Ghost, be with us all evermore. *Amen.*

Here endeth the Order of Evening Prayer
throughout the Year.

AT

MORNING PRAYER

Upon these Feasts; Christmas Day, *the* Epiphany, *Saint* Matthias, Easter Day, Ascension Day, Whitsunday, *Saint* John Baptist, *Saint* James, *Saint* Bartholomew, *Saint* Matthew, *Saint* Simon and *Saint* Jude, *Saint* Andrew, *and upon* Trinity Sunday, *shall be sung or said at Morning Prayer, instead of the Apostles' Creed, this Confession of our Christian Faith, commonly called the Creed of Saint Athanasius, by the Minister and people standing.*

QUICUNQUE VULT

WHOSOEVER will be saved: before all things it is necessary that he hold the Catholick Faith.

Which Faith except every one do keep whole and undefiled: without doubt he shall perish everlastingly.

And the Catholick Faith is this: That we worship one God in Trinity, and Trinity in Unity;

Neither confounding the Persons: nor dividing the Substance.

For there is one Person of the Father, another of the Son: and another of the Holy Ghost.

But the Godhead of the Father, of the Son, and of the Holy Ghost, is all one: the Glory equal, the Majesty co-eternal.

Such as the Father is, such is the Son: and such is the Holy Ghost.

The Father uncreate, the Son uncreate: and the Holy Ghost uncreate.

The Father incomprehensible, the Son incomprehensible: and the Holy Ghost incomprehensible.

The Father eternal, the Son eternal: and the Holy Ghost eternal.

And yet they are not three eternals: but one eternal.

As also there are not three incomprehensibles, nor three uncreated: but one uncreated, and one incomprehensible.

So likewise the Father is Almighty, the Son Almighty: and the Holy Ghost Almighty.

And yet they are not three Almighties: but one Almighty.

So the Father is God, the Son is God: and the Holy Ghost is God.

And yet they are not three Gods: but one God.

So likewise the Father is Lord, the Son Lord: and the Holy Ghost Lord.

And yet not three Lords: but one Lord.

For like as we are compelled by the Christian verity: to acknowledge every Person by himself to be God and Lord;

So are we forbidden by the Catholick Religion: to say there be three Gods, or three Lords.

The Father is made of none: neither created, nor begotten.

The Son is of the Father alone: not made, nor created, but begotten.

The Holy Ghost is of the Father and of the Son: neither made, nor created, nor begotten, but proceeding.

So there is one Father, not three Fathers; one Son, not three Sons: one Holy Ghost, not three Holy Ghosts.

And in this Trinity none is afore, or after other: none is greater, or less than another;

But the whole three Persons are co-eternal together: and co-equal.

So that in all things, as is aforesaid: the Unity in Trinity, and the Trinity in Unity is to be worshipped.

He therefore that will be saved: must thus think of the Trinity.

Furthermore it is necessary to everlasting salvation: that he also believe rightly the Incarnation of our Lord Jesus Christ.

For the right Faith is that we believe and confess: that our Lord Jesus Christ, the Son of God, is God and Man;

God, of the Substance of the Father, begotten before the worlds: and Man, of the Substance of his Mother, born in the world;

Perfect God, and Perfect Man: of a reasonable soul and human flesh subsisting;

Equal to the Father, as touching his Godhead: and inferior to the Father, as touching his Manhood.

Who although he be God and Man: yet he is not two, but one Christ;

One, not by conversion of the Godhead into flesh: but by taking of the Manhood into God;

One altogether, not by confusion of Substance: but by unity of Person.

For as the reasonable soul and flesh is one man: so God and Man is one Christ.

Who suffered for our salvation: descended into hell, rose again the third day from the dead.

He ascended into heaven, he sitteth on the right hand of the Father, God Almighty: from whence he shall come to judge the quick and the dead.

At whose coming all men shall rise again with their bodies: and shall give account for their own works.

And they that have done good shall go into life everlasting: and they that have done evil into everlasting fire.

This is the Catholick Faith: which except a man believe faithfully, he cannot be saved.

Glory be to the Father, and to the Son: and to the Holy Ghost;

As it was in the beginning, is now, and ever shall be: world without end. Amen.

THE LITANY

Here followeth the Litany, or General Supplication, to be sung or said after Morning Prayer, upon Sundays, Wednesdays, and Fridays, and at other times when it shall be commanded by the Ordinary.

O GOD the Father of heaven: have mercy upon us miserable sinners.

O God the Father of heaven: have mercy upon us miserable sinners.

O God the Son, Redeemer of the world: have mercy upon us miserable sinners.

O God the Son, Redeemer of the world: have mercy upon us miserable sinners.

O God the Holy Ghost, proceeding from the Father and the Son: have mercy upon us miserable sinners.

O God the Holy Ghost, proceeding from the Father and the Son: have mercy upon us miserable sinners.

O holy, blessed, and glorious Trinity, three Persons and one God: have mercy upon us miserable sinners.

O holy, blessed, and glorious Trinity, three Persons and one God: have mercy upon us miserable sinners.

Remember not, Lord, our offences, nor the offences of our forefathers; neither take thou vengeance of our sins: spare us, good Lord, spare thy people, whom thou hast redeemed with thy most precious blood, and be not angry with us for ever.

Spare us, good Lord.

From all evil and mischief; from sin, from the crafts and assaults of the devil; from thy wrath, and from everlasting damnation,

Good Lord, deliver us.

From all blindness of heart; from pride, vain-glory, and hypo-crisy; from envy, hatred, and malice, and all uncharitableness,

Good Lord, deliver us.

From fornication, and all other deadly sin; and from all the deceits of the world, the flesh, and the devil,

Good Lord, deliver us.

From lightning and tempest; from plague, pestilence, and famine; from battle and murder, and from sudden death,

Good Lord, deliver us.

From all sedition, privy conspiracy, and rebellion; from all false doctrine, heresy, and schism; from hardness of heart, and contempt of thy Word and Commandment,

Good Lord, deliver us.

By the mystery of thy holy Incarnation; by thy holy Nativity and Circumcision; by thy Baptism, Fasting, and Temptation,

Good Lord, deliver us.

By thine Agony and bloody Sweat; by thy Cross and Passion; by thy precious Death and Burial; by thy glorious Resurrection and Ascension; and by the coming of the Holy Ghost,

Good Lord, deliver us.

In all time of our tribulation; in all time of our wealth; in the hour of death, and in the day of judgement,

Good Lord, deliver us.

We sinners do beseech thee to hear us, O Lord God: and that it may please thee to rule and govern thy holy Church universal in the right way,

We beseech thee to hear us, good Lord.

That it may please thee to keep and strengthen in the true worshipping of thee, in righteousness and holiness of life, thy Servant *ELIZABETH*, our most gracious Queen and Governor,

We beseech thee to hear us, good Lord.

That it may please thee to rule her heart in thy faith, fear, and love, and that she may evermore have affiance in thee, and ever seek thy honour and glory,

We beseech thee to hear us, good Lord.

That it may please thee to be her defender and keeper, giving her the victory over all her enemies,

We beseech thee to hear us, good Lord.

That it may please thee to bless and preserve *Philip* Duke of *Edinburgh*, *Charles* Prince of *Wales*, and all the Royal Family,

We beseech thee to hear us, good Lord.

That it may please thee to illuminate all Bishops, Priests, and Deacons, with true knowledge and understanding of thy Word; and that both by their preaching and living they may set it forth and shew it accordingly,

We beseech thee to hear us, good Lord.

That it may please thee to endue the Lords of the Council, and all the Nobility, with grace, wisdom, and understanding,

We beseech thee to hear us, good Lord.

That it may please thee to bless and keep the Magistrates, giving them grace to execute justice, and to maintain truth,

We beseech thee to hear us, good Lord.

That it may please thee to bless and keep all thy people,

We beseech thee to hear us, good Lord.

That it may please thee to give to all nations unity, peace, and concord,

We beseech thee to hear us, good Lord.

That it may please thee to give us an heart to love and dread thee, and diligently to live after thy commandments,

We beseech thee to hear us, good Lord.

That it may please thee to give to all thy people increase of grace, to hear meekly thy Word, and to receive it with pure affection, and to bring forth the fruits of the Spirit,

We beseech thee to hear us, good Lord.

That it may please thee to bring into the way of truth all such as have erred, and are deceived,

We beseech thee to hear us, good Lord.

That it may please thee to strengthen such as do stand; and to comfort and help the weak-hearted; and to raise up them that fall; and finally to beat down Satan under our feet,

We beseech thee to hear us, good Lord.

That it may please thee to succour, help, and comfort all that are in danger, necessity, and tribulation,

We beseech thee to hear us, good Lord.

That it may please thee to preserve all that travel by land or by water, all women labouring of child, all sick persons, and young children; and to shew thy pity upon all prisoners and captives,

We beseech thee to hear us, good Lord.

That it may please thee to defend, and provide for, the fatherless children, and widows, and all that are desolate and oppressed

We beseech thee to hear us, good Lord.

That it may please thee to have mercy upon all men,

We beseech thee to hear us, good Lord.

That it may please thee to forgive our enemies, persecutors, and slanderers, and to turn their hearts,

We beseech thee to hear us, good Lord.

That it may please thee to give and preserve to our use the kindly fruits of the earth, so as in due time we may enjoy them,

We beseech thee to hear us, good Lord.

That it may please thee to give us true repentance; to forgive us all our sins, negligences, and ignorances; and to endue us with the grace of thy Holy Spirit, to amend our lives according to thy holy Word,

We beseech thee to hear us, good Lord.

Son of God: we beseech thee to hear us.

Son of God: we beseech thee to hear us.

O Lamb of God: that takest away the sins of the world;

Grant us thy peace.

O Lamb of God: that takest away the sins of the world;

Have mercy upon us.

O Christ, hear us.

O Christ, hear us.

Lord, have mercy upon us.

Lord, have mercy upon us.

Christ, have mercy upon us.

Christ, have mercy upon us.

Lord, have mercy upon us.

Lord, have mercy upon us.

Then shall the Priest, and the people with him, say the Lord's Prayer.

OUR Father which art in heaven, Hallowed be thy Name, Thy kingdom come, Thy will be done, in earth as it is in heaven. Give us this day our daily bread; And forgive us our trespasses,

As we forgive them that trespass against us; And lead us not into temptation, But deliver us from evil. Amen.

Priest. O Lord, deal not with us after our sins.

Answer. Neither reward us after our iniquities.

Let us pray.

O GOD, merciful Father, that despisest not the sighing of a contrite heart, nor the desire of such as be sorrowful: Mercifully assist our prayers that we make before thee in all our troubles and adversities, whensoever they oppress us; and graciously hear us, that those evils, which the craft and subtilty of the devil or man worketh against us, be brought to nought, and by the providence of thy goodness they may be dispersed; that we thy servants, being hurt by no persecutions, may evermore give thanks unto thee in thy holy Church; through Jesus Christ our Lord.

O Lord, arise, help us, and deliver us for thy Name's sake.

O GOD, we have heard with our ears, and our fathers have declared unto us, the noble works that thou didst in their days, and in the old time before them.

O Lord, arise, help us, and deliver us for thine honour.

Glory be to the Father, and to the Son: and to the Holy Ghost;

Answer. As it was in the beginning, is now, and ever shall be: world without end. Amen.

From our enemies defend us, O Christ.

Graciously look upon our afflictions.

Pitifully behold the sorrows of our hearts.

Mercifully forgive the sins of thy people.

Favourably with mercy hear our prayers.

O Son of David, have mercy upon us.

Both now and ever vouchsafe to hear us, O Christ.

Graciously hear us, O Christ; graciously hear us, O Lord Christ.

Priest. O Lord, let thy mercy be shewed upon us;

Answer. As we do put our trust in thee.

Let us pray.

WE humbly beseech thee, O Father, mercifully to look upon our infirmities; and for the glory of thy Name turn from us all those evils that we most righteously have deserved; and grant that in all our troubles we may put our whole trust and confidence in thy mercy, and evermore serve thee in holiness and pureness of living, to thy honour and glory; through our only Mediator and Advocate, Jesus Christ our Lord. *Amen.*

A Prayer of Saint Chrysostom.

ALMIGHTY God, who hast given us grace at this time with one accord to make our common supplications unto thee; and dost promise that when two or three are gathered together in thy Name thou wilt grant their requests: Fulfil now, O Lord, the desires and petitions of thy servants, as may be most expedient for them; granting us in this world knowledge of thy truth, and in the world to come life everlasting. *Amen.*

2 *Corinthians* 13.

THE grace of our Lord Jesus Christ, and the love of God, and the fellowship of the Holy Ghost, be with us all evermore. *Amen.*

Here endeth the Litany.

PRAYERS AND THANKSGIVINGS

Upon several occasions, to be used before the two final Prayers of the Litany, or of Morning and Evening Prayer.

PRAYERS

For Rain.

O GOD, heavenly Father, who by thy Son Jesus Christ hast promised to all them that seek thy kingdom, and the right-eousness thereof, all things necessary to their bodily sustenance: Send us, we beseech thee, in this our necessity, such moderate rain and showers, that we may receive the fruits of the earth to our comfort, and to thy honour; through Jesus Christ our Lord. *Amen.*

For fair Weather.

O ALMIGHTY Lord God, who for the sin of man didst once drown all the world, except eight persons, and afterward of thy great mercy didst promise never to destroy it so again: We humbly beseech thee, that although we for our iniquities have worthily deserved a plague of rain and waters, yet upon our true repentance thou wilt send us such weather, as that we may receive the fruits of the earth in due season; and learn both by thy punishment to amend our lives, and for thy clemency to give thee praise and glory; through Jesus Christ our Lord. *Amen.*

In the time of Dearth and Famine.

O GOD, heavenly Father, whose gift it is that the rain doth fall, the earth is fruitful, beasts increase, and fishes do multiply: Behold, we beseech thee, the afflictions of thy people; and grant that the scarcity and dearth, which we do now most justly suffer for our iniquity, may through thy goodness be mercifully turned into cheapness and plenty; for the love of Jesus Christ our Lord, to whom with thee and the Holy Ghost be all honour and glory, now and for ever. *Amen.*

Or this.

O GOD, merciful Father, who, in the time of Elisha the prophet, didst suddenly in Samaria turn great scarcity and dearth into plenty and cheapness: Have mercy upon us, that we, who are now for our sins punished with like adversity, may likewise find a seasonable relief: Increase the fruits of the earth by thy heavenly benediction; and grant that we, receiving thy bountiful liberality, may use the same to thy glory, the relief of those that are needy, and our own comfort; through Jesus Christ our Lord. *Amen.*

In the time of War and Tumults.

O ALMIGHTY God, King of all kings, and Governor of all things, whose power no creature is able to resist, to whom it belongeth justly to punish sinners, and to be merciful to them that truly repent: Save and deliver us, we humbly beseech thee, from the hands of our enemies; abate their pride, asswage their malice, and confound their devices; that we, being armed with thy defence, may be preserved evermore from all perils, to glorify thee, who art the only giver of all victory; through the merits of thy only Son, Jesus Christ our Lord. *Amen.*

In the time of any common Plague or Sickness.

O ALMIGHTY God, who in thy wrath didst send a plague upon thine own people in the wilderness, for their obstinate rebellion against Moses and Aaron; and also, in the time of king David, didst slay with the plague of pestilence threescore and ten thousand, and yet remembering thy mercy didst save the rest: Have pity upon us miserable sinners, who now are visited with great sickness and mortality; that like as thou didst then accept of an atonement, and didst command the destroying Angel to cease from punishing, so it may now please thee to withdraw from us this plague and grievous sickness; through Jesus Christ our Lord. *Amen.*

In the Ember Weeks, to be said every day, for those that are to be admitted into Holy Orders.

ALMIGHTY God, our heavenly Father, who hast purchased to thyself an universal Church by the precious blood of thy dear Son: Mercifully look upon the same, and at this time so guide and govern the minds of thy servants the Bishops and Pastors of thy flock, that they may lay hands suddenly on no man, but faithfully and wisely make choice of fit persons to serve in the sacred Ministry of thy Church. And to those which shall be ordained to any holy function give thy grace and heavenly benediction; that both by their life and doctrine they may set forth thy glory, and set forward the salvation of all men; through Jesus Christ our Lord. *Amen.*

Or this.

ALMIGHTY God, the giver of all good gifts, who of thy divine providence hast appointed divers Orders in thy Church: Give thy grace, we humbly beseech thee, to all those who are to be called to any office and administration in the same; and so replenish them with the truth of thy doctrine, and endue them with innocency of life, that they may faithfully serve before thee, to the glory of thy great Name, and the benefit of thy holy Church; through Jesus Christ our Lord. *Amen.*

A Prayer that may be said after any of the former.

O GOD, whose nature and property is ever to have mercy and to forgive, receive our humble petitions; and though we be tied and bound with the chain of our sins, yet let the pitifulness of thy great mercy loose us; for the honour of Jesus Christ, our Mediator and Advocate. *Amen.*

A Prayer for the High Court of Parliament, to be read during their Session.

MOST gracious God, we humbly beseech thee, as for this Kingdom in general, so especially for the High Court of Parliament, under our most religious and gracious Queen at this time assembled: That thou wouldest be pleased to direct and prosper all their consultations to the advancement of thy glory, the good of thy Church, the safety, honour, and welfare of our Sovereign and her Dominions; that all things may be so ordered and settled by their endeavours, upon the best and surest foundations, that peace and happiness, truth and justice, religion and piety, may be established among us for all generations. These and all other necessaries, for them, for us, and thy whole Church, we humbly beg in the Name and Mediation of Jesus Christ our most blessed Lord and Saviour. *Amen*.

A Collect or Prayer for all Conditions of men, to be used at such times when the Litany is not appointed to be said.

O GOD, the Creator and Preserver of all mankind, we humbly beseech thee for all sorts and conditions of men; that thou wouldest be pleased to make thy ways known unto them, thy saving health unto all nations. More especially we pray for the good estate of the Catholick Church; that it may be so guided and governed by thy good Spirit, that all who profess and call themselves Christians may be led into the way of truth, and hold the faith in unity of spirit, in the bond of peace, and in righteousness of life. Finally we commend to thy fatherly goodness all those, who are any ways afflicted or distressed in mind, body, or estate; [*especially those for whom our prayers are desired;*] that it may please thee to comfort and relieve them according to their several necessities, giving them patience under their sufferings, and a happy issue out of all their afflictions. And this we beg for Jesus Christ his sake. *Amen*.

*This to be said when any desire the Prayers of the Congregation.

THANKSGIVINGS

A General Thanksgiving.

ALMIGHTY God, Father of all mercies, we thine unworthy
servants do give thee most humble and hearty thanks for all thy
goodness and loving-kindness to us and to all men; [*particularly
to those who desire now to offer up their praises and thanksgivings
for thy late mercies vouchsafed unto them.*] We bless thee for our
creation, preservation, and all the blessings of this life; but above
all for thine inestimable love in the redemption of the world by
our Lord Jesus Christ, for the means of grace, and for the hope
of glory. And we beseech thee, give us that due sense of all thy
mercies, that our hearts may be unfeignedly thankful, and that
we shew forth thy praise, not only with our lips, but in our lives;
by giving up ourselves to thy service, and by walking before thee
in holiness and righteousness all our days; through Jesus Christ
our Lord, to whom with thee and the Holy Ghost be all honour
and glory, world without end. *Amen.*

For Rain.

O GOD our heavenly Father, who by thy gracious providence
dost cause the former and the latter rain to descend upon the
earth, that it may bring forth fruit for the use of man: We
give thee humble thanks that it hath pleased thee, in our great
necessity, to send us at the last a joyful rain upon thine inheritance, and to refresh it when it was dry, to the great comfort of
us thy unworthy servants, and to the glory of thy holy Name;
through thy mercies in Jesus Christ our Lord. *Amen.*

For fair Weather.

O LORD God, who hast justly humbled us by thy late plague
of immoderate rain and waters, and in thy mercy hast relieved
and comforted our souls by this seasonable and blessed change
of weather: We praise and glorify thy holy Name for this thy

This to be said when any that have been prayed for desire to return praise.

mercy, and will always declare thy loving-kindness from genera
tion to generation; through Jesus Christ our Lord. *Amen.*

For Plenty.

O MOST merciful Father, who of thy gracious goodness ha
heard the devout prayers of thy Church, and turned our deart
and scarcity into cheapness and plenty: We give thee humb
thanks for this thy special bounty; beseeching thee to continu
thy loving-kindness unto us, that our land may yield us her frui
of increase, to thy glory and our comfort; through Jesus Chri
our Lord. *Amen.*

For Peace and Deliverance from our Enemies.

O ALMIGHTY God, who art a strong tower of defenc
unto thy servants against the face of their enemies: We yiel
thee praise and thanksgiving for our deliverance from thos
great and apparent dangers wherewith we were compassed: W
acknowledge it thy goodness that we were not delivered over
a prey unto them; beseeching thee still to continue such th
mercies towards us, that all the world may know that thou a
our Saviour and mighty Deliverer; through Jesus Christ o
Lord. *Amen.*

For restoring Publick Peace at Home.

O ETERNAL God, our heavenly Father, who alone make
men to be of one mind in a house, and stillest the outrage of
violent and unruly people: We bless thy holy Name, that it hat
pleased thee to appease the seditious tumults which have bee
lately raised up amongst us: most humbly beseeching thee
grant to all of us grace, that we may henceforth obediently wal
in thy holy commandments; and leading a quiet and peaceabl
life, in all godliness and honesty, may continually offer unto the
our sacrifice of praise and thanksgiving for these thy mercie
towards us; through Jesus Christ our Lord. *Amen.*

For Deliverance from the Plague, or other common Sickness.

O LORD God, who hast wounded us for our sins, and consumed us for our transgressions, by thy late heavy and dreadful visitation; and now, in the midst of judgement remembering mercy, hast redeemed our souls from the jaws of death: We offer unto thy fatherly goodness ourselves, our souls and bodies which thou hast delivered, to be a living sacrifice unto thee, always praising and magnifying thy mercies in the midst of thy Church; through Jesus Christ our Lord. *Amen.*

Or this.

WE humbly acknowledge before thee, O most merciful Father, that all the punishments which are threatened in thy law might justly have fallen upon us, by reason of our manifold transgressions and hardness of heart: Yet seeing it hath pleased thee of thy tender mercy, upon our weak and unworthy humiliation, to asswage the contagious sickness wherewith we lately have been sore afflicted, and to restore the voice of joy and health into our dwellings: We offer unto thy Divine Majesty the sacrifice of praise and thanksgiving, lauding and magnifying thy glorious Name for such thy preservation and providence over us; through Jesus Christ our Lord. *Amen.*

THE
COLLECTS, EPISTLES, AND GOSPELS
TO BE USED THROUGHOUT THE YEAR

Note, that the Collect appointed for every Sunday, or for any Holy-day that hath a Vigil or Eve, shall be said at the Evening Service next before.

THE FIRST SUNDAY IN ADVENT

The Collect

ALMIGHTY God, give us grace that we may cast away the works of darkness, and put upon us the armour of light, now in the time of this mortal life, in which thy Son Jesus Christ came to visit us in great humility; that in the last day, when he shall come again in his glorious Majesty, to judge both the quick and the dead, we may rise to the life immortal; through him who liveth and reigneth with thee and the Holy Ghost, now and ever. *Amen.*

This Collect is to be repeated every day with the other Collects in Advent, until Christmas Eve.

The Epistle. Rom. 13. 8–end

OWE no man any thing, but to love one another: for he that loveth another hath fulfilled the law. For this, Thou shalt not commit adultery, Thou shalt not kill, Thou shalt not steal, Thou shalt not bear false witness, Thou shalt not covet; and if there be any other commandment, it is briefly comprehended in this saying, namely, Thou shalt love thy neighbour as thyself. Love worketh no ill to his neighbour; therefore love is the fulfilling of the law. And that, knowing the time, that now it is high time to awake out of sleep: for now is our salvation nearer than when we believed. The night is far spent, the day is at hand; let us therefore cast off the works of darkness, and let us put on the armour of light. Let us walk honestly as in the day; not in rioting and drunkenness, not in chambering and wantonness, not in strife and envying. But put ye on the Lord Jesus Christ, and make not provision for the flesh, to fulfil the lusts thereof.

The Gospel. S. Matth. 21. 1–13

WHEN they drew nigh unto Jerusalem, and were come to Bethphage, unto the mount of Olives, then sent Jesus two disciples, saying unto them, Go into the village over against you, and straightway ye shall find an ass tied, and a colt with her: loose them, and bring them unto me. And if any man say ought unto you, ye shall say, The Lord hath need of them; and straightway he will send them. All this was done, that it might be fulfilled which was spoken by the Prophet, saying, Tell ye the daughter of Sion, Behold, thy King cometh unto thee, meek, and sitting upon an ass, and a colt the foal of an ass. And the disciples went, and did as Jesus commanded them; and brought the ass, and the colt, and put on them their clothes, and they set him thereon. And a very great multitude spread their garments in the way; others cut down branches from the trees, and strawed them in the way. And the multitudes that went before, and that followed, cried, saying, Hosanna to the Son of David; Blessed is he that cometh in the Name of the Lord; Hosanna in the Highest. And when he was come into Jerusalem all the city was moved, saying, Who is this? And the multitude said, This is Jesus the Prophet of Nazareth of Galilee. And Jesus went into the temple of God, and cast out all them that sold and bought in the temple; and overthrew the tables of the money-changers, and the seats of them that sold doves; and said unto them, It is written, My house shall be called the house of prayer; but ye have made it a den of thieves.

THE SECOND SUNDAY IN ADVENT

The Collect

BLESSED Lord, who hast caused all holy Scriptures to be written for our learning: Grant that we may in such wise hear them, read, mark, learn, and inwardly digest them, that by patience and comfort of thy holy Word, we may embrace and ever hold fast the blessed hope of everlasting life, which thou hast given us in our Saviour Jesus Christ. *Amen.*

The Epistle. Rom. 15. 4–13

WHATSOEVER things were written aforetime were written for our learning; that we through patience and comfort of the Scriptures might have hope. Now the God of patience and consolation grant you to be like-minded one towards another, according to Christ Jesus: that ye may with one mind and one mouth glorify God, even the Father of our Lord Jesus Christ. Wherefore receive ye one another, as Christ also received us, to the glory of God. Now I say, that Jesus Christ was a minister of the circumcision for the truth of God, to confirm the promises made unto the fathers; and that the Gentiles might glorify God for his mercy; as it is written, For this cause I will confess to thee among the Gentiles, and sing unto thy Name. And again he saith, Rejoice, ye Gentiles, with his people. And again, Praise the Lord, all ye Gentiles, and laud him, all ye people. And again, Esaias saith, There shall be a root of Jesse, and he that shall rise to reign over the Gentiles, in him shall the Gentiles trust. Now the God of hope fill you with all joy and peace in believing, that ye may abound in hope, through the power of the Holy Ghost.

The Gospel. S. Luke 21. 25–33

AND there shall be signs in the sun, and in the moon, and in the stars; and upon the earth distress of nations, with perplexity, the sea and the waves roaring; men's hearts failing them for fear, and for looking after those things which are coming on the earth: for the powers of heaven shall be shaken. And then shall they see the Son of Man coming in a cloud with power and great glory. And when these things begin to come to pass, then look up, and lift up your heads; for your redemption draweth nigh. And he spake to them a parable; Behold the fig-tree, and all the trees; when they now shoot forth, ye see and know of your own selves that summer is now nigh at hand. So likewise ye, when ye see these things come to pass, know ye that the kingdom of God is nigh at hand. Verily I say unto you, This generation shall not pass away, till all be fulfilled: heaven and earth shall pass away; but my words shall not pass away.

THE THIRD SUNDAY IN ADVENT

The Collect

O LORD Jesus Christ, who at thy first coming didst send thy messenger to prepare thy way before thee: Grant that the ministers and stewards of thy mysteries may likewise so prepare and make ready thy way, by turning the hearts of the disobedient to the wisdom of the just, that at thy second coming to judge the world we may be found an acceptable people in thy sight, who livest and reignest with the Father and the Holy Spirit, ever one God, world without end. *Amen.*

The Epistle. 1 Cor. 4. 1–5

LET a man so account of us, as of the ministers of Christ, and stewards of the mysteries of God. Moreover, it is required in stewards, that a man be found faithful. But with me it is a very small thing that I should be judged of you, or of man's judgement: yea, I judge not mine own self. For I know nothing by myself, yet am I not hereby justified; but he that judgeth me is the Lord. Therefore judge nothing before the time, until the Lord come, who both will bring to light the hidden things of darkness, and will make manifest the counsels of the hearts; and then shall every man have praise of God.

The Gospel. S. Matth. 11. 2–10

NOW when John had heard in the prison the works of Christ, he sent two of his disciples, and said unto him, Art thou he that should come, or do we look for another? Jesus answered and said unto them, Go and shew John again those things which ye do hear and see: the blind receive their sight, and the lame walk, the lepers are cleansed, and the deaf hear, the dead are raised up, and the poor have the Gospel preached to them. And blessed is he whosoever shall not be offended in me. And as they departed, Jesus began to say unto the multitudes concerning John, What went ye out into the wilderness to see? a reed shaken with the wind? But what went ye out for to see? a man clothed in soft raiment? behold, they that wear soft clothing are in kings' houses. But what went ye out for to see? a prophet? yea, I say unto you, and more than a prophet. For this is he of whom it is written, Behold, I send my messenger before thy face, which shall prepare thy way before thee.

THE FOURTH SUNDAY IN ADVENT

The Collect

O LORD, raise up (we pray thee) thy power, and come among us, and with great might succour us; that whereas, through our sins and wickedness, we are sore let and hindered in running the race that is set before us, thy bountiful grace and mercy may speedily help and deliver us; through the satisfaction of thy Son our Lord, to whom with thee and the Holy Ghost be honour and glory, world without end. *Amen.*

The Epistle. Philip. 4. 4–7

REJOICE in the Lord alway, and again I say, Rejoice. Let your moderation be known unto all men. The Lord is at hand. Be careful for nothing: but in every thing, by prayer and supplication with thanksgiving, let your requests be made known unto God. And the peace of God, which passeth all understanding, shall keep your hearts and minds through Christ Jesus.

The Gospel. S. John 1. 19–28

THIS is the record of John, when the Jews sent Priests and Levites from Jerusalem to ask him, Who art thou? And he confessed, and denied not; but confessed, I am not the Christ. And they asked him, What then? Art thou Elias? And he saith, I am not. Art thou that Prophet? And he answered, No. Then said they unto him, Who art thou? that we may give an answer to them that sent us. What sayest thou of thyself? He said, I am the voice of one crying in the wilderness, Make straight the way of the Lord, as said the prophet Esaias. And they which were sent were of the Pharisees. And they asked him, and said unto him, Why baptizest thou then, if thou be not that Christ, nor Elias, neither that Prophet? John answered them, saying, I baptize with water: but there standeth one among you, whom ye know not: he it is who coming after me is preferred before me, whose shoe's latchet I am not worthy to unloose. These things were done in Bethabara beyond Jordan, where John was baptizing.

THE NATIVITY OF OUR LORD, OR THE BIRTH-DAY OF CHRIST COMMONLY CALLED

CHRISTMAS DAY*

The Collect

ALMIGHTY God, who hast given us thy only-begotten Son to take our nature upon him, and as at this time to be born of a pure Virgin: Grant that we being regenerate, and made thy children by adoption and grace, may daily be renewed by thy Holy Spirit; through the same our Lord Jesus Christ, who liveth and reigneth with thee and the same Spirit, ever one God, world without end. *Amen.*

The Epistle. Hebr. i. 1–12

GOD, who at sundry times and in divers manners spake in time past unto the fathers by the prophets, hath in these last days spoken unto us by his Son, whom he hath appointed heir of all things, by whom also he made the worlds; who being the brightness of his glory, and the express image of his person, and upholding all things by the word of his power, when he had by himself purged our sins, sat down on the right hand of the

*December 25.

Majesty on high; being made so much better than the angels, as he hath by inheritance obtained a more excellent name than they. For unto which of the angels said he at any time, Thou art my Son, this day have I begotten thee? And again, I will be to him a Father, and he shall be to me a Son? And again, when he bringeth in the first-begotten into the world, he saith, And let all the angels of God worship him. And of the angels he saith, Who maketh his angels spirits, and his ministers a flame of fire. But unto the Son he saith, Thy throne, O God, is for ever and ever; a sceptre of righteousness is the sceptre of thy kingdom: Thou hast loved righteousness, and hated iniquity; therefore God, even thy God, hath anointed thee with the oil of gladness above thy fellows. And, Thou, Lord, in the beginning hast laid the foundation of the earth; and the heavens are the works of thine hands: they shall perish, but thou remainest; and they all shall wax old as doth a garment; and as a vesture shalt thou fold them up, and they shall be changed; but thou art the same, and thy years shall not fail.

The Gospel. S. John 1. 1–14

IN the beginning was the Word, and the Word was with God, and the Word was God. The same was in the beginning with God. All things were made by him; and without him was not any thing made that was made. In him was life, and the life was the light of men. And the light shineth in darkness, and the darkness comprehended it not. There was a man sent from God, whose name was John. The same came for a witness, to bear witness of the light, that all men through him might believe. He was not that light, but was sent to bear witness of that light. That was the true light, which lighteth every man that cometh into the world. He was in the world, and the world was made by him, and the world knew him not. He came unto his own, and his own received him not. But as many as received him, to them gave he power to become the sons of God, even to them that believe on his Name: which were born, not of blood, nor of the will of the flesh, nor of the will of man, but of God. And the Word was made flesh, and dwelt among us (and we beheld his glory, the glory as of the only-begotten of the Father) full of grace and truth.

SAINT STEPHEN'S DAY*

The Collect

GRANT, O Lord, that in all our sufferings here upon earth, for the testimony of thy truth, we may stedfastly look up to heaven, and by faith behold the glory that shall be revealed; and, being filled with the Holy Ghost, may learn to love and bless our persecutors, by the example of thy first Martyr Saint Stephen, who prayed for his murderers to thee, O blessed Jesus, who standest at the right hand of God to succour all those that suffer for thee, our only Mediator and Advocate. *Amen.*

Then shall follow the Collect of the Nativity, which shall be said continually unto New-year's Eve.

For the Epistle. Acts 7. 55–end

STEPHEN, being full of the Holy Ghost, looked up stedfastly into heaven, and saw the glory of God, and Jesus standing on the right hand of God, and said, Behold, I see the heavens opened, and the Son of Man standing on the right hand of God. Then they cried out with a loud voice, and stopped their ears, and ran upon him with one accord, and cast him out of the city, and stoned him: and the witnesses laid down their clothes at a young man's feet, whose name was Saul. And they stoned Stephen, calling upon God, and saying, Lord Jesus, receive my spirit. And he kneeled down, and cried with a loud voice, Lord, lay not this sin to their charge. And when he had said this, he fell asleep.

The Gospel. S. Matth. 23. 34–end

BEHOLD, I send unto you prophets, and wise men, and scribes; and some of them ye shall kill and crucify; and some of them shall ye scourge in your synagogues, and persecute them from city to city; that upon you may come all the righteous

December 26.

blood shed upon the earth, from the blood of righteous Abel
unto the blood of Zacharias, son of Barachias, whom ye slew
between the temple and the altar. Verily I say unto you, All these
things shall come upon this generation. O Jerusalem, Jerusalem,
thou that killest the prophets, and stonest them which are sent
unto thee; how often would I have gathered thy children
together, even as a hen gathereth her chickens under her wings,
and ye would not! Behold, your house is left unto you desolate.
For I say unto you, Ye shall not see me henceforth, till ye shall
say, Blessed is he that cometh in the Name of the Lord.

SAINT JOHN THE EVANGELIST'S DAY*

The Collect

MERCIFUL Lord, we beseech thee to cast thy bright beams
of light upon thy Church, that it being enlightened by the doctrine of thy blessed Apostle and Evangelist Saint John may so
walk in the light of thy truth, that it may at length attain to the
light of everlasting life; through Jesus Christ our Lord. *Amen.*

The Epistle. 1 S. John 1. 1–end

THAT which was from the beginning, which we have heard,
which we have seen with our eyes, which we have looked upon,
and our hands have handled of the word of life; (for the life was
manifested, and we have seen it, and bear witness, and shew
unto you that eternal life, which was with the Father, and was
manifested unto us;) That which we have seen and heard declare
we unto you, that ye also may have fellowship with us; and truly
our fellowship is with the Father, and with his Son Jesus Christ.
And these things write we unto you, that your joy may be full.
This then is the message which we have heard of him, and
declare unto you, That God is light, and in him is no darkness
at all. If we say that we have fellowship with him, and walk in
darkness, we lie, and do not the truth: but if we walk in the
light, as he is in the light, we have fellowship one with another,
and the blood of Jesus Christ his Son cleanseth us from all sin.

*December 27.

If we say that we have no sin, we deceive ourselves, and the truth is not in us. If we confess our sins, he is faithful and just to forgive us our sins, and to cleanse us from all unrighteousness. If we say that we have not sinned, we make him a liar, and his word is not in us.

The Gospel. S. John 21. 19–end

JESUS said unto Peter, Follow me. Then Peter, turning about, seeth the disciple whom Jesus loved following; which also leaned on his breast at supper, and said, Lord, which is he that betrayeth thee? Peter seeing him saith to Jesus, Lord, and what shall this man do? Jesus saith unto him, If I will that he tarry till I come, what is that to thee? Follow thou me. Then went this saying abroad among the brethren, That that disciple should not die: yet Jesus said not unto him, He shall not die; but, If I will that he tarry till I come, what is that to thee? This is the disciple which testifieth of these things, and wrote these things, and we know that his testimony is true. And there are also many other things which Jesus did, the which if they should be written every one, I suppose, that even the world itself could not contain the books that should be written.

THE INNOCENTS' DAY*

The Collect

O ALMIGHTY God, who out of the mouths of babes and sucklings hast ordained strength, and madest infants to glorify thee by their deaths: Mortify and kill all vices in us, and so strengthen us by thy grace, that by the innocency of our lives, and constancy of our faith, even unto death, we may glorify thy holy Name; through Jesus Christ our Lord. *Amen.*

For the Epistle. Rev. 14. 1–5

I LOOKED, and lo, a Lamb stood on the mount Sion, and with him an hundred forty and four thousand, having his Father's Name written in their foreheads. And I heard a voice from

*December 28.

heaven, as the voice of many waters, and as the voice of a great thunder: and I heard the voice of harpers harping with their harps: and they sung as it were a new song before the throne, and before the four beasts, and the elders; and no man could learn that song, but the hundred and forty and four thousand, which were redeemed from the earth. These are they which were not defiled with women, for they are virgins: these are they which follow the Lamb whithersoever he goeth: these were redeemed from among men, being the first-fruits unto God, and to the Lamb. And in their mouth was found no guile; for they are without fault before the throne of God.

The Gospel. S. Matth. 2. 13–18

THE Angel of the Lord appeareth to Joseph in a dream, saying, Arise, and take the young child, and his mother, and flee into Egypt, and be thou there until I bring thee word; for Herod will seek the young child to destroy him. When he arose, he took the young child and his mother by night, and departed into Egypt, and was there until the death of Herod; that it might be fulfilled which was spoken of the Lord by the prophet, saying, Out of Egypt have I called my Son. Then Herod, when he saw that he was mocked of the wise men, was exceeding wroth; and sent forth, and slew all the children that were in Bethlehem, and in all the coasts thereof, from two years old and under, according to the time which he had diligently inquired of the wise men. Then was fulfilled that which was spoken by Jeremy the prophet, saying, In Rama was there a voice heard, lamentation, and weeping, and great mourning, Rachel weeping for her children, and would not be comforted, because they are not.

THE SUNDAY AFTER CHRISTMAS DAY

The Collect

ALMIGHTY God, who hast given us thy only-begotten Son to take our nature upon him, and as at this time to be born of a pure Virgin: Grant that we being regenerate, and made thy children by adoption and grace, may daily be renewed by thy

Holy Spirit; through the same our Lord Jesus Christ, who liveth and reigneth with thee and the same Spirit, ever one God, world without end. *Amen.*

The Epistle. Gal. 4. 1–7

NOW I say, that the heir, as long as he is a child, differeth nothing from a servant, though he be lord of all; but is under tutors and governors, until the time appointed of the father. Even so we, when we were children, were in bondage under the elements of the world: but when the fulness of the time was come, God sent forth his Son, made of a woman, made under the law, to redeem them that were under the law, that we might receive the adoption of sons. And because ye are sons, God hath sent forth the Spirit of his Son into your hearts, crying, Abba, Father. Wherefore thou art no more a servant, but a son; and if a son, then an heir of God through Christ.

The Gospel. S. Matth. 1. 18–21

THE birth of Jesus Christ was on this wise: When as his mother Mary was espoused to Joseph, before they came together she was found with child of the Holy Ghost. Then Joseph her husband, being a just man, and not willing to make her a publick example, was minded to put her away privily. But while he thought on these things, behold, the angel of the Lord appeared unto him in a dream, saying, Joseph thou son of David, fear not to take unto thee Mary thy wife; for that which is conceived in her is of the Holy Ghost: and she shall bring forth a Son, and thou shalt call his name JESUS; for he shall save his people from their sins. (Now all this was done, that it might be fulfilled which was spoken of the Lord by the prophet, saying, Behold, a Virgin shall be with child, and shall bring forth a Son, and they shall call his name Emmanuel, which being interpreted is, God with us.) Then Joseph, being raised from sleep, did as the angel of the Lord had bidden him, and took unto him his wife; and knew her not till she had brought forth her first-born son: and he called his name JESUS.

THE CIRCUMCISION OF CHRIST*

The Collect

ALMIGHTY God, who madest thy blessed Son to be circumcised, and obedient to the law for man: Grant us the true circumcision of the Spirit; that, our hearts, and all our members, being mortified from all worldly and carnal lusts, we may in all things obey thy blessed will; through the same thy Son Jesus Christ our Lord. *Amen.*

The Epistle. Rom. 4. 8–14

BLESSED is the man to whom the Lord will not impute sin. Cometh this blessedness then upon the circumcision only, or upon the uncircumcision also? For we say, that faith was reckoned to Abraham for righteousness. How was it then reckoned? when he was in circumcision, or in uncircumcision? Not in circumcision, but in uncircumcision. And he received the sign of circumcision, a seal of the righteousness of the faith which he had yet being uncircumcised; that he might be the father of all them that believe, though they be not circumcised; that righteousness might be imputed unto them also: And the father of circumcision to them who are not of the circumcision only, but also walk in the steps of that faith of our father Abraham, which he had being yet uncircumcised. For the promise, that he should be the heir of the world, was not to Abraham, or to his seed, through the law, but through the righteousness of faith. For if they which are of the law be heirs, faith is made void, and the promise made of none effect.

The Gospel. S. Luke 2. 15–21

AND it came to pass, as the angels were gone away from them into heaven, the shepherds said one to another, Let us now go even unto Bethlehem, and see this thing which is come to pass, which the Lord hath made known unto us. And they came with haste, and found Mary and Joseph, and the babe lying in a manger. And when they had seen it, they made known abroad the saying which was told them concerning this child. And all

*January 1.

hey that heard it wondered at those things which were told
hem by the shepherds. But Mary kept all these things, and
pondered them in her heart. And the shepherds returned, glori-
ying and praising God for all the things that they had heard
and seen, as it was told unto them. And when eight days were
accomplished for the circumcising of the child, his name was
called Jesus, which was so named of the angel before he was
conceived in the womb.

*The same Collect, Epistle, and Gospel shall serve for every day
after unto the Epiphany.*

THE EPIPHANY*
OR THE MANIFESTATION OF CHRIST
TO THE GENTILES

The Collect

O GOD, who by the leading of a star didst manifest thy only-
begotten Son to the Gentiles: Mercifully grant, that we, which
know thee now by faith, may after this life have the fruition of
thy glorious Godhead; through Jesus Christ our Lord. *Amen.*

The Epistle. Ephes. 3. 1–12

FOR this cause I Paul, the prisoner of Jesus Christ for you
Gentiles; if ye have heard of the dispensation of the grace of
God, which is given me to you-ward: How that by revelation he
made known unto me the mystery (as I wrote afore in few
words, whereby, when ye read, ye may understand my knowledge in the mystery of Christ) which in other ages was not
made known unto the sons of men, as it is now revealed unto
his holy Apostles and Prophets by the Spirit; That the Gentiles
should be fellow-heirs, and of the same body, and partakers of
his promise in Christ, by the Gospel: whereof I was made a
minister, according to the gift of the grace of God given unto
me by the effectual working of his power. Unto me, who am less
than the least of all saints, is this grace given, that I should

*January 6.

preach among the Gentiles the unsearchable riches of Christ
and to make all men see what is the fellowship of the mystery
which from the beginning of the world hath been hid in God
who created all things by Jesus Christ: to the intent, that now
unto the principalities and powers in heavenly places might be
known by the Church the manifold wisdom of God, according
to the eternal purpose which he purposed in Christ Jesus our
Lord: In whom we have boldness and access with confidence by
the faith of him.

The Gospel. S. Matth. 2. 1–12

WHEN Jesus was born in Bethlehem of Judæa, in the days of
Herod the king, behold, there came wise men from the east to
Jerusalem, saying, Where is he that is born King of the Jews?
for we have seen his star in the east, and are come to worship
him. When Herod the king had heard these things, he was
troubled, and all Jerusalem with him. And when he had
gathered all the chief priests and scribes of the people together,
he demanded of them, where Christ should be born. And they
said unto him, In Bethlehem of Judæa: for thus it is written by
the prophet, And thou, Bethlehem, in the land of Juda, art not
the least among the princes of Juda: for out of thee shall come a
Governor that shall rule my people Israel. Then Herod, when
he had privily called the wise men, inquired of them diligently
what time the star appeared. And he sent them to Bethlehem
and said, Go, and search diligently for the young child, and
when ye have found him, bring me word again, that I may come
and worship him also. When they had heard the king, they
departed; and lo, the star which they saw in the east went before
them, till it came and stood over where the young child was.
When they saw the star, they rejoiced with exceeding great joy.
And when they were come into the house, they saw the young
child with Mary his mother, and fell down and worshipped him:
and when they had opened their treasures, they presented unto
him gifts; gold, and frankincense, and myrrh. And being warned
of God in a dream that they should not return to Herod, they
departed into their own country another way.

THE FIRST SUNDAY AFTER THE EPIPHANY

The Collect

O LORD, we beseech thee mercifully to receive the prayers of thy people which call upon thee; and grant that they may both perceive and know what things they ought to do, and also may have grace and power faithfully to fulfil the same; through Jesus Christ our Lord. *Amen.*

The Epistle. Rom. 12. 1–5

I BESEECH you therefore, brethren, by the mercies of God, that ye present your bodies a living sacrifice, holy, acceptable unto God, which is your reasonable service. And be not conformed to this world; but be ye transformed by the renewing of your mind, that ye may prove what is that good, and acceptable, and perfect will of God. For I say, through the grace given unto me, to every man that is among you, not to think of himself more highly than he ought to think, but to think soberly, according as God hath dealt to every man the measure of faith. For as we have many members in one body, and all members have not the same office; so we, being many, are one body in Christ, and every one members one of another.

The Gospel. S. Luke 2. 41–end

NOW his parents went to Jerusalem every year at the feast of the passover. And when he was twelve years old, they went up to Jerusalem, after the custom of the feast. And when they had fulfilled the days, as they returned, the child Jesus tarried behind in Jerusalem; and Joseph and his mother knew not of it. But they, supposing him to have been in the company, went a day's journey, and they sought him among their kinsfolk and acquaintance. And when they found him not, they turned back again to Jerusalem, seeking him. And it came to pass, that after three days they found him in the temple, sitting in the midst of the doctors, both hearing them, and asking them questions. And all that heard him were astonished at his understanding and answers. And when they saw him, they were amazed: and his mother said unto him, Son, why hast thou thus dealt with us?

behold, thy father and I have sought thee sorrowing. And he said unto them, How is it that ye sought me? wist ye not that I must be about my Father's business? And they understood not the saying which he spake unto them. And he went down with them, and came to Nazareth, and was subject unto them: but his mother kept all these sayings in her heart. And Jesus increased in wisdom, and stature, and in favour with God and man.

THE SECOND SUNDAY AFTER THE EPIPHANY

The Collect

ALMIGHTY and everlasting God, who dost govern all things in heaven and earth: Mercifully hear the supplications of thy people, and grant us thy peace all the days of our life; through Jesus Christ our Lord. *Amen.*

The Epistle. Rom. 12. 6–16

HAVING then gifts differing according to the grace that is given to us, whether prophecy, let us prophesy according to the proportion of faith; or ministry, let us wait on our ministering; or he that teacheth, on teaching; or he that exhorteth, on exhortation: he that giveth, let him do it with simplicity; he that ruleth, with diligence; he that sheweth mercy, with cheerfulness. Let love be without dissimulation. Abhor that which is evil, cleave to that which is good. Be kindly affectioned one to another with brotherly love, in honour preferring one another: not slothful in business; fervent in spirit; serving the Lord; rejoicing in hope; patient in tribulation; continuing instant in prayer; distributing to the necessity of saints; given to hospitality. Bless them which persecute you; bless, and curse not. Rejoice with them that do rejoice, and weep with them that weep. Be of the same mind one towards another. Mind not high things, but condescend to men of low estate.

The Gospel. S. John 2. 1–11

AND the third day there was a marriage in Cana of Galilee, and the mother of Jesus was there. And both Jesus was called, nd his disciples, to the marriage. And when they wanted wine, he mother of Jesus saith unto him, They have no wine. Jesus aith unto her, Woman, what have I to do with thee? mine hour s not yet come. His mother saith unto the servants, Whatsoever e saith unto you, do it. And there were set there six water-pots f stone, after the manner of the purifying of the Jews, contain-ing two or three firkins apiece. Jesus saith unto them, Fill the ater-pots with water. And they filled them up to the brim. And he saith unto them, Draw out now, and bear unto the overnor of the feast. And they bare it. When the ruler of the east had tasted the water that was made wine, and knew not vhence it was, (but the servants which drew the water knew,) he governor of the feast called the bridegroom, and saith unto im, Every man at the beginning doth set forth good wine, and vhen men have well drunk, then that which is worse: but thou ast kept the good wine until now. This beginning of miracles id Jesus in Cana of Galilee, and manifested forth his glory, and is disciples believed on him.

THE THIRD SUNDAY AFTER THE EPIPHANY

The Collect

ALMIGHTY and everlasting God, mercifully look upon our nfirmities, and in all our dangers and necessities stretch forth ny right hand to help and defend us; through Jesus Christ our Lord. *Amen.*

The Epistle. Rom. 12. 16–end

BE not wise in your own conceits. Recompense to no man evil or evil. Provide things honest in the sight of all men. If it be ossible, as much as lieth in you, live peaceably with all men. Dearly beloved, avenge not yourselves, but rather give place nto wrath; for it is written, Vengeance is mine; I will repay, aith the Lord. Therefore if thine enemy hunger, feed him; if he nirst, give him drink: for in so doing thou shalt heap coals of re on his head. Be not overcome of evil, but overcome evil ith good.

The Gospel. S. Matth. 8. 1–13

WHEN he was come down from the mountain, great multi
tudes followed him. And behold, there came a leper and wor
shipped him, saying, Lord, if thou wilt, thou canst make m
clean. And Jesus put forth his hand, and touched him, saying,
will; be thou clean. And immediately his leprosy was cleansed
And Jesus saith unto him, See thou tell no man, but go th
way, shew thyself to the priest, and offer the gift that Mose
commanded, for a testimony unto them. And when Jesus wa
entered into Capernaum, there came unto him a centurio
beseeching him, and saying, Lord, my servant lieth at home sic
of the palsy, grievously tormented. And Jesus saith unto him,
will come and heal him. The centurion answered and said, Lord
I am not worthy that thou shouldest come under my roof; bu
speak the word only, and my servant shall be healed. For I am
man under authority, having soldiers under me: and I say unt
this man, Go, and he goeth; and to another, Come, and h
cometh; and to my servant, Do this, and he doeth it. Whe
Jesus heard it, he marvelled, and said to them that followed
Verily I say unto you, I have not found so great faith, no not i
Israel. And I say unto you, That many shall come from the eas
and west, and shall sit down with Abraham, and Isaac, an
Jacob, in the kingdom of heaven. But the children of the king
dom shall be cast out into outer darkness: there shall be weepin
and gnashing of teeth. And Jesus said unto the centurion, G
thy way, and as thou hast believed, so be it done unto thee. An
his servant was healed in the self-same hour.

THE FOURTH SUNDAY AFTER THE EPIPHANY

The Collect

O GOD, who knowest us to be set in the midst of so man
and great dangers, that by reason of the frailty of our nature w
cannot always stand upright: Grant to us such strength an
protection, as may support us in all dangers, and carry u
through all temptations; through Jesus Christ our Lord. *Amen.*

The Epistle. Rom. 13. 1–7

LET every soul be subject unto the higher powers; for there is no power but of God: the powers that be are ordained of God. Whosoever therefore resisteth the power resisteth the ordinance of God: and they that resist shall receive to themselves damnation. For rulers are not a terror to good works, but to the evil. Wilt thou then not be afraid of the power? do that which is good, and thou shalt have praise of the same: for he is the minister of God to thee for good. But if thou do that which is evil, be afraid; for he beareth not the sword in vain: for he is the minister of God, a revenger to execute wrath upon him that doeth evil. Wherefore ye must needs be subject, not only for wrath, but also for conscience sake. For for this cause pay ye tribute also; for they are God's ministers, attending continually upon this very thing. Render therefore to all their dues; tribute to whom tribute is due, custom to whom custom, fear to whom fear, honour to whom honour.

The Gospel. S. Matth. 8. 23–end

AND when he was entered into a ship, his disciples followed him. And behold, there arose a great tempest in the sea, insomuch that the ship was covered with the waves: but he was asleep. And his disciples came to him, and awoke him, saying, Lord, save us, we perish. And he saith unto them, Why are ye fearful, O ye of little faith? Then he arose, and rebuked the winds and the sea, and there was a great calm. But the men marvelled, saying, What manner of man is this, that even the winds and the sea obey him! And when he was come to the other side into the country of the Gergesenes, there met him two possessed with devils, coming out of the tombs, exceeding fierce, so that no man might pass by that way. And behold, they cried out, saying, What have we to do with thee, Jesus, thou Son of God? art thou come hither to torment us before the time? And there was a good way off from them an herd of many swine, feeding. So the devils besought him, saying, If thou cast us out, suffer us to go away into the herd of swine. And he said unto them, Go. And when they were come out, they went into

the herd of swine: and behold, the whole herd of swine ran
violently down a steep place into the sea, and perished in the
waters. And they that kept them fled, and went their ways into
the city, and told every thing, and what was befallen to the
possessed of the devils. And behold, the whole city came out to
meet Jesus: and when they saw him, they besought him that he
would depart out of their coasts.

THE FIFTH SUNDAY AFTER THE EPIPHANY

The Collect

O LORD, we beseech thee to keep thy Church and household
continually in thy true religion; that they who do lean only upon
the hope of thy heavenly grace may evermore be defended by
thy mighty power; through Jesus Christ our Lord. *Amen.*

The Epistle. Coloss. 3. 12–17

PUT on therefore, as the elect of God, holy and beloved,
bowels of mercies, kindness, humbleness of mind, meekness,
long-suffering; forbearing one another, and forgiving one
another, if any man have a quarrel against any; even as Christ
forgave you, so also do ye. And above all these things put on
charity, which is the bond of perfectness. And let the peace of
God rule in your hearts, to the which also ye are called in one
body; and be ye thankful. Let the word of Christ dwell in you
richly in all wisdom, teaching and admonishing one another in
psalms, and hymns, and spiritual songs, singing with grace in
your hearts to the Lord. And whatsoever ye do, in word or deed,
do all in the Name of the Lord Jesus, giving thanks to God and
the Father by him.

The Gospel. S. Matth. 13. 24–30

THE kingdom of heaven is likened unto a man which sowed
good seed in his field. But while men slept, his enemy came and
sowed tares among the wheat, and went his way. But when the
blade was sprung up, and brought forth fruit, then appeared the
tares also. So the servants of the householder came, and said
unto him, Sir, didst not thou sow good seed in thy field? from

whence then hath it tares? He said unto them, An enemy hath done this. The servants said unto him, Wilt thou then that we go and gather them up? But he said, Nay; lest while ye gather up the tares, ye root up also the wheat with them. Let both grow together until the harvest; and in the time of harvest I will say to the reapers, Gather ye together first the tares, and bind them in bundles to burn them: but gather the wheat into my barn.

THE SIXTH SUNDAY AFTER THE EPIPHANY

The Collect

O GOD, whose blessed Son was manifested that he might destroy the works of the devil, and make us the sons of God, and heirs of eternal life: Grant us, we beseech thee, that, having this hope, we may purify ourselves, even as he is pure; that, when he shall appear again with power and great glory, we may be made like unto him in his eternal and glorious kingdom; where with thee, O Father, and thee, O Holy Ghost, he liveth and reigneth, ever one God, world without end. *Amen.*

The Epistle. 1 S. John 3. 1–8

BEHOLD, what manner of love the Father hath bestowed upon us, that we should be called the sons of God: therefore the world knoweth us not, because it knew him not. Beloved, now are we the sons of God, and it doth not yet appear what we shall be: but we know that, when he shall appear, we shall be like him; for we shall see him as he is. And every man that hath this hope in him purifieth himself, even as he is pure. Whosoever committeth sin transgresseth also the law: for sin is the transgression of the law. And ye know that he was manifested to take away our sins; and in him is no sin. Whosoever abideth in him sinneth not: whosoever sinneth hath not seen him, neither known him. Little children, let no man deceive you: he that doeth righteousness is righteous, even as he is righteous. He that committeth sin is of the devil: for the devil sinneth from the beginning. For this purpose the Son of God was manifested, that he might destroy the works of the devil.

The Gospel. S. Matth. 24. 23–31

THEN if any man shall say unto you, Lo, here is Christ, or there; believe it not. For there shall arise false Christs, and false prophets, and shall shew great signs and wonders; insomuch that (if it were possible) they shall deceive the very elect. Behold, I have told you before. Wherefore, if they shall say unto you, Behold, he is in the desert; go not forth: Behold, he is in the secret chambers; believe it not. For as the lightning cometh out of the east, and shineth even unto the west; so shall also the coming of the Son of Man be. For wheresoever the carcase is, there will the eagles be gathered together. Immediately after the tribulation of those days shall the sun be darkened, and the moon shall not give her light, and the stars shall fall from heaven, and the powers of the heavens shall be shaken. And then shall appear the sign of the Son of Man in heaven: and then shall all the tribes of the earth mourn, and they shall see the Son of Man coming in the clouds of heaven, with power and great glory. And he shall send his angels with a great sound of a trumpet, and they shall gather together his elect from the four winds, from one end of heaven to the other.

THE SUNDAY CALLED SEPTUAGESIMA
OR THE THIRD SUNDAY BEFORE LENT

The Collect

O LORD, we beseech thee favourably to hear the prayers of thy people; that we, who are justly punished for our offences, may be mercifully delivered by thy goodness, for the glory of thy Name; through Jesus Christ our Saviour, who liveth and reigneth with thee and the Holy Ghost, ever one God, world without end. *Amen.*

The Epistle. 1 Cor. 9. 24–end

KNOW ye not that they which run in a race run all, but one receiveth the prize? So run that ye may obtain. And every man that striveth for the mastery is temperate in all things: now they do it to obtain a corruptible crown, but we an incorruptible.

I therefore so run, not as uncertainly; so fight I, not as one that beateth the air: but I keep under my body, and bring it into subjection, lest that by any means, when I have preached to others, I myself should be a cast-away.

The Gospel. S. Matth. 20. 1–16

THE kingdom of heaven is like unto a man that is an householder, which went out early in the morning to hire labourers into his vineyard. And when he had agreed with the labourers for a penny a day, he sent them into his vineyard. And he went out about the third hour, and saw others standing idle in the market-place, and said unto them, Go ye also into the vineyard, and whatsoever is right I will give you. And they went their way. Again he went out about the sixth and ninth hour, and did likewise. And about the eleventh hour he went out, and found others standing idle, and saith unto them, Why stand ye here all the day idle? They say unto him, Because no man hath hired us. He saith unto them, Go ye also into the vineyard, and whatsoever is right, that shall ye receive. So when even was come, the lord of the vineyard saith unto his steward, Call the labourers, and give them their hire, beginning from the last unto the first. And when they came that were hired about the eleventh hour, they received every man a penny. But when the first came, they supposed that they should have received more; and they likewise received every man a penny. And when they had received it, they murmured against the good-man of the house, saying, These last have wrought but one hour, and thou hast made them equal unto us, which have borne the burden and heat of the day. But he answered one of them, and said, Friend, I do thee no wrong; didst not thou agree with me for a penny? Take that thine is, and go thy way; I will give unto this last even as unto thee. Is it not lawful for me to do what I will with mine own? Is thine eye evil, because I am good? So the last shall be first, and the first last: for many be called, but few chosen.

THE SUNDAY CALLED SEXAGESIMA
OR THE SECOND SUNDAY BEFORE LENT

The Collect

O LORD God, who seest that we put not our trust in any thing that we do: Mercifully grant that by thy power we may be defended against all adversity; through Jesus Christ our Lord. *Amen.*

The Epistle. 2 Cor. 11. 19–31

YE suffer fools gladly, seeing ye yourselves are wise. For ye suffer if a man bring you into bondage, if a man devour you, if a man take of you, if a man exalt himself, if a man smite you on the face. I speak as concerning reproach, as though we had been weak: howbeit, whereinsoever any is bold, (I speak foolishly,) I am bold also. Are they Hebrews? so am I. Are they Israelites? so am I. Are they the seed of Abraham? so am I. Are they ministers of Christ? (I speak as a fool,) I am more: in labours more abundant; in stripes above measure; in prisons more frequent; in deaths oft. Of the Jews five times received I forty stripes save one; thrice was I beaten with rods; once was I stoned; thrice I suffered shipwreck; a night and a day I have been in the deep; in journeyings often; in perils of waters; in perils of robbers; in perils by mine own countrymen; in perils by the heathen; in perils in the city; in perils in the wilderness; in perils in the sea; in perils among false brethren; in weariness and painfulness; in watchings often; in hunger and thirst; in fastings often; in cold and nakedness; besides those things that are without, that which cometh upon me daily, the care of all the churches. Who is weak, and I am not weak? who is offended, and I burn not? If I must needs glory, I will glory of the things which concern mine infirmities. The God and Father of our Lord Jesus Christ, which is blessed for evermore, knoweth that I lie not.

The Gospel. S. Luke 8. 4–15

WHEN much people were gathered together, and were come to him out of every city, he spake by a parable: A sower went out to sow his seed; and as he sowed, some fell by the way-side, and it was trodden down, and the fowls of the air devoured it. And some fell upon a rock, and as soon as it was sprung up, it withered away, because it lacked moisture. And some fell among thorns, and the thorns sprang up with it, and choked it. And other fell on good ground, and sprang up, and bare fruit an hundred-fold. And when he had said these things, he cried, He that hath ears to hear, let him hear. And his disciples asked him, saying, What might this parable be? And he said, Unto you it is given to know the mysteries of the kingdom of God: but to others in parables; that seeing they might not see, and hearing they might not understand. Now the parable is this: The seed is the word of God. Those by the way-side are they that hear; then cometh the devil, and taketh away the word out of their hearts, lest they should believe, and be saved. They on the rock are they which, when they hear, receive the word with joy; and these have no root, which for a while believe, and in time of temptation fall away. And that which fell among thorns are they which, when they have heard, go forth, and are choked with cares, and riches, and pleasures of this life, and bring no fruit to perfection. But that on the good ground are they which in an honest and good heart, having heard the word, keep it, and bring forth fruit with patience.

THE SUNDAY CALLED QUINQUAGESIMA
OR THE NEXT SUNDAY BEFORE LENT

The Collect

O LORD, who hast taught us that all our doings without charity are nothing worth: Send thy Holy Ghost, and pour into our hearts that most excellent gift of charity, the very bond of peace and of all virtues, without which whosoever liveth is counted dead before thee: Grant this for thine only Son Jesus Christ's sake. *Amen.*

The Epistle. 1 Cor. 13. 1—end

THOUGH I speak with the tongues of men and of angels, and have not charity, I am become as sounding brass, or a tinkling cymbal. And though I have the gift of prophecy, and understand all mysteries, and all knowledge; and though I have all faith, so that I could remove mountains, and have not charity, I am nothing. And though I bestow all my goods to feed the poor, and though I give my body to be burned, and have not charity, it profiteth me nothing. Charity suffereth long, and is kind; charity envieth not; charity vaunteth not itself, is not puffed up, doth not behave itself unseemly, seeketh not her own, is not easily provoked, thinketh no evil, rejoiceth not in iniquity, but rejoiceth in the truth; beareth all things, believeth all things, hopeth all things, endureth all things. Charity never faileth: but whether there be prophecies, they shall fail; whether there be tongues, they shall cease; whether there be knowledge, it shall vanish away. For we know in part, and we prophesy in part. But when that which is perfect is come, then that which is in part shall be done away. When I was a child, I spake as a child, I understood as a child, I thought as a child; but when I became a man, I put away childish things. For now we see through a glass darkly; but then face to face: now I know in part; but then shall I know even as also I am known. And now abideth faith, hope, charity, these three: but the greatest of these is charity.

The Gospel. S. Luke 18. 31–end

THEN Jesus took unto him the twelve, and said unto them, Behold, we go up to Jerusalem, and all things that are written by the prophets concerning the Son of Man shall be accomplished. For he shall be delivered unto the Gentiles, and shall be mocked, and spitefully entreated, and spitted on: and they shall scourge him, and put him to death; and the third day he shall rise again. And they understood none of these things: and this saying was hid from them, neither knew they the things which were spoken. And it came to pass, that as he was come nigh unto Jericho, a certain blind man sat by the way-side begging: and hearing the multitude pass by, he asked what it meant. And they told him, that Jesus of Nazareth passeth by. And he cried, saying, Jesus, thou Son of David, have mercy on me. And they which went before rebuked him, that he should hold his peace: but he cried so much the more, Thou Son of David, have mercy on me. And Jesus stood, and commanded him to be brought unto him: and when he was come near, he asked him, saying, What wilt thou that I should do unto thee? And he said, Lord, that I may receive my sight. And Jesus said unto him, Receive thy sight; thy faith hath saved thee. And immediately he received his sight, and followed him, glorifying God: and all the people, when they saw it, gave praise unto God.

THE FIRST DAY OF LENT
COMMONLY CALLED

ASH WEDNESDAY

The Collect

ALMIGHTY and everlasting God, who hatest nothing that thou hast made, and dost forgive the sins of all them that are penitent: Create and make in us new and contrite hearts, that we worthily lamenting our sins, and acknowledging our wretchedness, may obtain of thee, the God of all mercy, perfect remission and forgiveness; through Jesus Christ our Lord. *Amen.*

This Collect is to be read every day in Lent after the Collect appointed for the Day.

For the Epistle. Joel 2. 12–17

TURN ye even to me, saith the Lord, with all your heart, and with fasting, and with weeping, and with mourning. And rend your heart, and not your garments, and turn unto the Lord your God: for he is gracious and merciful, slow to anger, and of great kindness, and repenteth him of the evil. Who knoweth if he will return, and repent, and leave a blessing behind him, even a meat-offering and a drink-offering unto the Lord your God? Blow the trumpet in Zion, sanctify a fast, call a solemn assembly, gather the people, sanctify the congregation, assemble the elders, gather the children, and those that suck the breasts; let the bridegroom go forth of his chamber, and the bride out of her closet; let the priests, the ministers of the Lord, weep between the porch and the altar, and let them say, Spare thy people, O Lord, and give not thine heritage to reproach, that the heathen should rule over them: wherefore should they say among the people, Where is their God?

The Gospel. S. Matth. 6. 16–21

WHEN ye fast, be not as the hypocrites, of a sad countenance: for they disfigure their faces, that they may appear unto men to fast. Verily I say unto you, They have their reward. But thou, when thou fastest, anoint thine head, and wash thy face, that thou appear not unto men to fast, but unto thy Father which is in secret; and thy Father, which seeth in secret, shall reward thee openly. Lay not up for yourselves treasures upon earth, where moth and rust doth corrupt, and where thieves break through and steal: but lay up for yourselves treasures in heaven, where neither moth nor rust doth corrupt, and where thieves do not break through nor steal: for where your treasure is, there will your heart be also.

THE FIRST SUNDAY IN LENT

The Collect

O LORD, who for our sake didst fast forty days and forty nights: Give us grace to use such abstinence, that, our flesh being subdued to the Spirit, we may ever obey thy godly motions in righteousness and true holiness, to thy honour and glory, who livest and reignest with the Father and the Holy Ghost, one God, world without end. *Amen.*

The Epistle. 2 Cor. 6. 1–10

WE then, as workers together with him, beseech you also, that ye receive not the grace of God in vain; (for he saith, I have heard thee in a time accepted, and in the day of salvation have I succoured thee: behold, now is the accepted time; behold, now is the day of salvation;) giving no offence in any thing, that the ministry be not blamed; but in all things approving ourselves as the ministers of God, in much patience, in afflictions, in necessities, in distresses, in stripes, in imprisonments, in tumults, in labours, in watchings, in fastings; by pureness, by knowledge, by long-suffering, by kindness, by the Holy Ghost, by love unfeigned, by the word of truth, by the power of God; by the armour of righteousness on the right hand and on the left; by honour and dishonour, by evil report and good report; as deceivers, and yet true; as unknown, and yet well known; as dying, and behold, we live; as chastened, and not killed; as sorrowful, yet alway rejoicing; as poor, yet making many rich; as having nothing, and yet possessing all things.

The Gospel. S. Matth. 4. 1–11

THEN was Jesus led up of the Spirit into the wilderness, to be tempted of the devil. And when he had fasted forty days and forty nights, he was afterward an-hungred. And when the tempter came to him, he said, If thou be the Son of God, command that these stones be made bread. But he answered and said, It is written, Man shall not live by bread alone, but by every word that proceedeth out of the mouth of God. Then the devil taketh him up into the holy city, and setteth him on a pinnacle of the temple, and saith unto him, If thou be the Son of God, cast thyself down; for it is written, He shall give his angels charge concerning thee, and in their hands they shall bear thee up, lest at any time thou dash thy foot against a stone. Jesus said unto him, It is written again, Thou shalt not tempt the Lord thy God. Again, the devil taketh him up into an exceeding high mountain, and sheweth him all the kingdoms of the world, and the glory of them; and saith unto him, All these things will I give thee, if thou wilt fall down and worship me. Then saith Jesus unto him, Get thee hence, Satan; for it is written, Thou shalt worship the Lord thy God, and him only shalt thou serve. Then the devil leaveth him, and behold, angels came and ministered unto him.

THE SECOND SUNDAY IN LENT

The Collect

ALMIGHTY God, who seest that we have no power of ourselves to help ourselves: Keep us both outwardly in our bodies, and inwardly in our souls; that we may be defended from all adversities which may happen to the body, and from all evil thoughts which may assault and hurt the soul; through Jesus Christ our Lord. *Amen.*

The Epistle. 1 Thess. 4. 1–8

WE beseech you, brethren, and exhort you by the Lord Jesus, that as ye have received of us how ye ought to walk, and to please God, so ye would abound more and more. For ye know what commandments we gave you by the Lord Jesus. For this is the will of God, even your sanctification, that ye should abstain from fornication; that every one of you should know how to possess his vessel in sanctification and honour; not in the lust of concupiscence, even as the Gentiles which know not God; that no man go beyond and defraud his brother in any matter; because that the Lord is the avenger of all such, as we also have forewarned you and testified. For God hath not called us unto uncleanness, but unto holiness. He therefore that despiseth despiseth not man, but God, who hath also given unto us his Holy Spirit.

The Gospel. S. Matth. 15. 21–8

JESUS went thence, and departed into the coasts of Tyre and Sidon. And behold, a woman of Canaan came out of the same coasts, and cried unto him, saying, Have mercy on me, O Lord, thou Son of David; my daughter is grievously vexed with a devil. But he answered her not a word. And his disciples came and besought him, saying, Send her away; for she crieth after us. But he answered and said, I am not sent, but unto the lost sheep of the house of Israel. Then came she and worshipped him, saying, Lord, help me. But he answered and said, It is not meet to take the children's bread, and to cast it to dogs. And she said, Truth, Lord; yet the dogs eat of the crumbs which fall from their masters' table. Then Jesus answered and said unto her, O woman, great is thy faith: be it unto thee even as thou wilt. And her daughter was made whole from that very hour.

THE THIRD SUNDAY IN LENT

The Collect

WE beseech thee, Almighty God, look upon the hearty desires of thy humble servants, and stretch forth the right hand of thy Majesty, to be our defence against all our enemies; through Jesus Christ our Lord. *Amen.*

The Epistle. Ephes. 5. 1–14

BE ye therefore followers of God, as dear children; and walk in love, as Christ also hath loved us, and hath given himself for us, an offering and a sacrifice to God for a sweet-smelling savour. But fornication, and all uncleanness, or covetousness, let it not be once named amongst you, as becometh saints; neither filthiness, nor foolish-talking, nor jesting, which are not convenient; but rather giving of thanks: for this ye know, that no whoremonger, nor unclean person, nor covetous man, who is an idolater, hath any inheritance in the kingdom of Christ, and of God. Let no man deceive you with vain words: for because of these things cometh the wrath of God upon the children of disobedience. Be not ye therefore partakers with them: for ye were sometimes darkness, but now are ye light in the Lord: walk as children of light; (for the fruit of the Spirit is in all goodness, and righteousness, and truth;) proving what is acceptable unto the Lord. And have no fellowship with the unfruitful works of darkness, but rather reprove them: for it is a shame even to speak of those things which are done of them in secret. But all things that are reproved are made manifest by the light: for whatsoever doth make manifest is light. Wherefore he saith, Awake, thou that sleepest, and arise from the dead, and Christ shall give thee light.

The Gospel. S. Luke 11. 14–28

JESUS was casting out a devil, and it was dumb. And it came to pass, when the devil was gone out, the dumb spake; and the people wondered. But some of them said, He casteth out devils through Beelzebub, the chief of the devils. And others, tempting him, sought of him a sign from heaven. But he, knowing their thoughts, said unto them, Every kingdom divided against itself is brought to desolation; and a house divided against a house falleth. If Satan also be divided against himself, how shall his kingdom stand? because ye say, that I cast out devils through Beelzebub. And if I by Beelzebub cast out devils, by whom do your sons cast them out? therefore shall they be your judges. But if I with the finger of God cast out devils, no doubt the kingdom of God is come upon you. When a strong man armed keepeth his palace, his goods are in peace; but when a stronger than he shall come upon him, and overcome him, he taketh from him all his armour wherein he trusted, and divideth his spoils. He that is not with me is against me: and he that gathereth not with me scattereth. When the unclean spirit is gone out of a man, he walketh through dry places, seeking rest; and finding none, he saith, I will return unto my house whence I came out. And when he cometh, he findeth it swept and garnished. Then goeth he and taketh to him seven other spirits more wicked than himself, and they enter in, and dwell there; and the last state of that man is worse than the first. And it came to pass, as he spake these things, a certain woman of the company lift up her voice, and said unto him, Blessed is the womb that bare thee, and the paps which thou hast sucked. But he said, Yea rather, blessed are they that hear the word of God, and keep it.

THE FOURTH SUNDAY IN LENT

The Collect

GRANT, we beseech thee, Almighty God, that we, who for our evil deeds do worthily deserve to be punished, by the comfort of thy grace may mercifully be relieved; through our Lord and Saviour Jesus Christ. *Amen.*

The Epistle. Gal. 4. 21–end

TELL me, ye that desire to be under the law, do ye not hear

he law? For it is written, that Abraham had two sons, the one by a bond-maid, the other by a free-woman. But he who was of he bond-woman was born after the flesh; but he of the free-woman was by promise. Which things are an allegory: for these are the two covenants; the one from the mount Sinai, which gendereth to bondage, which is Agar. For this Agar is mount Sinai in Arabia, and answereth to Jerusalem which now is, and is in bondage with her children. But Jerusalem which is above is free; which is the mother of us all. For it is written, Rejoice, thou barren that bearest not; break forth and cry, thou that travailest not: for the desolate hath many more children than she which hath an husband. Now we, brethren, as Isaac was, are the children of promise. But as then he that was born after the flesh persecuted him that was born after the Spirit; even so it is now. Nevertheless, what saith the Scripture? Cast out the bond-woman and her son; for the son of the bond-woman shall not be heir with the son of the free-woman. So then, brethren, we are not children of the bond-woman, but of the free.

The Gospel. S. John 6. 1–14

JESUS went over the sea of Galilee, which is the sea of Tiberias. And a great multitude followed him, because they saw his miracles which he did on them that were diseased. And Jesus went up into a mountain, and there he sat with his disciples. And the Passover, a feast of the Jews, was nigh. When Jesus then lift up his eyes, and saw a great company come unto him, he saith unto Philip, Whence shall we buy bread, that these may eat? (And this he said to prove him; for he himself knew what he would do.) Philip answered him, Two hundred penny-worth of bread is not sufficient for them, that every one of them may take a little. One of his disciples, Andrew, Simon Peter's brother, saith unto him, There is a lad here, which hath five barley-loaves, and two small fishes: but what are they among so many? And Jesus said, Make the men sit down. Now there was much grass in the place. So the men sat down, in number about five thousand. And Jesus took the loaves, and when he had given thanks, he distributed to the disciples, and the disciples to them that were set down; and likewise of the fishes, as much as the would. When they were filled, he said unto his disciples, Gathe up the fragments that remain, that nothing be lost. Therefore they gathered them together, and filled twelve baskets with the fragments of the five barley-loaves, which remained over and above unto them that had eaten. Then those men, when they had seen the miracle that Jesus did, said, This is of a truth that Prophet that should come into the world.

THE FIFTH SUNDAY IN LENT

The Collect

WE beseech thee, Almighty God, mercifully to look upon thy people; that by thy great goodness they may be governed and preserved evermore, both in body and soul; through Jesus Christ our Lord. *Amen.*

The Epistle. Hebr. 9. 11–15

CHRIST being come an High Priest of good things to come by a greater and more perfect tabernacle, not made with hands, that is to say, not of this building; neither by the blood of goats and calves; but by his own blood he entered in once into the holy place, having obtained eternal redemption for us. For if the blood of bulls and of goats, and the ashes of an heifer sprinkling the unclean, sanctifieth to the purifying of the flesh; how much more shall the blood of Christ, who, through the eternal Spirit offered himself without spot to God, purge your conscience from dead works to serve the living God? And for this cause he is the Mediator of the new testament, that by means of death for the redemption of the transgressions that were under the first testament, they which are called might receive the promise of eternal inheritance.

The Gospel. S. John 8. 46–end

JESUS said, Which of you convinceth me of sin? and if I say the truth, why do ye not believe me? He that is of God heareth God's words; ye therefore hear them not, because ye are not of God. Then answered the Jews, and said unto him, Say we not well, that thou art a Samaritan, and hast a devil? Jesus answered, I have not a devil; but I honour my Father, and ye do dishonour me. And I seek not mine own glory; there is one that seeketh and judgeth. Verily, verily, I say unto you, If a man keep my saying, he shall never see death. Then said the Jews unto him, Now we know that thou hast a devil: Abraham is dead, and the prophets; and thou sayest, If a man keep my saying, he shall never taste of death. Art thou greater than our father Abraham, which is dead? and the prophets are dead: whom makest thou thyself? Jesus answered, If I honour myself, my honour is nothing; it is my Father that honoureth me, of whom ye say, that he is your God: yet ye have not known him; but I know him: and if I should say, I know him not, I shall be a liar like unto you; but I know him, and keep his saying. Your father Abraham rejoiced to see my day, and he saw it, and was glad. Then said the Jews unto him, Thou art not yet fifty years old, and hast thou seen Abraham? Jesus said unto them, Verily, verily, I say unto you, Before Abraham was, I am. Then took they up stones to cast at him: but Jesus hid himself, and went out of the temple.

THE SUNDAY NEXT BEFORE EASTER

The Collect

ALMIGHTY and everlasting God, who, of thy tender love towards mankind, hast sent thy Son our Saviour Jesus Christ, to take upon him our flesh, and to suffer death upon the cross, that all mankind should follow the example of his great humility: Mercifully grant, that we may both follow the example of his patience, and also be made partakers of his resurrection; through the same Jesus Christ our Lord. *Amen.*

The Epistle. Philip. 2. 5–11

LET this mind be in you, which was also in Christ Jesus: who, being in the form of God, thought it not robbery to be equal with God; but made himself of no reputation, and took upon him the form of a servant, and was made in the likeness of men: and being found in fashion as a man, he humbled himself, and became obedient unto death, even the death of the cross. Wherefore God also hath highly exalted him, and given him a name which is above every name; that at the name of Jesus every knee should bow, of things in heaven, and things in earth, and things under the earth; and that every tongue should confess that Jesus Christ is Lord, to the glory of God the Father.

The Gospel. S. Matth. 27. 1–54

WHEN the morning was come, all the chief priests and elders of the people took counsel against Jesus, to put him to death. And when they had bound him, they led him away, and delivered him to Pontius Pilate the governor. Then Judas who had betrayed him, when he saw that he was condemned, repented himself, and brought again the thirty pieces of silver to the chief priests and elders, saying, I have sinned, in that I have betrayed the innocent blood. And they said, What is that to us? see thou to that. And he cast down the pieces of silver in the temple, and departed, and went and hanged himself. And the chief priests took the silver pieces, and said, it is not lawful for to put them into the treasury, because it is the price of blood. And they took counsel, and bought with them the potter's field, to bury strangers in. Wherefore that field was called, The field of blood, unto this day. (Then was fulfilled that which was spoken by Jeremy the prophet, saying, And they took the thirty pieces of silver, the price of him that was valued, whom they of the children of Israel did value, and gave them for the potter's field, as the Lord appointed me.) And Jesus stood before the governor; and the governor asked him, saying, Art thou the King of the Jews? And Jesus said unto him, Thou sayest. And when he was accused of the chief priests and elders, he answered nothing. Then saith Pilate unto him, Hearest thou not how many things they witness against thee? And he answered him to never a word, in so much that the governor marvelled greatly. Now at that feast the governor was wont to release unto the people a prisoner, whom they would. And they had then a not-able prisoner, called Barabbas. Therefore when they were gathered together, Pilate said unto them, Whom will ye that I release unto you? Barabbas, or Jesus which is called Christ? For he knew that for envy they had delivered him. When he was set down on the judgement-seat, his wife sent unto him, saying, Have thou nothing to do with that just man: for I have suffered many things this day in a dream because of him. But the chief priests and elders persuaded the multitude that they should ask Barabbas, and destroy Jesus. The governor answered and said unto them, Whether of the twain will ye that I release unto you? They said, Barabbas. Pilate saith unto them, What shall I do then with Jesus which is called Christ? They all say unto him, Let him be crucified. And the governor said, Why, what evil hath he done? But they cried out the more, saying, Let him be crucified. When Pilate saw that he could prevail nothing, but that rather a tumult was made, he took water, and washed his hands before the multitude, saying, I am innocent of the blood of this just person: see ye to it. Then answered all the people, and said, His blood be on us, and on our children. Then released he Barabbas unto them: and when he had scourged Jesus he delivered him to be crucified. Then the soldiers of the governor took Jesus into the common hall, and gathered unto him the whole band of soldiers. And they stripped him, and put on him a scarlet robe. And when they had platted a crown of thorns they put it upon his head, and a reed in his right hand: and they bowed the knee before him, and mocked him, saying, Hail, King of the Jews. And they spit upon him, and took the reed, and smote him on the head. And after that they had mocked him they took the robe off from him, and put his own raiment on him, and led him away to crucify him. And as they came out they found a man of Cyrene, Simon by name; him they compelled to bear his cross. And when they were come unto a place called Golgotha, that is to say, a place of a skull, they gave him vinegar to drink mingled with gall: and when he had tasted thereof, he would not drink. And they crucified him, and parted his garments, casting lots: that it might be fulfilled, which was spoken by the prophet, They parted my garments among them, and upon my vesture did they cast lots. And sitting down they watched him there; and set up over his head his accusation written, THIS IS JESUS THE KING OF THE JEWS. Then were there two thieves crucified with him; one on the right hand, and another on the left. And they that passed by reviled him, wagging their heads, and saying, Thou that destroyest the temple, and buildest it in three days, save thyself: if thou be the Son of God, come down from the cross. Likewise also the chef priests mocking him, with the scribes and elders, said, He saved others; himself he cannot save: if he be the King of Israel, let him now come down from the cross, and we will believe him. He trusted in God; let him deliver him now, if he will have him: for he said, I am the Son of God. The thieves also, which were crucified with him, cast the same in his teeth. Now from the sixth hour there was darkness over all the land unto the ninth hour. And about the ninth hour Jesus cried with a loud voice, saying, *Eli, Eli, lama sabachthani?* that is to say, My God, my God, why hast thou forsaken me? Some of them that stood there, when they heard that, said, This man calleth for Elias. And straightway one of them ran, and took a spunge, and filled it with vinegar, and put it on a reed, and gave him to drink. The rest said, Let be, let us see whether Elias will come to save him. Jesus, when he had cried again with a loud voice, yielded up the ghost. And behold, the vail of the temple was rent in twain from the top to the bottom, and the earth did quake, and the rocks rent, and the graves were opened, and many bodies of saints which slept arose, and came out of the graves after his resurrection, and went into the holy city, and appeared unto many. Now when the centurion and they that were with him, watching Jesus, saw the earthquake and those things that were done, they feared greatly, saying, Truly this was the Son of God.

MONDAY BEFORE EASTER

For the Epistle. Isai. 63. 1–end

WHO is this that cometh from Edom, with dyed garments from Bozrah? this that is glorious in his apparel, travelling in the greatness of his strength? I that speak in righteousness, mighty to save. Wherefore art thou red in thine apparel, and thy garments like him that treadeth in the wine-fat? I have trodden the wine-press alone, and of the people there was none with me: for I will tread them in mine anger, and trample them in my fury, and their blood shall be sprinkled upon my garments, and I will stain all my raiment. For the day of vengeance is in mine heart, and the year of my redeemed is come. And I looked, and there was none to help; and I wondered that there was none to uphold: therefore mine own arm brought salvation unto me, and my fury it upheld me. And I will tread down the people in mine anger, and make them drunk in my fury, and I will bring down their strength to the earth. I will mention the loving-kindnesses of the Lord, and the praises of the Lord, according to all that the Lord hath bestowed on us, and the great goodness towards the house of Israel, which he hath bestowed on them, according to his mercies, and according to the multitude of his loving-kindnesses. For he said, Surely they are my people, children that will not lie: so he was their Saviour. In all their affliction he was afflicted, and the angel of his presence saved them: in his love, and in his pity, he redeemed them, and he bare them, and carried them all the days of old. But they rebelled, and vexed his Holy Spirit; therefore he was turned to be their enemy, and he fought against them. Then he remembered the days of old, Moses and his people, saying, Where is he that brought them up out of the sea with the shepherd of his flock? where is he that put his Holy Spirit within him? that led them by the right hand of Moses, with his glorious arm, dividing the water before them, to make himself an everlasting name? that led them through the deep as an horse in the wilderness, that they should not stumble? As a beast goeth down into the valley, the Spirit of the Lord caused him to rest: so didst thou lead thy people, to make thyself a glorious name. Look down from heaven, and behold from the habitation of thy holiness and of thy glory; where is thy zeal and thy strength, the sounding of thy bowels, and of thy mercies towards me? Are they restrained? Doubtless thou art our Father, though Abraham be ignorant of us, and Israel acknowledge us not: Thou, O Lord, art our Father, our Redeemer, thy name is from everlasting. O Lord, why hast thou made us to err from

thy ways? and hardened our heart from thy fear? Return for thy
servants' sake, the tribes of thine inheritance. The people of thy
holiness have possessed it but a little while: our adversaries have
trodden down thy sanctuary. We are thine: thou never barest
rule over them; they were not called by thy name.

The Gospel. S. Mark 14. 1–end

AFTER two days was the feast of the passover, and of
unleavened bread: and the chief priests and the scribes sought
how they might take him by craft, and put him to death. But
they said, Not on the feast-day, lest there be an uproar of the
people. And being in Bethany, in the house of Simon the leper,
as he sat at meat, there came a woman having an alabaster box
of ointment of spikenard, very precious; and she brake the box,
and poured it on his head. And there were some that had indignation within themselves, and said, Why was this waste of the
ointment made? for it might have been sold for more than three
hundred pence, and have been given to the poor: and they
murmured against her. And Jesus said, Let her alone; why
trouble ye her? she hath wrought a good work on me: for ye
have the poor with you always, and whensoever ye will ye may
do them good; but me ye have not always. She hath done what
she could; she is come aforehand to anoint my body to the
burying. Verily I say unto you, Wheresoever this Gospel shall
be preached throughout the whole world, this also that she hath
done shall be spoken of for a memorial of her. And Judas
Iscariot, one of the twelve, went unto the chief priests to betray
him unto them. And when they heard it they were glad, and
promised to give him money. And he sought how he might
conveniently betray him. And the first day of unleavened bread,
when they killed the passover, his disciples said unto him,
Where wilt thou that we go and prepare, that thou mayest eat
the passover? And he sendeth forth two of his disciples, and
saith unto them, Go ye into the city, and there shall meet you a
man bearing a pitcher of water; follow him: and wheresoever he
shall go in, say ye to the good-man of the house, The Master
saith, Where is the guest-chamber, where I shall eat the

passover with my disciples? And he will shew you a large upper-room furnished and prepared: there make ready for us. And his disciples went forth, and came into the city, and found as he had said unto them: and they made ready the passover. And in the evening he cometh with the twelve. And as they sat, and did eat, Jesus said, Verily I say unto you, One of you which eateth with me shall betray me. And they began to be sorrowful, and to say unto him one by one, Is it I? and another said, Is it I? And he answered and said unto them, It is one of the twelve that dippeth with me in the dish. The Son of Man indeed goeth, as it is written of him: but woe to that man by whom the Son of Man is betrayed: good were it for that man if he had never been born. And as they did eat, Jesus took bread, and blessed, and brake it, and gave to them, and said, Take, eat: this is my body. And he took the cup, and when he had given thanks he gave it to them: and they all drank of it. And he said unto them, This is my blood of the new testament, which is shed for many. Verily I say unto you, I will drink no more of the fruit of the vine, until that day that I drink it new in the Kingdom of God. And when they had sung an hymn they went out into the mount of Olives. And Jesus saith unto them, All ye shall be offended because of me this night: for it is written, I will smite the shepherd, and the sheep shall be scattered. But, after that I am risen, I will go before you into Galilee. But Peter said unto him, Although all shall be offended, yet will not I. And Jesus saith unto him, Verily I say unto thee, That this day, even in this night, before the cock crow twice, thou shalt deny me thrice. But he spake the more vehemently, If I should die with thee, I will not deny thee in any wise. Likewise also said they all. And they came to a place which was named Gethsemane: and he saith to his disciples, Sit ye here, while I shall pray. And he taketh with him Peter and James and John, and began to be sore amazed, and to be very heavy, and saith unto them, My soul is exceeding sorrowful unto death; tarry ye here, and watch. And he went forward a little, and fell on the ground, and prayed that, if it were possible, the hour might pass from him. And he said, Abba, Father, all things are possible unto thee; take away this cup from me; nevertheless, not what I will, but what thou wilt. And he cometh and findeth them sleeping, and saith unto Peter, Simon, sleepest thou couldest not thou watch one hour? Watch ye and pray, lest ye enter into temptation: the spirit truly is ready, but the flesh is weak. And again he went away, and prayed, and spake the same words. And when he returned he found them asleep again, (for their eyes were heavy,) neither wist they what to answer him. And he cometh the third time, and saith unto them, Sleep on now, and take your rest: it is enough, the hour is come; behold the Son of Man is betrayed into the hands of sinners. Rise up, let us go; lo, he that betrayeth me is at hand. And immediately, while he yet spake, cometh Judas, one of the twelve, and with him a great multitude with swords and staves, from the chief priests and the scribes and the elders. And he that betrayed him had given them a token, saying, Whomsoever I shall kiss, that same is he; take him, and lead him away safely. And as soon as he was come he goeth straightway to him, and saith, Master, master; and kissed him. And they laid their hands on him, and took him. And one of them that stood by drew a sword, and smote a servant of the high priest, and cut off his ear. And Jesus answered, and said unto them, Are ye come out as against a thief, with swords and with staves, to take me? I was daily with you in the temple teaching, and ye took me not: but the Scriptures must be fulfilled. And they all forsook him, and fled. And there followed him a certain young man, having a linen cloth cast about his naked body; and the young men laid hold on him; and he left the linen cloth, and fled from them naked. And they led Jesus away to the high priest: and with him were assembled all the chief priests and the elders and the scribes. And Peter followed him afar off, even into the palace of the high priest; and he sat with the servants, and warmed himself at the fire. And the chief priests and all the council sought for witness against Jesus to put him to death; and found none. For many bare false witness against him, but their witness agreed not together. And there arose certain, and bare false witness against him, saying, We heard him say, I will destroy this temple that is made with hands, and within three days I will build another made without hands. But neither so did their witness agree together. And the high priest stood up in the midst, and asked Jesus, saying, Answerest thou nothing? what is it which these witness against thee? But he held his peace, and answered nothing. Again the high priest asked him, and said unto him, Art thou the Christ, the Son of the Blessed? And Jesus said, I am; and ye shall see the Son of Man sitting on the right hand of power, and coming in the clouds of heaven. Then the high priest rent his clothes, and saith, What need we any further witnesses? ye have heard the blasphemy: what think ye? And they all condemned him to be guilty of death. And some began to spit on him, and to cover his face, and to buffet him, and to say unto him, Prophesy: and the servants did strike him with the palms of their hands. And as Peter was beneath in the palace there cometh one of the maids of the high priest; and when she saw Peter warming himself she looked upon him, and said, And thou also wast with Jesus of Nazareth. But he denied, saying, I know not, neither understand I what thou sayest. And he went out into the porch; and the cock crew. And a maid saw him again, and began to say to them that stood by, This is one of them. And he denied it again. And a little after, they that stood by said again to Peter, Surely thou art one of them; for thou art a Galilæan, and thy speech agreeth thereto. But he began to curse and to swear, saying, I know not this man of whom ye speak. And the second time the cock crew. And Peter called to mind the word that Jesus said unto him, Before the cock crow twice, thou shalt deny me thrice. And when he thought thereon, he wept.

TUESDAY BEFORE EASTER

For the Epistle. Isai. 50. 5–end

THE Lord God hath opened mine ear, and I was not rebellious, neither turned away back. I gave my back to the smiters, and my cheeks to them that plucked off the hair: I hid not my face from shame and spitting. For the Lord God will help me, therefore shall I not be confounded: therefore have I set my face

like a flint, and I know that I shall not be ashamed. He is near
that justifieth me; who will contend with me? Let us stand
together; who is mine adversary? let him come near to me
Behold, the Lord God will help me; who is he that shall con
demn me? Lo, they all shall wax old as a garment: the moth
shall eat them up. Who is among you that feareth the Lord
that obeyeth the voice of his servant, that walketh in darkness
and hath no light? let him trust in the name of the Lord, and
stay upon his God. Behold, all ye that kindle a fire, that compass
yourselves about with sparks; walk in the light of your fire, and
in the sparks that ye have kindled. This shall ye have of mine
hand, ye shall lie down in sorrow.

The Gospel. S. Mark 15. 1–39

AND straightway in the morning the chief priests held a con
sultation with the elders and scribes and the whole council, and
bound Jesus, and carried him away, and delivered him to Pilate
And Pilate asked him, Art thou the King of the Jews? And he
answering said unto him, Thou sayest it. And the chief priests
accused him of many things: but he answered nothing. And
Pilate asked him again, saying, Answerest thou nothing? behold
how many things they witness against thee. But Jesus yet
answered nothing: so that Pilate marvelled. Now at that feast
he released unto them one prisoner, whomsoever they desired
And there was one named Barabbas, which lay bound with them
that had made insurrection with him, who had committed
murder in the insurrection. And the multitude, crying aloud
began to desire him to do as he had ever done unto them. But
Pilate answered them, saying, Will ye that I release unto you
the King of the Jews? For he knew that the chief priests had
delivered him for envy. But the chief priests moved the people
that he should rather release Barabbas unto them. And Pilate
answered, and said again unto them, What will ye then that I
shall do unto him whom ye call the King of the Jews? And they
cried out again, Crucify him. Then Pilate said unto them, Why
what evil hath he done? And they cried out the more exceed
ingly, Crucify him. And so Pilate, willing to content the people

released Barabbas unto them, and delivered Jesus, when he had scourged him, to be crucified. And the soldiers led him away into the hall, called Prætorium; and they call together the whole band. And they clothed him with purple, and platted a crown of thorns, and put it about his head: and began to salute him, Hail, King of the Jews. And they smote him on the head with a reed, and did spit upon him, and bowing their knees worshipped him. And when they had mocked him, they took off the purple from him, and put his own clothes on him, and led him out to crucify him. And they compel one Simon a Cyrenian, who passed by, coming out of the country, the father of Alexander and Rufus, to bear his cross. And they bring him unto the place Golgotha, which is, being interpreted, The place of a skull. And they gave him to drink wine mingled with myrrh; but he received it not. And when they had crucified him they parted his garments, casting lots upon them, what every man should take. And it was the third hour, and they crucified him. And the superscription of his accusation was written over, THE KING OF THE JEWS. And with him they crucify two thieves, the one on his right hand, and the other on his left. And the scripture was fulfilled, which saith, And he was numbered with the transgressors. And they that passed by railed on him, wagging their heads, and saying, Ah, thou that destroyest the temple, and buildest it in three days, save thyself, and come down from the cross. Likewise also the chief priests mocking said among themselves, with the scribes, He saved others; himself he cannot save. Let Christ the King of Israel descend now from the cross, that we may see and believe. And they that were crucified with him reviled him. And when the sixth hour was come, there was darkness over the whole land until the ninth hour. And at the ninth hour Jesus cried with a loud voice, saying, *Eloi, Eloi, lama sabachthani?* which is, being interpreted, My God, my God, why hast thou forsaken me? And some of them that stood by, when they heard it, said, Behold, he calleth Elias. And one ran and filled a spunge full of vinegar, and put it on a reed, and gave him to drink, saying, Let alone; let us see whether Elias will come to take him down. And Jesus cried with a loud voice, and gave up the ghost. And the vail of the temple was rent in twain from the top to the bottom. And when the centurion, which stood over against him, saw that he so cried out, and gave up the ghost, he said, Truly this man was the Son of God.

WEDNESDAY BEFORE EASTER

The Epistle. Hebr. 9. 16–end

WHERE a testament is, there must also of necessity be the death of the testator: for a testament is of force after men are dead; otherwise it is of no strength at all whilst the testator liveth. Whereupon, neither the first testament was dedicated without blood: for when Moses had spoken every precept to all the people, according to the law, he took the blood of calves and of goats, with water and scarlet wool and hyssop, and sprinkled both the book and all the people, saying, This is the blood of the testament, which God hath enjoined unto you. Moreover, he sprinkled with blood both the tabernacle and all the vessels of the ministry. And almost all things are by the law purged with blood; and without shedding of blood is no remission. It was therefore necessary that the patterns of things in the heavens should be purified with these; but the heavenly things themselves with better sacrifices than these. For Christ is not entered into the holy places made with hands, which are the figures of the true, but into heaven itself, now to appear in the presence of God for us; nor yet that he should offer himself often, as the high priest entereth into the holy place every year with blood of others: for then must he often have suffered since the foundation of the world; but now once in the end of the world hath he appeared to put away sin by the sacrifice of himself. And as it is appointed unto men once to die, but after this the judgement: so Christ was once offered to bear the sins of many; and unto them that look for him shall he appear the second time without sin unto salvation.

The Gospel. S. Luke 22. 1–end

NOW the feast of unleavened bread drew nigh, which is called the Passover. And the chief priests and scribes sought how they might kill him; for they feared the people. Then entered Satan into Judas surnamed Iscariot, being of the number of the twelve. And he went his way, and communed with the chief priests and captains, how he might betray him unto them. And they were glad, and covenanted to give him money. And he promised, and sought opportunity to betray him unto them in the absence of the multitude. Then came the day of unleavened bread, when the passover must be killed. And he sent Peter and John, saying, Go and prepare us the passover, that we may eat. And they said unto him, Where wilt thou that we prepare? And he said unto them, Behold, when ye are entered into the city, there shall a man meet you, bearing a pitcher of water; follow him into the house where he entereth in. And ye shall say unto the good-man of the house, The Master saith unto thee, Where is the guest-chamber, where I shall eat the passover with my disciples? And he shall shew you a large upper-room furnished; there make ready. And they went, and found as he had said unto them: and they made ready the passover. And when the hour was come he sat down, and the twelve Apostles with him. And he said unto them, With desire I have desired to eat this passover with you before I suffer: for I say unto you, I will not any more eat thereof, until it be fulfilled in the Kingdom of God. And he took the cup, and gave thanks, and said, Take this, and divide it among yourselves. For I say unto you, I will not drink of the fruit of the vine, until the Kingdom of God shall come. And he took bread, and gave thanks, and brake it, and gave unto them, saying, This is my body, which is given for you: this do in remembrance of me. Likewise also the cup after supper, saying, This cup is the new testament in my blood, which is shed for you. But behold, the hand of him that betrayeth me is with me on the table. And truly the Son of Man goeth as it was determined; but woe unto that man by whom he is betrayed. And they began to inquire among themselves, which of them it was that should do this thing. And there was also a strife among them, which of them should be accounted the greatest. And he said unto them, The kings of the Gentiles exercise lordship over them, and they that exercise authority upon them are called benefactors. But ye shall not be so: but he that is greatest among you, let him be as the younger; and he that is chief, as he that doth serve. For whether is greater, he that sitteth at meat, or he that serveth? is not he that sitteth at meat? but I am among you as he that serveth. Ye are they which have continued with me in my temptations. And I appoint unto you a kingdom, as my Father hath appointed unto me; that ye may eat and drink at my table in my kingdom, and sit on thrones, judging the twelve tribes of Israel. And the Lord said, Simon, Simon, behold, Satan hath desired to have you, that he may sift you as wheat: but I have prayed for thee, that thy faith fail not; and when thou art converted, strengthen thy brethren. And he said unto him, Lord, I am ready to go with thee both into prison and to death. And he said, I tell thee, Peter, the cock shall not crow this day, before that thou shalt thrice deny that thou knowest me. And he said unto them, When I sent you without purse, and scrip, and shoes, lacked ye any thing? And they said, Nothing. Then said he unto them, But now, he that hath a purse, let him take it, and likewise his scrip: and he that hath no sword, let him sell his garment, and buy one. For I say unto you, That this that is written must yet be accomplished in me, And he was reckoned among the transgressors: for the things concerning me have an end. And they said, Lord, behold, here are two swords. And he said unto them, It is enough. And he came out, and went, as he was wont, to the mount of Olives, and his disciples also followed him. And when he was at the place, he said unto them, Pray, that ye enter not into temptation. And he was withdrawn from them about a stone's cast, and kneeled down and prayed, saying, Father, if thou be willing, remove this cup from me: nevertheless, not my will, but thine be done. And there appeared an angel unto him from heaven, strengthening him. And being in an agony, he prayed more earnestly; and his sweat was as it were great drops of blood falling down to the ground. And when he rose up from prayer, and was come to his disciples, he found them sleeping for sorrow, and said unto them, Why sleep ye? rise and pray, lest ye enter into temptation. And while he yet pake, behold, a multitude, and he that was called Judas, one of he twelve, went before them, and drew near unto Jesus to kiss him. But Jesus said unto him, Judas, betrayest thou the Son of Man with a kiss? When they who were about him saw what would follow, they said unto him, Lord, shall we smite with the sword? And one of them smote the servant of the high priest, and cut off his right ear. And Jesus answered and said, Suffer ye thus far. And he touched his ear, and healed him. Then Jesus said unto the chief priests, and captains of the temple, and the elders who were come to him, Be ye come out as against a thief, with swords and staves? When I was daily with you in the temple, ye stretched forth no hands against me: but this is your hour, and the power of darkness. Then took they him, and led him, and brought him into the high priest's house: and Peter followed afar off. And when they had kindled a fire in the midst of the hall, and were set down together, Peter sat down among them. But a certain maid beheld him, as he sat by the fire, and earnestly looked upon him, and said, This man was also with him. And he denied him, saying, Woman, I know him not. And after a little while another saw him, and said, Thou art also of them. And Peter said, Man, I am not. And about the space of one hour after, another confidently affirmed, saying, Of a truth this fellow also was with him; for he is a Galilæan. And Peter said, Man, I know not what thou sayest. And immediately, while he yet spake, the cock crew. And the Lord turned, and looked upon Peter; and Peter remembered the word of the Lord, how he had said unto him, Before the cock crow, thou shalt deny me thrice. And Peter went out, and wept bitterly. And the men that held Jesus mocked him, and smote him. And when they had blindfolded him, they struck him on the face, and asked him, saying, Prophesy, who is it that smote thee? And many other things blasphemously spake they against him. And as soon as it was day, the elders of the people and the chief priests and the scribes came together, and led him into their council, saying, Art thou the Christ? tell us. And he said unto them, If I tell you, ye will not believe: and if I also ask you, ye will not answer me, nor let me go. Hereafter shall the Son of

Man sit on the right hand of the power of God. Then said the
all, Art thou then the Son of God? And he said unto them, Y
say that I am. And they said, What need we any further witness
for we ourselves have heard of his own mouth.

THURSDAY BEFORE EASTER

The Epistle. 1 Cor. 11. 17–end

IN this that I declare unto you, I praise you not; that ye com
together not for the better, but for the worse. For first of all
when ye come together in the church, I hear that there be divi
sions among you, and I partly believe it. For there must be also
heresies among you, that they who are approved may be mad
manifest among you. When ye come together therefore into on
place, this is not to eat the Lord's supper: for in eating every on
taketh before other his own supper; and one is hungry, an
another is drunken. What, have ye not houses to eat and t
drink in? or despise ye the church of God, and shame them tha
have not? What shall I say to you? shall I praise you in this?
praise you not. For I have received of the Lord that which als
I delivered unto you, That the Lord Jesus, the same night i
which he was betrayed, took bread; and when he had give
thanks, he brake it, and said, Take, eat; this is my body, whicl
is broken for you: this do in remembrance of me. After the sam
manner also he took the cup, when he had supped, saying, Thi
cup is the new testament in my blood: this do ye, as oft as y
drink it, in remembrance of me. For as often as ye eat this bread
and drink this cup, ye do shew the Lord's death till he come
Wherefore, whosoever shall eat this bread, and drink this cuj
of the Lord, unworthily, shall be guilty of the body and blood o
the Lord. But let a man examine himself, and so let him eat o
that bread, and drink of that cup. For he that eateth and drink
eth unworthily eateth and drinketh damnation to himself, no
discerning the Lord's body. For this cause many are weak an
sickly among you, and many sleep. For if we would judge our
selves, we should not be judged. But when we are judged, w
are chastened of the Lord, that we should not be condemne

with the world. Wherefore, my brethren, when ye come together to eat, tarry one for another. And if any man hunger, let him eat at home; that ye come not together unto condemnation. And the rest will I set in order when I come.

The Gospel. S. Luke 23. 1–49

THE whole multitude of them arose, and led him unto Pilate. And they began to accuse him, saying, We found this fellow perverting the nation, and forbidding to give tribute to Cæsar, saying, That he himself is Christ a King. And Pilate asked him, saying, Art thou the King of the Jews? And he answered him, and said, Thou sayest it. Then said Pilate to the chief priests and to the people, I find no fault in this man. And they were the more fierce, saying, He stirreth up the people, teaching throughout all Jewry, beginning from Galilee to this place. When Pilate heard of Galilee, he asked whether the man were a Galilæan. And as soon as he knew that he belonged unto Herod's jurisdiction, he sent him to Herod, who himself was also at Jerusalem at that time. And when Herod saw Jesus he was exceeding glad; for he was desirous to see him of a long season, because he had heard many things of him; and he hoped to have seen some miracle done by him. Then he questioned with him in many words; but he answered him nothing. And the chief priests and scribes stood and vehemently accused him. And Herod with his men of war set him at naught, and mocked him, and arrayed him in a gorgeous robe, and sent him again to Pilate. And the same day Pilate and Herod were made friends together; for before they were at enmity between themselves. And Pilate, when he had called together the chief priests and the rulers and the people, said unto them, Ye have brought this man unto me, as one that perverteth the people: and behold, I, having examined him before you, have found no fault in this man touching those things whereof ye accuse him: No, nor yet Herod: for I sent you to him; and lo, nothing worthy of death is done unto him. I will therefore chastise him, and release him. For of necessity he must release one unto them at the feast. And they cried out all at once, saying, Away with this man, and release unto us Barabbas: (who for a certain sedition made in the city, and for murder, was cast into prison.) Pilate therefore willing to release Jesus, spake again to them. But they cried saying, Crucify him, crucify him. And he said unto them the third time, Why, what evil hath he done? I have found no cause of death in him: I will therefore chastise him, and let him go And they were instant with loud voices, requiring that he might be crucified: and the voices of them and of the chief priests prevailed. And Pilate gave sentence that it should be as they required. And he released unto them him that for sedition and murder was cast into prison, whom they had desired; but he delivered Jesus to their will. And as they led him away, they laid hold upon one Simon a Cyrenian, coming out of the country and on him they laid the cross, that he might bear it after Jesus And there followed him a great company of people, and of women, which also bewailed and lamented him. But Jesus, turning unto them, said, Daughters of Jerusalem, weep not for me but weep for yourselves, and for your children. For behold, the days are coming, in the which they shall say, Blessed are the barren, and the wombs that never bare, and the paps which never gave suck. Then shall they begin to say to the mountains Fall on us; and to the hills, Cover us. For if they do these thing in a green tree, what shall be done in the dry? And there were also two other, malefactors, led with him to be put to death And when they were come to the place which is called Calvary there they crucified him; and the malefactors, one on the right hand, and the other on the left. Then said Jesus, Father, forgive them, for they know not what they do. And they parted his raiment, and cast lots. And the people stood beholding; and the rulers also with them derided him, saying, He saved others; let him save himself, if he be Christ, the chosen of God. And the soldiers also mocked him, coming to him, and offering him vinegar, and saying, If thou be the King of the Jews, save thyself And a superscription also was written over him in letters of Greek, and Latin, and Hebrew, THIS IS THE KING OF THE JEWS. And one of the malefactors, which were hanged, railed on him, saying, If thou be Christ, save thyself and us. But the other answering rebuked him, saying, Dost not thou fear God, seeing thou art in the same condemnation? And we indeed justly; for we receive the due reward of our deeds; but this man hath done nothing amiss. And he said unto Jesus, Lord, remember me when thou comest into thy kingdom. And Jesus said unto him, Verily I say unto thee, To-day shalt thou be with me in paradise. And it was about the sixth hour: and there was a darkness over all the earth until the ninth hour. And the sun was darkened, and the vail of the temple was rent in the midst. And when Jesus had cried with a loud voice, he said, Father, into thy hands I commend my spirit: and having said thus, he gave up the ghost. Now when the centurion saw what was done, he glorified God, saying, Certainly this was a righteous man. And all the people that came together to that sight, beholding the things that were done, smote their breasts and returned. And all his acquaintance, and the women that followed him from Galilee, stood afar off, beholding these things.

GOOD FRIDAY

The Collects

ALMIGHTY God, we beseech thee graciously to behold this thy family, for which our Lord Jesus Christ was contented to be betrayed, and given up into the hands of wicked men, and to suffer death upon the cross, who now liveth and reigneth with thee and the Holy Ghost, ever one God, world without end. *Amen.*

ALMIGHTY and everlasting God, by whose Spirit the whole body of the Church is governed and sanctified: Receive our supplications and prayers, which we offer before thee for all estates of men in thy holy Church, that every member of the same, in his vocation and ministry, may truly and godly serve thee; through our Lord and Saviour Jesus Christ. *Amen.*

O MERCIFUL God, who hast made all men, and hatest nothing that thou hast made, nor wouldest the death of a sinner, but rather that he should be converted and live: Have mercy upon all Jews, Turks, Infidels, and Hereticks, and take from them all ignorance, hardness of heart, and contempt of thy word; and so fetch them home, blessed Lord, to thy flock, that they may be saved among the remnant of the true Israelites, and be made one fold under one shepherd, Jesus Christ our Lord, who liveth and reigneth with thee and the Holy Spirit, one God, world without end. *Amen.*

The Epistle. Hebr. 10. 1–25

THE law having a shadow of good things to come, and not the very image of the things, can never with those sacrifices, which they offered year by year continually, make the comers thereunto perfect: for then would they not have ceased to be offered? because that the worshippers once purged should have had no more conscience of sins. But in those sacrifices there is a remembrance again made of sins every year. For it is not possible that the blood of bulls and of goats should take away sins. Wherefore, when he cometh into the world, he saith, Sacrifice and offering thou wouldest not, but a body hast thou prepared me: in burnt-offerings and sacrifices for sin thou hast had no pleasure: then said I, Lo, I come (in the volume of the book it is written of me) to do thy will, O God. Above when he said, Sacrifice and offering and burnt-offerings and offering for sin thou wouldest not, neither hadst pleasure therein, (which are offered by the law;) then said he, Lo, I come to do thy will, O God: he taketh away the first, that he may establish the second. By the which will we are sanctified, through the offering of the body of Jesus Christ once for all. And every priest standeth daily ministering, and offering oftentimes the same sacrifices, which can never take away sins. But this man, after he had offered one sacrifice for sins for ever, sat down on the right hand of God; from henceforth expecting till his enemies be made his foot-stool. For by one offering he hath perfected for ever them that are sanctified. Whereof the Holy Ghost also is a witness to us: for after that he had said before, This is the covenant that I will make with them after those days, saith the Lord, I will put my laws into their hearts, and in their minds will I write them; and their sins and iniquities will I remember no more. Now where remission of these is, there is no more offering for sin. Having therefore, brethren, boldness to enter into the holiest by the blood of Jesus, by a new and living way, which he hath consecrated for us, through the vail, that is to say, his flesh; and having an high Priest over the house of God; let us draw near with a true heart, in full assurance of faith, having our hearts sprinkled from an evil conscience, and our bodies washed with pure water. Let us hold fast the profession of our faith without wavering; (for he is faithful that promised;) and let us consider one another to provoke unto love, and to good works; not forsaking the assembling of ourselves together, as the manner of some is; but exhorting one another: and so much the more, as ye see the day approaching.

The Gospel. S. John 19. 1–37

PILATE therefore took Jesus, and scourged him. And the soldiers platted a crown of thorns, and put it on his head, and they put on him a purple robe, and said, Hail, King of the Jews: and they smote him with their hands. Pilate therefore went forth again, and saith unto them, Behold, I bring him forth to you, that ye may know that I find no fault in him. Then came Jesus forth, wearing the crown of thorns, and the purple robe. And Pilate saith unto them, Behold the man! When the chief priests therefore and officers saw him, they cried out, saying, Crucify him, crucify him. Pilate saith unto them, Take ye him, and crucify him: for I find no fault in him. The Jews answered him, We have a law, and by our law he ought to die, because he made himself the Son of God. When Pilate therefore heard that saying, he was the more afraid; and went again into the judgement-hall, and saith unto Jesus, Whence art thou? But Jesus gave him no answer. Then saith Pilate unto him, Speakest thou not unto me? knowest thou not that I have power to crucify thee, and have power to release thee? Jesus answered, Thou couldest have no power at all against me, except it were given thee from above: therefore he that delivered me unto thee hath the greater sin. And from thenceforth Pilate sought to release him: but the Jews cried out, saying, If thou let this man go, thou art not Cæsar's friend: whosoever maketh himself a king speaketh against Cæsar. When Pilate therefore heard that saying, he brought Jesus forth, and sat down in the judgement-seat, in a place that is called the Pavement, but in the Hebrew, Gabbatha. And it was the preparation of the passover, and about the sixth hour: and he saith unto the Jews, Behold your King! But they cried out, Away with him, away with him, crucify him. Pilate saith unto them, Shall I crucify your King? The chief priests answered, We have no king but Cæsar. Then delivered he him therefore unto them to be crucified: and they took Jesus, and led him away. And he, bearing his cross, went forth into a place called the place of a skull, which is called in the Hebrew, Golgotha: where they crucified him, and two other with him, on either side one, and Jesus in the midst. And Pilate wrote a title, and put it on the cross; and the writing was, JESUS OF NAZARETH THE KING OF THE JEWS. This title then read many of the Jews: for the place where Jesus was crucified was nigh to the city: and it was written in Hebrew, and Greek, and Latin. Then said the chief priests of the Jews to Pilate, Write not, The King of the Jews; but that he said, I am the King of the Jews. Pilate answered, What I have written, I have written. Then the soldiers, when they had crucified Jesus, took his garments, and made four parts, to every soldier a part; and also his coat: now the coat was without seam, woven from the top throughout. They said therefore among themselves, Let us not rend it, but cast lots for it, whose it shall be: that the Scripture might be fulfilled, which saith, They parted my raiment among them, and for my vesture they did cast lots. These things therefore the soldiers did. Now there stood by the cross of Jesus, his mother, and his mother's sister, Mary the wife of Cleophas, and Mary Magdalene. When Jesus therefore saw his mother, and the disciple standing by, whom he loved, he saith unto his mother, Woman, behold thy son. Then saith he to the disciple, Behold thy mother. And from that hour that disciple took her unto his own home. After this, Jesus, knowing that all things were now accomplished, that the Scripture might be fulfilled, saith, I thirst. Now there was set a vessel full of vinegar: and they filled a spunge with vinegar, and put it upon hyssop, and put it to his mouth. When Jesus therefore had received the vinegar, he said, It is finished: and he bowed his head, and gave up the ghost. The Jews therefore, because it was the preparation, that the bodies should not remain upon the cross on the sabbath-day, (for that sabbath-day was an high day,) besought Pilate that their legs might be broken, and that they might be taken away. Then came the soldiers, and brake the legs of the first, and of the other which was crucified with him. But when they came to Jesus, and saw that he was dead already, they brake not his legs. But one of the soldiers with a spear pierced his side, and forthwith came there out blood and water. And he that saw it bare record, and his record is true: and he knoweth that he saith true, that ye might believe. For these things were done that the Scripture should be fulfilled, A bone of him shall not be broken. And again another Scripture saith, They shall look on him whom they pierced.

EASTER EVEN

The Collect

GRANT, O Lord, that as we are baptized into the death of thy blessed Son our Saviour Jesus Christ, so by continual mortifying our corrupt affections we may be buried with him; and that, through the grave, and gate of death, we may pass to our joyful resurrection; for his merits, who died, and was buried, and rose again for us, thy Son Jesus Christ our Lord. *Amen.*

The Epistle. 1 S. Peter 3. 17–end

IT is better, if the will of God be so, that ye suffer for well-doing, than for evil-doing. For Christ also hath once suffered for sins, the just for the unjust, that he might bring us to God, being put to death in the flesh, but quickened by the Spirit: by which also he went and preached unto the spirits in prison; which sometime were disobedient, when once the long-suffering of God waited in the days of Noah, while the ark was a preparing; wherein few, that is, eight souls, were saved by water. The like figure whereunto, even baptism, doth also now save us, (not the putting away of the filth of the flesh, but the answer of a good conscience towards God,) by the resurrection of Jesus Christ: who is gone into heaven, and is on the right hand of God, angels and authorities and powers being made subject unto him.

The Gospel. S. Matth. 27. 57–end

WHEN the even was come, there came a rich man of Arimathæa, named Joseph, who also himself was Jesus' disciple. He went to Pilate, and begged the body of Jesus. Then Pilate commanded the body to be delivered. And when Joseph had taken the body, he wrapped it in a clean linen cloth, and laid it in his own new tomb, which he had hewn out in the rock; and he rolled a great stone to the door of the sepulchre, and departed. And there was Mary Magdalen, and the other Mary, sitting over against the sepulchre. Now the next day, that followed the day of the preparation, the chief priests and Pharisees came together unto Pilate, saying, Sir, we remember that that deceiver said, while he was yet alive, After three days I will rise again. Command therefore that the sepulchre be made sure until the third day, lest his disciples come by night and steal him away, and say unto the people, He is risen from the dead: so the last error shall be worse than the first. Pilate said unto them, Ye have a watch; go your way, make it as sure as you can. So they went and made the sepulchre sure, sealing the stone, and setting a watch.

EASTER DAY

At Morning Prayer, instead of the Psalm: O come, let us, &c. these Anthems shall be sung or said.

CHRIST our passover is sacrificed for us: therefore let us keep the feast;

Not with the old leaven, nor with the leaven of malice and wickedness: but with the unleavened bread of sincerity and truth.   1 *Cor.* 5. 7.

Christ being raised from the dead dieth no more: death hath no more dominion over him.

For in that he died, he died unto sin once: but in that he liveth, he liveth unto God.

Likewise reckon ye also yourselves to be dead indeed unto sin: but alive unto God, through Jesus Christ our Lord.

Rom. 6. 9.

Christ is risen from the dead: and become the first-fruits of them that slept.

For since by man came death: by man came also the resurrection of the dead.

For as in Adam all die: even so in Christ shall all be made alive. 1 *Cor.* 15. 20.

Glory be to the Father, and to the Son: and to the Holy Ghost;

Answer. As it was in the beginning, is now, and ever shall be: world without end. Amen.

The Collect

ALMIGHTY God, who through thine only-begotten Son Jesus Christ hast overcome death, and opened unto us the gate of everlasting life: We humbly beseech thee, that as by thy special grace preventing us thou dost put into our minds good desires, so by thy continual help we may bring the same to good effect; through Jesus Christ our Lord, who liveth and reigneth with thee and the Holy Ghost, ever one God, world without end. *Amen.*

The Epistle. Coloss. 3. 1–7

IF ye then be risen with Christ, seek those things which are above, where Christ sitteth on the right hand of God. Set your affection on things above, not on things on the earth. For ye are dead, and your life is hid with Christ in God. When Christ, who is our life, shall appear, then shall ye also appear with him in glory. Mortify therefore your members which are upon the earth; fornication, uncleanness, inordinate affection, evil concupiscence, and covetousness, which is idolatry: for which things' sake the wrath of God cometh on the children of disobedience: in the which ye also walked some time, when ye lived in them.

The Gospel. S. John 20. 1–10

THE first day of the week cometh Mary Magdalen early, when it was yet dark, unto the sepulchre, and seeth the stone taken away from the sepulchre. Then she runneth and cometh to Simon Peter, and to the other disciple whom Jesus loved, and saith unto them, They have taken away the Lord out of the sepulchre, and we know not where they have laid him. Peter therefore went forth, and that other disciple, and came to the sepulchre. So they ran both together; and the other disciple did outrun Peter, and came first to the sepulchre; and he, stooping down and looking in, saw the linen clothes lying; yet went he not in. Then cometh Simon Peter following him, and went into the sepulchre, and seeth the linen clothes lie; and the napkin that was about his head, not lying with the linen clothes, but wrapped together in a place by itself. Then went in also that other disciple which came first to the sepulchre, and he saw, and believed. For as yet they knew not the Scripture, that he must rise again from the dead. Then the disciples went away again unto their own home.

MONDAY IN EASTER WEEK

The Collect

ALMIGHTY God, who through thy only-begotten Son Jesus Christ hast overcome death, and opened unto us the gate of everlasting life: We humbly beseech thee, that as by thy special grace preventing us thou dost put into our minds good desires, so by thy continual help we may bring the same to good effect; through Jesus Christ our Lord, who liveth and reigneth with thee and the Holy Ghost, ever one God, world without end. *Amen.*

For the Epistle. Acts 10. 34–43

PETER opened his mouth, and said, Of a truth I perceive that God is no respecter of persons; but in every nation he that feareth him, and worketh righteousness, is accepted with him. The word which God sent unto the children of Israel, preaching peace by Jesus Christ; (he is Lord of all;) that word, I say, ye know, which was published throughout all Judæa, and began from Galilee, after the baptism which John preached: how God anointed Jesus of Nazareth with the Holy Ghost, and with power; who went about doing good, and healing all that were oppressed of the devil: for God was with him. And we are witnesses of all things which he did, both in the land of the Jews, and in Jerusalem; whom they slew, and hanged on a tree: him God raised up the third day, and shewed him openly; not to all the people, but unto witnesses chosen before of God, even to us, who did eat and drink with him after he rose from the dead. And he commanded us to preach unto the people, and to testify that it is he who was ordained of God to be the Judge of quick and dead. To him give all the prophets witness, that through his name whosoever believeth in him shall receive remission of sins.

The Gospel. S. Luke 24. 13–35

BEHOLD, two of his disciples went that same day to a village called Emmaus, which was from Jerusalem about threescore furlongs. And they talked together of all these things which had happened. And it came to pass, that while they communed together, and reasoned, Jesus himself drew near, and went with them. But their eyes were holden, that they should not know him. And he said unto them, What manner of communications are these that ye have one to another, as ye walk, and are sad? And the one of them, whose name was Cleopas, answering said unto him, Art thou only a stranger in Jerusalem, and hast not known the things which are come to pass there in these days? And he said unto them, What things? And they said unto him, Concerning Jesus of Nazareth, who was a prophet mighty in deed and word, before God and all the people: and how the chief priests and our rulers delivered him to be condemned to death, and have crucified him. But we trusted that it had been he which should have redeemed Israel: and beside all this, to-day is the third day since these things were done. Yea, and certain women also of our company made us astonished, which were early at the sepulchre; and when they found not his body, they came, saying that they had also seen a vision of angels, which said that he was alive. And certain of them which were with us went to the sepulchre, and found it even so as the women had said; but him they saw not. Then he said unto them, O fools, and slow of heart to believe all that the prophets have spoken: ought not Christ to have suffered these things, and to enter into his glory? And beginning at Moses, and all the prophets, he expounded unto them in all the Scriptures the things concerning himself. And they drew nigh unto the village whither they went; and he made as though he would have gone further: but they constrained him, saying, Abide with us: for it is towards evening, and the day is far spent. And he went in to tarry with them. And it came to pass, as he sat at meat with them, he took bread, and blessed it, and brake, and gave to them. And their eyes were opened, and they knew him; and he vanished out of their sight. And they said one to another, Did not our heart burn within us, while he talked with us by the way, and while he opened to us the Scriptures? And they rose up the same hour, and returned to Jerusalem, and found the eleven gathered together, and them that were with them, saying, The Lord is risen indeed, and hath appeared to Simon. And they told what things were done in the way, and how he was known of them in breaking of bread.

TUESDAY IN EASTER WEEK

The Collect

ALMIGHTY God, who through thy only-begotten Son Jesus Christ hast overcome death, and opened unto us the gate of everlasting life: We humbly beseech thee, that as by thy special grace preventing us thou dost put into our minds good desires, so by thy continual help we may bring the same to good effect; through Jesus Christ our Lord, who liveth and

reigneth with thee and the Holy Ghost, ever one God, world
without end. *Amen.*

For the Epistle. Acts 13. 26–41

MEN and brethren, children of the stock of Abraham, and
whosoever among you feareth God, to you is the word of this
salvation sent. For they that dwell at Jerusalem, and their rulers,
because they knew him not, nor yet the voices of the prophets
which are read every sabbath-day, they have fulfilled them in
condemning him. And though they found no cause of death in
him, yet desired they Pilate that he should be slain. And when
they had fulfilled all that was written of him, they took him
down from the tree, and laid him in a sepulchre. But God raised
him from the dead: and he was seen many days of them which
came up with him from Galilee to Jerusalem, who are his witnesses unto the people. And we declare unto you glad tidings,
how that the promise which was made unto the fathers, God
hath fulfilled the same unto us their children, in that he hath
raised up Jesus again; as it is also written in the second psalm,
Thou art my Son, this day have I begotten thee. And as concerning that he raised him up from the dead, now no more to
return to corruption, he said on this wise, I will give you the
sure mercies of David. Wherefore he saith also in another
psalm, Thou shalt not suffer thine Holy One to see corruption.
For David, after he had served his own generation by the will
of God, fell on sleep, and was laid unto his fathers, and saw
corruption: but he whom God raised again saw no corruption.
Be it known unto you therefore, men and brethren, that through
this man is preached unto you the forgiveness of sins: and by
him all that believe are justified from all things, from which ye
could not be justified by the law of Moses. Beware therefore,
lest that come upon you which is spoken of in the prophets;
Behold, ye despisers, and wonder, and perish: for I work a work
in your days, a work which ye shall in no wise believe, though a
man declare it unto you.

The Gospel. S. Luke 24. 36–48

JESUS himself stood in the midst of them, and saith unto

them, Peace be unto you. But they were terrified and affrighted, and supposed that they had seen a spirit. And he said unto them, Why are ye troubled, and why do thoughts arise in your hearts? Behold my hands and my feet, that it is I myself: handle me, and see; for a spirit hath not flesh and bones, as ye see me have. And when he had thus spoken, he shewed them his hands and his feet. And while they yet believed not for joy, and wondered, he said unto them, Have ye here any meat? And they gave him a piece of a broiled fish, and of an honey-comb. And he took it, and did eat before them. And he said unto them, These are the words which I spake unto you, while I was yet with you, that all things must be fulfilled which were written in the law of Moses, and in the prophets, and in the psalms concerning me. Then opened he their understanding, that they might understand the Scriptures, and said unto them, Thus it is written, and thus it behoved Christ to suffer, and to rise from the dead the third day; and that repentance and remission of sins should be preached in his name among all nations, beginning at Jerusalem. And ye are witnesses of these things.

THE FIRST SUNDAY AFTER EASTER

The Collect

ALMIGHTY Father, who hast given thine only Son to die for our sins, and to rise again for our justification: Grant us so to put away the leaven of malice and wickedness, that we may alway serve thee in pureness of living and truth; through the merits of the same thy Son Jesus Christ our Lord. *Amen.*

The Epistle. 1 S. John 5. 4–12

WHATSOEVER is born of God overcometh the world: and this is the victory that overcometh the world, even our faith. Who is he that overcometh the world, but he that believeth that Jesus is the Son of God? This is he that came by water and blood, even Jesus Christ; not by water only, but by water and blood: and it is the Spirit that beareth witness, because the Spirit is truth. For there are three that bear record in heaven, the Father, the Word, and the Holy Ghost: and these three are one. And there are three that bear witness in earth, the spirit, and the water, and the blood: and these three agree in one. If we receive the witness of men, the witness of God is greater: for this is the witness of God, which he hath testified of his Son. He that believeth on the Son of God hath the witness in himself: he that believeth not God hath made him a liar, because he believeth not the record that God gave of his Son. And this is the record, that God hath given to us eternal life; and this life is in his Son. He that hath the Son hath life; and he that hath not the Son hath not life.

The Gospel. S. John 20. 19–23

THE same day at evening, being the first day of the week, when the doors were shut, where the disciples were assembled for fear of the Jews, came Jesus and stood in the midst, and saith unto them, Peace be unto you. And when he had so said, he shewed unto them his hands and his side. Then were the disciples glad when they saw the Lord. Then said Jesus to them again, Peace be unto you: As my Father hath sent me, even so send I you. And when he had said this, he breathed on them, and saith unto them, Receive ye the Holy Ghost. Whosesoever sins ye remit, they are remitted unto them; and whosesoever sins ye retain, they are retained.

THE SECOND SUNDAY AFTER EASTER

The Collect

ALMIGHTY God, who hast given thine only Son to be unto us both a sacrifice for sin, and also an ensample of godly life: Give us grace that we may always most thankfully receive that his inestimable benefit, and also daily endeavour ourselves to follow the blessed steps of his most holy life; through the same Jesus Christ our Lord. *Amen.*

The Epistle. 1 S. Peter 2. 19–end

THIS is thank-worthy, if a man for conscience toward God

endure grief, suffering wrongfully. For what glory is it, if, when ye be buffeted for your faults, ye shall take it patiently? but if, when ye do well, and suffer for it, ye take it patiently; this is acceptable with God. For even hereunto were ye called: because Christ also suffered for us, leaving us an example, that ye should follow his steps: who did no sin, neither was guile found in his mouth: who, when he was reviled, reviled not again; when he suffered, he threatened not; but committed himself to him that judgeth righteously: who his own self bare our sins in his own body on the tree, that we, being dead to sins, should live unto righteousness: by whose stripes ye were healed. For ye were as sheep going astray; but are now returned unto the Shepherd and Bishop of your souls.

The Gospel. S. John 10. 11–16

JESUS said, I am the good shepherd: the good shepherd giveth his life for the sheep. But he that is an hireling, and not the shepherd, whose own the sheep are not, seeth the wolf coming, and leaveth the sheep, and fleeth; and the wolf catcheth them, and scattereth the sheep. The hireling fleeth, because he is an hireling, and careth not for the sheep. I am the good shepherd, and know my sheep, and am known of mine. As the Father knoweth me, even so know I the Father: and I lay down my life for the sheep. And other sheep I have, which are not of this fold; them also I must bring, and they shall hear my voice; and there shall be one fold, and one shepherd.

THE THIRD SUNDAY AFTER EASTER

The Collect

ALMIGHTY God, who shewest to them that be in error the light of thy truth, to the intent that they may return into the way of righteousness: Grant unto all them that are admitted into the fellowship of Christ's religion, that they may eschew those things that are contrary to their profession, and follow all such things as are agreeable to the same; through our Lord Jesus Christ. *Amen.*

The Epistle. 1 S. Peter 2. 11–17

DEARLY beloved, I beseech you as strangers and pilgrims, abstain from fleshly lusts, which war against the soul; having your conversation honest among the Gentiles; that, whereas they speak against you as evildoers, they may, by your good works which they shall behold, glorify God in the day of visitation. Submit yourselves to every ordinance of man for the Lord's sake; whether it be to the king, as supreme; or unto governors, as unto them that are sent by him, for the punishment of evildoers, and for the praise of them that do well. For so is the will of God, that with well-doing ye may put to silence the ignorance of foolish men: as free, and not using your liberty for a cloke of maliciousness; but as the servants of God. Honour all men. Love the brotherhood. Fear God. Honour the king.

The Gospel. S. John 16. 16–22

JESUS said to his disciples, A little while and ye shall not see me; and again a little while and ye shall see me; because I go to the Father. Then said some of his disciples among themselves, What is this that he saith unto us, A little while and ye shall not see me; and again a little while and ye shall see me; and, Because I go to the Father? They said therefore, What is this that he saith, A little while? we cannot tell what he saith. Now Jesus knew that they were desirous to ask him, and said unto them, Do ye inquire among yourselves of that I said, A little while and ye shall not see me; and again a little while and ye shall see me? Verily, verily I say unto you, that ye shall weep and lament, but the world shall rejoice: and ye shall be sorrowful, but your sorrow shall be turned into joy. A woman, when she is in travail, hath sorrow, because her hour is come: but as soon as she is delivered of the child, she remembereth no more the anguish, for joy that a man is born into the world. And ye now therefore have sorrow: but I will see you again, and your heart shall rejoice, and your joy no man taketh from you.

THE FOURTH SUNDAY AFTER EASTER

The Collect

O ALMIGHTY God, who alone canst order the unruly wills and affections of sinful men: Grant unto thy people, that they may love the thing which thou commandest, and desire that which thou dost promise; that so, among the sundry and manifold changes of the world, our hearts may surely there be fixed, where true joys are to be found; through Jesus Christ our Lord. *Amen.*

The Epistle. S. James 1. 17–21

EVERY good gift and every perfect gift is from above, and cometh down from the Father of lights, with whom is no variableness, neither shadow of turning. Of his own will begat he us with the word of truth, that we should be a kind of first-fruits of his creatures. Wherefore, my beloved brethren, let every man be swift to hear, slow to speak, slow to wrath; for the wrath of man worketh not the righteousness of God. Wherefore lay apart all filthiness and superfluity of naughtiness, and receive with meekness the engrafted word, which is able to save your souls.

The Gospel. S. John 16. 5–15

JESUS said unto his disciples, Now I go my way to him that sent me, and none of you asketh me, Whither goest thou? But, because I have said these things unto you, sorrow hath filled your heart. Nevertheless, I tell you the truth; it is expedient for you that I go away: for if I go not away, the Comforter will not come unto you; but if I depart, I will send him unto you. And when he is come, he will reprove the world of sin, and of righteousness, and of judgement: of sin, because they believe not on me; of righteousness, because I go to my Father, and ye see me no more; of judgement, because the prince of this world is judged. I have yet many things to say unto you, but ye cannot bear them now. Howbeit, when he, the Spirit of truth, is come, he will guide you into all truth: for he shall not speak of himself; but whatsoever he shall hear, that shall he speak: and he will shew you things to come. He shall glorify me: for he shall receive of mine, and shall shew it unto you. All things that the Father hath are mine: therefore said I, that he shall take of mine, and shall shew it unto you.

THE FIFTH SUNDAY AFTER EASTER

The Collect

O LORD, from whom all good things do come: Grant to us thy humble servants, that by thy holy inspiration we may think those things that be good, and by thy merciful guiding may perform the same; through our Lord Jesus Christ. *Amen.*

The Epistle. S. James i. 22—end

BE ye doers of the word, and not hearers only, deceiving your own selves. For if any be a hearer of the word, and not a doer, he is like unto a man beholding his natural face in a glass. For he beholdeth himself, and goeth his way, and straightway forgetteth what manner of man he was. But whoso looketh into the perfect law of liberty, and continueth therein, he being not a forgetful hearer, but a doer of the work, this man shall be blessed in his deed. If any man among you seem to be religious, and bridleth not his tongue, but deceiveth his own heart, this man's religion is vain. Pure religion and undefiled before God and the Father is this, To visit the fatherless and widows in their affliction, and to keep himself unspotted from the world.

The Gospel. S. John 16. 23—end

VERILY, verily I say unto you, Whatsoever ye shall ask the Father in my name, he will give it you. Hitherto have ye asked nothing in my name: ask, and ye shall receive, that your joy may be full. These things have I spoken unto you in proverbs: the time cometh when I shall no more speak unto you in proverbs, but I shall shew you plainly of the Father. At that day ye shall ask in my name: and I say not unto you, that I will pray the Father for you; for the Father himself loveth you, because ye have loved me, and have believed that I came out from God. I came forth from the Father, and am come into the world: again, I leave the world, and go to the Father. His disciples said unto

him, Lo, now speakest thou plainly, and speakest no proverb.
Now are we sure that thou knowest all things, and needest no
that any man should ask thee: by this we believe that thou
camest forth from God. Jesus answered them, Do ye now
believe? Behold, the hour cometh, yea, is now come, that ye
shall be scattered every man to his own, and shall leave me
alone: and yet I am not alone, because the Father is with me.
These things I have spoken unto you, that in me ye might have
peace. In the world ye shall have tribulation; but be of good
cheer, I have overcome the world.

THE ASCENSION DAY

The Collect

GRANT, we beseech thee, Almighty God, that like as we do
believe thy only begotten Son our Lord Jesus Christ to have
ascended into the heavens; so we may also in heart and mind
thither ascend, and with him continually dwell, who liveth and
reigneth with thee and the Holy Ghost, one God, world without end. *Amen.*

For the Epistle. Acts i. 1–11

THE former treatise have I made, O Theophilus, of all that
Jesus began both to do and teach, until the day in which he
was taken up, after that he through the Holy Ghost had given
commandments unto the Apostles whom he had chosen: to
whom also he shewed himself alive after his passion, by many
infallible proofs; being seen of them forty days, and speaking of
the things pertaining to the kingdom of God: and, being
assembled together with them, commanded them that they
should not depart from Jerusalem, but wait for the promise of
the Father, which, saith he, ye have heard of me. For John truly
baptized with water, but ye shall be baptized with the Holy
Ghost not many days hence. When they therefore were come
together, they asked of him, saying, Lord, wilt thou at this time
restore again the kingdom to Israel? And he said unto them, It
is not for you to know the times or the seasons, which the Father

ath put in his own power. But ye shall receive power after that he Holy Ghost is come upon you; and ye shall be witnesses unto me, both in Jerusalem, and in all Judæa, and in Samaria, and unto the uttermost part of the earth. And when he had spoken these things, while they beheld, he was taken up, and a cloud received him out of their sight. And while they looked stedfastly toward heaven, as he went up, behold, two men stood by them in white apparel; which also said, Ye men of Galilee, why stand ye gazing up into heaven? This same Jesus, which is taken up from you into heaven, shall so come, in like manner as ye have seen him go into heaven.

The Gospel. S. Mark 16. 14–end

JESUS appeared unto the eleven as they sat at meat, and upbraided them with their unbelief and hardness of heart, because they believed not them which had seen him after he was risen. And he said unto them, Go ye into all the world, and preach the Gospel to every creature. He that believeth and is baptized shall be saved; but he that believeth not shall be damned. And these signs shall follow them that believe: In my name shall they cast out devils; they shall speak with new tongues; they shall take up serpents; and if they drink any deadly thing, it shall not hurt them; they shall lay hands on the sick, and they shall recover. So then after the Lord had spoken unto them, he was received up into heaven, and sat on the right hand of God. And they went forth and preached every where, the Lord working with them, and confirming the word with signs following.

SUNDAY AFTER ASCENSION DAY

The Collect

O GOD the King of glory, who hast exalted thine only Son Jesus Christ with great triumph unto thy kingdom in heaven: We beseech thee, leave us not comfortless; but send to us thine Holy Ghost to comfort us, and exalt us unto the same place whither our Saviour Christ is gone before, who liveth and reigneth with thee and the Holy Ghost, one God, world without end. *Amen.*

The Epistle. 1 S. Peter 4. 7–11

THE end of all things is at hand; be ye therefore sober, and watch unto prayer. And above all things have fervent charity among yourselves: for charity shall cover the multitude of sins. Use hospitality one to another without grudging. As every man hath received the gift, even so minister the same one to another, as good stewards of the manifold grace of God. If any man speak, let him speak as the oracles of God: if any man minister, let him do it as of the ability which God giveth; that God in all things may be glorified through Jesus Christ, to whom be praise and dominion for ever and ever. Amen.

The Gospel. S. John 15. 26–end, and 16. 1–4

WHEN the Comforter is come, whom I will send unto you from the Father, even the Spirit of truth, which proceedeth from the Father, he shall testify of me: and ye also shall bear witness, because ye have been with me from the beginning. These things have I spoken unto you, that ye should not be offended. They shall put you out of the synagogues: yea, the time cometh, that whosoever killeth you will think that he doeth God service. And these things will they do unto you, because they have not known the Father, nor me. But these things have I told you, that, when the time shall come, ye may remember that I told you of them.

WHITSUNDAY

The Collect

GOD, who as at this time didst teach the hearts of thy faithful people, by the sending to them the light of thy Holy Spirit: Grant us by the same Spirit to have a right judgement in all things, and evermore to rejoice in his holy comfort; through the merits of Christ Jesus our Saviour, who liveth and reigneth with thee, in the unity of the same Spirit, one God, world without end. *Amen.*

For the Epistle. Acts 2. 1–11

WHEN the day of Pentecost was fully come, they were all with one accord in one place. And suddenly there came a sound from heaven, as of a rushing mighty wind, and it filled all the house where they were sitting. And there appeared unto them cloven tongues, like as of fire, and it sat upon each of them: and they were all filled with the Holy Ghost, and began to speak with other tongues, as the Spirit gave them utterance. And there were dwelling at Jerusalem Jews, devout men, out of every nation under heaven. Now when this was noised abroad, the multitude came together, and were confounded, because that every man heard them speak in his own language. And they were all amazed, and marvelled, saying one to another, Behold, are not all these which speak Galilæans? And how hear we every man in our own tongue wherein we were born? Parthians, and Medes, and Elamites, and the dwellers in Mesopotamia, and in Judæa, and Cappadocia, in Pontus, and Asia, Phrygia, and Pamphylia, in Egypt, and in the parts of Libya about Cyrene, and strangers of Rome, Jews and proselytes, Cretes and Arabians, we do hear them speak in our tongues the wonderful works of God.

The Gospel. S. John 14. 15–end

JESUS said unto his disciples, If ye love me, keep my commandments. And I will pray the Father, and he shall give you another Comforter, that he may abide with you for ever; even the Spirit of truth, whom the world cannot receive, because it seeth him not, neither knoweth him: but ye know him; for he dwelleth with you, and shall be in you. I will not leave you comfortless; I will come to you. Yet a little while, and the world seeth me no more; but ye see me: because I live, ye shall live also. At that day ye shall know that I am in my Father, and ye in me, and I in you. He that hath my commandments, and keepeth them, he it is that loveth me; and he that loveth me shall be loved of my Father, and I will love him, and will manifest myself to him. Judas saith unto him, (not Iscariot,) Lord, how is it that thou wilt manifest thyself unto us, and not unto the world? Jesus answered and said unto him, If a man love me, he will keep my words, and my Father will love him, and we will come unto him, and make our abode with him. He that loveth me not keepeth not my sayings: and the word which ye hear is not mine, but the Father's which sent me. These things have I spoken unto you, being yet present with you. But the Comforter, which is the Holy Ghost, whom the Father will send in my name, he shall teach you all things, and bring all things to your remembrance, whatsoever I have said unto you. Peace I leave with you, my peace I give unto you: not as the world giveth, give I unto you. Let not your heart be troubled, neither let it be afraid. Ye have heard how I said unto you, I go away, and come again unto you. If ye loved me, ye would rejoice, because I said, I go unto the Father: for my Father is greater than I. And now I have told you before it come to pass, that, when it is come to pass, ye might believe. Hereafter I will not talk much with you: for the prince of this world cometh, and hath nothing in me. But that the world may know that I love the Father; and as the Father gave me commandment, even so I do.

MONDAY IN WHITSUN WEEK

The Collect

GOD, who as at this time didst teach the hearts of thy faithful people, by the sending to them the light of thy Holy Spirit: Grant us by the same Spirit to have a right judgement in all things, and evermore to rejoice in his holy comfort; through the merits of Christ Jesus our Saviour, who liveth and reigneth with thee, in the unity of the same Spirit, one God, world without end. *Amen.*

For the Epistle. Acts 10. 34–end

THEN Peter opened his mouth, and said, Of a truth I perceive that God is no respecter of persons; but in every nation he that feareth him, and worketh righteousness, is accepted with him. The word which God sent unto the children of Israel, preaching peace by Jesus Christ; (he is Lord of all;) that word, I say, ye know, which was published throughout all Judæa, and began from Galilee, after the baptism which John preached: how God anointed Jesus of Nazareth with the Holy Ghost, and with power; who went about doing good, and healing all that were oppressed of the devil: for God was with him. And we are witnesses of all things which he did, both in the land of the Jews, and in Jerusalem; whom they slew, and hanged on a tree: him God raised up the third day, and shewed him openly: not to all the people, but unto witnesses chosen before of God, even to us, who did eat and drink with him after he rose from the dead. And he commanded us to preach unto the people, and to testify that it is he which was ordained of God to be the Judge of quick and dead. To him give all the prophets witness, that through his name whosoever believeth in him shall receive remission of sins. While Peter yet spake these words, the Holy Ghost fell on all them which heard the word. And they of the circumcision which believed were astonished, as many as came with Peter, because that on the Gentiles also was poured out the gift of the Holy Ghost. For they heard them speak with tongues, and magnify God. Then answered Peter, Can any man forbid water, that these should not be baptized, which have received the Holy Ghost as well as we? And he commanded them to be baptized in the name of the Lord. Then prayed they him to tarry certain days.

The Gospel. S. John 3. 16–21

GOD so loved the world, that he gave his only-begotten Son, that whosoever believeth in him should not perish, but have everlasting life. For God sent not his Son into the world to condemn the world, but that the world through him might be saved. He that believeth on him is not condemned: but he that believeth not is condemned already; because he hath not believed in the name of the only-begotten Son of God. And this is the condemnation, that light is come into the world, and men loved darkness rather than light, because their deeds were evil. For every one that doeth evil hateth the light, neither cometh to the light, lest his deeds should be reproved. But he that doeth truth cometh to the light, that his deeds may be made manifest, that they are wrought in God.

TUESDAY IN WHITSUN WEEK

The Collect

GOD, who as at this time didst teach the hearts of thy faithful people, by the sending to them the light of thy Holy Spirit: Grant us by the same Spirit to have a right judgement in all things, and evermore to rejoice in his holy comfort; through the merits of Christ Jesus our Saviour, who liveth and reigneth with thee, in the unity of the same Spirit, one God, world without end. *Amen.*

For the Epistle. Acts 8. 14–17

WHEN the Apostles, which were at Jerusalem, heard that Samaria had received the word of God, they sent unto them Peter and John; who, when they were come down, prayed for them, that they might receive the Holy Ghost: (for as yet he was fallen upon none of them; only they were baptized in the name of the Lord Jesus.) Then laid they their hands on them, and they received the Holy Ghost.

The Gospel. S. John 10. 1–10

VERILY, verily I say unto you, He that entereth not by the door into the sheepfold, but climbeth up some other way, the same is a thief and a robber. But he that entereth in by the door is the shepherd of the sheep: to him the porter openeth; and the sheep hear his voice, and he calleth his own sheep by name, and leadeth them out. And, when he putteth forth his own sheep, he goeth before them, and the sheep follow him; for they know his voice. And a stranger will they not follow; but will flee from him; for they know not the voice of strangers. This parable spake Jesus unto them: but they understood not what things they were which he spake unto them. Then said Jesus unto them again; Verily, verily I say unto you, I am the door of the sheep. All that ever came before me are thieves and robbers; but the sheep did not hear them. I am the door; by me if any man enter in, he shall be saved, and shall go in and out, and find pasture. The thief cometh not but for to steal, and to kill, and to destroy: I am come that they might have life, and that they might have it more abundantly.

TRINITY SUNDAY

The Collect

ALMIGHTY and everlasting God, who hast given unto us thy servants grace, by the confession of a true faith, to acknowledge the glory of the eternal Trinity, and in the power of the Divine Majesty to worship the Unity: We beseech thee, that thou wouldest keep us stedfast in this faith, and evermore defend us from all adversities, who livest and reignest, one God, world without end. *Amen.*

For the Epistle. Rev. 4. 1–end

AFTER this I looked, and behold, a door was opened in heaven: and the first voice which I heard was as it were of a trumpet talking with me; which said, come up hither, and I will shew thee things which must be hereafter. And immediately I was in the Spirit; and behold, a throne was set in heaven, and one sat on the throne: and he that sat was to look upon like a jasper and a sardine stone: and there was a rainbow round about the throne, in sight like unto an emerald. And round about the throne were four and twenty seats; and upon the seats I saw four and twenty elders sitting, clothed in white raiment; and they had on their heads crowns of gold: and out of the throne proceeded lightnings and thunderings and voices. And there were seven lamps of fire burning before the throne, which are the seven spirits of God. And before the throne there was a sea of glass like unto crystal: and in the midst of the throne, and round about the throne, were four beasts full of eyes before and behind. And the first beast was like a lion, and the second beast like a calf, and the third beast had a face as a man, and the fourth beast was like a flying eagle. And the four beasts had each of them six wings about him; and they were full of eyes within: and they rest not day and night, saying, Holy, holy, holy, Lord God Almighty, which was, and is, and is to come. And when those beasts give glory and honour and thanks to him that sat on the throne, who liveth for ever and ever, the four and twenty elders fall down before him that sat on the throne, and worship him that liveth for ever and ever, and cast their crowns before the throne, saying, Thou art worthy, O Lord, to receive glory and honour and power; for thou hast created all things, and for thy pleasure they are, and were created.

The Gospel. S. John 3. 1–15

THERE was a man of the Pharisees, named Nicodemus, a ruler of the Jews: the same came to Jesus by night, and said unto him, Rabbi, we know that thou art a teacher come from God: for no man can do these miracles that thou doest, except God be with him. Jesus answered and said unto him, Verily, verily I say unto thee, Except a man be born again, he cannot see the kingdom of God. Nicodemus saith unto him, How can a man be born when he is old? can he enter the second time into his mother's womb, and be born? Jesus answered, Verily, verily I say unto thee, Except a man be born of water and of the Spirit, he cannot enter into the kingdom of God. That which is born of the flesh is flesh; and that which is born of the Spirit is spirit. Marvel not that I said unto thee, Ye must be born again. The wind bloweth where it listeth, and thou hearest the sound thereof, but canst not tell whence it cometh, and whither it goeth; so is every one that is born of the Spirit. Nicodemus answered and said unto him, How can these things be? Jesus answered and said unto him, Art thou a master of Israel, and knowest not these things? Verily, verily I say unto thee, We speak that we do know, and testify that we have seen; and ye receive not our witness. If I have told you earthly things, and ye believe not; how shall ye believe, if I tell you of heavenly things? And no man hath ascended up to heaven, but he that came down from heaven, even the Son of man, who is in heaven. And as Moses lifted up the serpent in the wilderness, even so must the Son of man be lifted up: that whosoever believeth in him should not perish, but have eternal life.

THE FIRST SUNDAY AFTER TRINITY

The Collect

O GOD, the strength of all them that put their trust in thee, mercifully accept our prayers; and because through the weakness of our mortal nature we can do no good thing without thee, grant us the help of thy grace, that in keeping of thy commandments we may please thee both in will and deed; through Jesus Christ our Lord. *Amen.*

The Epistle. 1 S. John 4. 7—end

BELOVED, let us love one another: for love is of God, and every one that loveth is born of God, and knoweth God. He that loveth not knoweth not God; for God is love. In this was manifested the love of God towards us, because that God sent his only-begotten Son into the world, that we might live through him. Herein is love, not that we loved God, but that he loved us, and sent his Son to be the propitiation for our sins. Beloved, if God so loved us, we ought also to love one another. No man hath seen God at any time. If we love one another, God dwelleth in us, and his love is perfected in us. Hereby know we that we dwell in him, and he in us; because he hath given us of his Spirit. And we have seen, and do testify, that the Father sent the Son to be the Saviour of the world. Whosoever shall confess that Jesus is the Son of God, God dwelleth in him, and he in God. And we have known and believed the love that God hath to us. God is love; and he that dwelleth in love dwelleth in God, and God in him. Herein is our love made perfect, that we may have boldness in the day of judgement; because as he is, so are we in this world. There is no fear in love; but perfect love casteth out fear; because fear hath torment: he that feareth is not made perfect in love. We love him, because he first loved us. If a man say, I love God, and hateth his brother, he is a liar: for he that loveth not his brother whom he hath seen, how can he love God whom he hath not seen? And this commandment have we from him, that he who loveth God love his brother also.

The Gospel. S. Luke 16. 19–end

THERE was a certain rich man, which was clothed in purple and fine linen, and fared sumptuously every day. And there was a certain beggar named Lazarus, which was laid at his gate full of sores, and desiring to be fed with the crumbs which fell from the rich man's table: moreover the dogs came and licked his sores. And it came to pass, that the beggar died, and was carried by the angels into Abraham's bosom. The rich man also died, and was buried: and in hell he lift up his eyes, being in torments, and seeth Abraham afar off, and Lazarus in his bosom. And he cried and said, Father Abraham, have mercy on me, and send Lazarus, that he may dip the tip of his finger in water, and cool my tongue; for I am tormented in this flame. But Abraham said, Son, remember that thou in thy life-time receivedst thy good things, and likewise Lazarus evil things; but now he is comforted, and thou art tormented. And besides all this, between us and you there is a great gulf fixed: so that they who would pass from hence to you cannot; neither can they pass to us, that would come from thence. Then he said, I pray thee therefore, father, that thou wouldest send him to my father's house: for I have five brethren; that he may testify unto them, lest they also come into this place of torment. Abraham saith unto him, They have Moses and the prophets; let them hear them. And he said, Nay, father Abraham; but if one went unto them from the dead, they will repent. And he said unto him, If they hear not Moses and the prophets, neither will they be persuaded, though one rose from the dead.

THE SECOND SUNDAY AFTER TRINITY

The Collect

O LORD, who never failest to help and govern them whom thou dost bring up in thy stedfast fear and love: Keep us, we beseech thee, under the protection of thy good providence, and make us to have a perpetual fear and love of thy holy Name; through Jesus Christ our Lord. *Amen.*

The Epistle. 1 S. John 3. 13–end

MARVEL not, my brethren, if the world hate you. We know that we have passed from death unto life, because we love the brethren. He that loveth not his brother abideth in death. Whosoever hateth his brother is a murderer: and ye know that no murderer hath eternal life abiding in him. Hereby perceive we the love of God, because he laid down his life for us: and we ought to lay down our lives for the brethren. But whoso hath this world's good, and seeth his brother have need, and shutteth up his bowels of compassion from him; how dwelleth the love of God in him? My little children, let us not love in word, neither in tongue; but in deed, and in truth. And hereby we know that we are of the truth, and shall assure our hearts before him. For if our heart condemn us, God is greater than our heart, and knoweth all things. Beloved, if our heart condemn us not, then have we confidence towards God. And whatsoever we ask, we receive of him, because we keep his commandments, and do those things that are pleasing in his sight. And this is his commandment, That we should believe on the name of his Son Jesus Christ, and love one another, as he gave us commandment. And he that keepeth his commandments dwelleth in him, and he in him: and hereby we know that he abideth in us, by the Spirit which he hath given us.

The Gospel. S. Luke 14. 16–24

A CERTAIN man made a great supper, and bade many; and sent his servant at supper-time to say to them that were bidden, Come, for all things are now ready. And they all with one consent began to make excuse. The first said unto him, I have bought a piece of ground, and I must needs go and see it; I pray thee have me excused. And another said, I have bought five yoke of oxen, and I go to prove them; I pray thee have me excused. And another said, I have married a wife, and therefore I cannot come. So that servant came and shewed his lord these things. Then the master of the house being angry said to his servant,

Go out quickly into the streets and lanes of the city, and bring in hither the poor, and the maimed, and the halt, and the blind. And the servant said, Lord, it is done as thou hast commanded, and yet there is room. And the lord said unto the servant, Go out into the high-ways and hedges, and compel them to come in, that my house may be filled. For I say unto you, That none of those men which were bidden shall taste of my supper.

THE THIRD SUNDAY AFTER TRINITY

The Collect

O LORD, we beseech thee mercifully to hear us; and grant that we, to whom thou hast given an hearty desire to pray, may by thy mighty aid be defended and comforted in all dangers and adversities; through Jesus Christ our Lord. *Amen.*

The Epistle. 1 S. Peter 5. 5–11

ALL of you be subject one to another, and be clothed with humility: for God resisteth the proud, and giveth grace to the humble. Humble yourselves therefore under the mighty hand of God, that he may exalt you in due time; casting all your care upon him, for he careth for you. Be sober, be vigilant; because your adversary the devil, as a roaring lion, walketh about seeking whom he may devour: whom resist stedfast in the faith, knowing that the same afflictions are accomplished in your brethren that are in the world. But the God of all grace, who hath called us into his eternal glory by Christ Jesus, after that ye have suffered a while, make you perfect, stablish, strengthen, settle you. To him be glory and dominion for ever and ever. Amen.

The Gospel. S. Luke 15. 1–10

THEN drew near unto him all the Publicans and sinners for to hear him. And the Pharisees and Scribes murmured, saying, This man receiveth sinners, and eateth with them. And he spake this parable unto them, saying, What man of you having an hundred sheep, if he lose one of them, doth not leave the ninety and nine in the wilderness, and go after that which is lost, until e find it? And when he hath found it, he layeth it on his houlders, rejoicing. And when he cometh home, he calleth ogether his friends and neighbours, saying unto them, Rejoice vith me, for I have found my sheep which was lost. I say unto ou, that likewise joy shall be in heaven over one sinner that epenteth, more than over ninety and nine just persons, which eed no repentance. Either what woman having ten pieces of ilver, if she lose one piece, doth not light a candle, and sweep he house, and seek diligently till she find it? And when she ath found it, she calleth her friends and her neighbours ogether, saying, Rejoice with me, for I have found the piece vhich I had lost. Likewise, I say unto you, There is joy in the resence of the angels of God over one sinner that repenteth.

THE FOURTH SUNDAY AFTER TRINITY

The Collect

GOD, the protector of all that trust in thee, without whom othing is strong, nothing is holy: Increase and multiply upon s thy mercy; that, thou being our ruler and guide, we may so ass through things temporal, that we finally lose not the things ternal: Grant this, O heavenly Father, for Jesus Christ's sake ur Lord. *Amen.*

The Epistle. Rom. 8. 18–23

RECKON that the sufferings of this present time are not vorthy to be compared with the glory which shall be revealed n us. For the earnest expectation of the creature waiteth for the nanifestation of the sons of God. For the creature was made ubject to vanity, not willingly, but by reason of him who hath ubjected the same in hope: because the creature itself also shall e delivered from the bondage of corruption into the glorious berty of the children of God. For we know that the whole reation groaneth and travaileth in pain together until now. And ot only they, but ourselves also, which have the first-fruits of he Spirit, even we ourselves groan within ourselves, waiting for he adoption, to wit, the redemption of our body.

The Gospel. S. Luke 6. 36–42

BE ye therefore merciful, as your Father also is merciful. Judg
not, and ye shall not be judged: condemn not, and ye shall no
be condemned: forgive, and ye shall be forgiven: give, and
shall be given unto you; good measure, pressed down, an
shaken together, and running over, shall men give into you
bosom. For with the same measure that ye mete withal, it sha
be measured to you again. And he spake a parable unto then
Can the blind lead the blind? shall they not both fall into th
ditch? The disciple is not above his master; but every one tha
is perfect shall be as his master. And why beholdest thou th
mote that is in thy brother's eye, but perceivest not the bear
that is in thine own eye? Either how canst thou say to th
brother, Brother, let me pull out the mote that is in thine eye
when thou thyself beholdest not the beam that is in thine ow
eye? Thou hypocrite, cast out first the beam out of thine ow
eye, and then shalt thou see clearly to pull out the mote that
in thy brother's eye.

THE FIFTH SUNDAY AFTER TRINITY

The Collect

GRANT, O Lord, we beseech thee, that the course of thi
world may be so peaceably ordered by thy governance, that th
Church may joyfully serve thee in all godly quietness; throug
Jesus Christ our Lord. *Amen.*

The Epistle. 1 S. Peter 3. 8–15

BE ye all of one mind, having compassion one of another, lov
as brethren, be pitiful, be courteous; not rendering evil for evi
or railing for railing: but contrariwise blessing; knowing that y
are thereunto called, that ye should inherit a blessing. For h
that will love life, and see good days, let him refrain his tongu
from evil, and his lips that they speak no guile: let him eschev
evil, and do good; let him seek peace, and ensue it. For the eye
of the Lord are over the righteous, and his ears are open unt
their prayers: but the face of the Lord is against them that d

vil. And who is he that will harm you, if ye be followers of that which is good? But and if ye suffer for righteousness' sake, happy are ye: and be not afraid of their terror, neither be troubled; but sanctify the Lord God in your hearts.

The Gospel. S. Luke 5. 1–11

IT came to pass that as the people pressed upon him to hear the word of God, he stood by the lake of Gennesaret, and saw two ships standing by the lake; but the fishermen were gone out of them, and were washing their nets. And he entered into one of the ships, which was Simon's, and prayed him that he would thrust out a little from the land: and he sat down, and taught the people out of the ship. Now when he had left speaking, he said unto Simon, Launch out into the deep, and let down your nets for a draught. And Simon answering said unto him, Master, we have toiled all the night, and have taken nothing; nevertheless, at thy word I will let down the net. And when they had this done, they inclosed a great multitude of fishes, and their net brake. And they beckoned unto their partners which were in the other ship, that they should come and help them. And they came, and filled both the ships, so that they began to sink. When Simon Peter saw it, he fell down at Jesus' knees, saying, Depart from me, for I am a sinful man, O Lord. For he was astonished, and all that were with him, at the draught of the fishes which they had taken; and so was also James, and John, the sons of Zebedee, which were partners with Simon. And Jesus said unto Simon, Fear not, from henceforth thou shalt catch men. And when they had brought their ships to land, they forsook all, and followed him.

THE SIXTH SUNDAY AFTER TRINITY

The Collect

O GOD, who hast prepared for them that love thee such good things as pass man's understanding: Pour into our hearts such love toward thee, that we, loving thee above all things, may obtain thy promises, which exceed all that we can desire; through Jesus Christ our Lord. *Amen.*

The Epistle. Rom. 6. 3–11

KNOW ye not that so many of us as were baptized into Jesus Christ were baptized into his death? Therefore we are buried with him by baptism into death; that like as Christ was raised up from the dead by the glory of the Father, even so we also should walk in newness of life. For if we have been planted together in the likeness of his death, we shall be also in the likeness of his resurrection: knowing this, that our old man is crucified with him, that the body of sin might be destroyed, that henceforth we should not serve sin. For he that is dead is freed from sin. Now if we be dead with Christ, we believe that we shall also live with him; knowing that Christ being raised from the dead dieth no more; death hath no more dominion over him. For in that he died, he died unto sin once; but in that he liveth, he liveth unto God. Likewise reckon ye also yourselves to be dead indeed unto sin, but alive unto God through Jesus Christ our Lord.

The Gospel. S. Matth. 5. 20–26

JESUS said unto his disciples, Except your righteousness shall exceed the righteousness of the Scribes and Pharisees, ye shall in no case enter into the kingdom of heaven. Ye have heard that it was said by them of old time, Thou shalt not kill: and whosoever shall kill, shall be in danger of the judgement. But I say unto you, that whosoever is angry with his brother without a cause shall be in danger of the judgement: and whosoever shall say to his brother, Raca, shall be in danger of the council: but whosoever shall say, Thou fool, shall be in danger of hell-fire. Therefore if thou bring thy gift to the altar, and there rememberest that thy brother hath ought against thee; leave there thy gift before the altar, and go thy way, first be reconciled to thy brother, and then come and offer thy gift. Agree with thine adversary quickly, whiles thou art in the way with him; lest at any time the adversary deliver thee to the judge, and the judge deliver thee to the officer, and thou be cast into prison. Verily I say unto thee, Thou shalt by no means come out thence, till thou hast paid the uttermost farthing.

THE SEVENTH SUNDAY AFTER TRINITY

The Collect

LORD of all power and might, who art the author and giver of all good things: Graft in our hearts the love of thy name, increase in us true religion, nourish us with all goodness, and of thy great mercy keep us in the same; through Jesus Christ our Lord. *Amen.*

The Epistle. Rom. 6. 19–end

I SPEAK after the manner of men, because of the infirmity of your flesh: for as ye have yielded your members servants to uncleanness, and to iniquity, unto iniquity; even so now yield your members servants to righteousness, unto holiness. For when ye were the servants of sin, ye were free from righteousness. What fruit had ye then in those things whereof ye are now ashamed? for the end of those things is death. But now being made free from sin, and become servants to God, ye have your fruit unto holiness, and the end everlasting life. For the wages of sin is death: but the gift of God is eternal life, through Jesus Christ our Lord.

The Gospel. S. Mark 8. 1–9

IN those days the multitude being very great, and having nothing to eat, Jesus called his disciples unto him, and saith unto them, I have compassion on the multitude, because they have now been with me three days, and have nothing to eat: and if I send them away fasting to their own houses, they will faint by the way; for divers of them came from far. And his disciples answered him, From whence can a man satisfy these men with bread here in the wilderness? And he asked them, How many loaves have ye? And they said, Seven. And he commanded the people to sit down on the ground. And he took the seven loaves, and gave thanks, and brake, and gave to his disciples to set before them; and they did set them before the people. And they had a few small fishes; and he blessed, and commanded to set them also before them. So they did eat, and were filled: and they took up of the broken meat that was left seven baskets. And they that had eaten were about four thousand. And he sent them away.

THE EIGHTH SUNDAY AFTER TRINITY

The Collect

O GOD, whose never-failing providence ordereth all things both in heaven and earth: We humbly beseech thee to put away from us all hurtful things, and to give us those things which be profitable for us; through Jesus Christ our Lord. *Amen.*

The Epistle. Rom. 8. 12–17

BRETHREN, we are debtors, not to the flesh, to live after the flesh: for if ye live after the flesh, ye shall die; but if ye through the Spirit do mortify the deeds of the body, ye shall live. For as many as are led by the Spirit of God, they are the sons of God. For ye have not received the spirit of bondage again to fear; but ye have received the spirit of adoption, whereby we cry, Abba, Father. The Spirit itself beareth witness with our spirit, that we are the children of God: and if children, then heirs; heirs of God, and joint-heirs with Christ: if so be that we suffer with him, that we may be also glorified together.

The Gospel. S. Matth. 7. 15–21

BEWARE of false prophets, which come to you in sheep's clothing, but inwardly they are ravening wolves. Ye shall know them by their fruits. Do men gather grapes of thorns, or figs of thistles? Even so every good tree bringeth forth good fruit; but a corrupt tree bringeth forth evil fruit. A good tree cannot bring forth evil fruit; neither can a corrupt tree bring forth good fruit. Every tree that bringeth not forth good fruit is hewn down, and cast into the fire. Wherefore by their fruits ye shall know them. Not every one that saith unto me, Lord, Lord, shall enter into the kingdom of heaven; but he that doeth the will of my Father which is in heaven.

THE NINTH SUNDAY AFTER TRINITY

The Collect

GRANT to us, Lord, we beseech thee, the spirit to think and do always such things as be rightful; that we, who cannot do any thing that is good without thee, may by thee be enabled to live according to thy will; through Jesus Christ our Lord. *Amen.*

The Epistle. 1 Cor. 10. 1–13

BRETHREN, I would not that ye should be ignorant, how that all our fathers were under the cloud, and all passed through the sea; and were all baptized unto Moses in the cloud, and in the sea; and did all eat the same spiritual meat, and did all drink the same spiritual drink: for they drank of that spiritual rock that followed them; and that rock was Christ. But with many of them God was not well pleased; for they were overthrown in the wilderness. Now these things were our examples, to the intent we should not lust after evil things, as they also lusted. Neither be ye idolaters, as were some of them; as it is written, The people sat down to eat and drink, and rose up to play. Neither let us commit fornication, as some of them committed, and fell in one day three and twenty thousand. Neither let us tempt Christ, as some of them also tempted, and were destroyed of serpents. Neither murmur ye, as some of them also murmured, and were destroyed of the destroyer. Now all these things happened unto them for ensamples: and they are written for our admonition, upon whom the ends of the world are come. Wherefore let him that thinketh he standeth take heed lest he fall. There hath no temptation taken you, but such as is common to man: but God is faithful, who will not suffer you to be tempted above that ye are able; but will with the temptation also make a way to escape, that ye may be able to bear it.

The Gospel. S. Luke. 16. 1–9

JESUS said unto his disciples, There was a certain rich man which had a steward; and the same was accused unto him that he had wasted his goods. And he called him, and said unto him, How is it that I hear this of thee? Give an account of thy stewardship; for thou mayest be no longer steward. Then the steward said within himself, What shall I do? for my lord taketh away from me the stewardship: I cannot dig, to beg I am ashamed. I am resolved what to do, that, when I am put out of the stewardship, they may receive me into their houses. So he called every one of his lord's debtors unto him, and said unto the first, How much owest thou unto my lord? And he said, An hundred measures of oil. And he said unto him, Take thy bill, and sit down quickly, and write fifty. Then said he to another, And how much owest thou? And he said, An hundred measures of wheat. And he said unto him, Take thy bill, and write fourscore. And the lord commended the unjust steward, because he had done wisely: for the children of this world are in their generation wiser than the children of light. And I say unto you, Make to yourselves friends of the mammon of unrighteousness, that when ye fail, they may receive you into everlasting habitations.

THE TENTH SUNDAY AFTER TRINITY

The Collect

LET thy merciful ears, O Lord, be open to the prayers of thy humble servants; and that they may obtain their petitions make them to ask such things as shall please thee; through Jesus Christ our Lord. *Amen.*

The Epistle. 1 Cor. 12. 1–11

CONCERNING spiritual gifts, brethren, I would not have you ignorant. Ye know that ye were Gentiles, carried away unto these dumb idols, even as ye were led. Wherefore I give you to understand, that no man speaking by the Spirit of God calleth Jesus accursed; and that no man can say that Jesus is the Lord, but by the Holy Ghost. Now there are diversities of gifts, but the same Spirit. And there are differences of administrations, but the same Lord. And there are diversities of operations, but it is the same God, who worketh all in all. But the manifestation of the Spirit is given to every man to profit withal. For to one is given by the Spirit the word of wisdom; to another the word of knowledge by the same Spirit; to another faith by the same Spirit; to another the gifts of healing by the same Spirit; to another the working of miracles; to another prophecy; to another discerning of spirits; to another divers kinds of tongues; to another the interpretation of tongues. But all these worketh that one and the self-same Spirit, dividing to every man severally as he will.

The Gospel. S. Luke 19. 41-7

AND when he was come near, he beheld the city, and wept over it, saying, If thou hadst known, even thou, at least in this thy day, the things which belong unto thy peace! but now they are hid from thine eyes. For the days shall come upon thee, that thine enemies shall cast a trench about thee, and compass thee round, and keep thee in on every side, and shall lay thee even with the ground, and thy children within thee; and they shall not leave in thee one stone upon another; because thou knewest not the time of thy visitation. And he went into the temple, and began to cast out them that sold therein, and them that bought, saying unto them, It is written, My house is the house of prayer: but ye have made it a den of thieves. And he taught daily in the temple.

THE ELEVENTH SUNDAY AFTER TRINITY

The Collect

O GOD, who declarest thy almighty power most chiefly in shewing mercy and pity: Mercifully grant unto us such a measure of thy grace, that we, running the way of thy commandments, may obtain thy gracious promises, and be made partakers of thy heavenly treasure; through Jesus Christ our Lord. *Amen.*

The Epistle. 1 Cor. 15. 1-11

BRETHREN, I declare unto you the Gospel which I preached unto you, which also ye have received, and wherein ye stand: by which also ye are saved, if ye keep in memory what I preached unto you, unless ye have believed in vain. For I delivered unto you first of all, that which I also received, how that Christ died for our sins, according to the Scriptures; and that he was buried, and that he rose again the third day, according to the Scriptures; and that he was seen of Cephas; then of the twelve: after that, he was seen of above five hundred brethren at once; of whom the greater part remain unto this present, but some are fallen asleep: after that, he was seen of James; then of all the Apostles: and last of all, he was seen of me also, as of one born out of due time. For I am the least of the Apostles, that am not meet to be called an Apostle, because I persecuted the Church of God. But by the grace of God I am what I am: and his grace which was bestowed upon me was not in vain; but I laboured more abundantly than they all; yet not I, but the grace of God which was with me. Therefore whether it were I or they, so we preach, and so ye believed.

The Gospel. S. Luke 18. 9–14

JESUS spake this parable unto certain which trusted in themselves that they were righteous, and despised others: Two men went up into the temple to pray; the one a Pharisee, and the other a Publican. The Pharisee stood and prayed thus with himself, God, I thank thee that I am not as other men are, extortioners, unjust, adulterers, or even as this Publican: I fast twice in the week, I give tithes of all that I possess. And the Publican, standing afar off, would not lift up so much as his eyes unto heaven, but smote upon his breast, saying, God be merciful to me a sinner. I tell you, this man went down to his house justified rather than the other: for every one that exalteth himself shall be abased; and he that humbleth himself shall be exalted.

THE TWELFTH SUNDAY AFTER TRINITY

The Collect

ALMIGHTY and everlasting God, who art always more ready to hear than we to pray, and art wont to give more than either we desire or deserve: Pour down upon us the abundance of thy mercy; forgiving us those things whereof our conscience is afraid, and giving us those good things which we are not worthy to ask, but through the merits and mediation of Jesus Christ, thy Son, our Lord. *Amen.*

The Epistle. 2 Cor. 3. 4–9

SUCH trust have we through Christ to Godward: not that we are sufficient of ourselves to think any thing as of ourselves; but our sufficiency is of God: who also hath made us able ministers of the new testament; not of the letter, but of the spirit: for the letter killeth, but the spirit giveth life. But if the ministration of death written and engraven in stones was glorious, so that the children of Israel could not stedfastly behold the face of Moses for the glory of his countenance, which glory was to be done away; how shall not the ministration of the spirit be rather glorious? For if the ministration of condemnation be glory, much more doth the ministration of righteousness exceed in glory.

The Gospel. S. Mark 7. 31–end

JESUS, departing from the coasts of Tyre and Sidon, came unto the sea of Galilee, through the midst of the coasts of Decapolis. And they bring unto him one that was deaf, and had an impediment in his speech; and they beseech him to put his hand upon him. And he took him aside from the multitude, and put his fingers into his ears, and he spit, and touched his tongue; and looking up to heaven, he sighed, and saith unto him, *Ephphatha*, that is, Be opened. And straightway his ears were opened, and the string of his tongue was loosed, and he spake plain. And he charged them that they should tell no man: but the more he charged them, so much the more a great deal they published it; and were beyond measure astonished, saying, He hath done all things well; he maketh both the deaf to hear, and the dumb to speak.

THE THIRTEENTH SUNDAY AFTER TRINITY

The Collect

ALMIGHTY and merciful God, of whose only gift it cometh that thy faithful people do unto thee true and laudable service:

Grant, we beseech thee, that we may so faithfully serve thee in this life, that we fail not finally to attain thy heavenly promises; through the merits of Jesus Christ our Lord. *Amen.*

The Epistle. Gal. 3. 16–22

TO Abraham and his seed were the promises made. He saith not, And to seeds, as of many; but as of one, And to thy seed, which is Christ. And this I say, that the covenant that was confirmed before of God in Christ, the law, which was four hundred and thirty years after, cannot disannul, that it should make the promise of none effect. For if the inheritance be of the law, it is no more of promise; but God gave it to Abraham by promise. Wherefore then serveth the law? It was added because of transgressions, till the seed should come, to whom the promise was made; and it was ordained by angels in the hand of a mediator. Now a mediator is not a mediator of one; but God is one. Is the law then against the promises of God? God forbid: for if there had been a law given which could have given life, verily righteousness should have been by the law. But the Scripture hath concluded all under sin, that the promise by faith of Jesus Christ might be given to them that believe.

The Gospel. S. Luke 10. 23–37

BLESSED are the eyes which see the things that ye see. For I tell you, that many prophets and kings have desired to see those things which ye see, and have not seen them; and to hear those things which ye hear, and have not heard them. And behold, a certain Lawyer stood up, and tempted him, saying, Master, what shall I do to inherit eternal life? He said unto him, What is written in the law? how readest thou? And he answering said, Thou shalt love the Lord thy God with all thy heart, and with all thy soul, and with all thy strength, and with all thy mind; and thy neighbour as thyself. And he said unto him, Thou hast answered right; this do, and thou shalt live. But he, willing to justify himself, said unto Jesus, And who is my neighbour? And Jesus answering said, A certain man went down from Jerusalem to Jericho, and fell among thieves, which stripped him of his raiment, and wounded him, and departed, leaving him half dead. And by chance there came down a certain Priest that way, and, when he saw him, he passed by on the other side. And likewise a Levite, when he was at the place, came and looked on him, and passed by on the other side. But a certain Samaritan, as he journeyed, came where he was; and, when he saw him, he had compassion on him, and went to him, and bound up his wounds, pouring in oil and wine, and set him on his own beast, and brought him to an inn, and took care of him. And on the morrow, when he departed, he took out two pence, and gave them to the host, and said unto him, Take care of him; and whatsoever thou spendest more, when I come again, I will repay thee. Which now of these three, thinkest thou, was neighbour unto him that fell among the thieves? And he said, He that shewed mercy on him. Then said Jesus unto him, Go, and do thou likewise.

THE FOURTEENTH SUNDAY AFTER TRINITY

The Collect

ALMIGHTY and everlasting God, give unto us the increase of faith, hope, and charity; and, that we may obtain that which thou dost promise, make us to love that which thou dost command; through Jesus Christ our Lord. *Amen.*

The Epistle. Gal. 5. 16–24

I SAY then, Walk in the Spirit, and ye shall not fulfil the lust of the flesh. For the flesh lusteth against the Spirit, and the Spirit against the flesh; and these are contrary the one to the other; so that ye cannot do the things that ye would. But if ye be led by the Spirit, ye are not under the law. Now the works of the flesh are manifest, which are these: adultery, fornication, uncleanness, lasciviousness, idolatry, witchcraft, hatred, variance, emulations, wrath, strife, seditions, heresies, envyings, murders, drunkenness, revellings, and such like: of the which I tell you before, as I have also told you in time past, that they who do such things shall not inherit the kingdom of God. But the fruit of the Spirit is love, joy, peace, long-suffering, gentleness, goodness, faith, meekness, temperance: against such there is no law. And they that are Christ's have crucified the flesh, with the affections and lusts.

The Gospel. S. Luke 17. 11–19

AND it came to pass, as Jesus went to Jerusalem, that he passed through the midst of Samaria and Galilee. And as he entered into a certain village, there met him ten men that were lepers, which stood afar off: and they lifted up their voices, and said, Jesus, Master, have mercy on us. And when he saw them, he said unto them, Go, shew yourselves unto the priests. And it came to pass that, as they went, they were cleansed. And one of them, when he saw that he was healed, turned back, and with a loud voice glorified God, and fell down on his face at his feet, giving him thanks; and he was a Samaritan. And Jesus answering said, Were there not ten cleansed? but where are the nine? There are not found that returned to give glory to God, save this stranger. And he said unto him, Arise, go thy way, thy faith hath made thee whole.

THE FIFTEENTH SUNDAY AFTER TRINITY

The Collect

KEEP, we beseech thee, O Lord, thy Church with thy perpetual mercy; and, because the frailty of man without thee cannot but fall, keep us ever by thy help from all things hurtful, and lead us to all things profitable to our salvation; through Jesus Christ our Lord. *Amen.*

The Epistle. Gal. 6. 11–end

YE see how large a letter I have written unto you with mine own hand. As many as desire to make a fair shew in the flesh, they constrain you to be circumcised; only lest they should suffer persecution for the cross of Christ. For neither they themselves who are circumcised keep the law; but desire to have you circumcised, that they may glory in your flesh. But God forbid that I should glory, save in the cross of our Lord Jesus Christ, by whom the world is crucified unto me, and I unto the world. For in Christ Jesus neither circumcision availeth any thing, nor uncircumcision, but a new creature. And as many as walk according to this rule, peace be on them, and mercy, and upon the Israel of God. From henceforth let no man trouble me; for I bear in my body the marks of the Lord Jesus. Brethren, the grace of our Lord Jesus Christ be with your spirit. Amen.

The Gospel. S. Matth. 6. 24–end

NO man can serve two masters: for either he will hate the one, and love the other; or else he will hold to the one, and despise the other. Ye cannot serve God and Mammon. Therefore I say unto you, Take no thought for your life, what ye shall eat, or what ye shall drink; nor yet for your body, what ye shall put on. Is not the life more than meat, and the body than raiment? Behold the fowls of the air; for they sow not, neither do they reap, nor gather into barns; yet your heavenly Father feedeth them. Are ye not much better than they? Which of you by taking thought can add one cubit unto his stature? And why take ye thought for raiment? Consider the lilies of the field how they grow: they toil not, neither do they spin: and yet I say unto you, that even Solomon in all his glory was not arrayed like one of these. Wherefore, if God so clothe the grass of the field, which to-day is, and to-morrow is cast into the oven; shall he not much more clothe you, O ye of little faith? Therefore take no thought, saying, What shall we eat? or, What shall we drink? or, Wherewithal shall we be clothed? (For after all these things do the Gentiles seek:) for your heavenly Father knoweth that ye have need of all these things. But seek ye first the kingdom of God, and his righteousness; and all these things shall be added unto you. Take therefore no thought for the morrow; for the morrow shall take thought for the things of itself: sufficient unto the day is the evil thereof.

THE SIXTEENTH SUNDAY AFTER TRINITY

The Collect

O LORD, we beseech thee, let thy continual pity cleanse and defend thy Church; and, because it cannot continue in safety without thy succour, preserve it evermore by thy help and goodness; through Jesus Christ our Lord. *Amen.*

The Epistle. Ephes. 3. 13–end

I DESIRE that ye faint not at my tribulations for you, which is your glory. For this cause I bow my knees unto the Father of our Lord Jesus Christ, of whom the whole family in heaven and earth is named, that he would grant you, according to the riches of his glory, to be strengthened with might by his Spirit in the inner man; that Christ may dwell in your hearts by faith; that ye, being rooted and grounded in love, may be able to comprehend with all saints, what is the breadth, and length, and depth, and height; and to know the love of Christ, which passeth knowledge, that ye might be filled with all the fulness of God. Now unto him that is able to do exceeding abundantly above all that we ask or think, according to the power that worketh in us, unto him be glory in the Church by Christ Jesus, throughout all ages, world without end. Amen.

The Gospel. S. Luke 7. 11–17

AND it came to pass the day after, that Jesus went into a city called Nain; and many of his disciples went with him, and much people. Now when he came nigh to the gate of the city, behold, there was a dead man carried out, the only son of his mother, and she was a widow; and much people of the city was with her. And when the Lord saw her, he had compassion on her, and said unto her, Weep not. And he came and touched the bier; and they that bare him stood still: and he said, Young man, I say unto thee, Arise. And he that was dead sat up, and began to speak: and he delivered him to his mother. And there came a fear on all, and they glorified God, saying, that a great Prophet is risen up among us, and that God hath visited his people. And this rumour of him went forth throughout all Judæa, and throughout all the region round about.

THE SEVENTEENTH SUNDAY
AFTER TRINITY

The Collect

LORD, we pray thee that thy grace may always prevent and follow us, and make us continually to be given to all good works; through Jesus Christ our Lord. *Amen.*

The Epistle. Ephes. 4. 1–6

I THEREFORE the prisoner of the Lord beseech you, that ye walk worthy of the vocation wherewith ye are called, with all lowliness and meekness, with long-suffering, forbearing one another in love; endeavouring to keep the unity of the Spirit in the bond of peace. There is one body, and one Spirit, even as ye are called in one hope of your calling; one Lord, one faith, one baptism, one God and Father of all, who is above all, and through all, and in you all.

The Gospel. S. Luke 14. 1–11

IT came to pass, as Jesus went into the house of one of the chief Pharisees to eat bread on the sabbath-day, that they watched him. And behold, there was a certain man before him which had the dropsy. And Jesus answering spake unto the Lawyers and Pharisees, saying, Is it lawful to heal on the sabbath-day? And they held their peace. And he took him, and healed him, and let him go; and answered them, saying, Which of you shall have an ass, or an ox, fallen into a pit, and will not straightway pull him out on the sabbath-day? And they could not answer him again to these things. And he put forth a parable to those which were bidden, when he marked how they chose out the chief rooms, saying unto them, When thou art bidden of any man to a wedding, sit not down in the highest room; lest a more honourable man than thou be bidden of him; and he that bade thee and him come and say to thee, Give this man place; and thou begin with shame to take the lowest room. But when thou art bidden, go and sit down in the lowest room; that, when he that bade thee cometh, he may say unto thee, Friend, go up higher: then shalt thou have worship in the presence of them that sit at meat with thee. For whosoever exalteth himself shall be abased; and he that humbleth himself shall be exalted.

THE EIGHTEENTH SUNDAY AFTER TRINITY

The Collect

LORD, we beseech thee, grant thy people grace to withstand the temptations of the world, the flesh, and the devil, and with pure hearts and minds to follow thee the only God; through Jesus Christ our Lord. *Amen.*

The Epistle. 1 Cor. 1. 4–8

I THANK my God always on your behalf, for the grace of God which is given you by Jesus Christ; that in every thing ye are enriched by him, in all utterance, and in all knowledge; even as the testimony of Christ was confirmed in you; so that ye come behind in no gift; waiting for the coming of our Lord Jesus Christ, who shall also confirm you unto the end, that ye may be blameless in the day of our Lord Jesus Christ.

The Gospel. S. Matth. 22. 34–end

WHEN the Pharisees had heard that Jesus had put the Sadducees to silence, they were gathered together. Then one of them, who was a lawyer, asked him a question, tempting him, and saying, Master, which is the great commandment in the law? Jesus said unto him, Thou shalt love the Lord thy God with all thy heart, and with all thy soul, and with all thy mind. This is the first and great commandment. And the second is like unto it, Thou shalt love thy neighbour as thyself. On these two commandments hang all the law and the prophets. While the Pharisees were gathered together, Jesus asked them, saying, What think ye of Christ? whose son is he? They say unto him, The son of David. He saith unto them, How then doth David in spirit call him Lord, saying, the LORD said unto my Lord, Sit thou on my right hand, till I make thine enemies thy footstool? If David then call him Lord, how is he his son? And no man was able to answer him a word; neither durst any man from that day forth ask him any more questions.

THE NINETEENTH SUNDAY AFTER TRINITY

The Collect

O GOD, forasmuch as without thee we are not able to please thee; Mercifully grant, that thy Holy Spirit may in all things direct and rule our hearts; through Jesus Christ our Lord. *Amen.*

The Epistle. Ephes. 4. 17—end

THIS I say therefore, and testify in the Lord, that ye henceforth walk not as other Gentiles walk, in the vanity of their mind; having the understanding darkened, being alienated from the life of God through the ignorance that is in them, because of the blindness of their heart: who, being past feeling, have given themselves over unto lasciviousness, to work all uncleanness with greediness. But ye have not so learned Christ; if so be that ye have heard him, and have been taught by him, as the truth is in Jesus: that ye put off, concerning the former conversation, the old man, which is corrupt according to the deceitful lusts; and be renewed in the spirit of your mind; and that ye put on the new man, which after God is created in righteousness and true holiness. Wherefore, putting away lying, speak every man truth with his neighbour: for we are members one of another. Be ye angry and sin not: let not the sun go down upon your wrath: neither give place to the devil. Let him that stole steal no more; but rather let him labour, working with his hands the thing which is good, that he may have to give to him that needeth. Let no corrupt communication proceed out of your mouth, but that which is good to the use of edifying, that it may minister grace unto the hearers. And grieve not the Holy Spirit of God, whereby ye are sealed unto the day of redemption. Let all bitterness, and wrath, and anger, and clamour, and evil-speaking, be put away from you, with all malice. And be ye kind one to another, tender-hearted, forgiving one another, even as God for Christ's sake hath forgiven you.

The Gospel. S. Matth. 9. 1—8

JESUS entered into a ship, and passed over, and came into his own city. And behold, they brought to him a man sick of the palsy, lying on a bed. And Jesus, seeing their faith, said unto the sick of the palsy, Son, be of good cheer, thy sins be forgiven thee. And behold, certain of the Scribes said within themselves, This man blasphemeth. And Jesus, knowing their thoughts, said, Wherefore think ye evil in your hearts? For whether is easier, to say, Thy sins be forgiven thee? or to say, Arise, and walk? But that ye may know that the Son of man hath power on earth to forgive sins, (then saith he to the sick of the palsy,) Arise, take up thy bed, and go unto thine house. And he arose, and departed to his house. But when the multitude saw it, they marvelled, and glorified God, who had given such power unto men.

THE TWENTIETH SUNDAY AFTER TRINITY

The Collect

O ALMIGHTY and most merciful God, of thy bountiful goodness keep us, we beseech thee, from all things that may hurt us; that we, being ready both in body and soul, may cheerfully accomplish those things that thou wouldest have done; through Jesus Christ our Lord. *Amen.*

The Epistle. Ephes. 5. 15–21

SEE then that ye walk circumspectly, not as fools, but as wise, redeeming the time, because the days are evil. Wherefore be ye not unwise, but understanding what the will of the Lord is. And be not drunk with wine, wherein is excess; but be filled with the Spirit; speaking to yourselves in psalms, and hymns, and spiritual songs; singing and making melody in your heart to the Lord; giving thanks always for all things unto God and the Father, in the name of our Lord Jesus Christ; submitting yourselves one to another in the fear of God.

The Gospel. S. Matth. 22. 1–14

JESUS said, The kingdom of heaven is like unto a certain king, who made a marriage for his son; and sent forth his servants to call them that were bidden to the wedding; and they would not come. Again, he sent forth other servants, saying, Tell them which are bidden, Behold, I have prepared my dinner; my oxen and my fatlings are killed, and all things are ready; come unto the marriage. But they made light of it, and went their ways, one to his farm, another to his merchandise: and the remnant took his servants, and entreated them spitefully, and slew them. But when the king heard thereof, he was wroth; and he sent forth his armies, and destroyed those murderers, and burnt up their city. Then saith he to his servants, The wedding is ready, but they who were bidden were not worthy. Go ye therefore into the high-ways, and as many as ye shall find bid to the marriage. So those servants went out into the high-ways, and gathered together all, as many as they found, both bad and good; and the wedding was furnished with guests. And when the king came in to see the guests, he saw there a man which had not on a wedding-garment. And he saith unto him, Friend, how camest thou in hither, not having a wedding-garment? And he was speechless. Then said the king to the servants, Bind him hand and foot, and take him away, and cast him into outer darkness: there shall be weeping and gnashing of teeth. For many are called, but few are chosen.

THE TWENTY-FIRST SUNDAY
AFTER TRINITY

The Collect

GRANT, we beseech thee, merciful Lord, to thy faithful people pardon and peace; that they may be cleansed from all their sins, and serve thee with a quiet mind; through Jesus Christ our Lord. *Amen.*

The Epistle. Ephes. 6. 10–20

MY brethren, be strong in the Lord, and in the power of his might. Put on the whole armour of God, that ye may be able to stand against the wiles of the devil. For we wrestle not against flesh and blood, but against principalities, against powers, against the rulers of the darkness of this world, against spiritual wickedness in high places. Wherefore take unto you the whole armour of God, that ye may be able to withstand in the evil day, and, having done all, to stand. Stand therefore, having your loins girt about with truth; and having on the breast-plate of righteousness; and your feet shod with the preparation of the Gospel of peace; above all, taking the shield of faith, wherewith ye shall be able to quench all the fiery darts of the wicked: and take the helmet of salvation, and the sword of the Spirit, which is the word of God: praying always with all prayer and supplication in the Spirit, and watching thereunto with all perseverance, and supplication for all saints; and for me, that utterance may be given unto me, that I may open my mouth boldly, to make known the mystery of the Gospel, for which I am an ambassador in bonds; that therein I may speak boldly, as I ought to speak.

The Gospel. S. John 4. 46–end

THERE was a certain nobleman, whose son was sick at Capernaum. When he heard that Jesus was come out of Judæa into Galilee, he went unto him, and besought him that he would come down and heal his son; for he was at the point of death. Then said Jesus unto him, Except ye see signs and wonders, ye will not believe. The nobleman saith unto him, Sir, come down ere my child die. Jesus saith unto him, Go thy way, thy son liveth. And the man believed the word that Jesus had spoken unto him, and he went his way. And as he was now going down, his servants met him, and told him, saying, Thy son liveth. Then inquired he of them the hour when he began to amend: and they said unto him, Yesterday at the seventh hour the fever left him. So the father knew that it was at the same hour, in the which Jesus said unto him, Thy son liveth; and himself believed, and his whole house. This is again the second miracle that Jesus did, when he was come out of Judæa into Galilee.

THE TWENTY-SECOND SUNDAY AFTER TRINITY

The Collect

LORD, we beseech thee to keep thy household the Church in

continual godliness; that through thy protection it may be free from all adversities, and devoutly given to serve thee in good works, to the glory of thy name; through Jesus Christ our Lord. *Amen.*

The Epistle. Philip. i. 3–11

I THANK my God upon every remembrance of you, always in every prayer of mine for you all making request with joy, for your fellowship in the Gospel from the first day until now; being confident of this very thing, that he who hath begun a good work in you will perform it until the day of Jesus Christ; even as it is meet for me to think this of you all, because I have you in my heart, inasmuch as both in my bonds, and in the defence and confirmation of the Gospel, ye all are partakers of my grace. For God is my record, how greatly I long after you all in the bowels of Jesus Christ. And this I pray, that your love may abound yet more and more in knowledge and in all judgement: that ye may approve things that are excellent; that ye may be sincere, and without offence, till the day of Christ: being filled with the fruits of righteousness, which are by Jesus Christ unto the glory and praise of God.

The Gospel. S. Matth. 18. 21–end

PETER said unto Jesus, Lord, how oft shall my brother sin against me, and I forgive him? till seven times? Jesus saith unto him, I say not unto thee, until seven times; but until seventy times seven. Therefore is the kingdom of heaven likened unto a certain king, which would take account of his servants. And when he had begun to reckon, one was brought unto him, which owed him ten thousand talents. But forasmuch as he had not to pay, his lord commanded him to be sold, and his wife and children, and all that he had, and payment to be made. The servant therefore fell down and worshipped him, saying, Lord, have patience with me, and I will pay thee all. Then the lord of that servant was moved with compassion, and loosed him, and forgave him the debt. But the same servant went out, and found one of his fellow-servants, which owed him an hundred pence; and he laid hands on him, and took him by the throat, saying,

Pay me that thou owest. And his fellow-servant fell down at his feet, and besought him, saying, Have patience with me, and I will pay thee all. And he would not; but went and cast him into prison, till he should pay the debt. So when his fellow-servants saw what was done, they were very sorry, and came and told unto their lord all that was done. Then his lord, after that he had called him, said unto him, O thou wicked servant, I forgave thee all that debt, because thou desiredst me: shouldest not thou also have had compassion on thy fellow-servant, even as I had pity on thee? And his lord was wroth, and delivered him to the tormentors, till he should pay all that was due unto him. So likewise shall my heavenly Father do also unto you, if ye from your hearts forgive not every one his brother their trespasses.

THE TWENTY-THIRD SUNDAY AFTER TRINITY

The Collect

O GOD, our refuge and strength, who art the author of all godliness: Be ready, we beseech thee, to hear the devout prayers of thy Church; and grant that those things which we ask faithfully we may obtain effectually; through Jesus Christ our Lord. *Amen.*

The Epistle. Philip. 3. 17–end

BRETHREN, be followers together of me, and mark them which walk so as ye have us for an ensample. (For many walk, of whom I have told you often, and now tell you even weeping, that they are the enemies of the cross of Christ; whose end is destruction, whose god is their belly, and whose glory is in their shame, who mind earthly things.) For our conversation is in heaven; from whence also we look for the Saviour, the Lord Jesus Christ; who shall change our vile body, that it may be fashioned like unto his glorious body, according to the working whereby he is able even to subdue all things unto himself.

The Gospel. S. Matth. 22. 15–22

THEN went the Pharisees and took counsel how they might

entangle him in his talk. And they sent out unto him their disciples, with the Herodians, saying, Master, we know that thou art true, and teachest the way of God in truth, neither carest thou for any man: for thou regardest not the person of men. Tell us therefore, what thinkest thou? Is it lawful to give tribute unto Cæsar, or not? But Jesus perceived their wickedness, and said, Why tempt ye me, ye hypocrites? shew me the tribute-money. And they brought unto him a penny. And he saith unto them, Whose is this image and superscription? They say unto him, Cæsar's. Then saith he unto them, Render therefore unto Cæsar the things which are Cæsar's; and unto God the things that are God's. When they had heard these words, they marvelled, and left him, and went their way.

THE TWENTY-FOURTH SUNDAY AFTER TRINITY

The Collect

O LORD, we beseech thee, absolve thy people from their offences; that through thy bountiful goodness we may all be delivered from the bands of those sins, which by our frailty we have committed: Grant this, O heavenly Father, for Jesus Christ's sake, our blessed Lord and Saviour. *Amen.*

The Epistle. Coloss. 1. 3–12

WE give thanks to God and the Father of our Lord Jesus Christ, praying always for you, since we heard of your faith in Christ Jesus, and of the love which ye have to all the saints; for the hope which is laid up for you in heaven, whereof ye heard before in the word of the truth of the Gospel; which is come unto you, as it is in all the world, and bringeth forth fruit, as it doth also in you, since the day ye heard of it, and knew the grace of God in truth. As ye also learned of Epaphras, our dear fellow-servant, who is for you a faithful minister of Christ; who also declared unto us your love in the Spirit. For this cause we also, since the day we heard it, do not cease to pray for you, and to desire that ye might be filled with the knowledge of his will in all wisdom and spiritual understanding: that ye might walk worthy of the Lord unto all pleasing, being fruitful in every good work, and increasing in the knowledge of God; strengthened with all might, according to his glorious power, unto all patience and long-suffering with joyfulness; giving thanks unto the Father, which hath made us meet to be partakers of the inheritance of the saints in light.

The Gospel. S. Matth. 9. 18–26

WHILE Jesus spake these things unto John's disciples, behold, there came a certain ruler, and worshipped him, saying, My daughter is even now dead; but come and lay thy hand upon her, and she shall live. And Jesus arose, and followed him, and so did his disciples. (And behold, a woman, which was diseased with an issue of blood twelve years, came behind him, and touched the hem of his garment: for she said within herself, If I may but touch his garment, I shall be whole. But Jesus turned him about, and when he saw her, he said, Daughter, be of good comfort, thy faith hath made thee whole. And the woman was made whole from that hour.) And when Jesus came into the ruler's house, and saw the minstrels and the people making a noise, he said unto them, Give place; for the maid is not dead, but sleepeth. And they laughed him to scorn. But when the people were put forth, he went in, and took her by the hand, and the maid arose. And the fame hereof went abroad into all that land.

THE TWENTY-FIFTH SUNDAY AFTER TRINITY

The Collect

STIR up, we beseech thee, O Lord, the wills of thy faithful people; that they, plenteously bringing forth the fruit of good works, may of thee be plenteously rewarded; through Jesus Christ our Lord. *Amen.*

For the Epistle. Jer. 23. 5–8

BEHOLD, the days come, saith the Lord, that I will raise

unto David a righteous Branch, and a King shall reign and prosper, and shall execute judgement and justice in the earth. In his days Judah shall be saved, and Israel shall dwell safely: and this is his name whereby he shall be called, THE LORD OUR RIGHTEOUSNESS. Therefore behold, the days come, saith the Lord, that they shall no more say, The Lord liveth, which brought up the children of Israel out of the land of Egypt; but, The Lord liveth, which brought up, and which led the seed of the house of Israel out of the north-country, and from all countries whither I had driven them; and they shall dwell in their own land.

The Gospel. S. John 6. 5–14

WHEN Jesus then lift up his eyes, and saw a great company come unto him, he saith unto Philip, Whence shall we buy bread that these may eat? (And this he said to prove him; for he himself knew what he would do.) Philip answered him, Two hundred penny-worth of bread is not sufficient for them, that every one of them may take a little. One of his disciples, Andrew, Simon Peter's brother, saith unto him, There is a lad here, which hath five barley-loaves, and two small fishes; but what are they among so many? And Jesus said, Make the men sit down. Now there was much grass in the place. So the men sat down, in number about five thousand. And Jesus took the loaves, and when he had given thanks, he distributed to the disciples, and the disciples to them that were set down; and likewise of the fishes, as much as they would. When they were filled, he said unto his disciples, Gather up the fragments that remain, that nothing be lost. Therefore they gathered them together, and filled twelve baskets with the fragments of the five barley-loaves, which remained over and above unto them that had eaten. Then those men, when they had seen the miracle that Jesus did, said, This is of a truth that Prophet that should come into the world.

If there be any more Sundays before Advent Sunday, the Service of some of those Sundays that were omitted after the Epiphany shall be taken in to supply so many as are here wanting. And if there be fewer, the overplus may be omitted: Provided that this last Collect, Epistle, and Gospel shall always be used upon the Sunday next before Advent.

SAINT ANDREW'S DAY*

The Collect

ALMIGHTY God, who didst give such grace unto thy holy Apostle Saint Andrew, that he readily obeyed the calling of thy Son Jesus Christ, and followed him without delay: Grant unto us all, that we, being called by thy holy word, may forthwith give up ourselves obediently to fulfil thy holy commandments; through the same Jesus Christ our Lord. *Amen.*

The Epistle. Rom. 10. 9–end

IF thou shalt confess with thy mouth the Lord Jesus, and shalt believe in thine heart that God hath raised him from the dead, thou shalt be saved. For with the heart man believeth unto righteousness, and with the mouth confession is made unto salvation. For the Scripture saith, Whosoever believeth on him shall not be ashamed. For there is no difference between the Jew and the Greek: for the same Lord over all is rich unto all that call upon him. For whosoever shall call upon the name of the Lord shall be saved. How then shall they call on him, in whom they have not believed? And how shall they believe in him, of whom they have not heard? And how shall they hear without a preacher? And how shall they preach, except they be sent? As it is written, How beautiful are the feet of them that preach the Gospel of peace, and bring glad tidings of good things! But they have not all obeyed the Gospel. For Esaias saith, Lord, who hath believed our report? So then faith cometh by hearing, and hearing by the word of God. But I say, Have they not heard? Yes verily, their sound went into all the earth, and their words unto the ends of the world. But I say, Did not Israel know? First Moses saith, I will provoke you to jealousy by them that are no people, and by a foolish nation I will anger you. But Esaias is

*November 30.

very bold, and saith, I was found of them that sought me not; I was made manifest unto them that asked not after me. But to Israel he saith, All day long I have stretched forth my hands unto a disobedient and gainsaying people.

The Gospel. S. Matth. 4. 18–20

JESUS, walking by the sea of Galilee, saw two brethren, Simon called Peter, and Andrew his brother, casting a net into the sea, (for they were fishers;) and he saith unto them, Follow me; and I will make you fishers of men. And they straightway left their nets, and followed him. And going on from thence he saw other two brethren, James the son of Zebedee, and John his brother, in a ship with Zebedee their father, mending their nets; and he called them. And they immediately left the ship and their father, and followed him.

SAINT THOMAS THE APOSTLE*

The Collect

ALMIGHTY and everliving God, who for the more confirmation of the faith didst suffer thy holy Apostle Thomas to be doubtful in thy Son's resurrection: Grant us so perfectly, and without all doubt, to believe in thy Son Jesus Christ, that our faith in thy sight may never be reproved. Hear us, O Lord, through the same Jesus Christ, to whom, with thee and the Holy Ghost, be all honour and glory, now and for evermore. *Amen.*

The Epistle. Ephes. 2. 19–end

NOW therefore ye are no more strangers and foreigners, but fellow-citizens with the saints, and of the household of God; and are built upon the foundation of the Apostles and Prophets, Jesus Christ himself being the chief corner-stone; in whom all the building, fitly framed together, groweth unto an holy temple in the Lord; in whom ye also are builded together for an habitation of God through the Spirit.

*December 21.

The Gospel. S. John 20. 24–end

THOMAS, one of the twelve, called Didymus, was not with them when Jesus came. The other disciples therefore said unto him, We have seen the Lord. But he said unto them, Except I shall see in his hands the print of the nails, and put my finger into the print of the nails, and thrust my hand into his side, I will not believe. And after eight days again his disciples were within, and Thomas with them: then came Jesus, the doors being shut, and stood in the midst, and said, Peace be unto you. Then saith he to Thomas, Reach hither thy finger, and behold my hands; and reach hither thy hand, and thrust it into my side; and be not faithless, but believing. And Thomas answered and said unto him, My Lord, and my God. Jesus saith unto him, Thomas, because thou hast seen me, thou hast believed; blessed are they that have not seen, and yet have believed. And many other signs truly did Jesus in the presence of his disciples, which are not written in this book. But these are written, that ye might believe that Jesus is the Christ, the Son of God; and that believing ye might have life through his name.

THE CONVERSION OF SAINT PAUL*

The Collect

O GOD, who, through the preaching of the blessed Apostle Saint Paul, hast caused the light of the Gospel to shine throughout the world: Grant, we beseech thee, that we, having his wonderful conversion in remembrance, may shew forth our thankfulness unto thee for the same, by following the holy doctrine which he taught; through Jesus Christ our Lord. *Amen.*

For the Epistle. Acts 9. 1–22

AND Saul, yet breathing out threatenings and slaughter against the disciples of the Lord, went unto the high priest, and desired of him letters to Damascus to the synagogues, that if he found any of this way, whether they were men or women, he might bring them bound unto Jerusalem. And, as he journeyed,

*January 25.

he came near Damascus, and suddenly there shined round about him a light from heaven. And he fell to the earth, and heard a voice saying unto him, Saul, Saul, why persecutest thou me? And he said, Who art thou, Lord? And the Lord said, I am Jesus whom thou persecutest: it is hard for thee to kick against the pricks. And he, trembling and astonished, said, Lord, what wilt thou have me to do? And the Lord said unto him, Arise, and go into the city, and it shall be told thee what thou must do. And the men which journeyed with him stood speechless, hearing a voice, but seeing no man. And Saul arose from the earth, and when his eyes were opened he saw no man; but they led him by the hand, and brought him into Damascus. And he was three days without sight, and neither did eat nor drink. And there was a certain disciple at Damascus, named Ananias; and to him said the Lord in a vision, Ananias. And he said, Behold, I am here, Lord. And the Lord said unto him, Arise, and go into the street which is called Straight, and inquire in the house of Judas for one called Saul, of Tarsus: for behold, he prayeth, and hath seen in a vision a man named Ananias, coming in, and putting his hand on him, that he might receive his sight. Then Ananias answered, Lord, I have heard by many of this man, how much evil he hath done to thy saints at Jerusalem; and here he hath authority from the chief priests to bind all that call on thy name. But the Lord said unto him, Go thy way; for he is a chosen vessel unto me, to bear my name before the Gentiles, and kings, and the children of Israel: for I will shew him how great things he must suffer for my name's sake. And Ananias went his way, and entered into the house; and, putting his hands on him, said, Brother Saul, the Lord, (even Jesus that appeared unto thee in the way as thou camest,) hath sent me, that thou mightest receive thy sight, and be filled with the Holy Ghost. And immediately there fell from his eyes as it had been scales; and he received sight forthwith, and arose, and was baptized. And when he had received meat, he was strengthened. Then was Saul certain days with the disciples which were at Damascus. And straightway he preached Christ in the synagogues, that he is the Son of God. But all that heard him were amazed, and said, Is not this he that destroyed them which called on this name in Jerusalem, and came hither for that intent, that he might bring them bound unto the chief priests? But Saul increased the more in strength, and confounded the Jews which dwelt at Damascus, proving that this is very Christ.

The Gospel. S. Matth. 19. 27–end

PETER answered and said unto Jesus, Behold, we have forsaken all, and followed thee; what shall we have therefore? And Jesus said unto them, Verily I say unto you, that ye which have followed me, in the regeneration when the Son of man shall sit in the throne of his glory, ye also shall sit upon twelve thrones, judging the twelve tribes of Israel. And every one that hath forsaken houses, or brethren, or sisters, or father, or mother, or wife, or children, or lands, for my name's sake, shall receive an hundred-fold, and shall inherit everlasting life. But many that are first shall be last, and the last shall be first.

THE PRESENTATION OF CHRIST IN THE TEMPLE
COMMONLY CALLED
THE PURIFICATION OF SAINT MARY THE VIRGIN*

The Collect

ALMIGHTY and everliving God, we humbly beseech thy Majesty, that, as thy only-begotten Son was this day presented in the temple in substance of our flesh, so we may be presented unto thee with pure and clean hearts, by the same thy Son Jesus Christ our Lord. *Amen.*

For the Epistle. Mal. 3. 1–5

BEHOLD, I will send my messenger, and he shall prepare the way before me: and the Lord, whom ye seek, shall suddenly come to his temple; even the messenger of the covenant, whom ye delight in; behold, he shall come, saith the Lord of hosts. But who may abide the day of his coming? and who shall stand

*February 2.

when he appeareth? for he is like a refiner's fire, and like fullers' soap. And he shall sit as a refiner and purifier of silver; and he shall purify the sons of Levi, and purge them as gold and silver, that they may offer unto the Lord an offering in righteousness. Then shall the offerings of Judah and Jerusalem be pleasant unto the Lord, as in the days of old, and as in former years. And I will come near to you to judgement, and I will be a swift witness against the sorcerers, and against the adulterers, and against false swearers, and against those that oppress the hireling in his wages, the widow and the fatherless, and that turn aside the stranger from his right, and fear not me, saith the Lord of hosts.

The Gospel. S. Luke 2. 22–40

AND when the days of her purification, according to the law of Moses, were accomplished, they brought him to Jerusalem, to present him to the Lord; (as it is written in the law of the Lord, Every male that openeth the womb shall be called holy to the Lord;) and to offer a sacrifice, according to that which is said in the law of the Lord, A pair of turtle-doves, or two young pigeons. And behold, there was a man in Jerusalem, whose name was Simeon; and the same man was just and devout, waiting for the consolation of Israel: and the Holy Ghost was upon him. And it was revealed unto him by the Holy Ghost, that he should not see death, before he had seen the Lord's Christ. And he came by the Spirit into the temple; and when the parents brought in the child Jesus, to do for him after the custom of the law, then took he him up in his arms, and blessed God, and said, Lord, now lettest thou thy servant depart in peace, according to thy word: for mine eyes have seen thy salvation, which thou hast prepared before the face of all people; a light to lighten the Gentiles, and the glory of thy people Israel. And Joseph and his mother marvelled at those things which were spoken of him. And Simeon blessed them, and said unto Mary his mother, Behold, this child is set for the fall and rising again of many in Israel; and for a sign which shall be spoken against; (yea, a sword shall pierce through thy own soul also;) that the thoughts of many hearts may be revealed. And there was one Anna a proph etess, the daughter of Phanuel, of the tribe of Aser; she was of great age, and had lived with an husband seven years from he virginity: and she was a widow of about fourscore and four years which departed not from the temple, but served God with fastings and prayers night and day. And she coming in tha instant gave thanks likewise unto the Lord, and spake of him to all them that looked for redemption in Jerusalem. And when they had performed all things according to the law of the Lord they returned into Galilee to their own city Nazareth. And the child grew, and waxed strong in spirit, filled with wisdom; and the grace of God was upon him.

SAINT MATTHIAS'S DAY*

The Collect

O ALMIGHTY God, who into the place of the traitor Juda didst choose thy faithful servant Matthias to be of the numbe of the twelve Apostles: Grant that thy Church, being alway preserved from false Apostles, may be ordered and guided by faithful and true pastors; through Jesus Christ our Lord. *Amen.*

For the Epistle. Acts 1. 15–end

IN those days Peter stood up in the midst of the disciples, and said, (the number of the names together were about an hundred and twenty,) Men and brethren, this Scripture must needs have been fulfilled, which the Holy Ghost by the mouth of David spake before concerning Judas, which was guide to them that took Jesus: for he was numbered with us, and had obtained part of this ministry. Now this man purchased a field with the reward of iniquity; and falling headlong he burst asunder in the midst and all his bowels gushed out. And it was known unto all the dwellers at Jerusalem, in so much as that field is called in their proper tongue, Aceldama, that is to say, The field of blood. For it is written in the book of Psalms, Let his habitation be deso late, and let no man dwell therein; and, His bishoprick le

* *February 24.*

another take. Wherefore, of these men which have companied with us all the time that the Lord Jesus went in and out among us, beginning from the baptism of John, unto that same day that he was taken up from us, must one be ordained to be a witness with us of his resurrection. And they appointed two, Joseph called Barsabas, who was surnamed Justus, and Matthias. And they prayed, and said, Thou, Lord, which knowest the hearts of all men, shew whether of these two thou hast chosen; that he may take part of this ministry and apostleship, from which Judas by transgression fell, that he might go to his own place. And they gave forth their lots; and the lot fell upon Matthias, and he was numbered with the eleven Apostles.

The Gospel. S. Matth. 11. 25–end

AT that time Jesus answered and said, I thank thee, O Father, Lord of heaven and earth, because thou hast hid these things from the wise and prudent, and hast revealed them unto babes. Even so, Father, for so it seemed good in thy sight. All things are delivered unto me of my Father: and no man knoweth the Son, but the Father; neither knoweth any man the Father, save the Son, and he to whomsoever the Son will reveal him. Come unto me, all ye that labour and are heavy laden, and I will give you rest. Take my yoke upon you, and learn of me, for I am meek and lowly in heart: and ye shall find rest unto your souls. For my yoke is easy, and my burden is light.

THE ANNUNCIATION OF THE BLESSED VIRGIN MARY*

The Collect

WE beseech thee, O Lord, pour thy grace into our hearts; that, as we have known the incarnation of thy Son Jesus Christ by the message of an angel, so by his cross and passion we may be brought unto the glory of his resurrection; through the same Jesus Christ our Lord. *Amen.*

* *March 25.*

For the Epistle. Isai. 7. 10–15

MOREOVER, the Lord spake again unto Ahaz, saying, Ask thee a sign of the Lord thy God; ask it either in the depth, or in the height above. But Ahaz said, I will not ask, neither will I tempt the Lord. And he said, Hear ye now, O house of David; Is it a small thing for you to weary men, but will ye weary my God also? Therefore the Lord himself shall give you a sign; Behold, a Virgin shall conceive, and bear a son, and shall call his name Immanuel. Butter and honey shall he eat, that he may know to refuse the evil, and choose the good.

The Gospel. S. Luke 1. 26–38

AND in the sixth month the angel Gabriel was sent from God unto a city of Galilee named Nazareth, to a Virgin espoused to a man whose name was Joseph, of the house of David; and the Virgin's name was Mary. And the angel came in unto her, and said, Hail, thou that art highly favoured, the Lord is with thee; blessed art thou among women. And when she saw him she was troubled at his saying, and cast in her mind what manner of salutation this should be. And the angel said unto her, Fear not, Mary; for thou hast found favour with God. And behold, thou shalt conceive in thy womb, and bring forth a Son, and shalt call his name JESUS. He shall be great, and shall be called the Son of the Highest; and the Lord God shall give unto him the throne of his father David. And he shall reign over the house of Jacob for ever; and of his kingdom there shall be no end. Then said Mary unto the angel, How shall this be, seeing I know not a man? And the angel answered and said unto her, The Holy Ghost shall come upon thee, and the power of the Highest shall overshadow thee: therefore also that holy thing which shall be born of thee shall be called the Son of God. And behold, thy cousin Elisabeth, she hath also conceived a son in her old age; and this is the sixth month with her who was called barren: for with God nothing shall be impossible. And Mary said, Behold the handmaid of the Lord; be it unto me according to thy word. And the angel departed from her.

SAINT MARK'S DAY*

The Collect

O ALMIGHTY God, who hast instructed thy holy Church with the heavenly doctrine of thy Evangelist Saint Mark: Give us grace, that, being not like children carried away with every blast of vain doctrine, we may be established in the truth of thy holy Gospel; through Jesus Christ our Lord. *Amen.*

The Epistle. Ephes. 4. 7–16

UNTO every one of us is given grace, according to the measure of the gift of Christ. Wherefore he saith, When he ascended up on high, he led captivity captive, and gave gifts unto men. (Now that he ascended, what is it but that he also descended first into the lower parts of the earth? He that descended is the same also that ascended up far above all heavens, that he might fill all things.) And he gave some Apostles, and some Prophets, and some Evangelists, and some Pastors and Teachers; for the perfecting of the saints for the work of the ministry, for the edifying of the body of Christ; till we all come, in the unity of the faith and of the knowledge of the Son of God, unto a perfect man, unto the measure of the stature of the fulness of Christ: that we henceforth be no more children, tossed to and fro, and carried about with every wind of doctrine, by the sleight of men, and cunning craftiness, whereby they lie in wait to deceive; but speaking the truth in love, may grow up into him in all things, which is the head, even Christ: from whom the whole body fitly joined together and compacted by that which every joint supplieth, according to the effectual working in the measure of every part, maketh increase of the body, unto the edifying of itself in love.

The Gospel. S. John 15. 1–11

I AM the true vine, and my Father is the husbandman. Every branch in me that beareth not fruit he taketh away; and every branch that beareth fruit, he purgeth it, that it may bring forth more fruit. Now ye are clean through the word which

April 25.

I have spoken unto you. Abide in me, and I in you. As the branch cannot bear fruit of itself, except it abide in the vine; no more can ye, except ye abide in me. I am the vine, ye are the branches. He that abideth in me, and I in him, the same bringeth forth much fruit; for without me ye can do nothing. If a man abide not in me, he is cast forth as a branch, and is withered; and men gather them, and cast them into the fire, and they are burned. If ye abide in me, and my words abide in you, ye shall ask what ye will, and it shall be done unto you. Herein is my Father glorified, that ye bear much fruit; so shall ye be my disciples. As the Father hath loved me, so have I loved you: continue ye in my love. If ye keep my commandments, ye shall abide in my love; even as I have kept my Father's commandments, and abide in his love. These things have I spoken unto you, that my joy might remain in you, and that your joy might be full.

SAINT PHILIP AND SAINT JAMES'S DAY*

The Collect

O ALMIGHTY God, whom truly to know is everlasting life: Grant us perfectly to know thy Son Jesus Christ to be the way, the truth, and the life; that, following the steps of thy holy Apostles, Saint Philip and Saint James, we may stedfastly walk in the way that leadeth to eternal life; through the same thy Son Jesus Christ our Lord. *Amen.*

The Epistle. S. James i. 1–12

JAMES, a servant of God and of the Lord Jesus Christ, to the twelve tribes which are scattered abroad, greeting. My brethren, count it all joy when ye fall into divers temptations; knowing this, that the trying of your faith worketh patience. But let patience have her perfect work, that ye may be perfect and entire, wanting nothing. If any of you lack wisdom, let him ask of God, that giveth to all men liberally, and upbraideth not, and it shall be given him. But let him ask in faith, nothing wavering; for he that wavereth is like a wave of the sea, driven with the

May 1.

wind, and tossed. For let not that man think that he shall receive any thing of the Lord. A double-minded man is unstable in all his ways. Let the brother of low degree rejoice in that he is exalted; but the rich in that he is made low; because as the flower of the grass he shall pass away. For the sun is no sooner risen with a burning heat, but it withereth the grass, and the flower thereof falleth, and the grace of the fashion of it perisheth: so also shall the rich man fade away in his ways. Blessed is the man that endureth temptation; for when he is tried, he shall receive the crown of life, which the Lord hath promised to them that love him.

The Gospel. S. John 14. 1–14

AND Jesus said unto his disciples, Let not your heart be troubled; ye believe in God, believe also in me. In my Father's house are many mansions; if it were not so, I would have told you. I go to prepare a place for you: and if I go and prepare a place for you, I will come again, and receive you unto myself, that where I am, there ye may be also. And whither I go ye know, and the way ye know. Thomas saith unto him, Lord, we know not whither thou goest, and how can we know the way? Jesus saith unto him, I am the way, the truth, and the life: no man cometh unto the Father but by me. If ye had known me, ye should have known my Father also: and from henceforth ye know him, and have seen him. Philip saith unto him, Lord, shew us the Father, and it sufficeth us. Jesus saith unto him, Have I been so long time with you, and yet hast thou not known me, Philip? He that hath seen me hath seen the Father; and how sayest thou then, Shew us the Father? Believest thou not that I am in the Father, and the Father in me? The words that I speak unto you I speak not of myself; but the Father that dwelleth in me, he doeth the works. Believe me, that I am in the Father, and the Father in me, or else believe me for the very works' sake. Verily, verily I say unto you, He that believeth on me, the works that I do shall he do also; and greater works than these shall he do; because I go unto my Father. And whatsoever ye shall ask in my name, that will I do, that the Father may be glorified in the Son. If ye shall ask any thing in my name, I will do it.

SAINT BARNABAS THE APOSTLE*

The Collect

O LORD God Almighty, who didst endue thy holy Apostle Barnabas with singular gifts of the Holy Ghost: Leave us not, we beseech thee, destitute of thy manifold gifts, nor yet of grace to use them alway to thy honour and glory; through Jesus Christ our Lord. *Amen.*

For the Epistle. Acts 11. 22–end

TIDINGS of these things came unto the ears of the church which was in Jerusalem; and they sent forth Barnabas, that he should go as far as Antioch. Who, when he came, and had seen the grace of God, was glad; and exhorted them all, that with purpose of heart they would cleave unto the Lord. For he was a good man, and full of the Holy Ghost and of faith: and much people was added unto the Lord. Then departed Barnabas to Tarsus, for to seek Saul. And when he had found him, he brought him unto Antioch. And it came to pass, that a whole year they assembled themselves with the Church, and taught much people: and the disciples were called Christians first in Antioch. And in these days came prophets from Jerusalem unto Antioch. And there stood up one of them named Agabus, and signified by the Spirit, that there should be great dearth throughout all the world; which came to pass in the days of Claudius Cæsar. Then the disciples, every man according to his ability, determined to send relief unto the brethren which dwelt in Judæa: which also they did, and sent it to the elders by the hands of Barnabas and Saul.

The Gospel. S. John 15. 12–16

THIS is my commandment, that ye love one another, as I have loved you. Greater love hath no man than this, that a man lay

*June 11.

down his life for his friends. Ye are my friends, if ye do whatsoever I command you. Henceforth I call you not servants; for the servant knoweth not what his lord doeth: but I have called you friends; for all things that I have heard of my Father I have made known unto you. Ye have not chosen me, but I have chosen you, and ordained you, that ye should go and bring forth fruit, and that your fruit should remain: that whatsoever ye shall ask of the Father in my name, he may give it you.

SAINT JOHN BAPTIST'S DAY*

The Collect

ALMIGHTY God, by whose providence thy servant John Baptist was wonderfully born, and sent to prepare the way of thy Son our Saviour, by preaching of repentance: Make us so to follow his doctrine and holy life, that we may truly repent according to his preaching, and after his example constantly speak the truth, boldly rebuke vice, and patiently suffer for the truth's sake; through Jesus Christ our Lord. *Amen.*

For the Epistle. Isai. 40. 1–11

COMFORT ye, comfort ye my people, saith your God. Speak ye comfortably to Jerusalem, and cry unto her, that her warfare is accomplished, that her iniquity is pardoned: for she hath received of the Lord's hand double for all her sins. The voice of him that crieth in the wilderness, Prepare ye the way of the Lord, make straight in the desert a high-way for our God. Every valley shall be exalted, and every mountain and hill shall be made low, and the crooked shall be made straight, and the rough places plain. And the glory of the Lord shall be revealed, and all flesh shall see it together: for the mouth of the Lord hath spoken it. The voice said, Cry. And he said, What shall I cry? All flesh is grass, and all the goodliness thereof is as the flower of the field. The grass withereth, the flower fadeth, because the Spirit of the Lord bloweth upon it: surely the people is grass. The grass withereth, the flower fadeth; but the word of our God

June 24.

shall stand for ever. O Zion, that bringest good tidings, get thee up into the high mountain: O Jerusalem, that bringest good tidings, lift up thy voice with strength; lift it up, be not afraid: say unto the cities of Judah, Behold your God. Behold, the Lord God will come with strong hand, and his arm shall rule for him: behold, his reward is with him, and his work before him. He shall feed his flock like a shepherd; he shall gather the lambs with his arm, and carry them in his bosom, and shall gently lead those that are with young.

The Gospel. S. Luke 1. 57–end

ELISABETH's full time came that she should be delivered; and she brought forth a son. And her neighbours and her cousins heard how the Lord had shewed great mercy upon her; and they rejoiced with her. And it came to pass, that on the eighth day they came to circumcise the child; and they called him Zacharias, after the name of his father. And his mother answered and said, Not so; but he shall be called John. And they said unto her, there is none of thy kindred that is called by this name. And they made signs to his father, how he would have him called. And he asked for a writing-table, and wrote, saying, His name is John. And they marvelled all. And his mouth was opened immediately, and his tongue loosed, and he spake, and praised God. And fear came on all that dwelt round about them; and all these sayings were noised abroad throughout all the hill-country of Judæa. And all they that had heard them laid them up in their hearts, saying, What manner of child shall this be? And the hand of the Lord was with him. And his father Zacharias was filled with the Holy Ghost, and prophesied, saying, Blessed be the Lord God of Israel: for he hath visited and redeemed his people, and hath raised up an horn of salvation for us in the house of his servant David; as he spake by the mouth of his holy prophets, which have been since the world began; that we should be saved from our enemies, and from the hand of all that hate us; to perform the mercy promised to our fathers, and to remember his holy covenant; the oath which he sware to our father Abraham, that he would grant unto us, that we, being delivered out of the hands of our enemies, might serve him without fear, in holiness and righteousness before him all the days of our life. And thou, child, shalt be called the Prophet of the Highest: for thou shalt go before the face of the Lord to prepare his ways; to give knowledge of salvation unto his people, by the remission of their sins, through the tender mercy of our God, whereby the day-spring from on high hath visited us; to give light to them that sit in darkness and in the shadow of death; to guide our feet into the way of peace. And the child grew, and waxed strong in spirit; and was in the deserts till the day of his shewing unto Israel.

SAINT PETER'S DAY*

The Collect

O ALMIGHTY God, who by thy Son Jesus Christ didst give to thy Apostle Saint Peter many excellent gifts, and commandedst him earnestly to feed thy flock: Make, we beseech thee, all Bishops and Pastors diligently to preach thy holy Word, and the people obediently to follow the same, that they may receive the crown of everlasting glory; through Jesus Christ our Lord. *Amen.*

For the Epistle. Acts 12. 1–11

ABOUT that time Herod the king stretched forth his hands to vex certain of the Church. And he killed James the brother of John with the sword. And because he saw it pleased the Jews, he proceeded further to take Peter also. (Then were the days of unleavened bread.) And when he had apprehended him, he put him in prison, and delivered him to four quaternions of soldiers to keep him, intending after Easter to bring him forth to the people. Peter therefore was kept in prison; but prayer was made without ceasing of the Church unto God for him. And when Herod would have brought him forth, the same night Peter was sleeping between two soldiers, bound with two chains; and the keepers before the door kept the prison. And behold, the angel

*June 29.

of the Lord came upon him, and a light shined in the prison; and he smote Peter on the side, and raised him up, saying, Arise up quickly. And his chains fell off from his hands. And the angel said unto him, Gird thyself, and bind on thy sandals: and so he did. And he saith unto him, Cast thy garment about thee, and follow me. And he went out and followed him; and wist not that it was true which was done by the angel; but thought he saw a vision. When they were past the first and the second ward, they came unto the iron gate that leadeth unto the city, which opened to them of his own accord; and they went out, and passed on through one street, and forthwith the angel departed from him. And when Peter was come to himself, he said, Now I know of a surety, that the Lord hath sent his angel, and hath delivered me out of the hand of Herod, and from all the expectation of the people of the Jews.

The Gospel. S. Matth. 16. 13–19

WHEN Jesus came into the coasts of Cæsarea Philippi, he asked his disciples, saying, Whom do men say that I, the Son of man, am? And they said, Some say that thou art John the Baptist, some Elias, and others Jeremias, or one of the prophets. He saith unto them, But whom say ye that I am? And Simon Peter answered and said, Thou art Christ, the Son of the living God. And Jesus answered and said unto him, Blessed art thou, Simon Bar-jona: for flesh and blood hath not revealed it unto thee, but my Father which is in heaven. And I say also unto thee, that thou art Peter, and upon this rock I will build my Church; and the gates of hell shall not prevail against it. And I will give unto thee the keys of the kingdom of heaven: and whatsoever thou shalt bind on earth shall be bound in heaven; and whatsoever thou shalt loose on earth shall be loosed in heaven.

SAINT JAMES THE APOSTLE*

The Collect

GRANT, O merciful God, that as thine holy Apostle Saint

*July 25.

James, leaving his father and all that he had, without delay was obedient unto the calling of thy Son Jesus Christ, and followed him; so we, forsaking all worldly and carnal affections, may be evermore ready to follow thy holy commandments; through Jesus Christ our Lord. *Amen.*

For the Epistle. Acts 11. 27–end,
and 12. 1–3

IN those days came prophets from Jerusalem unto Antioch. And there stood up one of them named Agabus, and signified by the Spirit, that there should be great dearth throughout all the world; which came to pass in the days of Claudius Cæsar. Then the disciples, every man according to his ability, determined to send relief unto the brethren which dwelt in Judæa: which also they did, and sent it to the elders by the hands of Barnabas and Saul. Now about that time Herod the king stretched forth his hands to vex certain of the Church. And he killed James the brother of John with the sword. And because he saw it pleased the Jews, he proceeded further to take Peter also.

The Gospel. S. Matth. 20. 20–28

THEN came to him the mother of Zebedee's children with her sons, worshipping him, and desiring a certain thing of him. And he said unto her, What wilt thou? She saith unto him, Grant that these my two sons may sit, the one on thy right hand, and the other on the left, in thy kingdom. But Jesus answered and said, Ye know not what ye ask. Are ye able to drink of the cup that I shall drink of, and to be baptized with the baptism that I am baptized with? They say unto him, We are able. And he saith unto them, Ye shall drink indeed of my cup, and be baptized with the baptism that I am baptized with: but to sit on my right hand, and on my left, is not mine to give; but it shall be given to them for whom it is prepared of my Father. And when the ten heard it, they were moved with indignation against the two brethren. But Jesus called them unto him, and said, Ye know that the princes of the Gentiles exercise dominion over them, and they that are great exercise authority upon them. But it shall not be so among you: but whosoever

will be great among you, let him be your minister; and whosoever will be chief among you, let him be your servant: even as
the Son of man came not to be ministered unto, but to minister,
and to give his life a ransom for many.

SAINT BARTHOLOMEW THE APOSTLE*

The Collect

O ALMIGHTY and everlasting God, who didst give to
thine Apostle Bartholomew grace truly to believe and to preach
thy Word: Grant, we beseech thee, unto thy Church, to love
that Word which he believed, and both to preach and receive
the same; through Jesus Christ our Lord. *Amen.*

For the Epistle. Acts 5. 12–16

BY the hands of the Apostles were many signs and wonders
wrought among the people: (and they were all with one accord
in Solomon's porch: and of the rest durst no man join himself to
them: but the people magnified them: and believers were the
more added to the Lord, multitudes both of men and women:)
insomuch that they brought forth the sick into the streets, and
laid them on beds and couches, that at the least the shadow of
Peter passing by might overshadow some of them. There came
also a multitude out of the cities round about unto Jerusalem,
bringing sick folks, and them which were vexed with unclean
spirits; and they were healed every one.

The Gospel. S. Luke 22. 24–30

AND there was also a strife among them, which of them
should be accounted the greatest. And he said unto them, The
kings of the Gentiles exercise lordship over them; and they that
exercise authority upon them are called benefactors. But ye shall
not be so: but he that is greatest among you, let him be as the
younger; and he that is chief, as he that doth serve. For whether
is greater, he that sitteth at meat, or he that serveth? is not he
that sitteth at meat? but I am among you as he that serveth. Ye

*August 24.

are they which have continued with me in my temptations. And I appoint unto you a kingdom, as my Father hath appointed unto me; that ye may eat and drink at my table in my kingdom, and sit on thrones judging the twelve tribes of Israel.

SAINT MATTHEW THE APOSTLE*

The Collect

O ALMIGHTY God, who by thy blessed Son didst call Matthew from the receipt of custom to be an Apostle and Evangelist: Grant us grace to forsake all covetous desires and inordinate love of riches, and to follow the same thy Son Jesus Christ, who liveth and reigneth with thee and the Holy Ghost, one God, world without end. *Amen.*

The Epistle. 2 Cor. 4. 1–6

THEREFORE seeing we have this ministry, as we have received mercy, we faint not; but have renounced the hidden things of dishonesty, not walking in craftiness, nor handling the word of God deceitfully, but by manifestation of the truth commending ourselves to every man's conscience in the sight of God. But if our Gospel be hid, it is hid to them that are lost: in whom the god of this world hath blinded the minds of them which believe not, lest the light of the glorious Gospel of Christ, who is the image of God, should shine unto them. For we preach not ourselves but Christ Jesus the Lord; and ourselves your servants for Jesus' sake. For God, who commanded the light to shine out of darkness, hath shined in our hearts, to give the light of the knowledge of the glory of God, in the face of Jesus Christ.

The Gospel. S. Matth. 9. 9–13

AND as Jesus passed forth from thence, he saw a man named Matthew, sitting at the receipt of custom: and he saith unto him, Follow me. And he arose, and followed him. And it came to pass, as Jesus sat at meat in the house, behold, many publicans

* *September 21.*

and sinners came, and sat down with him and his disciples. And when the Pharisees saw it, They said unto his disciples, Why eateth your Master with publicans and sinners? But when Jesus heard that, he said unto them, They that be whole need not a physician, but they that are sick. But go ye and learn what that meaneth, I will have mercy, and not sacrifice: for I am not come to call the righteous, but sinners to repentance.

SAINT MICHAEL AND ALL ANGELS*

The Collect

O EVERLASTING God, who hast ordained and constituted the services of Angels and men in a wonderful order: Mercifully grant that, as thy holy Angels alway do thee service in heaven, so by thy appointment they may succour and defend us on earth; through Jesus Christ our Lord. *Amen.*

For the Epistle. Rev. 12. 7–12

THERE was war in heaven: Michael and his angels fought against the dragon; and the dragon fought and his angels, and prevailed not, neither was their place found any more in heaven. And the great dragon was cast out, that old serpent, called the devil and Satan, which deceiveth the whole world; he was cast out into the earth, and his angels were cast out with him. And I heard a loud voice saying in heaven, Now is come salvation, and strength, and the kingdom of our God, and the power of his Christ: for the accuser of our brethren is cast down, which accused them before our God day and night. And they overcame him by the blood of the Lamb, and by the word of their testimony; and they loved not their lives unto the death. Therefore rejoice, ye heavens, and ye that dwell in them. Woe to the inhabiters of the earth and of the sea: for the devil is come down unto you, having great wrath, because he knoweth that he hath but a short time.

* *September 29.*

The Gospel. S. Matth. 18. 1–10

AT the same time came the disciples unto Jesus, saying, Who is the greatest in the kingdom of heaven? And Jesus called a little child unto him, and set him in the midst of them, and said, Verily I say unto you, Except ye be converted, and become as little children, ye shall not enter into the kingdom of heaven. Whosoever therefore shall humble himself as this little child, the same is greatest in the kingdom of heaven. And whoso shall receive one such little child in my name, receiveth me. But whoso shall offend one of these little ones which believe in me, it were better for him that a mill-stone were hanged about his neck, and that he were drowned in the depth of the sea. Woe unto the world because of offences: for it must needs be that offences come: but woe to that man by whom the offence cometh. Wherefore if thy hand or thy foot offend thee, cut them off, and cast them from thee: it is better for thee to enter into life halt or maimed, rather than having two hands or two feet to be cast into everlasting fire. And if thine eye offend thee, pluck it out, and cast it from thee: it is better for thee to enter into life with one eye, rather than having two eyes to be cast into hell-fire. Take heed that ye despise not one of these little ones; for I say unto you, that in heaven their angels do always behold the face of my Father which is in heaven.

SAINT LUKE THE EVANGELIST*

The Collect

ALMIGHTY God, who calledst Luke the Physician, whose praise is in the Gospel, to be an Evangelist, and Physician of the soul: May it please thee that, by the wholesome medicines of the doctrine delivered by him, all the diseases of our souls may be healed; through the merits of thy Son Jesus Christ our Lord. *Amen.*

The Epistle. 2 Tim. 4. 5–15

WATCH thou in all things, endure afflictions, do the work of

* *October 18.*

an Evangelist, make full proof of thy ministry. For I am now ready to be offered, and the time of my departure is at hand. I have fought a good fight, I have finished my course, I have kept the faith. Henceforth there is laid up for me a crown of righteousness, which the Lord, the righteous Judge, shall give me at that day: and not to me only, but unto all them also that love his appearing. Do thy diligence to come shortly unto me: for Demas hath forsaken me, having loved this present world, and is departed unto Thessalonica; Crescens to Galatia, Titus unto Dalmatia. Only Luke is with me. Take Mark and bring him with thee: for he is profitable to me for the ministry. And Tychicus have I sent to Ephesus. The cloke that I left at Troas with Carpus, when thou comest, bring with thee; and the books, but especially the parchments. Alexander the copper-smith did me much evil: the Lord reward him according to his works. Of whom be thou ware also, for he hath greatly withstood our words.

The Gospel. S. Luke 10. 1–7

THE Lord appointed other seventy also, and sent them two and two before his face into every city and place whither he himself would come. Therefore said he unto them, The harvest truly is great, but the labourers are few; pray ye therefore the Lord of the harvest, that he would send forth labourers into his harvest. Go your ways; behold, I send you forth as lambs among wolves. Carry neither purse, nor scrip, nor shoes, and salute no man by the way. And into whatsoever house ye enter, first say, Peace be to this house. And if the son of peace be there, your peace shall rest upon it: if not, it shall turn to you again. And in the same house remain, eating and drinking such things as they give: for the labourer is worthy of his hire.

SAINT SIMON AND SAINT JUDE, APOSTLES*

The Collect

O ALMIGHTY God, who hast built thy Church upon the

*October 28.

foundation of the Apostles and Prophets, Jesus Christ himself being the head corner-stone: Grant us so to be joined together in unity of spirit by their doctrine, that we may be made an holy temple acceptable unto thee; through Jesus Christ our Lord. *Amen.*

The Epistle. S. Jude 1–8

JUDE, the servant of Jesus Christ, and brother of James, to them that are sanctified by God the Father, and preserved in Jesus Christ, and called: Mercy unto you, and peace, and love be multiplied. Beloved, when I gave all diligence to write unto you of the common salvation, it was needful for me to write unto you, and exhort you, that ye should earnestly contend for the faith which was once delivered unto the saints. For there are certain men crept in unawares, who were before of old ordained to this condemnation; ungodly men, turning the grace of our God into lasciviousness, and denying the only Lord God and our Lord Jesus Christ. I will therefore put you in remembrance, though ye once knew this, how that the Lord, having saved the people out of the land of Egypt, afterward destroyed them that believed not. And the angels which kept not their first estate, but left their own habitation, he hath reserved in everlasting chains under darkness unto the judgement of the great day. Even as Sodom and Gomorrha, and the cities about them, in like manner giving themselves over to fornication, and going after strange flesh, are set forth for an example, suffering the vengeance of eternal fire. Likewise also these filthy dreamers defile the flesh, despise dominion, and speak evil of dignities.

The Gospel. S. John 15. 17–end

THESE things I command you, that ye love one another. If the world hate you, ye know that it hated me before it hated you. If ye were of the world, the world would love his own: but because ye are not of the world, but I have chosen you out of the world, therefore the world hateth you. Remember the word that I said unto you, The servant is not greater than the lord: if they have persecuted me, they will also persecute you; if they have kept my saying, they will keep yours also. But all these things will they do unto you for my name's sake, because they know not him that sent me. If I had not come and spoken unto them, they had not had sin: but now they have no cloke for their sin. He that hateth me hateth my Father also. If I had not done among them the works which none other man did, they had not had sin; but now have they both seen and hated both me and my Father. But this cometh to pass, that the word might be fulfilled that is written in their law, They hated me without a cause. But when the Comforter is come, whom I will send unto you from the Father, even the Spirit of truth, which proceedeth from the Father, he shall testify of me: and ye also shall bear witness, because ye have been with me from the beginning.

ALL SAINTS' DAY*

The Collect

O ALMIGHTY God, who hast knit together thine elect in one communion and fellowship, in the mystical body of thy Son Christ our Lord: Grant us grace so to follow thy blessed Saints in all virtuous and godly living, that we may come to those unspeakable joys, which thou hast prepared for them that unfeignedly love thee; through Jesus Christ our Lord. *Amen.*

For the Epistle. Rev. 7. 2–12

AND I saw another angel ascending from the east, having the seal of the living God; and he cried with a loud voice to the four angels, to whom it was given to hurt the earth and the sea, saying, Hurt not the earth, neither the sea, nor the trees, till we have sealed the servants of our God in their foreheads. And I heard the number of them which were sealed; and there were sealed an hundred and forty and four thousand, of all the tribes of the children of Israel.

Of the tribe of Juda were sealed twelve thousand.
Of the tribe of Reuben were sealed twelve thousand.
Of the tribe of Gad were sealed twelve thousand.
Of the tribe of Aser were sealed twelve thousand.

*November 1.

Of the tribe of Nepthalim were sealed twelve thousand.
Of the tribe of Manasses were sealed twelve thousand.
Of the tribe of Simeon were sealed twelve thousand.
Of the tribe of Levi were sealed twelve thousand.
Of the tribe of Issachar were sealed twelve thousand.
Of the tribe of Zabulon were sealed twelve thousand.
Of the tribe of Joseph were sealed twelve thousand.
Of the tribe of Benjamin were sealed twelve thousand.

After this I beheld, and lo, a great multitude, which no man could number, of all nations, and kindreds, and people, and tongues, stood before the throne, and before the Lamb, clothed with white robes, and palms in their hands; and cried with a loud voice, saying, Salvation to our God which sitteth upon the throne, and unto the Lamb. And all the angels stood round about the throne, and about the elders, and the four beasts, and fell before the throne on their faces, and worshipped God, saying, Amen; Blessing, and glory, and wisdom, and thanksgiving, and honour, and power, and might, be unto our God for ever and ever. Amen.

Gospel. S. Matth. 5. 1–12

JESUS, seeing the multitudes, went up into a mountain; and when he was set, his disciples came unto him. And he opened his mouth, and taught them, saying, Blessed are the poor in spirit: for theirs is the kingdom of heaven. Blessed are they that mourn: for they shall be comforted. Blessed are the meek: for they shall inherit the earth. Blessed are they which do hunger and thirst after righteousness: for they shall be filled. Blessed are the merciful: for they shall obtain mercy. Blessed are the pure in heart: for they shall see God. Blessed are the peace-makers: for they shall be called the children of God. Blessed are they which are persecuted for righteousness' sake: for theirs is the kingdom of heaven. Blessed are ye, when men shall revile you, and persecute you, and shall say all manner of evil against you falsely for my sake. Rejoice, and be exceeding glad; for great is your reward in heaven: for so persecuted they the prophets which were before you.

THE ORDER
FOR THE ADMINISTRATION
OF

THE LORD'S
SUPPER
OR
HOLY COMMUNION

So many as intend to be partakers of the holy Communion shall signify their names to the Curate, at least some time the day before.

If a Minister be persuaded that any person who presents himself to be a partaker of the holy Communion ought not to be admitted thereunto by reason of malicious and open contention with his neighbours, or other grave and open sin without repentance, he shall give an account of the same to the Ordinary of the place, and therein obey his order and direction, but so as not to refuse the Sacrament to any person until in accordance with such order and direction he shall have called him and advertised him that in any wise he presume not to come to the Lord's Table; Provided that in case of grave and immediate scandal to the Congregation the Minister shall not admit such person, but shall give an account of the same to the Ordinary within seven days after at the latest and therein obey the order and direction given to him by the Ordinary; Provided also that before issuing his order and direction in relation to any such person the Ordinary shall afford to him an opportunity for interview.

The Table at the Communion time having a fair white linen cloth upon it, shall stand in the body of the Church, or in the

Chancel, where Morning and Evening Prayer are appointed to be said. And the Priest standing at the north side of the Table shall say the Lord's Prayer with the Collect following, the people kneeling.

OUR Father which art in heaven, Hallowed be thy Name, Thy kingdom come, Thy will be done, in earth as it is in heaven. Give us this day our daily bread; And forgive us our trespasses, As we forgive them that trespass against us; And lead us not into temptation, But deliver us from evil. Amen.

The Collect

ALMIGHTY God, unto whom all hearts be open, all desires known, and from whom no secrets are hid: Cleanse the thoughts of our hearts by the inspiration of thy Holy Spirit, that we may perfectly love thee, and worthily magnify thy holy Name; through Christ our Lord. *Amen.*

Then shall the Priest, turning to the people, rehearse distinctly all the TEN COMMANDMENTS: and the people still kneeling shall after every Commandment ask God mercy for their transgression thereof for the time past, and grace to keep the same for the time to come, as followeth.

Minister.

GOD spake these words, and said; I am the Lord thy God: Thou shalt have none other gods but me.

People. Lord, have mercy upon us, and incline our hearts to keep this law.

Minister. Thou shalt not make to thyself any graven image, nor the likeness of any thing that is in heaven above, or in the earth beneath, or in the water under the earth. Thou shalt not bow down to them, nor worship them. For I the Lord thy God am a jealous God, and visit the sins of the fathers upon the children unto the third and fourth generation of them that hate me, and shew mercy unto thousands in them that love me and keep my commandments.

People. Lord, have mercy upon us, and incline our hearts to keep this law.

Minister. Thou shalt not take the Name of the Lord thy God in vain: for the Lord will not hold him guiltless, that taketh his Name in vain.

People. Lord, have mercy upon us, and incline our hearts to keep this law.

Minister. Remember that thou keep holy the Sabbath day. Six days shalt thou labour, and do all that thou hast to do; but the seventh day is the Sabbath of the Lord thy God. In it thou shalt do no manner of work, thou, and thy son, and thy daughter, thy man-servant, and thy maid-servant, thy cattle, and the stranger that is within thy gates. For in six days the Lord made heaven and earth, the sea, and all that in them is, and rested the seventh day: wherefore the Lord blessed the seventh day, and hallowed it.

People. Lord, have mercy upon us, and incline our hearts to keep this law.

Minister. Honour thy father and thy mother; that thy days may be long in the land which the Lord thy God giveth thee.

People. Lord, have mercy upon us, and incline our hearts to keep this law.

Minister. Thou shalt do no murder.

People. Lord, have mercy upon us, and incline our hearts to keep this law.

Minister. Thou shalt not commit adultery.

People. Lord, have mercy upon us, and incline our hearts to keep this law.

Minister. Thou shalt not steal.

People. Lord, have mercy upon us, and incline our hearts to keep this law.

Minister. Thou shalt not bear false witness against thy neighbour.

People. Lord, have mercy upon us, and incline our hearts to keep this law.

Minister. Thou shalt not covet thy neighbour's house, thou shalt not covet thy neighbour's wife, nor his servant, nor his maid, nor his ox, nor his ass, nor any thing that is his.

People. Lord, have mercy upon us, and write all these thy laws in our hearts, we beseech thee.

Then shall follow one of these two Collects for the Queen, the Priest standing as before, and saying,

Let us pray.

ALMIGHTY God, whose kingdom is everlasting, and power infinite: Have mercy upon the whole Church; and so rule the heart of thy chosen servant *ELIZABETH*, our Queen and Governor, that she (knowing whose minister she is) may above all things seek thy honour and glory: and that we and all her subjects (duly considering whose authority she hath) may faithfully serve, honour, and humbly obey her, in thee, and for thee, according to thy blessed Word and ordinance; through Jesus Christ our Lord, who with thee and the Holy Ghost liveth and reigneth, ever one God, world without end. *Amen.*

Or,

ALMIGHTY and everlasting God, we are taught by thy holy Word, that the hearts of Kings are in thy rule and governance, and that thou dost dispose and turn them as it seemeth best to thy godly wisdom: We humbly beseech thee so to dispose and govern the heart of *ELIZABETH* thy servant, our Queen and Governor, that in all her thoughts, words, and works, she may ever seek thy honour and glory, and study to preserve thy people committed to her charge, in wealth, peace and godliness: Grant this, O merciful Father, for thy dear Son's sake, Jesus Christ our Lord. *Amen.*

Then shall be said the Collect of the Day. And immediately after the Collect the Priest shall read the Epistle, saying, The Epistle [*or,* The portion of Scripture appointed for the Epistle] is written in the —— Chapter of —— beginning at the —— Verse. *And the Epistle ended, he shall say,* Here endeth the Epistle. *Then shall he read the Gospel* (*the people all standing up*) *saying,* The holy Gospel is written in the —— Chapter of —— beginning at the —— Verse. *And the Gospel ended, shall be sung or said the Creed following, the people still standing as before.*

I BELIEVE in one God the Father Almighty, Maker of heaven and earth, And of all things visible and invisible:

And in one Lord Jesus Christ, the only-begotten Son of God, Begotten of his Father before all worlds, God of God, Light of Light, Very God of very God, Begotten, not made, Being of one substance with the Father, By whom all things were made: Who for us men and for our salvation came down from heaven, And was incarnate by the Holy Ghost of the Virgin Mary, And was made man, And was crucified also for us under Pontius Pilate. He suffered and was buried, And the third day he rose again according to the Scriptures, And ascended into heaven, And sitteth on the right hand of the Father. And he shall come again with glory to judge both the quick and the dead: Whose kingdom shall have no end.

And I believe in the Holy Ghost, The Lord and giver of life, Who proceedeth from the Father and the Son, Who with the Father and the Son together is worshipped and glorified, Who spake by the Prophets. And I believe one Catholick and Apostolick Church. I acknowledge one Baptism for the remission of sins. And I look for the Resurrection of the dead, And the life of the world to come. Amen.

Then the Curate shall declare unto the people what Holy-days, or Fasting-days, are in the week following to be observed. And then also (if occasion be) shall notice be given of the Communion; and Briefs, Citations, and Excommunications read. And nothing shall be proclaimed or published in the Church during the time of Divine Service, but by the Minister: nor by him any thing but what is prescribed in the Rules of this Book, or enjoined by the Queen, or by the Ordinary of the place.

Then shall follow the Sermon, or one of the Homilies already set forth, or hereafter to be set forth, by authority.

Then shall the Priest return to the Lord's Table, and begin the Offertory, saying one or more of these Sentences following, as he thinketh most convenient in his discretion.

LET your light so shine before men, that they may see your good works, and glorify your Father which is in heaven.

S. Matth. 5.

Lay not up for yourselves treasure upon the earth; where the rust and moth doth corrupt, and where thieves break through and steal: but lay up for yourselves treasures in heaven; where neither rust nor moth doth corrupt, and where thieves do not break through and steal. *S. Matth.* 6.

Whatsoever ye would that men should do unto you, even so do unto them; for this is the Law and the Prophets. *S. Matth.* 7.

Not every one that saith unto me, Lord, Lord, shall enter into the kingdom of heaven; but he that doeth the will of my Father which is in heaven. *S. Matth.* 7.

Zacchæus stood forth, and said unto the Lord, Behold, Lord, the half of my goods I give to the poor; and if I have done any wrong to any man, I restore four-fold. *S. Luke* 19.

Who goeth a warfare at any time of his own cost? who planteth a vineyard, and eateth not of the fruit thereof? or who feedeth a flock, and eateth not of the milk of the flock? 1 *Cor.* 9.

If we have sown unto you spiritual things, is it a great matter if we shall reap your worldly things? 1 *Cor.* 9.

Do ye not know that they who minister about holy things live of the sacrifice; and they who wait at the altar are partakers with the altar? Even so hath the Lord also ordained, that they who preach the Gospel should live of the Gospel. 1 *Cor.* 9.

He that soweth little shall reap little; and he that soweth plenteously shall reap plenteously. Let every man do according as he is disposed in his heart, not grudging, or of necessity; for God loveth a cheerful giver. 2 *Cor.* 9.

Let him that is taught in the word minister unto him that teacheth, in all good things. Be not deceived, God is not mocked: for whatsoever a man soweth that shall he reap. *Gal.* 6.

While we have time, let us do good unto all men; and specially unto them that are of the household of faith. *Gal.* 6.

Godliness is great riches, if a man be content with that he hath: for we brought nothing into the world, neither may we carry any thing out. 1 *Tim.* 6.

Charge them who are rich in this world, that they be ready to give, and glad to distribute; laying up in store for themselves a good foundation against the time to come, that they may attain eternal life. *1 Tim.* 6.

God is not unrighteous, that he will forget your works, and labour that proceedeth of love; which love ye have shewed for his name's sake, who have ministered unto the saints, and yet do minister. *Hebr.* 6.

To do good and to distribute forget not; for with such sacrifices God is pleased. *Hebr.* 13.

Whoso hath this world's good, and seeth his brother have need, and shutteth up his compassion from him, how dwelleth the love of God in him? *1 S. John* 3.

Give alms of thy goods, and never turn thy face from any poor man; and then the face of the Lord shall not be turned away from thee. *Tobit* 4.

Be merciful after thy power. If thou hast much, give plenteously; if thou hast little, do thy diligence gladly to give of that little; for so gatherest thou thyself a good reward in the day of necessity. *Tobit* 4.

He that hath pity upon the poor lendeth unto the Lord: and look, what he layeth out, it shall be paid him again. *Prov.* 19.

Blessed be the man that provideth for the sick and needy: the Lord shall deliver him in the time of trouble. *Psal.* 41.

Whilst these Sentences are in reading, the Deacons, Churchwardens, or other fit person appointed for that purpose, shall receive the Alms for the Poor, and other devotions of the people, in a decent bason to be provided by the Parish for that purpose; and reverently bring it to the Priest, who shall humbly present and place it upon the holy Table.

And when there is a Communion, the Priest shall then place upon the Table so much Bread and Wine as he shall think sufficient. After which done, the Priest shall say,

Let us pray for the whole state of Christ's
Church militant here in earth.

ALMIGHTY and everliving God, who by thy holy Apostle hast taught us to make prayers and supplications, and to give thanks, for all men: We humbly beseech thee most mercifully [*to accept our alms and oblations, and] to receive these our prayers, which we offer unto thy Divine Majesty; beseeching thee to inspire continually the universal Church with the spirit of truth, unity, and concord: And grant, that all they that do confess thy holy Name may agree in the truth of thy holy Word, and live in unity, and godly love. We beseech thee also to save and defend all Christian Kings, Princes, and Governors; and specially thy servant *ELIZABETH* our Queen; that under her we may be godly and quietly governed: And grant unto her whole Council, and to all that are put in authority under her, that they may truly and indifferently minister justice, to the punishment of wickedness and vice, and to the maintenance of thy true religion, and virtue. Give grace, O heavenly Father, to all Bishops and Curates, that they may both by their life and doctrine set forth thy true and lively Word, and rightly and duly administer thy holy Sacraments: And to all thy people give thy heavenly grace; and specially to this congregation here present; that, with meek heart and due reverence, they may hear, and receive thy holy Word; truly serving thee in holiness and righteousness all the days of their life. And we most humbly beseech thee of thy goodness, O Lord, to comfort and succour all them, who in this transitory life are in trouble, sorrow, need, sickness, or any other adversity. And we also bless thy holy Name for all thy servants departed this life in thy faith and fear; beseeching thee to give us grace so to follow their good examples, that with them we may be partakers of thy heavenly kingdom: Grant this, O Father, for Jesus Christ's sake, our only Mediator and Advocate. *Amen.*

When the Minister giveth warning for the Celebration of the holy Communion, (which he shall always do upon the Sunday, or some Holy-day, immediately preceding,) after the Sermon or Homily ended, he shall read this Exhortation following.

*If there be no alms or oblations, then shall the words [of accepting our alms and oblations] be left out unsaid.

DEARLY beloved, on —day next I purpose, through God's assistance, to administer to all such as shall be religiously and devoutly disposed the most comfortable Sacrament of the Body and Blood of Christ; to be by them received in remembrance of his meritorious Cross and Passion, whereby alone we obtain remission of our sins, and are made partakers of the kingdom of heaven. Wherefore it is our duty to render most humble and hearty thanks to Almighty God our heavenly Father, for that he hath given his Son our Saviour Jesus Christ, not only to die for us, but also to be our spiritual food and sustenance in that holy Sacrament. Which being so divine and comfortable a thing to them who receive it worthily, and so dangerous to them that will presume to receive it unworthily; my duty is to exhort you in the mean season to consider the dignity of that holy mystery, and the great peril of the unworthy receiving thereof; and so to search and examine your own consciences, and that not lightly, and after the manner of dissemblers with God: but so that ye may come holy and clean to such a heavenly Feast, in the marriage-garment required by God in holy Scripture, and be received as worthy partakers of that holy Table.

The way and means thereto is; First, to examine your lives and conversations by the rule of God's commandments; and whereinsoever ye shall perceive yourselves to have offended, either by will, word, or deed, there to bewail your own sinfulness, and to confess yourselves to Almighty God, with full purpose of amendment of life. And if ye shall perceive your offences to be such as are not only against God, but also against your neighbours; then ye shall reconcile yourselves unto them; being ready to make restitution and satisfaction, according to the uttermost of your powers, for all injuries and wrongs done by you to any other; and being likewise ready to forgive others that have offended you, as you would have forgiveness of your offences at God's hand; for otherwise the receiving of the holy Communion doth nothing else but increase your damnation. Therefore if any of you be a blasphemer of God, an hinderer or slanderer of his Word, an adulterer, or be in malice, or envy, or in any other grievous crime, repent you of your sins, or else come not to that holy Table; lest, after the taking of that holy Sacrament, the devil enter into you, as he entered into Judas, and fill you full of all iniquities, and bring you to destruction both of body and soul.

And because it is requisite, that no man should come to the holy Communion, but with a full trust in God's mercy, and with a quiet conscience; therefore if there be any of you, who by this means cannot quiet his own conscience herein, but requireth further comfort or counsel, let him come to me, or to some other discreet and learned Minister of God's Word, and open his grief; that by the ministry of God's holy Word he may receive the benefit of absolution, together with ghostly counsel and advice, to the quieting of his conscience, and avoiding of all scruple and doubtfulness.

Or, in case he shall see the people negligent to come to the holy Communion, instead of the former, he shall use this Exhortation.

DEARLY beloved brethren, on —— I intend, by God's grace, to celebrate the Lord's Supper: unto which, in God's behalf, I bid you all that are here present; and beseech you, for the Lord Jesus Christ's sake, that ye will not refuse to come thereto, being so lovingly called and bidden by God himself. Ye know how grievous and unkind a thing it is, when a man hath prepared a rich feast, decked his table with all kind of provision, so that there lacketh nothing but the guests to sit down; and yet they who are called (without any cause) most unthankfully refuse to come. Which of you in such a case would not be moved? Who would not think a great injury and wrong done unto him? Wherefore, most dearly beloved in Christ, take ye good heed, lest ye, withdrawing yourselves from this holy Supper, provoke God's indignation against you. It is an easy matter for a man to say, I will not communicate, because I am otherwise hindered with worldly business. But such excuses are not so easily accepted and allowed before God. If any man say, I am a grievous sinner, and therefore am afraid to come: wherefore then do ye not repent and amend? When God calleth you, are ye not

ashamed to say ye will not come? When ye should return to
God, will ye excuse yourselves, and say ye are not ready? Consider earnestly with yourselves how little such feigned excuses
will avail before God. They that refused the feast in the Gospel,
because they had bought a farm, or would try their yokes of
oxen, or because they were married, were not so excused, but
counted unworthy of the heavenly feast. I, for my part, shall be
ready; and, according to mine Office, I bid you in the Name of
God, I call you in Christ's behalf, I exhort you, as ye love your
own salvation, that ye will be partakers of this holy Communion. And as the Son of God did vouchsafe to yield up his soul
by death upon the Cross for your salvation; so it is your duty to
receive the Communion, in remembrance of the sacrifice of his
death, as he himself hath commanded: which if ye shall neglect
to do, consider with yourselves how great injury ye do unto God,
and how sore punishment hangeth over your heads for the same;
when ye wilfully abstain from the Lord's Table, and separate
from your brethren, who come to feed on the banquet of that
most heavenly food. These things if ye earnestly consider, ye
will by God's grace return to a better mind: for the obtaining
whereof we shall not cease to make our humble petitions unto
Almighty God our heavenly Father.

*At the time of the Celebration of the Communion, the Com-
municants being conveniently placed for the receiving of the
holy Sacrament, the Priest shall say this Exhortation.*

DEARLY beloved in the Lord, ye that mind to come to the
holy Communion of the Body and Blood of our Saviour Christ,
must consider how Saint Paul exhorteth all persons diligently to
try and examine themselves, before they presume to eat of that
Bread, and drink of that Cup. For as the benefit is great, if
with a true penitent heart and lively faith we receive that holy
Sacrament; (for then we spiritually eat the flesh of Christ, and
drink his blood; then we dwell in Christ, and Christ in us; we
are one with Christ, and Christ with us;) so is the danger great,
if we receive the same unworthily. For then we are guilty of the
Body and Blood of Christ our Saviour; we eat and drink our

own damnation, not considering the Lord's Body; we kindle
God's wrath against us; we provoke him to plague us with divers
diseases, and sundry kinds of death. Judge therefore yourselves,
brethren, that ye be not judged of the Lord; repent you truly for
your sins past; have a lively and stedfast faith in Christ our
Saviour; amend your lives, and be in perfect charity with all
men; so shall ye be meet partakers of those holy mysteries. And
above all things ye must give most humble and hearty thanks to
God, the Father, the Son, and the Holy Ghost, for the redemption of the world by the death and passion of our Saviour Christ,
both God and man; who did humble himself, even to the death
upon the Cross, for us miserable sinners, who lay in darkness
and the shadow of death; that he might make us the children of
God, and exalt us to everlasting life. And to the end that we
should alway remember the exceeding great love of our Master
and only Saviour Jesus Christ, thus dying for us, and the innumerable benefits which by his precious blood-shedding he hath
obtained to us; he hath instituted and ordained holy mysteries,
as pledges of his love, and for a continual remembrance of his
death, to our great and endless comfort. To him therefore, with
the Father and the Holy Ghost, let us give (as we are most
bounden) continual thanks; submitting ourselves wholly to his
holy will and pleasure, and studying to serve him in true holiness
and righteousness all the days of our life. *Amen.*

*Then shall the Priest say to them that come to receive the holy
Communion,*

YE that do truly and earnestly repent you of your sins, and are
in love and charity with your neighbours, and intend to lead a
new life, following the commandments of God, and walking
from henceforth in his holy ways: Draw near with faith, and
take this holy Sacrament to your comfort; and make your
humble confession to Almighty God, meekly kneeling upon
your knees.

*Then shall this general Confession be made, in the name of all
those that are minded to receive the holy Communion, by one*

of the Ministers: both he and all the people kneeling humbly upon their knees and saying,

ALMIGHTY God, Father of our Lord Jesus Christ, Maker of all things, Judge of all men: We acknowledge and bewail our manifold sins and wickedness, Which we from time to time most grievously have committed, By thought, word, and deed, Against thy Divine Majesty, Provoking most justly thy wrath and indignation against us. We do earnestly repent, And are heartily sorry for these our misdoings; The remembrance of them is grievous unto us; The burden of them is intolerable. Have mercy upon us, Have mercy upon us, most merciful Father; For thy Son our Lord Jesus Christ's sake, Forgive us all that is past; And grant that we may ever hereafter Serve and please thee In newness of life, To the honour and glory of thy Name; Through Jesus Christ our Lord. Amen.

Then shall the Priest (or the Bishop, being present,) stand up, and turning himself to the people, pronounce this Absolution

ALMIGHTY God, our heavenly Father, who of his great mercy hath promised forgiveness of sins to all them that with hearty repentance and true faith turn unto him; Have mercy upon you; pardon and deliver you from all your sins; confirm and strengthen you in all goodness; and bring you to everlasting life; through Jesus Christ our Lord. *Amen.*

Then shall the Priest say,

Hear what comfortable words our Saviour
Christ saith unto all that truly turn to him.

COME unto me all that travail and are heavy laden, and I will refresh you. *S. Matth.* 11. 28.

So God loved the world, that he gave his only-begotten Son, to the end that all that believe in him should not perish, but have everlasting life. *S. John* 3. 16.

Hear also what Saint Paul saith.

This is a true saying, and worthy of all men to be received, that Christ Jesus came into the world to save sinners.

1 *Tim.* 1. 15.

Hear also what Saint John saith.

If any man sin, we have an Advocate with the Father, Jesus Christ the righteous; and he is the propitiation for our sins.

1 *S. John* 2. 1.

After which the Priest shall proceed, saying,

Lift up your hearts.

Answer. We lift them up unto the Lord.

Priest. Let us give thanks unto our Lord God.

Answer. It is meet and right so to do.

Then shall the Priest turn to the Lord's Table and say,

IT is very meet, right, and our bounden duty, that we should at all times, and in all places, give thanks unto thee, O Lord, *Holy Father, Almighty, Everlasting God.

Here shall follow the proper Preface, according to the time, if there be any specially appointed: or else immediately shall follow,

THEREFORE with Angels and Archangels, and with all the company of heaven, we laud and magnify thy glorious Name; evermore praising thee, and saying: Holy, holy, holy, Lord God of hosts, heaven and earth are full of thy glory: Glory be to thee, O Lord most High. Amen.

Proper Prefaces

Upon Christmas Day, *and seven days after.*

BECAUSE thou didst give Jesus Christ thine only Son to be born as at this time for us; who, by the operation of the Holy Ghost, was made very man of the substance of the Virgin Mary his mother; and that without spot of sin, to make us clean from all sin. Therefore with Angels, *&c.*

These words [Holy Father] *must be omitted on* Trinity Sunday.

Upon Easter Day, *and seven days after.*

BUT chiefly are we bound to praise thee for the glorious Resurrection of thy Son Jesus Christ our Lord: for he is the very Paschal Lamb, which was offered for us, and hath taken away the sin of the world; who by his death hath destroyed death, and by his rising to life again hath restored to us everlasting life. Therefore with Angels, *&c.*

Upon Ascension Day, *and seven days after.*

THROUGH thy most dearly beloved Son Jesus Christ our Lord; who after his most glorious Resurrection manifestly appeared to all his Apostles, and in their sight ascended up into heaven to prepare a place for us; that where he is, thither we might also ascend, and reign with him in glory. Therefore with Angels, *&c.*

Upon Whitsunday, *and six days after.*

THROUGH Jesus Christ our Lord; according to whose most true promise, the Holy Ghost came down as at this time from heaven with a sudden great sound, as it had been a mighty wind, in the likeness of fiery tongues, lighting upon the Apostles, to teach them, and to lead them to all truth; giving them both the gift of divers languages, and also boldness with fervent zeal constantly to preach the Gospel unto all nations; whereby we have been brought out of darkness and error into the clear light and true knowledge of thee, and of thy Son Jesus Christ. Therefore with Angels, *&c.*

Upon the Feast of Trinity *only.*

WHO art one God, one Lord; not one only Person, but three Persons in one Substance. For that which we believe of the glory of the Father, the same we believe of the Son, and of the Holy Ghost, without any difference or inequality. Therefore with Angels, *&c.*

After each of which Prefaces shall immediately be sung or said,

THEREFORE with Angels and Archangels, and with all the company of heaven, we laud and magnify thy glorious Name;

evermore praising thee, and saying: Holy, holy, holy, Lord God of hosts, heaven and earth are full of thy glory: Glory be to thee, O Lord most High. Amen.

Then shall the Priest, kneeling down at the Lord's Table, say in the name of all them that shall receive the Communion this Prayer following.

WE do not presume to come to this thy Table, O merciful Lord, trusting in our own righteousness, but in thy manifold and great mercies. We are not worthy so much as to gather up the crumbs under thy Table. But thou art the same Lord, whose property is always to have mercy: Grant us therefore, gracious Lord, so to eat the flesh of thy dear Son Jesus Christ, and to drink his blood, that our sinful bodies may be made clean by his body, and our souls washed through his most precious blood, and that we may evermore dwell in him, and he in us. *Amen.*

When the Priest, standing before the Table, hath so ordered the Bread and Wine, that he may with the more readiness and decency break the Bread before the people, and take the Cup into his hands, he shall say the Prayer of Consecration, as followeth.

ALMIGHTY God, our heavenly Father, who of thy tender mercy didst give thine only Son Jesus Christ to suffer death upon the Cross for our redemption; who made there (by his one oblation of himself once offered) a full, perfect, and sufficient sacrifice, oblation, and satisfaction, for the sins of the whole world; and did institute, and in his holy Gospel command us to continue, a perpetual memory of that his precious death, until his coming again: Hear us, O merciful Father, we most humbly beseech thee; and grant that we receiving these thy creatures of bread and wine, according to thy Son our Saviour Jesus Christ's holy institution, in remembrance of his death and passion, may be partakers of his most blessed Body and Blood: who, in the same night that he was betrayed, ᵃtook Bread; and, when he had

a *Here the Priest is to take the Paten into his hands:*

given thanks, [b]he brake it, and gave it to his disciples, saying, Take, eat; [c]this is my Body which is given for you: Do this in remembrance of me. Likewise after supper [d]he took the Cup; and, when he had given thanks, he gave it to them, saying, Drink ye all of this; for [e]this is my Blood of the New Testament, which is shed for you and for many for the remission of sins: Do this, as oft as ye shall drink it, in remembrance of me. *Amen.*

Then shall the Minister first receive the Communion in both kinds himself, and then proceed to deliver the same to the Bishops, Priests, and Deacons, in like manner, (if any be present,) and after that to the people also in order, into their hands, all meekly kneeling. And, when he delivereth the Bread to any one, he shall say,

THE Body of our Lord Jesus Christ, which was given for thee, preserve thy body and soul unto everlasting life: Take and eat this in remembrance that Christ died for thee, and feed on him in thy heart by faith with thanksgiving.

And the Minister that delivereth the Cup to any one shall say,

THE Blood of our Lord Jesus Christ, which was shed for thee, preserve thy body and soul unto everlasting life: Drink this in remembrance that Christ's Blood was shed for thee, and be thankful.

If the consecrated Bread or Wine be all spent before all have communicated, the Priest is to consecrate more according to the Form before prescribed: Beginning at [Our Saviour Christ in the same night, &c.] *for the blessing of the Bread: and at* [Likewise after Supper, &c.] *for the blessing of the Cup.*

When all have communicated, the Minister shall return to the Lord's Table, and reverently place upon it what remaineth

b *And here to break the Bread:*
c *And here to lay his hand upon all the Bread.*
d *Here he is to take the Cup into his hand:*
e *And here to lay his hand upon every vessel (be it Chalice or Flagon) in which there is any Wine to be consecrated.*

of the consecrated Elements, covering the same with a fair linen cloth.

Then shall the Priest say the Lord's Prayer, the people repeating after him every petition.

OUR Father which art in heaven, Hallowed be thy Name, Thy kingdom come, Thy will be done, in earth as it is in heaven. Give us this day our daily bread; And forgive us our trespasses, As we forgive them that trespass against us; And lead us not into temptation, But deliver us from evil. For thine is the kingdom, the power, and the glory, For ever and ever. Amen.

After shall be said as followeth.

O LORD and heavenly Father, we thy humble servants entirely desire thy fatherly goodness mercifully to accept this our sacrifice of praise and thanksgiving; most humbly beseeching thee to grant, that by the merits and death of thy Son Jesus Christ, and through faith in his blood, we and all thy whole Church may obtain remission of our sins, and all other benefits of his passion. And here we offer and present unto thee, O Lord, ourselves, our souls and bodies, to be a reasonable, holy, and lively sacrifice unto thee; humbly beseeching thee, that all we, who are partakers of this holy Communion, may be fulfilled with thy grace and heavenly benediction. And although we be unworthy, through our manifold sins, to offer unto thee any sacrifice, yet we beseech thee to accept this our bounden duty and service; not weighing our merits, but pardoning our offences, through Jesus Christ our Lord; by whom, and with whom, in the unity of the Holy Ghost, all honour and glory be unto thee, O Father Almighty, world without end. *Amen.*

Or this.

ALMIGHTY and everliving God, we most heartily thank thee, for that thou dost vouchsafe to feed us, who have duly received these holy mysteries, with the spiritual food of the most precious Body and Blood of thy Son our Saviour Jesus Christ; and dost assure us thereby of thy favour and goodness towards us; and that we are very members incorporate in the mystical body of thy Son, which is the blessed company of all faithful people; and are also heirs through hope of thy everlasting kingdom, by the merits of the most precious death and passion of thy dear Son. And we most humbly beseech thee, O heavenly Father, so to assist us with thy grace, that we may continue in that holy fellowship, and do all such good works as thou hast prepared for us to walk in; through Jesus Christ our Lord, to whom, with thee and the Holy Ghost, be all honour and glory, world without end. *Amen.*

Then shall be said or sung,

GLORY be to God on high, and in earth peace, good will towards men. We praise thee, we bless thee, we worship thee, we glorify thee, we give thanks to thee for thy great glory, O Lord God, heavenly King, God the Father Almighty.

O Lord, the only-begotten Son, Jesu Christ; O Lord God, Lamb of God, Son of the Father, that takest away the sins of the world, have mercy upon us. Thou that takest away the sins of the world, have mercy upon us. Thou that takest away the sins of the world, receive our prayer. Thou that sittest at the right hand of God the Father, have mercy upon us.

For thou only art holy; thou only art the Lord; thou only, O Christ, with the Holy Ghost, art most high in the glory of God the Father. Amen.

Then the Priest (or Bishop if he be present) shall let them depart with this Blessing.

THE peace of God, which passeth all understanding, keep your hearts and minds in the knowledge and love of God, and of his Son Jesus Christ our Lord: And the blessing of God Almighty, the Father, the Son, and the Holy Ghost, be amongst you and remain with you always. *Amen.*

Collects to be said after the Offertory, when there is no Communion, every such day one or more; and the same may be said also, as often as occasion shall serve, after the Collects either of

Morning or Evening Prayer, Communion, or Litany, by the discretion of the Minister.

ASSIST us mercifully, O Lord, in these our supplications and prayers, and dispose the way of thy servants towards the attainment of everlasting salvation; that, among all the changes and chances of this mortal life, they may ever be defended by thy most gracious and ready help; through Jesus Christ our Lord. *Amen.*

O ALMIGHTY Lord, and everlasting God, vouchsafe, we beseech thee, to direct, sanctify, and govern, both our hearts and bodies, in the ways of thy laws, and in the works of thy commandments; that through thy most mighty protection, both here and ever, we may be preserved in body and soul; through our Lord and Saviour Jesus Christ. *Amen.*

GRANT, we beseech thee, Almighty God, that the words, which we have heard this day with our outward ears, may through thy grace be so grafted inwardly in our hearts, that they may bring forth in us the fruit of good living, to the honour and praise of thy Name; through Jesus Christ our Lord. *Amen.*

PREVENT us, O Lord, in all our doings with thy most gracious favour, and further us with thy continual help; that in all our works, begun, continued, and ended in thee, we may glorify thy holy Name, and finally by thy mercy obtain everlasting life; through Jesus Christ our Lord. *Amen.*

ALMIGHTY God, the fountain of all wisdom, who knowest our necessities before we ask, and our ignorance in asking: We beseech thee to have compassion upon our infirmities; and those things, which for our unworthiness we dare not, and for our blindness we cannot ask, vouchsafe to give us for the worthiness of thy Son Jesus Christ our Lord. *Amen.*

ALMIGHTY God, who hast promised to hear the petitions of them that ask in thy Son's Name: We beseech thee mercifully to incline thine ears to us that have made now our prayers and supplications unto thee; and grant that those things, which we have faithfully asked according to thy will, may effectually be obtained, to the relief of our necessity, and to the setting forth of thy glory; through Jesus Christ our Lord. *Amen.*

Upon the Sundays and other Holy-days (if there be no Communion) shall be said all that is appointed at the Communion, until the end of the general Prayer [For the whole state of Christ's Church militant here in earth] *together with one or more of these Collects last before rehearsed, concluding with the Blessing.*

And there shall be no Celebration of the Lord's Supper, except there be a convenient number to communicate with the Priest, according to his discretion.

And if there be not above twenty persons in the Parish of discretion to receive the Communion: yet there shall be no Communion, except four (or three at the least) communicate with the Priest.

And in Cathedral and Collegiate Churches, and Colleges, where there are many Priests and Deacons, they shall all receive the Communion with the Priest every Sunday at the least, except they have a reasonable cause to the contrary.

And to take away all occasion of dissension, and superstition, which any person hath or might have concerning the Bread and Wine, it shall suffice that the Bread be such as is usual to be eaten; but the best and purest Wheat Bread that conveniently may be gotten.

And if any of the Bread and Wine remain unconsecrated, the Curate shall have it to his own use: but if any remain of that which was consecrated, it shall not be carried out of the Church, but the Priest, and such other of the Communicants as he shall then call unto him, shall, immediately after the Blessing, reverently eat and drink the same.

The Bread and Wine for the Communion shall be provided by the Curate and the Church-wardens at the charges of the Parish.

And note, that every Parishioner shall communicate at the least three times in the year, of which Easter to be one. And yearly at Easter every Parishioner shall reckon with the Parson, Vicar, or Curate, or his or their Deputy or Deputies; and pay to them or him all Ecclesiastical Duties, accustomably due, then and at that time to be paid.

After the Divine Service ended, the money given at the Offertory shall be disposed of to such pious and charitable uses, as the Minister and Church-wardens shall think fit. Wherein if they disagree, it shall be disposed of as the Ordinary shall appoint.

Whereas it is ordained in this office for the Administration of the Lord's Supper, that the Communicants should receive the same kneeling; (which order is well meant, for a signification of our humble and grateful acknowledgement of the benefits of Christ therein given to all worthy Receivers, and for the avoiding of such profanation and disorder in the holy Communion, as might otherwise ensue;) yet, lest the same kneeling should by any persons, either out of ignorance and infirmity, or out of malice and obstinacy, be misconstrued and depraved: It is here declared, that thereby no Adoration is intended, or ought to be done, either unto the Sacramental Bread or Wine there bodily received, or unto any Corporal Presence of Christ's natural Flesh and Blood. For the Sacramental Bread and Wine remain still in their very natural substances, and therefore may not be adored; (for that were Idolatry, to be abhorred of all faithful Christians;) and the natural Body and Blood of our Saviour Christ are in Heaven, and not here; it being against the truth of Christ's natural Body to be at one time in more places than one.

THE MINISTRATION OF

PUBLICK BAPTISM
OF INFANTS

TO BE USED IN THE CHURCH

Due notice, normally of at least a week, shall be given before a Child is brought to the church to be baptized.

For every child to be baptized there shall be not fewer than three godparents, of whom at least two shall be of the same sex as the child and of whom at least one shall be of the opposite sex; save that, when three cannot conveniently be had, one godfather and one godmother shall suffice. Parents may be godparents for their own children provided that the child shall have at least one other godparent. The godparents shall be persons who have been baptized and confirmed and will faithfully fulfil their responsibilities both by their care for the child committed to their charge and by the example of their own godly living. Nevertheless the Minister shall have power to dispense with the requirement of confirmation in any case in which in his judgement need so requires.

The Minister shall instruct the parents or guardians of an infant to be admitted to Holy Baptism that the same responsibilities rest on them as are in the service of Holy Baptism required of the godparents.

No Minister shall refuse or, save for the purpose of preparing or instructing the parents or guardians or godparents, delay to baptize any infant within his cure that is brought to the church to be baptized, provided that due notice has been given and the provisions relating to godparents are observed. If the Minister shall refuse or unduly delay to baptize any such infant, the parents or guardians may apply to the Bishop of the diocese who shall, after consultation with the Minister, give such directions as he thinks fit.

The Minister, before proceeding to the Baptism, shall have satisfied himself that the child presented to him has not already been baptized.

At the time appointed the godfathers and godmothers and the parents or guardians with the child must be ready at the Font, and the Priest coming to the Font (which is then to be filled with pure Water,) and standing there, shall proceed as follows.

DEARLY beloved, forasmuch as all men are conceived and born in sin, and that our Saviour Christ saith, none can enter into the kingdom of God, except he be regenerate and born anew of Water and of the Holy Ghost: I beseech you to call upon God the Father, through our Lord Jesus Christ, that of his bounteous mercy he will grant to *this Child* that thing which by nature *he* cannot have; that *he* may be baptized with Water and the Holy Ghost, and received into Christ's holy Church, and be made *a lively member* of the same.

Then shall the Priest say,

Let us pray.

ALMIGHTY and everlasting God, who of thy great mercy didst save Noah and his family in the ark from perishing by water; and also didst safely lead the children of Israel thy people through the Red Sea, figuring thereby thy holy Baptism; and by the Baptism of thy well-beloved Son Jesus Christ, in the river Jordan, didst sanctify Water to the mystical washing away of sin: We beseech thee, for thine infinite mercies, that thou wilt mercifully look upon *this Child*; wash *him* and sanctify *him* with the Holy Ghost; that *he*, being delivered from thy wrath, may be received into the ark of Christ's Church; and being stedfast in faith, joyful through hope, and rooted in charity, may so pass the waves of this troublesome world, that finally *he* may come to the land of everlasting life, there to reign with thee world without end, through Jesus Christ our Lord. *Amen.*

ALMIGHTY and immortal God, the aid of all that need, the helper of all that flee to thee for succour, the life of them that believe, and the resurrection of the dead: We call upon thee for *this Infant*, that *he*, coming to thy holy Baptism, may receive remission of *his* sins by spiritual regeneration. Receive *him*, O Lord, as thou hast promised by thy well-beloved Son, saying, Ask, and ye shall have; seek, and ye shall find; knock, and it shall be opened unto you: So give now unto us that ask; let us that seek find; open the gate unto us that knock; that *this Infant* may enjoy the everlasting benediction of thy heavenly washing, and may come to the eternal kingdom which thou hast promised by Christ our Lord. *Amen.*

Then shall the people stand up, and the Priest shall say,

Hear the words of the Gospel, written by Saint Mark in the tenth chapter at the thirteenth verse.

THEY brought young children to Christ, that he should touch them; and his disciples rebuked those that brought them. But when Jesus saw it, he was much displeased, and said unto them, Suffer little children to come unto me, and forbid them not; for of such is the kingdom of God. Verily I say unto you, Whosoever shall not receive the kingdom of God as a little child, he shall not enter therein. And he took them up in his arms, put his hands upon them, and blessed them.

After the Gospel is read, the Minister shall make this brief exhortation upon the words of the Gospel.

BELOVED, ye hear in this Gospel the words of our Saviour Christ, that he commanded the children to be brought unto him; how he blamed those that would have kept them from him; how he exhorteth all men to follow their innocency. Ye perceive how by his outward gesture and deed he declared his good will toward them; for he embraced them in his arms, he laid his hands upon them, and blessed them. Doubt ye not therefore, but earnestly believe, that he will likewise favourably receive *this* present *Infant*; that he will embrace *him* with the arms of his mercy; that he will give unto *him* the blessing of eternal life, and make *him partaker* of his everlasting kingdom. Wherefore we being thus persuaded of the good will of our heavenly Father towards *this Infant*, declared by his Son Jesus Christ; and nothing doubting but that he favourably alloweth this charitable work of ours in bringing *this Infant* to his holy Baptism; let us faithfully and devoutly give thanks unto him, and say,

ALMIGHTY and everlasting God, heavenly Father, we give thee humble thanks that thou hast vouchsafed to call us to the knowledge of thy grace and faith in thee: Increase this know-ledge, and confirm this faith in us evermore. Give thy Holy Spirit to *this Infant*, that *he* may be born again, and be made *an heir* of everlasting salvation, through our Lord Jesus Christ, who liveth and reigneth with thee and the Holy Spirit, now and for ever. *Amen.*

Then shall the Priest speak unto the Godfathers and God-mothers on this wise.

DEARLY beloved, ye have brought *this Child* here to be bap-tized; ye have prayed that our Lord Jesus Christ would vouch-safe to receive *him*, to release *him* of *his* sins, to sanctify *him* with the Holy Ghost, to give *him* the kingdom of heaven and everlasting life. Ye have heard also that our Lord Jesus Christ hath promised in his Gospel, to grant all these things that ye have prayed for: which promise he, for his part, will most surely keep and perform. Wherefore, after this promise made by Christ, *this Infant* must also faithfully, for *his* part, promise by you that are *his* sureties, (until *he* come of age to take it upon *himself,*) that *he* will renounce the devil and all his works, and constantly believe God's holy Word, and obediently keep his commandments.

I demand therefore,

DOST thou, in the name of this Child, renounce the devil and all his works, the vain pomp and glory of the world, with all covetous desires of the same, and the carnal desires of the flesh, so that thou wilt not follow nor be led by them?

Answer. I renounce them all.

Minister.

DOST thou believe in God the Father Almighty, Maker of heaven and earth?

And in Jesus Christ his only-begotten Son our Lord? And that he was conceived by the Holy Ghost, born of the Virgin Mary; that he suffered under Pontius Pilate, was crucified, dead, and buried; that he went down into hell, and also did rise again the third day; that he ascended into heaven, and sitteth at the right hand of God the Father Almighty; and from thence shall come again at the end of the world, to judge the quick and the dead?

And dost thou believe in the Holy Ghost; the holy Catholick Church; the Communion of Saints; the Remission of sins; the Resurrection of the flesh; and everlasting life after death?

Answer. All this I stedfastly believe.

Minister.

WILT thou be baptized in this faith?

Answer. That is my desire.

Minister.

WILT thou then obediently keep God's holy will and commandments, and walk in the same all the days of thy life?

Answer. I will.

Then shall the Priest say,

O MERCIFUL God, grant that the old Adam in *this Child* may be so buried, that the new man may be raised up in *him*. *Amen.*

Grant that all carnal affections may die in *him*, and that all things belonging to the Spirit may live and grow in *him*. *Amen.*

Grant that *he* may have power and strength, to have victory, and to triumph against the devil, the world, and the flesh. *Amen.*

Grant that whosoever is here dedicated to thee by our office and ministry may also be endued with heavenly virtues, and everlastingly rewarded, through thy mercy, O blessed Lord God, who dost live, and govern all things, world without end. *Amen.*

ALMIGHTY everliving God, whose most dearly beloved Son Jesus Christ, for the forgiveness of our sins, did shed out of his most precious side both water and blood; and gave commandment to his disciples, that they should go teach all nations, and baptize them in the Name of the Father, and of the Son, and of the Holy Ghost: Regard, we beseech thee, the supplications of thy Congregation; sanctify this Water to the mystical washing away of sin; and grant that *this Child*, now to be baptized therein, may receive the fulness of thy grace, and ever remain in the number of thy faithful and elect children; through Jesus Christ our Lord. *Amen.*

Then the Priest shall take the Child into his hands, and shall say to the Godfathers and Godmothers, Name this Child. *And then naming it after them (if they shall certify him that the Child may well endure it) he shall dip it in the Water discreetly and warily, saying,*

N. I baptize thee in the Name of the Father, and of the Son, and of the Holy Ghost. Amen.

But if they certify that the Child is weak, it shall suffice to pour Water upon it, saying the foresaid words,

N. I baptize thee in the Name of the Father, and of the Son, and of the Holy Ghost. Amen.

Then the Priest shall say,

WE receive this Child into the Congregation of Christ's flock, *and do sign *him* with the sign of the Cross, in token that hereafter *he* shall not be ashamed to confess the faith of Christ crucified, and manfully to fight under his banner against sin, the

*Here the Priest shall make a Cross upon the Child's forehead.

world, and the devil, and to continue Christ's faithful soldier and servant unto *his* life's end. Amen.

Then shall the Priest say,

SEEING now, dearly beloved brethren, that *this Child is* regenerate and grafted into the body of Christ's Church, let us give thanks unto Almighty God for these benefits, and with one accord make our prayers unto him, that *this Child* may lead the rest of *his* life according to this beginning.

Then shall be said, all kneeling,

OUR Father which art in heaven, Hallowed be thy Name, Thy kingdom come, Thy will be done, in earth as it is in heaven. Give us this day our daily bread; And forgive us our trespasses, As we forgive them that trespass against us; And lead us not into temptation, But deliver us from evil. Amen.

Then shall the Priest say,

WE yield thee hearty thanks, most merciful Father, that it hath pleased thee to regenerate *this Infant* with thy Holy Spirit, to receive *him* for thine own *Child* by adoption, and to incorporate *him* into thy holy Church. And humbly we beseech thee to grant that *he* being dead unto sin, and living unto righteousness, and being buried with Christ in his death, may crucify the old man, and utterly abolish the whole body of sin; and that, as *he* is made *partaker* of the death of thy Son, *he* may also be *partaker* of his resurrection; so that finally, with the residue of thy holy Church, *he* may be *an inheritor* of thine everlasting kingdom; through Christ our Lord. *Amen.*

Then, all standing up, the Priest shall say to the Godfathers and Godmothers this exhortation following.

FORASMUCH as *this Child hath* promised by you *his* sureties to renounce the devil and all his works, to believe in God, and to serve him: Ye must remember that it is your parts and duties to see that *this Infant* be taught, so soon as *he* shall be able to learn, what a solemn vow, promise and profession *he hath* here made by you. And that *he* may know these things the better, ye shall call upon *him* to hear sermons; and chiefly ye shall provide that *he* may learn the Creed, the Lord's Prayer and the Ten Commandments in the vulgar tongue, and all other things which a Christian ought to know and believe to his soul's health; and that *this Child* may be virtuously brought up to lead a godly and a Christian life; remembering always, that Baptism doth represent unto us our profession; which is, to follow the example of our Saviour Christ, and to be made like unto him; that as he died and rose again for us, so should we, who are baptized, die from sin and rise again unto righteousness, continually mortifying all our evil and corrupt affections, and daily proceeding in all virtue and godliness of living.

Then shall he add and say,

YE are to take care that *this Child* be brought to the Bishop to be confirmed by him, so soon as *he* can say the Creed, the Lord's Prayer and the Ten Commandments in the vulgar tongue, and be further instructed in the Church Catechism set forth for that purpose.

It is certain by God's Word, that children which are baptized, dying before they commit actual sin, are undoubtedly saved.

To take away all scruple concerning the use of the sign of the Cross in Baptism; the true explication thereof, and the just reasons for the retaining of it, may be seen in the xxxth Canon, first published in the year MDCIV.

THE MINISTRATION OF
PRIVATE BAPTISM OF CHILDREN
IN HOUSES

The Minister of every parish shall warn the people that with-out great cause and necessity they procure not their children to be baptized at home in their houses. But when need shall compel them so to do, then Baptism shall be administered on this fashion.

First let the Minister of the Parish (or, in his absence, any other lawful Minister that can be procured) with them that are present call upon God, and say the Lord's Prayer, and so many of the Collects appointed to be said before in the form of Publick Baptism, as the time and present exigence will suffer. And then, the child being named by some one that is present, the Minister shall pour Water upon it, saying these words;

N. I baptize thee in the Name of the Father, and of the Son, and of the Holy Ghost. Amen.

Then, all kneeling down, the Minister shall give thanks unto God, and say,

WE yield thee hearty thanks, most merciful Father, that it hath pleased thee to regenerate this Infant with thy Holy Spirit, to receive *him* for thine own Child by adoption, and to incorporate *him* into thy holy Church. And we humbly beseech thee to grant, that as *he* is now made partaker of the death of thy Son, so *he* may be also of his resurrection; and that finally, with the residue of thy Saints, *he* may inherit thine everlasting kingdom; through the same thy Son Jesus Christ our Lord. *Amen.*

And let them not doubt, but that the Child so baptized is lawfully and sufficiently baptized, and ought not to be baptized again. Yet nevertheless, if the Child which is after this sort baptized do afterward live, it is expedient that it be brought into the Church, to the intent that, if the Minister of the same Parish did himself baptize that Child, the Congregation may be certified of the true form of Baptism, by him privately before used. In which case he shall say thus,

I CERTIFY you, that according to the due and prescribed Order of the Church, *at such a time, and at such a place*, before divers witnesses, I baptized this Child.

But if the Child were baptized by any other lawful Minister, then the Minister of the Parish, where the Child was born or christened, shall examine and try whether the Child be lawfully baptized, or no. In which case, if those that bring any Child to the Church do answer that the same Child is already baptized, then shall the Minister examine them further, saying,

BY whom was this Child baptized?

Who was present when this Child was baptized?

Because some things essential to this Sacrament may happen to be omitted through fear or haste, in such times of extremity; therefore I demand further of you,

With what matter was this Child baptized?

With what words was this Child baptized?

And if the Minister shall find by the answers of such as bring the Child, that all things were done as they ought to be; then shall not he christen the Child again, but shall receive him as one of the flock of true Christian people, saying thus,

I CERTIFY you, that in this case all is well done, and according unto due order, concerning the baptizing of this Child; who being born in original sin, and in the wrath of God, is now, by the laver of Regeneration in Baptism, received into the number of the children of God and heirs of everlasting life: for our

Lord Jesus Christ doth not deny his grace and mercy unto such infants, but most lovingly doth call them unto him, as the holy Gospel doth witness to our comfort on this wise.

S. Mark 10. 13

THEY brought young children to Christ, that he should touch them; and his disciples rebuked those that brought them. But when Jesus saw it, he was much displeased, and said unto them, Suffer the little children to come unto me, and forbid them not; for of such is the kingdom of God. Verily I say unto you, Whosoever shall not receive the kingdom of God as a little child, he shall not enter therein. And he took them up in his arms, put his hands upon them, and blessed them.

After the Gospel is read, the Minister shall make this brief exhortation upon the words of the Gospel.

BELOVED, ye hear in this Gospel the words of our Saviour Christ, that he commanded the children to be brought unto him; how he blamed those that would have kept them from him; how he exhorted all men to follow their innocency. Ye perceive how by his outward gesture and deed he declared his good will toward them; for he embraced them in his arms, he laid his hands upon them, and blessed them. Doubt ye not therefore, but earnestly believe, that he hath likewise favourably received this present Infant; that he hath embraced *him* with the arms of his mercy; and (as he hath promised in his holy Word) will give unto *him* the blessing of eternal life, and make *him* partaker of his everlasting kingdom. Wherefore, we being thus persuaded of the good will of our heavenly Father, declared by his Son Jesus Christ, towards this Infant, let us faithfully and devoutly give thanks unto him, and say the Prayer which the Lord himself taught us:

OUR Father which art in heaven, Hallowed be thy Name, Thy kingdom come, Thy will be done, in earth as it is in heaven. Give us this day our daily bread; And forgive us our trespasses, As we forgive them that trespass against us; And lead us not into temptation, But deliver us from evil. Amen.

ALMIGHTY and everlasting God, heavenly Father, we give thee humble thanks that thou hast vouchsafed to call us to the knowledge of thy grace and faith in thee: Increase this knowledge, and confirm this faith in us evermore. Give thy Holy Spirit to this Infant, that *he*, being born again, and being made an heir of everlasting salvation, through our Lord Jesus Christ, may continue thy servant, and attain thy promise; through the same our Lord Jesus Christ thy Son, who liveth and reigneth with thee and the Holy Spirit, now and for ever. *Amen.*

Then shall the Priest demand the Name of the Child; which being by the Godfathers and Godmothers pronounced, the Minister shall say,

DOST thou, in the name of this Child, renounce the devil and all his works, the vain pomp and glory of this world, with all covetous desires of the same, and the carnal desires of the flesh, so that thou wilt not follow nor be led by them?

Answer. I renounce them all.

Minister.

DOST thou believe in God the Father Almighty, Maker of heaven and earth?

And in Jesus Christ his only-begotten Son our Lord? And that he was conceived by the Holy Ghost, born of the Virgin Mary; that he suffered under Pontius Pilate, was crucified, dead, and buried; that he went down into hell, and also did rise again the third day; that he ascended into heaven, and sitteth at the right hand of God the Father Almighty; and from thence shall come again at the end of the world, to judge the quick and the dead?

And dost thou believe in the Holy Ghost; the holy Catholick Church; the Communion of Saints; the Remission of sins; the Resurrection of the flesh; and everlasting life after death?

Answer. All this I stedfastly believe.

Minister.

WILT thou then obediently keep God's holy will and commandments, and walk in the same all the days of thy life?

Answer. I will.

Then the Priest shall say,

WE receive this Child into the Congregation of Christ's flock, and do *sign *him* with the sign of the Cross, in token that hereafter *he* shall not be ashamed to confess the faith of Christ crucified, and manfully to fight under his banner against sin, the world, and the devil, and to continue Christ's faithful soldier and servant unto *his* life's end. Amen.

Then shall the Priest say,

SEEING now, dearly beloved brethren, that this Child is by Baptism regenerate and grafted into the body of Christ's Church, let us give thanks unto Almighty God for these benefits, and with one accord make our prayers unto him, that *he* may lead the rest of *his* life according to this beginning.

Then shall the Priest say,

WE yield thee most hearty thanks, most merciful Father, that it hath pleased thee to regenerate this Infant with thy Holy Spirit, to receive *him* for thine own Child by adoption, and to incorporate *him* into thy holy Church. And humbly we beseech thee to grant that *he* being dead unto sin, and living unto righteousness, and being buried with Christ in his death, may crucify the old man, and utterly abolish the whole body of sin; and that, as *he* is made partaker of the death of thy Son, *he* may also be partaker of his resurrection; so that finally, with the residue of thy holy Church, *he* may be an inheritor of thine everlasting kingdom; through Jesus Christ our Lord. *Amen.*

Then, all standing up, the Minister shall make this exhortation to the Godfathers and Godmothers.

FORASMUCH as this Child hath promised by you *his* sureties to renounce the devil and all his works, to believe in God, and to serve him: Ye must remember, that it is your parts and duties to see that this Infant be taught, so soon as *he* shall

* *The Priest shall make a Cross upon the Child's forehead.*

be able to learn, what a solemn vow, promise and profession *he* hath made by you. And that *he* may know these things the better, ye shall call upon *him* to hear sermons; and chiefly ye shall provide that *he* may learn the Creed, the Lord's Prayer and the Ten Commandments in the vulgar tongue, and all other things which a Christian ought to know and believe to his soul's health; and that this Child may be virtuously brought up to lead a godly and a Christian life; remembering alway, that Baptism doth represent unto us our profession; which is, to follow the example of our Saviour Christ, and be made like unto him; that as he died and rose again for us, so should we, who are baptized, die from sin and rise again unto righteousness, continually mortifying all our evil and corrupt affections, and daily proceeding in all virtue and godliness of living.

But if they which bring the Infant to the Church do make such uncertain answers to the Priest's questions, as that it cannot appear that the Child was baptized with Water, In the Name of the Father, and of the Son, and of the Holy Ghost, (which are essential parts of Baptism,) then let the Priest baptize it in the form before appointed for Publick Baptism of Infants: Saving that at the dipping of the Child in the Font, he shall use this form of words.

IF thou art not already baptized, *N.* I baptize thee in the Name of the Father, and of the Son, and of the Holy Ghost. Amen.

THE MINISTRATION OF
BAPTISM
TO SUCH AS ARE OF RIPER YEARS AND ABLE TO ANSWER FOR THEMSELVES

When any such person as is of riper years and able to answer for himself is to be baptized, the Minister shall instruct such person, or cause him to be instructed, in the principles of the Christian religion, and exhort him so to prepare himself with prayers and fasting that he may receive this Holy Sacrament with repentance and faith.

At least a week before any such baptism is to take place, the Minister shall give notice thereof to the Bishop of the Diocese or whomsoever he shall appoint for the purpose.

The person to be baptized shall choose three, or at least two, to be his sponsors, who shall be ready to present him at the Font and afterwards put him in mind of his Christian profession and duties. No person shall be admitted to be a sponsor who has not been baptized and confirmed. Nevertheless the Minister shall have power to dispense with the requirement of confirmation in any case in which in his judgement need so requires.

At the time appointed, the sponsors shall be ready to present the person to be baptized at the Font, and standing there the Priest shall ask whether the person presented be baptized or no, and if he shall answer, No, *then shall the Priest say thus.*

DEARLY beloved, forasmuch as all men are conceived and born in sin, (and that which is born of the flesh is flesh,) and they that are in the flesh cannot please God, but live in sin, committing many actual transgressions; and that our Saviour

Christ saith, none can enter into the kingdom of God, except he be regenerate and born anew of Water and of the Holy Ghost; I beseech you to call upon God the Father, through our Lord Jesus Christ, that of his bounteous goodness he will grant to *these persons* that which by nature *they* cannot have; that *they* may be baptized with Water and the Holy Ghost, and received into Christ's holy Church, and be made lively *members* of the same.

Then shall the Priest say,

Let us pray.

(And here all the Congregation shall kneel.)

ALMIGHTY and everlasting God, who of thy great mercy didst save Noah and his family in the ark from perishing by water; and also didst safely lead the children of Israel thy people through the Red Sea, figuring thereby thy holy Baptism; and by the Baptism of thy well-beloved Son Jesus Christ, in the river Jordan, didst sanctify the element of water to the mystical washing away of sin: We beseech thee, for thine infinite mercies, that thou wilt mercifully look upon *these* thy *servants*; wash *them* and sanctify *them* with the Holy Ghost; that *they*, being delivered from thy wrath, may be received into the ark of Christ's Church; and being stedfast in faith, joyful through hope, and rooted in charity, may so pass the waves of this troublesome world, that finally *they* may come to the land of everlasting life, there to reign with thee world without end, through Jesus Christ our Lord. *Amen.*

ALMIGHTY and immortal God, the aid of all that need, the helper of all that flee to thee for succour, the life of them that believe, and the resurrection of the dead: We call upon thee for *these persons*, that *they*, coming to thy holy Baptism, may receive remission of *their* sins by spiritual regeneration. Receive *them*, O Lord: and as thou hast promised by thy well-beloved Son, saying, Ask, and ye shall receive; seek, and ye shall find; knock, and it shall be opened unto you: So give now unto us that ask; let us that seek find; open the gate unto us that knock; that *these persons* may enjoy the everlasting benediction of thy heavenly washing, and may come to the eternal kingdom which thou hast promised by Christ our Lord. *Amen.*

Then shall the people stand up, and the Priest shall say,

Hear the words of the Gospel, written by Saint John in the third chapter, beginning at the first verse.

THERE was a man of the Pharisees, named Nicodemus, a ruler of the Jews. The same came to Jesus by night, and said unto him, Rabbi, we know that thou art a teacher come from God; for no man can do these miracles that thou doest, except God be with him. Jesus answered and said unto him, Verily, verily I say unto thee, Except a man be born again, he cannot see the kingdom of God. Nicodemus saith unto him, How can a man be born when he is old? Can he enter the second time into his mother's womb, and be born? Jesus answered, Verily, verily I say unto thee, Except a man be born of water and of the Spirit, he cannot enter into the kingdom of God. That which is born of the flesh is flesh; and that which is born of the Spirit is spirit. Marvel not that I said unto thee, Ye must be born again. The wind bloweth where it listeth, and thou hearest the sound thereof; but canst not tell whence it cometh, and whither it goeth: so is every one that is born of the Spirit.

After which he shall say this exhortation following.

BELOVED, ye hear in this Gospel the express words of our Saviour Christ, that except a man be born of water and of the Spirit, he cannot enter into the kingdom of God. Whereby ye may perceive the great necessity of this Sacrament, where it may be had. Likewise, immediately before his ascension into heaven, (as we read in the last chapter of Saint Mark's Gospel,) he gave command to his disciples, saying, Go ye into all the world, and preach the Gospel to every creature. He that believeth and is baptized shall be saved; but he that believeth not shall be damned. Which also sheweth unto us the great benefit we reap thereby. For which cause Saint Peter the Apostle, when upon his first preaching of the Gospel many were pricked at the heart, and said to him and the rest of the Apostles, Men and brethren, what shall we do? replied and said unto them, Repent, and be baptized every one of you for the remission of sins, and ye shall receive the gift of the Holy Ghost. For the promise is to you and your children, and to all that are afar off, even as many as the Lord our God shall call. And with many other words exhorted he them, saying, Save yourselves from this untoward generation. For (as the same Apostle testifieth in another place) even Baptism doth also now save us, (not the putting away of the filth of the flesh, but the answer of a good conscience towards God,) by the resurrection of Jesus Christ. Doubt ye not therefore, but earnestly believe, that he will favourably receive *these* present *persons*, truly repenting, and coming unto him by faith; that he will grant *them* remission of *their* sins, and bestow upon *them* the Holy Ghost; that he will give *them* the blessing of eternal life, and make *them partakers* of his everlasting kingdom. Wherefore we being thus persuaded of the good will of our heavenly Father towards *these persons*, declared by his Son Jesus Christ; let us faithfully and devoutly give thanks to him, and say,

ALMIGHTY and everlasting God, heavenly Father, we give thee humble thanks, for that thou hast vouchsafed to call us to the knowledge of thy grace and faith in thee: Increase this knowledge, and confirm this faith in us evermore. Give thy Holy Spirit to *these persons*, that *they* may be born again, and be made *heirs* of everlasting salvation, through our Lord Jesus Christ, who liveth and reigneth with thee and the Holy Spirit, now and for ever. *Amen.*

Then the Priest shall speak to the persons to be baptized on this wise.

WELL-BELOVED, who are come hither desiring to receive holy Baptism, *ye* have heard how the Congregation hath prayed that our Lord Jesus Christ would vouchsafe to receive you and bless you, to release you of your sins, to give you the kingdom of heaven and everlasting life. *Ye* have heard also that our Lord Jesus Christ hath promised in his holy Word, to grant all those things that we have prayed for; which promise he, for his part, will most surely keep and perform. Wherefore, after this promise made by Christ, *ye* must also faithfully, for your part, promise in the presence of these your witnesses, and this whole Congregation, that *ye* will renounce the devil and all his works, and constantly believe God's holy Word, and obediently keep his commandments.

Then shall the Priest demand of each of the persons to be baptized, severally, these Questions following.

Question.

DOST thou renounce the devil and all his works, the vain pomp and glory of the world, with all covetous desires of the same, and the carnal desires of the flesh, so that thou wilt not follow nor be led by them?

Answer. I renounce them all.

Question.

DOST thou believe in God the Father Almighty, Maker of heaven and earth?

And in Jesus Christ his only-begotten Son our Lord? And that he was conceived by the Holy Ghost, born of the Virgin Mary; that he suffered under Pontius Pilate, was crucified, dead, and buried; that he went down into hell, and also did rise again the third day; that he ascended into heaven, and sitteth at the right hand of God the Father Almighty; and from thence shall come again at the end of the world, to judge the quick and the dead?

And dost thou believe in the Holy Ghost; the holy Catholick Church; the Communion of Saints; the Remission of sins; the Resurrection of the flesh; and everlasting life after death?

Answer. All this I stedfastly believe.

Question.

WILT thou be baptized in this faith?

Answer. That is my desire.

Question.

WILT thou then obediently keep God's holy will and commandments, and walk in the same all the days of thy life?

Answer. I will endeavour so to do, God being my helper.

Then shall the Priest say,

O MERCIFUL God, grant that the old Adam in *these persons* may be so buried, that the new man may be raised up in *them. Amen.*

Grant that all carnal affections may die in *them*, and that all things belonging to the Spirit may live and grow in *them. Amen.*

Grant that *they* may have power and strength, to have victory, and to triumph against the devil, the world, and the flesh. *Amen.*

Grant that *they*, being here dedicated to thee by our office and ministry, may also be endued with heavenly virtues, and everlastingly rewarded, through thy mercy, O blessed Lord God, who dost live, and govern all things, world without end. *Amen.*

ALMIGHTY everliving God, whose most dearly beloved Son Jesus Christ, for the forgiveness of our sins, did shed out of his most precious side both water and blood; and gave commandment to his disciples, that they should go teach all nations, and baptize them in the Name of the Father, the Son, and the Holy Ghost: Regard, we beseech thee, the supplications of this Congregation; sanctify this Water to the mystical washing away of sin; and grant that the *persons* now to be baptized therein may receive the fulness of thy grace, and ever remain in the number of thy faithful and elect children; through Jesus Christ our Lord. *Amen.*

Then shall the Priest take each person to be baptized by the right hand, and placing him conveniently by the Font, according to his discretion, shall ask the Godfathers and Godmothers the Name; and then shall dip him in the water, or pour water upon him, saying,

N. I baptize thee, In the Name of the Father, and of the Son, and of the Holy Ghost. Amen.

Then shall the Priest say,

WE receive this person into the Congregation of Christ's flock; and *do sign *him* with the sign of the Cross, in token that hereafter *he* shall not be ashamed to confess the faith of Christ crucified, and manfully to fight under his banner against sin, the world, and the devil, and to continue Christ's faithful soldier and servant unto *his* life's end. Amen.

Then shall the Priest say,

SEEING now, dearly beloved brethren, that *these persons are* regenerate and grafted into the body of Christ's Church, let us give thanks unto Almighty God for these benefits, and with one accord make our prayers unto him, that *they* may lead the rest of *their* life according to this beginning.

Then shall be said the Lord's Prayer, all kneeling.

OUR Father which art in heaven, Hallowed be thy Name, Thy kingdom come, Thy will be done, in earth as it is in heaven. Give us this day our daily bread; And forgive us our trespasses, As we forgive them that trespass against us; And lead us not into temptation, But deliver us from evil. Amen.

WE yield thee humble thanks, O heavenly Father, that thou hast vouchsafed to call us to the knowledge of thy grace and faith in thee; Increase this knowledge, and confirm this faith in us evermore. Give thy Holy Spirit to *these persons*; that, being now born again, and made *heirs* of everlasting salvation, through our Lord Jesus Christ, *they* may continue thy *servants*, and attain thy promises; through the same Lord Jesus Christ thy Son, who liveth and reigneth with thee, in the unity of the same Holy Spirit, everlastingly. *Amen.*

Then, all standing up, the Priest shall use this exhortation following; speaking to the Godfathers and Godmothers first.

FORASMUCH as *these persons have* promised in your presence to renounce the devil and all his works, to believe in

---

* *Here the Priest shall make a Cross upon the person's forehead.*

God, and to serve him: Ye must remember that it is your part and duty to put *them* in mind, what a solemn vow, promise, and profession *they have* now made before this Congregation, and especially before you *their* chosen witnesses. And ye are also to call upon *them* to use all diligence to be rightly instructed in God's holy Word; that so *they* may grow in grace, and in the knowledge of our Lord Jesus Christ, and live godly, righteously, and soberly in this present world.

(*And then, speaking to the new baptized* persons, *he shall proceed, and say,*)

AND as for you, who have now by Baptism put on Christ, it is your part and duty also, being made the *children* of God and of the light by faith in Jesus Christ, to walk answerably to your Christian calling, and as becometh the children of light; remembering always, that Baptism representeth unto us our profession; which is, to follow the example of our Saviour Christ, and to be made like unto him; that as he died and rose again for us, so should we, who are baptized, die from sin and rise again unto righteousness, continually mortifying all our evil and corrupt affections, and daily proceeding in all virtue and godliness of living.

It is expedient that every person, thus baptized, should be confirmed by the Bishop so soon after his Baptism as conveniently may be; that so he may be admitted to the holy Communion.

If any persons not baptized in their infancy shall be brought to be baptized before they come to years of discretion to answer for themselves; it may suffice to use the Office for Publick Baptism of Infants, or (in case of extreme danger) the Office for Private Baptism; only changing the word [Infant] *for* [Child or Person] *as occasion requireth.*

A CATECHISM

THAT IS TO SAY

AN INSTRUCTION TO BE LEARNED OF EVERY PERSON BEFORE HE BE BROUGHT TO BE CONFIRMED BY THE BISHOP

QUESTION. What is your Name?

Answer. N. or M.

Question. Who gave you this Name?

Answer. My Godfathers and Godmothers in my Baptism; wherein I was made a member of Christ, the child of God, and an inheritor of the kingdom of heaven.

Question. What did your Godfathers and Godmothers then for you?

Answer. They did promise and vow three things in my name. First, that I should renounce the devil and all his works, the pomps and vanity of this wicked world, and all the sinful lusts of the flesh. Secondly, that I should believe all the articles of the Christian faith. And thirdly, that I should keep God's holy will and commandments, and walk in the same all the days of my life.

Question. Dost thou not think that thou art bound to believe, and to do, as they have promised for thee?

Answer. Yes verily: and by God's help so I will. And I heartily thank our heavenly Father, that he hath called me to this state of salvation, through Jesus Christ our Saviour. And I pray unto God to give me his grace, that I may continue in the same unto my life's end.

Catechist.

Rehearse the Articles of thy Belief.

Answer.

I BELIEVE in God the Father Almighty, Maker of heaven and earth:

And in Jesus Christ his only Son our Lord, Who was conceived by the Holy Ghost, Born of the Virgin Mary, Suffered under Pontius Pilate, Was crucified, dead, and buried: He descended into hell; The third day he rose again from the dead; He ascended into heaven, And sitteth at the right hand of God the Father Almighty; From thence he shall come to judge the quick and the dead.

I believe in the Holy Ghost; The holy Catholick Church; The Communion of Saints; The Forgiveness of sins; The Resurrection of the body, And the life everlasting. Amen.

Question. What dost thou chiefly learn in these Articles of thy Belief?

Answer. First, I learn to believe in God the Father, who hath made me, and all the world.

Secondly, in God the Son, who hath redeemed me, and all mankind.

Thirdly, in God the Holy Ghost, who sanctifieth me, and all the elect people of God.

Question.

You said that your Godfathers and Godmothers did promise for you, that you should keep God's Commandments. Tell me how many there be?

Answer. Ten.

Question. Which be they?

Answer.

THE same which God spake in the twentieth chapter of Exodus, saying, I am the Lord thy God, who brought thee out of the land of Egypt, out of the house of bondage.

I. Thou shalt have none other gods but me.

II. Thou shalt not make to thyself any graven image, nor the likeness of any thing that is in heaven above, or in the earth beneath, or in the water under the earth. Thou shalt not bow down to them, nor worship them. For I the Lord thy God am a jealous God, and visit the sins of the fathers upon the children unto the third and fourth generation of them that hate me, and shew mercy unto thousands in them that love me and keep my commandments.

III. Thou shalt not take the Name of the Lord thy God in vain: for the Lord will not hold him guiltless, that taketh his Name in vain.

IV. Remember that thou keep holy the Sabbath day. Six days shalt thou labour, and do all that thou hast to do; but the seventh day is the Sabbath of the Lord thy God. In it thou shalt do no manner of work, thou, and thy son, and thy daughter, thy man-servant, and thy maid-servant, thy cattle, and the stranger that is within thy gates. For in six days the Lord made heaven and earth, the sea, and all that in them is, and rested the seventh day: wherefore the Lord blessed the seventh day, and hallowed it.

V. Honour thy father and thy mother; that thy days may be long in the land which the Lord thy God giveth thee.

VI. Thou shalt do no murder.

VII. Thou shalt not commit adultery.

VIII. Thou shalt not steal.

IX. Thou shalt not bear false witness against thy neighbour.

X. Thou shalt not covet thy neighbour's house, thou shalt not covet thy neighbour's wife, nor his servant, nor his maid, nor his ox, nor his ass, nor any thing that is his.

Question.

What dost thou chiefly learn by these Commandments?

Answer. I learn two things: my duty towards God, and my duty towards my Neighbour.

Question. What is thy duty towards God?

Answer. My duty towards God is to believe in him, to fear him, and to love him, with all my heart, with all my mind, with all my soul, and with all my strength; to worship him, to give him thanks, to put my whole trust in him, to call upon him, to honour his holy Name and his Word, and to serve him truly all the days of my life.

Question. What is thy duty towards thy Neighbour?

Answer. My duty towards my Neighbour is to love him as myself, and to do to all men as I would they should do unto me: To love, honour, and succour my father and mother: To honour and obey the Queen, and all that are put in authority under her: To submit myself to all my governors, teachers, spiritual pastors and masters: To order myself lowly and reverently to all my betters: To hurt nobody by word nor deed: To be true and just in all my dealing: To bear no malice nor hatred in my heart: To keep my hands from picking and stealing, and my tongue from evil-speaking, lying, and slandering: To keep my body in temperance, soberness, and chastity: Not to covet nor desire other men's goods; but to learn and labour truly to get mine own living, and to do my duty in that state of life, unto which it shall please God to call me.

Catechist.

My good child, know this, that thou art not able to do these things of thyself, nor to walk in the commandments of God, and to serve him, without his special grace; which thou must learn at all times to call for by diligent prayer. Let me hear therefore if thou canst say the Lord's Prayer.

Answer.

OUR Father which art in heaven, Hallowed be thy Name, Thy kingdom come, Thy will be done, in earth as it is in heaven. Give us this day our daily bread; And forgive us our trespasses, As we forgive them that trespass against us; And lead us not into temptation, But deliver us from evil. Amen.

Question. What desirest thou of God in this Prayer?

Answer. I desire my Lord God our heavenly Father, who is the giver of all goodness, to send his grace unto me, and to all people, that we may worship him, serve him, and obey him, as we ought to do. And I pray unto God, that he will send us all things that be needful both for our souls and bodies; and that he will be merciful unto us, and forgive us our sins; and that it will please him to save and defend us in all dangers ghostly and bodily; and that he will keep us from all sin and wickedness, and from our ghostly enemy, and from everlasting death. And this I trust he will do of his mercy and goodness, through our Lord Jesus Christ. And therefore I say, Amen, So be it.

Question.

HOW many Sacraments hath Christ ordained in his Church?

Answer. Two only, as generally necessary to salvation; that is to say, Baptism, and the Supper of the Lord.

Question. What meanest thou by this word *Sacrament*?

Answer. I mean an outward and visible sign of an inward and spiritual grace given unto us, ordained by Christ himself, as a means whereby we receive the same, and a pledge to assure us thereof.

Question. How many parts are there in a Sacrament?

Answer. Two: the outward visible sign, and the inward spiritual grace.

Question. What is the outward visible sign or form in Baptism?

Answer. Water: wherein the person is baptized, *In the Name of the Father, and of the Son, and of the Holy Ghost.*

Question. What is the inward and spiritual grace?

Answer. A death unto sin, and a new birth unto righteousness: for being by nature born in sin, and the children of wrath, we are hereby made the children of grace.

Question. What is required of persons to be baptized?

Answer. Repentance, whereby they forsake sin: and faith, whereby they stedfastly believe the promises of God, made to them in that Sacrament.

Question. Why then are infants baptized, when by reason of their tender age they cannot perform them?

Answer. Because they promise them both by their sureties: which promise, when they come to age, themselves are bound to perform.

Question. Why was the Sacrament of the Lord's Supper ordained?

Answer. For the continual remembrance of the sacrifice of the death of Christ, and of the benefits which we receive thereby.

Question. What is the outward part or sign of the Lord's Supper?

Answer. Bread and Wine, which the Lord hath commanded to be received.

Question. What is the inward part, or thing signified?

Answer. The Body and Blood of Christ, which are verily and indeed taken and received by the faithful in the Lord's Supper.

Question. What are the benefits whereof we are partakers thereby?

Answer. The strengthening and refreshing of our souls by the Body and Blood of Christ, as our bodies are by the Bread and Wine.

Question. What is required of them who come to the Lord's Supper?

Answer. To examine themselves, whether they repent them truly of their former sins, stedfastly purposing to lead a new life; have a lively faith in God's mercy through Christ, with a thankful remembrance of his death; and be in charity with all men.

The Curate of every Parish shall diligently upon Sundays and Holy-days, after the second Lesson at Evening Prayer, openly in the Church instruct and examine so many Children of his Parish sent unto him, as he shall think convenient, in some part of this Catechism.

And all Fathers, Mothers, Masters, and Dames, shall cause their Children, Servants, and Prentices, (which have not learned their Catechism,) to come to the Church at the time appointed, and obediently to hear and be ordered by the Curate, until such time as they have learned all that is here appointed for them to learn.

So soon as Children are come to a competent age, and can say, in their mother tongue, the Creed, the Lord's Prayer, and the Ten Commandments; and also can answer to the other questions of this short Catechism; they shall be brought to the

Bishop: And every one shall have a Godfather, or a God-mother, as a witness of their Confirmation.

And whensoever the Bishop shall give knowledge for Children to be brought unto him for their Confirmation, the Curate of every Parish shall either bring or send in writing, with his hand subscribed thereunto, the names of all such persons within his Parish, as he shall think fit to be presented to the Bishop to be confirmed. And, if the Bishop approve of them, he shall confirm them in manner following.

THE ORDER OF

CONFIRMATION

OR LAYING ON OF HANDS UPON THOSE THAT ARE BAPTIZED AND COME TO YEARS OF DISCRETION

Upon the day appointed, all that are to be then confirmed, being placed, and standing in order before the Bishop; he (or some other Minister appointed by him) shall read this Preface following.

TO the end that Confirmation may be ministered to the more edifying of such as shall receive it, the Church hath thought good to order, That none hereafter shall be confirmed, but such as can say the Creed, the Lord's Prayer, and the Ten Commandments; and can also answer to such other Questions, as in the short Catechism are contained: which order is very convenient to be observed; to the end that children being now come to the years of discretion, and having learned what their Godfathers and Godmothers promised for them in Baptism, they may themselves, with their own mouth and consent, openly before the Church, ratify and confirm the same; and also promise, that by the grace of God they will evermore endeavour themselves faithfully to observe such things, as they by their own confession have assented unto.

Then shall the Bishop say,

DO ye here, in the presence of God, and of this Congregation, renew the solemn promise and vow that was made in your name at your Baptism; ratifying and confirming the same in your own persons, and acknowledging yourselves bound to believe and to do all those things, which your Godfathers and Godmothers then undertook for you?

And every one shall audibly answer,

I do.

The Bishop.

OUR help is in the Name of the Lord;
Answer. Who hath made heaven and earth.
Bishop. Blessed be the Name of the Lord;
Answer. Henceforth world without end.
Bishop. Lord, hear our prayers.
Answer. And let our cry come unto thee.

Bishop.

Let us pray.

ALMIGHTY and everliving God, who hast vouchsafed to regenerate these thy servants by Water and the Holy Ghost, and hast given unto them forgiveness of all their sins: Strengthen them, we beseech thee, O Lord, with the Holy Ghost the Comforter, and daily increase in them thy manifold gifts of grace; the spirit of wisdom and understanding; the spirit of counsel and ghostly strength; the spirit of knowledge and true godliness; and fill them, O Lord, with the spirit of thy holy fear, now and for ever. *Amen.*

Then all of them in order kneeling before the Bishop, he shall lay his hand upon the head of every one severally, saying,

DEFEND, O Lord, this thy Child [or *this thy Servant*] with thy heavenly grace, that *he* may continue thine for ever; and daily increase in thy Holy Spirit, more and more, until *he* come unto thy everlasting kingdom. Amen.

Then shall the Bishop say,
The Lord be with you.

Answer. And with thy spirit.

And (all kneeling down) the Bishop shall add,

Let us pray.

OUR Father which art in heaven, Hallowed be thy Name, Thy kingdom come, Thy will be done, in earth as it is in heaven. Give us this day our daily bread; And forgive us our trespasses, As we forgive them that trespass against us; And lead us not into temptation, But deliver us from evil. Amen.

And this Collect.

ALMIGHTY and everliving God, who makest us both to will and to do those things that be good and acceptable unto thy divine Majesty; We make our humble supplications unto thee for these thy servants, upon whom (after the example of thy holy Apostles) we have now laid our hands, to certify them (by this sign) of thy favour and gracious goodness towards them. Let thy fatherly hand, we beseech thee, ever be over them; let thy Holy Spirit ever be with them; and so lead them in the knowledge and obedience of thy Word, that in the end they may obtain everlasting life; through our Lord Jesus Christ, who with thee and the Holy Ghost liveth and reigneth, ever one God, world without end. *Amen.*

O ALMIGHTY Lord, and everlasting God, vouchsafe, we beseech thee, to direct, sanctify, and govern both our hearts and bodies, in the ways of thy laws, and in the works of thy commandments; that through thy most mighty protection, both here and ever, we may be preserved in body and soul; through our Lord and Saviour Jesus Christ. *Amen.*

Then the Bishop shall bless them, saying thus,

THE blessing of God Almighty, the Father, the Son, and the Holy Ghost, be upon you, and remain with you, for ever. *Amen.*

And there shall none be admitted to the holy Communion, until such time as he be confirmed, or be ready and desirous to be confirmed.

THE FORM
OF SOLEMNIZATION OF
MATRIMONY

First, the Banns of all that are to be married together must be published in the Church three several Sundays, during the time of Morning Service, or of Evening Service, (if there be no Morning Service,) immediately after the second Lesson; the Curate saying after the accustomed manner, I publish the Banns of Marriage between M. of — and N. of —. If any of you know cause, or just impediment, why these two persons should not be joined together in holy Matrimony, ye are to declare it. This is the first [*second*, or *third*] time of asking.

And if the persons that are to be married dwell in divers Parishes, the Banns must be asked in both Parishes; and the Curate of the one Parish shall not solemnize Matrimony betwixt them, without a Certificate of the Banns being thrice asked, from the Curate of the other Parish.

At the day and time appointed for solemnization of Matrimony, the persons to be married shall come into the Body of the Church with their friends and neighbours: and there standing together, the Man on the right hand, and the Woman on the left, the Priest shall say,

DEARLY beloved, we are gathered together here in the sight of God, and in the face of this Congregation, to join together this man and this woman in holy Matrimony; which is an honourable estate, instituted of God in the time of man's innocency, signifying unto us the mystical union that is betwixt Christ and his Church; which holy estate Christ adorned and beautified with his presence, and first miracle that he wrought, in Cana of Galilee; and is commended of Saint Paul to be honourable among all men: and therefore is not by any to be enterprized, nor taken in hand, unadvisedly, lightly, or wantonly, to satisfy men's carnal lusts and appetites, like brute beasts that have no understanding; but reverently, discreetly, advisedly, soberly, and in the fear of God; duly considering the causes for which Matrimony was ordained.

First, It was ordained for the procreation of children, to be brought up in the fear and nurture of the Lord, and to the praise of his holy Name.

Secondly, It was ordained for a remedy against sin, and to avoid fornication; that such persons as have not the gift of continency might marry, and keep themselves undefiled members of Christ's body.

Thirdly, It was ordained for the mutual society, help, and comfort, that the one ought to have of the other, both in prosperity and adversity. Into which holy estate these two persons present come now to be joined. Therefore if any man can shew any just cause, why they may not lawfully be joined together, let him now speak, or else hereafter for ever hold his peace.

And also, speaking unto the persons that shall be married, he shall say,

I REQUIRE and charge you both, as ye will answer at the dreadful day of judgement, when the secrets of all hearts shall be disclosed, that if either of you know any impediment, why ye may not be lawfully joined together in Matrimony, ye do now confess it. For be ye well assured, that so many as are coupled together otherwise than God's Word doth allow are not joined together by God; neither is their Matrimony lawful.

At which day of Marriage, if any man do allege and declare any impediment, why they may not be coupled together in Matrimony, by God's law, or the laws of this Realm; and will be bound, and sufficient sureties with him, to the parties; or else put in a caution (to the full value of such charges as the persons to be married do thereby sustain) to prove his allegation: then the solemnization must be deferred, until such time as the truth be tried.

If no impediment be alleged, then shall the Curate say unto the Man,

N. WILT thou have this woman to thy wedded wife, to live together after God's ordinance in the holy estate of Matrimony? Wilt thou love her, comfort her, honour, and keep her, in sickness and in health; and, forsaking all other, keep thee only unto her, so long as ye both shall live?

The Man shall answer,

I will.

Then shall the Priest say unto the Woman,

N. WILT thou have this man to thy wedded husband, to live together after God's ordinance in the holy estate of Matrimony? Wilt thou obey him, and serve him, love, honour, and keep him, in sickness and in health; and, forsaking all other, keep thee only unto him, so long as ye both shall live?

The Woman shall answer,

I will.

Then shall the Minister say,

Who giveth this woman to be married to this man?

Then shall they give their troth to each other in this manner.
The Minister, receiving the Woman at her father's or friend's hands, shall cause the Man with his right hand to take the Woman by her right hand, and to say after him as followeth.

I N. take thee N. to my wedded wife, to have and to hold from this day forward, for better for worse, for richer for poorer, in sickness and in health, to love and to cherish, till death us do part, according to God's holy ordinance; and thereto I plight thee my troth.

Then shall they loose their hands; and the Woman, with her right hand taking the Man by his right hand, shall likewise say after the Minister,

I *N*. take thee N. to my wedded husband, to have and to hold from this day forward, for better for worse, for richer for poorer, in sickness and in health, to love, cherish, and to obey, till death us do part, according to God's holy ordinance; and thereto I give thee my troth.

> *Then shall they again loose their hands; and the Man shall give unto the Woman a Ring, laying the same upon the book with the accustomed duty to the Priest and Clerk. And the Priest, taking the Ring, shall deliver it unto the Man, to put it upon the fourth finger of the Woman's left hand. And the Man holding the Ring there, and taught by the Priest, shall say,*

WITH this ring I thee wed, with my body I thee worship, and with all my worldly goods I thee endow: In the Name of the Father, and of the Son, and of the Holy Ghost. Amen.

> *Then the Man leaving the Ring upon the fourth finger of the Woman's left hand, they shall both kneel down, and the Minister shall say,*

Let us pray.

O ETERNAL God, Creator and Preserver of all mankind, Giver of all spiritual grace, the Author of everlasting life: Send thy blessing upon these thy servants, this man and this woman, whom we bless in thy Name; that, as Isaac and Rebecca lived faithfully together, so these persons may surely perform and keep the vow and covenant betwixt them made, (whereof this ring given and received is a token and pledge,) and may ever remain in perfect love and peace together, and live according to thy laws; through Jesus Christ our Lord. *Amen.*

> *Then shall the Priest join their right hands together, and say,*

Those whom God hath joined together let no man put asunder.

> *Then shall the Minister speak unto the people.*

FORASMUCH as N. and *N*. have consented together in holy wedlock, and have witnessed the same before God and this company, and thereto have given and pledged their troth either to other, and have declared the same by giving and receiving of a ring, and by joining of hands; I pronounce that they be man and wife together, In the Name of the Father, and of the Son, and of the Holy Ghost. Amen.

And the Minister shall add this Blessing.

GOD the Father, God the Son, God the Holy Ghost, bless, preserve, and keep you; the Lord mercifully with his favour look upon you, and so fill you with all spiritual benediction and grace, that ye may so live together in this life, that in the world to come ye may have life everlasting. *Amen.*

Then the Minister or Clerks, going to the Lord's Table, shall say or sing this Psalm following.

Beati omnes. Psalm 128

BLESSED are all they that fear the Lord: and walk in his ways.

For thou shalt eat the labour of thine hands: O well is thee, and happy shalt thou be.

Thy wife shall be as the fruitful vine: upon the walls of thy house;

Thy children like the olive branches: round about thy table.

Lo, thus shall the man be blessed: that feareth the Lord.

The Lord from out of Sion shall so bless thee: that thou shalt see Jerusalem in prosperity all thy life long;

Yea, that thou shalt see thy children's children: and peace upon Israel.

Glory be to the Father, and to the Son: and to the Holy Ghost;

As it was in the beginning, is now, and ever shall be: world without end. Amen.

Or this Psalm.

Deus misereatur. Psalm 67

GOD be merciful unto us, and bless us: and shew us the light of his countenance, and be merciful unto us:

That thy way may be known upon earth: thy saving health among all nations.

Let the people praise thee, O God: yea, let all the people praise thee.

O let the nations rejoice and be glad: for thou shalt judge the folk righteously, and govern the nations upon earth.

Let the people praise thee, O God: yea, let all the people praise thee.

Then shall the earth bring forth her increase: and God, even our own God, shall give us his blessing.

God shall bless us: and all the ends of the world shall fear him.

Glory be to the Father, and to the Son: and to the Holy Ghost;

As it was in the beginning, is now, and ever shall be: world without end. Amen.

The Psalm ended, and the Man and the Woman kneeling before the Lord's Table, the Priest standing at the Table, and turning his face towards them, shall say,

Lord, have mercy upon us.
Answer. Christ, have mercy upon us.
Minister. Lord, have mercy upon us.

OUR father which art in heaven, Hallowed be thy Name, Thy kingdom come, Thy will be done, in earth as it is in heaven. Give us this day our daily bread; And forgive us our trespasses, As we forgive them that trespass against us; And lead us not into temptation, But deliver us from evil. Amen.

Minister. O Lord, save thy servant, and thy handmaid;
Answer. Who put their trust in thee.
Minister. O Lord, send them help from thy holy place;
Answer. And evermore defend them.
Minister. Be unto them a tower of strength,
Answer. From the face of their enemy.
Minister. O Lord, hear our prayer;
Answer. And let our cry come unto thee.

Minister.

O GOD of Abraham, God of Isaac, God of Jacob, bless these thy servants, and sow the seed of eternal life in their hearts; that whatsoever in thy holy Word they shall profitably learn, they may in deed fulfil the same. Look, O Lord, mercifully upon them from heaven, and bless them. And as thou didst send thy blessing upon Abraham and Sarah, to their great comfort, so vouchsafe to send thy blessing upon these thy servants; that they obeying thy will, and alway being in safety under thy protection, may abide in thy love unto their lives' end; through Jesus Christ our Lord. *Amen.*

This Prayer next following shall be omitted, where the Woman is past child-bearing.

O MERCIFUL Lord, and heavenly Father, by whose gracious gift mankind is increased: We beseech thee, assist with thy blessing these two persons, that they may both be fruitful in procreation of children, and also live together so long in godly love and honesty, that they may see their children christianly and virtuously brought up, to thy praise and honour; through Jesus Christ our Lord. *Amen.*

O GOD, who by thy mighty power hast made all things of nothing; who also (after other things set in order) didst appoint, that out of man (created after thine own image and similitude) woman should take her beginning; and, knitting them together, didst teach that it should never be lawful to put asunder those whom thou by Matrimony hadst made one: O God, who hast consecrated the state of Matrimony to such an excellent mystery, that in it is signified and represented the spiritual marriage and unity betwixt Christ and his Church: Look mercifully upon these thy servants, that both this man may love his wife, according to thy Word, (as Christ did love his spouse the Church, who gave himself for it, loving and cherishing it even as his own flesh,) and also that this woman may be loving and amiable, faithful and obedient to her husband; and in all quietness, sobriety, and peace, be a follower of holy and godly matrons. O

Lord, bless them both, and grant them to inherit thy everlasting kingdom; through Jesus Christ our Lord. *Amen.*

Then shall the Priest say,

ALMIGHTY God, who at the beginning did create our first parents, Adam and Eve, and did sanctify and join them together in marriage; Pour upon you the riches of his grace, sanctify and bless you, that ye may please him both in body and soul, and live together in holy love unto your lives' end. *Amen.*

After which, if there be no Sermon declaring the duties of Man and Wife, the Minister shall read as followeth.

ALL ye that are married, or that intend to take the holy estate of Matrimony upon you, hear what the holy Scripture doth say as touching the duty of husbands towards their wives, and wives towards their husbands.

Saint Paul, in his Epistle to the Ephesians, the fifth Chapter, doth give this commandment to all married men; Husbands, love your wives, even as Christ also loved the Church, and gave himself for it, that he might sanctify and cleanse it with the washing of water, by the word; that he might present it to himself a glorious Church, not having spot, or wrinkle, or any such thing; but that it should be holy, and without blemish. So ought men to love their wives as their own bodies. He that loveth his wife loveth himself: for no man ever yet hated his own flesh, but nourisheth and cherisheth it, even as the Lord the Church: for we are members of his body, of his flesh, and of his bones. For this cause shall a man leave his father and mother, and shall be joined unto his wife; and they two shall be one flesh. This is a great mystery; but I speak concerning Christ and the Church. Nevertheless, let every one of you in particular so love his wife, even as himself.

Likewise the same Saint Paul, writing to the Colossians, speaketh thus to all men that are married; Husbands, love your wives, and be not bitter against them.

Hear also what Saint Peter, the Apostle of Christ, who was himself a married man, saith unto them that are married; Ye husbands, dwell with your wives according to knowledge; giving honour unto the wife, as unto the weaker vessel, and as being heirs together of the grace of life, that your prayers be not hindered.

Hitherto ye have heard the duty of the husband toward the wife. Now likewise, ye wives, hear and learn your duties toward your husbands, even as it is plainly set forth in holy Scripture.

Saint Paul, in the aforenamed Epistle to the Ephesians, teacheth you thus; Wives, submit yourselves unto your own husbands, as unto the Lord. For the husband is the head of the wife, even as Christ is the head of the Church: and he is the Saviour of the body. Therefore as the Church is subject unto Christ, so let the wives be to their own husbands in every thing. And again he saith, Let the wife see that she reverence her husband.

And in his Epistle to the Colossians, Saint Paul giveth you this short lesson; Wives, submit yourselves unto your own husbands, as it is fit in the Lord.

Saint Peter also doth instruct you very well, thus saying; Ye wives, be in subjection to your own husbands; that, if any obey not the word, they also may without the word be won by the conversation of the wives; while they behold your chaste conversation coupled with fear. Whose adorning, let it not be that outward adorning of plaiting the hair, and of wearing of gold, or of putting on of apparel; but let it be the hidden man of the heart, in that which is not corruptible; even the ornament of a meek and quiet spirit, which is in the sight of God of great price. For after this manner in the old time the holy women also, who trusted in God, adorned themselves, being in subjection unto their own husbands; even as Sarah obeyed Abraham, calling him lord; whose daughters ye are as long as ye do well, and are not afraid with any amazement.

It is convenient that the new-married persons should receive the holy Communion at the time of their Marriage, or at the first opportunity after their Marriage.

THE ORDER FOR
THE VISITATION
OF THE SICK

When any person is sick, notice shall be given thereof to the Minister of the Parish; who, coming into the sick person's house, shall say,

PEACE be to this house, and to all that dwell in it.

When he cometh into the sick man's presence he shall say, kneeling down,

REMEMBER not, Lord, our iniquities, nor the iniquities of our forefathers: Spare us, good Lord, spare thy people, whom thou hast redeemed with thy most precious blood, and be not angry with us for ever.

Answer. Spare us, good Lord.

Then the Minister shall say,

Let us pray.

Lord, have mercy upon us.
Christ, have mercy upon us.
Lord, have mercy upon us.

OUR Father which art in heaven, Hallowed be thy Name, Thy kingdom come, Thy will be done, in earth as it is in heaven. Give us this day our daily bread; And forgive us our trespasses, As we forgive them that trespass against us; And lead us not into temptation, But deliver us from evil. Amen.

Minister. O Lord, save thy servant;
Answer. Which putteth *his* trust in thee.
Minister. Send *him* help from thy holy place;
Answer. And evermore mightily defend *him*.
Minister. Let the enemy have no advantage of *him*;

Answer. Nor the wicked approach to hurt *him.*
Minister. Be unto *him,* O Lord, a strong tower,
Answer. From the face of *his* enemy.
Minister. O Lord, hear our prayers;
Answer. And let our cry come unto thee.

Minister.

O LORD, look down from heaven, behold, visit, and relieve this thy servant. Look upon *him* with the eyes of thy mercy, give *him* comfort and sure confidence in thee, defend *him* from the danger of the enemy, and keep *him* in perpetual peace and safety; through Jesus Christ our Lord. *Amen.*

HEAR us, Almighty and most merciful God and Saviour; extend thy accustomed goodness to this thy servant who is grieved with sickness. Sanctify, we beseech thee, this thy fatherly correction to *him*; that the sense of *his* weakness may add strength to *his* faith, and seriousness to *his* repentance: that, if it shall be thy good pleasure to restore *him* to *his* former health, *he* may lead the residue of *his* life in thy fear, and to thy glory: or else give *him* grace so to take thy visitation, that, after this painful life ended, *he* may dwell with thee in life everlasting; through Jesus Christ our Lord. *Amen.*

Then shall the Minister exhort the sick person after this form, or other like.

DEARLY beloved, know this, that Almighty God is the Lord of life and death, and of all things to them pertaining, as youth, strength, health, age, weakness, and sickness. Wherefore, whatsoever your sickness is, know you certainly, that it is God's visitation. And for what cause soever this sickness is sent unto you; whether it be to try your patience, for the example of others, and that your faith may be found in the day of the Lord laudable, glorious, and honourable, to the increase of glory and endless felicity; or else it be sent unto you to correct and amend in you whatsoever doth offend the eyes of your heavenly Father; know you certainly, that if you truly repent you of your sins, and bear your sickness patiently, trusting in God's mercy for his dear Son Jesus Christ's sake, and render unto him humble thanks for his fatherly visitation, submitting yourself wholly unto his will, it shall turn to your profit, and help you forward in the right way that leadeth unto everlasting life.

If the person visited be very sick, then the Curate may end his exhortation in this place, or else proceed.

TAKE therefore in good part the chastisement of the Lord: For (as Saint Paul saith in the twelfth chapter to the Hebrews) whom the Lord loveth he chasteneth, and scourgeth every son whom he receiveth. If ye endure chastening, God dealeth with you as with sons; for what son is he whom the father chasteneth not? But if ye be without chastisement, whereof all are partakers, then are ye bastards, and not sons. Furthermore, we have had fathers of our flesh, which corrected us, and we gave them reverence: shall we not much rather be in subjection unto the Father of spirits, and live? For they verily for a few days chastened us after their own pleasure; but he for our profit, that we might be partakers of his holiness. These words, good *brother*, are written in holy Scripture for our comfort and instruction, that we should patiently, and with thanksgiving, bear our heavenly Father's correction, whensoever by any manner of adversity it shall please his gracious goodness to visit us. And there should be no greater comfort to Christian persons, than to be made like unto Christ, by suffering patiently adversities, troubles, and sicknesses. For he himself went not up to joy, but first he suffered pain; he entered not into his glory before he was crucified. So truly our way to eternal joy is to suffer here with Christ; and our door to enter into eternal life is gladly to die with Christ; that we may rise again from death, and dwell with him in everlasting life. Now therefore, taking your sickness, which is thus profitable for you, patiently, I exhort you, in the name of God, to remember the profession which you made unto God in your Baptism. And forasmuch as after this life there is an account to be given unto the righteous Judge, by whom all must be judged without respect of persons, I require you to examine yourself and your

estate, both toward God and man; so that, accusing and condemning yourself for your own faults, you may find mercy at our
heavenly Father's hand for Christ's sake, and not be accused and
condemned in that fearful judgement. Therefore I shall rehearse
to you the Articles of our Faith, that you may know whether
you do believe as a Christian man should, or no.

*Here the Minister shall rehearse the Articles of the Faith, say-
ing thus,*

DOST thou believe in God the Father Almighty, Maker of
heaven and earth?

And in Jesus Christ his only-begotten Son our Lord? And
that he was conceived by the Holy Ghost, born of the Virgin
Mary; that he suffered under Pontius Pilate, was crucified, dead,
and buried; that he went down into hell, and also did rise again
the third day; that he ascended into heaven, and sitteth at the
right hand of God the Father Almighty; and from thence shall
come again at the end of the world, to judge the quick and
the dead?

And dost thou believe in the Holy Ghost; the holy Catholick
Church; the Communion of Saints; the Remission of sins; the
Resurrection of the flesh; and everlasting life after death?

The sick person shall answer,

All this I stedfastly believe.

*Then shall the Minister examine whether he repent him truly
of his sins, and be in charity with all the world; exhorting him
to forgive, from the bottom of his heart, all persons that have
offended him; and if he have offended any other, to ask them
forgiveness; and where he hath done injury or wrong to any
man, that he make amends to the uttermost of his power. And
if he have not before disposed of his goods, let him then be
admonished to make his Will, and to declare his debts, what
he oweth, and what is owing unto him; for the better dis-
charging of his conscience, and the quietness of his Executors.
But men should often be put in remembrance to take order for
the settling of their temporal estates whilst they are in health.*

These words before rehearsed may be said before the Minister begin his Prayer, as he shall see cause.

The Minister should not omit earnestly to move such sick persons as are of ability to be liberal to the poor.

Here shall the sick person be moved to make a special confession of his sins, if he feel his conscience troubled with any weighty matter. After which confession, the Priest shall absolve him (if he humbly and heartily desire it) after this sort.

OUR Lord Jesus Christ, who hath left power to his Church to absolve all sinners who truly repent and believe in him, of his great mercy forgive thee thine offences: And by his authority committed to me, I absolve thee from all thy sins, In the Name of the Father, and of the Son, and of the Holy Ghost. Amen.

And then the Priest shall say the Collect following.

Let us pray.

O MOST merciful God, who, according to the multitude of thy mercies, dost so put away the sins of those who truly repent, that thou rememberest them no more: Open thine eye of mercy upon this thy servant, who most earnestly desireth pardon and forgiveness. Renew in *him* (most loving Father) whatsoever hath been decayed by the fraud and malice of the devil, or by *his* own carnal will and frailness; preserve and continue this sick member in the unity of the Church; consider *his* contrition, accept *his* tears, asswage *his* pain, as shall seem to thee most expedient for *him*. And forasmuch as *he* putteth *his* full trust only in thy mercy, impute not unto *him his* former sins, but strengthen *him* with thy blessed Spirit; and, when thou art pleased to take *him* hence, take *him* unto thy favour, through the merits of thy most dearly beloved Son Jesus Christ our Lord. *Amen.*

Then shall the Minister say this Psalm.

In te, Domine, speravi. Psalm 71

IN thee, O Lord, have I put my trust; let me never be put to confusion: but rid me, and deliver me in thy righteousness; incline thine ear unto me, and save me.

Be thou my strong hold, whereunto I may alway resort: thou hast promised to help me; for thou art my house of defence, and my castle.

Deliver me, O my God, out of the hand of the ungodly: out of the hand of the unrighteous and cruel man.

For thou, O Lord God, art the thing that I long for: thou art my hope, even from my youth.

Through thee have I been holden up ever since I was born: thou art he that took me out of my mother's womb; my praise shall alway be of thee.

I am become as it were a monster unto many: but my sure trust is in thee.

O let my mouth be filled with thy praise: that I may sing of thy glory and honour all the day long.

Cast me not away in the time of age: forsake me not when my strength faileth me.

For mine enemies speak against me, and they that lay wait for my soul take their counsel together, saying: God hath forsaken him, persecute him, and take him; for there is none to deliver him.

Go not far from me, O God: my God, haste thee to help me.

Let them be confounded and perish that are against my soul: let them be covered with shame and dishonour that seek to do me evil.

As for me, I will patiently abide alway: and will praise thee more and more.

My mouth shall daily speak of thy righteousness and salvation: for I know no end thereof.

I will go forth in the strength of the Lord God: and will make mention of thy righteousness only.

Thou, O God, hast taught me from my youth up until now: therefore will I tell of thy wondrous works.

Forsake me not, O God, in mine old age, when I am gray-headed: until I have shewed thy strength unto this generation, and thy power to all them that are yet for to come.

Thy righteousness, O God, is very high, and great things are they that thou hast done: O God, who is like unto thee?

Glory be to the Father, and to the Son: and to the Holy Ghost;

As it was in the beginning, is now, and ever shall be: world without end. Amen.

Adding this.

O SAVIOUR of the world, who by thy Cross and precious Blood hast redeemed us: Save us, and help us, we humbly beseech thee, O Lord.

Then shall the Minister say,

THE Almighty Lord, who is a most strong tower to all them that put their trust in him, to whom all things in heaven, in earth, and under the earth, do bow and obey, be now and evermore thy defence; and make thee know and feel, that there is none other Name under heaven given to man, in whom, and through whom, thou mayest receive health and salvation, but only the Name of our Lord Jesus Christ. Amen.

And after that shall say,

UNTO God's gracious mercy and protection we commit thee. The Lord bless thee, and keep thee. The Lord make his face to shine upon thee, and be gracious unto thee. The Lord lift up his countenance upon thee, and give thee peace, both now and evermore. *Amen.*

A Prayer for a sick Child.

O ALMIGHTY God, and merciful Father, to whom alone belong the issues of life and death: Look down from heaven, we humbly beseech thee, with the eyes of mercy upon this child now lying upon the bed of sickness. Visit *him*, O Lord, with thy salvation; deliver *him* in thy good appointed time from *his* bodily pain, and save *his* soul for thy mercies' sake: that, if it shall be thy pleasure to prolong *his* days here on earth, *he* may live to thee, and be an instrument of thy glory, by serving thee faithfully, and doing good in *his* generation; or else receive *him* into those heavenly habitations, where the souls of them that sleep in the Lord Jesus enjoy perpetual rest and felicity. Grant this, O

Lord, for thy mercies' sake, in the same thy Son our Lord Jesus Christ, who liveth and reigneth with thee and the Holy Ghost, ever one God, world without end. Amen.

A Prayer for a sick person, when there appeareth small hope of recovery.

O FATHER of mercies, and God of all comfort, our only help in time of need: We fly unto thee for succour in behalf of this thy servant, here lying under thy hand in great weakness of body. Look graciously upon *him*, O Lord; and the more the outward man decayeth, strengthen *him*, we beseech thee, so much the more continually with thy grace and Holy Spirit in the inner man. Give *him* unfeigned repentance for all the errors of *his* life past, and stedfast faith in thy Son Jesus; that *his* sins may be done away by thy mercy, and *his* pardon sealed in heaven, before *he* go hence, and be no more seen. We know, O Lord, that there is no word impossible with thee; and that, if thou wilt, thou canst even yet raise *him* up, and grant *him* a longer continuance amongst us: Yet, forasmuch as in all appearance the time of *his* dissolution draweth near, so fit and prepare *him*, we beseech thee, against the hour of death, that after *his* departure hence in peace, and in thy favour, *his* soul may be received into thine everlasting kingdom, through the merits and mediation of Jesus Christ, thine only Son, our Lord and Saviour. *Amen.*

A commendatory Prayer for a sick person at the point of departure.

O ALMIGHTY God, with whom do live the spirits of just men made perfect, after they are delivered from their earthly prisons: We humbly commend the soul of this thy servant, our dear *brother*, into thy hands, as into the hands of a faithful Creator, and most merciful Saviour; most humbly beseeching thee that it may be precious in thy sight. Wash it, we pray thee, in the blood of that immaculate Lamb, that was slain to take away the sins of the world; that whatsoever defilements it may have contracted in the midst of this miserable and naughty world, through the lusts of the flesh or the wiles of Satan, being purged and done away, it may be presented pure and without spot before thee. And teach us who survive, in this and other like daily spectacles of mortality, to see how frail and uncertain our own condition is; and so to number our days, that we may seriously apply our hearts to that holy and heavenly wisdom, whilst we live here, which may in the end bring us to life ever-lasting, through the merits of Jesus Christ, thine only Son our Lord. *Amen.*

A Prayer for persons troubled in mind or in conscience.

O BLESSED Lord, the Father of mercies, and the God of all comforts: We beseech thee, look down in pity and compassion upon this thy afflicted servant. Thou writest bitter things against *him*, and makest *him* to possess *his* former iniquities; thy wrath lieth hard upon *him*, and *his* soul is full of trouble: But, O merciful God, who hast written thy holy Word for our learning, that we, through patience and comfort of thy holy Scriptures, might have hope; give *him* a right understanding of *himself*, and of thy threats and promises; that *he* may neither cast away *his* confidence in thee, nor place it any where but in thee. Give *him* strength against all *his* temptations, and heal all *his* distempers. Break not the bruised reed, nor quench the smoking flax. Shut not up thy tender mercies in displeasure; but make *him* to hear of joy and gladness, that the bones which thou hast broken may rejoice. Deliver *him* from fear of the enemy, and lift up the light of thy countenance upon *him*, and give *him* peace, through the merits and mediation of Jesus Christ our Lord. *Amen.*

THE
COMMUNION OF
THE SICK

*Forasmuch as all mortal men be subject to many sudden perils,
diseases and sicknesses, and ever uncertain what time they
shall depart out of this life; therefore, to the intent they may be
always in a readiness to die, whensoever it shall please
Almighty God to call them, the Curates shall diligently from
time to time (but especially in the time of pestilence, or other
infectious sickness) exhort their Parishioners to the often
receiving of the holy Communion of the Body and Blood of our
Saviour Christ, when it shall be publickly administered in the
Church; that so doing, they may, in case of sudden visitation,
have the less cause to be disquieted for lack of the same. But if
the sick person be not able to come to the Church, and yet is
desirous to receive the Communion in his house; then he must
give timely notice to the Curate, signifying also how many
there are to communicate with him, (which shall be three, or
two at the least,) and having a convenient place in the sick
man's house, with all things necessary so prepared, that the
Curate may reverently minister, he shall there celebrate the
holy Communion, beginning with the Collect, Epistle, and
Gospel here following.*

The Collect

ALMIGHTY everliving God, Maker of mankind, who dost
correct those whom thou dost love, and chastise every one
whom thou dost receive: We beseech thee to have mercy upon
this thy servant visited with thine hand; and to grant that *he*
may take *his* sickness patiently, and recover *his* bodily health, (if
it be thy gracious will,) and whensoever *his* soul shall depart
from the body, it may be without spot presented unto thee;
through Jesus Christ our Lord. *Amen.*

The Epistle. Hebr. 12. 5

MY son, despise not thou the chastening of the Lord, nor faint when thou art rebuked of him. For whom the Lord loveth he chasteneth, and scourgeth every son whom he receiveth.

The Gospel. S. John 5. 24

VERILY, verily I say unto you, He that heareth my word, and believeth on him that sent me, hath everlasting life, and shall not come into condemnation; but is passed from death unto life.

After which the Priest shall proceed according to the form before prescribed for the holy Communion, beginning at these words [Ye that do truly, &c.], p. 152.

At the time of the distribution of the holy Sacrament, the Priest shall first receive the Communion himself, and after minister unto them that are appointed to communicate with the sick; and last of all to the sick person.

But if a man, either by reason of extremity of sickness, or for want of warning in due time to the Curate, or for lack of company to receive with him, or by any other just impediment, do not receive the Sacrament of Christ's Body and Blood: the Curate shall instruct him that if he do truly repent him of his sins, and stedfastly believe that Jesus Christ hath suffered death upon the Cross for him, and shed his Blood for his redemption, earnestly remembering the benefits he hath thereby, and giving him hearty thanks therefore; he doth eat and drink the Body and Blood of our Saviour Christ profitably to his soul's health, although he do not receive the Sacrament with his mouth.

When the sick person is visited and receiveth the holy Communion all at one time, then the Priest, for more expedition, shall cut off the form of the Visitation at the Psalm [In thee, O Lord, have I put my trust] *and go straight to the Communion.*

In the time of the plague, sweat, or such other like contagious times of sickness or diseases, when none of the Parish or neighbours can be gotten to communicate with the sick in their houses, for fear of the infection, upon special request of the diseased, the Minister may only communicate with him.

THE ORDER FOR
THE BURIAL OF THE DEAD

Here is to be noted, that the Office ensuing is not to be used for any that die unbaptized, or excommunicate, or have laid violent hands upon themselves.

The Priest and Clerks meeting the corpse at the entrance of the Church-yard, and going before it, either into the Church, or towards the grave, shall say, or sing:

I AM the resurrection and the life, saith the Lord: he that believeth in me, though he were dead, yet shall he live: and whosoever liveth and believeth in me shall never die.

S. John 11. 25, 26.

I KNOW that my Redeemer liveth, and that he shall stand at the latter day upon the earth. And though after my skin worms destroy this body, yet in my flesh shall I see God: whom I shall see for myself, and mine eyes shall behold, and not another.

Job 19. 25, 26, 27.

WE brought nothing into this world, and it is certain we can carry nothing out. The Lord gave, and the Lord hath taken away; blessed be the name of the Lord.   1 *Tim.* 6. 7. *Job* 1. 21.

After they are come into the Church, shall be read one or both of these Psalms following.

Dixi, Custodiam. Psalm 39

I SAID, I will take heed to my ways: that I offend not in my tongue.

I will keep my mouth as it were with a bridle: while the ungodly is in my sight.

I held my tongue, and spake nothing: I kept silence, yea, even from good words; but it was pain and grief to me.

My heart was hot within me, and while I was thus musing the fire kindled: and at the last I spake with my tongue;

Lord, let me know mine end, and the number of my days: that I may be certified how long I have to live.

Behold, thou hast made my days as it were a span long: and mine age is even as nothing in respect of thee; and verily every man living is altogether vanity.

For man walketh in a vain shadow, and disquieteth himself in vain: he heapeth up riches, and cannot tell who shall gather them.

And now, Lord, what is my hope: truly my hope is even in thee.

Deliver me from all mine offences: and make me not a rebuke unto the foolish.

I became dumb, and opened not my mouth: for it was thy doing.

Take thy plague away from me: I am even consumed by means of thy heavy hand.

When thou with rebukes dost chasten man for sin, thou makest his beauty to consume away, like as it were a moth fretting a garment: every man therefore is but vanity.

Hear my prayer, O Lord, and with thine ears consider my calling: hold not thy peace at my tears.

For I am a stranger with thee: and a sojourner, as all my fathers were.

O spare me a little, that I may recover my strength: before I go hence, and be no more seen.

Glory be to the Father, and to the Son: and to the Holy Ghost;

As it was in the beginning, is now, and ever shall be: world without end. Amen.

Domine, refugium. Psalm 90

LORD, thou hast been our refuge: from one generation to another.

Before the mountains were brought forth, or ever the earth and the world were made: thou art God from everlasting, and world without end.

Thou turnest man to destruction: again thou sayest, Come again, ye children of men.

For a thousand years in thy sight are but as yesterday: seeing that is past as a watch in the night.

As soon as thou scatterest them, they are even as a sleep: and fade away suddenly like the grass.

In the morning it is green, and groweth up: but in the evening it is cut down, dried up, and withered.

For we consume away in thy displeasure: and are afraid at thy wrathful indignation.

Thou hast set our misdeeds before thee: and our secret sins in the light of thy countenance.

For when thou art angry, all our days are gone: we bring our years to an end, as it were a tale that is told.

The days of our age are threescore years and ten; and though men be so strong, that they come to fourscore years: yet is their strength then but labour and sorrow; so soon passeth it away, and we are gone.

But who regardeth the power of thy wrath: for even thereafter as a man feareth, so is thy displeasure.

O teach us to number our days: that we may apply our hearts unto wisdom.

Turn thee again, O Lord, at the last: and be gracious unto thy servants.

O satisfy us with thy mercy, and that soon: so shall we rejoice and be glad all the days of our life.

Comfort us again now after the time that thou hast plagued us: and for the years wherein we have suffered adversity.

Shew thy servants thy work: and their children thy glory.

And the glorious majesty of the Lord our God be upon us: prosper thou the work of our hands upon us, O prosper thou our handywork.

Glory be to the Father, and to the Son: and to the Holy Ghost;

As it was in the beginning, is now, and ever shall be: world without end. Amen.

Then shall follow the Lesson taken out of the fifteenth chapter
of the former Epistle of Saint Paul to the Corinthians.

1 Cor. 15. 20

NOW is Christ risen from the dead, and become the first-fruits of them that slept. For since by man came death, by man came also the resurrection of the dead. For as in Adam all die, even so in Christ shall all be made alive. But every man in his own order: Christ the first-fruits; afterward they that are Christ's, at his coming. Then cometh the end, when he shall have delivered up the kingdom to God, even the Father; when he shall have put down all rule, and all authority, and power. For he must reign, till he hath put all enemies under his feet. The last enemy that shall be destroyed is death. For he hath put all things under his feet. But when he saith, all things are put under him, it is manifest that he is excepted, which did put all things under him. And when all things shall be subdued unto him, then shall the Son also himself be subject unto him that put all things under him, that God may be all in all. Else what shall they do which are baptized for the dead, if the dead rise not at all? why are they then baptized for the dead? And why stand we in jeopardy every hour? I protest by your rejoicing, which I have in Christ Jesus our Lord, I die daily. If after the manner of men I have fought with beasts at Ephesus, what advantageth it me, if the dead rise not? Let us eat and drink, for to-morrow we die. Be not deceived: evil communications corrupt good manners. Awake to righteousness, and sin not: for some have not the knowledge of God: I speak this to your shame. But some man will say, How are the dead raised up? and with what body do they come? Thou fool, that which thou sowest is not quickened, except it die. And that which thou sowest, thou sowest not that body that shall be, but bare grain, it may chance of wheat, or of some other grain: but God giveth it a body, as it hath pleased him, and to every seed his own body. All flesh is not the same flesh; but there is one kind of flesh of men, another flesh of beasts, another of fishes, and another of birds. There are also celestial bodies, and bodies terrestrial; but the glory of the celestial is one, and the glory of the terrestrial is another. There is one glory of the sun, and another glory of the moon, and another glory of the stars; for one star differeth from another star in glory. So also is the resurrection of the dead. It is sown in corruption; it is raised in incorruption: it is sown in dishonour; it is raised in glory: it is sown in weakness; it is raised in power: it is sown a natural body; it is raised a spiritual body. There is a natural body, and there is a spiritual body. And so it is written, The first man Adam was made a living soul; the last Adam was made a quickening spirit. Howbeit, that was not first which is spiritual, but that which is natural; and afterward that which is spiritual. The first man is of the earth, earthy: the second man is the Lord from heaven. As is the earthy, such are they that are earthy: and as is the heavenly, such are they also that are heavenly. And as we have borne the image of the earthy, we shall also bear the image of the heavenly. Now this I say, brethren, that flesh and blood cannot inherit the kingdom of God; neither doth corruption inherit incorruption. Behold, I shew you a mystery: We shall not all sleep, but we shall all be changed, in a moment, in the twinkling of an eye, at the last trump: for the trumpet shall sound, and the dead shall be raised incorruptible, and we shall be changed. For this corruptible must put on incorruption, and this mortal must put on immortality. So when this corruptible shall have put on incorruption, and this mortal shall have put on immortality; then shall be brought to pass the saying that is written, Death is swallowed up in victory. O death, where is thy sting? O grave, where is thy victory? The sting of death is sin; and the strength of sin is the law. But thanks be to God, which giveth us the victory through our Lord Jesus Christ. Therefore, my beloved brethren, be ye stedfast, unmoveable, always abounding in the work of the Lord, forasmuch as ye know that your labour is not in vain in the Lord.

When they come to the grave, while the corpse is made ready to be laid into the earth, the Priest shall say, or the Priest and Clerks shall sing:

MAN that is born of a woman hath but a short time to live, and is full of misery. He cometh up, and is cut down, like a flower; he fleeth as it were a shadow, and never continueth in one stay.

In the midst of life we are in death: of whom may we seek for succour, but of thee, O Lord, who for our sins art justly displeased?

Yet, O Lord God most holy, O Lord most mighty, O holy and most merciful Saviour, deliver us not into the bitter pains of eternal death.

Thou knowest, Lord, the secrets of our hearts; shut not thy merciful ears to our prayer; but spare us, Lord most holy, O God most mighty, O holy and merciful Saviour, thou most worthy Judge eternal, suffer us not, at our last hour, for any pains of death, to fall from thee.

Then, while the earth shall be cast upon the body by some standing by, the Priest shall say,

FORASMUCH as it hath pleased Almighty God of his great mercy to take unto himself the soul of our dear *brother* here departed: we therefore commit *his* body to the ground; earth to earth, ashes to ashes, dust to dust; in sure and certain hope of the Resurrection to eternal life, through our Lord Jesus Christ; who shall change our vile body, that it may be like unto his glorious body, according to the mighty working, whereby he is able to subdue all things to himself.

Then shall be said or sung,

I HEARD a voice from heaven, saying unto me, Write, From henceforth blessed are the dead which die in the Lord: Even so, saith the Spirit, for they rest from their labours.

Then the Priest shall say,

Lord, have mercy upon us.
Christ, have mercy upon us.
Lord, have mercy upon us.

OUR Father which art in heaven, Hallowed be thy Name, Thy

kingdom come, Thy will be done, in earth as it is in heaven. Give us this day our daily bread; And forgive us our trespasses, As we forgive them that trespass against us; And lead us not into temptation, But deliver us from evil. Amen.

Priest.

ALMIGHTY God, with whom do live the spirits of them that depart hence in the Lord, and with whom the souls of the faithful, after they are delivered from the burden of the flesh, are in joy and felicity: We give thee hearty thanks, for that it hath pleased thee to deliver this our *brother* out of the miseries of this sinful world; beseeching thee that it may please thee, of thy gracious goodness, shortly to accomplish the number of thine elect, and to hasten thy kingdom; that we, with all those that are departed in the true faith of thy holy Name, may have our perfect consummation and bliss, both in body and soul, in thy eternal and everlasting glory; through Jesus Christ our Lord. *Amen.*

The Collect

O MERCIFUL God, the Father of our Lord Jesus Christ, who is the resurrection and the life; in whom whosoever believeth shall live, though he die; and whosoever liveth, and believeth in him, shall not die eternally; who also hath taught us (by his holy Apostle Saint Paul) not to be sorry, as men without hope, for them that sleep in him: We meekly beseech thee, O Father, to raise us from the death of sin unto the life of righteousness; that, when we shall depart this life, we may rest in him, as our hope is this our *brother* doth; and that, at the general Resurrection in the last day, we may be found acceptable in thy sight, and receive that blessing, which thy well-beloved Son shall then pronounce to all that love and fear thee, saying, Come, ye blessed children of my Father, receive the kingdom prepared for you from the beginning of the world: Grant this, we beseech thee, O merciful Father, through Jesus Christ, our Mediator and Redeemer. *Amen.*

THE grace of our Lord Jesus Christ, and the love of God, and the fellowship of the Holy Ghost, be with us all evermore. *Amen.*

THE THANKSGIVING OF
WOMEN AFTER CHILD-BIRTH
COMMONLY CALLED

THE CHURCHING
OF WOMEN

The Woman, at the usual time after her delivery, shall come into the Church decently apparelled, and there shall kneel down in some convenient place, as hath been accustomed, or as the Ordinary shall direct: And then the Priest shall say unto her,

FORASMUCH as it hath pleased Almighty God of his goodness to give you safe deliverance, and hath preserved you in the great danger of child-birth: You shall therefore give hearty thanks unto God, and say,

Then shall the Priest say the 116th Psalm.

Dilexi quoniam

I AM well pleased: that the Lord hath heard the voice of my prayer;

That he hath inclined his ear unto me: therefore will I call upon him as long as I live.

The snares of death compassed me round about: and the pains of hell gat hold upon me.

I found trouble and heaviness, and I called upon the name of the Lord: O Lord, I beseech thee, deliver my soul.

Gracious is the Lord, and righteous: yea, our God is merciful.

The Lord preserveth the simple: I was in misery, and he helped me.

Turn again then unto thy rest, O my soul: for the Lord hath rewarded thee.

And why? thou hast delivered my soul from death: mine eyes from tears, and my feet from falling.

I will walk before the Lord: in the land of the living.

I believed, and therefore will I speak; but I was sore troubled: I said in my haste, All men are liars.

What reward shall I give unto the Lord: for all the benefits that he hath done unto me?

I will receive the cup of salvation: and call upon the name of the Lord.

I will pay my vows now in the presence of all his people: in the courts of the Lord's house, even in the midst of thee, O Jerusalem. Praise the Lord.

Glory be to the Father, and to the Son: and to the Holy Ghost;

As it was in the beginning, is now, and ever shall be: world without end. Amen.

Or Psalm 127.

Nisi Dominus

EXCEPT the Lord build the house: their labour is but lost that build it.

Except the Lord keep the city: the watchman waketh but in vain.

It is but lost labour that ye haste to rise up early, and so late take rest, and eat the bread of carefulness: for so he giveth his beloved sleep.

Lo, children and the fruit of the womb: are an heritage and gift that cometh of the Lord.

Like as the arrows in the hand of the giant: even so are the young children.

Happy is the man that hath his quiver full of them: they shall not be ashamed when they speak with their enemies in the gate.

Glory be to the Father, and to the Son: and to the Holy Ghost;

As it was in the beginning, is now, and ever shall be: world without end. Amen.

Then the Priest shall say,

Let us pray.

Lord, have mercy upon us.
Christ, have mercy upon us.
Lord, have mercy upon us.

OUR Father which art in heaven, Hallowed be thy Name, Thy kingdom come, Thy will be done, in earth as it is in heaven. Give us this day our daily bread; And forgive us our trespasses, As we forgive them that trespass against us; And lead us not into temptation, But deliver us from evil. For thine is the kingdom, the power, and the glory, For ever and ever. Amen.

Minister. O Lord, save this woman thy servant;
Answer. Who putteth her trust in thee.
Minister. Be thou to her a strong tower;
Answer. From the face of her enemy.
Minister. Lord, hear our prayer.
Answer. And let our cry come unto thee.

Minister.

Let us pray.

O ALMIGHTY God, we give thee humble thanks for that thou hast vouchsafed to deliver this woman thy servant from the great pain and peril of child-birth: Grant, we beseech thee, most merciful Father, that she through thy help may both faithfully live and walk according to thy will, in this life present; and also may be partaker of everlasting glory in the life to come; through Jesus Christ our Lord. *Amen.*

The Woman, that cometh to give her thanks, must offer accustomed offerings; and, if there be a Communion, it is convenient that she receive the holy Communion.

A COMMINATION

OR DENOUNCING OF GOD'S ANGER AND JUDGEMENTS AGAINST SINNERS

WITH CERTAIN PRAYERS TO BE USED ON THE FIRST DAY OF LENT, AND AT OTHER TIMES, AS THE ORDINARY SHALL APPOINT

After Morning Prayer, the Litany ended, according to the accustomed manner, the Priest shall in the reading Pew or Pulpit say,

BRETHREN, in the primitive Church there was a godly discipline, that, at the beginning of Lent, such persons as stood convicted of notorious sin were put to open penance, and punished in this world, that their souls might be saved in the day of the Lord; and that others, admonished by their example, might be the more afraid to offend.

Instead whereof, until the said discipline may be restored again, (which is much to be wished,) it is thought good that at this time (in the presence of you all) should be read the general sentences of God's cursing against impenitent sinners, gathered out of the seven and twentieth chapter of Deuteronomy, and other places of Scripture; and that ye should answer to every sentence, *Amen:* To the intent that, being admonished of the great indignation of God against sinners, ye may the rather be moved to earnest and true repentance; and may walk more warily in these dangerous days; fleeing from such vices, for which ye affirm with your own mouths the curse of God to be due.

CURSED is the man that maketh any carved or molten image, to worship it.

And the people shall answer and say,
Amen.

Minister. Cursed is he that curseth his father or mother.
Answer. Amen.
Minister. Cursed is he that removeth his neighbour's landmark.
Answer. Amen.
Minister. Cursed is he that maketh the blind to go out of his way.
Answer. Amen.
Minister. Cursed is he that perverteth the judgement of the stranger, the fatherless, and widow.
Answer. Amen.
Minister. Cursed is he that smiteth his neighbour secretly.
Answer. Amen.
Minister. Cursed is he that lieth with his neighbour's wife.
Answer. Amen.
Minister. Cursed is he that taketh reward to slay the innocent.
Answer. Amen.
Minister. Cursed is he that putteth his trust in man, and taketh man for his defence, and in his heart goeth from the Lord.
Answer. Amen.
Minister. Cursed are the unmerciful, fornicators, and adulterers, covetous persons, idolaters, slanderers, drunkards, and extortioners.
Answer. Amen.

Minister.

NOW seeing that all they are accursed (as the prophet David beareth witness) who do err and go astray from the commandments of God; let us (remembering the dreadful judgement hanging over our heads, and always ready to fall upon us) return unto our Lord God with all contrition and meekness of heart; bewailing and lamenting our sinful life, acknowledging and confessing our offences, and seeking to bring forth worthy fruits of penance. For now is the axe put unto the root of the trees, so that every tree that bringeth not forth good fruit is hewn down, and cast into the fire. It is a fearful thing to fall into the hands of the living God: He shall pour down rain upon the sinners, snares, fire and brimstone, storm and tempest; this shall be their portion to drink. For lo, the Lord is come out of his place to visit the wickedness of such as dwell upon the earth. But who may abide the day of his coming? Who shall be able to endure when he appeareth? His fan is in his hand, and he will purge his floor, and gather his wheat into the barn; but he will burn the chaff with unquenchable fire. The day of the Lord cometh as a thief in the night: and when men shall say, Peace, and all things are safe, then shall sudden destruction come upon them, as sorrow cometh upon a woman travailing with child, and they shall not escape. Then shall appear the wrath of God in the day of vengeance, which obstinate sinners, through the stubbornness of their heart, have heaped unto themselves; which despised the goodness, patience, and long-sufferance of God, when he calleth them continually to repentance. Then shall they call upon me (saith the Lord) but I will not hear; they shall seek me early, but they shall not find me; and that, because they hated knowledge, and received not the fear of the Lord, but abhorred my counsel, and despised my correction. Then shall it be too late to knock, when the door shall be shut; and too late to cry for mercy, when it is the time of justice. O terrible voice of most just judgement, which shall be pronounced upon them, when it shall be said unto them, Go, ye cursed, into the fire everlasting, which is prepared for the devil and his angels. Therefore, brethren, take we heed betime, while the day of salvation lasteth; for the night cometh, when none can work: But let us, while we have the light, believe in the light, and walk as children of the light; that we be not cast into utter darkness, where is weeping and gnashing of teeth. Let us not abuse the goodness of God, who calleth us mercifully to amendment, and of his endless pity promiseth us forgiveness of that which is past, if with a perfect and true heart we return unto him. For though our sins be as red as scarlet, they shall be made white as snow; and though they be like purple, yet they shall be made white as wool. Turn ye (saith the Lord) from all your wickedness, and your sin shall not be your destruction: Cast away from you all your ungodliness that ye have done: Make you new hearts, and a new spirit: Wherefore will ye die, O ye house of Israel? seeing that I have no pleasure in the death of him that dieth, saith the Lord God. Turn ye then, and ye shall live. Although we have sinned, yet have we an Advocate with the Father, Jesus Christ the righteous; and he is the propitiation for our sins. For he was wounded for our offences, and smitten for our wickedness. Let us therefore return unto him, who is the merciful receiver of all true penitent sinners; assuring ourselves that he is ready to receive us, and most willing to pardon us, if we come unto him with faithful repentance; if we submit ourselves unto him, and from henceforth walk in his ways; if we will take his easy yoke and light burden upon us, to follow him in lowliness, patience, and charity, and be ordered by the governance of his Holy Spirit; seeking always his glory, and serving him duly in our vocation with thanksgiving. This if we do, Christ will deliver us from the curse of the law, and from the extreme malediction which shall light upon them that shall be set on the left hand; and he will set us on his right hand, and give us the gracious benediction of his Father, commanding us to take possession of his glorious kingdom: Unto which he vouchsafe to bring us all, for his infinite mercy. Amen.

Then shall they all kneel upon their knees, and the Priest and Clerks kneeling (in the place where they are accustomed to say the Litany) shall say this Psalm.

Miserere mei, Deus. Psalm 51

HAVE mercy upon me, O God, after thy great goodness: according to the multitude of thy mercies do away mine offences.

Wash me throughly from my wickedness: and cleanse me from my sin.

For I acknowledge my faults: and my sin is ever before me.

Against thee only have I sinned, and done this evil in thy sight: that thou mightest be justified in thy saying, and clear when thou art judged.

Behold, I was shapen in wickedness: and in sin hath my mother conceived me.

But lo, thou requirest truth in the inward parts: and shalt make me to understand wisdom secretly.

Thou shalt purge me with hyssop, and I shall be clean: thou shalt wash me, and I shall be whiter than snow.

Thou shalt make me hear of joy and gladness: that the bones which thou hast broken may rejoice.

Turn thy face away from my sins: and put out all my misdeeds.

Make me a clean heart, O God: and renew a right spirit within me.

Cast me not away from thy presence: and take not thy holy Spirit from me.

O give me the comfort of thy help again: and stablish me with thy free Spirit.

Then shall I teach thy ways unto the wicked: and sinners shall be converted unto thee.

Deliver me from blood-guiltiness, O God, thou that art the God of my health: and my tongue shall sing of thy righteousness.

Thou shalt open my lips, O Lord: and my mouth shall shew thy praise.

For thou desirest no sacrifice, else would I give it thee: but thou delightest not in burnt-offering.

The sacrifice of God is a troubled spirit: a broken and contrite heart, O God, shalt thou not despise.

O be favourable and gracious unto Sion: build thou the walls of Jerusalem.

Then shalt thou be pleased with the sacrifice of righteousness, with the burnt-offerings and oblations: then shall they offer young bullocks upon thine altar.

Glory be to the Father, and to the Son: and to the Holy Ghost;

Answer. As it was in the beginning, is now, and ever shall be: world without end. Amen.

Lord, have mercy upon us.

Christ, have mercy upon us.
Lord, have mercy upon us.

OUR Father which art in heaven, Hallowed be thy Name, Thy kingdom come, Thy will be done, in earth as it is in heaven. Give us this day our daily bread; And forgive us our trespasses, As we forgive them that trespass against us; And lead us not into temptation, But deliver us from evil. Amen.

Minister. O Lord, save thy servants;
Answer. That put their trust in thee.
Minister. Send unto them help from above.
Answer. And evermore mightily defend them.
Minister. Help us, O God our Saviour.
Answer. And for the glory of thy Name deliver us; be merciful unto us sinners, for thy Name's sake.
Minister. O Lord, hear our prayer.
Answer. And let our cry come unto thee.

Minister.

Let us pray.

O LORD, we beseech thee, mercifully hear our prayers, and spare all those who confess their sins unto thee; that they, whose consciences by sin are accused, by thy merciful pardon may be absolved; through Christ our Lord. *Amen.*

O MOST mighty God, and merciful Father, who hast compassion upon all men, and hatest nothing that thou hast made; who wouldest not the death of a sinner, but that he should rather turn from his sin, and be saved: Mercifully forgive us our trespasses; receive and comfort us, who are grieved and wearied with the burden of our sins. Thy property is always to have mercy; to thee only it appertaineth to forgive sins. Spare us therefore, good Lord, spare thy people, whom thou hast redeemed; enter not into judgement with thy servants, who are vile earth, and miserable sinners; but so turn thine anger from us, who meekly acknowledge our vileness, and truly repent us of our faults, and so make haste to help us in this world, that we may ever live with thee in the world to come; through Jesus Christ our Lord. *Amen.*

Then shall the people say this that followeth, after the Minister.

TURN thou us, O good Lord, and so shall we be turned. Be favourable, O Lord, Be favourable to thy people, Who turn to thee in weeping, fasting, and praying. For thou art a merciful God, Full of compassion, long-suffering, and of great pity. Thou sparest when we deserve punishment, And in thy wrath thinkest upon mercy. Spare thy people, good Lord, Spare them, and let not thine heritage be brought to confusion. Hear us, O Lord, for thy mercy is great, And after the multitude of thy mercies look upon us; Through the merits and mediation of thy blessed Son, Jesus Christ our Lord. Amen.

Then the Minister alone shall say,

THE Lord bless us, and keep us; the Lord lift up the light of his countenance upon us, and give us peace, now and for evermore. *Amen.*

THE
PSALMS OF DAVID

DAY 1. MORNING PRAYER

PSALM 1. *Beatus vir, qui non abiit, &c.*

BLESSED is the man that hath not walked in the counsel of the ungodly, nor stood in the way of sinners: and hath not sat in the seat of the scornful.

2 But his delight is in the law of the Lord: and in his law will he exercise himself day and night.

3 And he shall be like a tree planted by the water-side: that will bring forth his fruit in due season.

4 His leaf also shall not wither: and look, whatsoever he doeth, it shall prosper.

5 As for the ungodly, it is not so with them: but they are like the chaff, which the wind scattereth away from the face of the earth.

6 Therefore the ungodly shall not be able to stand in the judgement: neither the sinners in the congregation of the righteous.

7 But the Lord knoweth the way of the righteous: and the way of the ungodly shall perish.

PSALM 2. *Quare fremuerunt gentes?*

WHY do the heathen so furiously rage together: and why do the people imagine a vain thing?

2 The kings of the earth stand up, and the rulers take counsel together: against the Lord, and against his Anointed.

3 Let us break their bonds asunder: and cast away their cords from us.

4 He that dwelleth in heaven shall laugh them to scorn: the Lord shall have them in derision.

5 Then shall he speak unto them in his wrath: and vex them in his sore displeasure.

6 Yet have I set my King: upon my holy hill of Sion.

7 I will preach the law, whereof the Lord hath said unto me: Thou art my Son, this day have I begotten thee.

8 Desire of me, and I shall give thee the heathen for thine inheritance: and the utmost parts of the earth for thy possession.

9 Thou shalt bruise them with a rod of iron: and break them in pieces like a potter's vessel.

10 Be wise now therefore, O ye kings: be learned, ye that are judges of the earth.

11 Serve the Lord in fear: and rejoice unto him with reverence.

12 Kiss the Son, lest he be angry, and so ye perish from the right way: if his wrath be kindled, (yea, but a little,) blessed are all they that put their trust in him.

PSALM 3. *Domine, quid multiplicati?*

LORD, how are they increased that trouble me: many are they that rise against me.

2 Many one there be that say of my soul: There is no help for him in his God.

3 But thou, O Lord, art my defender: thou art my worship, and the lifter up of my head.

4 I did call upon the Lord with my voice: and he heard me out of his holy hill.

5 I laid me down and slept, and rose up again: for the Lord sustained me.

6 I will not be afraid for ten thousands of the people: that have set themselves against me round about.

7 Up, Lord, and help me, O my God: for thou smitest all mine enemies upon the cheek-bone; thou hast broken the teeth of the ungodly.

8 Salvation belongeth unto the Lord: and thy blessing is upon thy people.

PSALM 4. *Cum invocarem*

HEAR me when I call, O God of my righteousness: thou hast set me at liberty when I was in trouble; have mercy upon me, and hearken unto my prayer.

2 O ye sons of men, how long will ye blaspheme mine honour: and have such pleasure in vanity, and seek after leasing?

3 Know this also, that the Lord hath chosen to himself the man that is godly: when I call upon the Lord, he will hear me.

4 Stand in awe, and sin not: commune with your own heart, and in your chamber, and be still.

5 Offer the sacrifice of righteousness: and put your trust in the Lord.

6 There be many that say: Who will shew us any good?

7 Lord, lift thou up: the light of thy countenance upon us.

8 Thou hast put gladness in my heart: since the time that their corn and wine and oil increased.

9 I will lay me down in peace, and take my rest: for it is thou, Lord, only, that makest me dwell in safety.

PSALM 5. *Verba mea auribus*

PONDER my words, O Lord: consider my meditation.

2 O hearken thou unto the voice of my calling, my King, and my God: for unto thee will I make my prayer.

3 My voice shalt thou hear betimes, O Lord: early in the morning will I direct my prayer unto thee, and will look up.

4 For thou art the God that hast no pleasure in wickedness: neither shall any evil dwell with thee.

5 Such as be foolish shall not stand in thy sight: for thou hatest all them that work vanity.

6 Thou shalt destroy them that speak leasing: the Lord will abhor both the blood-thirsty and deceitful man.

7 But as for me, I will come into thine house, even upon the multitude of thy mercy: and in thy fear will I worship toward thy holy temple.

8 Lead me, O Lord, in thy righteousness, because of mine enemies: make thy way plain before my face.

9 For there is no faithfulness in his mouth: their inward parts are very wickedness.

10 Their throat is an open sepulchre: they flatter with their tongue.

11 Destroy thou them, O God; let them perish through their

own imaginations: cast them out in the multitude of their ungodliness; for they have rebelled against thee.

12 And let all them that put their trust in thee rejoice: they shall ever be giving of thanks, because thou defendest them; they that love thy Name shall be joyful in thee;

13 For thou, Lord, wilt give thy blessing unto the righteous: and with thy favourable kindness wilt thou defend him as with a shield.

DAY 1. EVENING PRAYER

Psalm 6. *Domine, ne in furore*

O LORD, rebuke me not in thine indignation: neither chasten me in thy displeasure.

2 Have mercy upon me, O Lord, for I am weak: O Lord, heal me, for my bones are vexed.

3 My soul also is sore troubled: but, Lord, how long wilt thou punish me?

4 Turn thee, O Lord, and deliver my soul: O save me for thy mercy's sake.

5 For in death no man remembereth thee: and who will give thee thanks in the pit?

6 I am weary of my groaning; every night wash I my bed: and water my couch with my tears.

7 My beauty is gone for very trouble: and worn away because of all mine enemies.

8 Away from me, all ye that work vanity: for the Lord hath heard the voice of my weeping.

9 The Lord hath heard my petition: the Lord will receive my prayer.

10 All mine enemies shall be confounded, and sore vexed: they shall be turned back, and put to shame suddenly.

Psalm 7. *Domine, Deus meus*

O LORD my God, in thee have I put my trust: save me from all them that persecute me, and deliver me;

2 Lest he devour my soul, like a lion, and tear it in pieces: while there is none to help.

3 O Lord my God, if I have done any such thing: or if there be any wickedness in my hands;

4 If I have rewarded evil unto him that dealt friendly with me: yea, I have delivered him that without any cause is mine enemy;

5 Then let mine enemy persecute my soul, and take me: yea, let him tread my life down upon the earth, and lay mine honour in the dust.

6 Stand up, O Lord, in thy wrath, and lift up thyself, because of the indignation of mine enemies: arise up for me in the judgement that thou hast commanded.

7 And so shall the congregation of the people come about thee: for their sakes therefore lift up thyself again.

8 The Lord shall judge the people; give sentence with me, O Lord: according to my righteousness, and according to the innocency that is in me.

9 O let the wickedness of the ungodly come to an end: but guide thou the just.

10 For the righteous God: trieth the very hearts and reins.

11 My help cometh of God: who preserveth them that are true of heart.

12 God is a righteous Judge, strong and patient: and God is provoked every day.

13 If a man will not turn, he will whet his sword: he hath bent his bow, and made it ready.

14 He hath prepared for him the instruments of death: he ordaineth his arrows against the persecutors.

15 Behold, he travaileth with mischief: he hath conceived sorrow, and brought forth ungodliness.

16 He hath graven and digged up a pit: and is fallen himself into the destruction that he made for other.

17 For his travail shall come upon his own head: and his wickedness shall fall on his own pate.

18 I will give thanks unto the Lord, according to his righteousness: and I will praise the Name of the Lord most High.

Psalm 8. *Domine, Dominus noster*

O LORD our Governor, how excellent is thy Name in all the world: thou that hast set thy glory above the heavens!

2 Out of the mouth of very babes and sucklings hast thou ordained strength, because of thine enemies: that thou mightest still the enemy and the avenger.

3 For I will consider thy heavens, even the works of thy fingers: the moon and the stars, which thou hast ordained.

4 What is man, that thou art mindful of him: and the son of man, that thou visitest him?

5 Thou madest him lower than the angels: to crown him with glory and worship.

6 Thou makest him to have dominion of the works of thy hands: and thou hast put all things in subjection under his feet;

7 All sheep and oxen: yea, and the beasts of the field;

8 The fowls of the air, and the fishes of the sea: and whatsoever walketh through the paths of the seas.

9 O Lord our Governor: how excellent is thy Name in all the world!

DAY 2. MORNING PRAYER

Psalm 9. *Confitebor tibi*

I WILL give thanks unto thee, O Lord, with my whole heart: I will speak of all thy marvellous works.

2 I will be glad and rejoice in thee: yea, my songs will I make of thy Name, O thou most Highest.

3 While mine enemies are driven back: they shall fall and perish at thy presence.

4 For thou hast maintained my right and my cause: thou art set in the throne that judgest right.

5 Thou hast rebuked the heathen, and destroyed the ungodly: thou hast put out their name for ever and ever.

6 O thou enemy, destructions are come to a perpetual end: even as the cities which thou hast destroyed, their memorial is perished with them.

7 But the Lord shall endure for ever: he hath also prepared his seat for judgement.

8 For he shall judge the world in righteousness: and minister true judgement unto the people.

9 The Lord also will be a defence for the oppressed: even a refuge in due time of trouble.

10 And they that know thy Name will put their trust in thee: for thou, Lord, hast never failed them that seek thee.

11 O praise the Lord which dwelleth in Sion: shew the people of his doings.

12 For when he maketh inquisition for blood, he remembereth them: and forgetteth not the complaint of the poor.

13 Have mercy upon me, O Lord; consider the trouble which I suffer of them that hate me: thou that liftest me up from the gates of death.

14 That I may shew all thy praises within the ports of the daughter of Sion: I will rejoice in thy salvation.

15 The heathen are sunk down in the pit that they made: in the same net which they hid privily, is their foot taken.

16 The Lord is known to execute judgement: the ungodly is trapped in the work of his own hands.

17 The wicked shall be turned into hell: and all the people that forget God.

18 For the poor shall not alway be forgotten: the patient abiding of the meek shall not perish for ever.

19 Up, Lord, and let not man have the upper hand: let the heathen be judged in thy sight.

20 Put them in fear, O Lord: that the heathen may know themselves to be but men.

Psalm 10. *Ut quid, Domine?*

WHY standest thou so far off, O Lord: and hidest thy face in the needful time of trouble?

2 The ungodly for his own lust doth persecute the poor: let them be taken in the crafty wiliness that they have imagined.

3 For the ungodly hath made boast of his own heart's desire: and speaketh good of the covetous, whom God abhorreth.

4 The ungodly is so proud, that he careth not for God: neither is God in all his thoughts.

5 His ways are alway grievous: thy judgements are far above out of his sight, and therefore defieth he all his enemies.

6 For he hath said in his heart, Tush, I shall never be cast down: there shall no harm happen unto me.

7 His mouth is full of cursing, deceit, and fraud: under his tongue is ungodliness and vanity.

8 He sitteth lurking in the thievish corners of the streets: and privily in his lurking dens doth he murder the innocent; his eyes are set against the poor.

9 For he lieth waiting secretly, even as a lion lurketh he in his den: that he may ravish the poor.

10 He doth ravish the poor: when he getteth him into his net.

11 He falleth down, and humbleth himself: that the congregation of the poor may fall into the hands of his captains.

12 He hath said in his heart, Tush, God hath forgotten: he hideth away his face, and he will never see it.

13 Arise, O Lord God, and lift up thine hand: forget not the poor.

14 Wherefore should the wicked blaspheme God: while he doth say in his heart, Tush, thou God carest not for it.

15 Surely thou hast seen it: for thou beholdest ungodliness and wrong.

16 That thou mayest take the matter into thy hand: the poor committeth himself unto thee; for thou art the helper of the friendless.

17 Break thou the power of the ungodly and malicious: take away his ungodliness, and thou shalt find none.

18 The Lord is King for ever and ever: and the heathen are perished out of the land.

19 Lord, thou hast heard the desire of the poor: thou preparest their heart, and thine ear hearkeneth thereto;

20 To help the fatherless and poor unto their right: that the man of the earth be no more exalted against them.

PSALM 11. *In Domino confido*

IN the Lord put I my trust: how say ye then to my soul, that she should flee as a bird unto the hill?

2 For lo, the ungodly bend their bow, and make ready their arrows within the quiver: that they may privily shoot at them which are true of heart.

3 For the foundations will be cast down: and what hath the righteous done?

4 The Lord is in his holy temple: the Lord's seat is in heaven.

5 His eyes consider the poor: and his eye-lids try the children of men.

6 The Lord alloweth the righteous: but the ungodly, and him that delighteth in wickedness, doth his soul abhor.

7 Upon the ungodly he shall rain snares, fire and brimstone, storm and tempest: this shall be their portion to drink.

8 For the righteous Lord loveth righteousness: his countenance will behold the thing that is just.

DAY 2. EVENING PRAYER

PSALM 12. *Salvum me fac*

HELP me, Lord, for there is not one godly man left: for the faithful are minished from among the children of men.

2 They talk of vanity every one with his neighbour: they do but flatter with their lips, and dissemble in their double heart.

3 The Lord shall root out all deceitful lips: and the tongue that speaketh proud things;

4 Which have said, With our tongue will we prevail: we are they that ought to speak, who is lord over us?

5 Now for the comfortless trouble's sake of the needy: and because of the deep sighing of the poor,

6 I will up, saith the Lord: and will help every one from him that swelleth against him, and will set him at rest.

7 The words of the Lord are pure words: even as the silver, which from the earth is tried, and purified seven times in the fire.

8 Thou shalt keep them, O Lord: thou shalt preserve him from this generation for ever.

9 The ungodly walk on every side: when they are exalted, the children of men are put to rebuke.

PSALM 13. *Usque quo, Domine?*

HOW long wilt thou forget me, O Lord, for ever: how long wilt thou hide thy face from me?

2 How long shall I seek counsel in my soul, and be so vexed in my heart: how long shall mine enemies triumph over me?

3 Consider, and hear me, O Lord my God: lighten mine eyes, that I sleep not in death.

4 Lest mine enemy say, I have prevailed against him: for if I be cast down, they that trouble me will rejoice at it.

5 But my trust is in thy mercy: and my heart is joyful in thy salvation.

6 I will sing of the Lord, because he hath dealt so lovingly with me: yea, I will praise the Name of the Lord most Highest.

PSALM 14. *Dixit insipiens*

THE fool hath said in his heart: There is no God.

2 They are corrupt, and become abominable in their doings: there is none that doeth good, no not one.

3 The Lord looked down from heaven upon the children of men: to see if there were any that would understand, and seek after God.

4 But they are all gone out of the way, they are altogether become abominable: there is none that doeth good, no not one.

5 Their throat is an open sepulchre, with their tongues have they deceived: the poison of asps is under their lips.

6 Their mouth is full of cursing and bitterness: their feet are swift to shed blood.

7 Destruction and unhappiness is in their ways, and the way of peace have they not known: there is no fear of God before their eyes.

8 Have they no knowledge, that they are all such workers of

mischief: eating up my people as it were bread, and call not upon the Lord?

9 There were they brought in great fear, even where no fear was: for God is in the generation of the righteous.

10 As for you, ye have made a mock at the counsel of the poor: because he putteth his trust in the Lord.

11 Who shall give salvation unto Israel out of Sion? When the Lord turneth the captivity of his people: then shall Jacob rejoice, and Israel shall be glad.

DAY 3. MORNING PRAYER

Psalm 15. *Domine, quis habitabit?*

LORD, who shall dwell in thy tabernacle: or who shall rest upon thy holy hill?

2 Even he that leadeth an uncorrupt life: and doeth the thing which is right, and speaketh the truth from his heart.

3 He that hath used no deceit in his tongue, nor done evil to his neighbour: and hath not slandered his neighbour.

4 He that setteth not by himself, but is lowly in his own eyes: and maketh much of them that fear the Lord.

5 He that sweareth unto his neighbour, and disappointeth him not: though it were to his own hindrance.

6 He that hath not given his money upon usury: nor taken reward against the innocent.

7 Whoso doeth these things: shall never fall.

Psalm 16. *Conserva me, Domine*

PRESERVE me, O God: for in thee have I put my trust.

2 O my soul, thou hast said unto the Lord: Thou art my God, my goods are nothing unto thee.

3 All my delight is upon the saints, that are in the earth: and upon such as excel in virtue.

4 But they that run after another god: shall have great trouble.

5 Their drink-offerings of blood will I not offer: neither make mention of their names within my lips.

6 The Lord himself is the portion of mine inheritance, and of my cup: thou shalt maintain my lot.

7 The lot is fallen unto me in a fair ground: yea, I have a goodly heritage.

8 I will thank the Lord for giving me warning: my reins also chasten me in the night-season.

9 I have set God always before me: for he is on my right hand, therefore I shall not fall.

10 Wherefore my heart was glad, and my glory rejoiced: my flesh also shall rest in hope.

11 For why? thou shalt not leave my soul in hell: neither shalt thou suffer thy Holy One to see corruption.

12 Thou shalt shew me the path of life; in thy presence is the fulness of joy: and at thy right hand there is pleasure for evermore.

Psalm 17. *Exaudi, Domine*

HEAR the right, O Lord, consider my complaint: and hearken unto my prayer, that goeth not out of feigned lips.

2 Let my sentence come forth from thy presence: and let thine eyes look upon the thing that is equal.

3 Thou hast proved and visited mine heart in the night-season; thou hast tried me, and shalt find no wickedness in me: for I am utterly purposed that my mouth shall not offend.

4 Because of men's works, that are done against the words of thy lips: I have kept me from the ways of the destroyer.

5 O hold thou up my goings in thy paths: that my footsteps slip not.

6 I have called upon thee, O God, for thou shalt hear me: incline thine ear to me, and hearken unto my words.

7 Shew thy marvellous loving-kindness, thou that art the Saviour of them which put their trust in thee: from such as resist thy right hand.

8 Keep me as the apple of an eye: hide me under the shadow of thy wings,

9 From the ungodly that trouble me: mine enemies compass me round about to take away my soul.

10 They are inclosed in their own fat: and their mouth speaketh proud things.

11 They lie waiting in our way on every side: turning their eyes down to the ground;

12 Like as a lion that is greedy of his prey: and as it were a lion's whelp, lurking in secret places.

13 Up, Lord, disappoint him, and cast him down: deliver my soul from the ungodly, which is a sword of thine;

14 From the men of thy hand, O Lord, from the men, I say, and from the evil world: which have their portion in this life, whose bellies thou fillest with thy hid treasure.

15 They have children at their desire: and leave the rest of their substance for their babes.

16 But as for me, I will behold thy presence in righteousness: and when I awake up after thy likeness, I shall be satisfied with it.

DAY 3. EVENING PRAYER

Psalm 18. *Diligam te, Domine*

I WILL love thee, O Lord, my strength; the Lord is my stony rock, and my defence: my Saviour, my God, and my might, in whom I will trust, my buckler, the horn also of my salvation, and my refuge.

2 I will call upon the Lord, which is worthy to be praised: so shall I be safe from mine enemies.

3 The sorrows of death compassed me: and the overflowings of ungodliness made me afraid.

4 The pains of hell came about me: the snares of death overtook me.

5 In my trouble I will call upon the Lord: and complain unto my God.

6 So shall he hear my voice out of his holy temple: and my complaint shall come before him, it shall enter even into his ears.

7 The earth trembled and quaked: the very foundations also of the hills shook, and were removed, because he was wroth.

8 There went a smoke out in his presence: and a consuming fire out of his mouth, so that coals were kindled at it.

9 He bowed the heavens also, and came down: and it was dark under his feet.

10 He rode upon the cherubins, and did fly: he came flying upon the wings of the wind.

11 He made darkness his secret place: his pavilion round about him, with dark water and thick clouds to cover him.

12 At the brightness of his presence his clouds removed: hail-stones, and coals of fire.

13 The Lord also thundered out of heaven, and the Highest gave his thunder: hail-stones, and coals of fire.

14 He sent out his arrows, and scattered them: he cast forth lightnings, and destroyed them.

15 The springs of waters were seen, and the foundations of the round world were discovered, at thy chiding, O Lord: at the blasting of the breath of thy displeasure.

16 He shall send down from on high to fetch me: and shall take me out of many waters.

17 He shall deliver me from my strongest enemy, and from them which hate me: for they are too mighty for me.

18 They prevented me in the day of my trouble: but the Lord was my upholder.

19 He brought me forth also into a place of liberty: he brought me forth, even because he had a favour unto me.

20 The Lord shall reward me after my righteous dealing: according to the cleanness of my hands shall he recompense me.

21 Because I have kept the ways of the Lord: and have not forsaken my God, as the wicked doth.

22 For I have an eye unto all his laws: and will not cast out his commandments from me.

23 I was also uncorrupt before him: and eschewed mine own wickedness.

24 Therefore shall the Lord reward me after my righteous dealing: and according unto the cleanness of my hands in his eye-sight.

25 With the holy thou shalt be holy: and with a perfect man thou shalt be perfect.

26 With the clean thou shalt be clean: and with the froward thou shalt learn frowardness.

27 For thou shalt save the people that are in adversity: and shalt bring down the high looks of the proud.

28 Thou also shalt light my candle: the Lord my God shall make my darkness to be light.

29 For in thee I shall discomfit an host of men: and with the help of my God I shall leap over the wall.

30 The way of God is an undefiled way: the word of the Lord also is tried in the fire; he is the defender of all them that put their trust in him.

31 For who is God, but the Lord: or who hath any strength, except our God?

32 It is God, that girdeth me with strength of war: and maketh my way perfect.

33 He maketh my feet like harts' feet: and setteth me up on high.

34 He teacheth mine hands to fight: and mine arms shall break even a bow of steel.

35 Thou hast given me the defence of thy salvation: thy right hand also shall hold me up, and thy loving correction shall make me great.

36 Thou shalt make room enough under me for to go: that my footsteps shall not slide.

37 I will follow upon mine enemies, and overtake them: neither will I turn again till I have destroyed them.

38 I will smite them, that they shall not be able to stand: but fall under my feet.

39 Thou hast girded me with strength unto the battle: thou shalt throw down mine enemies under me.

40 Thou hast made mine enemies also to turn their backs upon me: and I shall destroy them that hate me.

41 They shall cry, but there shall be none to help them: yea, even unto the Lord shall they cry, but he shall not hear them.

42 I will beat them as small as the dust before the wind: I will cast them out as the clay in the streets.

43 Thou shalt deliver me from the strivings of the people: and thou shalt make me the head of the heathen.

44 A people whom I have not known: shall serve me.

45 As soon as they hear of me, they shall obey me: but the strange children shall dissemble with me.

46 The strange children shall fail: and be afraid out of their prisons.

47 The Lord liveth, and blessed be my strong helper: and praised be the God of my salvation;

48 Even the God that seeth that I be avenged: and subdueth the people unto me.

49 It is he that delivereth me from my cruel enemies, and setteth me up above mine adversaries: thou shalt rid me from the wicked man.

50 For this cause will I give thanks unto thee, O Lord, among the Gentiles: and sing praises unto thy Name.

51 Great prosperity giveth he unto his King: and sheweth loving-kindness unto David his Anointed, and unto his seed for evermore.

DAY 4. MORNING PRAYER

Psalm 19. *Caeli enarrant*

THE heavens declare the glory of God: and the firmament sheweth his handywork.

2 One day telleth another: and one night certifieth another.

3 There is neither speech nor language: but their voices are heard among them.

4 Their sound is gone out into all lands: and their words into the ends of the world.

5 In them hath he set a tabernacle for the sun: which cometh forth as a bridegroom out of his chamber, and rejoiceth as a giant to run his course.

6 It goeth forth from the uttermost part of the heaven, and runneth about unto the end of it again: and there is nothing hid from the heat thereof.

7 The law of the Lord is an undefiled law, converting the soul:

the testimony of the Lord is sure, and giveth wisdom unto the simple.

8 The statutes of the Lord are right, and rejoice the heart: the commandment of the Lord is pure, and giveth light unto the eyes.

9 The fear of the Lord is clean, and endureth for ever: the judgements of the Lord are true, and righteous altogether.

10 More to be desired are they than gold, yea, than much fine gold: sweeter also than honey, and the honey-comb.

11 Moreover, by them is thy servant taught: and in keeping of them there is great reward.

12 Who can tell how oft he offendeth: O cleanse thou me from my secret faults.

13 Keep thy servant also from presumptuous sins, lest they get the dominion over me: so shall I be undefiled, and innocent from the great offence.

14 Let the words of my mouth, and the meditation of my heart: be alway acceptable in thy sight,

15 O Lord: my strength, and my redeemer.

Psalm 20. *Exaudiat te Dominus*

THE Lord hear thee in the day of trouble: the Name of the God of Jacob defend thee;

2 Send thee help from the sanctuary: and strengthen thee out of Sion;

3 Remember all thy offerings: and accept thy burnt-sacrifice;

4 Grant thee thy heart's desire: and fulfil all thy mind.

5 We will rejoice in thy salvation, and triumph in the Name of the Lord our God: the Lord perform all thy petitions.

6 Now know I that the Lord helpeth his Anointed, and will hear him from his holy heaven: even with the wholesome strength of his right hand.

7 Some put their trust in chariots, and some in horses: but we will remember the Name of the Lord our God.

8 They are brought down, and fallen: but we are risen, and stand upright.

9 Save, Lord, and hear us, O King of heaven: when we call upon thee.

Psalm 21. *Domine, in virtute tua*

THE King shall rejoice in thy strength, O Lord: exceeding glad shall he be of thy salvation.

2 Thou hast given him his heart's desire: and hast not denied him the request of his lips.

3 For thou shalt prevent him with the blessings of goodness: and shalt set a crown of pure gold upon his head.

4 He asked life of thee, and thou gavest him a long life: even for ever and ever.

5 His honour is great in thy salvation: glory and great worship shalt thou lay upon him.

6 For thou shalt give him everlasting felicity: and make him glad with the joy of thy countenance.

7 And why? because the King putteth his trust in the Lord: and in the mercy of the most Highest he shall not miscarry.

8 All thine enemies shall feel thine hand: thy right hand shall find out them that hate thee.

9 Thou shalt make them like a fiery oven in time of thy wrath: the Lord shall destroy them in his displeasure, and the fire shall consume them.

10 Their fruit shalt thou root out of the earth: and their seed from among the children of men.

11 For they intended mischief against thee: and imagined such a device as they are not able to perform.

12 Therefore shalt thou put them to flight: and the strings of thy bow shalt thou make ready against the face of them.

13 Be thou exalted, Lord, in thine own strength: so will we sing, and praise thy power.

DAY 4. EVENING PRAYER

Psalm 22. *Deus, Deus meus*

MY God, my God, look upon me; why hast thou forsaken me: and art so far from my health, and from the words of my complaint?

2 O my God, I cry in the day-time, but thou hearest not: and in the night-season also I take no rest.

3 And thou continuest holy: O thou worship of Israel.

4 Our fathers hoped in thee: they trusted in thee, and thou didst deliver them.

5 They called upon thee, and were holpen: they put their trust in thee, and were not confounded.

6 But as for me, I am a worm, and no man: a very scorn of men, and the outcast of the people.

7 All they that see me laugh me to scorn: they shoot out their lips, and shake their heads, saying,

8 He trusted in God, that he would deliver him: let him deliver him, if he will have him.

9 But thou art he that took me out of my mother's womb: thou wast my hope, when I hanged yet upon my mother's breasts.

10 I have been left unto thee ever since I was born: thou art my God, even from my mother's womb.

11 O go not from me, for trouble is hard at hand: and there is none to help me.

12 Many oxen are come about me: fat bulls of Basan close me in on every side.

13 They gape upon me with their mouths: as it were a ramping and a roaring lion.

14 I am poured out like water, and all my bones are out of joint: my heart also in the midst of my body is even like melting wax.

15 My strength is dried up like a potsherd, and my tongue cleaveth to my gums: and thou shalt bring me into the dust of death.

16 For many dogs are come about me: and the council of the wicked layeth siege against me.

17 They pierced my hands and my feet; I may tell all my bones: they stand staring and looking upon me.

18 They part my garments among them: and cast lots upon my vesture.

19 But be not thou far from me, O Lord: thou art my succour, haste thee to help me.

20 Deliver my soul from the sword: my darling from the power of the dog.

21 Save me from the lion's mouth: thou hast heard me also from among the horns of the unicorns.

22 I will declare thy Name unto my brethren: in the midst of the congregation will I praise thee.

23 O praise the Lord, ye that fear him: magnify him, all ye of the seed of Jacob, and fear him, all ye seed of Israel;

24 For he hath not despised, nor abhorred, the low estate of the poor: he hath not hid his face from him, but when he called unto him he heard him.

25 My praise is of thee in the great congregation: my vows will I perform in the sight of them that fear him.

26 The poor shall eat and be satisfied: they that seek after the Lord shall praise him; your heart shall live for ever.

27 All the ends of the world shall remember themselves, and be turned unto the Lord: and all the kindreds of the nations shall worship before him.

28 For the kingdom is the Lord's: and he is the Governor among the people.

29 All such as be fat upon earth: have eaten and worshipped.

30 All they that go down into the dust shall kneel before him: and no man hath quickened his own soul.

31 My seed shall serve him: they shall be counted unto the Lord for a generation.

32 They shall come, and the heavens shall declare his righteousness: unto a people that shall be born, whom the Lord hath made.

PSALM 23. *Dominus regit me*

THE Lord is my shepherd: therefore can I lack nothing.

2 He shall feed me in a green pasture: and lead me forth beside the waters of comfort.

3 He shall convert my soul: and bring me forth in the paths of righteousness, for his Name's sake.

4 Yea, though I walk through the valley of the shadow of death, I will fear no evil: for thou art with me; thy rod and thy staff comfort me.

5 Thou shalt prepare a table before me against them that trouble

me: thou hast anointed my head with oil, and my cup shall be full.

6 But thy loving-kindness and mercy shall follow me all the days of my life: and I will dwell in the house of the Lord for ever.

DAY 5. MORNING PRAYER

PSALM 24. *Domini est terra*

THE earth is the Lord's, and all that therein is: the compass of the world, and they that dwell therein.

2 For he hath founded it upon the seas: and prepared it upon the floods.

3 Who shall ascend into the hill of the Lord: or who shall rise up in his holy place?

4 Even he that hath clean hands, and a pure heart: and that hath not lift up his mind unto vanity, nor sworn to deceive his neighbour.

5 He shall receive the blessing from the Lord: and righteousness from the God of his salvation.

6 This is the generation of them that seek him: even of them that seek thy face, O Jacob.

7 Lift up your heads, O ye gates, and be ye lift up, ye everlasting doors: and the King of glory shall come in.

8 Who is the King of glory: it is the Lord strong and mighty, even the Lord mighty in battle.

9 Lift up your heads, O ye gates, and be ye lift up, ye everlasting doors: and the King of glory shall come in.

10 Who is the King of glory: even the Lord of hosts, he is the King of glory.

PSALM 25. *Ad te, Domine, levavi*

UNTO thee, O Lord, will I lift up my soul; my God, I have put my trust in thee: O let me not be confounded, neither let mine enemies triumph over me.

2 For all they that hope in thee shall not be ashamed: but such as transgress without a cause shall be put to confusion.

3 Shew me thy ways, O Lord: and teach me thy paths.

4 Lead me forth in thy truth, and learn me: for thou art the God of my salvation; in thee hath been my hope all the day long.

5 Call to remembrance, O Lord, thy tender mercies: and thy loving-kindnesses, which have been ever of old.

6 O remember not the sins and offences of my youth: but according to thy mercy think thou upon me, O Lord, for thy goodness.

7 Gracious and righteous is the Lord: therefore will he teach sinners in the way.

8 Them that are meek shall he guide in judgement: and such as are gentle, them shall he learn his way.

9 All the paths of the Lord are mercy and truth: unto such as keep his covenant and his testimonies.

10 For thy Name's sake, O Lord: be merciful unto my sin, for it is great.

11 What man is he that feareth the Lord: him shall he teach in the way that he shall choose.

12 His soul shall dwell at ease: and his seed shall inherit the land.

13 The secret of the Lord is among them that fear him: and he will shew them his covenant.

14 Mine eyes are ever looking unto the Lord: for he shall pluck my feet out of the net.

15 Turn thee unto me, and have mercy upon me: for I am desolate and in misery.

16 The sorrows of my heart are enlarged: O bring thou me out of my troubles.

17 Look upon my adversity and misery: and forgive me all my sin.

18 Consider mine enemies, how many they are: and they bear a tyrannous hate against me.

19 O keep my soul, and deliver me: let me not be confounded, for I have put my trust in thee.

20 Let perfectness and righteous dealing wait upon me: for my hope hath been in thee.

21 Deliver Israel, O God: out of all his troubles.

Psalm 26. *Judica me, Domine*

BE thou my Judge, O Lord, for I have walked innocently: my trust hath been also in the Lord, therefore shall I not fall.

2 Examine me, O Lord, and prove me: try out my reins and my heart.

3 For thy loving-kindness is ever before mine eyes: and I will walk in thy truth.

4 I have not dwelt with vain persons: neither will I have fellowship with the deceitful.

5 I have hated the congregation of the wicked: and will not sit among the ungodly.

6 I will wash my hands in innocency, O Lord: and so will I go to thine altar;

7 That I may shew the voice of thanksgiving: and tell of all thy wondrous works.

8 Lord, I have loved the habitation of thy house: and the place where thine honour dwelleth.

9 O shut not up my soul with the sinners: nor my life with the blood-thirsty;

10 In whose hands is wickedness: and their right hand is full of gifts.

11 But as for me, I will walk innocently: O deliver me, and be merciful unto me.

12 My foot standeth right: I will praise the Lord in the congregations.

DAY 5. EVENING PRAYER

Psalm 27. *Dominus illuminatio*

THE Lord is my light and my salvation; whom then shall I fear: the Lord is the strength of my life; of whom then shall I be afraid?

2 When the wicked, even mine enemies and my foes, came upon me to eat up my flesh: they stumbled and fell.

3 Though an host of men were laid against me, yet shall not my heart be afraid: and though there rose up war against me, yet will I put my trust in him.

4 One thing have I desired of the Lord, which I will require: even that I may dwell in the house of the Lord all the days of my life, to behold the fair beauty of the Lord, and to visit his temple.

5 For in the time of trouble he shall hide me in his tabernacle: yea, in the secret place of his dwelling shall he hide me, and set me up upon a rock of stone.

6 And now shall he lift up mine head: above mine enemies round about me.

7 Therefore will I offer in his dwelling an oblation with great gladness: I will sing, and speak praises unto the Lord.

8 Hearken unto my voice, O Lord, when I cry unto thee: have mercy upon me, and hear me.

9 My heart hath talked of thee, Seek ye my face: Thy face, Lord, will I seek.

10 O hide not thou thy face from me: nor cast thy servant away in displeasure.

11 Thou hast been my succour: leave me not, neither forsake me, O God of my salvation.

12 When my father and my mother forsake me: the Lord taketh me up.

13 Teach me thy way, O Lord: and lead me in the right way, because of mine enemies.

14 Deliver me not over into the will of mine adversaries: for there are false witnesses risen up against me, and such as speak wrong.

15 I should utterly have fainted: but that I believe verily to see the goodness of the Lord in the land of the living.

16 O tarry thou the Lord's leisure: be strong, and he shall comfort thine heart; and put thou thy trust in the Lord.

PSALM 28. *Ad te, Domine*

UNTO thee will I cry, O Lord my strength: think no scorn of me; lest, if thou make as though thou hearest not, I become like them that go down into the pit.

2 Hear the voice of my humble petitions, when I cry unto thee: when I hold up my hands towards the mercy-seat of thy holy temple.

3 O pluck me not away, neither destroy me, with the ungodly and wicked doers: which speak friendly to their neighbours, but imagine mischief in their hearts.

4 Reward them according to their deeds: and according to the wickedness of their own inventions.

5 Recompense them after the work of their hands: pay them that they have deserved.

6 For they regard not in their mind the works of the Lord, nor the operation of his hands: therefore shall he break them down, and not build them up.

7 Praised be the Lord: for he hath heard the voice of my humble petitions.

8 The Lord is my strength and my shield; my heart hath trusted in him, and I am helped: therefore my heart danceth for joy, and in my song will I praise him.

9 The Lord is my strength: and he is the wholesome defence of his Anointed.

10 O save thy people, and give thy blessing unto thine inheritance: feed them, and set them up for ever.

PSALM 29. *Afferte Domino*

BRING unto the Lord, O ye mighty, bring young rams unto the Lord: ascribe unto the Lord worship and strength.

2 Give the Lord the honour due unto his Name: worship the Lord with holy worship.

3 It is the Lord that commandeth the waters: it is the glorious God that maketh the thunder.

4 It is the Lord that ruleth the sea; the voice of the Lord is mighty in operation: the voice of the Lord is a glorious voice.

5 The voice of the Lord breaketh the cedar-trees: yea, the Lord breaketh the cedars of Libanus.

6 He maketh them also to skip like a calf: Libanus also, and Sirion, like a young unicorn.

7 The voice of the Lord divideth the flames of fire; the voice of the Lord shaketh the wilderness: yea, the Lord shaketh the wilderness of Cades.

8 The voice of the Lord maketh the hinds to bring forth young,

and discovereth the thick bushes: in his temple doth every man speak of his honour.

9 The Lord sitteth above the water-flood: and the Lord remaineth a King for ever.

10 The Lord shall give strength unto his people: the Lord shall give his people the blessing of peace.

DAY 6. MORNING PRAYER

PSALM 30. *Exaltabo te, Domine*

I WILL magnify thee, O Lord, for thou hast set me up: and not made my foes to triumph over me.

2 O Lord my God, I cried unto thee: and thou hast healed me.

3 Thou, Lord, hast brought my soul out of hell: thou hast kept my life from them that go down to the pit.

4 Sing praises unto the Lord, O ye saints of his: and give thanks unto him for a remembrance of his holiness.

5 For his wrath endureth but the twinkling of an eye, and in his pleasure is life: heaviness may endure for a night, but joy cometh in the morning.

6 And in my prosperity I said, I shall never be removed: thou, Lord, of thy goodness hast made my hill so strong.

7 Thou didst turn thy face from me: and I was troubled.

8 Then cried I unto thee, O Lord: and gat me to my Lord right humbly.

9 What profit is there in my blood: when I go down to the pit?

10 Shall the dust give thanks unto thee: or shall it declare thy truth?

11 Hear, O Lord, and have mercy upon me: Lord, be thou my helper.

12 Thou hast turned my heaviness into joy: thou hast put off my sackcloth, and girded me with gladness.

13 Therefore shall every good man sing of thy praise without ceasing: O my God, I will give thanks unto thee for ever.

PSALM 31. *In te, Domine, speravi*

IN thee, O Lord, have I put my trust: let me never be put to confusion, deliver me in thy righteousness.

2 Bow down thine ear to me: make haste to deliver me.

3 And be thou my strong rock, and house of defence: that thou mayest save me.

4 For thou art my strong rock, and my castle: be thou also my guide, and lead me for thy Name's sake.

5 Draw me out of the net that they have laid privily for me: for thou art my strength.

6 Into thy hands I commend my spirit: for thou hast redeemed me, O Lord, thou God of truth.

7 I have hated them that hold of superstitious vanities: and my trust hath been in the Lord.

8 I will be glad and rejoice in thy mercy: for thou hast considered my trouble, and hast known my soul in adversities.

9 Thou hast not shut me up into the hand of the enemy: but hast set my feet in a large room.

10 Have mercy upon me, O Lord, for I am in trouble: and mine eye is consumed for very heaviness; yea, my soul and my body.

11 For my life is waxen old with heaviness: and my years with mourning.

12 My strength faileth me, because of mine iniquity: and my bones are consumed.

13 I became a reproof among all mine enemies, but especially among my neighbours: and they of mine acquaintance were afraid of me; and they that did see me without conveyed themselves from me.

14 I am clean forgotten, as a dead man out of mind: I am become like a broken vessel.

15 For I have heard the blasphemy of the multitude: and fear is on every side, while they conspire together against me, and take their counsel to take away my life.

16 But my hope hath been in thee, O Lord: I have said, Thou art my God.

17 My time is in thy hand; deliver me from the hand of mine enemies: and from them that persecute me.

18 Shew thy servant the light of thy countenance: and save me for thy mercy's sake.

19 Let me not be confounded, O Lord, for I have called upon thee: let the ungodly be put to confusion, and be put to silence in the grave.

20 Let the lying lips be put to silence: which cruelly, disdainfully, and despitefully, speak against the righteous.

21 O how plentiful is thy goodness, which thou hast laid up for them that fear thee: and that thou hast prepared for them that put their trust in thee, even before the sons of men!

22 Thou shalt hide them privily by thine own presence from the provoking of all men: thou shalt keep them secretly in thy tabernacle from the strife of tongues.

23 Thanks be to the Lord: for he hath shewed me marvellous great kindness in a strong city.

24 And when I made haste, I said: I am cast out of the sight of thine eyes.

25 Nevertheless, thou heardest the voice of my prayer: when I cried unto thee.

26 O love the Lord, all ye his saints: for the Lord preserveth them that are faithful, and plenteously rewardeth the proud doer.

27 Be strong, and he shall establish your heart: all ye that put your trust in the Lord.

DAY 6. EVENING PRAYER

Psalm 32. *Beati, quorum*

BLESSED is he whose unrighteousness is forgiven: and whose sin is covered.

2 Blessed is the man unto whom the Lord imputeth no sin: and in whose spirit there is no guile.

3 For while I held my tongue: my bones consumed away through my daily complaining.

4 For thy hand is heavy upon me day and night: and my moisture is like the drought in summer.

5 I will acknowledge my sin unto thee: and mine unright-eousness have I not hid.

6 I said, I will confess my sins unto the Lord: and so thou forgavest the wickedness of my sin.

7 For this shall every one that is godly make his prayer unto thee, in a time when thou mayest be found: but in the great water-floods they shall not come nigh him.

8 Thou art a place to hide me in, thou shalt preserve me from trouble: thou shalt compass me about with songs of deliverance.

9 I will inform thee, and teach thee in the way wherein thou shalt go: and I will guide thee with mine eye.

10 Be ye not like to horse and mule, which have no understand-ing: whose mouths must be held with bit and bridle, lest they fall upon thee.

11 Great plagues remain for the ungodly: but whoso putteth his trust in the Lord, mercy embraceth him on every side.

12 Be glad, O ye righteous, and rejoice in the Lord: and be joyful, all ye that are true of heart.

PSALM 33. *Exultate, justi*

REJOICE in the Lord, O ye righteous: for it becometh well the just to be thankful.

2 Praise the Lord with harp: sing praises unto him with the lute, and instrument of ten strings.

3 Sing unto the Lord a new song: sing praises lustily unto him with a good courage.

4 For the word of the Lord is true: and all his works are faithful.

5 He loveth righteousness and judgement: the earth is full of the goodness of the Lord.

6 By the word of the Lord were the heavens made: and all the hosts of them by the breath of his mouth.

7 He gathereth the waters of the sea together, as it were upon an heap: and layeth up the deep, as in a treasure-house.

8 Let all the earth fear the Lord: stand in awe of him, all ye that dwell in the world.

9 For he spake, and it was done: he commanded, and it stood fast.

10 The Lord bringeth the counsel of the heathen to nought: and maketh the devices of the people to be of none effect, and casteth out the counsels of princes.

11 The counsel of the Lord shall endure for ever: and the thoughts of his heart from generation to generation.

12 Blessed are the people, whose God is the Lord Jehovah: and blessed are the folk, that he hath chosen to him to be his inheritance.

13 The Lord looked down from heaven, and beheld all the children of men: from the habitation of his dwelling he considereth all them that dwell on the earth.

14 He fashioneth all the hearts of them: and understandeth all their works.

15 There is no king that can be saved by the multitude of an host: neither is any mighty man delivered by much strength.

16 A horse is counted but a vain thing to save a man: neither shall he deliver any man by his great strength.

17 Behold, the eye of the Lord is upon them that fear him: and upon them that put their trust in his mercy;

18 To deliver their soul from death: and to feed them in the time of dearth.

19 Our soul hath patiently tarried for the Lord: for he is our help and our shield.

20 For our heart shall rejoice in him: because we have hoped in his holy Name.

21 Let thy merciful kindness, O Lord, be upon us: like as we do put our trust in thee.

Psalm 34. *Benedicam Domino*

I WILL alway give thanks unto the Lord: his praise shall ever be in my mouth.

2 My soul shall make her boast in the Lord: the humble shall hear thereof, and be glad.

3 O praise the Lord with me: and let us magnify his Name together.

4 I sought the Lord, and he heard me: yea, he delivered me out of all my fear.

5 They had an eye unto him, and were lightened: and their faces were not ashamed.

6 Lo, the poor crieth, and the Lord heareth him: yea, and saveth him out of all his troubles.

7 The angel of the Lord tarrieth round about them that fear him: and delivereth them.

8 O taste, and see, how gracious the Lord is: blessed is the man that trusteth in him.

9 O fear the Lord, ye that are his saints: for they that fear him lack nothing.

10 The lions do lack, and suffer hunger: but they who seek the Lord shall want no manner of thing that is good.

11 Come, ye children, and hearken unto me: I will teach you the fear of the Lord.

12 What man is he that lusteth to live: and would fain see good days?

13 Keep thy tongue from evil: and thy lips, that they speak no guile.

14 Eschew evil, and do good: seek peace, and ensue it.

15 The eyes of the Lord are over the righteous: and his ears are open unto their prayers.

16 The countenance of the Lord is against them that do evil: to root out the remembrance of them from the earth.

17 The righteous cry, and the Lord heareth them: and delivereth them out of all their troubles.

18 The Lord is nigh unto them that are of a contrite heart: and will save such as be of an humble spirit.

19 Great are the troubles of the righteous: but the Lord delivereth him out of all.

20 He keepeth all his bones: so that not one of them is broken.

21 But misfortune shall slay the ungodly: and they that hate the righteous shall be desolate.

22 The Lord delivereth the souls of his servants: and all they that put their trust in him shall not be destitute.

DAY 7. MORNING PRAYER

PSALM 35. *Judica, Domine*

PLEAD thou my cause, O Lord, with them that strive with me: and fight thou against them that fight against me.

2 Lay hand upon the shield and buckler: and stand up to help me.

3 Bring forth the spear, and stop the way against them that persecute me: say unto my soul, I am thy salvation.

4 Let them be confounded and put to shame, that seek after my soul: let them be turned back and brought to confusion, that imagine mischief for me.

5 Let them be as the dust before the wind: and the angel of the Lord scattering them.

6 Let their way be dark and slippery: and let the angel of the Lord persecute them.

7 For they have privily laid their net to destroy me without a cause: yea, even without a cause have they made a pit for my soul.

8 Let a sudden destruction come upon him unawares, and his net, that he hath laid privily, catch himself: that he may fall into his own mischief.

9 And, my soul, be joyful in the Lord: it shall rejoice in his salvation.

10 All my bones shall say, Lord, who is like unto thee, who deliverest the poor from him that is too strong for him: yea, the poor, and him that is in misery, from him that spoileth him?

11 False witnesses did rise up: they laid to my charge things that I knew not.

12 They rewarded me evil for good: to the great discomfort of my soul.

13 Nevertheless, when they were sick, I put on sackcloth, and humbled my soul with fasting: and my prayer shall turn into mine own bosom.

14 I behaved myself as though it had been my friend or my brother: I went heavily, as one that mourneth for his mother.

15 But in mine adversity they rejoiced, and gathered themselves together: yea, the very abjects came together against me unawares, making mouths at me, and ceased not.

16 With the flatterers were busy mockers: who gnashed upon me with their teeth.

17 Lord, how long wilt thou look upon this: O deliver my soul from the calamities which they bring on me, and my darling from the lions.

18 So will I give thee thanks in the great congregation: I will praise thee among much people.

19 O let not them that are mine enemies triumph over me ungodly: neither let them wink with their eyes that hate me without a cause.

20 And why? their communing is not for peace: but they imagine deceitful words against them that are quiet in the land.

21 They gaped upon me with their mouths, and said: Fie on thee, fie on thee, we saw it with our eyes.

22 This thou hast seen, O Lord: hold not thy tongue then, go not far from me, O Lord.

23 Awake, and stand up to judge my quarrel: avenge thou my cause, my God, and my Lord.

24 Judge me, O Lord my God, according to thy righteousness: and let them not triumph over me.

25 Let them not say in their hearts, There, there, so would we have it: neither let them say, We have devoured him.

26 Let them be put to confusion and shame together, that rejoice at my trouble: let them be clothed with rebuke and dishonour, that boast themselves against me.

27 Let them be glad and rejoice, that favour my righteous dealing: yea, let them say alway, Blessed be the Lord, who hath pleasure in the prosperity of his servant.

28 And as for my tongue, it shall be talking of thy righteousness: and of thy praise all the day long.

Psalm 36. *Dixit injustus*

MY heart sheweth me the wickedness of the ungodly: that there is no fear of God before his eyes.

2 For he flattereth himself in his own sight: until his abominable sin be found out.

3 The words of his mouth are unrighteous, and full of deceit: he hath left off to behave himself wisely, and to do good.

4 He imagineth mischief upon his bed, and hath set himself in no good way: neither doth he abhor any thing that is evil.

5 Thy mercy, O Lord, reacheth unto the heavens: and thy faithfulness unto the clouds.

6 Thy righteousness standeth like the strong mountains: thy judgements are like the great deep.

7 Thou, Lord, shalt save both man and beast; How excellent is thy mercy, O God: and the children of men shall put their trust under the shadow of thy wings.

8 They shall be satisfied with the plenteousness of thy house: and thou shalt give them drink of thy pleasures, as out of the river.

9 For with thee is the well of life: and in thy light shall we see light.

10 O continue forth thy loving-kindness unto them that know thee: and thy righteousness unto them that are true of heart.

11 O let not the foot of pride come against me: and let not the hand of the ungodly cast me down.

12 There are they fallen, all that work wickedness: they are cast down, and shall not be able to stand.

DAY 7. EVENING PRAYER

PSALM 37. *Noli aemulari*

FRET not thyself because of the ungodly: neither be thou envious against the evil-doers.

2 For they shall soon be cut down like the grass: and be withered even as the green herb.

3 Put thou thy trust in the Lord, and be doing good: dwell in the land, and verily thou shalt be fed.

4 Delight thou in the Lord: and he shall give thee thy heart's desire.

5 Commit thy way unto the Lord, and put thy trust in him: and he shall bring it to pass.

6 He shall make thy righteousness as clear as the light: and thy just dealing as the noon-day.

7 Hold thee still in the Lord, and abide patiently upon him: but grieve not thyself at him whose way doth prosper, against the man that doeth after evil counsels.

8 Leave off from wrath, and let go displeasure: fret not thyself, else shalt thou be moved to do evil.

9 Wicked doers shall be rooted out: and they that patiently abide the Lord, those shall inherit the land.

10 Yet a little while, and the ungodly shall be clean gone: thou shalt look after his place, and he shall be away.

11 But the meek-spirited shall possess the earth: and shall be refreshed in the multitude of peace.

12 The ungodly seeketh counsel against the just: and gnasheth upon him with his teeth.

13 The Lord shall laugh him to scorn: for he hath seen that his day is coming.

14 The ungodly have drawn out the sword, and have bent their bow: to cast down the poor and needy, and to slay such as are of a right conversation.

15 Their sword shall go through their own heart: and their bow shall be broken.

16 A small thing that the righteous hath: is better than great riches of the ungodly.

17 For the arms of the ungodly shall be broken: and the Lord upholdeth the righteous.

18 The Lord knoweth the days of the godly: and their inheritance shall endure for ever.

19 They shall not be confounded in the perilous time: and in the days of dearth they shall have enough.

20 As for the ungodly, they shall perish; and the enemies of the Lord shall consume as the fat of lambs: yea, even as the smoke shall they consume away.

21 The ungodly borroweth, and payeth not again: but the righteous is merciful and liberal.

22 Such as are blessed of God shall possess the land: and they that are cursed of him shall be rooted out.

23 The Lord ordereth a good man's going: and maketh his way acceptable to himself.

24 Though he fall, he shall not be cast away: for the Lord upholdeth him with his hand.

25 I have been young, and now am old: and yet saw I never the righteous forsaken, nor his seed begging their bread.

26 The righteous is ever merciful, and lendeth: and his seed is blessed.

27 Flee from evil, and do the thing that is good: and dwell for evermore.

28 For the Lord loveth the thing that is right: he forsaketh not his that be godly, but they are preserved for ever.

29 The unrighteous shall be punished: as for the seed of the ungodly, it shall be rooted out.

30 The righteous shall inherit the land: and dwell therein for ever.

31 The mouth of the righteous is exercised in wisdom: and his tongue will be talking of judgement.

32 The law of his God is in his heart: and his goings shall not slide.

33 The ungodly seeth the righteous: and seeketh occasion to slay him.

34 The Lord will not leave him in his hand: nor condemn him when he is judged.

35 Hope thou in the Lord, and keep his way, and he shall promote thee, that thou shalt possess the land: when the ungodly shall perish, thou shalt see it.

36 I myself have seen the ungodly in great power: and flourishing like a green bay-tree.

37 I went by, and lo, he was gone: I sought him, but his place could no where be found.

38 Keep innocency, and take heed unto the thing that is right: for that shall bring a man peace at the last.

39 As for the transgressors, they shall perish together: and the end of the ungodly is, they shall be rooted out at the last.

40 But the salvation of the righteous cometh of the Lord: who is also their strength in the time of trouble.

41 And the Lord shall stand by them, and save them: he shall deliver them from the ungodly, and shall save them, because they put their trust in him.

DAY 8. MORNING PRAYER
PSALM 38. *Domine, ne in furore*

PUT me not to rebuke, O Lord, in thine anger: neither chasten me in thy heavy displeasure.

2 For thine arrows stick fast in me: and thy hand presseth me sore.

3 There is no health in my flesh, because of thy displeasure: neither is there any rest in my bones, by reason of my sin.

4 For my wickednesses are gone over my head: and are like a sore burden, too heavy for me to bear.

5 My wounds stink, and are corrupt: through my foolishness.

6 I am brought into so great trouble and misery: that I go mourning all the day long.

7 For my loins are filled with a sore disease: and there is no whole part in my body.

8 I am feeble, and sore smitten: I have roared for the very disquietness of my heart.

9 Lord, thou knowest all my desire: and my groaning is not hid from thee.

10 My heart panteth, my strength hath failed me: and the sight of mine eyes is gone from me.

11 My lovers and my neighbours did stand looking upon my trouble: and my kinsmen stood afar off.

12 They also that sought after my life laid snares for me: and they that went about to do me evil talked of wickedness, and imagined deceit all the day long.

13 As for me, I was like a deaf man, and heard not: and as one that is dumb, who doth not open his mouth.

14 I became even as a man that heareth not: and in whose mouth are no reproofs.

15 For in thee, O Lord, have I put my trust: thou shalt answer for me, O Lord my God.

16 I have required that they, even mine enemies, should not triumph over me: for when my foot slipped, they rejoiced greatly against me.

17 And I, truly, am set in the plague: and my heaviness is ever in my sight.

18 For I will confess my wickedness: and be sorry for my sin.

19 But mine enemies live, and are mighty: and they that hate me wrongfully are many in number.

20 They also that reward evil for good are against me: because I follow the thing that good is.

21 Forsake me not, O Lord my God: be not thou far from me.

22 Haste thee to help me: O Lord God of my salvation.

PSALM 39. *Dixi, Custodiam*

I SAID, I will take heed to my ways: that I offend not in my tongue.

2 I will keep my mouth as it were with a bridle: while the ungodly is in my sight.

3 I held my tongue, and spake nothing: I kept silence, yea, even from good words; but it was pain and grief to me.

4 My heart was hot within me, and while I was thus musing the fire kindled: and at the last I spake with my tongue;

5 Lord, let me know mine end, and the number of my days: that I may be certified how long I have to live.

6 Behold, thou hast made my days as it were a span long: and mine age is even as nothing in respect of thee; and verily every man living is altogether vanity.

7 For man walketh in a vain shadow, and disquieteth himself in vain: he heapeth up riches, and cannot tell who shall gather them.

8 And now, Lord, what is my hope: truly my hope is even in thee.

9 Deliver me from all mine offences: and make me not a rebuke unto the foolish.

10 I became dumb, and opened not my mouth: for it was thy doing.

11 Take thy plague away from me: I am even consumed by the means of thy heavy hand.

12 When thou with rebukes dost chasten man for sin, thou makest his beauty to consume away, like as it were a moth fretting a garment: every man therefore is but vanity.

13 Hear my prayer, O Lord, and with thine ears consider my calling: hold not thy peace at my tears.

14 For I am a stranger with thee: and a sojourner, as all my fathers were.

15 O spare me a little, that I may recover my strength: before I go hence, and be no more seen.

PSALM 40. *Expectans expectavi*

I WAITED patiently for the Lord: and he inclined unto me, and heard my calling.

2 He brought me also out of the horrible pit, out of the mire and clay: and set my feet upon the rock, and ordered my goings.

3 And he hath put a new song in my mouth: even a thanksgiving unto our God.

4 Many shall see it, and fear: and shall put their trust in the Lord.

5 Blessed is the man that hath set his hope in the Lord: and turned not unto the proud, and to such as go about with lies.

6 O Lord my God, great are the wondrous works which thou hast done, like as be also thy thoughts which are to us-ward: and yet there is no man that ordereth them unto thee.

7 If I should declare them, and speak of them: they should be more than I am able to express.

8 Sacrifice and meat-offering thou wouldest not: but mine ears hast thou opened.

9 Burnt-offerings, and sacrifice for sin, hast thou not required: then said I, Lo, I come,

10 In the volume of the book it is written of me, that I should fulfil thy will, O my God: I am content to do it; yea, thy law is within my heart.

11 I have declared thy righteousness in the great congregation: lo, I will not refrain my lips, O Lord, and that thou knowest.

12 I have not hid thy righteousness within my heart: my talk hath been of thy truth and of thy salvation.

13 I have not kept back thy loving mercy and truth: from the great congregation.

14 Withdraw not thou thy mercy from me, O Lord: let thy loving-kindness and thy truth alway preserve me.

15 For innumerable troubles are come about me; my sins have taken such hold upon me that I am not able to look up: yea, they are more in number than the hairs of my head, and my heart hath failed me.

16 O Lord, let it be thy pleasure to deliver me: make haste, O Lord, to help me.

17 Let them be ashamed and confounded together, that seek after my soul to destroy it: let them be driven backward and put to rebuke, that wish me evil.

18 Let them be desolate, and rewarded with shame: that say unto me, Fie upon thee, fie upon thee.

19 Let all those that seek thee be joyful and glad in thee: and let such as love thy salvation say alway, The Lord be praised.

20 As for me, I am poor and needy: but the Lord careth for me.

21 Thou art my helper and redeemer: make no long tarrying, O my God.

DAY 8. EVENING PRAYER

Psalm 41. *Beatus qui intelligit*

BLESSED is he that considereth the poor and needy: the Lord shall deliver him in the time of trouble.

2 The Lord preserve him, and keep him alive, that he may be blessed upon earth: and deliver not thou him into the will of his enemies.

3 The Lord comfort him, when he lieth sick upon his bed: make thou all his bed in his sickness.

4 I said, Lord, be merciful unto me: heal my soul, for I have sinned against thee.

5 Mine enemies speak evil of me: When shall he die, and his name perish?

6 And if he come to see me, he speaketh vanity: and his heart conceiveth falsehood within himself, and when he cometh forth he telleth it.

7 All mine enemies whisper together against me: even against me do they imagine this evil.

8 Let the sentence of guiltiness proceed against him: and now that he lieth, let him rise up no more.

9 Yea, even mine own familiar friend, whom I trusted: who did also eat of my bread, hath laid great wait for me.

10 But be thou merciful unto me, O Lord: raise thou me up again, and I shall reward them.

11 By this I know thou favourest me: that mine enemy doth not triumph against me.

12 And when I am in my health, thou upholdest me: and shalt set me before thy face for ever.

13 Blessed be the Lord God of Israel: world without end. Amen.

Psalm 42. *Quemadmodum*

LIKE as the hart desireth the water-brooks: so longeth my soul after thee, O God.

2 My soul is athirst for God, yea, even for the living God: when shall I come to appear before the presence of God?

3 My tears have been my meat day and night: while they daily say unto me, Where is now thy God?

4 Now when I think thereupon, I pour out my heart by myself: for I went with the multitude, and brought them forth into the house of God;

5 In the voice of praise and thanksgiving: among such as keep holy-day.

6 Why art thou so full of heaviness, O my soul: and why art thou so disquieted within me?

7 Put thy trust in God: for I will yet give him thanks for the help of his countenance.

8 My God, my soul is vexed within me: therefore will I remember thee concerning the land of Jordan, and the little hill of Hermon.

9 One deep calleth another, because of the noise of the water-pipes: all thy waves and storms are gone over me.

10 The Lord hath granted his loving-kindness in the day-time: and in the night-season did I sing of him, and made my prayer unto the God of my life.

11 I will say unto the God of my strength, Why hast thou forgotten me: why go I thus heavily, while the enemy oppresseth me?

12 My bones are smitten asunder as with a sword: while mine enemies that trouble me cast me in the teeth;

13 Namely, while they say daily unto me: Where is now thy God?

14 Why art thou so vexed, O my soul: and why art thou so disquieted within me?

15 O put thy trust in God: for I will yet thank him, which is the help of my countenance, and my God.

PSALM 43. *Judica me, Deus*

GIVE sentence with me, O God, and defend my cause against the ungodly people: O deliver me from the deceitful and wicked man.

2 For thou art the God of my strength, why hast thou put me from thee: and why go I so heavily, while the enemy oppresseth me?

3 O send out thy light and thy truth, that they may lead me: and bring me unto thy holy hill, and to thy dwelling.

4 And that I may go unto the altar of God, even unto the God of my joy and gladness: and upon the harp will I give thanks unto thee, O God, my God.

5 Why art thou so heavy, O my soul: and why art thou so disquieted within me?

6 O put thy trust in God: for I will yet give him thanks, which is the help of my countenance, and my God.

DAY 9. MORNING PRAYER

PSALM 44. *Deus, auribus*

WE have heard with our ears, O God, our fathers have told us: what thou hast done in their time of old;

2 How thou hast driven out the heathen with thy hand, and planted them in: how thou hast destroyed the nations and cast them out.

3 For they gat not the land in possession through their own sword: neither was it their own arm that helped them;

4 But thy right hand, and thine arm, and the light of thy countenance: because thou hadst a favour unto them.

5 Thou art my King, O God: send help unto Jacob.

6 Through thee will we overthrow our enemies: and in thy Name will we tread them under, that rise up against us.

7 For I will not trust in my bow: it is not my sword that shall help me;

8 But it is thou that savest us from our enemies: and puttest them to confusion that hate us.

9 We make our boast of God all day long: and will praise thy Name for ever.

10 But now thou art far off, and puttest us to confusion: and goest not forth with our armies.

11 Thou makest us to turn our backs upon our enemies: so that they which hate us spoil our goods.

12 Thou lettest us be eaten up like sheep: and hast scattered us among the heathen.

13 Thou sellest thy people for nought: and takest no money for them.

14 Thou makest us to be rebuked of our neighbours: to be laughed to scorn, and had in derision of them that are round about us.

15 Thou makest us to be a by-word among the heathen: and that the people shake their heads at us.

16 My confusion is daily before me: and the shame of my face hath covered me;

17 For the voice of the slanderer and blasphemer: for the enemy and avenger.

18 And though all this be come upon us, yet do we not forget thee: nor behave ourselves frowardly in thy covenant.

19 Our heart is not turned back: neither our steps gone out of thy way;

20 No, not when thou hast smitten us into the place of dragons: and covered us with the shadow of death.

21 If we have forgotten the Name of our God, and holden up our hands to any strange god: shall not God search it out? for he knoweth the very secrets of the heart.

22 For thy sake also are we killed all the day long: and are counted as sheep appointed to be slain.

23 Up, Lord, why sleepest thou: awake, and be not absent from us for ever.

24 Wherefore hidest thou thy face: and forgettest our misery and trouble?

25 For our soul is brought low, even unto the dust: our belly cleaveth unto the ground.

26 Arise, and help us: and deliver us for thy mercy's sake.

PSALM 45. *Eructavit cor meum*

MY heart is inditing of a good matter: I speak of the things which I have made unto the King.

2 My tongue is the pen: of a ready writer.

3 Thou art fairer than the children of men: full of grace are thy lips, because God hath blessed thee for ever.

4 Gird thee with thy sword upon thy thigh, O thou most Mighty: according to thy worship and renown.

5 Good luck have thou with thine honour: ride on, because of the word of truth, of meekness, and righteousness; and thy right hand shall teach thee terrible things.

6 Thy arrows are very sharp, and the people shall be subdued unto thee: even in the midst among the King's enemies.

7 Thy seat, O God, endureth for ever: the sceptre of thy kingdom is a right sceptre.

8 Thou hast loved righteousness, and hated iniquity: wherefore God, even thy God, hath anointed thee with the oil of gladness above thy fellows.

9 All thy garments smell of myrrh, aloes, and cassia: out of the ivory palaces, whereby they have made thee glad.

10 Kings' daughters were among thy honourable women: upon

thy right hand did stand the queen in a vesture of gold, wrought about with divers colours.

11 Hearken, O daughter, and consider, incline thine ear: forget also thine own people, and thy father's house.

12 So shall the King have pleasure in thy beauty: for he is thy Lord God, and worship thou him.

13 And the daughter of Tyre shall be there with a gift: like as the rich also among the people shall make their supplication before thee.

14 The King's daughter is all glorious within: her clothing is of wrought gold.

15 She shall be brought unto the King in raiment of needle-work: the virgins that be her fellows shall bear her company, and shall be brought unto thee.

16 With joy and gladness shall they be brought: and shall enter into the King's palace.

17 Instead of thy fathers thou shalt have children: whom thou mayest make princes in all lands.

18 I will remember thy Name from one generation to another: therefore shall the people give thanks unto thee, world without end.

PSALM 46. *Deus noster refugium*

GOD is our hope and strength: a very present help in trouble.

2 Therefore will we not fear, though the earth be moved: and though the hills be carried into the midst of the sea;

3 Though the waters thereof rage and swell: and though the mountains shake at the tempest of the same.

4 The rivers of the flood thereof shall make glad the city of God: the holy place of the tabernacle of the most Highest.

5 God is in the midst of her, therefore shall she not be removed: God shall help her, and that right early.

6 The heathen make much ado, and the kingdoms are moved: but God hath shewed his voice, and the earth shall melt away.

7 The Lord of hosts is with us: the God of Jacob is our refuge.

8 O come hither, and behold the works of the Lord: what destruction he hath brought upon the earth.

9 He maketh wars to cease in all the world: he breaketh the bow, and knappeth the spear in sunder, and burneth the chariots in the fire.

10 Be still then, and know that I am God: I will be exalted among the heathen, and I will be exalted in the earth.

11 The Lord of hosts is with us: the God of Jacob is our refuge.

DAY 9. EVENING PRAYER

PSALM 47. *Omnes gentes, plaudite*

O CLAP your hands together, all ye people: O Sing unto God with the voice of melody.

2 For the Lord is high, and to be feared: he is the great King upon all the earth.

3 He shall subdue the people under us: and the nations under our feet.

4 He shall choose out an heritage for us: even the worship of Jacob, whom he loved.

5 God is gone up with a merry noise: and the Lord with the sound of the trump.

6 O sing praises, sing praises unto our God: O sing praises, sing praises unto our King.

7 For God is the King of all the earth: sing ye praises with understanding.

8 God reigneth over the heathen: God sitteth upon his holy seat.

9 The princes of the people are joined unto the people of the God of Abraham: for God, which is very high exalted, doth defend the earth, as it were with a shield.

PSALM 48. *Magnus Dominus*

GREAT is the Lord, and highly to be praised: in the city of our God, even upon his holy hill.

2 The hill of Sion is a fair place, and the joy of the whole earth: upon the north-side lieth the city of the great King; God is well known in her palaces as a sure refuge.

3 For lo, the kings of the earth: are gathered, and gone by together.

4 They marvelled to see such things: they were astonished, and suddenly cast down.

5 Fear came there upon them, and sorrow: as upon a woman in her travail.

6 Thou shalt break the ships of the sea: through the east-wind.

7 Like as we have heard, so have we seen in the city of the Lord of hosts, in the city of our God: God upholdeth the same for ever.

8 We wait for thy loving-kindness, O God: in the midst of thy temple.

9 O God, according to thy Name, so is thy praise unto the world's end: thy right hand is full of righteousness.

10 Let the mount Sion rejoice, and the daughters of Judah be glad: because of thy judgements.

11 Walk about Sion, and go round about her: and tell the towers thereof.

12 Mark well her bulwarks, set up her houses: that ye may tell them that come after.

13 For this God is our God for ever and ever: he shall be our guide unto death.

PSALM 49. *Audite haec, omnes*

O HEAR ye this, all ye people: ponder it with your ears, all ye that dwell in the world;

2 High and low, rich and poor: one with another.

3 My mouth shall speak of wisdom: and my heart shall muse of understanding.

4 I will incline mine ear to the parable: and shew my dark speech upon the harp.

5 Wherefore should I fear in the days of wickedness: and when the wickedness of my heels compasseth me round about?

6 There be some that put their trust in their goods: and boast themselves in the multitude of their riches.

7 But no man may deliver his brother: nor make agreement unto God for him;

8 For it cost more to redeem their souls: so that he must let that alone for ever;

9 Yea, though he live long: and see not the grave.

10 For he seeth that wise men also die, and perish together: as well as the ignorant and foolish, and leave their riches for other.

11 And yet they think that their houses shall continue for ever: and that their dwelling-places shall endure from one generation to another; and call the lands after their own names.

12 Nevertheless, man will not abide in honour: seeing he may be compared unto the beasts that perish; this is the way of them.

13 This is their foolishness: and their posterity praise their saying.

14 They lie in the hell like sheep, death gnaweth upon them, and the righteous shall have domination over them in the morning: their beauty shall consume in the sepulchre out of their dwelling.

15 But God hath delivered my soul from the place of hell: for he shall receive me.

16 Be not thou afraid, though one be made rich: or if the glory of his house be increased;

17 For he shall carry nothing away with him when he dieth: neither shall his pomp follow him.

18 For while he lived, he counted himself an happy man: and so long as thou doest well unto thyself, men will speak good of thee.

19 He shall follow the generation of his fathers: and shall never see light.

20 Man being in honour hath no understanding: but is compared unto the beasts that perish.

DAY 10. MORNING PRAYER

PSALM 50. *Deus deorum*

THE Lord, even the most mighty God, hath spoken: and called the world, from the rising up of the sun unto the going down thereof.

2 Out of Sion hath God appeared: in perfect beauty.

3 Our God shall come, and shall not keep silence: there shall go before him a consuming fire, and a mighty tempest shall be stirred up round about him.

4 He shall call the heaven from above: and the earth, that he may judge his people.

5 Gather my saints together unto me: those that have made a covenant with me with sacrifice.

6 And the heavens shall declare his righteousness: for God is Judge himself.

7 Hear, O my people, and I will speak: I myself will testify against thee, O Israel; for I am God, even thy God.

8 I will not reprove thee because of thy sacrifices, or for thy burnt-offerings: because they were not alway before me.

9 I will take no bullock out of thine house: nor he-goat out of thy folds.

10 For all the beasts of the forest are mine: and so are the cattle upon a thousand hills.

11 I know all the fowls upon the mountains: and the wild beasts of the field are in my sight.

12 If I be hungry, I will not tell thee: for the whole world is mine, and all that is therein.

13 Thinkest thou that I will eat bulls' flesh: and drink the blood of goats?

14 Offer unto God thanksgiving: and pay thy vows unto the most Highest.

15 And call upon me in the time of trouble: so will I hear thee, and thou shalt praise me.

16 But unto the ungodly said God: Why dost thou preach my laws, and takest my covenant in thy mouth;

17 Whereas thou hatest to be reformed: and hast cast my words behind thee?

18 When thou sawest a thief, thou consentedst unto him: and hast been partaker with the adulterers.

19 Thou hast let thy mouth speak wickedness: and with thy tongue thou hast set forth deceit.

20 Thou satest, and spakest against thy brother: yea, and hast slandered thine own mother's son.

21 These things hast thou done, and I held my tongue, and thou thoughtest wickedly, that I am even such a one as thyself: but I will reprove thee, and set before thee the things that thou hast done.

22 O consider this, ye that forget God: lest I pluck you away, and there be none to deliver you.

23 Whoso offereth me thanks and praise, he honoureth me: and to him that ordereth his conversation right will I shew the salvation of God.

Psalm 51. *Miserere mei, Deus*

HAVE mercy upon me, O God, after thy great goodness: according to the multitude of thy mercies do away mine offences.

2 Wash me throughly from my wickedness: and cleanse me from my sin.

3 For I acknowledge my faults: and my sin is ever before me.

4 Against thee only have I sinned, and done this evil in thy sight: that thou mightest be justified in thy saying, and clear when thou art judged.

5 Behold, I was shapen in wickedness: and in sin hath my mother conceived me.

6 But lo, thou requirest truth in the inward parts: and shalt make me to understand wisdom secretly.

7 Thou shalt purge me with hyssop, and I shall be clean: thou shalt wash me, and I shall be whiter than snow.

8 Thou shalt make me hear of joy and gladness: that the bones which thou hast broken may rejoice.

9 Turn thy face from my sins: and put out all my misdeeds.

10 Make me a clean heart, O God: and renew a right spirit within me.

11 Cast me not away from thy presence: and take not thy holy Spirit from me.

12 O give me the comfort of thy help again: and stablish me with thy free Spirit.

13 Then shall I teach thy ways unto the wicked: and sinners shall be converted unto thee.

14 Deliver me from blood-guiltiness, O God, thou that art the God of my health: and my tongue shall sing of thy righteousness.

15 Thou shalt open my lips, O Lord: and my mouth shall shew thy praise.

16 For thou desirest no sacrifice, else would I give it thee: but thou delightest not in burnt-offerings.

17 The sacrifice of God is a troubled spirit: a broken and contrite heart, O God, shalt thou not despise.

18 O be favourable and gracious unto Sion: build thou the walls of Jerusalem.

19 Then shalt thou be pleased with the sacrifice of righteousness, with the burnt-offerings and oblations: then shall they offer young bullocks upon thine altar.

PSALM 52. *Quid gloriaris?*

WHY boastest thou thyself, thou tyrant: that thou canst do mischief;

2 Whereas the goodness of God: endureth yet daily?

3 Thy tongue imagineth wickedness: and with lies thou cuttest like a sharp rasor.

4 Thou hast loved unrighteousness more than goodness: and to talk of lies more than righteousness.

5 Thou hast loved to speak all words that may do hurt: O thou false tongue.

6 Therefore shall God destroy thee for ever: he shall take thee, and pluck thee out of thy dwelling, and root thee out of the land of the living.

7 The righteous also shall see this, and fear: and shall laugh him to scorn;

8 Lo, this is the man that took not God for his strength: but trusted unto the multitude of his riches, and strengthened himself in his wickedness.

9 As for me, I am like a green olive-tree in the house of God: my trust is in the tender mercy of God for ever and ever.

10 I will always give thanks unto thee for that thou hast done: and I will hope in thy Name, for thy saints like it well.

DAY 10. EVENING PRAYER

PSALM 53. *Dixit insipiens*

THE foolish body hath said in his heart: There is no God.

2 Corrupt are they, and become abominable in their wickedness: there is none that doeth good.

3 God looked down from heaven upon the children of men: to see if there were any that would understand, and seek after God.

4 But they are all gone out of the way, they are altogether become abominable: there is also none that doeth good, no not one.

5 Are not they without understanding, that work wickedness: eating up my people as if they would eat bread? they have not called upon God.

6 They were afraid where no fear was: for God hath broken the bones of him that besieged thee; thou hast put them to confusion, because God hath despised them.

7 O that the salvation were given unto Israel out of Sion: O that the Lord would deliver his people out of captivity!

8 Then should Jacob rejoice: and Israel should be right glad.

PSALM 54. *Deus, in nomine*

SAVE me, O God, for thy Name's sake: and avenge me in thy strength.

2 Hear my prayer, O God: and hearken unto the words of my mouth.

3 For strangers are risen up against me: and tyrants, which have not God before their eyes, seek after my soul.

4 Behold, God is my helper: the Lord is with them that uphold my soul.

5 He shall reward evil unto mine enemies: destroy thou them in thy truth.

6 An offering of a free heart will I give thee, and praise thy Name, O Lord: because it is so comfortable.

7 For he hath delivered me out of all my trouble: and mine eye hath seen his desire upon mine enemies.

Psalm 55. *Exaudi, Deus*

HEAR my prayer, O God: and hide not thyself from my petition.

2 Take heed unto me, and hear me: how I mourn in my prayer, and am vexed.

3 The enemy crieth so, and the ungodly cometh on so fast: for they are minded to do me some mischief; so maliciously are they set against me.

4 My heart is disquieted within me: and the fear of death is fallen upon me.

5 Fearfulness and trembling are come upon me: and an horrible dread hath overwhelmed me.

6 And I said, O that I had wings like a dove: for then would I flee away, and be at rest.

7 Lo, then would I get me away far off: and remain in the wilderness.

8 I would make haste to escape: because of the stormy wind and tempest.

9 Destroy their tongues, O Lord, and divide them: for I have spied unrighteousness and strife in the city.

10 Day and night they go about within the walls thereof: mischief also and sorrow are in the midst of it.

11 Wickedness is therein: deceit and guile go not out of their streets.

12 For it is not an open enemy, that hath done me this dishonour: for then I could have borne it.

13 Neither was it mine adversary, that did magnify himself against me: for then peradventure I would have hid myself from him.

14 But it was even thou, my companion: my guide, and mine own familiar friend.

15 We took sweet counsel together: and walked in the house of God as friends.

16 Let death come hastily upon them, and let them go down quick into hell: for wickedness is in their dwellings, and among them.

17 As for me, I will call upon God: and the Lord shall save me.

18 In the evening, and morning, and at noon-day will I pray, and that instantly: and he shall hear my voice.

19 It is he that hath delivered my soul in peace from the battle that was against me: for there were many with me.

20 Yea, even God, that endureth for ever, shall hear me, and bring them down: for they will not turn, nor fear God.

21 He laid his hands upon such as be at peace with him: and he brake his covenant.

22 The words of his mouth were softer than butter, having war in his heart: his words were smoother than oil, and yet be they very swords.

23 O cast thy burden upon the Lord, and he shall nourish thee: and shall not suffer the righteous to fall for ever.

24 And as for them: thou, O God, shalt bring them into the pit of destruction.

25 The blood-thirsty and deceitful men shall not live out half their days: nevertheless, my trust shall be in thee, O Lord.

DAY 11. MORNING PRAYER

Psalm 56. *Miserere mei, Deus*

BE merciful unto me, O God, for man goeth about to devour me: he is daily fighting, and troubling me.

2 Mine enemies are daily in hand to swallow me up: for they be many that fight against me, O thou most Highest.

3 Nevertheless, though I am sometime afraid: yet put I my trust in thee.

4 I will praise God, because of his word: I have put my trust in God, and will not fear what flesh can do unto me.

5 They daily mistake my words: all that they imagine is to do me evil.

6 They hold all together, and keep themselves close: and mark my steps, when they lay wait for my soul.

7 Shall they escape for their wickedness: thou, O God, in thy displeasure shalt cast them down.

8 Thou tellest my flittings; put my tears into thy bottle: are not these things noted in thy book?

9 Whensoever I call upon thee, then shall mine enemies be put to flight: this I know; for God is on my side.

10 In God's word will I rejoice: in the Lord's word will I comfort me.

11 Yea, in God have I put my trust: I will not be afraid what man can do unto me.

12 Unto thee, O God, will I pay my vows: unto thee will I give thanks.

13 For thou hast delivered my soul from death, and my feet from falling: that I may walk before God in the light of the living.

Psalm 57. *Miserere mei, Deus*

BE merciful unto me, O God, be merciful unto me, for my soul trusteth in thee: and under the shadow of thy wings shall be my refuge, until this tyranny be over-past.

2 I will call unto the most high God: even unto the God that shall perform the cause which I have in hand.

3 He shall send from heaven: and save me from the reproof of him that would eat me up.

4 God shall send forth his mercy and truth: my soul is among lions.

5 And I lie even among the children of men, that are set on fire: whose teeth are spears and arrows, and their tongue a sharp sword.

6 Set up thyself, O God, above the heavens: and thy glory above all the earth.

7 They have laid a net for my feet, and pressed down my soul: they have digged a pit before me, and are fallen into the midst of it themselves.

8 My heart is fixed, O God, my heart is fixed: I will sing, and give praise.

9 Awake up, my glory; awake, lute and harp: I myself will awake right early.

10 I will give thanks unto thee, O Lord, among the people: and I will sing unto thee among the nations.

11 For the greatness of thy mercy reacheth unto the heavens: and thy truth unto the clouds.

12 Set up thyself, O God, above the heavens: and thy glory above all the earth.

PSALM 58. *Si vere utique*

ARE your minds set upon righteousness, O ye congregation: and do ye judge the thing that is right, O ye sons of men?

2 Yea, ye imagine mischief in your heart upon the earth: and your hands deal with wickedness.

3 The ungodly are froward, even from their mother's womb: as soon as they are born, they go astray, and speak lies.

4 They are as venomous as the poison of a serpent: even like the deaf adder that stoppeth her ears;

5 Which refuseth to hear the voice of the charmer: charm he never so wisely.

6 Break their teeth, O God, in their mouths; smite the jaw-bones of the lions, O Lord: let them fall away like water that runneth apace; and when they shoot their arrows let them be rooted out.

7 Let them consume away like a snail, and be like the untimely fruit of a woman: and let them not see the sun.

8 Or ever your pots be made hot with thorns: so let indignation vex him, even as a thing that is raw.

9 The righteous shall rejoice when he seeth the vengeance: he shall wash his footsteps in the blood of the ungodly.

10 So that a man shall say, Verily there is a reward for the righteous: doubtless there is a God that judgeth the earth.

DAY 11. EVENING PRAYER

PSALM 59. *Eripe me de inimicis*

DELIVER me from mine enemies, O God: defend me from them that rise up against me.

2 O deliver me from the wicked doers: and save me from the blood-thirsty men.

3 For lo, they lie waiting for my soul: the mighty men are gathered against me, without any offence or fault of me, O Lord.

4 They run and prepare themselves without my fault: arise thou therefore to help me, and behold.

5 Stand up, O Lord God of hosts, thou God of Israel, to visit all the heathen: and be not merciful unto them that offend of malicious wickedness.

6 They go to and fro in the evening: they grin like a dog, and run about through the city.

7 Behold, they speak with their mouth, and swords are in their lips: for who doth hear?

8 But thou, O Lord, shalt have them in derision: and thou shalt laugh all the heathen to scorn.

9 My strength will I ascribe unto thee: for thou art the God of my refuge.

10 God sheweth me his goodness plenteously: and God shall let me see my desire upon mine enemies.

11 Slay them not, lest my people forget it: but scatter them abroad among the people, and put them down, O Lord, our defence.

12 For the sin of their mouth, and for the words of their lips, they shall be taken in their pride: and why? their preaching is of cursing and lies.

13 Consume them in thy wrath, consume them, that they may perish: and know that it is God that ruleth in Jacob, and unto the ends of the world.

14 And in the evening they will return: grin like a dog, and will go about the city.

15 They will run here and there for meat: and grudge if they be not satisfied.

16 As for me, I will sing of thy power, and will praise thy mercy betimes in the morning: for thou hast been my defence and refuge in the day of my trouble.

17 Unto thee, O my strength, will I sing: for thou, O God, art my refuge, and my merciful God.

Psalm 60. *Deus, repulisti nos*

O GOD, thou hast cast us out, and scattered us abroad: thou hast also been displeased; O turn thee unto us again.

2 Thou hast moved the land, and divided it: heal the sores thereof, for it shaketh.

3 Thou hast shewed thy people heavy things: thou hast given us a drink of deadly wine.

4 Thou hast given a token for such as fear thee: that they may triumph because of the truth.

5 Therefore were thy beloved delivered: help me with thy right hand, and hear me.

6 God hath spoken in his holiness, I will rejoice, and divide Sichem: and mete out the valley of Succoth.

7 Gilead is mine, and Manasses is mine: Ephraim also is the strength of my head; Judah is my law-giver;

8 Moab is my wash-pot; over Edom will I cast out my shoe: Philistia, be thou glad of me.

9 Who will lead me into the strong city: who will bring me into Edom?

10 Hast not thou cast us out, O God: wilt not thou, O God, go out with our hosts?

11 O be thou our help in trouble: for vain is the help of man.

12 Through God will we do great acts: for it is he that shall tread down our enemies.

Psalm 61. *Exaudi, Deus*

HEAR my crying, O God: give ear unto my prayer.

2 From the ends of the earth will I call upon thee: when my heart is in heaviness.

3 O set me up upon the rock that is higher than I: for thou hast been my hope, and a strong tower for me against the enemy.

4 I will dwell in thy tabernacle for ever: and my trust shall be under the covering of thy wings.

5 For thou, O Lord, hast heard my desires: and hast given an heritage unto those that fear thy Name.

6 Thou shalt grant the King a long life: that his years may endure throughout all generations.

7 He shall dwell before God for ever: O prepare thy loving mercy and faithfulness, that they may preserve him.

8 So will I always sing praise unto thy Name: that I may daily perform my vows.

DAY 12. MORNING PRAYER

Psalm 62. *Nonne Deo?*

MY soul truly waiteth still upon God: for of him cometh my salvation.

2 He verily is my strength and my salvation: he is my defence, so that I shall not greatly fall.

3 How long will ye imagine mischief against every man: ye shall be slain all the sort of you; yea, as a tottering wall shall ye be, and like a broken hedge.

4 Their device is only how to put him out whom God will exalt: their delight is in lies; they give good words with their mouth, but curse with their heart.

5 Nevertheless, my soul, wait thou still upon God: for my hope is in him.

6 He truly is my strength and my salvation: he is my defence, so that I shall not fall.

7 In God is my health, and my glory: the rock of my might, and in God is my trust.

8 O put your trust in him alway, ye people: pour out your hearts before him, for God is our hope.

9 As for the children of men, they are but vanity: the children of men are deceitful upon the weights, they are altogether lighter than vanity itself.

10 O trust not in wrong and robbery, give not yourselves unto vanity: if riches increase, set not your heart upon them.

11 God spake once, and twice I have also heard the same: that power belongeth unto God;

12 And that thou, Lord, art merciful: for thou rewardest every man according to his work.

Psalm 63. *Deus, Deus meus*

O GOD, thou art my God: early will I seek thee.

2 My soul thirsteth for thee, my flesh also longeth after thee: in a barren and dry land where no water is.

3 Thus have I looked for thee in holiness: that I might behold thy power and glory.

4 For thy loving-kindness is better than the life itself: my lips shall praise thee.

5 As long as I live will I magnify thee on this manner: and lift up my hands in thy Name.

6 My soul shall be satisfied, even as it were with marrow and fatness: when my mouth praiseth thee with joyful lips.

7 Have I not remembered thee in my bed: and thought upon thee when I was waking?

8 Because thou hast been my helper: therefore under the shadow of thy wings will I rejoice.

9 My soul hangeth upon thee: thy right hand hath upholden me.

10 These also that seek the hurt of my soul: they shall go under the earth.

11 Let them fall upon the edge of the sword: that they may be a portion for foxes.

12 But the King shall rejoice in God; all they also that swear by him shall be commended: for the mouth of them that speak lies shall be stopped.

Psalm 64. *Exaudi, Deus*

HEAR my voice, O God, in my prayer: preserve my life from fear of the enemy.

2 Hide me from the gathering together of the froward: and from the insurrection of wicked doers;

3 Who have whet their tongue like a sword: and shoot out their arrows, even bitter words;

4 That they may privily shoot at him that is perfect: suddenly do they hit him, and fear not.

5 They encourage themselves in mischief: and commune among themselves how they may lay snares, and say that no man shall see them.

6 They imagine wickedness, and practise it: that they keep secret among themselves, every man in the deep of his heart.

7 But God shall suddenly shoot at them with a swift arrow: that they shall be wounded.

8 Yea, their own tongues shall make them fall: insomuch that whoso seeth them shall laugh them to scorn.

9 And all men that see it shall say, This hath God done: for they shall perceive that it is his work.

10 The righteous shall rejoice in the Lord, and put his trust in him: and all they that are true of heart shall be glad.

DAY 12. EVENING PRAYER

PSALM 65. *Te decet hymnus*

THOU, O God, art praised in Sion: and unto thee shall the vow be performed in Jerusalem.

2 Thou that hearest the prayer: unto thee shall all flesh come.

3 My misdeeds prevail against me: O be thou merciful unto our sins.

4 Blessed is the man whom thou choosest, and receivest unto thee: he shall dwell in thy court, and shall be satisfied with the pleasures of thy house, even of thy holy temple.

5 Thou shalt shew us wonderful things in thy righteousness, O God of our salvation: thou that art the hope of all the ends of the earth, and of them that remain in the broad sea.

6 Who in his strength setteth fast the mountains: and is girded about with power.

7 Who stilleth the raging of the sea: and the noise of his waves, and the madness of the people.

8 They also that dwell in the uttermost parts of the earth shall be afraid at thy tokens: thou that makest the outgoings of the morning and evening to praise thee.

9 Thou visitest the earth, and blessest it: thou makest it very plenteous.

10 The river of God is full of water: thou preparest their corn, for so thou providest for the earth.

11 Thou waterest her furrows, thou sendest rain into the little valleys thereof: thou makest it soft with the drops of rain, and blessest the increase of it.

12 Thou crownest the year with thy goodness: and thy clouds drop fatness.

13 They shall drop upon the dwellings of the wilderness: and the little hills shall rejoice on every side.

14 The folds shall be full of sheep: the valleys also shall stand so thick with corn, that they shall laugh and sing.

PSALM 66. *Jubilate Deo*

O BE joyful in God, all ye lands: sing praises unto the honour of his Name, make his praise to be glorious.

2 Say unto God, O how wonderful art thou in thy works: through the greatness of thy power shall thine enemies be found liars unto thee.

3 For all the world shall worship thee: sing of thee, and praise thy Name.

4 O come hither, and behold the works of God: how wonderful he is in his doing toward the children of men.

5 He turned the sea into dry land: so that they went through the water on foot; there did we rejoice thereof.

6 He ruleth with his power for ever; his eyes behold the people: and such as will not believe shall not be able to exalt themselves.

7 O praise our God, ye people: and make the voice of his praise to be heard;

8 Who holdeth our soul in life: and suffereth not our feet to slip.

9 For thou, O God, hast proved us: thou also hast tried us, like as silver is tried.

10 Thou broughtest us into the snare: and laidest trouble upon our loins.

11 Thou sufferedst men to ride over our heads: we went through fire and water, and thou broughtest us out into a wealthy place.

12 I will go into thine house with burnt-offerings: and will pay thee my vows, which I promised with my lips, and spake with my mouth, when I was in trouble.

13 I will offer unto thee fat burnt-sacrifices, with the incense of rams: I will offer bullocks and goats.

14 O come hither, and hearken, all ye that fear God: and I will tell you what he hath done for my soul.

15 I called unto him with my mouth: and gave him praises with my tongue.

16 If I incline unto wickedness with mine heart: the Lord will not hear me.

17 But God hath heard me: and considered the voice of my prayer.

18 Praised be God, who hath not cast out my prayer: nor turned his mercy from me.

PSALM 67. *Deus misereatur*

GOD be merciful unto us, and bless us: and shew us the light of his countenance, and be merciful unto us:

2 That thy way may be known upon earth: thy saving health among all nations.

3 Let the people praise thee, O God: yea, let all the people praise thee.

4 O let the nations rejoice and be glad: for thou shalt judge the folk righteously, and govern the nations upon earth.

5 Let the people praise thee, O God: let all the people praise thee.

6 Then shall the earth bring forth her increase: and God, even our own God, shall give us his blessing.

7 God shall bless us: and all the ends of the world shall fear him.

DAY 13. MORNING PRAYER

PSALM 68. *Exurgat Deus*

LET God arise, and let his enemies be scattered: let them also that hate him flee before him.

2 Like as the smoke vanisheth, so shalt thou drive them away: and like as wax melteth at the fire, so let the ungodly perish at the presence of God.

3 But let the righteous be glad and rejoice before God: let them also be merry and joyful.

4 O sing unto God, and sing praises unto his Name: magnify him that rideth upon the heavens, as it were upon an horse; praise him in his Name JAH, and rejoice before him.

5 He is a father of the fatherless, and defendeth the cause of the widows: even God in his holy habitation.

6 He is the God that maketh men to be of one mind in an house, and bringeth the prisoners out of captivity: but letteth the runagates continue in scarceness.

7 O God, when thou wentest forth before the people: when thou wentest through the wilderness;

8 The earth shook, and the heavens dropped at the presence of God: even as Sinai also was moved at the presence of God, who is the God of Israel.

9 Thou, O God, sentest a gracious rain upon thine inheritance: and refreshedst it when it was weary.

10 Thy congregation shall dwell therein: for thou, O God, hast of thy goodness prepared for the poor.

11 The Lord gave the word: great was the company of the preachers.

12 Kings with their armies did flee, and were discomfited: and they of the household divided the spoil.

13 Though ye have lien among the pots, yet shall ye be as the wings of a dove: that is covered with silver wings, and her feathers like gold.

14 When the Almighty scattered kings for their sake: then were they as white as snow in Salmon.

15 As the hill of Basan, so is God's hill: even an high hill, as the hill of Basan.

16 Why hop ye so, ye high hills? this is God's hill, in the which it pleaseth him to dwell: yea, the Lord will abide in it for ever.

17 The chariots of God are twenty thousand, even thousands of angels: and the Lord is among them, as in the holy place of Sinai.

18 Thou art gone up on high, thou hast led captivity captive, and received gifts for men: yea, even for thine enemies, that the Lord God might dwell among them.

19 Praised be the Lord daily: even the God who helpeth us, and poureth his benefits upon us.

20 He is our God, even the God of whom cometh salvation: God is the Lord, by whom we escape death.

21 God shall wound the head of his enemies: and the hairy scalp of such a one as goeth on still in his wickedness.

22 The Lord hath said, I will bring my people again, as I did from Basan: mine own will I bring again, as I did sometime from the deep of the sea.

23 That thy foot may be dipped in the blood of thine enemies: and that the tongue of thy dogs may be red through the same.

24 It is well seen, O God, how thou goest: how thou, my God and King, goest in the sanctuary.

25 The singers go before, the minstrels follow after: in the midst are the damsels playing with the timbrels.

26 Give thanks, O Israel, unto God the Lord in the congregations: from the ground of the heart.

27 There is little Benjamin their ruler, and the princes of Judah their counsel: the princes of Zabulon, and the princes of Nephthali.

28 Thy God hath sent forth strength for thee: stablish the thing, O God, that thou hast wrought in us,

29 For thy temple's sake at Jerusalem: so shall kings bring presents unto thee.

30 When the company of the spear-men, and multitude of the mighty are scattered abroad among the beasts of the people, so that they humbly bring pieces of silver: and when he hath scattered the people that delight in war;

31 Then shall the princes come out of Egypt: the Morians' land shall soon stretch out her hands unto God.

32 Sing unto God, O ye kingdoms of the earth: O sing praises unto the Lord;

33 Who sitteth in the heavens over all from the beginning: lo, he doth send out his voice, yea, and that a mighty voice.

34 Ascribe ye the power to God over Israel: his worship and strength is in the clouds.

35 O God, wonderful art thou in thy holy places: even the God of Israel, he will give strength and power unto his people; blessed be God.

DAY 13. EVENING PRAYER

PSALM 69. *Salvum me fac*

SAVE me, O God: for the waters are come in, even unto my soul.

2 I stick fast in the deep mire, where no ground is: I am come into deep waters, so that the floods run over me.

3 I am weary of crying; my throat is dry: my sight faileth me for waiting so long upon my God.

4 They that hate me without a cause are more than the hairs of my head: they that are mine enemies, and would destroy me guiltless, are mighty.

5 I paid them the things that I never took: God, thou knowest my simpleness, and my faults are not hid from thee.

6 Let not them that trust in thee, O Lord God of hosts, be ashamed for my cause: let not those that seek thee be confounded through me, O Lord God of Israel.

7 And why? for thy sake have I suffered reproof: shame hath covered my face.

8 I am become a stranger unto my brethren: even an alien unto my mother's children.

9 For the zeal of thine house hath even eaten me: and the rebukes of them that rebuked thee are fallen upon me.

10 I wept, and chastened myself with fasting: and that was turned to my reproof.

11 I put on sackcloth also: and they jested upon me.

12 They that sit in the gate speak against me: and the drunkards make songs upon me.

13 But, Lord, I make my prayer unto thee: in an acceptable time.

14 Hear me, O God, in the multitude of thy mercy: even in the truth of thy salvation.

15 Take me out of the mire, that I sink not: O let me be delivered from them that hate me, and out of the deep waters.

16 Let not the water-flood drown me, neither let the deep swallow me up: and let not the pit shut her mouth upon me.

17 Hear me, O Lord, for thy loving-kindness is comfortable:

turn thee unto me according to the multitude of thy mercies.

18 And hide not thy face from thy servant, for I am in trouble: O haste thee, and hear me.

19 Draw nigh unto my soul, and save it: O deliver me, because of mine enemies.

20 Thou hast known my reproof, my shame, and my dishonour: mine adversaries are all in thy sight.

21 Thy rebuke hath broken my heart; I am full of heaviness: I looked for some to have pity on me, but there was no man, neither found I any to comfort me.

22 They gave me gall to eat: and when I was thirsty they gave me vinegar to drink.

23 Let their table be made a snare to take themselves withal: and let the things that should have been for their wealth be unto them an occasion of falling.

24 Let their eyes be blinded, that they see not: and ever bow thou down their backs.

25 Pour out thine indignation upon them: and let thy wrathful displeasure take hold of them.

26 Let their habitation be void: and no man to dwell in their tents.

27 For they persecute him whom thou hast smitten: and they talk how they may vex them whom thou hast wounded.

28 Let them fall from one wickedness to another: and not come into thy righteousness.

29 Let them be wiped out of the book of the living: and not be written among the righteous.

30 As for me, when I am poor and in heaviness: thy help, O God, shall lift me up.

31 I will praise the Name of God with a song: and magnify it with thanksgiving.

32 This also shall please the Lord: better than a bullock that hath horns and hoofs.

33 The humble shall consider this, and be glad: seek ye after God, and your soul shall live.

34 For the Lord heareth the poor: and despiseth not his prisoners.

35 Let heaven and earth praise him: the sea, and all that moveth therein.

36 For God will save Sion, and build the cities of Judah: that men may dwell there, and have it in possession.

37 The posterity also of his servants shall inherit it: and they that love his Name shall dwell therein.

Psalm 70. *Deus, in adjutorium*

HASTE thee, O God, to deliver me: make haste to help me, O Lord.

2 Let them be ashamed and confounded that seek after my soul: let them be turned backward and put to confusion that wish me evil.

3 Let them for their reward be soon brought to shame: that cry over me, There, there.

4 But let all those that seek thee be joyful and glad in thee: and let all such as delight in thy salvation say alway, The Lord be praised.

5 As for me, I am poor and in misery: haste thee unto me, O God.

6 Thou art my helper and my redeemer: O Lord, make no long tarrying.

DAY 14. MORNING PRAYER

Psalm 71. *In te, Domine, speravi*

IN thee, O Lord, have I put my trust, let me never be put to confusion: but rid me and deliver me in thy righteousness, incline thine ear unto me, and save me.

2 Be thou my strong hold, whereunto I may alway resort: thou hast promised to help me, for thou art my house of defence and my castle.

3 Deliver me, O my God, out of the hand of the ungodly: out of the hand of the unrighteous and cruel man.

4 For thou, O Lord God, art the thing that I long for: thou art my hope, even from my youth.

5 Through thee have I been holden up ever since I was born:

thou art he that took me out of my mother's womb; my praise shall be always of thee.

6 I am become as it were a monster unto many: but my sure trust is in thee.

7 O let my mouth be filled with thy praise: that I may sing of thy glory and honour all the day long.

8 Cast me not away in the time of age: forsake me not when my strength faileth me.

9 For mine enemies speak against me, and they that lay wait for my soul take their counsel together, saying: God hath forsaken him; persecute him, and take him, for there is none to deliver him.

10 Go not far from me, O God: my God, haste thee to help me.

11 Let them be confounded and perish that are against my soul: let them be covered with shame and dishonour that seek to do me evil.

12 As for me, I will patiently abide alway: and will praise thee more and more.

13 My mouth shall daily speak of thy righteousness and salvation: for I know no end thereof.

14 I will go forth in the strength of the Lord God: and will make mention of thy righteousness only.

15 Thou, O God, hast taught me from my youth up until now: therefore will I tell of thy wondrous works.

16 Forsake me not, O God, in mine old age, when I am gray-headed: until I have shewed thy strength unto this generation, and thy power to all them that are yet for to come.

17 Thy righteousness, O God, is very high: and great things are they that thou hast done; O God, who is like unto thee?

18 O what great troubles and adversities hast thou shewed me, and yet didst thou turn and refresh me: yea, and broughtest me from the deep of the earth again.

19 Thou hast brought me to great honour: and comforted me on every side.

20 Therefore will I praise thee and thy faithfulness, O God, playing upon an instrument of musick: unto thee will I sing upon the harp, O thou Holy One of Israel.

21 My lips will be fain when I sing unto thee: and so will my soul whom thou hast delivered.

22 My tongue also shall talk of thy righteousness all the day long: for they are confounded and brought unto shame that seek to do me evil.

Psalm 72. *Deus, judicium*

GIVE the King thy judgements, O God: and thy righteousness unto the King's son.

2 Then shall he judge thy people according unto right: and defend the poor.

3 The mountains also shall bring peace: and the little hills righteousness unto the people.

4 He shall keep the simple folk by their right: defend the children of the poor, and punish the wrong-doer.

5 They shall fear thee, as long as the sun and moon endureth: from one generation to another.

6 He shall come down like the rain into a fleece of wool: even as the drops that water the earth.

7 In his time shall the righteous flourish: yea, and abundance of peace, so long as the moon endureth.

8 His dominion shall be also from the one sea to the other: and from the flood unto the world's end.

9 They that dwell in the wilderness shall kneel before him: his enemies shall lick the dust.

10 The kings of Tharsis and of the isles shall give presents: the kings of Arabia and Saba shall bring gifts.

11 All kings shall fall down before him: all nations shall do him service.

12 For he shall deliver the poor when he crieth: the needy also, and him that hath no helper.

13 He shall be favourable to the simple and needy: and shall preserve the souls of the poor.

14 He shall deliver their souls from falsehood and wrong: and dear shall their blood be in his sight.

15 He shall live, and unto him shall be given of the gold of

Arabia: prayer shall be made ever unto him, and daily shall he be praised.

16 There shall be an heap of corn in the earth, high upon the hills: his fruit shall shake like Libanus, and shall be green in the city like grass upon the earth.

17 His Name shall endure for ever; his Name shall remain under the sun among the posterities: which shall be blessed through him; and all the heathen shall praise him.

18 Blessed be the Lord God, even the God of Israel: which only doeth wondrous things;

19 And blessed be the Name of his majesty for ever: and all the earth shall be filled with his majesty. Amen, Amen.

DAY 14. EVENING PRAYER

PSALM 73. *Quam bonus Israel!*

TRULY God is loving unto Israel: even unto such as are of a clean heart.

2 Nevertheless, my feet were almost gone: my treadings had well-nigh slipt.

3 And why? I was grieved at the wicked: I do also see the ungodly in such prosperity.

4 For they are in no peril of death: but are lusty and strong.

5 They come in no misfortune like other folk: neither are they plagued like other men.

6 And this is the cause that they are so holden with pride: and overwhelmed with cruelty.

7 Their eyes swell with fatness: and they do even what they lust.

8 They corrupt other, and speak of wicked blasphemy: their talking is against the most High.

9 For they stretch forth their mouth unto the heaven: and their tongue goeth through the world.

10 Therefore fall the people unto them: and thereout suck they no small advantage.

11 Tush, say they, how should God perceive it: is there knowledge in the most High?

12 Lo, these are the ungodly, these prosper in the world, and

these have riches in possession: and I said, Then have I cleansed my heart in vain, and washed mine hands in innocency.

13 All the day long have I been punished: and chastened every morning.

14 Yea, and I had almost said even as they: but lo, then I should have condemned the generation of thy children.

15 Then thought I to understand this: but it was too hard for me,

16 Until I went into the sanctuary of God: then understood I the end of these men;

17 Namely, how thou dost set them in slippery places: and castest them down, and destroyest them.

18 O how suddenly do they consume: perish, and come to a fearful end!

19 Yea, even like as a dream when one awaketh: so shalt thou make their image to vanish out of the city.

20 Thus my heart was grieved: and it went even through my reins.

21 So foolish was I, and ignorant: even as it were a beast before thee.

22 Nevertheless, I am alway by thee: for thou hast holden me by my right hand.

23 Thou shalt guide me with thy counsel: and after that receive me with glory.

24 Whom have I in heaven but thee: and there is none upon earth that I desire in comparison of thee.

25 My flesh and my heart faileth: but God is the strength of my heart, and my portion for ever.

26 For lo, they that forsake thee shall perish: thou hast destroyed all them that commit fornication against thee.

27 But it is good for me to hold me fast by God, to put my trust in the Lord God: and to speak of all thy works in the gates of the daughter of Sion.

PSALM 74. *Ut quid, Deus?*

O GOD, wherefore art thou absent from us so long: why is thy wrath so hot against the sheep of thy pasture?

2 O think upon thy congregation: whom thou hast purchased and redeemed of old.

3 Think upon the tribe of thine inheritance: and mount Sion, wherein thou hast dwelt.

4 Lift up thy feet, that thou mayest utterly destroy every enemy: which hath done evil in thy sanctuary.

5 Thine adversaries roar in the midst of thy congregations: and set up their banners for tokens.

6 He that hewed timber afore out of the thick trees: was known to bring it to an excellent work.

7 But now they break down all the carved work thereof: with axes and hammers.

8 They have set fire upon thy holy places: and have defiled the dwelling-place of thy Name, even unto the ground.

9 Yea, they said in their hearts, Let us make havock of them altogether: thus have they burnt up all the houses of God in the land.

10 We see not our tokens, there is not one prophet more: no, not one is there among us, that understandeth any more.

11 O God, how long shall the adversary do this dishonour: how long shall the enemy blaspheme thy Name, for ever?

12 Why withdrawest thou thy hand: why pluckest thou not thy right hand out of thy bosom to consume the enemy?

13 For God is my King of old: the help that is done upon earth he doeth it himself.

14 Thou didst divide the sea through thy power: thou brakest the heads of the dragons in the waters.

15 Thou smotest the heads of Leviathan in pieces: and gavest him to be meat for the people in the wilderness.

16 Thou broughtest out fountains and waters out of the hard rocks: thou driedst up mighty waters.

17 The day is thine, and the night is thine: thou hast prepared the light and the sun.

18 Thou hast set all the borders of the earth: thou hast made summer and winter.

19 Remember this, O Lord, how the enemy hath rebuked: and how the foolish people hath blasphemed thy Name.

20 O deliver not the soul of thy turtle-dove unto the multitude of the enemies: and forget not the congregation of the poor for ever.

21 Look upon the covenant: for all the earth is full of darkness and cruel habitations.

22 O let not the simple go away ashamed: but let the poor and needy give praise unto thy Name.

23 Arise, O God, maintain thine own cause: remember how the foolish man blasphemeth thee daily.

24 Forget not the voice of thine enemies: the presumption of them that hate thee increaseth ever more and more.

DAY 15. MORNING PRAYER

Psalm 75. *Confitebimur tibi*

UNTO thee, O God, do we give thanks: yea, unto thee do we give thanks.

2 Thy Name also is so nigh: and that do thy wondrous works declare.

3 When I receive the congregation: I shall judge according unto right.

4 The earth is weak, and all the inhabiters thereof: I bear up the pillars of it.

5 I said unto the fools, Deal not so madly: and to the ungodly, Set not up your horn.

6 Set not up your horn on high: and speak not with a stiff neck.

7 For promotion cometh neither from the east, nor from the west: nor yet from the south.

8 And why? God is the Judge: he putteth down one, and setteth up another.

9 For in the hand of the Lord there is a cup, and the wine is red: it is full mixed, and he poureth out of the same.

10 As for the dregs thereof: all the ungodly of the earth shall drink them, and suck them out.

11 But I will talk of the God of Jacob: and praise him for ever.

12 All the horns of the ungodly also will I break: and the horns of the righteous shall be exalted.

Psalm 76. *Notus in Judaea*

IN Jewry is God known: his Name is great in Israel.

2 At Salem is his tabernacle: and his dwelling in Sion.

3 There brake he the arrows of the bow: the shield, the sword, and the battle.

4 Thou art of more honour and might: than the hills of the robbers.

5 The proud are robbed, they have slept their sleep: and all the men whose hands were mighty have found nothing.

6 At thy rebuke, O God of Jacob: both the chariot and horse are fallen.

7 Thou, even thou art to be feared: and who may stand in thy sight when thou art angry?

8 Thou didst cause thy judgement to be heard from heaven: the earth trembled, and was still;

9 When God arose to judgement: and to help all the meek upon earth.

10 The fierceness of man shall turn to thy praise: and the fierceness of them shalt thou refrain.

11 Promise unto the Lord your God, and keep it, all ye that are round about him: bring presents unto him that ought to be feared.

12 He shall refrain the spirit of princes: and is wonderful among the kings of the earth.

Psalm 77. *Voce mea ad Dominum*

I WILL cry unto God with my voice: even unto God will I cry with my voice, and he shall hearken unto me.

2 In the time of my trouble I sought the Lord: my sore ran and ceased not in the night-season; my soul refused comfort.

3 When I am in heaviness, I will think upon God: when my heart is vexed, I will complain.

4 Thou holdest mine eyes waking: I am so feeble, that I cannot speak.

5 I have considered the days of old: and the years that are past.

6 I call to remembrance my song: and in the night I commune with mine own heart, and search out my spirits.

7 Will the Lord absent himself for ever: and will he be no more intreated?

8 Is his mercy clean gone for ever: and is his promise come utterly to an end for evermore?

9 Hath God forgotten to be gracious: and will he shut up his loving-kindness in displeasure?

10 And I said, It is mine own infirmity: but I will remember the years of the right hand of the most Highest.

11 I will remember the works of the Lord: and call to mind thy wonders of old time.

12 I will think also of all thy works: and my talking shall be of thy doings.

13 Thy way, O God, is holy: who is so great a God as our God?

14 Thou art the God that doeth wonders: and hast declared thy power among the people.

15 Thou hast mightily delivered thy people: even the sons of Jacob and Joseph.

16 The waters saw thee, O God, the waters saw thee, and were afraid: the depths also were troubled.

17 The clouds poured out water, the air thundered: and thine arrows went abroad.

18 The voice of thy thunder was heard round about: the lightnings shone upon the ground; the earth was moved, and shook withal.

19 Thy way is in the sea, and thy paths in the great waters: and thy footsteps are not known.

20 Thou leddest thy people like sheep: by the hand of Moses and Aaron.

DAY 15. EVENING PRAYER
Psalm 78. *Attendite, popule*

HEAR my law, O my people: incline your ears unto the words of my mouth.

2 I will open my mouth in a parable: I will declare hard sentences of old;

3 Which we have heard and known: and such as our fathers have told us;

4 That we should not hide them from the children of the generations to come: but to shew the honour of the Lord, his mighty and wonderful works that he hath done.

5 He made a covenant with Jacob, and gave Israel a law: which he commanded our forefathers to teach their children;

6 That their posterity might know it: and the children which were yet unborn;

7 To the intent that when they came up: they might shew their children the same;

8 That they might put their trust in God: and not to forget the works of God, but to keep his commandments;

9 And not to be as their forefathers, a faithless and stubborn generation: a generation that set not their heart aright, and whose spirit cleaveth not stedfastly unto God;

10 Like as the children of Ephraim: who being harnessed, and carrying bows, turned themselves back in the day of battle.

11 They kept not the covenant of God: and would not walk in his law;

12 But forgat what he had done: and the wonderful works that he had shewed for them.

13 Marvellous things did he in the sight of our forefathers, in the land of Egypt: even in the field of Zoan.

14 He divided the sea, and let them go through: he made the waters to stand on an heap.

15 In the day-time also he led them with a cloud: and all the night through with a light of fire.

16 He clave the hard rocks in the wilderness: and gave them drink thereof, as it had been out of the great depth.

17 He brought waters out of the stony rock: so that it gushed out like the rivers.

18 Yet for all this they sinned more against him: and provoked the most Highest in the wilderness.

19 They tempted God in their hearts: and required meat for their lust.

20 They spake against God also, saying: Shall God prepare a table in the wilderness?

21 He smote the stony rock indeed, that the waters gushed out,

and the streams flowed withal: but can he give bread also, or provide flesh for his people?

22 When the Lord heard this, he was wroth: so the fire was kindled in Jacob, and there came up heavy displeasure against Israel;

23 Because they believed not in God: and put not their trust in his help.

24 So he commanded the clouds above: and opened the doors of heaven.

25 He rained down manna also upon them for to eat: and gave them food from heaven.

26 So man did eat angels' food: for he sent them meat enough.

27 He caused the east-wind to blow under heaven: and through his power he brought in the south-west-wind.

28 He rained flesh upon them as thick as dust: and feathered fowls like as the sand of the sea.

29 He let it fall among their tents: even round about their habitation.

30 So they did eat and were well filled, for he gave them their own desire: they were not disappointed of their lust.

31 But while the meat was yet in their mouths, the heavy wrath of God came upon them, and slew the wealthiest of them: yea, and smote down the chosen men that were in Israel.

32 But for all this they sinned yet more: and believed not his wondrous works.

33 Therefore their days did he consume in vanity: and their years in trouble.

34 When he slew them, they sought him: and turned them early, and inquired after God.

35 And they remembered that God was their strength: and that the high God was their redeemer.

36 Nevertheless, they did but flatter him with their mouth: and dissembled with him in their tongue.

37 For their heart was not whole with him: neither continued they stedfast in his covenant.

38 But he was so merciful, that he forgave their misdeeds: and destroyed them not.

39 Yea, many a time turned he his wrath away: and would not suffer his whole displeasure to arise.

40 For he considered that they were but flesh: and that they were even a wind that passeth away, and cometh not again.

41 Many a time did they provoke him in the wilderness: and grieved him in the desert.

42 They turned back, and tempted God: and moved the Holy One in Israel.

43 They thought not of his hand: and of the day when he delivered them from the hand of the enemy;

44 How he had wrought his miracles in Egypt: and his wonders in the field of Zoan.

45 He turned their waters into blood: so that they might not drink of the rivers.

46 He sent lice among them, and devoured them up: and frogs to destroy them.

47 He gave their fruit unto the caterpillar: and their labour unto the grasshopper.

48 He destroyed their vines with hail-stones: and their mulberry trees with the frost.

49 He smote their cattle also with hail-stones: and their flocks with hot thunderbolts.

50 He cast upon them the furiousness of his wrath, anger, displeasure, and trouble: and sent evil angels among them.

51 He made a way to his indignation, and spared not their soul from death: but gave their life over to the pestilence;

52 And smote all the first-born in Egypt: the most principal and mightiest in the dwellings of Ham.

53 But as for his own people, he led them forth like sheep: and carried them in the wilderness like a flock.

54 He brought them out safely, that they should not fear: and overwhelmed their enemies with the sea.

55 And brought them within the borders of his sanctuary: even to his mountain which he purchased with his right hand.

56 He cast out the heathen also before them: caused their land to be divided among them for an heritage, and made the tribes of Israel to dwell in their tents.

57 So they tempted and displeased the most high God: and kept not his testimonies;

58 But turned their backs, and fell away like their forefathers: starting aside like a broken bow.

59 For they grieved him with their hill-altars: and provoked him to displeasure with their images.

60 When God heard this, he was wroth: and took sore displeasure at Israel.

61 So that he forsook the tabernacle in Silo: even the tent that he had pitched among men.

62 He delivered their power into captivity: and their beauty into the enemy's hand.

63 He gave his people over also unto the sword: and was wroth with his inheritance.

64 The fire consumed their young men: and their maidens were not given to marriage.

65 Their priests were slain with the sword: and there were no widows to make lamentation.

66 So the Lord awaked as one out of sleep: and like a giant refreshed with wine.

67 He smote his enemies in the hinder parts: and put them to a perpetual shame.

68 He refused the tabernacle of Joseph: and chose not the tribe of Ephraim;

69 But chose the tribe of Judah: even the hill of Sion which he loved.

70 And there he built his temple on high: and laid the foundation of it like the ground which he hath made continually.

71 He chose David also his servant: and took him away from the sheep-folds.

72 As he was following the ewes great with young ones he took him: that he might feed Jacob his people, and Israel his inheritance.

73 So he fed them with a faithful and true heart: and ruled them prudently with all his power.

DAY 16. MORNING PRAYER

Psalm 79. *Deus, venerunt*

O GOD, the heathen are come into thine inheritance: thy holy temple have they defiled, and made Jerusalem an heap of stones.

2 The dead bodies of thy servants have they given to be meat unto the fowls of the air: and the flesh of thy saints unto the beasts of the land.

3 Their blood have they shed like water on every side of Jerusalem: and there was no man to bury them.

4 We are become an open shame to our enemies: a very scorn and derision unto them that are round about us.

5 Lord, how long wilt thou be angry: shall thy jealousy burn like fire for ever?

6 Pour out thine indignation upon the heathen that have not known thee: and upon the kingdoms that have not called upon thy Name.

7 For they have devoured Jacob: and laid waste his dwelling-place.

8 O remember not our old sins, but have mercy upon us, and that soon: for we are come to great misery.

9 Help us, O God of our salvation, for the glory of thy Name: O deliver us, and be merciful unto our sins, for thy Name's sake.

10 Wherefore do the heathen say: Where is now their God?

11 O let the vengeance of thy servants' blood that is shed: be openly shewed upon the heathen in our sight.

12 O let the sorrowful sighing of the prisoners come before thee: according to the greatness of thy power, preserve thou those that are appointed to die.

13 And for the blasphemy wherewith our neighbours have blasphemed thee: reward thou them, O Lord, seven-fold into their bosom.

14 So we, that are thy people, and sheep of thy pasture, shall give thee thanks for ever: and will alway be shewing forth thy praise from generation to generation.

PSALM 80. *Qui regis Israel*

HEAR, O thou Shepherd of Israel, thou that leadest Joseph like a sheep: shew thyself also, thou that sittest upon the cherubims.

2 Before Ephraim, Benjamin, and Manasses: stir up thy strength, and come, and help us.

3 Turn us again, O God: shew the light of thy countenance, and we shall be whole.

4 O Lord God of hosts: how long wilt thou be angry with thy people that prayeth?

5 Thou feedest them with the bread of tears: and givest them plenteousness of tears to drink.

6 Thou hast made us a very strife unto our neighbours: and our enemies laugh us to scorn.

7 Turn us again, thou God of hosts: shew the light of thy countenance, and we shall be whole.

8 Thou hast brought a vine out of Egypt: thou hast cast out the heathen, and planted it.

9 Thou madest room for it: and when it had taken root it filled the land.

10 The hills were covered with the shadow of it: and the boughs thereof were like the goodly cedar-trees.

11 She stretched out her branches unto the sea: and her boughs unto the river.

12 Why hast thou then broken down her hedge: that all they that go by pluck off her grapes?

13 The wild boar out of the wood doth root it up: and the wild beasts of the field devour it.

14 Turn thee again, thou God of hosts, look down from heaven: behold, and visit this vine;

15 And the place of the vineyard that thy right hand hath planted: and the branch that thou madest so strong for thyself.

16 It is burnt with fire, and cut down: and they shall perish at the rebuke of thy countenance.

17 Let thy hand be upon the man of thy right hand: and upon the son of man, whom thou madest so strong for thine own self.

18 And so will not we go back from thee: O let us live, and we shall call upon thy Name.

19 Turn us again, O Lord God of hosts: shew the light of thy countenance, and we shall be whole.

Psalm 81. *Exultate Deo*

SING we merrily unto God our strength: make a cheerful noise unto the God of Jacob.

2 Take the psalm, bring hither the tabret: the merry harp with the lute.

3 Blow up the trumpet in the new-moon: even in the time appointed, and upon our solemn feast-day.

4 For this was made a statute for Israel: and a law of the God of Jacob.

5 This he ordained in Joseph for a testimony: when he came out of the land of Egypt, and had heard a strange language.

6 I eased his shoulder from the burden: and his hands were delivered from making the pots.

7 Thou calledst upon me in troubles, and I delivered thee: and heard thee what time as the storm fell upon thee.

8 I proved thee also: at the waters of strife.

9 Hear, O my people, and I will assure thee, O Israel: if thou wilt hearken unto me,

10 There shall no strange god be in thee: neither shalt thou worship any other god.

11 I am the Lord thy God, who brought thee out of the land of Egypt: open thy mouth wide, and I shall fill it.

12 But my people would not hear my voice: and Israel would not obey me.

13 So I gave them up unto their own hearts' lusts: and let them follow their own imaginations.

14 O that my people would have hearkened unto me: for if Israel had walked in my ways,

15 I should soon have put down their enemies: and turned my hand against their adversaries.

16 The haters of the Lord should have been found liars: but their time should have endured for ever.

17 He should have fed them also with the finest wheat-flour: and with honey out of the stony rock should I have satisfied thee.

DAY 16. EVENING PRAYER

Psalm 82. *Deus stetit*

GOD standeth in the congregation of princes: he is a Judge among gods.

2 How long will ye give wrong judgement: and accept the persons of the ungodly?

3 Defend the poor and fatherless: see that such as are in need and necessity have right.

4 Deliver the outcast and poor: save them from the hand of the ungodly.

5 They will not be learned nor understand, but walk on still in darkness: all the foundations of the earth are out of course.

6 I have said, Ye are gods: and ye are all the children of the most Highest.

7 But ye shall die like men: and fall like one of the princes.

8 Arise, O God, and judge thou the earth: for thou shalt take all heathen to thine inheritance.

Psalm 83. *Deus, quis similis?*

HOLD not thy tongue, O God, keep not still silence: refrain not thyself, O God.

2 For lo, thine enemies make a murmuring: and they that hate thee have lift up their head.

3 They have imagined craftily against thy people: and taken counsel against thy secret ones.

4 They have said, Come, and let us root them out, that they be no more a people: and that the name of Israel may be no more in remembrance.

5 For they have cast their heads together with one consent: and are confederate against thee;

6 The tabernacles of the Edomites, and the Ismaelites: the Moabites and Hagarenes;

7 Gebal, and Ammon, and Amalek: the Philistines, with them that dwell at Tyre.

8 Assur also is joined with them: and have holpen the children of Lot.

9 But do thou to them as unto the Madianites: unto Sisera, and unto Jabin at the brook of Kison;

10 Who perished at Endor: and became as the dung of the earth.

11 Make them and their princes like Oreb and Zeb: yea, make all their princes like as Zeba and Salmana;

12 Who say, Let us take to ourselves: the houses of God in possession.

13 O my God, make them like unto a wheel: and as the stubble before the wind;

14 Like as the fire that burneth up the wood: and as the flame that consumeth the mountains.

15 Persecute them even so with thy tempest: and make them afraid with thy storm.

16 Make their faces ashamed, O Lord: that they may seek thy Name.

17 Let them be confounded and vexed ever more and more: let them be put to shame, and perish.

18 And they shall know that thou, whose Name is Jehovah: art only the most Highest over all the earth.

PSALM 84. *Quam dilecta!*

O HOW amiable are thy dwellings: thou Lord of hosts!

2 My soul hath a desire and longing to enter into the courts of the Lord: my heart and my flesh rejoice in the living God.

3 Yea, the sparrow hath found her an house, and the swallow a nest where she may lay her young: even thy altars, O Lord of hosts, my King and my God.

4 Blessed are they that dwell in thy house: they will be alway praising thee.

5 Blessed is the man whose strength is in thee: in whose heart are thy ways.

6 Who going through the vale of misery use it for a well: and the pools are filled with water.

7 They will go from strength to strength: and unto the God of gods appeareth every one of them in Sion.

8 O Lord God of hosts, hear my prayer: hearken, O God of Jacob.

9 Behold, O God our defender: and look upon the face of thine Anointed.

10 For one day in thy courts: is better than a thousand.

11 I had rather be a door-keeper in the house of my God: than to dwell in the tents of ungodliness.

12 For the Lord God is a light and defence: the Lord will give grace and worship, and no good thing shall he withhold from them that live a godly life.

13 O Lord God of hosts: blessed is the man that putteth his trust in thee.

Psalm 85. *Benedixisti, Domine*

LORD, thou art become gracious unto thy land: thou hast turned away the captivity of Jacob.

2 Thou hast forgiven the offence of thy people: and covered all their sins.

3 Thou hast taken away all thy displeasure: and turned thyself from thy wrathful indignation.

4 Turn us then, O God our Saviour: and let thine anger cease from us.

5 Wilt thou be displeased at us for ever: and wilt thou stretch out thy wrath from one generation to another?

6 Wilt thou not turn again, and quicken us: that thy people may rejoice in thee?

7 Shew us thy mercy, O Lord: and grant us thy salvation.

8 I will hearken what the Lord God will say concerning me: for he shall speak peace unto his people, and to his saints, that they turn not again.

9 For his salvation is nigh them that fear him: that glory may dwell in our land.

10 Mercy and truth are met together: righteousness and peace have kissed each other.

11 Truth shall flourish out of the earth: and righteousness hath looked down from heaven.

12 Yea, the Lord shall shew loving-kindness: and our land shall give her increase.

13 Righteousness shall go before him: and he shall direct his going in the way.

DAY 17. MORNING PRAYER

Psalm 86. *Inclina, Domine*

Bow down thine ear, O Lord, and hear me: for I am poor, and in misery.

2 Preserve thou my soul, for I am holy: my God, save thy servant that putteth his trust in thee.

3 Be merciful unto me, O Lord: for I will call daily upon thee.

4 Comfort the soul of thy servant: for unto thee, O Lord, do I lift up my soul.

5 For thou, Lord, art good and gracious: and of great mercy unto all them that call upon thee.

6 Give ear, Lord, unto my prayer: and ponder the voice of my humble desires.

7 In the time of my trouble I will call upon thee: for thou hearest me.

8 Among the gods there is none like unto thee, O Lord: there is not one that can do as thou doest.

9 All nations whom thou hast made shall come and worship thee, O Lord: and shall glorify thy Name.

10 For thou art great, and doest wondrous things: thou art God alone.

11 Teach me thy way, O Lord, and I will walk in thy truth: O knit my heart unto thee, that I may fear thy Name.

12 I will thank thee, O Lord my God, with all my heart: and will praise thy Name for evermore.

13 For great is thy mercy toward me: and thou hast delivered my soul from the nethermost hell.

14 O God, the proud are risen against me: and the congregations of naughty men have sought after my soul, and have not set thee before their eyes.

15 But thou, O Lord God, art full of compassion and mercy: long-suffering, plenteous in goodness and truth.

16 O turn thee then unto me, and have mercy upon me: give thy strength unto thy servant, and help the son of thine handmaid.

17 Shew some token upon me for good, that they who hate me may see it and be ashamed: because thou, Lord, hast holpen me and comforted me.

Psalm 87. *Fundamenta ejus*

HER foundations are upon the holy hills: the Lord loveth the gates of Sion more than all the dwellings of Jacob.

2 Very excellent things are spoken of thee: thou city of God.

3 I will think upon Rahab and Babylon: with them that know me.

4 Behold ye the Philistines also: and they of Tyre, with the Morians; lo, there was he born.

5 And of Sion it shall be reported that he was born in her: and the most High shall stablish her.

6 The Lord shall rehearse it when he writeth up the people: that he was born there.

7 The singers also and trumpeters shall he rehearse: All my fresh springs shall be in thee.

Psalm 88. *Domine Deus*

O LORD God of my salvation, I have cried day and night before thee: O let my prayer enter into thy presence, incline thine ear unto my calling.

2 For my soul is full of trouble: and my life draweth nigh unto hell.

3 I am counted as one of them that go down into the pit: and I have been even as a man that hath no strength.

4 Free among the dead, like unto them that are wounded, and lie in the grave: who are out of remembrance, and are cut away from thy hand.

5 Thou hast laid me in the lowest pit: in a place of darkness, and in the deep.

6 Thine indignation lieth hard upon me: and thou hast vexed me with all thy storms.

7 Thou hast put away mine acquaintance far from me: and made me to be abhorred of them.

8 I am so fast in prison: that I cannot get forth.

9 My sight faileth for very trouble: Lord, I have called daily upon thee, I have stretched forth my hands unto thee.

10 Dost thou shew wonders among the dead: or shall the dead rise up again, and praise thee?

11 Shall thy loving-kindness be shewed in the grave: or thy faithfulness in destruction?

12 Shall thy wondrous works be known in the dark: and thy righteousness in the land where all things are forgotten?

13 Unto thee have I cried, O Lord: and early shall my prayer come before thee.

14 Lord, why abhorrest thou my soul: and hidest thou thy face from me?

15 I am in misery, and like unto him that is at the point to die: even from my youth up thy terrors have I suffered with a troubled mind.

16 Thy wrathful displeasure goeth over me: and the fear of thee hath undone me.

17 They came round about me daily like water: and compassed me together on every side.

18 My lovers and friends hast thou put away from me: and hid mine acquaintance out of my sight.

DAY 17. EVENING PRAYER

Psalm 89. *Misericordias Domini*

MY song shall be alway of the loving-kindness of the Lord: with my mouth will I ever be shewing thy truth from one generation to another.

2 For I have said, Mercy shall be set up for ever: thy truth shalt thou stablish in the heavens.

3 I have made a covenant with my chosen: I have sworn unto David my servant;

4 Thy seed will I stablish for ever: and set up thy throne from one generation to another.

5 O Lord, the very heavens shall praise thy wondrous works: and thy truth in the congregation of the saints.

6 For who is he among the clouds: that shall be compared unto the Lord?

7 And what is he among the gods: that shall be like unto the Lord?

8 God is very greatly to be feared in the council of the saints: and to be had in reverence of all them that are round about him.

9 O Lord God of hosts, who is like unto thee: thy truth, most mighty Lord, is on every side.

10 Thou rulest the raging of the sea: thou stillest the waves thereof when they arise.

11 Thou hast subdued Egypt, and destroyed it: thou hast scattered thine enemies abroad with thy mighty arm.

12 The heavens are thine, the earth also is thine: thou hast laid the foundation of the round world, and all that therein is.

13 Thou hast made the north and the south: Tabor and Hermon shall rejoice in thy Name.

14 Thou hast a mighty arm: strong is thy hand, and high is thy right hand.

15 Righteousness and equity are the habitation of thy seat: mercy and truth shall go before thy face.

16 Blessed is the people, O Lord, that can rejoice in thee: they shall walk in the light of thy countenance.

17 Their delight shall be daily in thy Name: and in thy righteousness shall they make their boast.

18 For thou art the glory of their strength: and in thy loving-kindness thou shalt lift up our horns.

19 For the Lord is our defence: the Holy One of Israel is our King.

20 Thou spakest sometime in visions unto thy saints, and saidst: I have laid help upon one that is mighty; I have exalted one chosen out of the people.

21 I have found David my servant: with my holy oil have I anointed him.

22 My hand shall hold him fast: and my arm shall strengthen him.

23 The enemy shall not be able to do him violence: the son of wickedness shall not hurt him.

24 I will smite down his foes before his face: and plague them that hate him.

25 My truth also and my mercy shall be with him: and in my Name shall his horn be exalted.

26 I will set his dominion also in the sea: and his right hand in the floods.

27 He shall call me, Thou art my Father: my God, and my strong salvation.

28 And I will make him my first-born: higher than the kings of the earth.

29 My mercy will I keep for him for evermore: and my covenant shall stand fast with him.

30 His seed also will I make to endure for ever: and his throne as the days of heaven.

31 But if his children forsake my law: and walk not in my judgements;

32 If they break my statutes, and keep not my commandments: I will visit their offences with the rod, and their sin with scourges.

33 Nevertheless, my loving-kindness will I not utterly take from him: nor suffer my truth to fail.

34 My covenant will I not break, nor alter the thing that is gone out of my lips: I have sworn once by my holiness, that I will not fail David.

35 His seed shall endure for ever: and his seat is like as the sun before me.

36 He shall stand fast for evermore as the moon: and as the faithful witness in heaven.

37 But thou hast abhorred and forsaken thine Anointed: and art displeased at him.

38 Thou hast broken the covenant of thy servant: and cast his crown to the ground.

39 Thou hast overthrown all his hedges: and broken down his strong holds.

40 All they that go by spoil him: and he is become a reproach to his neighbours.

41 Thou hast set up the right hand of his enemies: and made all his adversaries to rejoice.

42 Thou hast taken away the edge of his sword: and givest him not victory in the battle.

43 Thou hast put out his glory: and cast his throne down to the ground.

44 The days of his youth hast thou shortened: and covered him with dishonour.

45 Lord, how long wilt thou hide thyself, for ever: and shall thy wrath burn like fire?

46 O remember how short my time is: wherefore hast thou made all men for nought?

47 What man is he that liveth, and shall not see death: and shall he deliver his soul from the hand of hell?

48 Lord, where are thy old loving-kindnesses: which thou swarest unto David in thy truth?

49 Remember, Lord, the rebuke that thy servants have: and how I do bear in my bosom the rebukes of many people;

50 Wherewith thine enemies have blasphemed thee, and slandered the footsteps of thine Anointed: Praised be the Lord for evermore. Amen, and Amen.

DAY 18. MORNING PRAYER
Psalm 90. *Domine, refugium*

LORD, thou hast been our refuge: from one generation to another.

2 Before the mountains were brought forth, or ever the earth and the world were made: thou art God from everlasting, and world without end.

3 Thou turnest man to destruction: again thou sayest, Come again, ye children of men.

4 For a thousand years in thy sight are but as yesterday: seeing that is past as a watch in the night.

5 As soon as thou scatterest them they are even as a sleep: and fade away suddenly like the grass.

6 In the morning it is green, and groweth up: but in the evening it is cut down, dried up, and withered.

7 For we consume away in thy displeasure: and are afraid at thy wrathful indignation.

8 Thou hast set our misdeeds before thee: and our secret sins in the light of thy countenance.

9 For when thou art angry all our days are gone: we bring our years to an end, as it were a tale that is told.

10 The days of our age are threescore years and ten; and though men be so strong that they come to fourscore years: yet is their strength then but labour and sorrow; so soon passeth it away, and we are gone.

11 But who regardeth the power of thy wrath: for even thereafter as a man feareth, so is thy displeasure.

12 So teach us to number our days: that we may apply our hearts unto wisdom.

13 Turn thee again, O Lord, at the last: and be gracious unto thy servants.

14 O satisfy us with thy mercy, and that soon: so shall we rejoice and be glad all the days of our life.

15 Comfort us again now after the time that thou hast plagued us: and for the years wherein we have suffered adversity.

16 Shew thy servants thy work: and their children thy glory.

17 And the glorious majesty of the Lord our God be upon us: prosper thou the work of our hands upon us, O prosper thou our handywork.

Psalm 91. *Qui habitat*

WHOSO dwelleth under the defence of the most High: shall abide under the shadow of the Almighty.

2 I will say unto the Lord, Thou art my hope, and my strong hold: my God, in him will I trust.

3 For he shall deliver thee from the snare of the hunter: and from the noisome pestilence.

4 He shall defend thee under his wings, and thou shalt be safe under his feathers: his faithfulness and truth shall be thy shield and buckler.

5 Thou shalt not be afraid for any terror by night: nor for the arrow that flieth by day;

6 For the pestilence that walketh in darkness: nor for the sickness that destroyeth in the noon-day.

7 A thousand shall fall beside thee, and ten thousand at thy right hand: but it shall not come nigh thee.

8 Yea, with thine eyes shalt thou behold: and see the reward of the ungodly.

9 For thou, Lord, art my hope: thou hast set thine house of defence very high.

10 There shall no evil happen unto thee: neither shall any plague come nigh thy dwelling.

11 For he shall give his angels charge over thee: to keep thee in all thy ways.

12 They shall bear thee in their hands: that thou hurt not thy foot against a stone.

13 Thou shalt go upon the lion and adder: the young lion and the dragon shalt thou tread under thy feet.

14 Because he hath set his love upon me, therefore will I deliver him: I will set him up, because he hath known my Name.

15 He shall call upon me, and I will hear him: yea, I am with him in trouble; I will deliver him, and bring him to honour.

16 With long life will I satisfy him: and shew him my salvation.

Psalm 92. *Bonum est confiteri*

IT is a good thing to give thanks unto the Lord: and to sing praises unto thy Name, O most Highest;

2 To tell of thy loving-kindness early in the morning: and of thy truth in the night-season;

3 Upon an instrument of ten strings, and upon the lute: upon a loud instrument, and upon the harp.

4 For thou, Lord, hast made me glad through thy works: and I will rejoice in giving praise for the operations of thy hands.

5 O Lord, how glorious are thy works: thy thoughts are very deep.

6 An unwise man doth not well consider this: and a fool doth not understand it.

7 When the ungodly are green as the grass, and when all the workers of wickedness do flourish: then shall they be destroyed for ever; but thou, Lord, art the most Highest for evermore.

8 For lo, thine enemies, O Lord, lo, thine enemies shall perish: and all the workers of wickedness shall be destroyed.

9 But mine horn shall be exalted like the horn of an unicorn: for I am anointed with fresh oil.

10 Mine eye also shall see his lust of mine enemies: and mine ear shall hear his desire of the wicked that arise up against me.

11 The righteous shall flourish like a palm-tree: and shall spread abroad like a cedar in Libanus.

12 Such as are planted in the house of the Lord: shall flourish in the courts of the house of our God.

13 They also shall bring forth more fruit in their age: and shall be fat and well-liking.

14 That they may shew how true the Lord my strength is: and that there is no unrighteousness in him.

DAY 18. EVENING PRAYER
Psalm 93. *Dominus regnavit*

THE Lord is King, and hath put on glorious apparel: the Lord hath put on his apparel, and girded himself with strength.

2 He hath made the round world so sure: that it cannot be moved.

3 Ever since the world began hath thy seat been prepared: thou art from everlasting.

4 The floods are risen, O Lord, the floods have lift up their voice: the floods lift up their waves.

5 The waves of the sea are mighty, and rage horribly: but yet the Lord, who dwelleth on high, is mightier.

6 Thy testimonies, O Lord, are very sure: holiness becometh thine house for ever.

Psalm 94. *Deus ultionum*

O LORD God, to whom vengeance belongeth: thou God, to whom vengeance belongeth, shew thyself.

2 Arise, thou Judge of the world: and reward the proud after their deserving.

3 Lord, how long shall the ungodly: how long shall the ungodly triumph?

4 How long shall all wicked doers speak so disdainfully: and make such proud boasting?

5 They smite down thy people, O Lord: and trouble thine heritage.

6 They murder the widow and the stranger: and put the fatherless to death.

7 And yet they say, Tush, the Lord shall not see: neither shall the God of Jacob regard it.

8 Take heed, ye unwise among the people: O ye fools, when will ye understand?

9 He that planted the ear, shall he not hear: or he that made the eye, shall he not see?

10 Or he that nurtureth the heathen: it is he that teacheth man knowledge, shall not he punish?

11 The Lord knoweth the thoughts of man: that they are but vain.

12 Blessed is the man whom thou chastenest, O Lord: and teachest him in thy law;

13 That thou mayest give him patience in time of adversity: until the pit be digged up for the ungodly.

14 For the Lord will not fail his people: neither will he forsake his inheritance;

15 Until righteousness turn again unto judgement: all such as are true in heart shall follow it.

16 Who will rise up with me against the wicked: or who will take my part against the evil-doers?

17 If the Lord had not helped me: it had not failed but my soul had been put to silence.

18 But when I said, My foot hath slipt: thy mercy, O Lord, held me up.

19 In the multitude of the sorrows that I had in my heart: thy comforts have refreshed my soul.

20 Wilt thou have any thing to do with the stool of wickedness: which imagineth mischief as a law?

21 They gather them together against the soul of the righteous: and condemn the innocent blood.

22 But the Lord is my refuge: and my God is the strength of my confidence.

23 He shall recompense them their wickedness, and destroy them in their own malice: yea, the Lord our God shall destroy them.

DAY 19. MORNING PRAYER

Psalm 95. *Venite, exultemus*

O COME, let us sing unto the Lord: let us heartily rejoice in the strength of our salvation.

2 Let us come before his presence with thanksgiving: and shew ourselves glad in him with psalms.

3 For the Lord is a great God: and a great King above all gods.

4 In his hand are all the corners of the earth: and the strength of the hills is his also.

5 The sea is his, and he made it: and his hands prepared the dry land.

6 O come, let us worship and fall down: and kneel before the Lord our Maker.

7 For he is the Lord our God: and we are the people of his pasture, and the sheep of his hand.

8 To-day if ye will hear his voice, harden not your hearts: as in the provocation, and as in the day of temptation in the wilderness;

9 When your fathers tempted me: proved me, and saw my works.

10 Forty years long was I grieved with this generation, and said: It is a people that do err in their hearts, for they have not known my ways;

11 Unto whom I sware in my wrath: that they should not enter into my rest.

PSALM 96. *Cantate Domino*

O SING unto the Lord a new song: sing unto the Lord, all the whole earth.

2 Sing unto the Lord, and praise his Name: be telling of his salvation from day to day.

3 Declare his honour unto the heathen: and his wonders unto all people.

4 For the Lord is great, and cannot worthily be praised: he is more to be feared than all gods.

5 As for all the gods of the heathen, they are but idols: but it is the Lord that made the heavens.

6 Glory and worship are before him: power and honour are in his sanctuary.

7 Ascribe unto the Lord, O ye kindreds of the people: ascribe unto the Lord worship and power.

8 Ascribe unto the Lord the honour due unto his Name: bring presents, and come into his courts.

9 O worship the Lord in the beauty of holiness: let the whole earth stand in awe of him.

10 Tell it out among the heathen that the Lord is King: and that it is he who hath made the round world so fast that it cannot be moved; and how that he shall judge the people righteously.

11 Let the heavens rejoice, and let the earth be glad: let the sea make a noise, and all that therein is.

12 Let the field be joyful, and all that is in it: then shall all the trees of the wood rejoice before the Lord.

13 For he cometh, for he cometh to judge the earth: and with righteousness to judge the world, and the people with his truth.

PSALM 97. *Dominus regnavit*

THE Lord is King, the earth may be glad thereof: yea, the multitude of the isles may be glad thereof.

2 Clouds and darkness are round about him: righteousness and judgement are the habitation of his seat.

3 There shall go a fire before him: and burn up his enemies on every side.

4 His lightnings gave shine unto the world: the earth saw it, and was afraid.

5 The hills melted like wax at the presence of the Lord: at the presence of the Lord of the whole earth.

6 The heavens have declared his righteousness: and all the people have seen his glory.

7 Confounded be all they that worship carved images, and that delight in vain gods: worship him, all ye gods.

8 Sion heard of it, and rejoiced: and the daughters of Judah were glad, because of thy judgements, O Lord.

9 For thou, Lord, art higher than all that are in the earth: thou art exalted far above all gods.

10 O ye that love the Lord, see that ye hate the thing which is evil: the Lord preserveth the souls of his saints; he shall deliver them from the hand of the ungodly.

11 There is sprung up a light for the righteous: and joyful gladness for such as are true-hearted.

12 Rejoice in the Lord, ye righteous: and give thanks for a remembrance of his holiness.

DAY 19. EVENING PRAYER

Psalm 98. *Cantate Domino*

O SING unto the Lord a new song: for he hath done marvellous things.

2 With his own right hand, and with his holy arm: hath he gotten himself the victory.

3 The Lord declared his salvation: his righteousness hath he openly shewed in the sight of the heathen.

4 He hath remembered his mercy and truth toward the house of Israel: and all the ends of the world have seen the salvation of our God.

5 Shew yourselves joyful unto the Lord, all ye lands: sing, rejoice, and give thanks.

6 Praise the Lord upon the harp: sing to the harp with a psalm of thanksgiving.

7 With trumpets also and shawms: O shew yourselves joyful before the Lord the King.

8 Let the sea make a noise, and all that therein is: the round world, and they that dwell therein.

9 Let the floods clap their hands, and let the hills be joyful together before the Lord: for he is come to judge the earth.

10 With righteousness shall he judge the world: and the people with equity.

Psalm 99. *Dominus regnavit*

THE Lord is King, be the people never so unpatient: he sitteth between the cherubims, be the earth never so unquiet.

2 The Lord is great in Sion: and high above all people.

3 They shall give thanks unto thy Name: which is great, wonderful, and holy.

4 The King's power loveth judgement; thou hast prepared equity: thou hast executed judgement and righteousness in Jacob.

5 O magnify the Lord our God: and fall down before his footstool, for he is holy.

6 Moses and Aaron among his priests, and Samuel among such as call upon his Name: these called upon the Lord, and he heard them.

7 He spake unto them out of the cloudy pillar: for they kept his testimonies, and the law that he gave them.

8 Thou heardest them, O Lord our God: thou forgavest them, O God, and punishedst their own inventions.

9 O magnify the Lord our God, and worship him upon his holy hill: for the Lord our God is holy.

Psalm 100. *Jubilate Deo*

O BE joyful in the Lord, all ye lands: serve the Lord with gladness, and come before his presence with a song.

2 Be ye sure that the Lord he is God: it is he that hath made us, and not we ourselves; we are his people, and the sheep of his pasture.

3 O go your way into his gates with thanksgiving, and into his courts with praise: be thankful unto him, and speak good of his Name.

4 For the Lord is gracious, his mercy is everlasting: and his truth endureth from generation to generation.

Psalm 101. *Misericordiam et judicium*

MY song shall be of mercy and judgement: unto thee, O Lord, will I sing.

2 O let me have understanding: in the way of godliness.

3 When wilt thou come unto me: I will walk in my house with a perfect heart.

4 I will take no wicked thing in hand; I hate the sins of unfaithfulness: there shall no such cleave unto me.

5 A froward heart shall depart from me: I will not know a wicked person.

6 Whoso privily slandereth his neighbour: him will I destroy.

7 Whoso hath also a proud look and high stomach: I will not suffer him.

8 Mine eyes look upon such as are faithful in the land: that they may dwell with me.

9 Whoso leadeth a godly life: he shall be my servant.

10 There shall no deceitful person dwell in my house: he that telleth lies shall not tarry in my sight.

11 I shall soon destroy all the ungodly that are in the land: that I may root out all wicked doers from the city of the Lord.

DAY 20. MORNING PRAYER

Psalm 102. *Domine, exaudi*

HEAR my prayer, O Lord: and let my crying come unto thee.

2 Hide not thy face from me in the time of my trouble: incline thine ear unto me when I call; O hear me, and that right soon.

3 For my days are consumed away like smoke: and my bones are burnt up as it were a fire-brand.

4 My heart is smitten down, and withered like grass: so that I forget to eat my bread.

5 For the voice of my groaning: my bones will scarce cleave to my flesh.

6 I am become like a pelican in the wilderness: and like an owl that is in the desert.

7 I have watched, and am even as it were a sparrow: that sitteth alone upon the house-top.

8 Mine enemies revile me all the day long: and they that are mad upon me are sworn together against me.

9 For I have eaten ashes as it were bread: and mingled my drink with weeping;

10 And that because of thine indignation and wrath: for thou hast taken me up, and cast me down.

11 My days are gone like a shadow: and I am withered like grass.

12 But thou, O Lord, shalt endure for ever: and thy remembrance throughout all generations.

13 Thou shalt arise, and have mercy upon Sion: for it is time that thou have mercy upon her, yea, the time is come.

14 And why? thy servants think upon her stones: and it pitieth them to see her in the dust.

15 The heathen shall fear thy Name, O Lord: and all the kings of the earth thy majesty;

16 When the Lord shall build up Sion: and when his glory shall appear;

17 When he turneth him unto the prayer of the poor destitute: and despiseth not their desire.

18 This shall be written for those that come after: and the people which shall be born shall praise the Lord.

19 For he hath looked down from his sanctuary: out of the heaven did the Lord behold the earth;

20 That he might hear the mournings of such as are in captivity: and deliver the children appointed unto death;

21 That they may declare the Name of the Lord in Sion: and his worship at Jerusalem;

22 When the people are gathered together: and the kingdoms also, to serve the Lord.

23 He brought down my strength in my journey: and shortened my days.

24 But I said, O my God, take me not away in the midst of mine age: as for thy years, they endure throughout all generations.

25 Thou, Lord, in the beginning hast laid the foundation of the earth: and the heavens are the work of thy hands.

26 They shall perish, but thou shalt endure: they all shall wax old as doth a garment;

27 And as a vesture shalt thou change them, and they shall be changed: but thou art the same, and thy years shall not fail.

28 The children of thy servants shall continue: and their seed shall stand fast in thy sight.

PSALM 103. *Benedic, anima mea*

PRAISE the Lord, O my soul: and all that is within me praise his holy Name.

2 Praise the Lord, O my soul: and forget not all his benefits;

3 Who forgiveth all thy sin: and healeth all thine infirmities;

4 Who saveth thy life from destruction: and crowneth thee with mercy and loving-kindness;

5 Who satisfieth thy mouth with good things: making thee young and lusty as an eagle.

6 The Lord executeth righteousness and judgement: for all them that are oppressed with wrong.

7 He shewed his ways unto Moses: his works unto the children of Israel.

8 The Lord is full of compassion and mercy: long-suffering, and of great goodness.

9 He will not alway be chiding: neither keepeth he his anger for ever.

10 He hath not dealt with us after our sins: nor rewarded us according to our wickednesses.

11 For look how high the heaven is in comparison of the earth: so great is his mercy also toward them that fear him.

12 Look how wide also the east is from the west: so far hath he set our sins from us.

13 Yea, like as a father pitieth his own children: even so is the Lord merciful unto them that fear him.

14 For he knoweth whereof we are made: he remembereth that we are but dust.

15 The days of man are but as grass: for he flourisheth as a flower of the field.

16 For as soon as the wind goeth over it, it is gone: and the place thereof shall know it no more.

17 But the merciful goodness of the Lord endureth for ever and ever upon them that fear him: and his righteousness upon children's children;

18 Even upon such as keep his covenant: and think upon his commandments to do them.

19 The Lord hath prepared his seat in heaven: and his kingdom ruleth over all.

20 O praise the Lord, ye angels of his, ye that excel in strength: ye that fulfil his commandment, and hearken unto the voice of his words.

21 O praise the Lord, all ye his hosts: ye servants of his that do his pleasure.

22 O speak good of the Lord, all ye works of his, in all places of his dominion: praise thou the Lord, O my soul.

DAY 20. EVENING PRAYER

Psalm 104. *Benedic, anima mea*

PRAISE the Lord, O my soul: O Lord my God, thou art become exceeding glorious; thou art clothed with majesty and honour.

2 Thou deckest thyself with light as it were with a garment: and spreadest out the heavens like a curtain.

3 Who layeth the beams of his chambers in the waters: and maketh the clouds his chariot, and walketh upon the wings of the wind.

4 He maketh his angels spirits: and his ministers a flaming fire.

5 He laid the foundations of the earth: that it never should move at any time.

6 Thou coveredst it with the deep like as with a garment: the waters stand in the hills.

7 At thy rebuke they flee: at the voice of thy thunder they are afraid.

8 They go up as high as the hills, and down to the valleys beneath: even unto the place which thou hast appointed for them.

9 Thou hast set them their bounds which they shall not pass: neither turn again to cover the earth.

10 He sendeth the springs into the rivers: which run among the hills.

11 All beasts of the field drink thereof: and the wild asses quench their thirst.

12 Beside them shall the fowls of the air have their habitation: and sing among the branches.

13 He watereth the hills from above: the earth is filled with the fruit of thy works.

14 He bringeth forth grass for the cattle: and green herb for the service of men;

15 That he may bring food out of the earth, and wine that maketh glad the heart of man: and oil to make him a cheerful countenance, and bread to strengthen man's heart.

16 The trees of the Lord also are full of sap: even the cedars of Libanus which he hath planted;

17 Wherein the birds make their nests: and the fir-trees are a dwelling for the stork.

18 The high hills are a refuge for the wild goats: and so are the stony rocks for the conies.

19 He appointed the moon for certain seasons: and the sun knoweth his going down.

20 Thou makest darkness that it may be night: wherein all the beasts of the forest do move.

21 The lions roaring after their prey: do seek their meat from God.

22 The sun ariseth, and they get them away together: and lay them down in their dens.

23 Man goeth forth to his work, and to his labour: until the evening.

24 O Lord, how manifold are thy works: in wisdom hast thou made them all; the earth is full of thy riches.

25 So is the great and wide sea also: wherein are things creeping innumerable, both small and great beasts.

26 There go the ships, and there is that Leviathan: whom thou hast made to take his pastime therein.

27 These wait all upon thee: that thou mayest give them meat in due season.

28 When thou givest it them they gather it: and when thou openest thy hand they are filled with good.

29 When thou hidest thy face they are troubled: when thou takest away their breath they die, and are turned again to their dust.

30 When thou lettest thy breath go forth they shall be made: and thou shalt renew the face of the earth.

31 The glorious majesty of the Lord shall endure for ever: the Lord shall rejoice in his works.

32 The earth shall tremble at the look of him: if he do but touch the hills, they shall smoke.

33 I will sing unto the Lord as long as I live: I will praise my God while I have my being.

34 And so shall my words please him: my joy shall be in the Lord.

35 As for sinners, they shall be consumed out of the earth, and the ungodly shall come to an end: praise thou the Lord, O my soul, praise the Lord.

DAY 21. MORNING PRAYER

Psalm 105. *Confitemini Domino*

O GIVE thanks unto the Lord, and call upon his Name: tell the people what things he hath done.

2 O let your songs be of him, and praise him: and let your talking be of all his wondrous works.

3 Rejoice in his holy Name: let the heart of them rejoice that seek the Lord.

4 Seek the Lord and his strength: seek his face evermore.

5 Remember the marvellous works that he hath done: his wonders, and the judgements of his mouth,

6 O ye seed of Abraham his servant: ye children of Jacob his chosen.

7 He is the Lord our God: his judgements are in all the world.

8 He hath been alway mindful of his covenant and promise: that he made to a thousand generations;

9 Even the covenant that he made with Abraham: and the oath that he sware unto Isaac;

10 And appointed the same unto Jacob for a law: and to Israel for an everlasting testament;

11 Saying, Unto thee will I give the land of Canaan: the lot of your inheritance;

12 When there were yet but a few of them: and they strangers in the land;

13 What time as they went from one nation to another: from one kingdom to another people;

14 He suffered no man to do them wrong: but reproved even kings for their sakes;

15 Touch not mine Anointed: and do my prophets no harm.

16 Moreover, he called for a dearth upon the land: and destroyed all the provision of bread.

17 But he had sent a man before them: even Joseph, who was sold to be a bond-servant;

18 Whose feet they hurt in the stocks: the iron entered into his soul;

19 Until the time came that his cause was known: the word of the Lord tried him.

20 The king sent, and delivered him: the prince of the people let him go free.

21 He made him lord also of his house: and ruler of all his substance;

22 That he might inform his princes after his will: and teach his senators wisdom.

23 Israel also came into Egypt: and Jacob was a stranger in the land of Ham.

24 And he increased his people exceedingly: and made them stronger than their enemies;

25 Whose heart turned, so that they hated his people: and dealt untruly with his servants.

26 Then sent he Moses his servant: and Aaron whom he had chosen.

27 And these shewed his tokens among them: and wonders in the land of Ham.

28 He sent darkness, and it was dark: and they were not obedient unto his word.

29 He turned their waters into blood: and slew their fish.

30 Their land brought forth frogs: yea, even in their kings' chambers.

31 He spake the word, and there came all manner of flies: and lice in all their quarters.

32 He gave them hail-stones for rain: and flames of fire in their land.

33 He smote their vines also and fig-trees: and destroyed the trees that were in their coasts.

34 He spake the word, and the grasshoppers came, and caterpillars innumerable: and did eat up all the grass in their land, and devoured the fruit of their ground.

35 He smote all the first-born in their land: even the chief of all their strength.

36 He brought them forth also with silver and gold: there was not one feeble person among their tribes.

37 Egypt was glad at their departing: for they were afraid of them.

38 He spread out a cloud to be a covering: and fire to give light in the night-season.

39 At their desire he brought quails: and he filled them with the bread of heaven.

40 He opened the rock of stone, and the waters flowed out: so that rivers ran in the dry places.

41 For why? he remembered his holy promise: and Abraham his servant.

42 And he brought forth his people with joy: and his chosen with gladness;

43 And gave them the lands of the heathen: and they took the labours of the people in possession;

44 That they might keep his statutes: and observe his laws.

DAY 21. EVENING PRAYER

Psalm 106. *Confitemini Domino*

O GIVE thanks unto the Lord, for he is gracious: and his mercy endureth for ever.

2 Who can express the noble acts of the Lord: or shew forth all his praise?

3 Blessed are they that alway keep judgement: and do righteousness.

4 Remember me, O Lord, according to the favour that thou bearest unto thy people: O visit me with thy salvation;

5 That I may see the felicity of thy chosen: and rejoice in the gladness of thy people, and give thanks with thine inheritance.

6 We have sinned with our fathers: we have done amiss, and dealt wickedly.

7 Our fathers regarded not thy wonders in Egypt, neither kept they thy great goodness in remembrance: but were disobedient at the sea, even at the Red sea.

8 Nevertheless, he helped them for his Name's sake: that he might make his power to be known.

9 He rebuked the Red sea also, and it was dried up: so he led them through the deep, as through a wilderness.

10 And he saved them from the adversaries' hand: and delivered them from the hand of the enemy.

11 As for those that troubled them, the waters overwhelmed them: there was not one of them left.

12 Then believed they his words: and sang praise unto him.

13 But within a while they forgat his works: and would not abide his counsel.

14 But lust came upon them in the wilderness: and they tempted God in the desert.

15 And he gave them their desire: and sent leanness withal into their soul.

16 They angered Moses also in the tents: and Aaron the saint of the Lord.

17 So the earth opened, and swallowed up Dathan: and covered the congregation of Abiram.

18 And the fire was kindled in their company: the flame burnt up the ungodly.

19 They made a calf in Horeb: and worshipped the molten image.

20 Thus they turned their glory: into the similitude of a calf that eateth hay.

21 And they forgat God their Saviour: who had done so great things in Egypt;

22 Wondrous works in the land of Ham: and fearful things by the Red sea.

23 So he said, he would have destroyed them, had not Moses his chosen stood before him in the gap: to turn away his wrathful indignation, lest he should destroy them.

24 Yea, they thought scorn of that pleasant land: and gave no credence unto his word;

25 But murmured in their tents: and hearkened not unto the voice of the Lord.

26 Then lift he up his hand against them: to overthrow them in the wilderness;

27 To cast out their seed among the nations: and to scatter them in the lands.

28 They joined themselves unto Baal-peor: and ate the offerings of the dead.

29 Thus they provoked him to anger with their own inventions: and the plague was great among them.

30 Then stood up Phinees and prayed: and so the plague ceased.

31 And that was counted unto him for righteousness: among all posterities for evermore.

32 They angered him also at the waters of strife: so that he punished Moses for their sakes;

33 Because they provoked his spirit: so that he spake unadvisedly with his lips.

34 Neither destroyed they the heathen: as the Lord commanded them;

35 But were mingled among the heathen: and learned their works.

36 Insomuch that they worshipped their idols, which turned to their own decay: yea, they offered their sons and their daughters unto devils;

37 And shed innocent blood, even the blood of their sons and of their daughters: whom they offered unto the idols of Canaan; and the land was defiled with blood.

38 Thus were they stained with their own works: and went a whoring with their own inventions.

39 Therefore was the wrath of the Lord kindled against his people: insomuch that he abhorred his own inheritance.

40 And he gave them over into the hands of the heathen: and they that hated them were lords over them.

41 Their enemies oppressed them: and had them in subjection.

42 Many a time did he deliver them: but they rebelled against him with their own inventions, and were brought down in their wickedness.

43 Nevertheless, when he saw their adversity: he heard their complaint.

44 He thought upon his covenant, and pitied them according unto the multitude of his mercies: yea, he made all those that led them away captive to pity them.

45 Deliver us, O Lord our God, and gather us from among the heathen: that we may give thanks unto thy holy Name, and make our boast of thy praise.

46 Blessed be the Lord God of Israel from everlasting and world without end: and let all the people say, Amen.

DAY 22. MORNING PRAYER

Psalm 107. *Confitemini Domino*

O GIVE thanks unto the Lord, for he is gracious: and his mercy endureth for ever.

2 Let them give thanks whom the Lord hath redeemed: and delivered from the hand of the enemy;

3 And gathered them out of the lands, from the east and from the west: from the north and from the south.

4 They went astray in the wilderness out of the way: and found no city to dwell in;

5 Hungry and thirsty: their soul fainted in them.

6 So they cried unto the Lord in their trouble: and he delivered them from their distress.

7 He led them forth by the right way: that they might go to the city where they dwelt.

8 O that men would therefore praise the Lord for his goodness: and declare the wonders that he doeth for the children of men!

9 For he satisfieth the empty soul: and filleth the hungry soul with goodness.

10 Such as sit in darkness, and in the shadow of death: being fast bound in misery and iron;

11 Because they rebelled against the words of the Lord: and lightly regarded the counsel of the most Highest;

12 He also brought down their heart through heaviness: they fell down, and there was none to help them.

13 So when they cried unto the Lord in their trouble: he delivered them out of their distress.

14 For he brought them out of darkness, and out of the shadow of death: and brake their bonds in sunder.

15 O that men would therefore praise the Lord for his goodness: and declare the wonders that he doeth for the children of men!

16 For he hath broken the gates of brass: and smitten the bars of iron in sunder.

17 Foolish men are plagued for their offence: and because of their wickedness.

18 Their soul abhorred all manner of meat: and they were even hard at death's door.

19 So when they cried unto the Lord in their trouble: he delivered them out of their distress.

20 He sent his word, and healed them: and they were saved from their destruction.

21 O that men would therefore praise the Lord for his goodness: and declare the wonders that he doeth for the children of men!

22 That they would offer unto him the sacrifice of thanksgiving: and tell out his works with gladness!

23 They that go down to the sea in ships: and occupy their business in great waters;

24 These men see the works of the Lord: and his wonders in the deep.

25 For at his word the stormy wind ariseth: which lifteth up the waves thereof.

26 They are carried up to the heaven, and down again to the deep: their soul melteth away because of the trouble.

27 They reel to and fro, and stagger like a drunken man: and are at their wits' end.

28 So when they cry unto the Lord in their trouble: he delivereth them out of their distress.

29 For he maketh the storm to cease: so that the waves thereof are still.

30 Then are they glad, because they are at rest: and so he bringeth them unto the haven where they would be.

31 O that men would therefore praise the Lord for his goodness: and declare the wonders that he doeth for the children of men!

32 That they would exalt him also in the congregation of the people: and praise him in the seat of the elders!

33 Who turneth the floods into a wilderness: and drieth up the water-springs.

34 A fruitful land maketh he barren: for the wickedness of them that dwell therein.

35 Again, he maketh the wilderness a standing water: and water-springs of a dry ground.

36 And there he setteth the hungry: that they may build them a city to dwell in;

37 That they may sow their land, and plant vineyards: to yield them fruits of increase.

38 He blesseth them so that they multiply exceedingly: and suffereth not their cattle to decrease.

39 And again, when they are minished and brought low: through oppression, through any plague or trouble;

40 Though he suffer them to be evil intreated through tyrants: and let them wander out of the way in the wilderness;

41 Yet helpeth he the poor out of misery: and maketh him households like a flock of sheep.

42 The righteous will consider this, and rejoice: and the mouth of all wickedness shall be stopped.

43 Whoso is wise will ponder these things: and they shall understand the loving-kindness of the Lord.

DAY 22. EVENING PRAYER

Psalm 108. *Paratum cor meum*

O GOD, my heart is ready, my heart is ready: I will sing and give praise with the best member that I have.

2 Awake, thou lute, and harp: I myself will awake right early.

3 I will give thanks unto thee, O Lord, among the people: I will sing praises unto thee among the nations.

4 For thy mercy is greater than the heavens: and thy truth reacheth unto the clouds.

5 Set up thyself, O God, above the heavens: and thy glory above all the earth.

6 That thy beloved may be delivered: let thy right hand save them, and hear thou me.

7 God hath spoken in his holiness: I will rejoice therefore, and divide Sichem, and mete out the valley of Succoth.

8 Gilead is mine, and Manasses is mine: Ephraim also is the strength of my head.

9 Judah is my law-giver, Moab is my wash-pot: over Edom will I cast out my shoe, upon Philistia will I triumph.

10 Who will lead me into the strong city: and who will bring me into Edom?

11 Hast not thou forsaken us, O God: and wilt not thou, O God, go forth with our hosts?

12 O help us against the enemy: for vain is the help of man.

13 Through God we shall do great acts: and it is he that shall tread down our enemies.

PSALM 109. *Deus, laudem*

HOLD not thy tongue, O God of my praise: for the mouth of the ungodly, yea, the mouth of the deceitful is opened upon me.

2 And they have spoken against me with false tongues: they compassed me about also with words of hatred, and fought against me without a cause.

3 For the love that I had unto them, lo, they take now my contrary part: but I give myself unto prayer.

4 Thus have they rewarded me evil for good: and hatred for my good will.

5 Set thou an ungodly man to be ruler over him: and let Satan stand at his right hand.

6 When sentence is given upon him, let him be condemned: and let his prayer be turned into sin.

7 Let his days be few: and let another take his office.

8 Let his children be fatherless: and his wife a widow.

9 Let his children be vagabonds, and beg their bread: let them seek it also out of desolate places.

10 Let the extortioner consume all that he hath: and let the stranger spoil his labour.

11 Let there be no man to pity him: nor to have compassion upon his fatherless children.

12 Let his posterity be destroyed: and in the next generation let his name be clean put out.

13 Let the wickedness of his fathers be had in remembrance in the sight of the Lord: and let not the sin of his mother be done away.

14 Let them alway be before the Lord: that he may root out the memorial of them from off the earth.

15 And that, because his mind was not to do good: but persecuted the poor helpless man, that he might slay him that was
vexed at the heart.

16 His delight was in cursing, and it shall happen unto him: he
loved not blessing, therefore shall it be far from him.

17 He clothed himself with cursing, like as with a raiment: and
it shall come into his bowels like water, and like oil into his
bones.

18 Let it be unto him as the cloke that he hath upon him: and
as the girdle that he is alway girded withal.

19 Let it thus happen from the Lord unto mine enemies: and
to those that speak evil against my soul.

20 But deal thou with me, O Lord God, according unto thy
Name: for sweet is thy mercy.

21 O deliver me, for I am helpless and poor: and my heart is
wounded within me.

22 I go hence like the shadow that departeth: and am driven
away as the grasshopper.

23 My knees are weak through fasting: my flesh is dried up for
want of fatness.

24 I became also a reproach unto them: they that looked upon
me shaked their heads.

25 Help me, O Lord my God: O save me according to thy
mercy.

26 And they shall know, how that this is thy hand: and that
thou, Lord, hast done it.

27 Though they curse, yet bless thou: and let them be confounded that rise up against me; but let thy servant rejoice.

28 Let mine adversaries be clothed with shame: and let them
cover themselves with their own confusion, as with a cloke.

29 As for me, I will give great thanks unto the Lord with my
mouth: and praise him among the multitude.

30 For he shall stand at the right hand of the poor: to save his
soul from unrighteous judges.

DAY 23. MORNING PRAYER

Psalm 110. *Dixit Dominus*

THE Lord said unto my Lord: Sit thou on my right hand, until I make thine enemies thy footstool.

2 The Lord shall send the rod of thy power out of Sion: be thou ruler, even in the midst among thine enemies.

3 In the day of thy power shall the people offer thee free-will offerings with an holy worship: the dew of thy birth is of the womb of the morning.

4 The Lord sware, and will not repent: Thou art a priest for ever after the order of Melchisedech.

5 The Lord upon thy right hand: shall wound even kings in the day of his wrath.

6 He shall judge among the heathen; he shall fill the places with the dead bodies: and smite in sunder the heads over divers countries.

7 He shall drink of the brook in the way: therefore shall he lift up his head.

Psalm 111. *Confitebor tibi*

I WILL give thanks unto the Lord with my whole heart: secretly among the faithful, and in the congregation.

2 The works of the Lord are great: sought out of all them that have pleasure therein.

3 His work is worthy to be praised and had in honour: and his righteousness endureth for ever.

4 The merciful and gracious Lord hath so done his marvellous works: that they ought to be had in remembrance.

5 He hath given meat unto them that fear him: he shall ever be mindful of his covenant.

6 He hath shewed his people the power of his works: that he may give them the heritage of the heathen.

7 The works of his hands are verity and judgement: all his commandments are true.

8 They stand fast for ever and ever: and are done in truth and equity.

9 He sent redemption unto his people: he hath commanded his covenant for ever; holy and reverend is his Name.

10 The fear of the Lord is the beginning of wisdom: a good understanding have all they that do thereafter; the praise of it endureth for ever.

PSALM 112. *Beatus vir*

BLESSED is the man that feareth the Lord: he hath great delight in his commandments.

2 His seed shall be mighty upon earth: the generation of the faithful shall be blessed.

3 Riches and plenteousness shall be in his house: and his righteousness endureth for ever.

4 Unto the godly there ariseth up light in the darkness: he is merciful, loving, and righteous.

5 A good man is merciful, and lendeth: and will guide his words with discretion.

6 For he shall never be moved: and the righteous shall be had in everlasting remembrance.

7 He will not be afraid of any evil tidings: for his heart standeth fast, and believeth in the Lord.

8 His heart is established, and will not shrink: until he see his desire upon his enemies.

9 He hath dispersed abroad, and given to the poor: and his righteousness remaineth for ever; his horn shall be exalted with honour.

10 The ungodly shall see it, and it shall grieve him: he shall gnash with his teeth, and consume away; the desire of the ungodly shall perish.

PSALM 113. *Laudate, pueri*

PRAISE the Lord, ye servants: O praise the Name of the Lord.

2 Blessed be the Name of the Lord: from this time forth for evermore.

3 The Lord's Name is praised: from the rising up of the sun unto the going down of the same.

4 The Lord is high above all heathen: and his glory above the heavens.

5 Who is like unto the Lord our God, that hath his dwelling so high: and yet humbleth himself to behold the things that are in heaven and earth?

6 He taketh up the simple out of the dust: and lifteth the poor out of the mire;

7 That he may set him with the princes: even with the princes of his people.

8 He maketh the barren woman to keep house: and to be a joyful mother of children.

DAY 23. EVENING PRAYER

PSALM 114. *In exitu Israel*

WHEN Israel came out of Egypt: and the house of Jacob from among the strange people,

2 Judah was his sanctuary: and Israel his dominion.

3 The sea saw that, and fled: Jordan was driven back.

4 The mountains skipped like rams: and the little hills like young sheep.

5 What aileth thee, O thou sea, that thou fleddest: and thou Jordan, that thou wast driven back?

6 Ye mountains, that ye skipped like rams: and ye little hills, like young sheep?

7 Tremble, thou earth, at the presence of the Lord: at the presence of the God of Jacob;

8 Who turned the hard rock into a standing water: and the flint-stone into a springing well.

PSALM 115. *Non nobis, Domine*

NOT unto us, O Lord, not unto us, but unto thy Name give the praise: for thy loving mercy and for thy truth's sake.

2 Wherefore shall the heathen say: Where is now their God?

3 As for our God, he is in heaven: he hath done whatsoever pleased him.

4 Their idols are silver and gold: even the work of men's hands.

5 They have mouths, and speak not: eyes have they, and see not.
6 They have ears, and hear not: noses have they, and smell not.
7 They have hands, and handle not; feet have they, and walk not: neither speak they through their throat.
8 They that make them are like unto them: and so are all such as put their trust in them.
9 But thou, house of Israel, trust thou in the Lord: he is their succour and defence.
10 Ye house of Aaron, put your trust in the Lord: he is their helper and defender.
11 Ye that fear the Lord, put your trust in the Lord: he is their helper and defender.
12 The Lord hath been mindful of us, and he shall bless us: even he shall bless the house of Israel, he shall bless the house of Aaron.
13 He shall bless them that fear the Lord: both small and great.
14 The Lord shall increase you more and more: you and your children.
15 Ye are the blessed of the Lord: who made heaven and earth.
16 All the whole heavens are the Lord's: the earth hath he given to the children of men.
17 The dead praise not thee, O Lord: neither all they that go down into silence.
18 But we will praise the Lord: from this time forth for evermore. Praise the Lord.

DAY 24. MORNING PRAYER

Psalm 116. *Dilexi, quoniam*

I AM well pleased: that the Lord hath heard the voice of my prayer;
2 That he hath inclined his ear unto me: therefore will I call upon him as long as I live.
3 The snares of death compassed me round about: and the pains of hell gat hold upon me.
4 I shall find trouble and heaviness, and I will call upon the Name of the Lord: O Lord, I beseech thee, deliver my soul.

5 Gracious is the Lord, and righteous: yea, our God is merciful.

6 The Lord preserveth the simple: I was in misery, and he helped me.

7 Turn again then unto thy rest, O my soul: for the Lord hath rewarded thee.

8 And why? thou hast delivered my soul from death: mine eyes from tears, and my feet from falling.

9 I will walk before the Lord: in the land of the living.

10 I believed, and therefore will I speak; but I was sore troubled: I said in my haste, All men are liars.

11 What reward shall I give unto the Lord: for all the benefits that he hath done unto me?

12 I will receive the cup of salvation: and call upon the Name of the Lord.

13 I will pay my vows now in the presence of all his people: right dear in the sight of the Lord is the death of his saints.

14 Behold, O Lord, how that I am thy servant: I am thy servant, and the son of thine handmaid; thou hast broken my bonds in sunder.

15 I will offer to thee the sacrifice of thanksgiving: and will call upon the Name of the Lord.

16 I will pay my vows unto the Lord, in the sight of all his people: in the courts of the Lord's house, even in the midst of thee, O Jerusalem. Praise the Lord.

PSALM 117. *Laudate Dominum*

O PRAISE the Lord, all ye heathen: praise him, all ye nations.

2 For his merciful kindness is ever more and more towards us: and the truth of the Lord endureth for ever. Praise the Lord.

PSALM 118. *Confitemini Domino*

O GIVE thanks unto the Lord, for he is gracious: because his mercy endureth for ever.

2 Let Israel now confess that he is gracious: and that his mercy endureth for ever.

3 Let the house of Aaron now confess: that his mercy endureth for ever.

4 Yea, let them now that fear the Lord confess: that his mercy endureth for ever.

5 I called upon the Lord in trouble: and the Lord heard me at large.

6 The Lord is on my side: I will not fear what man doeth unto me.

7 The Lord taketh my part with them that help me: therefore shall I see my desire upon mine enemies.

8 It is better to trust in the Lord: than to put any confidence in man.

9 It is better to trust in the Lord: than to put any confidence in princes.

10 All nations compassed me round about: but in the Name of the Lord will I destroy them.

11 They kept me in on every side, they kept me in, I say, on every side: but in the Name of the Lord will I destroy them.

12 They came about me like bees, and are extinct even as the fire among the thorns: for in the Name of the Lord I will destroy them.

13 Thou hast thrust sore at me, that I might fall: but the Lord was my help.

14 The Lord is my strength, and my song: and is become my salvation.

15 The voice of joy and health is in the dwellings of the righteous: the right hand of the Lord bringeth mighty things to pass.

16 The right hand of the Lord hath the pre-eminence: the right hand of the Lord bringeth mighty things to pass.

17 I shall not die, but live: and declare the works of the Lord.

18 The Lord hath chastened and corrected me: but he hath not given me over unto death.

19 Open me the gates of righteousness: that I may go into them, and give thanks unto the Lord.

20 This is the gate of the Lord: the righteous shall enter into it.

21 I will thank thee, for thou hast heard me: and art become my salvation.

22 The same stone which the builders refused: is become the head-stone in the corner.

23 This is the Lord's doing: and it is marvellous in our eyes.

24 This is the day which the Lord hath made: we will rejoice and be glad in it.

25 Help me now, O Lord: O Lord, send us now prosperity.

26 Blessed be he that cometh in the Name of the Lord: we have wished you good luck, ye that are of the house of the Lord.

27 God is the Lord who hath shewed us light: bind the sacrifice with cords, yea, even unto the horns of the altar.

28 Thou art my God, and I will thank thee: thou art my God, and I will praise thee.

29 O give thanks unto the Lord, for he is gracious: and his mercy endureth for ever.

DAY 24. EVENING PRAYER

PSALM 119. *Beati immaculati*

BLESSED are those that are undefiled in the way: and walk in the law of the Lord.

2 Blessed are they that keep his testimonies: and seek him with their whole heart.

3 For they who do no wickedness: walk in his ways.

4 Thou hast charged: that we shall diligently keep thy commandments.

5 O that my ways were made so direct: that I might keep thy statutes!

6 So shall I not be confounded: while I have respect unto all thy commandments.

7 I will thank thee with an unfeigned heart: when I shall have learned the judgements of thy righteousness.

8 I will keep thy ceremonies: O forsake me not utterly.

In quo corriget?

WHEREWITHAL shall a young man cleanse his way: even by ruling himself after thy word.

10 With my whole heart have I sought thee: O let me not go wrong out of thy commandments.

11 Thy words have I hid within my heart: that I should not sin against thee.

12 Blessed art thou, O Lord: O teach me thy statutes.

13 With my lips have I been telling: of all the judgements of thy mouth.

14 I have had as great delight in the way of thy testimonies: as in all manner of riches.

15 I will talk of thy commandments: and have respect unto thy ways.

16 My delight shall be in thy statutes: and I will not forget thy word.

Retribue servo tuo

O DO well unto thy servant: that I may live, and keep thy word.

18 Open thou mine eyes: that I may see the wondrous things of thy law.

19 I am a stranger upon earth: O hide not thy commandments from me.

20 My soul breaketh out for the very fervent desire: that it hath alway unto thy judgements.

21 Thou hast rebuked the proud: and cursed are they that do err from thy commandments.

22 O turn from me shame and rebuke: for I have kept thy testimonies.

23 Princes also did sit and speak against me: but thy servant is occupied in thy statutes.

24 For thy testimonies are my delight: and my counsellors.

Adhaesit pavimento

MY soul cleaveth to the dust: O quicken thou me, according to thy word.

26 I have acknowledged my ways, and thou heardest me: O teach me thy statutes.

27 Make me to understand the way of thy commandments: and so shall I talk of thy wondrous works.

28 My soul melteth away for very heaviness: comfort thou me according unto thy word.

29 Take from me the way of lying: and cause thou me to make much of thy law.

30 I have chosen the way of truth: and thy judgements have I laid before me.

31 I have stuck unto thy testimonies: O Lord, confound me not.

32 I will run the way of thy commandments: when thou hast set my heart at liberty.

DAY 25. MORNING PRAYER

Legem pone

TEACH me, O Lord, the way of thy statutes: and I shall keep it unto the end.

34 Give me understanding, and I shall keep thy law: yea, I shall keep it with my whole heart.

35 Make me to go in the path of thy commandments: for therein is my desire.

36 Incline my heart unto thy testimonies: and not to covetousness.

37 O turn away mine eyes, lest they behold vanity: and quicken thou me in thy way.

38 O stablish thy word in thy servant: that I may fear thee.

39 Take away the rebuke that I am afraid of: for thy judgements are good.

40 Behold, my delight is in thy commandments: O quicken me in thy righteousness.

Et veniat super me

LET thy loving mercy come also unto me, O Lord: even thy salvation, according unto thy word.

42 So shall I make answer unto my blasphemers: for my trust is in thy word.

43 O take not the word of thy truth utterly out of my mouth: for my hope is in thy judgements.

44 So shall I alway keep thy law: yea, for ever and ever.

45 And I will walk at liberty: for I seek thy commandments.

46 I will speak of thy testimonies also, even before kings: and will not be ashamed.

47 And my delight shall be in thy commandments: which I have loved.

48 My hands also will I lift up unto thy commandments, which I have loved: and my study shall be in thy statutes.

Memor esto servi tui

O THINK upon thy servant, as concerning thy word: wherein thou hast caused me to put my trust.

50 The same is my comfort in my trouble: for thy word hath quickened me.

51 The proud have had me exceedingly in derision: yet have I not shrinked from thy law.

52 For I remembered thine everlasting judgements, O Lord: and received comfort.

53 I am horribly afraid: for the ungodly that forsake thy law.

54 Thy statutes have been my songs: in the house of my pilgrimage.

55 I have thought upon thy Name, O Lord, in the night-season: and have kept thy law.

56 This I had: because I kept thy commandments.

Portio mea, Domine

THOU art my portion, O Lord: I have promised to keep thy law.

58 I made my humble petition in thy presence with my whole heart: O be merciful unto me, according to thy word.

59 I called mine own ways to remembrance: and turned my feet unto thy testimonies.

60 I made haste, and prolonged not the time: to keep thy commandments.

61 The congregations of the ungodly have robbed me: but I have not forgotten thy law.

62 At midnight I will rise to give thanks unto thee: because of thy righteous judgements.

63 I am a companion of all them that fear thee: and keep thy commandments.

64 The earth, O Lord, is full of thy mercy: O teach me thy statutes.

Bonitatem fecisti

O LORD, thou hast dealt graciously with thy servant: according unto thy word.

66 O learn me true understanding and knowledge: for I have believed thy commandments.

67 Before I was troubled, I went wrong: but now have I kept thy word.

68 Thou art good and gracious: O teach me thy statutes.

69 The proud have imagined a lie against me: but I will keep thy commandments with my whole heart.

70 Their heart is as fat as brawn: but my delight hath been in thy law.

71 It is good for me that I have been in trouble: that I may learn thy statutes.

72 The law of thy mouth is dearer unto me: than thousands of gold and silver.

DAY 25. EVENING PRAYER

Manus tuae fecerunt me

THY hands have made me and fashioned me: O give me understanding, that I may learn thy commandments.

74 They that fear thee will be glad when they see me: because I have put my trust in thy word.

75 I know, O Lord, that thy judgements are right: and that thou of very faithfulness hast caused me to be troubled.

76 O let thy merciful kindness be my comfort: according to thy word unto thy servant.

77 O let thy loving mercies come unto me, that I may live: for thy law is my delight.

78 Let the proud be confounded, for they go wickedly about to destroy me: but I will be occupied in thy commandments.

79 Let such as fear thee, and have known thy testimonies: be turned unto me.

80 O let my heart be sound in thy statutes: that I be not ashamed.

Defecit anima mea

MY soul hath longed for thy salvation: and I have a good hope because of thy word.

82 Mine eyes long sore for thy word: saying, O when wilt thou comfort me?

83 For I am become like a bottle in the smoke: yet do I not forget thy statutes.

84 How many are the days of thy servant: when wilt thou be avenged of them that persecute me?

85 The proud have digged pits for me: which are not after thy law.

86 All thy commandments are true: they persecute me falsely; O be thou my help.

87 They had almost made an end of me upon earth: but I forsook not thy commandments.

88 O quicken me after thy loving-kindness: and so shall I keep the testimonies of thy mouth.

In aeternum, Domine

O LORD, thy word: endureth for ever in heaven.

90 Thy truth also remaineth from one generation to another: thou hast laid the foundation of the earth, and it abideth.

91 They continue this day according to thine ordinance: for all things serve thee.

92 If my delight had not been in thy law: I should have perished in my trouble.

93 I will never forget thy commandments: for with them thou hast quickened me.

94 I am thine, O save me: for I have sought thy commandments.

95 The ungodly laid wait for me to destroy me: but I will consider thy testimonies.

96 I see that all things come to an end: but thy commandment is exceeding broad.

Quomodo dilexi!

LORD, what love have I unto thy law: all the day long is my study in it.

98 Thou through thy commandments hast made me wiser than mine enemies: for they are ever with me.

99 I have more understanding than my teachers: for thy testimonies are my study.

100 I am wiser than the aged: because I keep thy commandments.

101 I have refrained my feet from every evil way: that I may keep thy word.

102 I have not shrunk from thy judgements: for thou teachest me.

103 O how sweet are thy words unto my throat: yea, sweeter than honey unto my mouth.

104 Through thy commandments I get understanding: therefore I hate all evil ways.

DAY 26. MORNING PRAYER

Lucerna pedibus meis

THY word is a lantern unto my feet: and a light unto my paths.

106 I have sworn, and am stedfastly purposed: to keep thy righteous judgements.

107 I am troubled above measure: quicken me, O Lord, according to thy word.

108 Let the free-will offerings of my mouth please thee, O Lord: and teach me thy judgements.

109 My soul is alway in my hand: yet do I not forget thy law.

110 The ungodly have laid a snare for me: but yet I swerved not from thy commandments.

111 Thy testimonies have I claimed as mine heritage for ever: and why? they are the very joy of my heart.

112 I have applied my heart to fulfil thy statutes alway: even unto the end.

Iniquos odio habui

I HATE them that imagine evil things: but thy law do I love.

114 Thou art my defence and shield: and my trust is in thy word.

115 Away from me, ye wicked: I will keep the commandments of my God.

116 O stablish me according to thy word, that I may live: and let me not be disappointed of my hope.

117 Hold thou me up, and I shall be safe: yea, my delight shall be ever in thy statutes.

118 Thou hast trodden down all them that depart from thy statutes: for they imagine but deceit.

119 Thou puttest away all the ungodly of the earth like dross: therefore I love thy testimonies.

120 My flesh trembleth for fear of thee: and I am afraid of thy judgements.

Feci judicium

I DEAL with the thing that is lawful and right: O give me not over unto mine oppressors.

122 Make thou thy servant to delight in that which is good: that the proud do me no wrong.

123 Mine eyes are wasted away with looking for thy health: and for the word of thy righteousness.

124 O deal with thy servant according unto thy loving mercy: and teach me thy statutes.

125 I am thy servant, O grant me understanding: that I may know thy testimonies.

126 It is time for thee, Lord, to lay to thine hand: for they have destroyed thy law.

127 For I love thy commandments: above gold and precious stone.

128 Therefore hold I straight all thy commandments: and all false ways I utterly abhor.

Mirabilia

THY testimonies are wonderful: therefore doth my soul keep them.

130 When thy word goeth forth: it giveth light and understanding unto the simple.

131 I opened my mouth, and drew in my breath: for my delight was in thy commandments.

132 O look thou upon me, and be merciful unto me: as thou usest to do unto those that love thy Name.

133 Order my steps in thy word: and so shall no wickedness have dominion over me.

134 O deliver me from the wrongful dealings of men: and so shall I keep thy commandments.

135 Shew the light of thy countenance upon thy servant: and teach me thy statutes.

136 Mine eyes gush out with water: because men keep not thy law.

Justus es, Domine

RIGHTEOUS art thou, O Lord: and true is thy judgement.

138 The testimonies that thou hast commanded: are exceeding righteous and true.

139 My zeal hath even consumed me: because mine enemies have forgotten thy words.

140 Thy word is tried to the uttermost: and thy servant loveth it.

141 I am small, and of no reputation: yet do I not forget thy commandments.

142 Thy righteousness is an everlasting righteousness: and thy law is the truth.

143 Trouble and heaviness have taken hold upon me: yet is my delight in thy commandments.

144 The righteousness of thy testimonies is everlasting: O grant me understanding, and I shall live.

DAY 26. EVENING PRAYER

Clamavi in toto corde meo

I CALL with my whole heart: hear me, O Lord, I will keep thy statutes.

146 Yea, even unto thee do I call: help me, and I shall keep thy testimonies.

147 Early in the morning do I cry unto thee: for in thy word is my trust.

148 Mine eyes prevent the night-watches: that I might be occupied in thy words.

149 Hear my voice, O Lord, according unto thy loving-kindness: quicken me, according as thou art wont.

150 They draw nigh that of malice persecute me: and are far from thy law.

151 Be thou nigh at hand, O Lord: for all thy commandments are true.

152 As concerning thy testimonies, I have known long since: that thou hast grounded them for ever.

Vide humilitatem

O CONSIDER mine adversity, and deliver me: for I do not forget thy law.

154 Avenge thou my cause, and deliver me: quicken me, according to thy word.

155 Health is far from the ungodly: for they regard not thy statutes.

156 Great is thy mercy, O Lord: quicken me, as thou art wont.

157 Many there are that trouble me, and persecute me: yet do I not swerve from thy testimonies.

158 It grieveth me when I see the transgressors: because they keep not thy law.

159 Consider, O Lord, how I love thy commandments: O quicken me, according to thy loving-kindness.

160 Thy word is true from everlasting: all the judgements of thy righteousness endure for evermore.

Principes persecuti sunt

PRINCES have persecuted me without a cause: but my heart standeth in awe of thy word.

162 I am as glad of thy word: as one that findeth great spoils.

163 As for lies, I hate and abhor them: but thy law do I love.

164 Seven times a day do I praise thee: because of thy righteous judgements.

165 Great is the peace that they have who love thy law: and they are not offended at it.

166 Lord, I have looked for thy saving health: and done after thy commandments.

167 My soul hath kept thy testimonies: and loved them exceedingly.

168 I have kept thy commandments and testimonies: for all my ways are before thee.

Appropinquet deprecatio

LET my complaint come before thee, O Lord: give me understanding, according to thy word.

170 Let my supplication come before thee: deliver me, according to thy word.

171 My lips shall speak of thy praise: when thou hast taught me thy statutes.

172 Yea, my tongue shall sing of thy word: for all thy commandments are righteous.

173 Let thine hand help me: for I have chosen thy commandments.

174 I have longed for thy saving health, O Lord: and in thy law is my delight.

175 O let my soul live, and it shall praise thee: and thy judgements shall help me.

176 I have gone astray like a sheep that is lost: O seek thy servant, for I do not forget thy commandments.

DAY 27. MORNING PRAYER

PSALM 120. *Ad Dominum*

WHEN I was in trouble I called upon the Lord: and he heard me.

2 Deliver my soul, O Lord, from lying lips: and from a deceitful tongue.

3 What reward shall be given or done unto thee, thou false tongue: even mighty and sharp arrows, with hot burning coals.

4 Woe is me, that I am constrained to dwell with Mesech: and to have my habitation among the tents of Kedar.

5 My soul hath long dwelt among them: that are enemies unto peace.

6 I labour for peace, but when I speak unto them thereof: they make them ready to battle.

PSALM 121. *Levavi oculos*

I WILL lift up mine eyes unto the hills: from whence cometh my help.

2 My help cometh even from the Lord: who hath made heaven and earth.

3 He will not suffer thy foot to be moved: and he that keepeth thee will not sleep.

4 Behold, he that keepeth Israel: shall neither slumber nor sleep.

5 The Lord himself is thy keeper: the Lord is thy defence upon thy right hand;

6 So that the sun shall not burn thee by day: neither the moon by night.

7 The Lord shall preserve thee from all evil: yea, it is even he that shall keep thy soul.

8 The Lord shall preserve thy going out, and thy coming in: from this time forth for evermore.

PSALM 122. *Laetatus sum*

I WAS glad when they said unto me: We will go into the house of the Lord.

2 Our feet shall stand in thy gates: O Jerusalem.

3 Jerusalem is built as a city: that is at unity in itself.

4 For thither the tribes go up, even the tribes of the Lord: to testify unto Israel, to give thanks unto the Name of the Lord.

5 For there is the seat of judgement: even the seat of the house of David.

6 O pray for the peace of Jerusalem: they shall prosper that love thee.

7 Peace be within thy walls: and plenteousness within thy palaces.

8 For my brethren and companions' sakes: I will wish thee prosperity.

9 Yea, because of the house of the Lord our God: I will seek to do thee good.

PSALM 123. *Ad te levavi oculos meos*

UNTO thee lift I up mine eyes: O thou that dwellest in the heavens.

2 Behold, even as the eyes of servants look unto the hand of their masters, and as the eyes of a maiden unto the hand of her mistress: even so our eyes wait upon the Lord our God, until he have mercy upon us.

3 Have mercy upon us, O Lord, have mercy upon us: for we are utterly despised.

4 Our soul is filled with the scornful reproof of the wealthy: and with the despitefulness of the proud.

PSALM 124. *Nisi quia Dominus*

IF the Lord himself had not been on our side, now may Israel say: if the Lord himself had not been on our side, when men rose up against us;

2 They had swallowed us up quick: when they were so wrathfully displeased at us.

3 Yea, the waters had drowned us: and the stream had gone over our soul.

4 The deep waters of the proud: had gone even over our soul.

5 But praised be the Lord: who hath not given us over for a prey unto their teeth.

6 Our soul is escaped even as a bird out of the snare of the fowler: the snare is broken, and we are delivered.

7 Our help standeth in the Name of the Lord: who hath made heaven and earth.

Psalm 125. *Qui confidunt*

THEY that put their trust in the Lord shall be even as the mount Sion: which may not be removed, but standeth fast for ever.

2 The hills stand about Jerusalem: even so standeth the Lord round about his people, from this time forth for evermore.

3 For the rod of the ungodly cometh not into the lot of the righteous: lest the righteous put their hand unto wickedness.

4 Do well, O Lord: unto those that are good and true of heart.

5 As for such as turn back unto their own wickedness: the Lord shall lead them forth with the evil-doers; but peace shall be upon Israel.

DAY 27. EVENING PRAYER

Psalm 126. *In convertendo*

WHEN the Lord turned again the captivity of Sion: then were we like unto them that dream.

2 Then was our mouth filled with laughter: and our tongue with joy.

3 Then said they among the heathen: The Lord hath done great things for them.

4 Yea, the Lord hath done great things for us already: whereof we rejoice.

5 Turn our captivity, O Lord: as the rivers in the south.

6 They that sow in tears: shall reap in joy.

7 He that now goeth on his way weeping, and beareth forth good seed: shall doubtless come again with joy, and bring his sheaves with him.

Psalm 127. *Nisi Dominus*

EXCEPT the Lord build the house: their labour is but lost that build it.

2 Except the Lord keep the city: the watchman waketh but in vain.

3 It is but lost labour that ye haste to rise up early, and so late take rest, and eat the bread of carefulness: for so he giveth his beloved sleep.

4 Lo, children and the fruit of the womb: are an heritage and gift that cometh of the Lord.

5 Like as the arrows in the hand of the giant: even so are the young children.

6 Happy is the man that hath his quiver full of them: they shall not be ashamed when they speak with their enemies in the gate.

Psalm 128. *Beati omnes*

BLESSED are all they that fear the Lord: and walk in his ways.

2 For thou shalt eat the labours of thine hands: O well is thee, and happy shalt thou be.

3 Thy wife shall be as the fruitful vine: upon the walls of thine house.

4 Thy children like the olive-branches: round about thy table.

5 Lo, thus shall the man be blessed: that feareth the Lord.

6 The Lord from out of Sion shall so bless thee: that thou shalt see Jerusalem in prosperity all thy life long.

7 Yea, that thou shalt see thy children's children: and peace upon Israel.

Psalm 129. *Saepe expugnaverunt*

MANY a time have they fought against me from my youth up: may Israel now say.

2 Yea, many a time have they vexed me from my youth up: but they have not prevailed against me.

3 The plowers plowed upon my back: and made long furrows.

4 But the righteous Lord: hath hewn the snares of the ungodly in pieces.

5 Let them be confounded and turned backward: as many as have evil will at Sion.

6 Let them be even as the grass growing upon the house-tops: which withereth afore it be plucked up;

7 Whereof the mower filleth not his hand: neither he that bindeth up the sheaves his bosom.

8 So that they who go by say not so much as, The Lord prosper you: we wish you good luck in the Name of the Lord.

PSALM 130. *De profundis*

OUT of the deep have I called unto thee, O Lord: Lord, hear my voice.

2 O let thine ears consider well: the voice of my complaint.

3 If thou, Lord, wilt be extreme to mark what is done amiss: O Lord, who may abide it?

4 For there is mercy with thee: therefore shalt thou be feared.

5 I look for the Lord; my soul doth wait for him: in his word is my trust.

6 My soul fleeth unto the Lord: before the morning watch, I say, before the morning watch.

7 O Israel, trust in the Lord, for with the Lord there is mercy: and with him is plenteous redemption.

8 And he shall redeem Israel: from all his sins.

PSALM 131. *Domine, non est*

LORD, I am not high-minded: I have no proud looks.

2 I do not exercise myself in great matters: which are too high for me.

3 But I refrain my soul, and keep it low, like as a child that is weaned from his mother: yea, my soul is even as a weaned child.

4 O Israel, trust in the Lord: from this time forth for evermore.

DAY 28. MORNING PRAYER

PSALM 132. *Memento, Domine*

LORD, remember David: and all his trouble;

2 How he sware unto the Lord: and vowed a vow unto the Almighty God of Jacob;

3 I will not come within the tabernacle of mine house: nor climb up into my bed;

4 I will not suffer mine eyes to sleep, nor mine eye-lids to slumber: neither the temples of my head to take any rest;

5 Until I find out a place for the temple of the Lord: an habitation for the mighty God of Jacob.

6 Lo, we heard of the same at Ephrata: and found it in the wood.

7 We will go into his tabernacle: and fall low on our knees before his footstool.

8 Arise, O Lord, into thy resting-place: thou, and the ark of thy strength.

9 Let thy priests be clothed with righteousness: and let thy saints sing with joyfulness.

10 For thy servant David's sake: turn not away the presence of thine Anointed.

11 The Lord hath made a faithful oath unto David: and he shall not shrink from it;

12 Of the fruit of thy body: shall I set upon thy seat.

13 If thy children will keep my covenant, and my testimonies that I shall learn them: their children also shall sit upon thy seat for evermore.

14 For the Lord hath chosen Sion to be an habitation for himself: he hath longed for her.

15 This shall be my rest for ever: here will I dwell, for I have a delight therein.

16 I will bless her victuals with increase: and will satisfy her poor with bread.

17 I will deck her priests with health: and her saints shall rejoice and sing.

18 There shall I make the horn of David to flourish: I have ordained a lantern for mine Anointed.

19 As for his enemies, I shall clothe them with shame: but upon himself shall his crown flourish.

Psalm 133. *Ecce, quam bonum!*

BEHOLD, how good and joyful a thing it is: brethren, to dwell together in unity!

2 It is like the precious ointment upon the head, that ran down unto the beard: even unto Aaron's beard, and went down to the skirts of his clothing.

3 Like as the dew of Hermon: which fell upon the hill of Sion.

4 For there the Lord promised his blessing: and life for evermore.

Psalm 134. *Ecce nunc*

BEHOLD now, praise the Lord: all ye servants of the Lord;

2 Ye that by night stand in the house of the Lord: even in the courts of the house of our God.

3 Lift up your hands in the sanctuary: and praise the Lord.

4 The Lord that made heaven and earth: give thee blessing out of Sion.

Psalm 135. *Laudate Nomen*

O PRAISE the Lord, laud ye the Name of the Lord: praise it, O ye servants of the Lord;

2 Ye that stand in the house of the Lord: in the courts of the house of our God.

3 O praise the Lord, for the Lord is gracious: O sing praises unto his Name, for it is lovely.

4 For why? the Lord hath chosen Jacob unto himself: and Israel for his own possession.

5 For I know that the Lord is great: and that our Lord is above all gods.

6 Whatsoever the Lord pleased, that did he in heaven and in earth: and in the sea, and in all deep places.

7 He bringeth forth the clouds from the ends of the world: and sendeth forth lightnings with the rain, bringing the winds out of his treasures.

8 He smote the first-born of Egypt: both of man and beast.

9 He hath sent tokens and wonders into the midst of thee, O thou land of Egypt: upon Pharaoh, and all his servants.

10 He smote divers nations: and slew mighty kings;

11 Sehon king of the Amorites, and Og the king of Basan: and all the kingdoms of Canaan;

12 And gave their land to be an heritage: even an heritage unto Israel his people.

13 Thy Name, O Lord, endureth for ever: so doth thy memorial, O Lord, from one generation to another.

14 For the Lord will avenge his people: and be gracious unto his servants.

15 As for the images of the heathen, they are but silver and gold: the work of men's hands.

16 They have mouths, and speak not: eyes have they, but they see not.

17 They have ears, and yet they hear not: neither is there any breath in their mouths.

18 They that make them are like unto them: and so are all they that put their trust in them.

19 Praise the Lord, ye house of Israel: praise the Lord, ye house of Aaron.

20 Praise the Lord, ye house of Levi: ye that fear the Lord, praise the Lord.

21 Praised be the Lord out of Sion: who dwelleth at Jerusalem.

DAY 28. EVENING PRAYER

Psalm 136. *Confitemini*

O GIVE thanks unto the Lord, for he is gracious: and his mercy endureth for ever.

2 O give thanks unto the God of all gods: for his mercy endureth for ever.

3 O thank the Lord of all lords: for his mercy endureth for ever.

4 Who only doeth great wonders: for his mercy endureth for ever.

5 Who by his excellent wisdom made the heavens: for his mercy endureth for ever.

6 Who laid out the earth above the waters: for his mercy endureth for ever.

7 Who hath made great lights: for his mercy endureth for ever;

8 The sun to rule the day: for his mercy endureth for ever;

9 The moon and the stars to govern the night: for his mercy endureth for ever.

10 Who smote Egypt with their first-born: for his mercy endureth for ever;

11 And brought out Israel from among them: for his mercy endureth for ever;

12 With a mighty hand, and stretched out arm: for his mercy endureth for ever.

13 Who divided the Red sea in two parts: for his mercy endureth for ever;

14 And made Israel to go through the midst of it: for his mercy endureth for ever.

15 But as for Pharaoh and his host, he overthrew them in the Red sea: for his mercy endureth for ever.

16 Who led his people through the wilderness: for his mercy endureth for ever.

17 Who smote great kings: for his mercy endureth for ever;

18 Yea, and slew mighty kings: for his mercy endureth for ever;

19 Sehon king of the Amorites: for his mercy endureth for ever;

20 And Og the king of Basan: for his mercy endureth for ever;

21 And gave away their land for an heritage: for his mercy endureth for ever;

22 Even for an heritage unto Israel his servant: for his mercy endureth for ever.

23 Who remembered us when we were in trouble: for his mercy endureth for ever;

24 And hath delivered us from our enemies: for his mercy endureth for ever.

25 Who giveth food to all flesh: for his mercy endureth for ever.

26 O give thanks unto the God of heaven: for his mercy endureth for ever.

27 O give thanks unto the Lord of lords: for his mercy endureth for ever.

PSALM 137. *Super flumina*

BY the waters of Babylon we sat down and wept: when we remembered thee, O Sion.

2 As for our harps, we hanged them up: upon the trees that are therein.

3 For they that led us away captive required of us then a song, and melody in our heaviness: Sing us one of the songs of Sion.

4 How shall we sing the Lord's song: in a strange land?

5 If I forget thee, O Jerusalem: let my right hand forget her cunning.

6 If I do not remember thee, let my tongue cleave to the roof of my mouth: yea, if I prefer not Jerusalem in my mirth.

7 Remember the children of Edom, O Lord, in the day of Jerusalem: how they said, Down with it, down with it, even to the ground.

8 O daughter of Babylon, wasted with misery: yea, happy shall he be that rewardeth thee, as thou hast served us.

9 Blessed shall he be that taketh thy children: and throweth them against the stones.

PSALM 138. *Confitebor tibi*

I WILL give thanks unto thee, O Lord, with my whole heart: even before the gods will I sing praise unto thee.

2 I will worship toward thy holy temple, and praise thy Name, because of thy loving-kindness and truth: for thou hast magnified thy Name and thy word above all things.

3 When I called upon thee, thou heardest me: and enduedst my soul with much strength.

4 All the kings of the earth shall praise thee, O Lord: for they have heard the words of thy mouth.

5 Yea, they shall sing in the ways of the Lord: that great is the glory of the Lord.

6 For though the Lord be high, yet hath he respect unto the lowly: as for the proud, he beholdeth them afar off.

7 Though I walk in the midst of trouble, yet shalt thou refresh me: thou shalt stretch forth thy hand upon the furiousness of mine enemies, and thy right hand shall save me.

8 The Lord shall make good his loving-kindness toward me: yea, thy mercy, O Lord, endureth for ever; despise not then the works of thine own hands.

DAY 29. MORNING PRAYER

Psalm 139. *Domine, probasti*

O LORD, thou hast searched me out and known me: thou knowest my down-sitting and mine up-rising, thou understandest my thoughts long before.

2 Thou art about my path, and about my bed: and spiest out all my ways.

3 For lo, there is not a word in my tongue: but thou, O Lord, knowest it altogether.

4 Thou hast fashioned me behind and before: and laid thine hand upon me.

5 Such knowledge is too wonderful and excellent for me: I cannot attain unto it.

6 Whither shall I go then from thy Spirit: or whither shall I go then from thy presence?

7 If I climb up into heaven, thou art there: if I go down to hell, thou art there also.

8 If I take the wings of the morning: and remain in the uttermost parts of the sea;

9 Even there also shall thy hand lead me: and thy right hand shall hold me.

10 If I say, Peradventure the darkness shall cover me: then shall my night be turned to day.

11 Yea, the darkness is no darkness with thee, but the night is as clear as the day: the darkness and light to thee are both alike.

12 For my reins are thine: thou hast covered me in my mother's womb.

13 I will give thanks unto thee, for I am fearfully and wonderfully made: marvellous are thy works, and that my soul knoweth right well.

14 My bones are not hid from thee: though I be made secretly, and fashioned beneath in the earth.

15 Thine eyes did see my substance, yet being unperfect: and in thy book were all my members written;

16 Which day by day were fashioned: when as yet there was none of them.

17 How dear are thy counsels unto me, O God: O how great is the sum of them!

18 If I tell them, they are more in number than the sand: when I wake up I am present with thee.

19 Wilt thou not slay the wicked, O God: depart from me, ye blood-thirsty men.

20 For they speak unrighteously against thee: and thine enemies take thy Name in vain.

21 Do not I hate them, O Lord, that hate thee: and am not I grieved with those that rise up against thee?

22 Yea, I hate them right sore: even as though they were mine enemies.

23 Try me, O God, and seek the ground of my heart: prove me, and examine my thoughts.

24 Look well if there be any way of wickedness in me: and lead me in the way everlasting.

PSALM 140. *Eripe me, Domine*

DELIVER me, O Lord, from the evil man: and preserve me from the wicked man.

2 Who imagine mischief in their hearts: and stir up strife all the day long.

3 They have sharpened their tongues like a serpent: adders' poison is under their lips.

4 Keep me, O Lord, from the hands of the ungodly: preserve me from the wicked men, who are purposed to overthrow my goings.

5 The proud have laid a snare for me, and spread a net abroad with cords: yea, and set traps in my way.

6 I said unto the Lord, Thou art my God: hear the voice of my prayers, O Lord.

7 O Lord God, thou strength of my health: thou hast covered my head in the day of battle.

8 Let not the ungodly have his desire, O Lord: let not his mischievous imagination prosper, lest they be too proud.

9 Let the mischief of their own lips fall upon the head of them: that compass me about.

10 Let hot burning coals fall upon them: let them be cast into the fire and into the pit, that they never rise up again.

11 A man full of words shall not prosper upon the earth: evil shall hunt the wicked person to overthrow him.

12 Sure I am that the Lord will avenge the poor: and maintain the cause of the helpless.

13 The righteous also shall give thanks unto thy Name: and the just shall continue in thy sight.

Psalm 141. *Domine, clamavi*

LORD, I call upon thee, haste thee unto me: and consider my voice when I cry unto thee.

2 Let my prayer be set forth in thy sight as the incense: and let the lifting up of my hands be an evening sacrifice.

3 Set a watch, O Lord, before my mouth: and keep the door of my lips.

4 O let not mine heart be inclined to any evil thing: let me not be occupied in ungodly works with the men that work wickedness, lest I eat of such things as please them.

5 Let the righteous rather smite me friendly: and reprove me.

6 But let not their precious balms break my head: yea, I will pray yet against their wickedness.

7 Let their judges be overthrown in stony places: that they may hear my words, for they are sweet.

8 Our bones lie scattered before the pit: like as when one breaketh and heweth wood upon the earth.

9 But mine eyes look unto thee, O Lord God: in thee is my trust, O cast not out my soul.

10 Keep me from the snare that they have laid for me: and from the traps of the wicked doers.

11 Let the ungodly fall into their own nets together: and let me ever escape them.

DAY 29. EVENING PRAYER

Psalm 142. *Voce mea ad Dominum*

I CRIED unto the Lord with my voice: yea, even unto the Lord did I make my supplication.

2 I poured out my complaints before him: and shewed him of my trouble.

3 When my spirit was in heaviness thou knewest my path: in the way wherein I walked have they privily laid a snare for me.

4 I looked also upon my right hand: and saw there was no man that would know me.

5 I had no place to flee unto: and no man cared for my soul.

6 I cried unto thee, O Lord, and said: Thou art my hope, and my portion in the land of the living.

7 Consider my complaint: for I am brought very low.

8 O deliver me from my persecutors: for they are too strong for me.

9 Bring my soul out of prison, that I may give thanks unto thy Name: which thing if thou wilt grant me, then shall the righteous resort unto my company.

Psalm 143. *Domine, exaudi*

HEAR my prayer, O Lord, and consider my desire: hearken unto me for thy truth and righteousness' sake.

2 And enter not into judgement with thy servant: for in thy sight shall no man living be justified.

3 For the enemy hath persecuted my soul; he hath smitten my life down to the ground: he hath laid me in the darkness, as the men that have been long dead.

4 Therefore is my spirit vexed within me: and my heart within me is desolate.

5 Yet do I remember the time past; I muse upon all thy works: yea, I exercise myself in the works of thy hands.

6 I stretch forth my hands unto thee: my soul gaspeth unto thee as a thirsty land.

7 Hear me, O Lord, and that soon, for my spirit waxeth faint:

hide not thy face from me, lest I be like unto them that go down into the pit.

8 O let me hear thy loving-kindness betimes in the morning, for in thee is my trust: shew thou me the way that I should walk in, for I lift up my soul unto thee.

9 Deliver me, O Lord, from mine enemies: for I flee unto thee to hide me.

10 Teach me to do the thing that pleaseth thee, for thou art my God: let thy loving Spirit lead me forth into the land of righteousness.

11 Quicken me, O Lord, for thy Name's sake: and for thy right-eousness' sake bring my soul out of trouble.

12 And of thy goodness slay mine enemies: and destroy all them that vex my soul; for I am thy servant.

DAY 30. MORNING PRAYER

Psalm 144. *Benedictus Dominus*

BLESSED be the Lord my strength: who teacheth my hands to war, and my fingers to fight;

2 My hope and my fortress, my castle and deliverer, my defender in whom I trust: who subdueth my people that is under me.

3 Lord, what is man, that thou hast such respect unto him: or the son of man, that thou so regardest him?

4 Man is like a thing of nought: his time passeth away like a shadow.

5 Bow thy heavens, O Lord, and come down: touch the moun-tains, and they shall smoke.

6 Cast forth thy lightning, and tear them: shoot out thine arrows, and consume them.

7 Send down thine hand from above: deliver me, and take me out of the great waters, from the hand of strange children;

8 Whose mouth talketh of vanity: and their right hand is a right hand of wickedness.

9 I will sing a new song unto thee, O God: and sing praises unto thee upon a ten-stringed lute.

10 Thou hast given victory unto kings: and hast delivered David thy servant from the peril of the sword.

11 Save me, and deliver me from the hand of strange children: whose mouth talketh of vanity, and their right hand is a right hand of iniquity.

12 That our sons may grow up as the young plants: and that our daughters may be as the polished corners of the temple.

13 That our garners may be full and plenteous with all manner of store: that our sheep may bring forth thousands and ten thousands in our streets.

14 That our oxen may be strong to labour, that there be no decay: no leading into captivity, and no complaining in our streets.

15 Happy are the people that are in such a case: yea, blessed are the people who have the Lord for their God.

PSALM 145. *Exaltabo te, Deus*

I WILL magnify thee, O God, my King: and I will praise thy Name for ever and ever.

2 Every day will I give thanks unto thee: and praise thy Name for ever and ever.

3 Great is the Lord, and marvellous worthy to be praised: there is no end of his greatness.

4 One generation shall praise thy works unto another: and declare thy power.

5 As for me, I will be talking of thy worship: thy glory, thy praise, and wondrous works;

6 So that men shall speak of the might of thy marvellous acts: and I will also tell of thy greatness.

7 The memorial of thine abundant kindness shall be shewed: and men shall sing of thy righteousness.

8 The Lord is gracious and merciful: long-suffering and of great goodness.

9 The Lord is loving unto every man: and his mercy is over all his works.

10 All thy works praise thee, O Lord: and thy saints give thanks unto thee.

11 They shew the glory of thy kingdom: and talk of thy power;

12 That thy power, thy glory, and mightiness of thy kingdom: might be known unto men.

13 Thy kingdom is an everlasting kingdom: and thy dominion endureth throughout all ages.

14 The Lord upholdeth all such as fall: and lifteth up all those that are down.

15 The eyes of all wait upon thee, O Lord: and thou givest them their meat in due season.

16 Thou openest thine hand: and fillest all things living with plenteousness.

17 The Lord is righteous in all his ways: and holy in all his works.

18 The Lord is nigh unto all them that call upon him: yea, all such as call upon him faithfully.

19 He will fulfil the desire of them that fear him: he also will hear their cry, and will help them.

20 The Lord preserveth all them that love him: but scattereth abroad all the ungodly.

21 My mouth shall speak the praise of the Lord: and let all flesh give thanks unto his holy Name for ever and ever.

Psalm 146. *Lauda, anima mea*

PRAISE the Lord, O my soul; while I live will I praise the Lord: yea, as long as I have any being, I will sing praises unto my God.

2 O put not your trust in princes, nor in any child of man: for there is no help in them.

3 For when the breath of man goeth forth he shall turn again to his earth: and then all his thoughts perish.

4 Blessed is he that hath the God of Jacob for his help: and whose hope is in the Lord his God;

5 Who made heaven and earth, the sea, and all that therein is: who keepeth his promise for ever;

6 Who helpeth them to right that suffer wrong: who feedeth the hungry.

7 The Lord looseth men out of prison: the Lord giveth sight to the blind.

8 The Lord helpeth them that are fallen: the Lord careth for the righteous.

9 The Lord careth for the strangers, he defendeth the fatherless and widow: as for the way of the ungodly, he turneth it upside down.

10 The Lord thy God, O Sion, shall be King for evermore: and throughout all generations.

DAY 30. EVENING PRAYER

PSALM 147. *Laudate Dominum*

O PRAISE the Lord, for it is a good thing to sing praises unto our God: yea, a joyful and pleasant thing it is to be thankful.

2 The Lord doth build up Jerusalem: and gather together the out-casts of Israel.

3 He healeth those that are broken in heart: and giveth medicine to heal their sickness.

4 He telleth the number of the stars: and calleth them all by their names.

5 Great is our Lord, and great is his power: yea, and his wisdom is infinite.

6 The Lord setteth up the meek: and bringeth the ungodly down to the ground.

7 O sing unto the Lord with thanksgiving: sing praises upon the harp unto our God;

8 Who covereth the heaven with clouds, and prepareth rain for the earth: and maketh the grass to grow upon the mountains, and herb for the use of men;

9 Who giveth fodder unto the cattle: and feedeth the young ravens that call upon him.

10 He hath no pleasure in the strength of an horse: neither delighteth he in any man's legs.

11 But the Lord's delight is in them that fear him: and put their trust in his mercy.

12 Praise the Lord, O Jerusalem: praise thy God, O Sion.

13 For he hath made fast the bars of thy gates: and hath blessed thy children within thee.

14 He maketh peace in thy borders: and filleth thee with the flour of wheat.

15 He sendeth forth his commandment upon earth: and his word runneth very swiftly.

16 He giveth snow like wool: and scattereth the hoar-frost like ashes.

17 He casteth forth his ice like morsels: who is able to abide his frost?

18 He sendeth out his word, and melteth them: he bloweth with his wind, and the waters flow.

19 He sheweth his word unto Jacob: his statutes and ordinances unto Israel.

20 He hath not dealt so with any nation: neither have the heathen knowledge of his laws.

Psalm 148. *Laudate Dominum*

O PRAISE the Lord of heaven: praise him in the height.

2 Praise him, all ye angels of his: praise him, all his host.

3 Praise him, sun and moon: praise him, all ye stars and light.

4 Praise him, all ye heavens: and ye waters that are above the heavens.

5 Let them praise the Name of the Lord: for he spake the word, and they were made; he commanded, and they were created.

6 He hath made them fast for ever and ever: he hath given them a law which shall not be broken.

7 Praise the Lord upon earth: ye dragons, and all deeps;

8 Fire and hail, snow and vapours: wind and storm, fulfilling his word;

9 Mountains and all hills: fruitful trees and all cedars;

10 Beasts and all cattle: worms and feathered fowls;

11 Kings of the earth and all people: princes and all judges of the world;

12 Young men and maidens, old men and children, praise the Name of the Lord: for his Name only is excellent, and his praise above heaven and earth.

13 He shall exalt the horn of his people; all his saints shall praise him: even the children of Israel, even the people that serveth him.

PSALM 149. *Cantate Domino*

O SING unto the Lord a new song: let the congregation of saints praise him.

2 Let Israel rejoice in him that made him: and let the children of Sion be joyful in their King.

3 Let them praise his Name in the dance: let them sing praises unto him with tabret and harp.

4 For the Lord hath pleasure in his people: and helpeth the meek-hearted.

5 Let the saints be joyful with glory: let them rejoice in their beds.

6 Let the praises of God be in their mouth: and a two-edged sword in their hands;

7 To be avenged of the heathen: and to rebuke the people;

8 To bind their kings in chains: and their nobles with links of iron.

9 That they may be avenged of them, as it is written: Such honour have all his saints.

PSALM 150. *Laudate Dominum*

O PRAISE God in his holiness: praise him in the firmament of his power.

2 Praise him in his noble acts: praise him according to his excellent greatness.

3 Praise him in the sound of the trumpet: praise him upon the lute and harp.

4 Praise him in the cymbals and dances: praise him upon the strings and pipe.

5 Praise him upon the well-tuned cymbals: praise him upon the loud cymbals.

6 Let every thing that hath breath: praise the Lord.

FORMS OF PRAYER
TO BE
USED AT SEA

The Morning and Evening Service to be used daily at Sea shall be the same which is appointed in the Book of Common Prayer.

These two following Prayers are to be also used in her Majesty's Navy every day.

O ETERNAL Lord God, who alone spreadest out the heavens, and rulest the raging of the sea; who hast compassed the waters with bounds until day and night come to an end: Be pleased to receive into thy Almighty and most gracious protection the persons of us thy servants, and the Fleet in which we serve. Preserve us from the dangers of the sea, and from the violence of the enemy; that we may be a safeguard unto our most gracious Sovereign Lady, Queen *ELIZABETH*, and her Dominions, and a security for such as pass on the seas upon their lawful occasions; that the inhabitants of our Island may in peace and quietness serve thee our God; and that we may return in safety to enjoy the blessings of the land, with the fruits of our labours; and with a thankful remembrance of thy mercies to praise and glorify thy holy Name; through Jesus Christ our Lord. *Amen.*

The Collect

PREVENT us, O Lord, in all our doings, with thy most gracious favour, and further us with thy continual help; that in all our works begun, continued, and ended in thee, we may glorify thy holy Name, and finally by thy mercy obtain everlasting life; through Jesus Christ our Lord. *Amen.*

Prayers to be used in Storms at Sea.

O MOST powerful and glorious Lord God, at whose

command the winds blow, and lift up the waves of the sea, and who stillest the rage thereof: We thy creatures, but miserable sinners, do in this our great distress cry unto thee for help: Save, Lord, or else we perish. We confess, when we have been safe, and seen all things quiet about us, we have forgot thee our God, and refused to hearken to the still voice of thy word, and to obey thy commandments: But now we see how terrible thou art in all thy works of wonder; the great God to be feared above all: And therefore we adore thy Divine Majesty, acknowledging thy power, and imploring thy goodness. Help, Lord, and save us for thy mercy's sake in Jesus Christ thy Son, our Lord. *Amen.*

Or this:

O MOST glorious and gracious Lord God, who dwellest in heaven, but beholdest all things below: Look down, we beseech thee, and hear us, calling out of the depth of misery, and out of the jaws of this death, which is ready now to swallow us up: Save, Lord, or else we perish. The living, the living shall praise thee. O send thy word of command to rebuke the raging winds, and the roaring sea; that we, being delivered from this distress, may live to serve thee, and to glorify thy Name all the days of our life. Hear, Lord, and save us, for the infinite merits of our blessed Saviour, thy Son, our Lord Jesus Christ. *Amen.*

The Prayer to be said before a Fight at Sea against any Enemy.

O MOST powerful and glorious Lord God, the Lord of hosts, that rulest and commandest all things: Thou sittest in the throne judging right, and therefore we make our address to thy Divine Majesty in this our necessity, that thou wouldest take the cause into thine own hand, and judge between us and our enemies. Stir up thy strength, O Lord, and come and help us; for thou givest not alway the battle to the strong, but canst save by many or by few. O let not our sins now cry against us for vengeance; but hear us thy poor servants begging mercy, and imploring thy help, and that thou wouldest be a defence unto us against the face of the enemy. Make it appear that thou art our Saviour and mighty Deliverer; through Jesus Christ our Lord. *Amen.*

General Prayers.

Short Prayers for single persons that cannot meet to join in Prayer with others, by reason of the Fight, or Storm.

LORD, be merciful to us sinners, and save us for thy mercy's sake.

Thou art the great God, that hast made and rulest all things: O deliver us for thy Name's sake.

Thou art the great God to be feared above all: O save us, that we may praise thee.

Special Prayers with respect to the Enemy.

THOU, O Lord, art just and powerful: O defend our cause against the face of the enemy.

O God, thou art a strong tower of defence to all that flee unto thee: O save us from the violence of the enemy.

O Lord of hosts, fight for us, that we may glorify thee.

O suffer us not to sink under the weight of our sins, or the violence of the enemy.

O Lord, arise, help us, and deliver us for thy Name's sake.

Short Prayers in respect of a Storm.

THOU, O Lord, that stillest the raging of the sea: hear, hear us, and save us, that we perish not.

O blessed Saviour, that didst save thy disciples ready to perish in a storm: hear us, and save us, we beseech thee.

> Lord, have mercy upon us.
> Christ, have mercy upon us.
> Lord, have mercy upon us.
> O Lord, hear us.
> O Christ, hear us.

God the Father, God the Son, God the Holy Ghost, have mercy upon us, save us now and evermore. Amen.

OUR Father which art in heaven, Hallowed be thy Name, Thy kingdom come, Thy will be done, in earth as it is in heaven. Give us this day our daily bread; And forgive us our trespasses, As we forgive them that trespass against us; And lead us not into temptation, But deliver us from evil. For thine is the kingdom, the power, and the glory, For ever and ever. Amen.

When there shall be imminent danger, as many as can be spared from necessary service in the Ship shall be called together, and make an humble Confession of their sin to God: In which every one ought seriously to reflect upon those particular sins of which his conscience shall accuse him: saying as followeth.

The Confession

ALMIGHTY God, Father of our Lord Jesus Christ, Maker of all things, Judge of all men: We acknowledge and bewail our manifold sins and wickedness, Which we from time to time most grievously have committed, By thought, word, and deed, Against thy Divine Majesty, Provoking most justly thy wrath and indignation against us. We do earnestly repent, And are heartily sorry for these our misdoings; The remembrance of them is grievous unto us; The burden of them is intolerable. Have mercy upon us, Have mercy upon us, most merciful Father; For thy Son our Lord Jesus Christ's sake, Forgive us all that is past; And grant that we may ever hereafter Serve and please thee In newness of life, To the honour and glory of thy Name; Through Jesus Christ our Lord. Amen.

Then shall the Priest, if there be any in the Ship, pronounce this Absolution.

ALMIGHTY God, our heavenly Father, who of his great mercy hath promised forgiveness of sins to all them that with hearty repentance and true faith turn unto him; Have mercy upon you; pardon and deliver you from all your sins; confirm and strengthen you in all goodness; and bring you to everlasting life; through Jesus Christ our Lord. *Amen.*

Thanksgiving after a Storm.

Jubilate Deo. Psalm 66

O BE joyful in God, all ye lands: sing praises unto the honour of his Name, make his praise to be glorious.

Say unto God, O how wonderful art thou in thy works: through the greatness of thy power shall thine enemies be found liars unto thee.

For all the world shall worship thee: sing of thee, and praise thy Name.

O come hither, and behold the works of God: how wonderful he is in his doing toward the children of men.

He turned the sea into dry land: so that they went through the water on foot; there did we rejoice thereof.

He ruleth with his power for ever; his eyes behold the people: and such as will not believe shall not be able to exalt themselves.

O praise our God, ye people: and make the voice of his praise to be heard;

Who holdeth our soul in life: and suffereth not our feet to slip.

For thou, O God, hast proved us: thou also hast tried us, like as silver is tried.

Thou broughtest us into the snare: and laidest trouble upon our loins.

Thou sufferedst men to ride over our heads: we went through fire and water, and thou broughtest us out into a wealthy place.

I will go into thine house with burnt-offerings: and will pay thee my vows, which I promised with my lips, and spake with my mouth, when I was in trouble.

I will offer unto thee fat burnt-sacrifices, with the incense of rams: I will offer bullocks and goats.

O come hither, and hearken, all ye that fear God: and I will tell you what he hath done for my soul.

I called unto him with my mouth: and gave him praises with my tongue.

If I incline unto wickedness with mine heart: the Lord will not hear me.

But God hath heard me: and considered the voice of my prayer.

Praised be God, who hath not cast out my prayer: nor turned his mercy from me.

Glory be to the Father, and to the Son: and to the Holy Ghost;

As it was in the beginning, is now, and ever shall be: world without end. Amen.

Confitemini Domino. Psalm 107

O GIVE thanks unto the Lord, for he is gracious: and his mercy endureth for ever.

Let them give thanks whom the Lord hath redeemed: and delivered from the hand of the enemy;

And gathered them out of the lands, from the east and from the west: from the north and from the south.

They went astray in the wilderness out of the way: and found no city to dwell in;

Hungry and thirsty: their soul fainted in them.

So they cried unto the Lord in their trouble: and he delivered them from their distress.

He led them forth by the right way: that they might go to the city where they dwelt.

O that men would therefore praise the Lord for his goodness: and declare the wonders that he doeth for the children of men!

For he satisfieth the empty soul: and filleth the hungry soul with goodness.

Such as sit in darkness, and in the shadow of death: being fast bound in misery and iron;

Because they rebelled against the words of the Lord: and lightly regarded the counsel of the most Highest;

He also brought down their heart through heaviness: they fell down, and there was none to help them up.

So when they cried unto the Lord in their trouble: he delivered them out of their distress.

For he brought them out of darkness, and out of the shadow of death: and brake their bonds in sunder.

O that men would therefore praise the Lord for his goodness: and declare the wonders that he doeth for the children of men!

For he hath broken the gates of brass: and smitten the bars of iron in sunder.

Foolish men are plagued for their offence: and because of their wickedness.

Their soul abhorred all manner of meat: and they were even hard at death's door.

So when they cried unto the Lord in their trouble: he delivered them out of their distress.

He sent his word, and healed them: and they were saved from their destruction.

O that men would therefore praise the Lord for his goodness: and declare the wonders that he doeth for the children of men!

That they would offer unto him the sacrifice of thanksgiving: and tell out his works with gladness!

They that go down to the sea in ships: and occupy their business in great waters;

These men see the works of the Lord: and his wonders in the deep.

For at his word the stormy wind ariseth: which lifteth up the waves thereof.

They are carried up to the heaven, and down again to the deep: their soul melteth away because of the trouble.

They reel to and fro, and stagger like a drunken man: and are at their wits' end.

So when they cry unto the Lord in their trouble: he delivereth them out of their distress.

For he maketh the storm to cease: so that the waves thereof are still.

Then are they glad, because they are at rest: and so he bringeth them unto the haven where they would be.

O that men would therefore praise the Lord for his goodness: and declare the wonders that he doeth for the children of men!

That they would exalt him also in the congregation of the people: and praise him in the seat of the elders!

Who turneth the floods into a wilderness: and drieth up the water-springs.

A fruitful land maketh he barren: for the wickedness of them that dwell therein.

Again, he maketh the wilderness a standing water: and water-springs of a dry ground.

And there he setteth the hungry: that they may build them a city to dwell in;

That they may sow their land, and plant vineyards: to yield them fruits of increase.

He blesseth them, so that they multiply exceedingly: and suffereth not their cattle to decrease.

And again, when they are minished and brought low: through oppression, through any plague or trouble;

Though he suffer them to be evil intreated through tyrants: and let them wander out of the way in the wilderness;

Yet helpeth he the poor out of misery: and maketh him households like a flock of sheep.

The righteous will consider this, and rejoice: and the mouth of all wickedness shall be stopped.

Whoso is wise will ponder these things: and they shall understand the loving-kindness of the Lord.

Glory be to the Father, and to the Son: and to the Holy Ghost;

As it was in the beginning, is now, and ever shall be: world without end. Amen.

Collects of Thanksgiving.

O MOST blessed and glorious Lord God, who art of infinite goodness and mercy: We thy poor creatures, whom thou hast made and preserved, holding our souls in life, and now rescuing us out of the jaws of death, humbly present ourselves again before thy Divine Majesty, to offer a sacrifice of praise and thanksgiving, for that thou heardest us when we called in our trouble, and didst not cast out our prayer, which we made before thee in our great distress: Even when we gave all for lost, our ship, our goods, our lives, then didst thou mercifully look upon us, and wonderfully command a deliverance; for which we, now being in safety, do give all praise and glory to thy holy Name; through Jesus Christ our Lord. *Amen.*

Or this:

O MOST mighty and gracious good God, thy mercy is over all thy works, but in special manner hath been extended toward us, whom thou hast so powerfully and wonderfully defended. Thou hast shewed us terrible things, and wonders in the deep, that we might see how powerful and gracious a God thou art; how able and ready to help them that trust in thee. Thou hast shewed us how both winds and seas obey thy command; that we may learn, even from them, hereafter to obey thy voice, and to do thy will. We therefore bless and glorify thy Name, for this thy mercy in saving us, when we were ready to perish. And, we beseech thee, make us as truly sensible now of thy mercy, as we were then of the danger: and give us hearts always ready to express our thankfulness, not only by words, but also by our lives, in being more obedient to thy holy commandments. Continue, we beseech thee, this thy goodness to us; that we, whom thou hast saved, may serve thee in holiness and righteousness all the days of our life; through Jesus Christ our Lord and Saviour. *Amen.*

A Hymn of Praise and Thanksgiving after a dangerous Tempest.

O COME, let us give thanks unto the Lord, for he is gracious: and his mercy endureth for ever.

Great is the Lord, and greatly to be praised; let the redeemed of the Lord say so: whom he hath delivered from the merciless rage of the sea.

The Lord is gracious and full of compassion: slow to anger, and of great mercy.

He hath not dealt with us according to our sins: neither rewarded us according to our iniquities.

But as the heaven is high above the earth: so great hath been his mercy towards us.

We found trouble and heaviness: we were even at death's door.

The waters of the sea had well-nigh covered us: the proud waters had well-nigh gone over our soul.

The sea roared: and the stormy wind lifted up the waves thereof.

We were carried up as it were to heaven, and then down again into the deep: our soul melted within us, because of trouble;

Then cried we unto thee, O Lord: and thou didst deliver us out of our distress.

Blessed be thy Name, who didst not despise the prayer of thy servants: but didst hear our cry, and hast saved us.

Thou didst send forth thy commandment: and the windy storm ceased, and was turned into a calm.

O let us therefore praise the Lord for his goodness: and declare the wonders that he hath done, and still doeth, for the children of men.

Praised be the Lord daily: even the Lord that helpeth us, and poureth his benefits upon us.

He is our God, even the God of whom cometh salvation: God is the Lord by whom we have escaped death.

Thou, Lord, hast made us glad through the operation of thy hands: and we will triumph in thy praise.

Blessed be the Lord God: even the Lord God, who only doeth wondrous things;

And blessed be the Name of his majesty for ever: and let every one of us say, Amen, Amen.

Glory be to the Father, and to the Son: and to the Holy Ghost;

As it was in the beginning, is now, and ever shall be: world without end. Amen.

2 *Corinthians* 13.

THE grace of our Lord Jesus Christ, and the love of God, and the fellowship of the Holy Ghost, be with us all evermore. *Amen.*

After Victory or Deliverance from an Enemy.

A Psalm or Hymn of Praise and Thanksgiving after Victory.

IF the Lord had not been on our side, now may we say: if the Lord himself had not been on our side, when men rose up against us;

They had swallowed us up quick: when they were so wrath-fully displeased at us.

Yea, the waters had drowned us, and the stream had gone over our soul: the deep waters of the proud had gone over our soul.

But praised be the Lord: who hath not given us over as a prey unto them.

The Lord hath wrought: a mighty salvation for us.

We gat not this by our own sword, neither was it our own arm that saved us: but thy right hand, and thine arm, and the light of thy countenance, because thou hadst a favour unto us.

The Lord hath appeared for us: the Lord hath covered our heads, and made us to stand in the day of battle.

The Lord hath appeared for us: the Lord hath overthrown our enemies, and dashed in pieces those that rose up against us.

Therefore not unto us, O Lord, not unto us: but unto thy Name be given the glory.

The Lord hath done great things for us: the Lord hath done great things for us, for which we rejoice.

Our help standeth in the Name of the Lord: who hath made heaven and earth.

Blessed be the Name of the Lord: from this time forth for evermore.

Glory be to the Father, and to the Son: and to the Holy Ghost;

As it was in the beginning, is now, and ever shall be: world without end. Amen.

After this Hymn may be sung the TE DEUM.

Then this Collect.

O ALMIGHTY God, the Sovereign Commander of all the world, in whose hand is power and might which none is able to withstand: We bless and magnify thy great and glorious Name for this happy Victory, the whole glory whereof we do ascribe to thee, who art the only giver of Victory. And, we beseech thee, give us grace to improve this great mercy to thy glory, the advancement of thy Gospel, the honour of our Sovereign, and, as much as in us lieth, to the good of all mankind. And, we beseech thee, give us such a sense of this great mercy, as may engage us to a true thankfulness, such as may appear in our lives by an humble, holy, and obedient walking before thee all our days, through Jesus Christ our Lord; to whom with thee and the Holy Spirit, as for all thy mercies, so in particular for this Victory and Deliverance, be all glory and honour, world without end. *Amen.*

2 *Corinthians* 13.

THE grace of our Lord Jesus Christ, and the love of God, and the fellowship of the Holy Ghost, be with us all evermore. *Amen.*

AT THE BURIAL OF THEIR DEAD AT SEA

The Office in the Common-Prayer-Book may be used: only instead of these words [We therefore commit his body to the ground, earth to earth, &c.] *say,*

WE therefore commit his body to the deep, to be turned into corruption, looking for the resurrection of the body, (when the Sea shall give up her dead,) and the life of the world to come, through our Lord Jesus Christ; who at his coming shall change our vile body, that it may be like his glorious body, according to the mighty working, whereby he is able to subdue all things to himself.

THE FORM AND MANNER OF MAKING, ORDAINING, AND CONSECRATING OF

BISHOPS, PRIESTS, AND DEACONS

ACCORDING TO THE ORDER OF THE CHURCH OF ENGLAND

THE PREFACE

IT is evident unto all men diligently reading holy Scripture and ancient Authors, that from the Apostles' time there have been these Orders of Ministers in Christ's Church; Bishops, Priests, and Deacons. Which offices were evermore had in such reverend estimation, that no man might presume to execute any of them, except he were first called, tried, examined, and known to have such qualities as are requisite for the same; and also by publick Prayer, with Imposition of Hands, were approved and admitted thereunto by lawful authority. And therefore, to the intent that these Orders may be continued, and reverently used and esteemed, in the Church of England; No man shall be accounted or taken to be a lawful Bishop, Priest, or Deacon in the Church of England, or suffered to execute any of the said functions, except he be called, tried, examined, and admitted thereunto, according to the Form hereafter following, or hath had formerly Episcopal Consecration or Ordination.

And none shall be admitted a Deacon, except he be full twenty-three years of age unless he have a Faculty. And every man which is to be admitted a Priest shall be full twenty-four years of age, unless being over twenty-three years of age he have a Faculty. And every man which is to be ordained or consecrated Bishop shall be full thirty years of age.

And the Bishop, knowing either by himself or by sufficient testimony any person to be a person of virtuous conversation and without crime, and after examination and trial finding him to possess the qualifications required by law and sufficiently instructed in holy Scripture may on the Sundays immediately following the Ember Weeks or on the Feast of Saint Michael and All Angels or of Saint Thomas the Apostle, or on such other days as shall be provided by Canon, in the face of the Church, admit him a Deacon in such manner and form as hereafter followeth.

THE FORM AND MANNER OF
MAKING OF
DEACONS

When the day appointed by the Bishop is come; after Morning Prayer is ended, there shall be a Sermon or Exhortation, declaring the duty and office of such as come to be admitted Deacons; how necessary that Order is in the Church of Christ; and also how the people ought to esteem them in their office.

First, the Archdeacon, or his Deputy, or such other persons as by ancient custom have the right so to do, shall present unto the Bishop (sitting in his chair near to the holy Table) such as desire to be ordained Deacons (each of them being decently habited,) saying these words.

REVEREND Father in God, I present unto you these persons present, to be admitted Deacons.

The Bishop.

TAKE heed that the persons, whom ye present unto us, be apt and meet, for their learning and godly conversation, to exercise their ministry duly, to the honour of God, and the edifying of his Church.

The Archdeacon shall answer,

I HAVE enquired of them, and also examined them; and think them so to be.

Then the Bishop shall say unto the people:

BRETHREN, if there be any of you who knoweth any impediment or notable crime in any of these persons presented to be ordered Deacons, for the which he ought not to be admitted to that office; Let him come forth in the Name of God, and shew what the crime or impediment is.

And if any great crime or impediment be objected, the Bishop shall surcease from ordering that person, until such time as the party accused shall be found clear of that crime.

Then the Bishop (commending such as shall be found meet to be ordered to the prayers of the Congregation) shall, with the Clergy and people present, sing or say the Litany, with the Prayers, as followeth.

The Litany and Suffrages

O GOD the Father of heaven: have mercy upon us miserable sinners.

O God the Father of heaven: have mercy upon us miserable sinners.

O God the Son, Redeemer of the world: have mercy upon us miserable sinners.

O God the Son, Redeemer of the world: have mercy upon us miserable sinners.

O God the Holy Ghost, proceeding from the Father and the Son: have mercy upon us miserable sinners.

O God the Holy Ghost, proceeding from the Father and the Son: have mercy upon us miserable sinners.

O holy, blessed, and glorious Trinity, three Persons and one God: have mercy upon us miserable sinners.

O holy, blessed, and glorious Trinity, three Persons and one God: have mercy upon us miserable sinners.

Remember not, Lord, our offences, nor the offences of our forefathers; neither take thou vengeance of our sins: spare us, good Lord, spare thy people, whom thou hast redeemed with thy most precious blood, and be not angry with us for ever.

Spare us, good Lord.

From all evil and mischief; from sin, from the crafts and assaults of the devil; from thy wrath, and from everlasting damnation,

Good Lord, deliver us.

From all blindness of heart; from pride, vain-glory, and hypocrisy; from envy, hatred, and malice, and all uncharitableness,

Good Lord, deliver us.

From fornication, and all other deadly sin; and from all the deceits of the world, the flesh, and the devil,

Good Lord, deliver us.

From lightning and tempest; from plague, pestilence, and famine; from battle and murder, and from sudden death,

Good Lord, deliver us.

From all sedition, privy conspiracy, and rebellion; from all false doctrine, heresy, and schism; from hardness of heart, and contempt of thy Word and Commandment,

Good Lord, deliver us.

By the mystery of thy holy Incarnation; by thy holy Nativity and Circumcision; by thy Baptism, Fasting, and Temptation,

Good Lord, deliver us.

By thine Agony and bloody Sweat; by thy Cross and Passion; by thy precious Death and Burial; by thy glorious Resurrection and Ascension; and by the coming of the Holy Ghost,

Good Lord, deliver us.

In all time of our tribulation; in all time of our wealth; in the hour of death, and in the day of judgement,

Good Lord, deliver us.

We sinners do beseech thee to hear us, O Lord God: and that it may please thee to rule and govern thy holy Church universal in the right way,

We beseech thee to hear us, good Lord.

That it may please thee to keep and strengthen in the true worshipping of thee, in righteousness and holiness of life, thy Servant *ELIZABETH*, our most gracious Queen and Governor,

We beseech thee to hear us, good Lord.

That it may please thee to rule her heart in thy faith, fear, and love, and that she may evermore have affiance in thee, and ever seek thy honour and glory,

We beseech thee to hear us, good Lord.

That it may please thee to be her defender and keeper, giving her the victory over all her enemies,

We beseech thee to hear us, good Lord.

That it may please thee to bless and preserve *Philip* Duke of *Edinburgh*, *Charles* Prince of *Wales*, and all the Royal Family,

We beseech thee to hear us, good Lord.

That it may please thee to illuminate all Bishops, Priests, and Deacons, with true knowledge and understanding of thy Word; and that both by their preaching and living they may set it forth and shew it accordingly,

We beseech thee to hear us, good Lord.

That it may please thee to bless these thy servants, now to be admitted to the Order of Deacons, [*or* Priests,] and to pour thy grace upon them; that they may duly execute their office, to the edifying of thy Church, and the glory of thy holy Name,

We beseech thee to hear us, good Lord.

That it may please thee to endue the Lords of the Council, and all the Nobility, with grace, wisdom, and understanding,

We beseech thee to hear us, good Lord.

That it may please thee to bless and keep the Magistrates, giving them grace to execute justice, and to maintain truth,

We beseech thee to hear us, good Lord.

That it may please thee to bless and keep all thy people,

We beseech thee to hear us, good Lord.

That it may please thee to give to all nations unity, peace, and concord,

We beseech thee to hear us, good Lord.

That it may please thee to give us an heart to love and dread thee, and diligently to live after thy commandments,

We beseech thee to hear us, good Lord.

That it may please thee to give to all thy people increase of grace, to hear meekly thy Word, and to receive it with pure affection, and to bring forth the fruits of the Spirit,

We beseech thee to hear us, good Lord.

That it may please thee to bring into the way of truth all such as have erred, and are deceived,

We beseech thee to hear us, good Lord.

That it may please thee to strengthen such as do stand; and to comfort and help the weak-hearted; and to raise up them that fall; and finally to beat down Satan under our feet,

We beseech thee to hear us, good Lord.

That it may please thee to succour, help, and comfort all that are in danger, necessity, and tribulation,

We beseech thee to hear us, good Lord.

That it may please thee to preserve all that travel by land or by water, all women labouring of child, all sick persons, and young children; and to shew thy pity upon all prisoners and captives,

We beseech thee to hear us, good Lord.

That it may please thee to defend, and provide for, the fatherless children, and widows, and all that are desolate and oppressed,

We beseech thee to hear us, good Lord.

That it may please thee to have mercy upon all men,

We beseech thee to hear us, good Lord.

That it may please thee to forgive our enemies, persecutors, and slanderers, and to turn their hearts,

We beseech thee to hear us, good Lord.

That it may please thee to give and preserve to our use the kindly fruits of the earth, so as in due time we may enjoy them,

We beseech thee to hear us, good Lord.

That it may please thee to give us true repentance; to forgive us all our sins, negligences, and ignorances; and to endue us with the grace of thy Holy Spirit, to amend our lives according to thy holy Word,

We beseech thee to hear us, good Lord.

Son of God: we beseech thee to hear us.

Son of God: we beseech thee to hear us.

O Lamb of God: that takest away the sins of the world;

Grant us thy peace.

O Lamb of God: that takest away the sins of the world;

Have mercy upon us.

O Christ, hear us.

O Christ, hear us.

Lord, have mercy upon us.

Lord, have mercy upon us.

Christ, have mercy upon us.

Christ, have mercy upon us.

Lord, have mercy upon us.

Lord, have mercy upon us.

Then shall the Priest, and the people with him, say the Lord's Prayer.

OUR Father which art in heaven, Hallowed be thy Name, Thy kingdom come, Thy will be done, in earth as it is in heaven. Give us this day our daily bread; And forgive us our trespasses, As we forgive them that trespass against us; And lead us not into temptation, But deliver us from evil. Amen.

Priest. O Lord, deal not with us after our sins.

Answer. Neither reward us after our iniquities.

Let us pray.

O GOD, merciful Father, that despisest not the sighing of a contrite heart, nor the desire of such as be sorrowful: Mercifully assist our prayers that we make before thee in all our troubles and adversities, whensoever they oppress us; and graciously hear us, that those evils, which the craft and subtilty of the devil or man worketh against us, be brought to nought, and by the providence of thy goodness they may be dispersed; that we thy servants, being hurt by no persecutions, may evermore give thanks unto thee in thy holy Church; through Jesus Christ our Lord.

O Lord, arise, help us, and deliver us for thy Name's sake.

O GOD, we have heard with our ears, and our fathers have declared unto us, the noble works that thou didst in their days, and in the old time before them.

O Lord, arise, help us, and deliver us for thine honour.

Glory be to the Father, and to the Son: and to the Holy Ghost;

Answer. As it was in the beginning, is now, and ever shall be: world without end. Amen.

From our enemies defend us, O Christ.
Graciously look upon our afflictions.
Pitifully behold the sorrows of our hearts.
Mercifully forgive the sins of thy people.
Favourably with mercy hear our prayers.

O Son of David, have mercy upon us.
Both now and ever vouchsafe to hear us, O Christ.
Graciously hear us, O Christ; graciously hear us, O Lord Christ.
Priest. O Lord, let thy mercy be shewed upon us;
Answer. As we do put our trust in thee.

Let us pray.

WE humbly beseech thee, O Father, mercifully to look upon our infirmities; and for the glory of thy Name turn from us all those evils that we most righteously have deserved; and grant that in all our troubles we may put our whole trust and confidence in thy mercy, and evermore serve thee in holiness and pureness of living, to thy honour and glory; through our only Mediator and Advocate, Jesus Christ our Lord. *Amen.*

Then shall be sung or said the Service for the Communion, with the Collect, Epistle, and Gospel as followeth.

The Collect

ALMIGHTY God, who by thy divine providence hast appointed divers Orders of Ministers in thy Church, and didst inspire thine Apostles to choose into the Order of Deacons the first Martyr Saint Stephen, with others: Mercifully behold these thy servants now called to the like office and administration; replenish them so with the truth of thy doctrine, and adorn them with innocency of life, that, both by word and good example, they may faithfully serve thee in this office, to the glory of thy Name, and the edification of thy Church; through the merits of our Saviour Jesus Christ, who liveth and reigneth with thee and the Holy Ghost, now and for ever. *Amen.*

The Epistle. 1 S. Tim. 3. 8

LIKEWISE must the deacons be grave, not double-tongued, not given to much wine, not greedy of filthy lucre; holding the mystery of the faith in a pure conscience. And let these also first be proved; then let them use the office of a deacon, being found blameless. Even so must their wives be grave, not slanderers, sober, faithful in all things. Let the deacons be the husbands of one wife, ruling their children and their own houses well. For they that have used the office of a deacon well purchase to themselves a good degree, and great boldness in the faith which is in Christ Jesus.

Or else this, out of the sixth of the Acts of the Apostles.

Acts 6. 2

THEN the twelve called the multitude of the disciples unto them, and said, It is not reason that we should leave the word of God, and serve tables. Wherefore, brethren, look ye out among you seven men of honest report, full of the Holy Ghost and wisdom, whom we may appoint over this business. But we will give ourselves continually to prayer, and to the ministry of the word. And the saying pleased the whole multitude: and they chose Stephen, a man full of faith and of the Holy Ghost, and Philip, and Prochorus, and Nicanor, and Timon, and Parmenas, and Nicolas a proselyte of Antioch: whom they set before the apostles: and when they had prayed, they laid their hands on them. And the word of God increased; and the number of the disciples multiplied in Jerusalem greatly; and a great company of the priests were obedient to the faith.

And before the Gospel, the Bishop, sitting in his Chair, shall examine every one of them that are to be ordered, in the presence of the people, after this manner following.

DO you trust that you are inwardly moved by the Holy Ghost to take upon you this office and ministration, to serve God, for the promoting of his glory, and the edifying of his people?
Answer. I trust so.

The Bishop.

DO you think that you are truly called, according to the will of our Lord Jesus Christ, and the due order of this Realm, to the Ministry of the Church?
Answer. I think so.

The Bishop.

DO you unfeignedly believe all the Canonical Scriptures of the Old and New Testament?

Answer. I do believe them.

The Bishop.

WILL you diligently read the same unto the people assembled in the Church where you shall be appointed to serve?

Answer. I will.

The Bishop.

IT appertaineth to the office of a Deacon, in the Church where he shall be appointed to serve, to assist the Priest in Divine Service, and specially when he ministereth the holy Communion, and to help him in the distribution thereof, and to read holy Scriptures and Homilies in the Church; and to instruct the youth in the Catechism; in the absence of the Priest to baptize infants; and to preach, if he be admitted thereto by the Bishop. And furthermore, it is his office, where provision is so made, to search for the sick, poor, and impotent people of the Parish, to intimate their estates, names, and places where they dwell, unto the Curate, that by his exhortation they may be relieved with the alms of the Parishioners, or others. Will you do this gladly and willingly?

Answer. I will so do, by the help of God.

The Bishop.

WILL you apply all your diligence to frame and fashion your own lives, and the lives of your families, according to the doctrine of Christ; and to make both yourselves and them, as much as in you lieth, wholesome examples of the flock of Christ?

Answer. I will so do, the Lord being my helper.

The Bishop.

WILL you reverently obey your Ordinary, and other chief Ministers of the Church, and them to whom the charge and government over you is committed, following with a glad mind and will their godly admonitions?

Answer. I will endeavour myself, the Lord being my helper.

Then the Bishop laying his hands severally upon the head of every one of them, humbly kneeling before him, shall say,

TAKE thou authority to execute the office of a Deacon in the Church of God committed unto thee; In the Name of the Father, and of the Son, and of the Holy Ghost. Amen.

Then shall the Bishop deliver to every one of them the New Testament, saying,

TAKE thou authority to read the Gospel in the Church of God, and to preach the same, if thou be thereto licensed by the Bishop himself.

Then one of them, appointed by the Bishop, shall read

The Gospel. S. Luke 12. 35

LET your loins be girded about, and your lights burning; and ye yourselves like unto men that wait for their lord, when he will return from the wedding; that when he cometh and knocketh, they may open unto him immediately. Blessed are those servants, whom the lord when he cometh shall find watching. Verily I say unto you, that he shall gird himself; and make them to sit down to meat, and will come forth and serve them. And if he shall come in the second watch, or come in the third watch, and find them so, blessed are those servants.

Then shall the Bishop proceed in the Communion: and all that are ordered shall tarry, and receive the holy Communion the same day with the Bishop.

The Communion ended, after the last Collect, and immediately before the Benediction, shall be said these Collects following.

ALMIGHTY God, giver of all good things, who of thy great goodness hast vouchsafed to accept and take these thy servants unto the office of Deacons in thy Church: Make them, we beseech thee, O Lord, to be modest, humble, and constant in their ministration; to have a ready will to observe all spiritual discipline; that they having always the testimony of a good conscience, and continuing ever stable and strong in thy Son Christ, may so well behave themselves in this inferior office, that they may be found worthy to be called unto the higher ministries in thy Church; through the same thy Son our Saviour Jesus Christ, to whom be glory and honour world without end. *Amen.*

PREVENT us, O Lord, in all our doings with thy most gracious favour, and further us with thy continual help; that in all our works, begun, continued, and ended in thee, we may glorify thy holy Name, and finally by thy mercy obtain everlasting life; through Jesus Christ our Lord. *Amen.*

THE peace of God, which passeth all understanding, keep your hearts and minds in the knowledge and love of God, and of his Son Jesus Christ our Lord: And the blessing of God Almighty, the Father, the Son, and the Holy Ghost, be amongst you and remain with you always. *Amen.*

And here it must be declared unto the Deacon, that he must continue in that office of a Deacon the space of a whole year (except for reasonable causes which shall otherwise seem good unto the Bishop) to the intent that he may be perfect and well expert in the things appertaining to the Ecclesiastical Administration. In executing whereof if he be found faithful and diligent, he may be admitted by his Diocesan to the Order of Priesthood on the Sundays immediately following the Ember Weeks or on the Feast of Saint Michael and All Angels or of Saint Thomas the Apostle, or on such other days as shall be provided by Canon, in the face of the Church, in such manner and form as hereafter followeth.

THE FORM AND MANNER OF
ORDERING OF PRIESTS

When the day appointed by the Bishop is come; after Morning Prayer is ended, there shall be a Sermon or Exhortation, declaring the duty and office of such as come to be admitted Priests; how necessary that Order is in the Church of Christ; and also how the people ought to esteem them in their office.

First, the Archdeacon, or, in his absence, one appointed in his stead, or such other person as by ancient custom have the right so to do, shall present unto the Bishop (sitting in his chair near to the holy Table) all them that shall receive the Order of Priesthood that day (each of them being decently habited) and say,

REVEREND Father in God, I present unto you these persons present, to be admitted to the Order of Priesthood.

The Bishop.

TAKE heed that the persons, whom ye present unto us, be apt and meet, for their learning and godly conversation, to exercise their ministry duly, to the honour of God, and the edifying of his Church.

The Archdeacon shall answer,

I HAVE enquired of them, and also examined them; and think them so to be.

Then the Bishop shall say unto the people:

GOOD people, these are they whom we purpose, God willing, to receive this day unto the holy office of Priesthood: For after due examination we find not to the contrary, but that they be lawfully called to their function and ministry, and that they be persons meet for the same. But yet if there be any of you, who knoweth any impediment or notable crime in any of them, for the which he ought not to be received into this holy ministry; Let him come forth in the Name of God, and shew what the crime or impediment is.

And if any great crime or impediment be objected, the Bishop shall surcease from ordering that person, until such time as the party accused shall be found clear of that crime.

Then the Bishop (commending such as shall be found meet to be ordered to the prayers of the Congregation) shall, with the Clergy and people present, sing or say the Litany, with the Prayers, as is before appointed in the Form of Ordering Deacons; save only, that, in the proper Suffrage there added, the word [Deacons] *shall be omitted, and the word* [Priests] *inserted instead of it.*

Then shall be sung or said the Service for the Communion, with the Collect, Epistle, and Gospel, as followeth.

The Collect

ALMIGHTY God, giver of all good things, who by thy Holy Spirit hast appointed divers Orders of Ministers in thy Church: Mercifully behold these thy servants now called to the office of Priesthood; and replenish them so with the truth of thy doctrine, and adorn them with innocency of life, that, both by word and good example, they may faithfully serve thee in this office, to the glory of thy Name, and the edification of thy Church; through the merits of our Saviour Jesus Christ, who liveth and reigneth with thee and the Holy Ghost, world without end. *Amen.*

The Epistle. Ephes. 4. 7

UNTO every one of us is given grace, according to the measure of the gift of Christ. Wherefore he saith, When he ascended up on high, he led captivity captive, and gave gifts unto men. (Now that he ascended, what is it but that he also descended first into the lower parts of the earth? He that descended is the same also that ascended up far above all heavens, that he might fill all things.) And he gave some Apostles, and some Prophets, and some Evangelists, and some Pastors and Teachers; for the perfecting of the saints for the work of the ministry, for the edifying of the body of Christ; till we all come, in the unity of the faith and of the knowledge of the Son of God, unto a perfect man, unto the measure of the stature of the fulness of Christ.

After this shall be read for the Gospel part of the ninth chapter of Saint Matthew, as followeth.

S. Matth. 9. 36

WHEN Jesus saw the multitudes, he was moved with compassion on them, because they fainted, and were scattered abroad, as sheep having no shepherd. Then saith he unto his disciples, The harvest truly is plenteous, but the labourers are few; pray ye therefore the Lord of the harvest, that he will send forth labourers into his harvest.

Or else this that followeth, out of the tenth chapter of Saint John.

S. John 10. 1

VERILY, verily I say unto you, He that entereth not by the door into the sheep-fold, but climbeth up some other way, the same is a thief and a robber. But he that entereth in by the door is the shepherd of the sheep. To him the porter openeth; and the sheep hear his voice: and he calleth his own sheep by name, and leadeth them out. And when he putteth forth his own sheep, he goeth before them, and the sheep follow him: for they know his voice. And a stranger will they not follow, but will flee from him: for they know not the voice of strangers. This parable spake Jesus unto them, but they understood not what things they were which he spake unto them. Then said Jesus unto them again, Verily, verily I say unto you, I am the door of the sheep. All that ever came before me are thieves and robbers: but the sheep did not hear them. I am the door: by me if any man enter in, he shall be saved, and shall go in and out, and find pasture. The thief cometh not but for to steal, and to kill, and to destroy: I am come that they might have life, and that they might have it more abundantly. I am the good shepherd: the good shepherd giveth his life for the sheep. But he that is an hireling, and not the shepherd, whose own the sheep are not, seeth the wolf coming, and leaveth the sheep, and fleeth: and the wolf catcheth them, and scattereth the sheep. The hireling fleeth, because he is an hireling, and careth not for the sheep. I am the good shepherd, and know my sheep, and am known of mine. As the Father knoweth me, even so know I the Father: and I lay down my life for the sheep. And other sheep I have, which are not of this fold: them also I must bring, and they shall hear my voice; and there shall be one fold, and one shepherd.

Then the Bishop, sitting in his Chair, shall say unto them as hereafter followeth.

YOU have heard, brethren, as well in your private examination, as in the exhortation which was now made to you, and in the holy Lessons taken out of the Gospel and the writings of the Apostles, of what dignity and of how great importance this office is, whereunto ye are called. And now again we exhort you, in the Name of our Lord Jesus Christ, that you have in remembrance, into how high a dignity, and to how weighty an office and charge ye are called: that is to say, to be messengers, watchmen, and stewards of the Lord; to teach and to premonish, to feed and provide for the Lord's family; to seek for Christ's sheep that are dispersed abroad, and for his children who are in the midst of this naughty world, that they may be saved through Christ for ever.

Have always therefore printed in your remembrance, how great a treasure is committed to your charge. For they are the sheep of Christ, which he bought with his death, and for whom he shed his blood. The Church and Congregation whom you must serve, is his spouse and his body. And if it shall happen the same Church, or any member thereof, to take any hurt or hindrance by reason of your negligence, ye know the greatness of the fault, and also the horrible punishment that will ensue. Wherefore consider with yourselves the end of your ministry towards the children of God, towards the spouse and body of Christ; and see that you never cease your labour, your care and diligence, until you have done all that lieth in you, according to your bounden duty, to bring all such as are or shall be committed to your charge, unto that agreement in the faith and knowledge of God, and to that ripeness and perfectness of age in Christ, that there be no place left among you, either for error in religion, or for viciousness in life.

Forasmuch then as your office is both of so great excellency and of so great difficulty, ye see with how great care and study ye ought to apply yourselves, as well that ye may shew yourselves dutiful and thankful unto that Lord, who hath placed you in so high a dignity; as also to beware that neither you yourselves offend, nor be occasion that others offend. Howbeit, ye cannot have a mind and will thereto of yourselves; for that will and ability is given of God alone. Therefore ye ought, and have need, to pray earnestly for his Holy Spirit. And seeing that you cannot by any other means compass the doing of so weighty a work, pertaining to the salvation of man, but with doctrine and exhortation taken out of the holy Scriptures, and with a life agreeable to the same; consider how studious ye ought to be in reading and learning the Scriptures, and in framing the manners both of yourselves, and of them that specially pertain unto you, according to the rule of the same Scriptures: and for this self-same cause, how ye ought to forsake and set aside (as much as you may) all worldly cares and studies.

We have good hope that you have well weighed and pondered these things with yourselves long before this time; and that you have clearly determined, by God's grace, to give yourselves wholly to this office, whereunto it hath pleased God to call you: so that, as much as lieth in you, you will apply yourselves wholly to this one thing, and draw all your cares and studies this way; and that you will continually pray to God the Father, by the mediation of our only Saviour Jesus Christ, for the heavenly assistance of the Holy Ghost; that, by daily reading and weighing of the Scriptures, ye may wax riper and stronger in your ministry; and that ye may so endeavour yourselves from time to time to sanctify the lives of you and yours, and to fashion them after the rule and doctrine of Christ, that ye may be wholesome and godly examples and patterns for the people to follow.

And now, that this present Congregation of Christ here assembled may also understand your minds and wills in these things, and that this your promise may the more move you to do your duties, ye shall answer plainly to these things, which we, in the Name of God, and of his Church, shall demand of you touching the same.

DO you think in your heart that you be truly called, according to the will of our Lord Jesus Christ, and the order of this Church of *England,* to the Order and Ministry of Priesthood?

Answer. I think it.

The Bishop.

ARE you persuaded that the holy Scriptures contain sufficiently all doctrine required of necessity for eternal salvation through faith in Jesus Christ? And are you determined out of the said Scriptures to instruct the people committed to your charge, and to teach nothing (as required of necessity to eternal salvation) but that which you shall be persuaded may be concluded and proved by the Scripture?

Answer. I am so persuaded, and have so determined by God's grace.

The Bishop.

WILL you then give your faithful diligence always so to minister the doctrine and sacraments, and the discipline of Christ, as the Lord hath commanded, and as this Church and Realm hath received the same, according to the commandments of God; so that you may teach the people committed to your cure and charge with all diligence to keep and observe the same?

Answer. I will so do, by the help of the Lord.

The Bishop

WILL you be ready, with all faithful diligence, to banish and drive away all erroneous and strange doctrines contrary to God's Word; and to use both publick and private monitions and exhortations, as well to the sick as to the whole, within your cures, as need shall require, and occasion shall be given?

Answer. I will, the Lord being my helper.

The Bishop.

WILL you be diligent in prayers, and in reading of the holy Scriptures, and in such studies as help to the knowledge of the same, laying aside the study of the world and the flesh?

Answer. I will endeavour myself so to do, the Lord being my helper.

The Bishop.

WILL you be diligent to frame and fashion your own selves, and your families, according to the doctrine of Christ; and to make both yourselves and them, as much as in you lieth, whole-some examples and patterns to the flock of Christ?

Answer. I will apply myself thereto, the Lord being my helper.

The Bishop.

WILL you maintain and set forwards, as much as lieth in you, quietness, peace, and love, among all Christian people, and specially among them that are or shall be committed to your charge?

Answer. I will so do, the Lord being my helper.

The Bishop.

WILL you reverently obey your Ordinary, and other chief Ministers, unto whom is committed the charge and govern-ment over you; following with a glad mind and will their godly admonitions, and submitting yourselves to their godly judgements?

Answer. I will so do, the Lord being my helper.

Then shall the Bishop, standing up, say,

ALMIGHTY God, who hath given you this will to do all these things; Grant also unto you strength and power to perform the same; that he may accomplish his work which he hath begun in you; through Jesus Christ our Lord. *Amen.*

After this, the Congregation shall be desired, secretly in their prayers, to make their humble supplications to God for all these things: for the which prayers there shall be silence kept for a space.

After which shall be sung or said by the Bishop (the persons to be ordained Priests all kneeling) Veni, Creator Spiritus; the Bishop beginning, and the Priests, and others that are present, answering by verses, as followeth.

COME, Holy Ghost, our souls inspire,
And lighten with celestial fire.
Thou the anointing Spirit art,
Who dost thy seven-fold gifts impart.
Thy blessed Unction from above
Is comfort, life, and fire of love.
Enable with perpetual light
The dulness of our blinded sight.
Anoint and cheer our soiled face
With the abundance of thy grace.
Keep far our foes, give peace at home:
Where thou art guide, no ill can come.
Teach us to know the Father, Son,
And thee, of both, to be but One.
That, through the ages all along,
This may be our endless song:
  Praise to thy eternal merit,
  Father, Son, and Holy Spirit.

Or this:

COME, Holy Ghost, eternal God, proceeding from above,
Both from the Father and the Son, the God of peace and love;

Visit our minds, into our hearts thy heavenly grace inspire;
That truth and godliness we may pursue with full desire.

Thou art the very Comforter in grief and all distress;
The heav'nly gift of God most high, no tongue can it express;

The fountain and the living spring of joy celestial;
The fire so bright, the love so sweet, the Unction spiritual.

Thou in thy gifts art manifold, by them Christ's Church doth
stand:
In faithful hearts thou writ'st thy law, the finger of God's hand.

According to thy promise, Lord, thou givest speech with grace;
That through thy help God's praises may resound in every place.

O Holy Ghost, into our minds send down thy heav'nly light;
Kindle our hearts with fervent zeal to serve God day and night.

Our weakness strengthen and confirm, (for, Lord, thou know'st
us frail;)
That neither devil, world, nor flesh, against us may prevail.

Put back our enemy far from us, and help us to obtain
Peace in our hearts with God and man, (the best, the truest gain;)

And grant that thou being, O Lord, our leader and our guide,
We may escape the snares of sin, and never from thee slide.

Such measures of thy powerful grace grant, Lord, to us, we pray;
That thou may'st be our Comforter at the last dreadful day.

Of strife and of dissension dissolve, O Lord, the bands,
And knit the knots of peace and love throughout all Christian lands.

Grant us the grace that we may know the Father of all might,
That we of his beloved Son may gain the blissful sight;

And that we may with perfect faith ever acknowledge thee,
The Spirit of Father, and of Son, One God in Persons Three.

To God the Father laud and praise, and to his blessed Son,
And to the Holy Spirit of grace, co-equal Three in One.

And pray we, that our only Lord would please his Spirit to send
On all that shall profess his Name, from hence to the world's end.
    Amen.

That done, the Bishop shall pray in this wise, and say,

Let us pray.

ALMIGHTY God and heavenly Father, who of thine infinite love and goodness towards us hast given to us thy only and
most dearly beloved Son Jesus Christ, to be our Redeemer and
the Author of everlasting life; who, after he had made perfect
our redemption by his death, and was ascended into heaven,
sent abroad into the world his Apostles, Prophets, Evangelists,
Doctors, and Pastors, by whose labour and ministry he gathered
together a great flock in all the parts of the world, to set forth
the eternal praise of thy holy Name: For these so great benefits
of thy eternal goodness, and for that thou hast vouchsafed to call
these thy servants here present to the same office and ministry,
appointed for the salvation of mankind; we render unto thee
most hearty thanks, we praise and worship thee, and we humbly
beseech thee, by the same thy blessed Son, to grant unto all,
which either here or elsewhere call upon thy holy Name, that
we may continue to shew ourselves thankful unto thee for these
and all other thy benefits; and that we may daily increase and go
forwards in the knowledge and faith of thee and thy Son, by the
Holy Spirit. So that as well by these thy Ministers, as by them
over whom they shall be appointed thy Ministers, thy holy
Name may be for ever glorified, and thy blessed kingdom
enlarged; through the same thy Son Jesus Christ our Lord, who
liveth and reigneth with thee in the unity of the same Holy
Spirit, world without end. *Amen.*

*When this prayer is done, the Bishop with the Priests present
shall lay their hands severally upon the head of every one
that receiveth the Order of Priesthood; the receivers humbly
kneeling upon their knees, and the Bishop saying,*

RECEIVE the Holy Ghost for the office and work of a Priest
in the Church of God, now committed unto thee by the

imposition of our hands. Whose sins thou dost forgive, they are forgiven; and whose sins thou dost retain, they are retained. And be thou a faithful dispenser of the Word of God, and of his holy Sacraments; In the Name of the Father, and of the Son, and of the Holy Ghost. Amen.

Then the Bishop shall deliver to every one of them kneeling the Bible into his hand, saying,

TAKE thou authority to preach the Word of God, and to minister the holy Sacraments in the Congregation, where thou shalt be lawfully appointed thereunto.

When this is done, the Nicene Creed shall be sung or said; and the Bishop shall after that go on in the Service of the Communion, which all they that receive Orders shall take together, and remain in the same place where hands were laid upon them, until such time as they have received the Communion.

The Communion being done, after the last Collect, and imme-diately before the Benediction, shall be said these Collects.

MOST merciful Father, we beseech thee to send upon these thy servants thy heavenly blessing, that they may be clothed with righteousness, and that thy Word spoken by their mouths may have such success, that it may never be spoken in vain. Grant also that we may have grace to hear and receive what they shall deliver out of thy most holy Word, or agreeable to the same, as the means of our salvation; that in all our words and deeds we may seek thy glory, and the increase of thy kingdom; through Jesus Christ our Lord. *Amen.*

PREVENT us, O Lord, in all our doings with thy most gracious favour, and further us with thy continual help; that in all our works, begun, continued, and ended in thee, we may glorify thy holy Name, and finally by thy mercy obtain everlast-ing life; through Jesus Christ our Lord. *Amen.*

THE peace of God, which passeth all understanding, keep

your hearts and minds in the knowledge and love of God, and of his Son Jesus Christ our Lord: And the blessing of God Almighty, the Father, the Son, and the Holy Ghost, be amongst you and remain with you always. *Amen.*

And if on the same day the Order of Deacons be given to some, and the Order of Priesthood to others; the Deacons shall be first presented, and then the Priests: and it shall suffice that the Litany be once said for both. The Collects shall both be used; first that for Deacons, then that for Priests. The Epistle shall be Ephes. 4. 7–13, as before in this Office. Immediately after which they that are to be made Deacons shall be examined and ordained, as is above prescribed. Then one of them having read the Gospel (which shall be either out of S. Matth. 9. 36–38, as before in this Office; or else S. Luke 12. 35–38, as before in the Form for the Ordering of Deacons,) they that are to be made Priests shall likewise be examined and ordained, as is in this Office before appointed.

THE FORM OF ORDAINING OR CONSECRATING OF AN
ARCHBISHOP OR BISHOP

WHICH IS ALWAYS TO BE PERFORMED UPON SOME SUNDAY OR HOLY DAY UNLESS FOR WEIGHTY AND URGENT REASONS SOME OTHER DAY BE APPOINTED

When all things are duly prepared in the Church, and set in order; after Morning Prayer is ended, the Archbishop (or some other Bishop appointed) shall begin the Communion Service: in which this shall be

The Collect

ALMIGHTY God, who by thy Son Jesus Christ didst give to thy holy Apostles many excellent gifts, and didst charge them to feed thy flock: Give grace, we beseech thee, to all Bishops, the Pastors of thy Church, that they may diligently preach thy Word, and duly administer the godly discipline thereof; and grant to the people, that they may obediently follow the same; that all may receive the crown of everlasting glory; through Jesus Christ our Lord. *Amen.*

And another Bishop shall read

The Epistle. 1 S. Tim. 3. 1

THIS is a true saying, If a man desire the office of a bishop, he desireth a good work. A bishop then must be blameless, the husband of one wife, vigilant, sober, of good behaviour, given to hospitality, apt to teach; not given to wine, no striker, not greedy of filthy lucre; but patient, not a brawler, not covetous; one that ruleth well his own house, having his children in subjection with all gravity; (for if a man know not how to rule his own house, how shall he take care of the Church of God?) Not a novice, lest being lifted up with pride he fall into the condemnation of the devil. Moreover, he must have a good report of them which are without; lest he fall into reproach and the snare of the devil.

Or this.

For the Epistle. Acts 20. 17

FROM Miletus Paul sent to Ephesus, and called the elders of the Church. And when they were come to him, he said unto them, Ye know, from the first day that I came into Asia, after what manner I have been with you at all seasons, serving the Lord with all humility of mind, and with many tears, and temptations, which befel me by the lying in wait of the Jews: and how I kept back nothing that was profitable unto you, but have shewed you, and have taught you publickly, and from house to house, testifying both to the Jews, and also to the Greeks, repentance toward God, and faith toward our Lord Jesus Christ. And now behold, I go bound in the spirit unto Jerusalem, not knowing the things that shall befal me there; save that the Holy Ghost witnesseth in every city, saying that bonds and afflictions abide me. But none of these things move me, neither count I my life dear unto myself, so that I might finish my course with joy, and the ministry which I have received of the Lord Jesus, to testify the Gospel of the grace of God. And now behold, I know that ye all, among whom I have gone preaching the kingdom of God, shall see my face no more. Wherefore I take you to record this day, that I am pure from the blood of all men. For I have not shunned to declare unto you all the counsel of God. Take heed therefore unto yourselves, and to all the flock over the which the Holy Ghost hath made you overseers, to feed the Church of God, which he hath purchased with his own blood. For I know this, that after my departing shall grievous wolves enter in among you, not sparing the flock. Also of your own selves shall men arise speaking perverse things, to draw away disciples after them. Therefore watch, and remember that by the space of three years I ceased not to warn every one night and day with tears. And now, brethren, I commend you to God, and to the word of his grace, which is able to build you up, and to give you an inheritance among all them which are sanctified. I have coveted no man's silver, or gold, or apparel: yea, ye yourselves know, that these hands have ministered unto my necessities, and to them that were with me. I have shewed you all things, how that so labouring ye ought to support the weak; and to remember the words of the Lord Jesus, how he said, It is more blessed to give than to receive.

Then another Bishop shall read

The Gospel. S. John 21. 15

JESUS saith to Simon Peter, Simon, son of Jonas, lovest thou me more than these? He saith unto him, Yea, Lord, thou knowest that I love thee. He saith unto him, Feed my lambs. He saith to him again the second time, Simon, son of Jonas, lovest thou me? He saith unto him, Yea, Lord, thou knowest that I love thee. He saith unto him, Feed my sheep. He saith unto him the third time, Simon, son of Jonas, lovest thou me? Peter was grieved because he said unto him the third time, Lovest thou me? And he said unto him, Lord, thou knowest all things; thou knowest that I love thee. Jesus saith unto him, Feed my sheep.

Or else this.

S. John 20. 19

THE same day at evening, being the first day of the week, when the doors were shut where the disciples were assembled for fear of the Jews, came Jesus and stood in the midst, and saith unto them, Peace be unto you. And when he had so said, he shewed unto them his hands and his side. Then were the disciples glad, when they saw the Lord. Then said Jesus to them again, Peace be unto you: As my Father hath sent me, even so send I you. And when he had said this, he breathed on them, and saith unto them, Receive ye the Holy Ghost. Whose soever sins ye remit, they are remitted unto them; and whose soever sins ye retain, they are retained.

Or this.

S. Matth. 28. 18

JESUS came and spake unto them, saying, All power is given unto me in heaven and in earth. Go ye therefore and teach all nations, baptizing them in the Name of the Father, and of the Son, and of the Holy Ghost; teaching them to observe all things whatsoever I have commanded you: and lo, I am with you alway, even unto the end of the world.

After the Gospel, and the Nicene Creed, and the Sermon are ended, the elected Bishop (vested, with his Rochet) shall be presented by two Bishops unto the Archbishop of that province, (or to some other Bishop appointed by lawful commission,) the Archbishop sitting in his Chair, near the holy Table, and the Bishops that present him saying,

MOST reverend Father in God, we present unto you this godly and well-learned man to be ordained and consecrated Bishop.

Then shall the Archbishop demand the Queen's Mandate for the Consecration, and cause it to be read. And then shall be ministered unto them the Oath of due obedience to the Archbishop, as followeth.

The Oath of due obedience to the Archbishop

IN the Name of God, Amen. I *N.* chosen Bishop of the Church and See of *N.* do profess and promise all due reverence and obedience to the Archbishop and to the Metropolitical Church of *N.* and to their Successors: So help me God, through Jesus Christ.

This Oath shall not be made at the Consecration of an Archbishop.

Then the Archbishop shall move the Congregation present to pray, saying thus to them:

BRETHREN, it is written in the Gospel of Saint Luke, that

our Saviour Christ continued the whole night in prayer, before he did choose and send forth his twelve Apostles. It is written also in the Acts of the Apostles, that the disciples who were at Antioch did fast and pray, before they laid hands on Paul and Barnabas, and sent them forth. Let us therefore, following the example of our Saviour Christ and his Apostles, first fall to prayer, before we admit and send forth this person presented unto us, to the work whereunto we trust the Holy Ghost hath called him.

And then shall be said the Litany, as before in the Form of Ordering Deacons, save only that after this place, That it may please thee to illuminate all Bishops, *&c. the proper Suffrage there following shall be omitted, and this inserted instead of it;*

THAT it may please thee to bless this our Brother elected, and to send thy grace upon him, that he may duly execute the office whereunto he is called, to the edifying of thy Church, and to the honour, praise and glory of thy Name,
    Answer. We beseech thee to hear us, good Lord.

Then shall be said this Prayer following.

ALMIGHTY God, giver of all good things, who by thy Holy Spirit hast appointed divers Orders of Ministers in thy Church: Mercifully behold this thy servant now called to the work and ministry of a Bishop; and replenish him so with the truth of thy doctrine, and adorn him with innocency of life, that both by word and deed he may faithfully serve thee in this office, to the glory of thy Name, and the edifying and well-governing of thy Church; through the merits of our Saviour Jesus Christ, who liveth and reigneth with thee and the Holy Ghost, world without end. *Amen.*

Then the Archbishop, sitting in his Chair, shall say to him that is to be consecrated,

BROTHER, forasmuch as the holy Scripture and the ancient Canons command that we should not be hasty in laying on hands, and admitting any person to government in the Church of Christ, which he hath purchased with no less price than the effusion of his own blood: Before I admit you to this administration, I will examine you in certain articles, to the end that the Congregation present may have a trial, and bear witness, how you be minded to behave yourself in the Church of God.

ARE you persuaded that you be truly called to this ministration, according to the will of our Lord Jesus Christ, and the order of this Realm?

Answer. I am so persuaded.

The Archbishop.

ARE you persuaded that the holy Scriptures contain sufficiently all doctrine required of necessity for eternal salvation through faith in Jesus Christ? And are you determined out of the same holy Scriptures to instruct the people committed to your charge, and to teach or maintain nothing as required of necessity to eternal salvation, but that which you shall be persuaded may be concluded and proved by the same?

Answer. I am so persuaded and determined, by God's grace.

The Archbishop.

WILL you then faithfully exercise yourself in the same holy Scriptures, and call upon God by prayer, for the true understanding of the same; so as ye may be able by them to teach and exhort with wholesome doctrine, and to withstand and convince the gainsayers?

Answer. I will so do, by the help of God.

The Archbishop.

BE you ready, with all faithful diligence, to banish and drive away all erroneous and strange doctrine contrary to God's Word; and both privately and openly to call upon and encourage others to the same?

Answer. I am ready, the Lord being my helper.

The Archbishop.

WILL you deny all ungodliness and worldly lusts, and live soberly, righteously and godly in this present world; that you may shew yourself in all things an example of good works unto others, that the adversary may be ashamed, having nothing to say against you?

Answer. I will so do, the Lord being my helper.

The Archbishop.

WILL you maintain and set forward (as much as shall lie in you) quietness, peace, and love among all men; and such as be unquiet, disobedient and criminous within your Diocese, correct and punish, according to such authority as ye have by God's Word, and as to you shall be committed by the Ordinance of this Realm?

Answer. I will so do, by the help of God.

The Archbishop.

WILL you be faithful in ordaining, sending, or laying hands upon others?

Answer. I will so be, by the help of God.

The Archbishop.

WILL you shew yourself gentle, and be merciful for Christ's sake to poor and needy people, and to all strangers destitute of help?

Answer. I will so shew myself, by God's help.

Then the Archbishop, standing up, shall say,

ALMIGHTY God, our heavenly Father, who hath given you a good will to do all these things; Grant also unto you strength and power to perform the same; that he accomplishing in you the good work which he hath begun, ye may be found perfect and irreprehensible at the latter day; through Jesus Christ our Lord. *Amen.*

Then shall the Bishop elect put on the rest of the Episcopal habit; and kneeling down, Veni, Creator Spiritus, shall be sung or said over him, the Archbishop beginning, and the Bishops, with others that are present, answering by verses, as followeth.

COME, Holy Ghost, our souls inspire,
And lighten with celestial fire.
Thou the anointing Spirit art,
Who dost thy seven-fold gifts impart.
Thy blessed Unction from above
Is comfort, life, and fire of love.
Enable with perpetual light
The dulness of our blinded sight.
Anoint and cheer our soiled face
With the abundance of thy grace.
Keep far our foes, give peace at home:
Where thou art guide, no ill can come.
Teach us to know the Father, Son,
And thee, of both, to be but One.
That, through the ages all along,
This may be our endless song:
  Praise to thy eternal merit,
  Father, Son, and Holy Spirit.

Or this:

COME, Holy Ghost, eternal God, *&c.*

*As before in the Form for Ordering Priests.
That ended, the Archbishop shall say,*

Lord, hear our prayer.
Answer. And let our cry come unto thee.

Let us pray.

ALMIGHTY God and most merciful Father, who of thine infinite goodness hast given thine only and dearly beloved Son Jesus Christ, to be our Redeemer and the Author of everlasting life; who, after that he had made perfect our redemption by his death, and was ascended into heaven, poured down his gifts abundantly upon men, making some Apostles, some Prophets, some Evangelists, some Pastors and Doctors, to the edifying and making perfect his Church: Grant, we beseech thee, to this thy servant such grace, that he may evermore be ready to spread abroad thy Gospel, the glad tidings of reconciliation with thee; and use the authority given him, not to destruction, but to salvation; not to hurt, but to help: so that as a wise and faithful servant, giving to thy family their portion in due season, he may at last be received into everlasting joy; through Jesus Christ our Lord, who with thee and the Holy Ghost liveth and reigneth, one God, world without end. *Amen.*

Then the Archbishop and Bishops present shall lay their hands upon the head of the elected Bishop kneeling before them upon his knees, the Archbishop saying,

RECEIVE the Holy Ghost for the office and work of a Bishop in the Church of God, now committed unto thee by the imposition of our hands; In the Name of the Father, and of the Son, and of the Holy Ghost. Amen. And remember that thou stir up the grace of God which is given thee by this imposition of our hands: for God hath not given us the spirit of fear, but of power, and love, and soberness.

Then the Archbishop shall deliver him the Bible, saying,

GIVE heed unto reading, exhortation, and doctrine. Think upon the things contained in this Book. Be diligent in them, that the increase coming thereby may be manifest unto all men. Take heed unto thyself, and to doctrine, and be diligent in doing them: for by so doing thou shalt both save thyself and them that hear thee. Be to the flock of Christ a shepherd, not a wolf; feed them, devour them not. Hold up the weak, heal the sick, bind up the broken, bring again the outcasts, seek the lost. Be so merciful, that ye be not too remiss; so minister discipline, that you forget not mercy: that when the chief Shepherd shall appear ye may receive the never-fading crown of glory; through Jesus Christ our Lord. *Amen.*

Then the Archbishop shall proceed in the Communion-Service; with whom the new consecrated Bishop (with others) shall also communicate.

And for the last Collect, immediately before the Benediction, shall be said these Prayers.

MOST merciful Father, we beseech thee to send down upon this thy servant thy heavenly blessing; and so endue him with thy Holy Spirit, that he, preaching thy Word, may not only be earnest to reprove, beseech, and rebuke with all patience and doctrine; but also may be to such as believe a wholesome example, in word, in conversation, in love, in faith, in chastity, and in purity; that, faithfully fulfilling his course, at the latter day he may receive the crown of righteousness laid up by the Lord the righteous Judge, who liveth and reigneth one God with the Father and the Holy Ghost, world without end. *Amen.*

PREVENT us, O Lord, in all our doings with thy most gracious favour, and further us with thy continual help; that in all our works, begun, continued, and ended in thee, we may glorify thy holy Name, and finally by thy mercy obtain everlasting life; through Jesus Christ our Lord. *Amen.*

THE peace of God, which passeth all understanding, keep your hearts and minds in the knowledge and love of God, and of his Son Jesus Christ our Lord: And the blessing of God Almighty, the Father, the Son, and the Holy Ghost, be amongst you and remain with you always. *Amen.*

FORMS OF PRAYER
WITH THANKSGIVING TO ALMIGHTY GOD

For use in all Churches and Chapels within this Realm, every Year, upon the Anniversary of the day of the Accession of the Reigning Sovereign, or upon such other day as shall be appointed by Authority.

I

At Mattins and Evensong the following Psalms, Lessons, Suffrages, and Collects may be used.

Proper Psalms, 20, 101, 121.

Proper Lessons.
The First, Joshua 1 to verse 10, *or* Proverbs 8 to verse 17.
The Second, Rom. 13 to verse 11, *or* Rev. 21. 22–22. 4.

The Suffrages next after the Creed.

Priest.

O LORD, shew thy mercy upon us.
  Answer. And grant us thy salvation.
  Priest. O Lord, save the Queen;
  Answer. Who putteth her trust in thee.
  Priest. Send her help from thy holy place.
  Answer. And evermore mightily defend her.
  Priest. Be unto her, O Lord, a strong tower;
  Answer. From the face of her enemies.
  Priest. Endue thy Ministers with righteousness.
  Answer. And make thy chosen people joyful.
  Priest. O Lord, save thy people.
  Answer. And bless thine inheritance.
  Priest. Give peace in our time, O Lord.

Answer. Because there is none other that fighteth for us, but only thou, O God.

Priest. O Lord, hear our prayer;

Answer. And let our cry come unto thee.

After the first Collect, at Morning or Evening Prayer, the following Collect.

O GOD, who providest for thy people by thy power, and rulest over them in love: Vouchsafe so to bless thy Servant our Queen, that under her this nation may be wisely governed, and thy Church may serve thee in all godly quietness; and grant that she being devoted to thee with her whole heart, and persevering in good works unto the end, may, by thy guidance, come to thine everlasting kingdom; through Jesus Christ thy Son our Lord, who liveth and reigneth with thee and the Holy Ghost, ever one God, world without end. *Amen.*

If the Litany be sung or said, these Prayers immediately after the Prayer, We humbly beseech thee: *and if the Litany be not said, then these Prayers instead of the Prayers for the Queen and for the Royal Family at Mattins or Evensong.*

O LORD our God, who upholdest and governest all things by the word of thy power: Receive our humble prayers for our Sovereign Lady *ELIZABETH, as on this day,* set over us by thy grace and providence to be our Queen; and, together with her, bless, we beseech thee, *Philip* Duke of *Edinburgh, Charles* Prince of *Wales,* and all the Royal Family; that they, ever trusting in thy goodness, protected by thy power, and crowned with thy gracious and endless favour, may long continue before thee in peace and safety, joy and honour, and after death may obtain everlasting life and glory, by the merits and mediation of Christ Jesus our Saviour, who with thee and the Holy Ghost liveth and reigneth ever one God, world without end. *Amen.*

ALMIGHTY God, who rulest over all the kingdoms of the world, and dost order them according to thy good pleasure: We yield thee unfeigned thanks, for that thou wast pleased, *as on this day*, to set thy Servant our Sovereign Lady, Queen *ELIZA-BETH*, upon the Throne of this Realm. Let thy wisdom be her guide, and let thine arm strengthen her; let truth and justice, holiness and righteousness, peace and charity, abound in her days; direct all her counsels and endeavours to thy glory, and the welfare of her subjects; give us grace to obey her cheerfully for conscience sake, and let her always possess the hearts of her people; let her reign be long and prosperous, and crown her with everlasting life in the world to come; through Jesus Christ our Lord. *Amen*.

A Prayer for Unity.

O GOD the Father of our Lord Jesus Christ, our only Saviour, the Prince of Peace: Give us grace seriously to lay to heart the great dangers we are in by our unhappy divisions. Take away all hatred and prejudice, and whatsoever else may hinder us from godly union and concord: that, as there is but one Body, and one Spirit, and one hope of our calling, one Lord, one faith, one baptism, one God and Father of us all; so we may henceforth be all of one heart, and of one soul, united in one holy bond of truth and peace, of faith and charity, and may with one mind and one mouth glorify thee; through Jesus Christ our Lord. *Amen*.

II
THE COMMUNION

In the Order of the Administration of Holy Communion, in place of the Collect, Epistle, and Gospel of the day, shall be said the following.

The Collect

O GOD, who providest for thy people by thy power, and rulest over them in love: Vouchsafe so to bless thy Servant our Queen, that under her this nation may be wisely governed, and thy Church may serve thee in all godly quietness; and grant that she being devoted to thee with her whole heart, and persevering in good works unto the end, may, by thy guidance, come to thine everlasting kingdom; through Jesus Christ thy Son our Lord, who liveth and reigneth with thee and the Holy Ghost, ever one God, world without end. *Amen.*

The Epistle. 1 S. Peter 2. 11

DEARLY beloved, I beseech you as strangers and pilgrims, abstain from fleshly lusts, which war against the soul; having your conversation honest among the Gentiles; that, whereas they speak against you as evil-doers, they may, by your good works which they shall behold, glorify God in the day of visitation. Submit yourselves to every ordinance of man for the Lord's sake; whether it be to the king, as supreme; or unto governors, as unto them that are sent by him, for the punishment of evil-doers, and for the praise of them that do well. For so is the will of God, that with well-doing ye may put to silence the ignorance of foolish men: as free, and not using your liberty for a cloke of maliciousness; but as the servants of God. Honour all men. Love the brotherhood. Fear God. Honour the king.

The Gospel. S. Matth. 22. 16

AND they sent out unto him their disciples, with the Herodians, saying, Master, we know that thou art true, and teachest the way of God in truth, neither carest thou for any man: for thou regardest not the person of men. Tell us therefore, What thinkest thou? Is it lawful to give tribute unto Cæsar, or not? But Jesus perceived their wickedness, and said, Why tempt ye me, ye hypocrites? shew me the tribute-money. And they brought unto him a penny. And he saith unto them, Whose is this image and superscription? They say unto him, Cæsar's. Then saith he unto them, Render therefore unto Cæsar the things which are Cæsar's; and unto God the things that are God's. When they had heard these words, they marvelled, and left him, and went their way.

If this day should fall on a Sunday or other Holy-day, the

Collect, Epistle, and Gospel of the day shall be used, and the Collect, O God, who providest, *shall be said after the Collect of the day.*

III

The following Service may also be used on the same day at any convenient time.

TE DEUM LAUDAMUS

WE praise thee, O God: we acknowledge thee to be the Lord.

All the earth doth worship thee: the Father everlasting.

To thee all Angels cry aloud: the heavens and all the powers therein.

To thee Cherubin and Seraphin: continually do cry,

Holy, Holy, Holy: Lord God of Sabaoth;

Heaven and earth are full of the Majesty: of thy glory.

The glorious company of the Apostles: praise thee.

The goodly fellowship of the Prophets: praise thee.

The noble army of Martyrs: praise thee.

The holy Church throughout all the world: doth acknowledge thee;

The Father: of an infinite Majesty;

Thine honourable, true: and only Son;

Also the Holy Ghost: the Comforter.

THOU art the King of glory: O Christ.

Thou art the everlasting Son: of the Father.

When thou tookest upon thee to deliver man: thou didst not abhor the Virgin's womb.

When thou hadst overcome the sharpness of death: thou didst open the kingdom of heaven to all believers.

Thou sittest at the right hand of God: in the glory of the Father.

We believe that thou shalt come: to be our Judge.

We therefore pray thee, help thy servants: whom thou hast redeemed with thy precious blood.

Make them to be numbered with thy Saints: in glory everlasting.

O LORD, save thy people: and bless thine heritage.
Govern them: and lift them up for ever.
Day by day: we magnify thee;
And we worship thy Name: ever world without end.
Vouchsafe, O Lord: to keep us this day without sin.
O Lord, have mercy upon us: have mercy upon us.
O Lord, let thy mercy lighten upon us: as our trust is in thee.
O Lord, in thee have I trusted: let me never be confounded.

Then the Priest shall say,

The Lord be with you.
Answer. And with thy spirit.

Let us pray.

Lord, have mercy upon us.
Christ, have mercy upon us.
Lord, have mercy upon us.

OUR Father which art in heaven, Hallowed be thy Name, Thy kingdom come, Thy will be done, in earth as it is in heaven. Give us this day our daily bread; And forgive us our trespasses, As we forgive them that trespass against us; And lead us not into temptation, But deliver us from evil. Amen.

Then the Priest standing up shall say,

O Lord, save the Queen;
Answer. Who putteth her trust in thee.
Priest. Send her help from thy holy place.
Answer. And evermore mightily defend her.
Priest. Let her enemies have no advantage of her.
Answer. Nor the wicked approach to hurt her.
Priest. O Lord, hear our prayer;
Answer. And let our cry come unto thee.

Let us pray.

O GOD, who providest for thy people by thy power, and rulest over them in love: Vouchsafe so to bless thy Servant our Queen, that under her this nation may be wisely governed, and thy Church may serve thee in all godly quietness; and grant that she being devoted to thee with her whole heart, and persevering in good works unto the end, may, by thy guidance, come to thine everlasting kingdom; through Jesus Christ thy Son our Lord, who liveth and reigneth with thee and the Holy Ghost, ever one God, world without end. *Amen.*

O LORD our God, who upholdest and governest all things by the word of thy power: Receive our humble prayers for our Sovereign Lady *ELIZABETH*, *as on this day*, set over us by thy grace and providence to be our Queen; and, together with her, bless, we beseech thee, *Philip* Duke of *Edinburgh*, the Prince of *Wales*, and all the Royal Family; that they, ever trusting in thy goodness, protected by thy power, and crowned with thy gracious and endless favour, may long continue before thee in peace and safety, joy and honour, and after death may obtain everlasting life and glory, by the merits and mediation of Christ Jesus our Saviour, who with thee and the Holy Ghost liveth and reigneth ever one God, world without end. *Amen.*

ALMIGHTY God, who rulest over all the kingdoms of the world, and dost order them according to thy good pleasure: We yield thee unfeigned thanks, for that thou wast pleased, *as on this day*, to set thy Servant our Sovereign Lady, Queen *ELIZA-BETH*, upon the Throne of this Realm. Let thy wisdom be her guide, and let thine arm strengthen her; let truth and justice, holiness and righteousness, peace and charity, abound in her days; direct all her counsels and endeavours to thy glory, and the welfare of her subjects; give us grace to obey her cheerfully for conscience sake, and let her always possess the hearts of her people; let her reign be long and prosperous, and crown her with everlasting life in the world to come; through Jesus Christ our Lord. *Amen.*

A Prayer for Unity.

O GOD the Father of our Lord Jesus Christ, our only Saviour, the Prince of Peace: Give us grace seriously to lay to heart the great dangers we are in by our unhappy divisions. Take away all hatred and prejudice, and whatsoever else may hinder us from godly union and concord: that, as there is but one Body, and one Spirit, and one hope of our calling, one Lord, one faith, one baptism, one God and Father of us all; so we may henceforth be all of one heart, and of one soul, united in one holy bond of truth and peace, of faith and charity, and may with one mind and one mouth glorify thee; through Jesus Christ our Lord. *Amen.*

ALMIGHTY God, the fountain of all wisdom, who knowest our necessities before we ask, and our ignorance in asking: We beseech thee to have compassion upon our infirmities; and those things, which for our unworthiness we dare not, and for our blindness we cannot ask, vouchsafe to give us for the worthiness of thy Son Jesus Christ our Lord. *Amen.*

THE blessing of God Almighty, the Father, the Son, and the Holy Ghost, be amongst you and remain with you always. *Amen.*

"ELIZABETH R.

"WHEREAS by Our Royal Warrant dated the Twelfth day "of June, One thousand nine hundred and fifty-three, certain "Forms of Prayer and Service were made for the Sixth day of "February and commanded to be printed and published and "annexed to the Book of Common Prayer and Liturgy of the "Church of England to be used yearly in all Churches and "Chapels within the Provinces of Canterbury and York:

"NOW Our Will and Pleasure is that Our said Royal "Warrant be revoked, and that the use of the said Forms of Prayer "and Service be discontinued; and that the Forms of Prayer and "Service hereunto annexed be forthwith printed and published "and annexed to the Book of Common Prayer and Liturgy of "the Church of England to be used yearly on the Sixth day of "February in all Churches and Chapels within the Provinces of "Canterbury and York.

"GIVEN at Our Court at Saint James's the Twenty-sixth "day of July, 1958; In the Seventh Year of Our Reign.

"By Her Majesty's Command.

"R. A. BUTLER."

ARTICLES

AGREED UPON BY THE
ARCHBISHOPS AND BISHOPS OF
BOTH PROVINCES AND THE
WHOLE CLERGY IN THE
CONVOCATION HOLDEN AT
LONDON IN THE YEAR 1562 FOR
THE AVOIDING OF DIVERSITIES
OF OPINIONS AND FOR THE
ESTABLISHING OF CONSENT
TOUCHING TRUE RELIGION

REPRINTED
BY COMMAND OF HIS MAJESTY
KING CHARLES I
WITH HIS ROYAL DECLARATION
PREFIXED THEREUNTO

HIS MAJESTY'S DECLARATION

BEING by God's Ordinance, according to Our just Title, Defender of the Faith, and Supreme Governor of the Church, within these Our Dominions, We hold it most agreeable to this Our Kingly Office, and Our own religious Zeal, to conserve and maintain the Church committed to Our Charge, in Unity of true Religion, and in the Bond of Peace; and not to suffer unnecessary Disputations, Altercations, or Questions to be raised, which may nourish Faction both in the Church and Commonwealth. We have therefore, upon mature Deliberation, and with the Advice of so many of Our Bishops as might conveniently be called together, thought fit to make this Declaration following:

That the Articles of the Church of England (which have been allowed and authorized heretofore, and which Our Clergy generally have subscribed unto) do contain the true Doctrine of the Church of England agreeable to God's Word: which We do therefore ratify and confirm, requiring all Our loving Subjects to continue in the uniform Profession thereof, and prohibiting the least difference from the said Articles; which to that End We command to be new printed, and this Our Declaration to be published therewith.

That We are Supreme Governor of the Church of England: And that if any difference arise about the external Policy, concerning the Injunctions, Canons, and other Constitutions whatsoever thereto belonging, the Clergy in their Convocation is to order and settle them, having first obtained leave under Our Broad Seal so to do: and We approving their said Ordinances and Constitutions; providing that none be made contrary to the Laws and Customs of the Land.

That out of Our Princely Care that the Churchmen may do the Work which is proper unto them, the Bishops and Clergy, from time to time in Convocation, upon their humble Desire, shall have Licence under Our Broad Seal to deliberate of, and to do all such Things, as, being made plain by them, and assented unto by Us, shall concern the settled Continuance of the Doctrine and Discipline of the Church of England now established; from which We will not endure any varying or departing in the least Degree.

That for the present, though some differences have been ill raised, yet We take comfort in this, that all Clergymen within Our Realm have always most willingly subscribed to the Articles established; which is an argument to Us, that they all agree in the true, usual, literal meaning of the said Articles; and that even in those curious points, in which the present differences lie, men of all sorts take the Articles of the Church of England to be for them; which is an argument again, that none of them intend any desertion of the Articles established.

That therefore in these both curious and unhappy differences, which have for so many hundred years, in different times and places, exercised the Church of Christ, We will, that all further curious search be laid aside, and these disputes shut up in God's promises, as they be generally set forth to us in the holy Scriptures, and the general meaning of the Articles of the Church of England according to them. And that no man hereafter shall either print, or preach, to draw the Article aside any way, but shall submit to it in the plain and full meaning thereof: and shall not put his own sense or comment to be the meaning of the Article, but shall take it in the literal and grammatical sense.

That if any publick Reader in either of Our Universities, or any Head or Master of a College, or any other person respectively in either of them, shall affix any new sense to any Article, or shall publickly read, determine, or hold any publick Disputation, or suffer any such to be held either way, in either the Universities or Colleges respectively; or if any Divine in the Universities shall preach or print any thing either way, other than is already established in Convocation with Our Royal Assent; he, or they the Offenders, shall be liable to Our displeasure, and the Church's censure in Our Commission Ecclesiastical, as well as any other: And We will see there shall be due Execution upon them.

ARTICLES OF RELIGION

A TABLE OF THE ARTICLES

I. *Of Faith in the Holy Trinity*

THERE is but one living and true God, everlasting, without body, parts, or passions; of infinite power, wisdom, and goodness; the Maker, and Preserver of all things both visible and invisible. And in unity of this Godhead there be three Persons, of one substance, power, and eternity; the Father, the Son, and the Holy Ghost.

II. *Of the Word or Son of God, which was made very Man*

THE Son, which is the Word of the Father, begotten from everlasting of the Father, the very and eternal God, and of one substance with the Father, took Man's nature in the womb of the blessed Virgin, of her substance: so that two whole and perfect Natures, that is to say, the Godhead and Manhood, were joined together in one Person, never to be divided, whereof is one Christ, very God, and very Man; who truly suffered, was crucified, dead, and buried, to reconcile his Father to us, and to be a sacrifice, not only for original guilt, but also for all actual sins of men.

III. *Of the going down of Christ into Hell*

AS Christ died for us, and was buried, so also is it to be believed, that he went down into Hell.

IV. *Of the Resurrection of Christ*

CHRIST did truly rise again from death, and took again his body, with flesh, bones, and all things appertaining to the perfection of Man's nature; wherewith he ascended into Heaven, and there sitteth, until he return to judge all Men at the last day.

V. *Of the Holy Ghost*

THE Holy Ghost, proceeding from the Father and the Son, is of one substance, majesty, and glory, with the Father and the Son, very and eternal God.

VI. *Of the Sufficiency of the holy Scriptures for salvation*

HOLY Scripture containeth all things necessary to salvation: so that whatsoever is not read therein, nor may be proved thereby, is not to be required of any man, that it should be believed as an article of the Faith, or be thought requisite or necessary to salvation. In the name of the holy Scripture we do understand those Canonical Books of the Old and New Testament, of whose authority was never any doubt in the Church.

Of the Names and Number of the Canonical Books

Genesis,	Exodus,	Leviticus,	Numbers,
Deuteronomy,	Joshua,	Judges,	Ruth,

The First Book of Samuel,
The Second Book of Samuel,
The First Book of Kings,
The Second Book of Kings,
The First Book of Chronicles,
The Second Book of Chronicles,
The First Book of Esdras,
The Second Book of Esdras,   The Book of Esther,
The Book of Job,   The Psalms,
The Proverbs,   Ecclesiastes or Preacher,
Cantica, or Songs of Solomon,
Four Prophets the greater,
Twelve Prophets the less.

And the other Books (as *Hierome* saith) the Church doth read for example of life and instruction of manners; but yet doth it not apply them to establish any doctrine; such are these following:

The Third Book of
Esdras,
The Fourth Book of
Esdras,
The Book of Tobias,
The Book of Judith,
The rest of the Book of
Esther,
The Book of Wisdom,
Jesus the Son of Sirach,

Baruch the Prophet,
The Song of the Three
Children,
The Story of Susanna,
Of Bel and the Dragon,
The Prayer of Manasses,
The First Book of
Maccabees,
The Second Book of
Maccabees.

All the Books of the New Testament, as they are commonly received, we do receive, and account them Canonical.

VII. *Of the Old Testament*

THE Old Testament is not contrary to the New: for both in the Old and New Testament everlasting life is offered to Mankind by Christ, who is the only Mediator between God and Man, being both God and Man. Wherefore they are not to be heard, which feign that the old Fathers did look only for transitory promises. Although the Law given from God by Moses, as touching Ceremonies and Rites, do not bind Christian men, nor the Civil precepts thereof ought of necessity to be received in any commonwealth; yet notwithstanding, no Christian man whatsoever is free from the obedience of the Commandments which are called Moral.

VIII. *Of the Three Creeds*

THE Three Creeds, *Nicene* Creed, *Athanasius's* Creed, and that which is commonly called the *Apostles'* Creed, ought thoroughly to be received and believed: for they may be proved by most certain warrants of holy Scripture.

IX. *Of Original or Birth-sin*

ORIGINAL Sin standeth not in the following of *Adam*, (as the *Pelagians* do vainly talk;) but it is the fault and corruption of the Nature of every man, that naturally is ingendered of the offspring of *Adam*; whereby man is very far gone from original righteousness, and is of his own nature inclined to evil, so that the flesh lusteth always contrary to the spirit; and therefore in every person born into this world, it deserveth God's wrath and damnation. And this infection of nature doth remain, yea in them that are regenerated; whereby the lust of the flesh, called in the Greek, *Φρόνημα σαρκός*, which some do expound the wisdom, some sensuality, some the affection, some the desire, of the flesh, is not subject to the Law of God. And although there is no condemnation for them that believe and are baptized, yet the Apostle doth confess, that concupiscence and lust hath of itself the nature of sin.

X. *Of Free-Will*

THE condition of Man after the fall of *Adam* is such, that he cannot turn and prepare himself, by his own natural strength and good works, to faith, and calling upon God: Wherefore we have no power to do good works pleasant and acceptable to God, without the grace of God by Christ preventing us, that we may have a good will, and working with us, when we have that good will.

XI. *Of the Justification of Man*

WE are accounted righteous before God, only for the merit of our Lord and Saviour Jesus Christ by Faith, and not for our own works or deservings: Wherefore, that we are justified by Faith only is a most wholesome Doctrine, and very full of comfort, as more largely is expressed in the Homily of Justification.

XII. *Of Good Works*

ALBEIT that Good Works, which are the fruits of Faith, and follow after Justification, cannot put away our sins, and endure the severity of God's Judgement; yet are they pleasing and acceptable to God in Christ, and do spring out necessarily of a true and lively Faith; insomuch that by them a lively Faith may be as evidently known as a tree discerned by the fruit.

XIII. *Of Works before Justification*

WORKS done before the grace of Christ, and the Inspiration of his Spirit, are not pleasant to God, forasmuch as they spring not of faith in Jesus Christ, neither do they make men meet to receive grace, or (as the School-authors say) deserve grace of congruity: yea rather, for that they are not done as God hath willed and commanded them to be done, we doubt not but they have the nature of sin.

XIV. *Of Works of Supererogation*

VOLUNTARY Works besides, over, and above, God's Commandments, which they call Works of Supererogation, cannot be taught without arrogancy and impiety: for by them men do declare, that they do not only render unto God as much as they are bound to do, but that they do more for his sake, than of bounden duty is required: whereas Christ saith plainly, When ye have done all that are commanded to you, say, We are unprofitable servants.

XV. *Of Christ alone without Sin*

CHRIST in the truth of our nature was made like unto us in all things, sin only except, from which he was clearly void, both in his flesh, and in his spirit. He came to be the Lamb without spot, who, by sacrifice of himself once made, should take away the sins of the world, and sin, as Saint *John* saith, was not in him. But all we the rest, although baptized, and born again in Christ, yet offend in many things; and if we say we have no sin, we deceive ourselves, and the truth is not in us.

XVI. *Of Sin after Baptism*

NOT every deadly sin willingly committed after Baptism is sin against the Holy Ghost, and unpardonable. Wherefore the grant of repentance is not to be denied to such as fall into sin after Baptism. After we have received the Holy Ghost, we may depart from grace given, and fall into sin, and by the grace of God we may arise again, and amend our lives. And therefore they are to be condemned, which say, they can no more sin as long as they live here, or deny the place of forgiveness to such as truly repent.

XVII. *Of Predestination and Election*

PREDESTINATION to Life is the everlasting purpose of God, whereby (before the foundations of the world were laid) he hath constantly decreed by his counsel secret to us, to deliver from curse and damnation those whom he hath chosen in Christ out of mankind, and to bring them by Christ to everlasting salvation, as vessels made to honour. Wherefore, they which be endued with so excellent a benefit of God be called according to God's purpose by his Spirit working in due season: they through Grace obey the calling: they be justified freely: they be made sons of God by adoption: they be made like the image of his only-begotten Son Jesus Christ: they walk religiously in good works, and at length, by God's mercy, they attain to everlasting felicity.

As the godly consideration of Predestination, and our Election in Christ, is full of sweet, pleasant, and unspeakable comfort to godly persons, and such as feel in themselves the working of the Spirit of Christ, mortifying the works of the flesh, and their earthly members, and drawing up their mind to high and heavenly things, as well because it doth greatly establish and confirm their faith of eternal Salvation to be enjoyed through Christ, as because it doth fervently kindle their love towards God: So, for curious and carnal persons, lacking the Spirit of Christ, to have continually before their eyes the sentence of God's Predestination, is a most dangerous downfal, whereby the Devil doth thrust them either into desperation, or into wretchlessness of most unclean living, no less perilous than desperation.

Furthermore, we must receive God's promises in such wise, as they be generally set forth to us in holy Scripture: and, in our doings, that Will of God is to be followed, which we have expressly declared unto us in the Word of God.

XVIII. *Of obtaining eternal Salvation only by the Name of Christ*

THEY also are to be had accursed that presume to say, That every man shall be saved by the Law or Sect which he professeth, so that he be diligent to frame his life according to that Law, and the light of Nature. For holy Scripture doth set out unto us only the Name of Jesus Christ, whereby men must be saved.

XIX. *Of the Church*

THE visible Church of Christ is a congregation of faithful men, in the which the pure Word of God is preached, and the Sacraments be duly ministered according to Christ's ordinance in all those things that of necessity are requisite to the same.

As the Church of *Jerusalem*, *Alexandria*, and *Antioch*, have erred; so also the Church of *Rome* hath erred, not only in their living and manner of Ceremonies, but also in matters of Faith.

XX. *Of the Authority of the Church*

THE Church hath power to decree Rites or Ceremonies, and authority in Controversies of Faith: And yet it is not lawful for the Church to ordain any thing that is contrary to God's Word written, neither may it so expound one place of Scripture, that it be repugnant to another. Wherefore, although the Church be a witness and a keeper of holy Writ, yet, as it ought not to decree any thing against the same, so besides the same ought it not to enforce any thing to be believed for necessity of Salvation.

XXI. *Of the Authority of General Councils*

GENERAL Councils may not be gathered together without the commandment and will of Princes. And when they be gathered together, (forasmuch as they be an assembly of men, whereof all be not governed with the Spirit and Word of God,) they may err, and sometimes have erred, even in things pertaining unto God. Wherefore things ordained by them as necessary to salvation have neither strength nor authority, unless it may be declared that they be taken out of holy Scripture.

XXII. *Of Purgatory*

THE Romish Doctrine concerning Purgatory, Pardons, Worshipping, and Adoration, as well of Images as of Reliques, and also invocation of Saints, is a fond thing vainly invented, and grounded upon no warranty of Scripture, but rather repugnant to the Word of God.

XXIII. *Of Ministering in the Congregation*

IT is not lawful for any man to take upon him the office of publick preaching, or ministering the Sacraments in the Congregation, before he be lawfully called, and sent to execute the same. And those we ought to judge lawfully called and sent, which be chosen and called to this work by men who have publick authority given unto them in the Congregation, to call and send Ministers into the Lord's vineyard.

XXIV. *Of speaking in the Congregation in such a tongue as the people understandeth*

IT is a thing plainly repugnant to the Word of God, and the custom of the Primitive Church, to have publick Prayer in the Church, or to minister the Sacraments in a tongue not understanded of the people.

XXV. *Of the Sacraments*

SACRAMENTS ordained of Christ be not only badges or tokens of Christian men's profession, but rather they be certain sure witnesses, and effectual signs of grace, and God's good will towards us, by the which he doth work invisibly in us, and doth not only quicken, but also strengthen and confirm our Faith in him.

There are two Sacraments ordained of Christ our Lord in the Gospel, that is to say, Baptism, and the Supper of the Lord.

Those five commonly called Sacraments, that is to say, Confirmation, Penance, Orders, Matrimony, and extreme Unction, are not to be counted for Sacraments of the Gospel, being such as have grown partly of the corrupt following of the Apostles, partly are states of life allowed in the Scriptures; but yet have not like nature of Sacraments with Baptism, and the Lord's Supper, for that they have not any visible sign or ceremony ordained of God.

The Sacraments were not ordained of Christ to be gazed upon, or to be carried about, but that we should duly use them. And in such only as worthily receive the same they have a wholesome effect or operation: but they that receive them unworthily purchase to themselves damnation, as Saint *Paul* saith.

XXVI. *Of the Unworthiness of the Ministers, which hinders not the effect of the Sacrament*

ALTHOUGH in the visible Church the evil be ever mingled with the good, and sometimes the evil have chief authority in the Ministration of the Word and Sacraments, yet forasmuch as they do not the same in their own name, but in Christ's, and do minister by his commission and authority, we may use their Ministry, both in hearing the Word of God, and in receiving of the Sacraments. Neither is the effect of Christ's ordinance taken away by their wickedness, nor the grace of God's gifts diminished from such as by faith and rightly do receive the Sacraments ministered unto them; which be effectual, because of Christ's institution and promise, although they be ministered by evil men.

Nevertheless, it appertaineth to the discipline of the Church, that inquiry be made of evil Ministers, and that they be accused by those that have knowledge of their offences; and finally being found guilty, by just judgement be deposed.

XXVII. *Of Baptism*

BAPTISM is not only a sign of profession, and mark of difference, whereby Christian men are discerned from others that be not christened, but it is also a sign of Regeneration or new Birth, whereby, as by an instrument, they that receive Baptism rightly are grafted into the Church; the promises of forgiveness of sin, and of our adoption to be the sons of God by the Holy Ghost, are visibly signed and sealed; Faith is confirmed, and

Grace increased by virtue of prayer unto God. The Baptism of young Children is in any wise to be retained in the Church, as most agreeable with the institution of Christ.

XXVIII. *Of the Lord's Supper*

THE Supper of the Lord is not only a sign of the love that Christians ought to have among themselves one to another; but rather is a Sacrament of our Redemption by Christ's death: insomuch that to such as rightly, worthily, and with faith, receive the same, the Bread which we break is a partaking of the Body of Christ; and likewise the Cup of Blessing is a partaking of the Blood of Christ.

Transubstantiation (or the change of the substance of Bread and Wine) in the Supper of the Lord, cannot be proved by holy Writ; but is repugnant to the plain words of Scripture, overthroweth the nature of a Sacrament, and hath given occasion to many superstitions.

The Body of Christ is given, taken, and eaten, in the Supper, only after an heavenly and spiritual manner. And the mean whereby the Body of Christ is received and eaten in the Supper is Faith.

The Sacrament of the Lord's Supper was not by Christ's ordinance reserved, carried about, lifted up, or worshipped.

XXIX. *Of the Wicked which eat not the Body of Christ in the use of the Lord's Supper*

THE Wicked, and such as be void of a lively faith, although they do carnally and visibly press with their teeth (as Saint *Augustine* saith) the Sacrament of the Body and Blood of Christ, yet in no wise are they partakers of Christ: but rather, to their condemnation, do eat and drink the sign or Sacrament of so great a thing.

XXX. *Of both kinds*

THE Cup of the Lord is not to be denied to the Lay-people: for both the parts of the Lord's Sacrament, by Christ's ordinance and commandment, ought to be ministered to all Christian men alike.

XXXI. *Of the one Oblation of Christ finished upon the Cross*

THE Offering of Christ once made is that perfect redemption, propitiation, and satisfaction, for all the sins of the whole world, both original and actual; and there is none other satisfaction for sin, but that alone. Wherefore the sacrifices of Masses, in the which it was commonly said, that the Priest did offer Christ for the quick and the dead, to have remission of pain or guilt, were blasphemous fables, and dangerous deceits.

XXXII. *Of the Marriage of Priests*

BISHOPS, Priests, and Deacons, are not commanded by God's Law, either to vow the estate of single life, or to abstain from marriage: therefore it is lawful for them, as for all other Christian men, to marry at their own discretion, as they shall judge the same to serve better to godliness.

XXXIII. *Of Excommunicate Persons, how they are to be avoided*

THAT person which by open denunciation of the Church is rightly cut off from the unity of the Church, and excommunicated, ought to be taken of the whole multitude of the faithful, as an Heathen and Publican, until he be openly reconciled by penance, and received into the Church by a Judge that hath authority thereunto.

XXXIV. *Of the Traditions of the Church*

IT is not necessary that Traditions and Ceremonies be in all places one, and utterly like; for at all times they have been divers, and may be changed according to the diversities of countries, times, and men's manners, so that nothing be ordained against God's Word. Whosoever through his private judgement, willingly and purposely, doth openly break the traditions and ceremonies of the Church, which be not repugnant to the Word of God, and be ordained and approved by common authority, ought to be rebuked openly, (that others may fear to do the like,) as he that offendeth against the common order of the Church, and hurteth the authority of the Magistrate, and woundeth the consciences of the weak brethren.

Every particular or national Church hath authority to ordain, change, and abolish, ceremonies or rites of the Church ordained only by man's authority, so that all things be done to edifying.

XXXV. *Of the Homilies*

THE second Book of Homilies, the several titles whereof we have joined under this Article, doth contain a godly and whole-some Doctrine, and necessary for these times, as doth the former Book of Homilies, which were set forth in the time of *Edward* the Sixth; and therefore we judge them to be read in Churches by the Ministers, diligently and distinctly, that they may be understanded of the people.

Of the Names of the Homilies

1. Of the right Use of the Church.
2. Against peril of Idolatry.
3. Of repairing and keeping clean of Churches.
4. Of good Works: first of Fasting.
5. Against Gluttony and Drunkenness.
6. Against Excess of Apparel.
7. Of Prayer.
8. Of the Place and Time of Prayer.
9. That Common Prayers and Sacraments ought to be minis-tered in a known tongue.
10. Of the reverend estimation of God's Word.
11. Of Alms-doing.
12. Of the Nativity of Christ.
13. Of the Passion of Christ.
14. Of the Resurrection of Christ.
15. Of the worthy receiving of the Sacrament of the Body and Blood of Christ.
16. Of the Gifts of the Holy Ghost.
17. For the Rogation-days.
18. Of the State of Matrimony.
19. Of Repentance.
20. Against Idleness.
21. Against Rebellion.

XXXVI. *Of Consecration of Bishops and Ministers*

THE Book of Consecration of Archbishops and Bishops, and Ordering of Priests and Deacons, lately set forth in the time of *Edward* the Sixth, and confirmed at the same time by authority of Parliament, doth contain all things necessary to such Consecration and Ordering: neither hath it any thing, that of itself is superstitious and ungodly. And therefore whosoever are consecrated or ordered according to the Rites of that Book, since the second year of the forenamed King *Edward* unto this time, or hereafter shall be consecrated or ordered according to the same Rites; we decree all such to be rightly, orderly, and lawfully consecrated and ordered.

XXXVII. *Of the Civil Magistrates*

THE King's Majesty hath the chief power in this Realm of *England*, and other his Dominions, unto whom the chief Government of all Estates of this Realm, whether they be Ecclesiastical or Civil, in all causes doth appertain, and is not, nor ought to be, subject to any foreign Jurisdiction.

Where we attribute to the King's Majesty the chief government, by which Titles we understand the minds of some slanderous folks to be offended; we give not to our Princes the ministering either of God's Word, or of the Sacraments, the which thing the Injunctions also lately set forth by *Elizabeth* our Queen do most plainly testify; but that only prerogative, which we see to have been given always to all godly Princes in holy Scriptures by God himself; that is, that they should rule all estates and degrees committed to their charge by God, whether they be Ecclesiastical or Temporal, and restrain with the civil sword the stubborn and evil-doers.

The Bishop of *Rome* hath no jurisdiction in this Realm of *England*.

The Laws of the Realm may punish Christian men with death, for heinous and grievous offences.

It is lawful for Christian men, at the commandment of the Magistrate, to wear weapons, and serve in the wars.

XXXVIII. *Of Christian men's Goods, which are not common*

THE Riches and Goods of Christians are not common, as touching the right, title, and possession of the same, as certain Anabaptists do falsely boast. Notwithstanding, every man ought, of such things as he possesseth, liberally to give alms to the poor, according to his ability.

XXXIX. *Of a Christian man's Oath*

AS we confess that vain and rash Swearing is forbidden Christian men by our Lord Jesus Christ, and *James* his Apostle, so we judge, that Christian Religion doth not prohibit, but that a man may swear when the Magistrate requireth, in a cause of faith and charity, so it be done according to the Prophet's teaching, in justice, judgement, and truth.

THE RATIFICATION

THIS Book of Articles before rehearsed, is again approved, and allowed to be holden and executed within the Realm, by the assent and consent of our Sovereign Lady ELIZABETH, by the grace of God, of England, France, and Ireland, Queen, Defender of the Faith, &c. Which Articles were deliberately read, and confirmed again by the subscription of the hands of the Archbishop and Bishops of the Upper-house, and by the subscription of the whole Clergy of the Nether-house in their Convocation, in the Year of our Lord 1571.

A TABLE OF
KINDRED AND AFFINITY

WHEREIN WHOSOEVER ARE RELATED ARE FORBIDDEN BY THE CHURCH OF ENGLAND TO MARRY TOGETHER

A man may not marry his:	*A woman may not marry her:*
Mother	Father
Daughter	Son
Father's mother	Father's father
Mother's mother	Mother's father
Son's daughter	Son's son
Daughter's daughter	Daughter's son
Sister	Brother
Father's daughter	Father's son
Mother's daughter	Mother's son
Wife's mother	Husband's father
Wife's daughter	Husband's son
Father's wife	Mother's husband
Son's wife	Daughter's husband
Father's father's wife	Father's mother's husband
Mother's father's wife	Mother's mother's husband
Wife's father's mother	Husband's father's father
Wife's mother's mother	Husband's mother's father
Wife's son's daughter	Husband's son's son
Wife's daughter's daughter	Husband's daughter's son
Son's son's wife	Son's daughter's husband
Daughter's son's wife	Daughter's daughter's husband
Father's sister	Father's brother
Mother's sister	Mother's brother
Brother's daughter	Brother's son
Sister's daughter	Sister's son

APPENDIX 1

THE SUPPER OF THE LORD AND THE HOLY COMMUNION

COMMONLY CALLED

THE MASS

THE ORDER FOR THE BURIAL OF THE DEAD

[From *The Book of Common Prayer*, 1549]

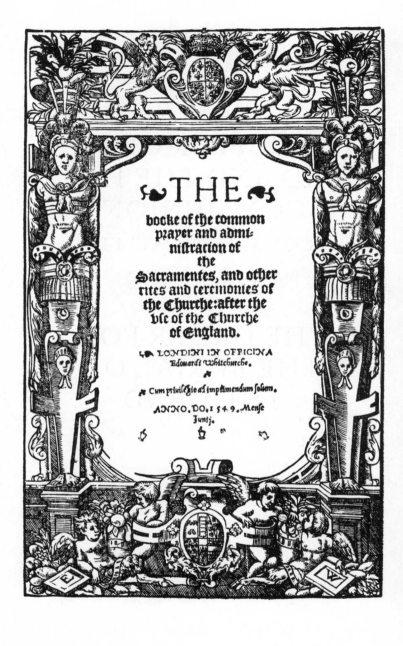

THE

booke of the common
prayer and admi-
nistracion of
the
Sacramentes, and other
rites and ceremonies of
the Churche: after the
vse of the Churche
of England.

LONDINI IN OFFICINA
Edouardi VVhitchurche.

Cum priuilegio ad imprimendum solum.

ANNO. DO. 1 5 4 9. Mense
Iunij.

✠THE SUPPER OF THE LORD

AND

THE HOLY COMMUNION

COMMONLY CALLED

THE MASS

*S*O many as intend to be partakers of the holy Communion, shall signify their names to the Curate over night, or else in the morning, afore the beginning of Mattins, or immediately after.

¶ *And if any of those be an open and notorious evil liver, so that the congregation by him is offended, or have done any wrong to his neighbours by word or deed; the Curate shall call him and advertise him in any wise not to presume to the Lord's Table, until he have openly declared himself to have truly repented and amended his former naughty life, that the congregation may thereby be satisfied, which afore were offended; and that he have recompensed the parties, whom he hath done wrong unto, or at the least be in full purpose so to do, as soon as he conveniently may.*

¶ *The same order shall the Curate use with those betwixt whom he perceiveth malice and hatred to reign; not suffering them to be partakers of the Lord's Table, until he know them to be reconciled. And if one of the parties so at variance be content to forgive from the bottom of his heart all that the other hath trespassed against him, and to make amends for that he himself hath offended; and the other party will not be persuaded to a godly unity, but remain still in his frowardness and malice: the Minister in that case ought to admit the penitent person to the holy Communion, and not him that is obstinate.*

¶ *Upon the day, and at the time appointed for the ministration of the holy Communion, the Priest that shall execute the holy ministry, shall put upon him the vesture appointed for that ministration, that is to say, a white Albe plain, with a Vestment or Cope. And where there be many Priests, or Deacons, there so many shall be ready to help the Priest in the ministration, as shall be requisite; and shall have upon them likewise the vestures appointed for their ministry, that is to say, Albes with Tunacles. Then shall the Clerks sing in English, for the Office or Introit, (as they call it,) a Psalm appointed for that day.*

The Priest, standing humbly afore the midst of the Altar, shall say the Lord's Prayer, with this Collect.

ALMIGHTY God, unto whom all hearts be open, and all desires known, and from whom no secrets are hid; Cleanse the thoughts of our hearts by the inspiration of thy Holy Spirit, that we may perfectly love thee, and worthily magnify thy holy Name; through Christ our Lord. Amen.

Then shall he say a Psalm appointed for the Introit: which Psalm ended, the Priest shall say, or else the Clerks shall sing,

iii. Lord have mercy upon us.
iii. Christ have mercy upon us.
iii. Lord have mercy upon us.

Then the Priest, standing at God's board, shall begin,

Glory be to God on high.

The Clerks.

And in earth peace, good will towards men.

We praise thee, we bless thee, we worship thee, we glorify thee, we give thanks to thee for thy great glory, O Lord God, heavenly King, God the Father Almighty.

O Lord, the only-begotten Son, Jesu Christ, O Lord God, Lamb of God, Son of the Father, that takest away the sins of the world, have mercy upon us: thou that takest away the sins of the world, receive our prayer.

Thou that sittest at the right hand of God the Father, have mercy upon us; for thou only art holy, thou only art the Lord. Thou only, (O Christ,) with the Holy Ghost, art most high in the glory of God the Father. Amen.

Then the Priest shall turn him to the people, and say,
The Lord be with you.

The Answer.
And with thy spirit.

The Priest.
Let us pray.

Then shall follow the Collect of the day, with one of these two Collects following, for the king.

ALMIGHTY God, whose kingdom is everlasting, and power infinite; Have mercy upon the whole congregation; and so rule the heart of thy chosen servant Edward the Sixth, our king and governor, that he (knowing whose minister he is) may above all things seek thy honour and glory: and that we, his subjects, (duly considering whose authority he hath,) may faithfully serve, honour, and humbly obey him, in thee, and for thee, according to thy blessed word and ordinance; through Jesus Christ our Lord, who with thee and the Holy Ghost liveth and reigneth, ever one God, world without end, Amen.

ALMIGHTY and everlasting God, we be taught by thy holy word, that the hearts of kings are in thy rule and governance, and that thou dost dispose and turn them as it seemeth best to thy godly wisdom: we humbly beseech thee so to dispose and govern the heart of Edward the Sixth, thy servant, our king and governor, that in all his thoughts, words, and works, he may ever seek thy honour and glory, and study to preserve thy people committed to his charge, in wealth, peace, and godliness: Grant this, O merciful Father, for thy dear Son's sake, Jesus Christ our Lord. Amen.

The Collects ended, the Priest, or he that is appointed, shall read the Epistle in a place assigned for the purpose, saying,

The Epistle of Saint Paul, written in the — chapiter of — to the —

The Minister then shall read the Epistle. Immediately after the Epistle ended, the Priest, or one appointed to read the Gospel, shall say,

The holy Gospel, written in the — chapiter of —

The Clerks and people shall answer,

Glory be to thee, O Lord.

The Priest or Deacon then shall read the Gospel. After the Gospel ended, the Priest shall begin,

I BELIEVE in One God.

The Clerks shall sing the rest.

The Father Almighty, Maker of heaven and earth, And of all things visible and invisible: And in one Lord Jesu Christ, the only-begotten Son of God, Begotten of his Father before all worlds, God of God, Light of Light, Very God of very God, Begotten, not made, Being of one Substance with the Father, By whom all things were made: Who for us men, and for our salvation, came down from heaven, And was incarnate by the Holy Ghost of the Virgin Mary, And was made man, And was crucified also for us under Poncius Pilate. He suffered and was buried, And the third day he arose again according to the Scriptures, And ascended into heaven, And sitteth at the right hand of the Father. And he shall come again with glory to judge both the quick and the dead.

And I believe in the Holy Ghost, the Lord and Giver of life, Who proceedeth from the Father and the Son, Who with the Father and the Son together is worshipped and glorified, Who spake by the prophets. And I believe one Catholic and Apostolic

Church. I acknowledge one Baptism for the remission of sins, And I look for the Resurrection of the dead, And the life of the world to come. Amen.

¶ *After the Creed ended, shall follow the Sermon or Homily, or some portion of one of the Homilies, as they shall be hereafter divided: wherein if the people be not exhorted to the worthy receiving of the holy Sacrament of the Body and Blood of our Saviour Christ, then shall the Curate give this exhortation to those that be minded to receive the same.*

DEARLY beloved in the Lord, ye that mind to come to the holy Communion of the Body and Blood of our Saviour Christ, must consider what S. Paul writeth to the Corinthians, how he exhorteth all persons diligently to try and examine themselves, before they presume to eat of that Bread and drink of that Cup. For as the benefit is great, if with a truly penitent heart and lively faith we receive that holy Sacrament; (for then we spiritually eat the flesh of Christ, and drink his Blood; then we dwell in Christ, and Christ in us; we be made one with Christ, and Christ with us;) so is the danger great, if we receive the same unworthily. For then we become guilty of the Body and Blood of Christ our Saviour; we eat and drink our own damnation, not considering the Lord's Body; we kindle God's wrath over us; we provoke him to plague us with divers diseases, and sundry kinds of death. Therefore, if any here be a blasphemer, advouterer, or be in malice, or envy, or in any other grievous crime, (except he be truly sorry therefore, and earnestly minded to leave the same vices, and do trust himself to be reconciled to Almighty God, and in charity with all the world,) let him bewail his sins, and not come to that holy Table, lest after the taking of that most blessed Bread, the devil enter into him, as he did into Judas, to fill him full of all iniquity, and bring him to destruction, both of body and soul. Judge therefore yourselves, (brethren,) that ye be not judged of the Lord. Let your mind be without desire to sin; repent you truly for your sins past; have an earnest and lively faith in Christ our Saviour; be in perfect charity with all men; so shall ye be meet partakers of those holy Mysteries. And above all things ye must give most humble and hearty thanks to God the Father, the Son, and the Holy Ghost, for the redemption of the world by the Death and Passion of our Saviour Christ, both God and man; who did humble himself, even to the death upon the Cross, for us, miserable sinners; which lay in darkness and shadow of death, that he might make us the children of God, and exalt us to everlasting life. And to the end that we should alway remember the exceeding love of our Master, and only Saviour, Jesu Christ, thus dying for us, and the innumerable benefits which (by his precious blood-shedding) he hath obtained to us; he hath left in those holy Mysteries, as a pledge of his love, and a continual remembrance of the same, his own blessed Body and precious Blood, for us to feed upon spiritually, to our endless comfort and consolation. To him therefore, with the Father and the Holy Ghost, let us give (as we are most bounden) continual thanks; submitting ourselves wholly to his holy will and pleasure, and studying to serve him in true holiness and righteousness all the days of our life. Amen.

¶ *In Cathedral Churches, or other places where there is daily Communion, it shall be sufficient to read this exhortation above written once in a month. And in Parish Churches, upon the week days, it may be left unsaid.*

¶ *And if upon the Sunday or Holy-day the people be negligent to come to the Communion, then shall the Priest earnestly exhort his Parishioners to dispose themselves to the receiving of the holy Communion more diligently, saying these or like words unto them.*

DEAR friends, and you especially upon whose souls I have cure and charge, on — next I do intend, by God's grace, to offer to all such as shall be godly disposed the most comfortable Sacrament of the Body and Blood of Christ, to be taken of them in the remembrance of his most fruitful and glorious Passion: by the which Passion we have obtained remission of our sins, and be made partakers of the kingdom of heaven; whereof we be assured and ascertained, if we come to the said Sacrament with hearty repentance for our offences, stedfast faith in God's mercy, and earnest mind to obey God's will, and to offend no more. Wherefore our duty is to come to these holy Mysteries with most hearty thanks to be given to Almighty God for his infinite mercy and benefits given and bestowed upon us his unworthy servants, for whom he hath not only given his Body to death, and shed his Blood, but also doth vouchsafe, in a Sacrament and Mystery, to give us his said Body and Blood to feed upon spiritually. The which Sacrament being so divine and holy a thing, and so comfortable to them which receive it worthily, and so dangerous to them that will presume to take the same unworthily: my duty is to exhort you, in the mean season, to consider the greatness of the thing, and to search and examine your own consciences, and that not lightly, nor after the manner of dissimulers with God, but as they which should come to a most godly and heavenly banquet; not to come but in the marriage garment required of God in Scripture; that you may (so much as lieth in you) be found worthy to come to such a Table. The ways and means thereto is,

First, that you be truly repentant of your former evil life; and that you confess with an unfeigned heart to Almighty God, your sins and unkindness towards his Majesty committed, either by will, word, or deed, infirmity or ignorance; and that with inward sorrow and tears you bewail your offences, and require of Almighty God mercy and pardon, promising to him (from the bottom of your hearts) the amendment of your former life. And emonges all others, I am commanded of God especially to move and exhort you to reconcile yourselves to your neighbours, whom you have offended, or who hath offended you, putting out of your hearts all hatred and malice against them, and to be in love and charity with all the world, and to forgive other as you would that God should forgive you. And if any man have done wrong to any other, let him make satisfaction and due restitution of all lands and goods wrongfully taken away or withholden, before he come to God's board; or at the least be in full mind and purpose so to do, as soon as he is able; or else let him not come to this holy Table, thinking to deceive God, who seeth all men's hearts. For neither the Absolution of the Priest can any thing avail them, nor the receiving of this holy Sacrament doth any thing but increase their damnation. And if there be any of you whose conscience is troubled and grieved in any thing, lacking comfort or counsel, let him come to me, or to some other discreet and learned Priest, taught in the law of God, and confess and open his sin and grief secretly, that he may receive such ghostly counsel, advice, and comfort, that his conscience may be relieved, and that of us (as of the Ministers of God and of the Church) he may receive comfort and Absolution, to the satisfaction of his mind, and avoiding of all scruple and doubtfulness; requiring such as shall be satisfied with a general Confession not to be offended with them that do use, to their further satisfying, the auricular and secret Confession to the Priest; nor those also which think needful or convenient, for the quietness of their own consciences, particularly to open their sins to the Priest, to be offended with them that are satisfied with their humble confession to God, and the general Confession to the Church: but in all things to follow and keep the rule of charity; and every man to be satisfied with his own conscience, not judging other men's minds or consciences; whereas he hath no warrant of God's Word to the same.

¶ Then shall follow for the Offertory one or more of these sentences of holy Scripture, to be sung whiles the people do offer; or else one of them to be said by the Minister immediately afore the offering.

LET your light so shine before men, that they may see your good works, and glorify your Father which is in heaven.

Math. v.

Lay not up for yourselves treasure upon the earth, where the rust and moth doth corrupt, and where thieves break through and steal: but lay up for yourselves treasures in heaven, where neither rust nor moth doth corrupt, and where thieves do not break through nor steal. *Math.* vi.

Whatsoever you would that men should do unto you, even so do you unto them: for this is the law and the prophets.

Math. vii.

Not every one that saith unto me, Lord, Lord, shall enter into the kingdom of heaven: but he that doeth the will of my Father which is in heaven. *Math.* vii.

Zache stood forth, and said unto the Lord, Behold, Lord, the half of my goods I give to the poor; and if I have done any wrong to any man, I restore four-fold. *Luc.* xix.

Who goeth a warfare at any time at his own cost? who planteth a vineyard, and eateth not of the fruit thereof? or who feedeth a flock, and eateth not of the milk of the flock? *i. Cor.* ix.

If we have sown unto you spiritual things, is it a great matter if we shall reap your worldly things? *i. Cor.* ix.

Do ye not know, that they which minister about holy things live of the sacrifice? they which wait of the altar are partakers with the altar? Even so hath the Lord also ordained that they which preach the gospel should live of the gospel. *i. Cor.* ix.

He which soweth little shall reap little; and he that soweth plenteously shall reap plenteously. Let every man do according as he is disposed in his heart; not grudgingly or of necessity: for God loveth a cheerful giver. *ii. Cor.* ix.

Let him that is taught in the word minister unto him that teacheth in all good things. Be not deceived; God is not mocked: for whatsoever a man soweth, that shall he reap. *Gala.* vi.

While we have time, let us do good unto all men, and specially unto them which are of the household of faith. *Gala.* vi.

Godliness is great riches, if a man be contented with that he hath. For we brought nothing into the world, neither may we carry any thing out. *i. Timo.* vi.

Charge them which are rich in this world, that they be ready to give, and glad to distribute; laying up in store for themselves a good foundation against the time to come, that they may attain eternal life. *i. Timo.* vi.

God is not unrighteous that he will forget your works and labour that proceedeth of love, which love ye have shewed for his Name's sake, which have ministered unto the saints and yet do minister. *Hebre.* vi.

To do good and to distribute forget not, for with such sacrifices God is pleased. *Hebre.* xiii.

Whoso hath this world's good, and seeth his brother have need, and shutteth up his compassion from him, how dwelleth the love of God in him? *i. John* iii.

Give almose of thy goods, and turn never thy face from any poor man, and then the face of the Lord shall not be turned away from thee. *Toby* iv.

Be merciful after thy power. If thou hast much, give plenteously; if thou hast little, do thy diligence gladly to give of that little; for so gatherest thou thyself a good reward in the day of necessity. *Toby* iv.

He that hath pity upon the poor lendeth unto the Lord; and look, what he layeth out shall be paid him again. *Prover.* xix.

Blessed be the man that provideth for the sick and needy; the Lord shall deliver him in the time of trouble. *Psal.* xli.

Where there be Clerks, they shall sing one or many of the sentences above written, according to the length and shortness of the time that the people be offering.

In the mean time, whiles the Clerks do sing the Offertory, so many as are disposed shall offer to the poor men's box every one according to his habilitie and charitable mind. And at the offering days appointed, every man and woman shall pay to the Curate the due and accustomed offerings.

Then so many as shall be partakers of the Holy Communion shall tarry still in the Quire, or in some convenient place nigh the Quire, the men on the one side, and the women on the other side. All other (that mind not to receive the said Holy Communion) shall depart out of the Quire, except the Ministers and Clerks.

Then shall the Minister take so much Bread and Wine as shall suffice for the persons appointed to receive the Holy Communion, laying the Bread upon the Corporas, or else in the Paten, or in some other comely thing prepared for that purpose: and putting the Wine into the Chalice, or else in some fair or convenient cup prepared for that use, (if the Chalice will not serve,) putting thereto a little pure and clean Water, and

setting both the Bread and Wine upon the Altar. Then the
Priest shall say,

The Lord be with you.

Answer.

And with thy spirit.

Priest.

Lift up your hearts.

Answer.

We lift them up unto the Lord.

Priest.

Let us give thanks to our Lord God.

Answer.

It is meet and right so to do.

The Priest.

It is very meet, right, and our bounden duty, that we should
at all times and in all places give thanks to thee, O Lord, holy
Father, Almighty Everlasting God.

¶ *Here shall follow the proper Preface, according to the time,*
(if there be any specially appointed,) or else immediately shall
follow,

Therefore with Angels, &c.

✠PROPER PREFACES

¶ UPON CHRISTMAS DAY.

BECAUSE thou diddest give Jesus Christ thine only Son to be born as this day for us; who, by the operation of the Holy Ghost, was made very man of the substance of the Virgin Mary his Mother; and that without spot of sin, to make us clean from all sin. Therefore &c.

¶ UPON EASTER DAY.

BUT chiefly are we bound to praise thee for the glorious Resurrection of thy Son Jesus Christ our Lord: for he is the very Paschal Lamb, which was offered for us, and hath taken away the sin of the world; who by his Death hath destroyed death, and by his rising to life again hath restored to us everlasting Life. Therefore &c.

¶ UPON THE ASCENSION DAY.

THROUGH thy most dear beloved Son Jesus Christ our Lord; who, after his most glorious Resurrection, manifestly appeared to all his disciples, and in their sight ascended up into Heaven to prepare a place for us; that where he is, thither might we also ascend, and reign with him in glory. Therefore &c.

¶ UPON WHITSUNDAY.

THROUGH Jesus Christ our Lord; according to whose most true promise the Holy Ghost came down this day from Heaven with a sudden great sound, as it had been a mighty wind, in the likeness of fiery tongues, lighting upon the Apostles, to teach them, and to lead them to all truth, giving them both the gift of divers languages, and also boldness with fervent zeal constantly to preach the gospel unto all nations; whereby we are brought out of darkness and error into the clear light and true knowledge of thee, and of thy Son Jesus Christ. Therefore &c.

¶ UPON THE FEAST OF THE TRINITY.

IT is very meet, right, and our bounden duty, that we should at all times, and in all places, give thanks to thee, O Lord, Almighty, Everlasting God, which art One God, One Lord; not one only Person, but three Persons in One Substance. For that which we believe of the glory of the Father, the same we believe of the Son, and of the Holy Ghost, without any difference or inequality. Whom the Angels &c.

After which Preface shall follow immediately,

Therefore with Angels and Archangels, and with all the holy company of Heaven, we laud and magnify thy glorious Name: evermore praising thee, and saying,

¶ Holy, holy, holy, Lord God of hosts, Heaven and earth are full of thy glory. Osanna in the highest. Blessed is he that cometh in the Name of the Lord. Glory be to thee, O Lord, in the highest.

This the Clerks shall also sing.

¶ *When the Clerks have done singing, then shall the Priest or Deacon turn him to the people, and say,*

Let us pray for the whole state of Christ's Church.

¶ *Then the Priest, turning him to the Altar, shall say or sing, plainly and distinctly, this prayer following:*

ALMIGHTY and everliving God, which by thy holy Apostle hast taught us to make prayers and supplications, and to give

thanks for all men; We humbly beseech thee most mercifully to
receive these our prayers, which we offer unto thy divine Majesty; beseeching thee to inspire continually the universal Church
with the spirit of truth, unity, and concord: and grant, that all
they that do confess thy holy Name may agree in the truth of
thy holy Word, and live in unity and godly love. Specially we
beseech thee to save and defend thy servant Edward our king;
that under him we may be godly and quietly governed: and grant
unto his whole Council, and to all that be put in authority under
him, that they may truly and indifferently minister justice, to
the punishment of wickedness and vice, and to the maintenance
of God's true religion and virtue. Give grace (O heavenly
Father) to all Bishops, Pastors, and Curates, that they may both
by their life and doctrine set forth thy true and lively word, and
rightly and duly administer thy holy Sacraments. And to all thy
people give thy heavenly grace; that with meek heart and due
reverence, they may hear and receive thy holy Word, truly
serving thee in holiness and righteousness all the days of their
life. And we most humbly beseech thee of thy goodness (O
Lord) to comfort and succour all them, which in this transitory
life be in trouble, sorrow, need, sickness, or any other adversity.
And especially we commend unto thy merciful goodness this
congregation, which is here assembled in thy Name, to celebrate
the commemoration of the most glorious Death of thy Son.
And here we do give unto thee most high praise, and hearty
thanks, for the wonderful grace and virtue declared in all thy
Saints, from the beginning of the world; and chiefly in the glorious and most blessed Virgin Mary, Mother of thy Son Jesu
Christ our Lord and God; and in the holy Patriarchs, Prophets,
Apostles, and Martyrs, whose examples (O Lord) and stead-
fastness in thy faith, and keeping thy holy commandments,
grant us to follow. We commend unto thy mercy (O Lord) all
other thy servants, which are departed hence from us with the
sign of faith, and now do rest in the sleep of peace: grant unto
them, we beseech thee, thy mercy and everlasting peace; and
that, at the day of the general Resurrection, we and all they
which be of the Mystical Body of thy Son, may altogether be

set on his right hand, and hear that his most joyful voice: Come unto me, O ye that be blessed of my Father, and possess the kingdom, which is prepared for you from the beginning of the world. Grant this, O Father, for Jesus Christ's sake, our only Mediator and Advocate.

O God, heavenly Father, which of thy tender mercy diddest give thine only Son Jesu Christ to suffer death upon the Cross for our redemption; who made there (by his one oblation once offered) a full, perfect, and sufficient sacrifice, oblation, and satisfaction, for the sins of the whole world; and did institute, and in his holy Gospel command us to celebrate a perpetual memory of that his precious Death, until his coming again: Hear us (O merciful Father) we beseech thee; and with thy Holy Spirit and word vouchsafe to bl✠ess and sanc✠tify these thy gifts and creatures of Bread and Wine, that they may be unto us the Body and Blood of thy most dearly beloved Son Jesus Christ: Who, in the same night that he was betrayed, took Bread;* and when he had blessed, and given thanks, he brake it, and gave it to his disciples, saying, Take, eat; This is My Body which is given for you: Do this in remembrance of Me.

Likewise after supper he took the Cup,† and when he had given thanks, he gave it to them, saying, Drink ye all of this; this is My Blood of the new Testament, which is shed for you and for many for remission of sins: Do this, as oft as you shall drink it, in remembrance of Me.

These words before rehearsed are to be said, turning still to the Altar, without any elevation or shewing the Sacrament to the people.

WHEREFORE, O Lord and heavenly Father, according to the institution of thy dearly beloved Son our Saviour Jesu Christ, we thy humble servants do celebrate and make here before thy divine Majesty, with these thy holy gifts, the memorial which thy Son hath willed us to make; having in remembrance his blessed Passion, mighty Resurrection, and glorious

* Here the Priest must take the Bread into his hands.
† Here the Priest shall take the Cup into his hands.

Ascension: rendering unto thee most hearty thanks for the innumerable benefits procured unto us by the same; entirely desiring thy fatherly goodness mercifully to accept this our Sacrifice of praise and thanksgiving; most humbly beseeching thee to grant, that by the Merits and Death of thy Son Jesus Christ, and through faith in his Blood, we and all thy whole Church may obtain remission of our sins, and all other benefits of his Passion. And here we offer and present unto thee (O Lord) ourself, our souls and bodies, to be a reasonable, holy, and lively sacrifice unto thee; humbly beseeching thee, that whosoever shall be partakers of this holy Communion may worthily receive the most precious Body and Blood of thy Son Jesus Christ; and be fulfilled with thy grace and heavenly benediction, and made one body with thy Son Jesu Christ, that he may dwell in them, and they in him. And although we be unworthy (through our manifold sins) to offer unto thee any Sacrifice, yet we beseech thee to accept this our bounden duty and service, and command these our prayers and supplications, by the ministry of thy holy Angels, to be brought up into thy holy Tabernacle before the sight of thy divine Majesty; not weighing our merits, but pardoning our offences, through Christ our Lord; by whom, and with whom, in the unity of the Holy Ghost, all honour and glory be unto thee, O Father Almighty, world without end. Amen.

Let us pray.

As our Saviour Christ hath commanded and taught us, we are bold to say: Our Father, which art in heaven, hallowed be thy Name. Thy kingdom come. Thy will be done in earth, as it is in heaven. Give us this day our daily bread. And forgive us our trespasses, as we forgive them that trespass against us. And lead us not into temptation.

The answer.

But deliver us from evil. Amen.

Then shall the Priest say,

The peace of the Lord be alway with you.

The Clerks.

And with thy spirit.

The Priest.

Christ our Paschal Lamb is offered up for us once for all, when he bare our sins on his Body upon the Cross; for he is the very Lamb of God that taketh away the sins of the world: wherefore let us keep a joyful and holy feast with the Lord.

Here the Priest shall turn him toward those that come to the holy Communion, and shall say,

YOU that do truly and earnestly repent you of your sins to Almighty God, and be in love and charity with your neighbours, and intend to lead a new life, following the commandments of God, and walking from henceforth in his holy ways; Draw near, and take this holy Sacrament to your comfort; make your humble confession to Almighty God, and to his holy Church here gathered together in his Name, meekly kneeling upon your knees.

Then shall this general Confession be made, in the name of all those that are minded to receive the holy Communion, either by one of them, or else by one of the Ministers, or by the Priest himself, all kneeling humbly upon their knees.

ALMIGHTY God, Father of our Lord Jesus Christ, Maker of all things, Judge of all men; we knowledge and bewail our manifold sins and wickedness, which we, from time to time, most grievously have committed, by thought, word, and deed, against thy divine Majesty, provoking most justly thy wrath and indignation against us. We do earnestly repent, and be heartily sorry for these our misdoings; the remembrance of them is grievous unto us; the burthen of them is intolerable. Have mercy upon us, have mercy upon us, most merciful Father; for thy Son our Lord Jesus Christ's sake, forgive us all that is past; and grant that we may ever hereafter serve and please thee in newness of life, to the honour and glory of thy Name; through Jesus Christ our Lord.

Then shall the Priest stand up, and turning himself to the people, say thus:

ALMIGHTY God, our heavenly Father, who of his great mercy hath promised forgiveness of sins to all them which with hearty repentance and true faith turn unto him; Have mercy upon you; pardon and deliver you from all your sins; confirm and strengthen you in all goodness; and bring you to everlasting life; through Jesus Christ our Lord. Amen.

Then shall the Priest also say,

Hear what comfortable words our Saviour Christ saith to all that truly turn to him.

COME unto me all that travail, and be heavy laden, and I shall refresh you. So God loved the world, that he gave his only-begotten Son, to the end that all that believe in him should not perish, but have life everlasting.

Hear also what Saint Paul saith.

This is a true saying, and worthy of all men to be received, that Jesus Christ came into this world to save sinners.

Hear also what Saint John saith.

If any man sin, we have an Advocate with the Father, Jesus Christ the righteous; and he is the propitiation for our sins.

Then shall the Priest, turning him to God's board, kneel down, and say in the name of all them that shall receive the Communion, this prayer following:

WE do not presume to come to this thy Table (O merciful Lord) trusting in our own righteousness, but in thy manifold and great mercies: We be not worthy so much as to gather up the crumbs under thy Table; but thou art the same Lord whose property is always to have mercy: Grant us therefore (gracious Lord) so to eat the flesh of thy dear Son Jesus Christ, and to drink his Blood, in these holy Mysteries, that we may continually dwell in him, and he in us, that our sinful bodies may be made clean by his Body, and our souls washed through his most precious Blood. Amen.

¶ Then shall the Priest first receive the Communion in both kinds himself, and next deliver it to other Ministers, if any be there present, (that they may be ready to help the chief Minister,) and after to the people.

¶ And when he delivereth the Sacrament of the Body of Christ, he shall say to every one these words:

The Body of our Lord Jesus Christ, which was given for thee, preserve thy body and soul unto everlasting life.

And the Minister delivering the Sacrament of the Blood, and giving every one to drink once, and no more, shall say,

The Blood of our Lord Jesus Christ, which was shed for thee, preserve thy body and soul unto everlasting life.

If there be a Deacon or other Priest, then shall he follow with the Chalice; and as the Priest ministereth the Sacrament of the Body, so shall he (for more expedition) minister the Sacrament of the Blood, in form before written.

In the Communion time the Clerks shall sing,

ii. O Lamb of God, that takest away the sins of the world: Have mercy upon us.

O Lamb of God, that takest away the sins of the world: Grant us thy peace.

Beginning so soon as the Priest doth receive the holy Communion: and when the Communion is ended, then shall the Clerks sing the post-Communion.

¶ Sentences of holy Scripture to be said or sung, every day one, after the holy Communion, called the post-Communion.

IF any man will follow me, let him forsake himself, and take up his cross and follow me.   *Math.* xvi.

Whosoever shall endure unto the end, he shall be saved.
                                                    Mar. xiii.

Praised be the Lord God of Israel; for he hath visited and redeemed his people. Therefore let us serve him all the days of our life, in holiness and righteousness accepted before him.

Luc. i.

Happy are those servants whom the Lord (when he cometh) shall find waking. *Luc.* xii.

Be ye ready, for the Son of Man will come at an hour when ye think not. *Luc.* xii.

The servant that knoweth his master's will, and hath not prepared himself, neither hath done according to his will, shall be beaten with many stripes. *Luc.* xii.

The hour cometh, and now it is, when true worshippers shall worship the Father in spirit and truth. *John* iv.

Behold, thou art made whole; sin no more, lest any worse thing happen unto thee. *John* v.

If ye shall continue in my word, then are ye my very disciples; and ye shall know the truth, and the truth shall make you free.

John viii.

While ye have light, believe on the light, that ye may be the children of light. *John* xii.

He that hath my commandments, and keepeth them, the same is he that loveth me. *John* xiv.

If any man love me, he will keep my word; and my Father will love him, and we will come unto him, and dwell with him.

John xiv.

If ye shall bide in me, and my word shall abide in you, ye shall ask what ye will, and it shall be done to you. *John* xv.

Herein is my Father glorified, that ye bear much fruit, and become my disciples. *John* xv.

This is my commandment, that you love together, as I have loved you. *John* xv.

If God be on our side, who can be against us? which did not spare his own Son, but gave him for us all. *Roma.* viii.

Who shall lay any thing to the charge of God's chosen? it is God that justifieth; who is he that can condemn? *Roma.* viii.

The night is past, and the day is at hand; let us therefore cast away the deeds of darkness, and put on the armour of light.

Roma. xiii.

Christ Jesus is made of God unto us wisdom, and

righteousness, and sanctifying, and redemption: that (according as it is written) He which rejoiceth should rejoice in the Lord.

i. Corin. i.

Know ye not that ye are the temple of God, and that the Spirit of God dwelleth in you? If any man defile the temple of God, him shall God destroy.   *i. Corin.* iii.

Ye are dearly bought; therefore glorify God in your bodies, and in your spirits, for they belong to God.   *i. Corin.* vi.

Be you followers of God, as dear children; and walk in love, even as Christ loved us, and gave himself for us an offering and a sacrifice of a sweet savour to God.   *Ephes.* v.

Then the Priest shall give thanks to God, in the name of all them that have communicated, turning him first to the people, and saying,

The Lord be with you.

The Answer.

And with thy spirit.

The Priest.

Let us pray.

ALMIGHTY and everliving God, we most heartily thank thee, for that thou hast vouchsafed to feed us in these holy Mysteries, with the spiritual food of the most precious Body and Blood of thy Son our Saviour Jesus Christ; and hast assured us (duly receiving the same) of thy favour and goodness toward us; and that we be very members incorporate in thy Mystical Body, which is the blessed company of all faithful people, and heirs through hope of thy everlasting kingdom, by the merits of the most precious Death and Passion of thy dear Son. We therefore most humbly beseech thee, O heavenly Father, so to assist us with thy grace, that we may continue in that holy fellowship, and do all such good works as thou hast prepared for us to walk in; through Jesus Christ our Lord, to whom, with thee and the Holy Ghost, be all honour and glory, world without end.

Then the Priest, turning him to the people, shall let them depart with this blessing:

THE peace of God (which passeth all understanding) keep your hearts and minds in the knowledge and love of God, and of his Son Jesus Christ our Lord. And the blessing of God Almighty, the Father, the Son, and the Holy Ghost, be emonges you, and remain with you alway.

Then the people shall answer,

Amen.

Where there are no Clerks, there the Priest shall say all things appointed here for them to sing.

When the holy Communion is celebrate on the workday, or in private houses, then may be omitted the Gloria in Excelsis, the Creed, the Homily, and the exhortation, beginning,

Dearly beloved, &c.

Collects to be said after the Offertory, when there is no Communion, every such day one.

ASSIST us mercifully, O Lord, in these our supplications and prayers, and dispose the way of thy servants toward the attainment of everlasting salvation; that, emong all the changes and chances of this mortal life, they may ever be defended by thy most gracious and ready help; through Christ our Lord. Amen.

O ALMIGHTY Lord, and everliving God, vouchsafe, we beseech thee, to direct, sanctify, and govern, both our hearts and bodies, in the ways of thy laws, and in the works of thy commandments; that through thy most mighty protection, both here and ever, we may be preserved in body and soul; through our Lord and Saviour Jesus Christ. Amen.

GRANT, we beseech thee, Almighty God, that the words which we have heard this day with our outward ears, may through thy grace be so grafted inwardly in our hearts, that they may bring forth in us the fruit of good living, to the honour and praise of thy Name; through Jesus Christ our Lord. Amen.

PREVENT us, O Lord, in all our doings with thy most gracious favour, and further us with thy continual help; that in all our works begun, continued, and ended in thee, we may glorify thy holy Name, and finally by thy mercy obtain everlasting life; through &c.

ALMIGHTY God, the fountain of all wisdom, which knowest our necessities before we ask, and our ignorance in asking; We beseech thee to have compassion upon our infirmities; and those things, which for our unworthiness we dare not, and for our blindness we cannot ask, vouchsafe to give us, for the worthiness of thy Son Jesu Christ our Lord. Amen.

ALMIGHTY God, which hast promised to hear the petitions of them that ask in thy Son's Name; We beseech thee mercifully to incline thine ears to us that have made now our prayers and supplications unto thee; and grant that those things which we have faithfully asked according to thy will, may effectually be obtained, to the relief of our necessity, and to the setting forth of thy glory; through Jesus Christ our Lord.

For rain.

O GOD, heavenly Father, which by thy Son Jesu Christ hast promised to all them that seek thy kingdom, and the righteousness thereof, all things necessary to the bodily sustenance; Send us (we beseech thee) in this our necessity, such moderate rain and showers, that we may receive the fruits of the earth to our comfort and to thy honour; through Jesus Christ our Lord.

For fair weather.

O LORD God, which for the sin of man, didst once drown all the world, except eight persons, and afterward, of thy great mercy, didst promise never to destroy it so again; We humbly beseech thee, that although we for our iniquities have worthily deserved this plague of rain and waters, yet, upon our true repentance, thou wilt send us such weather whereby we may receive the fruits of the earth in due season, and learn both by thy punishment to amend our lives, and by the granting of our petition, to give thee praise and glory; through Jesu Christ our Lord.

¶ *Upon Wednesdays and Fridays the English Litany shall be said or sung in all places, after such form as is appointed by the king's majesty's Injunctions; or as is or shall be otherwise appointed by his Highness. And though there be none to communicate with the Priest, yet these days (after the Litany ended) the Priest shall put upon him a plain Albe or Surplice, with a Cope, and say all things at the Altar, (appointed to be said at the celebration of the Lord's Supper,) until after the Offertory: And then shall add one or two of the Collects afore written, as occasion shall serve, by his discretion. And then, turning him to the people, shall let them depart with the accustomed Blessing.*

And the same order shall be used all other days, whensoever the people be customably assembled to pray in the Church, and none disposed to communicate with the Priest.

Likewise in Chapels annexed, and all other places, there shall be no celebration of the Lord's Supper, except there be some to communicate with the Priest. And in such Chapels annexed, where the people hath not been accustomed to pay any holy Bread, there they must either make some charitable provision for the bearing of the charges of the Communion, or else (for receiving of the same) resort to their Parish Church.

For avoiding of all matters and occasion of dissension, it is meet that the Bread prepared for the Communion be made throughout all this Realm after one sort and fashion; that is to say, unleavened, and round, as it was afore, but without all manner of print, and something more larger and thicker than it was, so that it may be aptly divided in divers pieces; and every one shall be divided in two pieces at the least, or more, by the discretion of the Minister, and so distributed. And men must not think less to be received in part than in the whole, but in each of them the whole Body of our Saviour Jesu Christ.

And forsomuch as the Pastors and Curates within this Realm shall continually find at their costs and charges in their Cures, sufficient Bread and Wine for the Holy Communion, (as oft as their Parishioners shall be disposed for their spiritual comfort to receive the same,) it is therefore ordered, that in recompense of such costs and charges the Parishioners of every Parish shall offer every Sunday, at the time of the Offertory, the just valour and price of the holy loaf, (with all such money and other things as were wont to be offered with the same,) to the use of their Pastors and Curates, and that in such order and course as they were wont to find and pay the said holy loaf.

Also, that the receiving of the Sacrament of the blessed Body and Blood of Christ may be most agreeable to the institution thereof, and to the usage of the primitive Church; in all Cathedral and Collegiate Churches there shall always some communicate with the Priest that ministereth. And that the same may be also observed every where abroad in the country, some one at the least of that house in every Parish, to whom by course, after the ordinance herein made, it appertaineth to offer for the charges of the Communion, or some other whom they shall provide to offer for them, shall receive the holy Communion with the Priest: the which may be the better done, for that they know before when their course cometh, and may therefore dispose themselves to the worthy receiving of the Sacrament. And with him or them who doth so offer the charges of the Communion, all other who be then godly disposed thereunto, shall likewise receive the Communion. And by this means the Minister, having always some to communicate with him, may accordingly solemnize so high and holy Mysteries with all the Suffrages and due order appointed for the same. And the Priest on the week day shall forbear to celebrate the Communion, except he have some that will communicate with him.

Furthermore, every man and woman to be bound to hear and

be at the Divine Service, in the Parish Church where they be resident, and there with devout prayer, or godly silence and meditation, to occupy themselves; there to pay their Duties, to communicate once in the year at the least, and there to receive and take all other Sacraments and Rites in this Book appointed. And whosoever willingly, upon no just cause, doth absent themselves, or doth ungodly in the Parish Church occupy themselves; upon proof thereof, by the Ecclesiastical laws of the Realm to be excommunicate, or suffer other punishment, as shall to the Ecclesiastical Judge (according to his discretion) seem convenient.

And although it be read in ancient writers that the people many years past received at the Priest's hands the Sacrament of the Body of Christ in their own hands, and no commandment of Christ to the contrary; yet forasmuch as they many times conveyed the same secretly away, kept it with them, and diversely abused it to superstition and wickedness: lest any such thing hereafter should be attempted, and that an uniformity might be used throughout the whole Realm, it is thought convenient the people commonly receive the Sacrament of Christ's Body in their mouths, at the Priest's hand.

✠ THE ORDER FOR

THE BURIAL OF
THE DEAD

The Priest, meeting the Corpse at the Church stile, shall say,
or else the Priests and Clerks shall sing, and so go either into
the Church, or towards the Grave.

I AM the Resurrection and the life, (saith the Lord:) he that
believeth in me, yea, though he were dead, yet shall he live: and
whosoever liveth and believeth in me shall not die for ever.

John xi.

I KNOW that my Redeemer liveth, and that I shall rise out of
the earth in the last day, and shall be covered again with my
skin, and shall see God in my flesh: yea, and I myself shall
behold him, not with other but with these same eyes.　*Job.* xix.

WE brought nothing into this world, neither may we carry
any thing out of this world. The Lord giveth, and the Lord
taketh away. Even as it pleaseth the Lord, so cometh things to
pass. Blessed be the Name of the Lord.　　　ı *Timo.* vi. *Job.* i.

When they come at the Grave, whiles the Corpse is made ready
to be laid into the earth, the Priest shall say, or else the Priests
and Clerks shall sing,

MAN that is born of a woman hath but a short time to live,
and is full of misery. He cometh up, and is cut down, like a
flower; he flieth as it were a shadow, and never continueth in
one stay.　　　　　　　　　　　　　　　　　　　*Job.* ix.

¶ In the midst of life we be in death: of whom may we seek for
succour, but of thee, O Lord, which for our sins justly art
moved? Yet, O Lord God most holy, O Lord most mighty, O
holy and most merciful Saviour, deliver us not into the bitter
pains of eternal death. Thou knowest, Lord, the secrets of our

hearts; shut not up thy merciful eyes to our prayers; but spare us, Lord most holy, O God most mighty, O holy and merciful Saviour, thou most worthy Judge eternal, suffer us not, at our last hour, for any pains of death, to fall from thee.

Then the Priest, casting earth upon the Corpse, shall say,

I COMMEND thy soul to God the Father Almighty, and thy body to the ground; earth to earth, ashes to ashes, dust to dust; in sure and certain hope of resurrection to eternal life, through our Lord Jesus Christ; who shall change our vile body, that it may be like to his glorious body, according to the mighty working, whereby he is able to subdue all things to himself.

Then shall be said or sung,

I HEARD a voice from heaven, saying unto me: Write, Blessed are the dead which die in the Lord: even so saith the Spirit; that they rest from their labours.   *Apoc.* xiv.

Let us pray.

WE commend into thy hands of mercy (most merciful Father) the soul of this our brother departed, N. And his body we commit to the earth; beseeching thine infinite goodness to give us grace to live in thy fear and love, and to die in thy favour: that when the Judgment shall come, which thou hast committed to thy well-beloved Son, both this our brother and we may be found acceptable in thy sight, and receive that blessing which thy well-beloved Son shall then pronounce to all that love and fear thee, saying, Come, ye blessed children of my Father, receive the kingdom prepared for you before the beginning of the world. Grant this, merciful Father, for the honour of Jesu Christ our only Saviour, Mediator, and Advocate. Amen.

This prayer shall also be added.

ALMIGHTY God, we give thee hearty thanks for this thy servant, whom thou hast delivered from the miseries of this wretched world, from the body of death, and all temptation; and, as we trust, hast brought his soul, which he committed into thy holy hands, into sure consolation and rest. Grant, we beseech thee, that at the day of Judgment his soul, and all the souls of thy elect departed out of this life, may with us and we with them, fully receive thy promises, and be made perfect altogether through the glorious resurrection of thy Son Jesus Christ our Lord.

These Psalms, with other suffrages following, are to be said in the Church, either before or after the burial of the Corpse.

Dilexi, quoniam. Psal. cxvi.

I AM well pleased that the Lord hath heard the voice of my prayer.

That he hath enclined his ear unto me: therefore will I call upon him as long as I live.

The snares of death compassed me round about, and the pains of hell gat hold upon me: I shall find trouble and heaviness, and I shall call upon the Name of the Lord, (O Lord) I beseech thee, deliver my soul.

Gracious is the Lord, and righteous: yea, our God is merciful.

The Lord preserveth the simple: I was in misery, and he helped me.

Turn again then unto thy rest, O my soul: for the Lord hath rewarded thee.

And why? thou hast delivered my soul from death: mine eyes from tears, and my feet from falling.

I will walk before the Lord: in the land of the living.

I believed, and therefore will I speak: but I was sore troubled.

I said in my haste: all men are liars.

What reward shall I give unto the Lord: for all the benefits that he hath done unto me?

I will receive the cup of salvation: and call upon the Name of the Lord.

I will pay my vows now in the presence of all his people: right dear in the sight of the Lord is the death of his saints.

Behold (O Lord) how that I am thy servant: I am thy servant, and the son of thy handmaid; thou hast broken my bonds in sunder.

I will offer to thee the sacrifice of thanksgiving: and will call upon the Name of the Lord.

I will pay my vows unto the Lord in the sight of all his people: in the courts of the Lord's house, even in the midst of thee, O Hierusalem.

Glory be to the Father, &c.

As it was in the beginning, &c.

Domine, probasti. Psal. cxxxix.

O LORD, thou hast searched me out, and known me.

Thou knowest my down-sitting and mine up-rising: thou understandest my thoughts long before.

Thou art about my path and about my bed: and spiest out all my ways.

For lo, there is not a word in my tongue: but thou (O Lord) knowest it altogether.

Thou hast fashioned me behind and before: and laid thine hand upon me.

Such knowledge is too wonderful and excellent for me: I cannot attain unto it.

Whither shall I go then from thy Spirit: or whither shall I go then from thy Presence?

If I climb up into heaven, thou art there: if I go down to hell, thou art there also.

If I take the wings of the morning: and remain in the uttermost parts of the sea;

Even there also shall thy hand lead me: and thy right hand shall hold me.

If I say, Peradventure the darkness shall cover me: then shall my night be turned to day.

Yea, the darkness is no darkness with thee: but the night is all clear as the day, the darkness and light to thee are both alike.

For my reins are thine, thou hast covered me in my mother's womb, I will give thanks unto thee: for I am fearfully and wondrously made, marvellous are thy works, and that my soul knoweth right well.

My bones are not hid from thee: though I be made secretly, and fashioned beneath in the earth.

Thine eyes did see my substance, yet being unperfect: and in thy book were all my members written;

Which day by day were fashioned: when as yet there was none of them.

How dear are thy counsels unto me, O God: O how great is the sum of them.

If I tell them, they are moe in number than the sand: when I wake up I am present with thee.

Wilt thou not slay the wicked, O God: depart from me, ye bloodthirsty men.

For they speak unrighteously against thee: and thine enemies take thy Name in vain.

Do not I hate them, O Lord, that hate thee: and am not I grieved with those that rise up against thee?

Yea, I hate them right sore: even as though they were mine enemies.

Try me, O God, and seek the ground of mine heart: prove me, and examine my thoughts.

Look well if there be any way of wickedness in me: and lead me in the way everlasting.

Glory be to the Father, &c.

As it was in the beginning, &c.

Lauda, anima mea. Psal. cxlvi.

PRAISE the Lord, (O my soul;) while I live will I praise the Lord: yea, as long as I have any being I will sing praises unto my God.

O put not your trust in princes, nor in any child of man: for there is no help in them.

For when the breath of man goeth forth he shall turn again to his earth: and then all his thoughts perish.

Blessed is he that hath the God of Jacob for his help: and whose hope is in the Lord his God;

Which made heaven and earth, the sea, and all that therein is: which keepeth his promise for ever;

Which helpeth them to right that suffer wrong: which feedeth the hungry.

The Lord looseth men out of prison: the Lord giveth sight to the blind.

The Lord helpeth them up that are fallen: the Lord careth for the righteous.

The Lord careth for the strangers; he defendeth the fatherless and widow: as for the way of the ungodly, he turneth it upside down.

The Lord thy God, O Zion, shall be King for evermore: and throughout all generations.

Glory be to the Father, &c.

As it was in the beginning, &c.

Then shall follow this Lesson, taken out of the xv. chapter to the Corinthians, the first Epistle.

CHRIST is risen from the dead, and become the first fruits of them that slept. For by a man came death, and by a man came the resurrection of the dead. For as by Adam all die, even so by Christ shall all be made alive. But every man in his own order: the first is Christ, then they that are Christ's at his coming. Then cometh the end, when he hath delivered up the kingdom to God the Father; when he hath put down all rule, and all authority, and power. For he must reign, till he have put all his enemies under his feet. The last enemy that shall be destroyed is death. For he hath put all things under his feet. But when he saith, all things are put under him, it is manifest that he is excepted, which did put all things under him. When all things are subdued unto him, then shall the Son also himself be subject unto him that put all things under him, that God may be all in all. Else what do they which are baptized over the dead, if the dead rise not at all? Why are they then baptized over them? yea, and why stand we alway then in jeopardy? By our rejoicing which I have in Christ Jesu our Lord, I die daily. That I have fought with beasts at Ephesus after the manner of men, what advantageth it me, if the dead rise not again? Let us eat and drink, for to-morrow we shall die. Be not ye deceived: evil words corrupt good manners. Awake truly out of sleep, and sin not; for some have not the knowledge of God. I speak this to your shame. But some man will say, How arise the dead? with what body shall they come? Thou fool, that which thou sowest is not quickened, except it die. And what sowest thou? Thou sowest not that body that shall be, but bare corn, as of wheat or of some other: but God giveth it a body at his pleasure, to every seed his own body. All flesh is not one manner of flesh; but there is one manner of flesh of men, another manner of flesh of beasts, another of fishes, and another of birds. There are also celestial bodies, and there are bodies terrestrial; but the glory of the celestial is one, and the glory of the terrestrial is another. There is one manner of glory of the sun, and another glory of the moon, and another glory of the stars; for one star differeth from another in glory. So is the resurrection of the dead: it is sown in corruption; it riseth again in incorruption: it is sown in dishonour; it riseth again in honour: it is sown in weakness; it riseth again in power: it is sown a natural body; it riseth again a spiritual body. There is a natural body, and there is a spiritual body: as it is also written, The first man Adam was made a living soul; and the last Adam was made a quickening spirit. Howbeit, that is not first which is spiritual, but that which is natural; and then that which is spiritual. The first man is of the earth, earthy: the second man is the Lord from heaven (heavenly). As is the earthy, such are they that are earthy: and as is the heavenly, such are they that are heavenly. And as we have borne the image of the earthy, so shall we bear the image of the heavenly. This say I, brethren, that flesh and blood cannot inherit the kingdom of God; neither doth corruption inherit uncorruption. Behold, I shew you a mystery: we shall not all sleep, but we shall all be changed, and that in a moment, in the twinkling of an eye, by the last trump; for the trump shall blow, and the dead shall rise incorruptible, and we shall be changed. For this corruptible must put on incorruption, and this mortal must put on immortality. When this corruptible hath put on incorruption, and this mortal hath put on immortality; then shall be brought to pass the saying that is written, Death is swallowed up in victory. Death, where is thy sting? Hell, where is thy victory? The sting of death is sin, and the strength of sin is the law. But thanks be unto God, which hath given us victory through our Lord Jesus Christ. Therefore, my dear brethren, be ye steadfast and unmoveable, always rich in the work of the Lord, forasmuch as ye know how that your labour is not in vain in the Lord.

The Lesson ended, then shall the Priest say,

Lord, have mercy upon us.
Christ, have mercy upon us.
Lord, have mercy upon us.
¶ Our Father, which art in heaven, &c.
And lead us not into temptation.

Answer.

But deliver us from evil. Amen.

Priest.

Enter not (O Lord) into judgment with thy servant.

Answer.

For in thy sight no living creature shall be justified.

Priest.

From the gates of hell.

Answer.

Deliver their souls, O Lord.

Priest.

I believe to see the goodness of the Lord.

Answer.

In the land of the living.

Priest.

O Lord, graciously hear my prayer.

Answer.

And let my cry come unto thee.

Let us pray.

O LORD, with whom do live the spirits of them that be dead, and in whom the souls of them that be elected, after they be delivered from the burden of the flesh, be in joy and felicity; Grant unto this thy servant, that the sins which he committed in this world be not imputed unto him; but that he, escaping the gates of hell, and pains of eternal darkness, may ever dwell in the region of light, with Abraham, Isaac, and Jacob, in the place where is no weeping, sorrow, nor heaviness; and when that dreadful Day of the general Resurrection shall come, make him to rise also with the just and righteous, and receive this body again to glory, then made pure and incorruptible. Set him on the right hand of thy Son Jesus Christ, among thy holy and elect, that then he may hear with them these most sweet and comfortable words; Come to me, ye blessed of my Father, possess the kingdom which hath been prepared for you from the beginning of the world. Grant this, we beseech thee, O merciful Father, through Jesus Christ our Mediator and Redeemer. Amen.

APPENDIX 2

A FORM OF PRAYER
WITH THANKSGIVING TO BE USED YEARLY UPON THE FIFTH DAY OF NOVEMBER

A FORM OF PRAYER
TO BE USED YEARLY UPON THE THIRTIETH DAY OF JANUARY

A FORM OF PRAYER
WITH THANKSGIVING TO BE USED YEARLY UPON THE NINE AND TWENTIETH DAY OF MAY

[Appendix to the 1662 edition, omitted since 1859]

CHARLES R.

OUR will and pleasure is, That these Three
Forms of Prayer and Service made for the Fifth
of November, the Thirtieth of January, and the
Twenty ninth of May, be forthwith Printed and
Published, and for the future annexed to the Book
of Common Prayer and Liturgy of the Church of
England, to be used yearly on the said days, in all
Cathedral and Collegiate Churches and Chap-
pels, in all Chappels of Colledges and Halls
within both Our Universities, and of Our Col-
ledges of Eaton and Winchester, and in all Parish-
Churches and Chappels within Our Kingdom of
England, Dominion of Wales, and Town of
Berwick upon Tweed.

Given at Our Court at White-Hall the 2^d day of
May, in the 14th year of Our Reign.

By His Majesties Command.

EDW. NICHOLAS.

A FORM OF
PRAYER WITH THANKSGIVING
TO BE USED YEARLY UPON THE FIFTH DAY OF NOVEMBER.

FOR THE HAPPY DELIVERANCE OF THE KING, AND THE THREE ESTATES OF THE REALM, FROM THE MOST TRAITEROUS AND BLOUDY INTENDED MASSACRE BY GUN-POWDER.

¶ *The Service shall be the same with the usual Office for Holidays in all things; Except where it is hereafter otherwise appointed.*

¶ *If this day shall happen to be Sunday, only the Collect proper for that Sunday, shall be added to this Office in its place.*

¶ *Morning Prayer shall begin with one of these Sentences.*

TURN thy face away from our sins, O Lord; and blot out all our offences. Psal. li. 9.

Correct us, O Lord, but with judgment, not in thine anger; lest thou bring us to nothing. Jere. x. 24.

I will go to my father, and will say unto him; Father, I have sinned against heaven, and before thee; and am no more worthy to be called thy son. S. Luke xx. 18, 19.

¶ Proper Psalms, xxxv. lxiv. cxxiv. cxxix.

¶ Proper Lessons, { The first, 2 Sam. xxii. The second, Acts xxiii.

¶ *In the Suffrages after the Creed, there shall be inserted and used for the King.*

Priest.

O Lord, save the King;

People.

Who putteth his trust in thee.

Priest.

Send him help from thy holy place.

People.

And evermore mightily defend him.

Priest.

Let his enemies have no advantage against him.

People.

Let not the wicked approach to hurt him.

¶ *Instead of the first Collect at Morning Prayer, shall these two be used.*

ALMIGHTY God, who hast in all ages shewed thy power and mercy in the miraculous and gracious deliverances of thy Church, and in the protection of righteous and religious Kings and States, professing thy holy and eternal truth, from the wicked conspiracies, and malicious practices of all the enemies thereof; We yield thee our unfeigned thanks and praise, for the wonderful and mighty deliverance of our late gracious Sovereign King James, the Queen, the Prince, and all the Royal Branches, with the Nobility, Clergy, and Commons of this Realm, then assembled in Parliament, by Popish treachery appointed as sheep to the slaughter, in a most barbarous, and savage manner, beyond the examples of former ages. From this unnatural conspiracy, not our merit, but thy mercy; not our foresight, but thy providence delivered us: And therefore, not unto us, O Lord, not unto us; but unto thy Name be ascribed all honour and glory in all Churches of the saints, from generation to generation, through Jesus Christ our Lord. *Amen.*

O LORD, who didst this day discover the snares of death that were laid for us, and didst wonderfully deliver us from the same; Be thou still our mighty Protector, and scatter our enemies that delight in blood. Infatuate and defeat their counsels, abate their pride, asswage their malice, and confound their devices. Strengthen the hands of our gracious King Charles, and all that are put in authority under him, with Judgment and justice, to cut off all such workers of iniquity, as turn religion into rebellion, and faith into faction; that they may never prevail against us, or triumph in the ruine of thy Church among us: But that our gracious Soveraign and his Realms, being preserved in thy true Religion, and by thy merciful goodness protected in the same, we may all duly serve thee, and give thee thanks in thy holy congregation, through Jesus Christ our Lord. *Amen.*

¶ *In the end of the Litany (which shall always this day be used after the Collect* [We humbly beseech thee, O Father, etc.] *shall this be said which followeth.*

ALMIGHTY God, and heavenly Father, who of thy gracious providence, and tender mercy towards us, didst prevent the malice and imaginations of our enemies, by discovering and confounding their horrible and wicked enterprise, plotted, and intended this day to be executed against the King, and the whole State of this Realm, for the subversion of the Government, and Religion established amongst us; We most humbly praise and magnifie thy glorious Name for this thine infinite gracious goodness towards us. We confess, it was thy mercy, thy mercy alone, that we were not then consumed. For our sins cried to heaven against us; and our iniquities justly called for vengeance upon us. But thou hast not dealt with us after our sins, nor rewarded us after our iniquities; nor given us over, as we deserved, to be a prey to our enemies; but didst in mercy deliver us from their malice, and preserve us from death and destruction. Let the consideration of this thy goodness, O Lord, work in us true repentance, that iniquity may not be our ruine. And increase in us more and more a lively faith, and fruitful love in all holy obedience, that thou maist continue thy favour, with the light of thy Gospel to us and our posterity for evermore; and that for thy dear Sons sake, Jesus Christ our only Mediatour and Advocate. Amen.

¶ *In the Communion Service, instead of the Collect for the day, shall this which followeth, be used.*

ETERNAL God, and our most mighty protector, we thy unworthy servants do humbly present our selves before thy Majesty, acknowledging thy power, wisdom, and goodness in preserving the King, and the three Estates of this Realm assembled in Parliament, from the destruction this day intended against them. Make us, we beseech thee, truly thankful for this thy great mercy towards us. Protect and defend our Soveraign Lord the King, and all the Royal Family from all treasons and conspiracies: Preserve them in thy faith, fear, and love; prosper his Reign with long happiness here on earth; and crown him with everlasting glory hereafter in the kingdom of heaven; through Jesus Christ our only Saviour and Redeemer. Amen.

The Epistle.

LET every soul be subject unto the higher powers. For there is no power but of God: the powers that be, are ordained of God. Whosoever therefore resisteth the power, resisteth the ordinance of God: and they that resist, shall receive to themselves damnation. For rulers are not a terrour to good works, but to the evil. Wilt thou then not be afraid of the power? do that which is good, and thou shalt have praise of the same: For he is the minister of God to thee for good. But if thou do that which is evil, be afraid; for he beareth not the sword in vain: for he is the minister of God, a revenger to execute wrath upon him that doth evil. Wherefore ye must needs be subject, not only for wrath, but also for conscience sake. For, for this cause pay you tribute also: for they are Gods ministers, attending continually upon this very thing. Render therefore to all their dues; tribute to whom tribute is due, custom to whom custom, fear to whom fear, honour to whom honour.

Rom. xiii. 1.

The Gospel.

WHEN the morning was come, all the chief priests and elders of the people took counsel against Jesus to put him to death. And when they had bound him, they led him away, and delivered him to Pontius Pilate the governour. Then Judas which had betrayed him, when he saw that he was condemned, repented himself, and brought again the thirty pieces of silver to the chief priests and elders, saying, I have sinned, in that I have

S. Matth.
xxvii. 1.

betrayed the innocent bloud. And they said, What is that to us? see thou to that. And he cast down the pieces of silver in the temple, and departed, and went and hanged himself. And the chief priests took the silver pieces, and said, It is not lawful for to put them into the treasury, because it is the price of bloud. And they took counsel, and bought with them the potters field, to bury strangers in. Wherefore that field was called, The field of bloud unto this day. Then was fulfilled that which was spoken by Jeremy the prophet, saying, And they took the thirty pieces of silver, the price of him that was valued, whom they of the children of Israel did value; and gave them for the potters field, as the Lord appointed me.

¶ *After the Creed, if there be no Sermon, shall be read one of the six Homilies against Rebellion.*

¶ *This sentence is to be read at the Offertory.*

WHATSOEVER ye would that men should do to you, do ye even so to them; for this is the law, and the prophets.

S. Matth. vii. 12.

A FORM OF COMMON PRAYER,

TO BE USED YEARLY UPON THE XXX. DAY OF JANUARY, BEING THE DAY OF THE MARTYRDOM OF K. CHARLES THE FIRST.

¶ *If this day shall happen to be Sunday, this form of Service shall be used the next day following.*

¶ *The Service shall be the same with the usual Office for Holidays in all things; except where it is hereafter otherwise appointed.*

THE ORDER FOR MORNING PRAYER.

¶ *He that ministereth, shall begin with one of these sentences.*

CORRECT us, O Lord, but with judgment, not in thine anger: lest thou bring us to nothing. Jere. x. 24.

Rent your heart, and not your garments, and turn to the Lord your God: for he is gracious and merciful; slow to anger, and of great kindness; and repenteth him of the evil. Joel ii. 13.

Lam. iii. 22. It is of the Lords mercies, that we are not consumed; because his compassions fail not.

¶ Instead of Venite, exultemus shall this Psalm following be used, one verse by the Priest, and another by the Clerk and People.

Psal. xcv. 6. O COME, let us worship, and fall down: and kneel before the Lord our maker.

Acts iii. 19. Let us repent, and turn from our wickedness: and our sins shall be forgiven us.

Jonah iii. 8, 9. Let us turn every one from his evil way: and the Lord will turn from his fierce anger, and we shall not perish.

Psal. li. 3. We acknowledge our faults: and our sins are ever before us.

Lam. iii. 42. We have provoked thine anger, O Lord: but
Psal. cxxx. 4. there is mercy with thee, therefore shalt thou be feared.

Psal. xxvi. 9. O shut not up our souls with sinners: nor our life with the bloud-thirsty.

Psal. lxv. 24. Thou hast promised, O Lord, that before we call, thou wilt answer: and whiles we are yet speaking, thou wilt hear.

Baruch. iii. 1. And now in the anguish of our souls we cry unto thee: Hear, Lord, and have mercy.

Psal. vi. 1. O Lord, rebuke us not in thine indignation: neither chasten us in thy displeasure.

Psal. xxv. 10. For thy Names sake be merciful to our sin: for it is great.

Psal. li. 9. Turn thy face from our sins: and put out all our misdeeds.

10. Make us clean hearts, O God: and renew a right spirit within us.

14. Deliver us from bloud-guiltiness, O God: thou that art the God of our salvation.

Psal. lxxix. 9. O deliver us, and be merciful to our sins: for thy Names sake.

O be favourable and gracious unto Sion: build Psal. li. 18. thou the walls of Jerusalem.

So we that are thy people, and sheep of thy Psal. lxxix. 14. pasture, shall give thee thanks for ever: and will alway be shewing forth thy praise from generation to generation.

Glory be to the Father, and to the Son: and to the Holy Ghost;

As it was in the beginning, is now, and ever shall be: world without end. Amen.

¶ Proper Psalms, vii. ix. x. xi.

¶ Proper Lessons, $\begin{cases} \text{The first, 2 Sam. i.} \\ \text{The second, S. Matth. xxvii.} \end{cases}$

¶ Instead of the first Collect at Morning Prayer, this which followeth shall be used.

O MOST mighty God, terrible in thy judgments, and wonderful in thy doings towards the children of men, who in thy heavy displeasure didst suffer the life of our late gracious Soveraign to be this day taken away by wicked hands; We, thy unworthy servants, humbly confess, that the sins of this Nation have been the cause which hath brought this heavy judgment upon us. But, O gracious God, when thou makest inquisition for bloud, lay not the guilt of this innocent bloud, (the shedding whereof nothing but the bloud of thy Son can expiate) lay it not to the charge of the people of this Land, nor let it ever be required of us, or our posterity. Be merciful, be merciful unto thy people, whom thou hast redeemed; and be not angry with us for ever; but pardon us for thy mercies sake, through the merits of thy Son our Lord Jesus Christ. Amen.

¶ In the end of the Litany (which shall always this day be used) after the Collect, We humbly

beseech thee, O Father, etc. *These three Collects are to be used.*

O LORD, we beseech thee, mercifully hear our
prayers, and spare all those who confess their sins
unto thee, that they whose consciences by sin are
accused, by thy merciful pardon may be absolved,
through Christ our Lord. Amen.

O MOST mighty God, and merciful Father,
who hast compassion upon all men, and hatest
nothing that thou hast made, who wouldest not
the death of a sinner, but that he should rather
turn from his sin, and be saved; Mercifully forgive
us our trespasses, receive and comfort us, who are
grieved and wearied with the burthen of our sins.
Thy property is always to have mercy, to thee only
it appertaineth to forgive sins; Spare us therefore
good Lord, spare thy people whom thou hast
redeemed; enter not into judgment with thy servants, who are vile earth, and miserable sinners:
but so turn thine anger from us, who meekly
acknowledge our vileness, and truly repent us of
our faults; and so make haste to help us in this
world, that we may ever live with thee in the world
to come, through Jesus Christ our Lord. Amen.

¶ *Then shall the people say this that followeth,
after the Minister.*

TURN thou us, O good Lord, and so shall we
be turned: Be favourable, O Lord, Be favourable
to thy people, Who turn to thee in weeping, fasting and praying: For thou art a merciful God, Full
of compassion, Long-suffering, and of great pity.
Thou sparest, when we deserve punishment, And
in thy wrath thinkest upon mercy. Spare thy
people, good Lord, spare them, And let not thine
heritage be brought to confusion. Hear us, O

Lord, for thy mercy is great, And after the multitude of thy mercies look upon us; Through the
merits and mediation of thy blessed Son Jesus
Christ our Lord. Amen.

¶ *In the Communion Service, immediately
after the Commandments shall this Collect be
used.*

O ALMIGHTY Lord, and everlasting God;
Vouchsafe, we beseech thee, to direct, sanctifie,
and govern both our hearts and bodies in the ways
of thy laws, and in the works of thy commandments; that through thy most mighty protection
both here and ever, we may be preserved in body
and soul; through our Lord and Saviour Jesus
Christ. Amen.

¶ *Then shall follow the Prayer for the King,*
[Almighty God, whose Kingdom is everlasting, etc.] *And after that, these two Collects
instead of that for the day.*

BLESSED Lord, in whose sight the death of
thy saints is precious; We magnifie thy Name for
that abundant grace bestowed on our late Mar-
tyred Soveraign; by which he was enabled so
chearfully to follow the steps of his blessed Master
and Saviour, in a constant meek suffering of all
barbarous indignities, and at last resisting unto
bloud; and even then, according to the same pat-
tern, praying for his murtherers. Let his memory,
O Lord, be ever blessed among us, that we may
follow the example of his patience, and charity:
And grant, that this our Land may be freed from
the vengeance of his bloud, and thy mercy glorified in the forgiveness of our sins; and all for Jesus
Christ his sake. Amen.

GRANT, Lord, we beseech thee, that the course of this world may be so peaceably ordered by thy governance, that thy Church may joyfully serve thee in all godly quietness, through Jesus Christ. Amen.

The Epistle.

1 S. Pet. ii. 13.

SUBMIT your selves to every ordinance of man for the Lords sake; whether it be to the King as supream; or unto governours, as unto them that are sent by him for the punishment of evil doers, and for the praise of them that do well. For so is the will of God, that with wel-doing ye may put to silence the ignorance of foolish men: As free, and not using your liberty for a cloak of maliciousness, but as the servants of God. Honour all men. Love the brotherhood. Fear God. Honour the King. Servants be subject to your masters with all fear, not only to the good and gentle, but also to the froward. For this is thank-worthy, if a man for conscience toward God endure grief, suffering wrongfully. For what glory is it, if when ye be buffeted for your faults, ye shall take it patiently? but if when ye do well, and suffer for it, ye take it patiently; this is acceptable with God. For even hereunto were ye called; because Christ also suffered for us, leaving us an example, that ye should follow his steps; who did no sin, neither was guile found in his mouth.

The Gospel.

S. Matth. xxi. 33.

THERE was a certain housholder which planted a vineyard, and hedged it round about, and digged a wine-press in it, and built a tower, and let it out to husbandmen, and went into a far countrey. And when the time of the fruit drew near, he sent his servants to the husbandmen, that they might receive the fruits of it. And the husbandmen took his servants, and beat one, and killed another, and stoned another. Again, he sent other servants, moe than the first: and they did unto them likewise. But last of all, he sent unto them his son, saying, They will reverence my son. But when the husbandmen saw the son, they said among themselves, This is the heir, come, let us kill him, and let us seise on his inheritance. And they caught him, and cast him out of the vineyard, and slew him. When the lord therefore of the vineyard cometh, what will he do unto those husbandmen? They say unto him, He will miserably destroy those wicked men, and will let out his vineyard unto other husbandmen, which shall render him the fruits in their seasons.

¶ *After the Prayer,* [For the whole state of Christs Church, etc.] *this Collect shall be used.*

O LORD, our heavenly Father, who dost not punish us as our sins have deserved, but hast in the midst of judgment remembred mercy; We acknowledge it thy special favour, that though for our many and great provocations thou didst suffer thine Anointed to fall this day into the hands of violent and bloud-thirsty men, and barbarously to be murthered by them; yet thou didst not leave us for ever as sheep without a shepherd, but by thy gracious providence didst miraculously preserve the undoubted heir of his Crown, our most gracious Soveraign King CHARLES the Second, from his bloudy enemies, hiding him under the shadow of thy wings, until their tyranny was overpast, and bringing him back in thy good appointed time to sit in peace upon the throne of his Father, and to exercise that authority over us, which of thy special grace thou hadst committed unto him. For these thy great and unspeakable mercies we render thee most humble thanks from the bottom of our hearts, beseeching thee still to continue thy gracious protection over him, and to grant him a long and a happy reign over us: So we that are thy people, will give thee thanks for ever, and will alway be shewing forth thy praise from generation to generation, through Jesus Christ our Lord. Amen.

THE ORDER FOR EVENING PRAYER.

¶ Proper Psalms, xxxviii. lxiv. cxliii.

¶ Proper Lessons, { The first Jere. xli. or Dan. ix to v. 22. The second Heb. xi. v. 32 to cap. xii, v. 7.

¶ *Instead of the first Collect at Evening Prayer, use these two which follow.*

O BLESSED Lord God, who by thy wisdom not only guidest and orderest all things most suitably to thine own justice, but also performest thy pleasure in such a manner, that we cannot but acknowledge thee to be righteous in all thy ways, and holy in all thy works; We thy sinful people fall down before thee, confessing that thy judgments were right in permitting cruel men, sons of Belial, this day to imbrue their hands in the bloud of thine Anointed; we having drawn down the same upon our selves, by the great and long provocations of our sins against thee; For which we do therefore here humble our selves before thee, imploring thy mercy for the pardon of them all; and that thou wouldst deliver this Nation from bloud-guiltiness (that of this day especially) and turn from us and our posterity all those judgments which we by our sins have deserved: Grant this for the all-sufficient merits of thy Son, our Saviour Jesus Christ. Amen.

BLESSED God, just, and powerful, who didst permit thy dear servant, our late dread Soveraign, to be this day given up to the violent out-rages of wicked men, to be despightfully used, and at last murthered by them; Though we cannot reflect upon so foul an act but with horrour and astonishment; yet do we most gratefully commemorate the glories of thy grace, which then shined forth in thine Anointed, whom thou wert pleased, even at the hour of death, to endue with an eminent measure of exemplary patience, meekness, and charity, before the face of his cruel enemies. And albeit, thou didst suffer them to proceed to such a height of violence against him, as to kill his person, and take possession of his throne; yet didst thou in great mercy preserve his son, whose right it was, and at length by a wonderful providence bring him back, and set him thereon, to restore thy true Religion, and to settle peace amongst us: For which, we glorifie thy Name, through Jesus Christ our blessed Saviour. Amen.

¶ *Immediately before the Prayer of S. Chrysostom, shall this Collect be used.*

ALMIGHTY and everlasting God, whose righteousness is like the strong mountains, and thy judgments like the great deep; and who, by that barbarous murder this day committed upon the sacred person of thine Anointed, our late

Soveraign, hast taught us, that neither the greatest of kings, nor the best of men are more secure from violence, than from natural death; Teach us also hereby so to number our days, that we may apply our hearts unto wisdom. And grant that neither the splendour of any thing that is great, nor the conceit of any thing that is good in us, may any way withdraw our eyes from looking upon our selves as sinful dust and ashes; but that (according to the example of this thy blessed Martyr) we may press forward towards the prize of the high calling that is before us, in faith and patience, humility and meekness, mortification and self-denial, charity and constant perseverance unto the end: And all this for thy Son our Lord Jesus Christs sake; To whom, with thee, and the holy Ghost be all honour, and glory, world without end. Amen.

A FORM OF

PRAYER WITH THANKSGIVING

TO BE USED YEARLY UPON THE XXIX. DAY OF MAY; BEING THE DAY OF HIS MAJESTIES BIRTH, AND HAPPY RETURN TO HIS KINGDOMS.

¶ *The Service shall be the same with the usual Office for Holidays in all things; except, where it is hereafter otherwise appointed.*

¶ *If this day shall happen to be Ascension-day, Whitsunday, or Trinity-Sunday, only the Collects of this Office are to be added to the several Services for those festivals in their proper places. If it shall happen to be any other Sunday, or to be Munday, or Tuesday in Whitsunweek, the Collects shall be used as before, and also the proper Psalms here appointed, instead of those of ordinary course, and all the rest of this Office omitted.*

¶ *Morning Prayer shall begin with this Sentence.*

I EXHORT, that first of all supplications, prayers, intercessions, and giving of thanks be made for all men; for Kings, and all that are in Authority, that we may lead a quiet and peaceable

1 Tim. ii. 1, 2, 3.

life in all godliness and honesty: For this is good
and acceptable in the sight of God our Saviour.

¶ *Instead of Venite, exultemus, shall be sung or*
said this Hymn following; one Verse by the
Priest, and another by the Clerk and people.

Psal. xcv. 1.   O COME let us sing unto the Lord: let us
heartily rejoyce in the strength of our salvation.

2.   Let us come before his presence with thanksgiving: and shew our selves glad in him with
psalms.

3.   For the Lord is a great God: and a great King
above all gods.

Psal. xcviii. 2.   With his own right hand, and with his holy
arm: hath he gotten himself the victory.

3.   The Lord declared his salvation: his righteousness hath he openly shewed in the sight of
the heathen.

4.   He hath remembered his mercy and truth
towards the house of Israel: and all the ends of the
world have seen the salvation of our God.

Psal. lxxxix. 21.   For he hath found David his servant: with his
holy oyl hath he anointed him.

Psal. lxxxix. 22.   His hand hath held him fast: and his arm hath
strengthned him.

23.   The enemy hath not been able to do him
violence: the son of wickedness hath not hurt him.

24.   He hath smitten down his foes before his face:
and plagued them that hated him.

25.   His truth also, and his mercy hath been with
him: and in his Name is his horn exalted.

26.   He hath set his dominion also in the sea: and
his right hand in the flouds.

Psal. cxxxviii. 4.   Therefore all the Kings of the earth shall praise
thee, O Lord: for they have heard the words of
thy mouth.

Yea, they shall sing in the ways of the Lord: 5.
that great is the glory of the Lord.

My mouth also shall speak the praise of the Psal. cxlv. 21.
Lord: and let all flesh give thanks unto his holy
Name for ever and ever.

Glory be to the Father, and to the Son: and to
the Holy Ghost;

As it was in the beginning, is now, and ever
shall be: world without end. Amen.

¶ Proper Psalms, xx. xxi. lxxxv. cxviii.

¶ Proper Lessons, {The first 2 Sam. xix. v. 9.
{The second Rom. xiii.

¶ *In the Suffrages after the Creed these shall be
inserted and used for the King.*

Priest.
O Lord, save the King.
People.
Who putteth his trust in thee.
Priest.
Send him help from thy holy place.
People.
And evermore mightily defend him.
Priest.
Let his enemies have no advantage against him.
People.
Let not the wicked approach to hurt him.

¶ *Instead of the first Collect for Morning
Prayer these two shall be used.*

O LORD God of our salvation, who hast been
exceedingly gracious unto this land, and by thy
miraculous providence hast delivered us out of our
late miserable confusions, by restoring to us our
dread Soveraign Lord, thy servant, King
CHARLES; We are now here before thee with

all due thankfulness to acknowledge thine unspeakable goodness this day shewed unto us, and to offer up our sacrifices of praise unto thy glorious Name; humbly beseeching thee to accept this our unfeigned, though unworthy oblation of our selves; vowing all holy obedience in thought, word, and work unto thy divine Majesty; and promising in thee, and for thee all loyal and dutiful allegiance to thine Anointed servant, and to his heirs after him: whom we beseech thee to bless with all encrease of grace, honour, and happiness in this world, and to crown with immortality and glory in the world to come; for Jesus Christ his sake, our only Lord and Saviour. Amen.

O GOD, who by thy divine providence and goodness didst this day first bring into the world, and didst this day also bring back and restore to us, and to his own just and undoubted rights our most gracious Soveraign Lord thy servant King CHARLES; Preserve his life, and establish his throne, we beseech thee. Be unto him a helmet of salvation against the face of his enemies, and a strong tower of defence in the time of trouble. Let his Reign be prosperous, and his days many. Let justice, truth, and holiness; let peace, and love, and all Christian vertues flourish in his time. Let his people serve him with honour and obedience; and let him so duly serve thee on earth, that he may hereafter everlastingly reign with thee in heaven, through Jesus Christ our Lord. Amen.

¶ *In the end of the Litany (which shall always this day be used) after the Collect,* [We humbly beseech thee, O Father, etc.] *shall this be said which followeth.*

O LORD God, most merciful Father, who of

thine especial grace and favour didst this day bring home unto us thy servant King CHARLES our Soveraign, and place him in the throne of this Kingdom, thereby restoring to us the publick and free profession of thy true Religion and worship, to the great comfort and joy of our hearts; We thine unworthy servants, here assembled together to celebrate the memory of this thy mercy, most humbly beseech thee to grant us grace, that we may always shew our selves truly and unfeignedly thankful unto thee for the same: And that our gracious King may through thy mercy continue his Reign over us in all vertue, godliness, and honour, many, and many years; and that we dutifully obeying him, as faithful and loyal subjects, may long enjoy him with the continuance of thy great blessings, which by him thou hast vouchsafed unto us, through Jesus Christ our Lord. Amen.

¶ *Immediately before the prayer of S. Chrysostom, use the Collect of Thanksgiving,* [For Peace, and Deliverance from our enemies.]

O ALMIGHTY God, who art a strong tower of defence unto thy servants against the face of their enemies; We yield thee praise and thanksgiving for our deliverance from those great and apparent dangers wherewith we were compassed. We acknowledge it thy goodness that we were not delivered over as a prey unto them; beseeching thee still to continue such thy mercies towards us, that all the world may know that thou art our Saviour and mighty deliverer, through Jesus Christ our Lord. Amen.

¶ *In the Communion Service between the Commandments and the Epistle, shall these two Collects be used, instead of the Collect for the King, and that of the day.*

O MOST gracious God, and merciful Father, who hast by thy infinite power and goodness safely and quietly, after so many and great troubles and adversities, setled thy servant our Soveraign Lord King CHARLES in the throne of his Fathers, (notwithstanding all the power and malice of his enemies) restoring unto us with him, and by him the free profession of thy sacred truth and Gospel, together with our former peace and prosperity; We beseech thee to grant him the defence of thy salvation, and to shew forth thy loving kindness, and mercy to him; and to stir up continually in our hearts all faithful duty and loyalty towards him, with a religious obedience, and thankfulness unto thee for these and all other thy mercies, through Jesus Christ our Lord. Amen.

GRANT, we beseech thee, Almighty God, that our Soveraign Lord the King, whom thou didst this day happily bring home, and restore to us, may be a mighty protector of his people, a religious defender of thy sacred Faith, and of thy holy Church among us, a glorious conquerour over all his enemies, a gracious governour unto all his subjects, and a happy father of many children to rule this Nation by succession in all ages, through Jesus Christ our Lord. Amen.

The Epistle.

1 S. Pet. ii. 11.　DEARLY beloved, I beseech you as strangers and pilgrims, abstain from fleshly lusts, which war against the soul; having your conversation honest among the Gentiles: that whereas they speak against you as evil-doers, they may by your good works which they shall behold, glorifie God in the day of visitation. Submit your selves to every ordinance of man for the Lords sake; whether it

be to the King, as supream; or unto governours, as unto them that are sent by him for the punishment of evil-doers, and for the praise of them that do well. For so is the will of God, that with welldoing ye may put to silence the ignorance of foolish men: As free, and not using your liberty for a cloak of maliciousness, but as the servants of God. Honour all men. Love the brotherhood. Fear God. Honour the King.

The Gospel.

AND they sent out unto him their disciples, with the Herodians, saying, Master, we know that thou art true, and teachest the way of God in truth, neither carest thou for any man; for thou regardest not the person of men. Tell us therefore, What thinkest thou? Is it lawful to give tribute unto Cesar, or not? But Jesus perceived their wickedness, and said, Why tempt ye me, ye hypocrites? Shew me the tribute-money. And they brought unto him a peny. And he saith unto them, Whose is this image and superscription? They say unto him, Cesars. Then saith he unto them, Render therefore unto Cesar, the things which are Cesars; and unto God, the things that are Gods. When they had heard these words, they marvelled, and left him, and went their way.

S. Matth. xxii. 16.

¶ *After the Prayer,* [For the whole state of Christs Church, etc.] *this Collect following shall be used.*

O LORD our God, who upholdest and governest all things in heaven and earth; Receive our humble prayers with our thanksgivings for our Soveraign Lord CHARLES, set over us by thy grace and providence to be our King: And so, together with him, bless the whole Royal Family with the dew of thy heavenly Spirit, that they, ever trusting in thy goodness, protected by thy power, and crowned with thy gracious and endless favour, may continue before thee in health, peace, joy, and honour, a long and happy life upon earth, and after death obtain everlasting life and glory in the kingdom of heaven, by the merits and mediation of Christ Jesus our Saviour; who with the Father, and the holy Spirit, liveth and reigneth ever one God, world without end. Amen.

FINIS.